Selected Issues in Equal Treatment Law: a Multi-Layered Comparison of European, English and Dutch Law

Selected Issues in Equal Treatment Law: a Multi-Layered Comparison of European, English and Dutch Law

THESIS

to obtain the degree of Doctor
at Maastricht University,
on the authority of the Rector Magnificus,
Prof. dr. G.P.M.F. Mols
in accordance with the decision of the Board of Deans,
to be defended in public
on Wednesday 13 December 2006, at 16.00 hours

by

Marianne Henriëtte Simone Gijzen

Supervisors:

Prof. dr. A.W. Heringa
Prof. dr. L. Waddington

Assessment Committee:

Prof. dr. H. Schneider (chairperson)
Dr. M. Bell (University of Leicester)
Prof. dr. I. Boerefijn (Universiteit Utrecht, Universiteit Maastricht)
Prof. dr. C. McCrudden (University of Oxford)
Prof. dr. J. Gerards (Universiteit Leiden)

A commercial edition of this PhD-thesis will be published by Intersentia in the Ius Commune Europaeum Series, no. 61 under ISBN-13: 978-90-5095-629-1.

To my beloved parents

ACKNOWLEDGEMENTS

It has been both a delight and a challenge to write this book! Special thanks are due to many. First and foremost, I am thankful to my parents to whom I dedicate this work. Without their unwavering and generous support in many ways the writing of this book would have been so much more difficult and arduous. I wish also to express gratitude to the other members of my immediate family, in particular to my brother Jeroen and my sister Marcella, who were always keen to learn about the progress of this work.

This book was written at the Maastricht Institute for Transnational Legal Research (METRO, the University of Maastricht, Faculty of Law). I am indebted to my colleagues at the faculty, in particular at METRO and also at the department of European and International law both of which transpired to be pleasant and vibrant academic environments. Firstly, and specifically, I am grateful to my supervisors Aalt Willem Heringa and Lisa Waddington for their generous support and knowledgeable academic feedback. Special thanks is also due to Niels and Ida both of whom are great friends and colleagues at the same time, to Hildegard Schneider for her interest in this work and her encouragement all through and to Michael Faure, academic director of METRO. Furthermore, I am grateful to Nettie Litjens who was willing to edit this book into its current literary format in a very short period of time and to everybody at my publisher, Intersentia. Thanks also to Ciara Clerx and Anita Jolink for helping me edit the footnotes and bibliography.

I am especially also appreciative to the members of the jury: Mark Bell, Ineke Boerefijn, Christopher McCrudden, Janneke Gerards and Hildegard Schneider. Many thanks to you all for reading an earlier version of this thesis and for your valuable and thought provoking commentaries.

Parts of this book were written during visiting research stays at King's College London and the University of Oxford. I owe special thanks to Maleiha Malik (King's College) and Christopher McCrudden (Oxford) who have been very helpful and kind in facilitating these research visits. While in Oxford, I received warm friendship from my housemates Intesar and Yanru who were a real joy to live with!

I wish also to thank the members of the Group of Independent Experts in Anti-Discrimination Matters and the Group of Independent Experts on Disability both set up by the European Commission for the enlightening debates we used to have.

I am equally indebted to Rikki Holtmaat, Kees Waaldijk and Jacqueline Schoonheim for reading and commenting on earlier versions of Chapters 4, 7 and 8, respectively. Thanks also to Jakob van der Velde for his useful comments on the law stemming from the European Convention on Human Rights.

I wish to say particular thanks also to Pam Karimbeik who has been tremendously helpful in commenting on my English language skills and who showed a tireless support!

Beyond the academic environment I take the opportunity to express a special thanks to all my friends for their constant and generous support and for the many happy moments we share together. Thanks to you all!

Finally, thanks to Ceriel for his unabated patience, loyalty and love throughout.

This book contains the law up to 1 July 2006 at least.

My work was supported by a grant from the Dutch Association for Academic Research (grant 015.000.063).

TABLE OF CONTENTS

LIST OF ABBREVIATIONS

AET w/m	Act on Equal Treatment between Women and Men
AETA	Age Equal Treatment Act
AETD	Amended Equal Treatment Directive
CA	Court of Appeal
CRE	Commission for Racial Equality
DDA	Disability Discrimination Act
DETA	Disability Equal Treatment Act
DRC	Disability Rights Commission
EAT	Employment Appeal Tribunal
ECJ	European Court of Justice
ECtHR	European Court of Human Rights
EFD	Employment Framework Directive
EOC	Equal Opportunities Commission
ET	Employment Tribunal
ETC	Equal Treatment Commission
ETD	Equal Treatment Directive
GC	Grand Chamber
GETA	General Equal Treatment Act
HL	House of Lords
HR	Hoge Raad (Dutch Supreme Court)
HRA	Human Rights Act
R&B Regulations	Religion and Belief Regulations
RD	Race Directive
RRA	Race Relations Act
S.O. Regulations	Sexual Orientation Regulations
SDA	Sex Discrimination Act

PART I

SETTING THE SCENE

Chapter 1

INTRODUCTION

1. Introduction

'Equality', writes Fletcher, 'is at once the simplest and the most complex idea that shapes the evolution of the law'.[1] The complexity of equality, rather than its falsely perceived simplicity, has been widely analysed, not only by lawyers, but also by social and political scientists, economists and philosophers. Since this book comprises yet another analysis of the principles of equality and non-discrimination[2] the question arises as to what it adds to the existing debate. I will answer this question in stages. Similar to other works, this book adopts the perspective of 'equality' and 'non-discrimination' as fundamental human rights principles. However, unlike other books, this book follows a multi-layered comparative approach to substantive issues of equality and non-discrimination in the context of law. Its implications shall be sketched in this introductory chapter. Initially, the research that led to this book took the starting-point of a so-called 'cross-fertilisation'[3] approach to selected issues

1 Fletcher, Basic concepts of legal thought, New York/Oxford 1996, p. 121, cited by Alkema and Rop 2002, p. 32, footnote 3.

2 Equality is a multi-facetted concept. The various meanings of this concept will be clarified throughout this book as a whole. It appears however useful to clarify at the outset the relationship between the principle of equality on the one hand, and the non-discrimination principle, on the other. These two principles are not synonymous. However, they are clearly inter-related concepts. The non-discrimination principle is a negative subset of the principle of equality. It is negative, for the principle is framed by law as a negative prohibition to use (directly or indirectly) unlawful, status-based, criteria such as race, sex, disability etc. in a given decision-making process. The non-discrimination principle fits in with the negative, reactive, strategy to combat discrimination. In contrast, equality goes beyond a mere prohibition against discrimination. Equality is proactive: it calls for positive steps to be taken with the objective of redressing disadvantage and promoting equality. See Fredman 2001a; Hirsch Ballin 2003. See also McCrudden 2003a, who has rightly observed that it was only after the 1990s that academic analysis has felt a need to marry both approaches.

3 See also Parmar 2004, p. 135, who has used the term 'reflexive cross-fertilisation'. She has employed this term in the context of an analysis which examined the reflexive links between EC gender equality law and EC race equality law. It might be useful to note that one of the first areas in which a cross-fertilisation approach was adopted by academic lawyers is that of →

in equal treatment law. Accordingly, the original idea was to analyse a process of cross-pollination of legal norms and their interpretations at five distinct[4] levels. However, for reasons that I will note below, the analysis of cross-fertilisation did not prove possible to the extent I envisaged at the outset. Therefore, the focus of research progressively shifted from a study into cross-fertilisation issues to an original, multi-layered comparative analysis of European, English and Dutch equal treatment law. Cross-fertilisation issues will still be addressed, albeit in a tentative way and wherever it appears relevant. As referenced before, the analysis of 'cross-fertilisation' I had foreseen in the realms of 'equality' and 'non-discrimination' was meant to be made with reference to five different levels. These have not lost their importance in the final format of this book and will be explained at this juncture. To come to the point, these levels, in conjunction, constitute the 'multi-layered' comparative exercise that is central to the scrutiny of this book. The interplay between the layers or levels takes different forms. First of all, supranational anti-discrimination and equality law bears a great impact upon regulatory and interpretative approaches to 'equality' and 'non-discrimination' in the Member States. The current European Community (EC)[5] anti-discrimination and equality framework embraces a wide range of discrimination grounds which were previously not covered. In other words, the Community's competencies in the areas of non-discrimination and equality have widened considerably in recent times. *Inter alia* this reflects a trend towards a 'constitutionalisation' of equality and non-discrimination at the supranational level. The widening of the Community's competence in the areas of equality and non-discrimination calls for changes to the legal and policy frameworks at the level of the Member States. Furthermore, the national courts in their capacity of *juges de droit commun* are

European administrative law. See especially the pioneering academic work by Schwarze (e.g. Schwarze 1996, Schwarze 1993, Schwarze 1992).

4 The various levels will be referred to in the main-text hereafter. They are identified for purposes of academic analysis. In practice, however, these levels might not be easily distinguishable and are arguably in constant interaction.

5 Where I refer to 'EC' law, I refer to the law of the European Community (i.e. 'first pillar' law). The, for this book, most relevant provisions in the EC Treaty have been amended and/or inserted into the Treaty by the Treaty of Amsterdam (ToA) (viz., *infra* note 35). Where I refer to 'EU' law, I refer to the law of the European Union in a wider sense including especially, EC law, Title I of the Treaty on the European Union (TEU) regarding 'Common Provisions' and the non-binding Charter of Fundamental Rights of the European Union. The latter document was solemnly proclaimed at the Nice summit in December 2000 [Charter of Fundamental Rights of the European Union, Solemn Proclamation by the Presidents of the European Parliament, the European Commission and the Council of Ministers, Nice, 7 December 2000, [2000] *OJ* C364/1]. The Charter forms an integral Part of the Treaty establishing a Constitution for Europe ([2004] *OJ* C310/1) which, however, has not entered into force and is unlikely to do so in the near future. It is to be noted that other important aspects of the TEU such as the law stemming from the so-called second ('common foreign and security policy') and third ('police and judicial cooperation in criminal matters') 'pillars' are irrelevant to the subject-matter analysed in this book and will thus not be comprised by the term 'EU' law. For a general account of the process of European integration and of the adoption and general content of the various treaties, I refer to Craig and de Búrca, 2003. See moreover, Lenaerts and van Nuffel, 2005, Part I. See moreover Chalmers, Hadjiemmanuil, Monti and Tomkins 2006.

under a duty to give full effectiveness to EC equality law when administering justice in a Community law context.[6] In summary: supranational Community law exercises what I will call a 'top-down' influence on domestic equality law and I will examine this type of influence by comparing regulatory and judicial approaches pre- and post-implementation of EC law. Secondly, one can compare different national approaches and practices among themselves, and in particular the different shapes national equal treatment laws take post-implementation of EC law, i.e. once Member States have brought their laws into conformity with EC equal treatment law. Such an exercise will provide insights into diverse regulatory strategies with respect to 'equality' and 'non-discrimination' across different Member States. Thirdly, a comparative analysis of equal treatment law can be conducted at the level of grounds of discrimination. This involves a comparative study into the intrinsic nature of different discrimination grounds. Such an exercise is valuable, for it provides insights into the question whether the regulatory approach to discrimination ground *x* (for example, 'sex') can set an example for that of discrimination ground *y* (for example, 'race' or 'disability'). It will be argued that, in view of the different logic of different grounds of discrimination this will not always be the case. To the contrary, the distinct underlying values of different grounds of discrimination may call for divergent regulatory strategies (and judicial approaches) with a view to optimising the protective scope of the principle of equality. In this book, a thorough comparative exercise will be made of the underlying values of different grounds of discrimination. Fourthly, existing domestic approaches to issues of equality, non-discrimination and the law may set an example (good or bad) of how EC anti-discrimination and equality law should (not) be framed and/or interpreted by the Community legislator and the European Court of Justice (henceforth: ECJ) respectively. To this end, it will be valuable to map and examine in detail certain aspects of national equal treatment law that can (or has) form(ed) a source of inspiration (in the positive or negative sense) for the development of supranational law. Indeed, as Article 6(2) of the EU Treaty provides 'The Union shall respect fundamental rights (...) as they result from the constitutional traditions common to the Member States'.[7] If the ECJ or the Community legislator feels inspired by domestic (constitutional) approaches while, respectively, interpreting or framing EC anti-discrimination law, this will eventually bear an impact upon the law of all Member States, given the supranational character of EC

6 It should be noted that the domestic courts perform a dual role. When administering justice in matters that are merely governed by the internal law of the Member State, domestic courts form part and parcel of the national legal framework. However, when adjudicating on matters which fall within the scope of Community law, functionally perceived national judges form part of the supranational legal framework. Grévisse and Bonichot have spoken of a '*dichotomie, une sorte the dualisme jurisdictionel dans la personne de même juge, selon qu'il statue à titre nationale ou à titre communautaire*'. (Grévisse and Bonichot, 'Les incidences du droit communautaire sur l'organisation et l'exercise de la fonction jurisdictionelle dans les Etats Membres ', in: Dalloz (ed.), *Europe et le Droit, Mélanges en Hommage de J. Boulois*, p. 310, cited by Kakouris 1997, p. 1392-1393.

7 See also Article 6(1) of the EU Treaty which provides as follows: 'The Union is founded on the principles of liberty, democracy, respect for human rights and fundamental freedoms, and the rule of law, principles which are common to the Member States.'

law.[8] In other words, via the roundabout route of Community law, the law of Member State *X* will be influenced by the law of Member State *Y*, if the legal approach adopted by the latter provides a model for the shaping of EC equality law.[9] This amounts to a 'bottom-up' influence of domestic law upon EC law. Unlike the aforementioned 'top-down' ascendancy, 'bottom-up' influences do not have a mandatory character. The fifth layer of interplay concerns the relationship between and influence of different 'European' jurisdictions. Although the ECJ is not formally bound by judicial reasoning of the European Court of Human Rights (henceforth: ECtHR, or 'Strasbourg Court') and *vice versa*, both Courts may nonetheless draw inspiration from one another whilst interpreting equal treatment law. Article 6(2) of the EU Treaty provides in this respect that 'the Union shall respect fundamental rights, as guaranteed by the [European Convention on Human Rights] (...)'.[10] In a similar fashion can domestic equal treatment law be analysed in light of relevant ECHR law. The comparison of EC and domestic equal treatment law with relevant Convention law will be addressed in this book although, it is stressed at the outset, this will only be done to a limited extent. All in all, this book is a hybrid that seeks to combine substantive issues of equality and non-discrimination law with the exercise of drawing a multi-layered comparison. In particular, the latter is carried out with a view to fertilising the discussion on the substantive issues.

Earlier, it was stated that the focus on 'cross-fertilisation' gradually diminished to the benefit of drawing a multi-layered comparison. Whilst conducting this research, I incrementally learned that advancing scientific proof of 'cross-fertilisation' between legal norms, interpretations and practices is markedly difficult for at least three reasons that ultimately led me to adapt the objectives of this book, in order not to exceed the boundaries in terms of time and space that are intrinsic to a doctoral research. First of all, proving cross-fertilisation in the context of law presupposes a comprehensive knowledge of a wide range of legal systems across Europe (or even

8 Already in the 1974 judgment in *Nold, Kohlen und Baustoffgrosshandlung v. Commission of the European Communities* (Case 4-73) ECR 1974, p. 00491, the Court held as follows: 'In safeguarding [fundamental rights], the Court is bound to draw inspiration from constitutional traditions common to the Member States and it cannot therefore uphold measures which are incompatible with fundamental rights recognised and protected by the Constitutions of these States' (paragraph 13). See also *Marguerite Johnston v. Chief Constable of the Royal Ulster Constabulary* (Case 222/84) ECR 1986, p. 01651, paragraph 18 (in the context of the right to an effective judicial remedy).

9 In the context of (European) administrative law (*inter alia*) Haibach has referred to so-called '*wertender Rechtsvergleich*' ('evaluative comparative law [approach]'; MG) as a method adopted by the ECJ with a view to filling perceived lacuna in Community law. This means that the Court when interpreting EC law has sometimes made excursions into the (common) constitutional or legal traditions of the Member States. See Haibach 1998, p. 456.

10 See also the Court's judgments in *Nold* and *Johnston* (referred to in footnote 8 above) in which the ECJ explicitly referred to, respectively, 'international Treaties for the Protection of Human Rights (...) [which] can supply guidelines which should be followed within the framework of Community law' (paragraph 13), and to the 'European Convention for the Protection of Human Rights and Fundamental Freedoms (...)'. According to the ECJ in *Johnston* '(...) the principles on which that Convention is based must be taken into consideration in Community Law' (paragraph 18).

the world), for otherwise there is the risk of producing a speculative overview of 'cross-fertilisation'. The mere conclusion that there is a congruity in the regulation of 'equality' and 'non-discrimination' by two or three different jurisdictions is arguably insufficient to validate definite conclusions on the question of 'cross-fertilisation'. This congruity may indeed have been influenced by other factors, for instance by developments in U.S. or international law. In summary, even if it is possible to discern forms of mutual influence between the legal systems covered in this book (i.e. the EU, English and Dutch legal systems),[11] it would not be academically justifiable to extrapolate this information to the much wider question of 'cross-fertilisation'. Secondly, an analysis of 'cross-fertilisation' between legal norms and approaches to their interpretation can arguably not be limited to a bare *legal* analysis. The latter would need to be complemented by a research into the political context of the legal systems concerned. Notably, a detailed study into the processes of political lobbying and negotiation that led to the enactment of equal treatment law at both the EC and the domestic levels would be required. Arguably, a combined legal-political analysis, which would include the provision of 'contextual evidence' (i.e. evidence stemming from e.g. Council minutes, government consultation papers or interviews with government officials), would help us understand better the precise nature of 'cross-fertilisation'.[12] Thirdly, in the particular context of EC equal treatment law, an analysis of 'cross-fertilisation' issues would arguably require a profound study into EC nationality discrimination law. As will become clear in section 4 hereafter, nationality discrimination law falls, however, outside the scope of this book.[13] Suffice it to note that 'nationality' (Article 12 EC) and 'sex' (Article 141 EC) are the sole grounds of discrimination that have been regulated in EC law since 1957, when the then called EEC Treaty[14] was signed. The well-known reason for the early regulation of these two grounds is that they show a close connection with internal market law.[15] Given the early birth of EC nationality discrimination law, it is not unlikely that this will have an arguably great impact on the approach adopted by the ECJ in discrimination cases concerning other grounds of discrimination. This form of influence, however, will not be addressed in further detail throughout this book.

Up until this juncture, I have provided insights into the evolution of the research that led to this book. Hereafter, I will clarify in further detail its *raison d'être*, including the practical and academic objectives that it pursues. In section 2, I will define in exact terms the five research questions this book seeks to address. From these it will become more clear in what respects this book can be distinguished from other works in the areas of equality and non-discrimination law. In section 3, I will explain the methodology employed in carrying out my analysis. Section 4 will clarify

11 In section 4 hereafter, I will elaborate in detail on the scope and structure of the present book.

12 I am grateful to Dr. Mark Bell for this point.

13 See for further analysis of EC nationality discrimination law the following contributions: Chalmers, Hadjiemmanuil, Monti and Tomkins 2006, Chapter 16; Schneider (ed.) 2005 (with contributions by a number of authors); Bell 2002, Chapter 2.

14 See footnote 22 *infra*.

15 An extensive overview of the evolution of the principles of equality and non-discrimination in the context of *inter alia* EU law will be provided in Chapter 2 hereafter.

the scope of this research and will give a brief outline of every chapter to follow. In section 5, I will outline which socio-political and, notably, which legal factors prompted me to write this book. In that section I will also explain the academic importance of this book.

2. Research Questions and Purposes

As stated, the comparative law analysis of selected issues in equal treatment law is multi-layered. It embraces dimensions that I will refer to as 'top-down', 'cross-country', 'cross-ground' and 'bottom-up' dimensions. In addition, EC and domestic equal treatment law will be perceived in light of relevant ECHR law, although the latter will not be explored in an exhaustive fashion.[16] At the basis of the multi-facetted comparative exercise are three major research-questions, but also two minor ones that the book addresses. To start with the three major research-questions, they are the following:

1. If, and in what respects has the process of constitutionalisation of equality and on-discrimination in EC law forced changes in domestic equal treatment law and to what degree has this created shifts in domestic approaches and practices? This question concerns 'top-down' effects that can be evidenced in domestic equal treatment laws when comparing their shape pre-and post-implementation of EC law.
2. To what extent do national legal approaches differ from one another pre- and post-implementation of EC law? This question involves a 'cross-country' comparison of English and Dutch equal treatment law, against the background of supranational equality standards.
3. What are the intrinsic values underlying the different grounds of discrimination that are covered in this book? Do these values differ from one another? If so, what consequences do or should such differences have for the regulatory approach of 'equality' and 'non-discrimination' in relation to these different grounds? ('cross-ground' comparison).

In addition, the following two minor research questions will be addressed at appropriate junctures:

4. Has EC equal treatment law been inspired, or should it be inspired in the future, by (long-standing) national approaches and practices? This question involves a 'bottom-up' analysis of EC equal treatment law in light of domestic law ('bottom-up comparison').

16 The reasons for this will be clarified at the outset of Part IV entitled 'Stretching the Scope of Non-Discrimination and Equality Law'.

5. If and in what respects could EC and domestic equal treatment law draw inspiration from the fundamental rights approach adopted by the Strasbourg Court in the context of the ECHR (and *vice versa*)?[17]

The analysis of the above research questions serves both academic (theoretical) and practical purposes. The academic purpose is foremost to map the dynamics of the exercise of comparative law in the EU multi-level system. In this book this aspect will be scrutinised from the specific angle of anti-discrimination and equality law. The practical purposes are essentially three-fold. First, this book gives a detailed and analytical overview of the current state of EC anti-discrimination and equality law in selected subject-areas. Secondly, it analyses the modus of implementation of EC equal treatment law by domestic governments as well as the question of whether implementation has correctly occurred. Thirdly, this book provides critical insights into different approaches, practices and interpretations in respect of the legal principles of equality and non-discrimination at a number of different levels. As such it can provide guidance to law and policy-makers, as well as to (semi) judicial bodies, including the ECJ, when interpreting equality and non-discrimination as legal principles. In a more general fashion this book seeks to enrich the minds of all others who have an interest in equality and non-discrimination, including legal practitioners, academics and students.

3. Methodology

The methodology adopted is that of comparative law.[18] The research questions mentioned above all involve a comparative exercise, albeit at different (intertwined) levels. The 'top-down', 'cross-country', and 'bottom-up' comparisons, as well as the comparison between both EC and domestic approaches with Strasbourg Convention law are captured by the analytical task comparative lawyers traditionally perform, namely comparing different legal systems.[19] In light of the classical doctrine of supremacy,[20] which stipulates that EC law takes precedence over domestic law unless the latter falls outside the scope of the former, 'top-down' influence is largely obligatory in kind. In other words, the Member States are required to bring national equality and

17 For reasons to be explained at the outset of Part IV this research question will merely be addressed in Chapters 6 and 7.

18 For a sound analysis of what is meant by comparative law and of its various aims and functions, I refer to the classical work by Zweigert & Kötz 1998. See moreover, Kahn-Freund 1974.

19 Zweigert & Kötz 1998, p. 4: 'Comparative lawyers compare the legal systems of different nations.' Although the EU can and must not be equated with a 'nation' there is nothing which precludes the EU from being captured by a comparative law analysis. This applies *eo ipso* to the law which has emerged under the auspices of the Council of Europe, notably the law contained in the ECHR.

20 See the early and ground breaking judgments by the ECJ in *Van Gend & Loos (NV Algemene Transporten Expeditie Onderneming) v. Nederlandse Administratie der Belastingen* (Case 26/62) [1963] ECR 1, which established the principle of 'direct effect' of Community law and in *Costa (Flaminio) v. ENEL* (Case 6/64) [1964] ECR 585 in which the Court established the doctrine of supremacy.

non-discrimination law into conformity with EC law. Besides, the domestic legislator or judge may decide to adopt the 'Community' solution even to a matter of national law where, from a Community law perspective, he is not under an obligation to do so. Hence, 'top down' influence can also be the result of a discretionary choice. Mapping 'top-down' influence presupposes a comparison between EU and national law on a given subject matter in a given policy area.

The 'cross-country' comparison essentially seeks to reveal different national solutions, approaches and practices pre- and post-implementation of the relevant norms of contemporary EC equality law. Indeed, even post-implementation of EC law, the common overarching objectives of EC equality and non-discrimination law, especially those contained in equality Directives, can be achieved by the Member States in different ways, without however transcending what is permitted by Community law.[21] It should be noted that EC Directives are binding as to the legal result to be achieved with their transposition into domestic law. *How* to implement a Directive is largely a matter for the Member States to decide. In light of this, domestic approaches can show divergent patterns notwithstanding that they develop under the wings of Community law.

The 'bottom-up' comparison reflects the opposite effect of the 'top-down' comparison, given that it seeks to discern a possible influence of national law upon both the development and interpretation of EC law. As stated earlier, drawing the 'bottom-up' comparison will be done to a limited extent only. It is submitted that a fully-fledged analysis of bottom-up influence would call for a concise knowledge of the anti-discrimination frameworks of all EC Member States which, needless to say, would go beyond the scope of a Ph.D. research. Therefore, 'bottom-up' influence will be illustrated in an anecdotal fashion only and no aspirations will be made to be complete, firm and all-inclusive. At appropriate junctures throughout this book, I will pay attention to if and in what ways EC equality law has or could be inspired by domestic models.

With respect to the comparison of EC and ECHR law in Chapters 6 and 7 it is vital to note that the current EC anti-discrimination and equality '*acquis*' reflects more than ever a 'constitutionalised' approach. The parameters of this approach will be elaborated in detail in Chapter 2. Suffice it to say here that it is not unlikely that EC equal treatment law will increasingly pay attention to established case law by the Strasbourg Court in comparable cases (and *vice versa*).

In contrast to the foregoing four comparative exercises, the 'cross-ground' comparison does not involve a comparison of legal systems but rather one of the intrinsic character underpinning different grounds of discrimination, e.g. religion, age or disability. In this sense, it falls outside the exercise of 'comparative law' in the conventional meaning of the word. Nonetheless, carrying out the cross-ground comparison is a valuable exercise, given that the conclusions with respect to this part of the research form an important benchmark for the considerations that the law should take into account when concerned with a particular ground of discrimination. In other words, the cross-ground comparison sheds light on the question whether or not

21 See Article 249 EC.

'equality' requires the adoption of different legal approaches for different grounds of discrimination. The conclusions with respect to this aspect of the research will be related to the EC anti-discrimination framework, as well as to the legal frameworks of the Member States.

4. Scope and Structure

With a view to providing answers to the above research questions the *modus operandi* will be the following. In this book I will analyse issues of equality and non-discrimination in respect of eight discrimination grounds, namely *sex, racial and ethnic origin, religion and belief, disability, age* and *sexual orientation*. These grounds are contained in Article 13 EC[22] which, as will be explained in section 5 to follow, has formed the legal impetus for this research. Rather than being all-inclusive, this book adopts an *illustrative* approach. Each of the research questions formulated above will be examined with reference to (1) a selected number of key issues which are relevant in the area of equality and non-discrimination law, (2) a selected number of legal systems and (3) a specific policy area (i.e. employment). This is a legitimate way of working not only for the obvious reasons of space and time but also, and more critically, in light of the approach adopted in this book, namely analysing substantive issues of equality and non-discrimination on the basis of a multi-layered comparison. Therefore, with a view to drawing conclusions on the above research questions, it will not be necessary to provide for an exhaustive analysis of all relevant aspects of EC and domestic equality law.

With respect to the choice of legal systems the following should be said. The book is limited to the legal systems of the Netherlands, England[23] and the EU. The choice of these instead of other legal systems can be rationalised as follows. The choice of the EU is self-explanatory, not only in light of the legal and socio-political impetus[24] for this book, but also because of the supranational character of EU/EC law and the precedence it takes over domestic law.[25] Supranational Community law constitutes a vital marker of the analysis of (notably) 'top-down' influence. The Dutch legal system is examined not only for practical reasons (the author being a Dutch lawyer) but, moreover, in light of long-standing experiences in the Netherlands with issues regarding equality and non-discrimination. Given that Dutch equal treatment law is comparatively mature it could serve as an example for other jurisdictions.

22 Consolidated version of the Treaty establishing the European Community, 10 November 1997, [1997] *OJ* C 340/3. The Treaty had been adopted in its original format in 1957 when it was still called the EEC Treaty (Treaty establishing the European Economic Community, 25 March 1957, 298 U.N.T.S. 11 (also known as the 'Rome Treaty').

23 It is stressed that only English law will be considered and thus not United Kingdom law. Hence, the analysis excludes the law of Northern Ireland and Scotland which in the areas of equality and non-discrimination differs from the English approach in various (important) respects.

24 The socio-political impetus for this research project will be explained in further detail in section 5 hereafter.

25 See footnote 20 *supra*.

This is all the more the case, given that Dutch equal treatment law has evolved in a constitutional law context and therefore embeds a fundamental rights approach. The choice of the law of England has been inspired by various facts. Firstly, like the Netherlands, England has a well-established equality framework (at least in respect of a number of (selected) discrimination grounds) which could set examples (good and bad ones) for others. Furthermore, a comparison with English law is interesting for the following reason: the English anti-discrimination framework has essentially developed in the context of industrial and labour law relations, rather than within a framework of constitutional law (given the absence of a written Constitution in England).[26] This contrasts with the Dutch model which reflects a 'balancing exercise' of various constitutional rights and freedoms, including the right to equality and non-discrimination.[27] The English model also contrasts with current trends in EU law which, I argue, increasingly reflect the 'constitutionalisation' of 'equality' and 'non-discrimination' as general principles of EU law. It is acknowledged that the classical distinction in legal families, i.e. 'civil law' *v.* 'common law' has been less at a premium in the context of this book, which essentially focuses upon statutory anti-discrimination law. It therefore should be observed that the Common Law might only bear an impact upon those fields of equality and non-discrimination which are not governed by statutory Acts of Parliament or by Regulations enacted by the government.[28] However, as will become clear in Chapter 2, all aspects of discrimination that will be addressed in this book have indeed been regulated within either a Statutory Act or a Regulation. Thus, English equality and non-discrimination law has been instigated by the legislator rather than the courts and has predominantly been moulded by statutory instruments which (like in the Netherlands) are subject to judicial interpretation. A last point which has been important in the choice of legal systems is that both Dutch and English law appear to have had a rather strong influence upon the shaping of contemporary EC equality law.[29]

This book is limited to the area of employment. This should, however, not be taken to mean that it is about employment. It means that the various themes and concepts of equality and non-discrimination law are illustrated, where appropriate, in the context of employment to the exclusion of other policy areas. Employment has been the area in which the Community's competence to act is least contested (in comparison with for example, education, health care or the realm of social security) and it is the only area which is covered both by the Article 13 EC 'Race Directive'[30] and the 'Employment Framework Directive'.[31] Moreover, and not least, discrimination in the labour market is still widespread and being at work is a (if not the

26 Fredman 2003, p. 202.

27 Goldschmidt 2003, p. 105.

28 See McColgan 2001, p. 215-241, especially p. 218-224 with further references; Jowell 1994, p. 1-18 (with a particular focus on the role of Equality and the English unwritten Constitution).

29 See also Geddes and Guiraudon 2004, who have argued that the EC race equality law has received 'strong Anglo-Dutch intellectual influences' (p. 341) and that 'an anti-discrimination Directive [was adopted] with a distinct Anglo-Dutch flavour' (p. 350).

30 See section 5 hereafter and footnote 48.

31 See section 5 hereafter and footnote 49.

most) crucial factor in fostering a sense of social inclusion and cohesion for under-represented groups.[32]

Hereafter, I will present my analysis as follows. For easy reference the book has been divided into 5 constituent Parts each of which contains one or more chapters. Part I (Setting the Scene) contains this introductory chapter and Chapter 2, the purpose of which is to sketch the necessary background information on the anti-discrimination frameworks in the three legal systems considered. This will include a number of theoretical observations, which help us grasp the evolution of the principles of equality and non-discrimination in the three legal systems considered. In Part II (Concepts of Discrimination) I will analyse two important concepts which present themselves generally in the realm of equality and non-discrimination law. Hence, Chapter 3 analyses the concept of 'indirect discrimination' whereas Chapter 4 examines the legal intricacies of 'harassment'. A selection has been made to confine these two chapters to the discrimination grounds 'race', 'sex' and 'disability'. The concept of direct discrimination will not be analysed in an in-depth fashion but will be addressed briefly at the outset of Part II, as well as in the analyses of Chapters 3 and 4. 'Direct discrimination', unlike 'indirect discrimination' and 'harassment' is a less recent and far less contentious concept. This is one reason why it has not been prioritised for a comprehensive examination in Part II. Moreover, and as will be illustrated in greater detail in Chapter 3, the way in which 'indirect discrimination' has been formulated in modern EC equal treatment law has eroded the theoretical premises of the concept. As far as harassment is concerned, it is interesting to note that the introduction of this concept in contemporary EC law has diminished the so-called 'comparative' approach to the principle of equality in favour of a freestanding approach to justice. This correlates with the 'constitutionalised' approach to equality and non-discrimination that is apparent in current EC equal treatment law and that will be examined in more detail in Chapter 2. Part III (Proactive Strategies) looks at positive strategies employed in the quest for equality. This Part consists of Chapter 5 which seeks to analyse positive action as a tool for realising equality in practice. In Part IV (Stretching the Scope of Non-Discrimination and Equality Law), I will make separate analyses of discrimination on the following grounds: 'religion and belief' (Chapter 6), 'sexual orientation' (Chapter 7), 'disability' (Chapter 8) (which will *inter alia* examine the concept of 'reasonable accommodation') and 'age' (Chapter 9). Although 'race' and 'sex' will be referred to, no separate studies will be made of these two grounds of discrimination. This exclusion is justified in view of the following. In the first place, in all three jurisdictions scrutinised, i.e. the EC, English and Dutch legal system, 'sex' is a classic ground of discrimination that has traditionally received great attention in academic analysis, particularly in the context of employment and

32 Recital No. 9 of the Employment Framework Directive which prohibits discrimination on a number of grounds in the area of employment provides as follows: 'Employment and occupation are key elements in guaranteeing equal opportunities for all and contribute strongly to the full participation of citizens in economic, cultural and social life and to realising their potential.'

occupation.[33] A further analysis could not substantially add to the academic discussion. Secondly, while 'race' and 'ethnicity' (as well as 'sex') were the only grounds of discrimination that had been regulated in *both* English *and* Dutch law pre-implementation of the RD and EFD, and while admittedly, in the context of EC law, race discrimination law is novel and has only existed since 2000, the regulation of 'race' and 'ethnicity' (as well as 'sex') in supranational equality law goes far beyond 'employment'. An effective and inclusive analysis of EC race discrimination law therefore calls for a separate research project that extends the limits of the present one. Part V (Concluding Observations) consists of Chapter 10 in which answers will be given to the research questions formulated above. This Part will also include a synthesis analysis, the aim of which will be to present an overview of the various values underlying different discrimination grounds. This will be instrumental to answering the question whether equality calls for different legal approaches for different target groups.

The foregoing chapter indication shows that no distinct theoretical analysis will be presented on the principles of equality and non-discrimination. In many legal analyses on equality and non-discrimination a theoretical overview or framework is provided prior to the discussion of substantive aspects.[34] In contrast, I have opted to interlace theoretical comments with the various substantive analyses. Such an integrated approach has the advantage that a given theoretical notion of equality is immediately tied up with the substantive aspect to which that notion fits best. In addition to paying attention to the theory of equality and non-discrimination, I will moreover look at theoretical issues and models which present themselves in the context of the various discrimination grounds considered. This will *eo ipso* be done in an intertwined fashion.

5. The Legal and Socio-Political Impetus for this Research

It does not appear an exaggeration to hold that but for the adoption of Article 13 EC, introduced by the Treaty of Amsterdam (ToA),[35] the current book would not have been written, at least not in its present format. Article 13(1) EC provides as follows: 'Without prejudice to the other provisions of this Treaty and within the limits of the powers conferred by it upon the Community, the Council, acting unanimously on a proposal from the Commission and after consulting the European Parliament, may take appropriate action to combat discrimination based on sex, racial or ethnic origin,

33 See, for example, Ellis 1998; Hervey and O'Keeffe (eds.) 1996 (with contributions by a number of authors).

34 Other works are wholly centred on theoretical issues regarding (*inter alia*) equality and non-discrimination. See notably Rawls 1971; Dworkin 2000; Raz 1986 (Chapter 9); Sen 1992; Loenen 1992.

35 Treaty of Amsterdam amending the Treaty on European Union, the Treaties establishing the European Communities and certain related acts, 2 October 1997, [1997] *OJ* C. 340/1. The ToA entered into force on 1 May 1999.

religion or belief, disability, age or sexual orientation'.[36] Article 13 EC introduces for the first time in the history of the EU an explicit legal basis upon which the Community legislator can act with a view to combating discrimination on the listed grounds.[37] Some authors have labelled Article 13 EC as a potential 'harbinger of change'[38] and as a 'vanguard' moment in the constitutionalisation of equality at EU level.[39] I will argue that Article 13 EC is of great importance in shaping a human rights dimension to 'equality' in the context of EU law.[40] Currently, EU equality provisions denote a moral human rights-based character quite detached from the economic and market-based rationales which have traditionally featured EC equality law in the context of sex and nationality.[41] This submission can be substantiated with reference to the following. First, and most recently, in the (to equal treatment lawyers) well-known judgment of *Mangold v. Helm*[42] the ECJ buttressed the ethical rationale underlying the principle of equality by holding that the 'principle of non-discrimination on grounds of age must be regarded as a general principle of Community law'. In casu this meant that Mr Mangold could directly rely upon this 'meta-legal' principle against Mr Helm in a private party dispute. Secondly, the constitutional dimension of equality is reflected by the large list of grounds which features in Article 13 EC. Thirdly, it is mirrored by the increased attention which equality as a principle has been receiving from the Commission, the Council, the Parliament, the ECJ and academics in recent times.[43] Fourthly, evidence for an increasingly constitutionalised approach to equality can be found in the adoption of Article II-81 of the Treaty establishing a Constitution for Europe notwithstanding that the process of ratification of the Treaty was thwarted by domestic referenda in the Netherlands and France.[44] Article II-81 contains a general anti-discrimination clause in respect of a wide range of

36 It is noted that Article 13 EC as introduced by the ToA consisted of only 1 paragraph. However, it was complemented by a second paragraph by the Treaty of Nice. The second paragraph reads as follows: 'By way of derogation from paragraph 1, when the Council adopts Community incentive measures, excluding any harmonisation of the laws and regulations of the Member States, to support action by the Member States in order to contribute to the achievement of objectives referred to in paragraph 1, it will act in accordance with the procedure referred to in Article 251'. Hence, 'incentive measures' can be taken via the procedure of co-decision enshrined in Article 251 EC.

37 Article 13 EC also includes the ground sex. Only with regard to this ground did the Treaty already contain a legal basis, namely Article 141 EC (old Article 119 EC).

38 Waddington, 1999.

39 Somek 1999. Others have discerned a trend towards a constitutionalisation of EU labour law in the wider sense, see for example Barnard 1997a, p. 275.

40 Also McColdrick 1999, p. 253.

41 This argument does not hold true for that area of Community non-discrimination law which deals with the prohibition of discriminatory measures in the areas of the free movement of goods (Articles 28 and 29 EC, old Articles 30 and 34 EC) and services (Article 49 EC, old Article 59 EC). These aspects of European non-discrimination law, as well as non-discrimination provisions applied to producers and consumers in the agricultural field (Article 34(2) EC, old Article 40(3) EC) fall entirely outside the scope of this book.

42 *Mangold v. Helm* (Case C-144/04) of 22 November 2005 available at <www.europa.eu.int>. The constitutional implications of this case will be considered in great detail in Chapter 9.

43 I am grateful to Professor Lisa Waddington for this point.

44 Schmidt 2005, p. 519.

grounds. The gradual shift in EC law from equality as a principle intrinsic to 'market-based' strategies to a constitutional principle seeking greater moral justice for members of disadvantaged groups will be illustrated in further detail in Chapter 2.

It follows that prior to the adoption of Article 13 EC, discrimination on grounds other than sex and nationality was more or less overlooked at the supranational level of the EC. The protection by EC law against nationality and sex discrimination has been largely characterised by a formalistic and economically inspired approach.

The situation at the supranational level differed from the state of affairs at the domestic level. Indeed, when I started writing this book the legal orders of the then 15 Member States of the EU contained provisions regarding the principles of equality and non-discrimination, although the scope and degree of enforceability diverged from one Member State to the other.[45] Moreover, equality and non-discrimination provisions have long been contained in international human rights documents, including the ECHR and the International Covenant for Civil and Political Rights (ICCPR). Therefore, prior to the adoption of Article 13 EC national and international legal instruments constituted the principal tools to combat discrimination and to foster equality. The fact that in current times this situation has fundamentally changed in part explains the interest for this research.

Article 13 EC is not a generic supranational anti-discrimination clause which is directly effective in the same fashion as are Article 12 EC (on nationality discrimination) and Article 141 EC (on sex discrimination).[46] Article 13 EC rather functions as a judicial basis upon which the Community legislator can act within the limits set by the Article itself. Article 13 EC is therefore an 'enabling clause' rather than an autonomous provision capable of conferring rights without more ado. When I started writing this book four measures had been adopted already on the basis of Article 13 EC: (1) a communication on certain Community measures to combat discrimination;[47] (2) Council Directive 2000/43/EC of 29 June 2000 implementing the principle of equal treatment between persons irrespective of racial or ethnic origin[48] (henceforth: the RD (Race Directive); (3) Council Directive 2000/78/EC of 27 November 2000 establishing a general framework for equal treatment in employment and occupation[49] (henceforth: the EFD (Employment Framework Directive); (4) and a Council decision establishing a Community action programme to combat discrimination 2001-

45 See for an overview the following report by the European Commission *Report on Member States' legal provisions to combat discrimination,* European Commission DG Employment and Social Affairs, 2000.

46 See, however, the recent judgment by the ECJ in *Mangold v. Helm* (Case C-144/04) of 22 November 2005 available at <www.europa.eu.int> in which the ECJ seems to have accorded *'de facto'* direct effect to Article 13 EC. This argument will be taken further in Chapter 9 concerning discrimination on grounds of age.

47 COM (1999) 564 final.

48 Council Directive 2000/43/EC of 29 June 2000 implementing the principle of equal treatment between persons irrespective of racial or ethnic origin, *OJ* L 180/22, 19 July 2000.

49 Council Directive 2000/78/EC of 27 November 2000 establishing a general framework for equal treatment in employment and occupation, *OJ* L 303/16, 02 December 2000.

2006.[50] Moreover, the Article 13 EC *acquis* currently comprises Council Directive 2004/113/EC of 13 December 2004 implementing the principle of equal treatment between men and women in the areas of access to and supply of goods and services.[51] The Article 13 EC Race and Framework Directive, on the one hand, have been inspired by the existing sex equality acquis and, on the other, have exercised a positive influence upon that *acquis*. Indeed, existing EC sex equality law has been 'streamlined' in light of the guarantees contained in the RD and EFD. This has been achieved by the adoption of Directive 2002/73/EC[52] which has amended Directive 76/207/EEC[53] (henceforth: AETD (Amended Equal Treatment Directive).[54] The RD prohibits discrimination on grounds of race and ethnicity in a wide range of areas of social life, including employment. The EFD and AETD prohibit, respectively, discrimination in employment on grounds of religion and belief, disability, age and sexual orientation, and discrimination on grounds of sex in employment. At the start of this research, implementation of these Directives had yet to occur, whereas they have currently been transposed into both Dutch and English law.[55] Moreover, case law by the ECJ and by domestic (semi)judicial bodies has emerged. Both developments allow for reflections on different approaches and on the way in which the new legal framework is applied and interpreted in concrete cases that have reached the courts. This book is among the first to consider issues of equality and non-discrimination on the basis of the multi-layered comparative exercise described earlier. As such it will hopefully be a source of inspiration to all with an interest in equality and non-discrimination law.

50 EC Council Decision 2000/750 of 27 November 2000 establishing a Community Action Programme to combat discrimination (2001-2006), [2000] *OJ* L 303/23. The Action Programme's objectives are essentially three-fold: 1. Increased comprehension of issues related to discrimination; 2. developing the capacity to tackle discrimination effectively and, 3. the promotion of the values underlying the fight against discrimination. For further information on the main purposes of the Action Programme I refer to 'Gelijkheid en non-discriminatie', Jaarrapport 2003. This report is available (both in Dutch and in English) at <http://europa.eu.int/comm/employment_social/fundamental_rights/public/pubst_en.htm#annual>.

51 *OJ* L 373, of 21 December 2004. This Directive will not be covered but is merely mentioned here for purposes of completeness.

52 Council Directive 2002/73/EC of 23 September 2002, *OJ* L 269/15, 23 September 2002.

53 Directive 76/207/EEC on Equal Treatment for Men and Women as regards Access to Employment, Vocational Training and Promotion and Working Conditions, *OJ* 1976, L 39/40.

54 The 'AETD' thus refers to Council Directive 76/207/EEC as amended by Council Directive 2002/73/EC of 23 September 2002 *OJ* L 269/15, 23 September 2002. Mention should moreover be made of the so-called 'Recast Directive', Directive 2006/54/EC of the European Parliament and of the Council of 5 July 2006 on the implementation of the principle of equal opportunities and equal treatment of men and women in matters of employment and occupation, *OJ* L 204/23. This Directive consolidates the provisions of the existing EC sex equality directives, including established case law by the ECJ, into a single text.

55 With the exception of the ground 'age' as far as English law is concerned. The English implementing legislation with respect to this ground will only take legal force on October 1 2006.

Chapter 2

PLACING EQUALITY LAW IN CONTEXT

1. Introduction

Hereafter, I will give a general account of the evolution of the anti-discrimination and equality law frameworks of the EU, the Netherlands and England and of the present state of affairs, including any particularities and specifics, in each of these legal systems. This will be done in sections 2 till 4 respectively hereafter. My aim will not be to present an extensive and in-depth overview of the historical developments of equality in the respective legal systems concerned.[1] However, providing some insights into the evolution of 'equality' and 'non-discrimination' in the legal systems considered appears to be of value in light of the following. Firstly, it helps us explain why certain grounds of discrimination are and others are not covered by the legal framework in a particular jurisdiction. Secondly, the historical and socio-political context helps us understand why, for example, anti-discrimination law in the context of the EC was initially merely embedded within the economic framework of market-integration, whilst in the Netherlands the principles of equality and non-discrimination have traditionally reflected a constitutional value and why, in England, these principles have been moulded in the context of labour law. The aim of this chapter will be to outline different developments in the respective legal systems concerned. This is necessary for a sound comprehension of the themes to be analysed in the remainder of this book.

1 For a historical account of equality and the rights of minority groups, I refer to the following: Heirbout 2002, p. 13-30; in the context of English law I refer to the excellent and classic analysis by Lester and Bindman, 1972, notably part I. For historical perspectives of discrimination against women, I refer to Fredman 1997a, notably Chapters 2 and 3.

2. Equality and Non-Discrimination in the Context of EU Law

2.1. *From Early Economic Sex Equality Ideals to Equality as a Rights-Based Value*

The introduction of Article 13 EC and the subsequent adoption of the RD[2] and the EFD[3] heralded a new stage in EU equality law which arguably strengthened the 'constitutionalisation' of the principles of equality and non-discrimination at the supranational level. The adoption of binding provisions which prohibit discrimination on grounds of race and ethnicity (RD) and religion, belief, disability, age and sexual orientation (EFD) mirrors a constitutional novelty in EU law and finally meets long-standing and widely voiced critiques regarding the absence in Community law of legal measures to combat discrimination on these grounds.[4] The constitutional dimension of equality is reinforced *inter alia* by the (non-binding) Charter of Fundamental Rights of the EU[5] which contains a separate Chapter on Equality (Articles 20-26 of the Charter) and which provides in Article 1 that 'human dignity is inviolable [and that it; MG] must be respected and protected'.

The stark absence, until the ToA, of EC competence in the above-mentioned areas contrasts with the long-standing commitment by the Community in securing equal opportunities and equal treatment between the sexes. Indeed, the old Article 119 EC (i.e. current Article 141 EC), which seeks to secure equal pay between women and men, was inserted into the Rome Treaty at the dawn of the integration project.[6]

2 Council Directive 2000/43/EC of 29 June 2000 implementing the principle of equal treatment between persons irrespective of racial or ethnic origin, *OJ* L 180/22, 19 July 2000 ('Race Directive').

3 Council Directive 2000/78/EC of 27 November 2000 establishing a general framework for equal treatment in employment and occupation, *OJ* L 303/16, 02 December 2000 ('Employment Framework Directive').

4 These critiques have mainly and initially focused upon the absence in Community law of legal measures directed at outlawing racial discrimination and xenophobia. In this context mention is to be made of the 1995 Final Report written by the Consultative Commission on Racism and Xenophobia (known as the 'Kahn Commission') which was established at the European Council in Corfu in 1994 (See Final Report 6906/95 Rev 1 Limite Raxen 24 p. 1-64). In this report the Ad hoc Working Party on Treaty Amendment and Institutional Questions, which formed part of the Kahn Commission, reached the conclusion that '(...) amendment of the Treaty to provide explicitly for Community competence must be regarded as an essential element in any serious European strategy aimed at combating racism and xenophobia'. I am grateful to Professor K. Groenendijk for providing me with this report. For further analysis on the specific matter of race, ethnicity and religious discrimination in EU law, I refer to Gearty 1999, p. 327-358.

5 Charter of Fundamental Rights of the European Union, Solemn Proclamation by the Presidents of the European Parliament, the European Commission and the Council of Ministers, Nice, 7 December 2000, [2000] *OJ* C364/1. Detailed information, including the text of the Charter, can be found at <http://www.europarl.eu.int/charter/default_en.htm> (last visited on 15-04-06). The Charter is non-binding and forms an integral part of the Treaty establishing a Constitution for Europe ([2004] *OJ* C310/1) which has, however, not entered into force. See for an analysis of equality and the EU Constitution, Bell 2004a, p. 242-260.

6 For background information to the origins of Article 119 EC I refer to Deakin 1996, p. 63-93; Barnard 1996a, p. 321-334.

On the basis of Article 119 EC a wide range of sex equality measures have been enacted which will not all be elaborated upon.[7] However, and this is well-known, Article 119 EC must not be perceived against any background of seeking greater social and moral justice for women.[8] It was therefore far detached from an ethical cause. In light of the economic nature, intrinsic to the project of European integration in the 1950s, the Community's concern over matters of sex equality was chiefly rationalised by economic reasons of competition in the internal market.[9] The economic rationale for equality has meant that the Community's engagement in this field has been limited in, at least, three inter-related respects. Firstly, EC level intervention

7 It should be noted that EC sex equality law has been elaborated upon in numerous legislative measures, both in the realm of employment and in the area of social security. The principle of equal pay between the sexes is contained in Article 141 EC and Directive 75/117/EC on Equal Pay for Men and Women, *OJ* 1975, L 45/19; sex equality in employment is regulated in Directive 76/207/EEC on Equal Treatment for Men and Women as regards Access to Employment, Vocational Training and Promotion and Working Conditions, *OJ* 1976, L 39/40. This first 'Equal Treatment Directive' (ETD) has been amended by Directive 2002/73/EC of 23 September 2002, *OJ* 2002, L 269/15 with a view to 'updating' sex equality legislation in light of the standards contained in the RD and EFD. In addition, there is Directive 86/613/EEC on Equal Treatment between Men and Women engaged in an activity, including agriculture, in a self-employed capacity, and on the protection of self-employed women during pregnancy and motherhood, *OJ* 1986, L 359/56. Equal Treatment in social security matters is regulated in the following Directives: Directive 79/7/EEC on Equal Treatment for Men and Women in matters of social security, *OJ* 1979, L6/24 and Directive 86/378/EEC on Equal Treatment for Men and Women in Occupational Social Security Schemes, *OJ* 1986, L 225/40, as amended by Directive 96/97 *OJ* 1997, L 46/20. Lately, on the basis of Article 13 EC, a Directive has been adopted regarding sex equality in the area of goods and service provision (Directive 2004/113/EC of 13 December 2004 implementing the principle of equal treatment between men and women in the access to and supply of goods and services, *OJ* L 373, of 21 December 2004). Most recently, the 'Recast Directive', Directive 2006/54/EC of the European Parliament and of the Council of 5 July 2006 on the implementation of the principle of equal opportunities and equal treatment of men and women in matters of employment and occupation, *OJ* L 204/23, has been adopted. This Directive consolidates the provisions of the existing EC sex equality directives, including established case law by the ECJ, into a single text. Moreover, Council Directive 92/85/EEC on the introduction of measures to encourage improvements in the safety and health at work of pregnant workers and workers who have recently given birth or are breastfeeding (*OJ* 1992, L 348/1) contains special guarantees for pregnant workers. In addition, there is the Parental Leave Directive containing the framework agreement on parental leave concluded by the European Social Partners (i.e. UNICE, CEEP and the ETUC) (Directive 96/34/EC, *OJ* 1996, L 145/4) and the Burden of Proof Directive regarding the burden of proof in cases of discrimination based on sex (Directive 97/80/EC, *OJ* 1998, L 14/6). A concise overview of EC sex equality guarantees is given by Barnard 2001, p. 955-977 under I. See moreover McColgan 2005, p. 19-22.

8 Article 119 (141) EC has been formulated in neutral terms and affords protection from discrimination to both women and men alike. However, as a matter of social reality women, not men, are the disadvantaged category.

9 Indeed, Article 119 EC was inserted into the Rome Treaty at the instigation of France in light of France's high level of labour protection standards. French legislation already contained the principle of equal pay between the sexes and therefore France feared being placed at a competitive disadvantage in the internal market, compared with Member States with low labour protection guarantees. See for example, Barnard 2001, p. 958. Also, Ellis 1998, p. 59-64.

has predominantly been concerned with those grounds of discrimination, namely gender and nationality,[10] which possibly bear an impeding impact upon the aim of market-integration.[11] Thus, writes de Búrca in respect of nationality,

> '(...) The Treaty provisions which embody a rule prohibiting discrimination on grounds of nationality do not seem to be based primarily on the desire to prevent racism or prejudice on ethnic or other arbitrary and exclusionary grounds. They are largely market-integration provisions and thus not inspired principally by the aim of promoting the values of tolerance, diversity or multi-culturalism'.[12]

The limited number of prohibited grounds in the original Treaty contrasts with more extensive lists of grounds in national Constitutions which guarantee protection from discrimination for all groups which have suffered historical disadvantage.[13] Secondly, the fight against discrimination has largely been confined to the realm of employment and employment-related areas (e.g. social security) to the exclusion of other policy areas. Thirdly, the principle of sex equality has been criticised for being applied in a formal, rather than a substantive fashion,[14] although elements of substantive equality are traceable in EC indirect discrimination law.[15] The distinction between formal equality *v.* substantive equality will be clarified throughout this book as a whole. Basically, the principle of formal equality requires the equal treatment of equal cases, without paying attention to material differences. This means in practice that the principle of formal equality is not concerned with the aim of fostering the social inclusion of persons who are members of disadvantaged groups.[16] The principle of formal equality could be understood as being a subset of rationality: it is

10 Article 12 EC (old Article 6 EC).

11 The prohibition of nationality discrimination in Article 12 EC can merely be invoked by those who possess the nationality of one of the EU Member States. It has been an essential tool to facilitate the free movement of workers (Article 39 EC, old Article 48 EC). As such it has been essentially economically inspired. However, the Citizenship provisions of the EC Treaty (i.e. Articles 17-22 EC, introduced by Maastricht) have facilitated moves to transcend the economic interpretation of equality and non-discrimination in relation to nationality. Such moves are for example apparent in the Case of *Martinez Sala v. Freistaat Bayern* (Case C-85-96), [1998] ECR I-2691, discussed *inter alia* by Barnard 1999, p. 375-394 (with further references). Nationality is not enshrined in the list of grounds contained in Article 13 EC and will not be further analysed in the remainder of this book. For further discussion, I refer to d'Oliveira 1999, p. 395-412.

12 De Búrca, 'The role of Equality in European Community Law', in: A. Dashwood and S. O'Leary, *The Principle of Equality in EC Law*, London 1997, p. 27, cited by Alkema & Rop, 2002, p. 62, footnote 122.

13 Barbera 2002, p. 84.

14 Fredman 1992, p. 110-134; More 1993, p. 45; Hervey and Shaw 1998, p. 43.

15 This point will be dealt with in further detail in Chapter 3. It may be worth noting at this juncture that the recognition by EC law of a concept of indirect discrimination simultaneously implies a recognition of the existence of social inequality between members of disadvantaged (e.g. women) and advantaged (e.g. men) groups. Perceived in this way, concerns over substantive inequalities *are* reflected in the case law by the ECJ which, as will be illustrated is, however, primarily concerned with creating equal *opportunities*, rather than equal *outcomes*.

16 For further discussion, I refer to Collins 2003.

irrational, because inconsistent, to treat equal cases unequally in the absence of sound reasons therefore.[17] 'Formal equality' presupposes that 'advantage' is symmetrically spread across society and therefore, formal equality perceives discrimination against (e.g.) men as being as reprehensible as discrimination against women. This approach deviates, however, from the social reality that women are the principal victims of sex discrimination[18] and it is therefore misleading.

In contrast to the principle of formal equality, the principle of substantive equality takes account of material differences between persons and groups of persons. It requires not only the equal treatment of equal cases, but also the unequal treatment of unequal cases. As such it seeks to bring about *de facto* equality, rather than merely equality in form. A substantive equality model takes, e.g. account of the different socio-economic position of women, compared to men, and does therefore not assume that women 'assimilate' to the dominant male standard.[19] For example, the dominant male standard is insensitive to childcare and domestic family responsibilities which tend to be carried out by women.

Another problem with the formal equality paradigm is that it is indifferent to the question whether 'justice' improves or declines.[20] This means that 'formal equality' is achieved, not only where advantage has traditionally been enjoyed by, e.g. whites and is then equally afforded to black persons ('progressive equality') but also, where these advantages are taken away from the white majority, in order to achieve 'consistent treatment' ('regressive equality').[21] Simply put: 'equally well treatment' amounts to formal equality, as well as 'equally bad treatment'.[22] A substantive equality model, in contrast, requires progressive equality.

It follows that the economic cause for EC equality law has resulted in a rather narrow picture of equality which does not receive support from the present author. In terms of models of justice it fits in with what Quinn has called a 'relative, or com-

17 This information was gained in a course organised by the Netherlands Research School of Women's Studies (NOV) coordinated by Professor dr. Magda Michielsens and in which the author participated in March 2004. The 'consistency' aspect of the principle of equality is often cited as the distinguishing criterion between formal *v.* substantive readings of 'equality'. For further analysis, I refer to Gerards 2005 (with numerous references to theoretical studies on the equality principle).

18 More than with any other ground is it difficult to establish who is the oppressed/dominant group in the context of age discrimination. The reason for this is, as observed by Veldman, that with regard to 'age' one may distinguish between many different groups (50+/50-/25+/30-/young people/old people). See Veldman 2003, p. 363.

19 As Barnard concludes with reference to feminist legal literature, '(...) while formal equality requires women to be treated like men it can assist only the minority who are able to conform to the male stereotype' (Barnard 1999, p. 386).

20 Also Fredman 2002, p. 8.

21 See for example *Smith v. Advel* (Case C-408/92) 1994] ECR I-4435 and where the ECJ expressed itself as follows: 'Article 119 of the Treaty does not preclude measures which achieve equal treatment by reducing the advantages of the persons previously favoured' (para. 21 of the judgment). Also, *Barber v. Guardian Royal Exchange Assurance* (Case C-262/88) [1990] ECR I-1889 (cited by Waddington 2005, footnote 113). See moreover Fredman 2002, p. 8.

22 See also *De Weerd* (Case C-343/92) [1994] ECR I-571.

parative approach to justice'.[23] Others have simply called it the 'anti-discrimination model'.[24] In such a model, 'justice' is not absolute, but it is instead perceived to be 'relative to' the degree of justice meted out to another person or group. This is popularly expressed by the Aristotelian dogma that 'likes should be treated alike' which, among others, has been strongly rejected by Westen in his famous Article on the 'empty idea of equality'.[25] In Westen's view, equality is 'empty', for it does not provide for clues or yardsticks which tell us which persons are 'likes' and what treatment is 'like' treatment.[26] Hence, equality remains an empty shell, as long as it remains obscure when or through what features two, or more, persons or cases should be considered equal. Indeed, argues Westen, this is to be determined by external, [substantive; MG] moral values. However, as soon as these values have been found, the principle of equality becomes superfluous.[27] The limits of the 'comparative model of justice' will be illustrated throughout some of the chapters to follow. It is submitted that a single-sided focus upon 'comparability' bears the risk that the various substantive causes of inequality are neglected in the legal analysis.[28]

The formal equality paradigm largely dominates EC, Dutch and English equality law, although, in some respects a substantive justice approach creeps into the legal framework. If the legal framework is premised upon formal equality, this will mean that the approach adopted by the law is essentially 'negatively' oriented. This 'negative' orientation underpins the principle of non-discrimination, whereas a 'positive' orientation underlies the principle of equality. It should be noted that up until the ToA the EC equality and non-discrimination framework had been largely 'negatively' oriented. Little emphasis had been placed upon the need for positive steps with a view to promoting equality in a proactive manner.[29] Proactive approaches will be considered in Chapter 5 and will not be elaborated on in more detail at this juncture.

23 Quinn 2004, p. 9-10.

24 Barbera 2002, p. 83 with reference to the work and classification by G. Calabresi, 'I dirritti fondamentali in quattro tipi di constituzione: quale è il modello americano?', in: M. Bonazzi (ed.), *La Constituzione statunitense* , (Il Mulino, 1988) 232.

25 Westen 1982, p. 537-596.

26 Westen 1982, p. 18: '(…) equality is entirely 'circular'. It tells us to treat people alike; but when we ask who 'like people' are, we are told that they are 'people who should be treated alike'. Westen draws this conclusion by citing the philosophical work by John Locke.

27 Westen, p. 547. Quinn has voiced a similar stance: '(..) it is hard to imagine a purely comparative theory of justice in complete isolation from substance. Substance creeps back into the equation when considering, for example, whether individuals are similarly situated.' (Quinn 2004, p. 9). See in particular also Gerards, who has argued that equal treatment as an instrumental right does not have an autonomous value of its own. She has, however, stressed at the same time that equality does have an added value at a more abstract (meta-legal) level in the sense that the equality principle gives expression to the equal worth and dignity of all, and, that it places an obligation upon the state to treat all persons with equal care and respect. See Gerards 2004, p. 1 and para. 2, footnote 18.

28 See also Prechal 2004, who has characterised the comparative approach as puzzling and who has moreover argued that it weakens the potential of the non-discrimination principle (p. 543-544).

29 Alkema and Rop have in this context drawn the conclusion that the objective of substantive justice is pursued by means of an inappropriate legal framework. Alkema & Rop 2002, p. 36.

The limited ambitions of 'formal equality' have also been mirrored in the ECJ's case law, although sometimes the Court has shown itself to be a proponent of substantive justice. That 'comparability' constitutes a central tenet of EC sex equality law follows from the definition of discrimination by the ECJ. In *Hill & Stapleton* the ECJ defined the concept as follows: 'discrimination can arise only through the application of different rules to comparable situations or the application of the same rule to different situations'[30] [unless the treatment can be justified; MG]. However, as Tobler has stressed correctly, in practice there has been a strong focus upon the first limb of this expression.[31] The second limb has foremost stayed rhetorical.[32] It has only been in very limited circumstances, of which pregnancy constitutes the pivotal example, that the ECJ has departed from the comparative exercise simply by reason that no relevant parallel (men cannot get pregnant!) can be found.[33]

Up until this junction, a particularly narrow vision of 'equality' has been outlined in the context of EC law. It has been argued that a nexus exists between this scant equality ideal, on the one hand, and the economic inspirations which laid behind it in the early decades of Community law, on the other. It is submitted that, once the economic rationale makes room for a 'constitutional and rights based approach',[34] the scope of equality may fundamentally change.[35] Prechal has indicated two factors which are characteristic of a human rights standard and which are useful to mention here: (1) a rights-based standard should offer legal protection in a wide range of situations and to a wide group of persons; (2) the human rights-based standard must be paid particular attention to in cases concerning conflicting rights.[36] If this is taken seriously, it will mean that concerns over human rights have more potential to trump internal-market ideas than has hitherto been the case.[37] Eventually, such an approach would reinterpret the underlying framework to equality. Indeed, the 'relative' approach to justice would make space for, what Quinn has called, the 'deontological' justice model which echoes the tenets of substantive equality.[38]

30 *Hill & Stapleton* (C-243/95), [1998] ECR I-3739 (sex discrimination). A similar vision had already been expressed by the Court in non sex discrimination cases. See *Schumacker* (Case C-279/93) [1995] ECR I-225 (fiscal law), and, *Ruckdeschel & Co* (Joined Cases 117/76 and 16/77), [1977] ECR 1753 (agriculture).

31 Tobler 2003, p. 18.

32 A substantive approach to equality was, e.g. adopted by the ECJ in *Thibault* (Case C-136/95) [1998] ECR I-2011, paragraph 26; *P v. S* (Case C-13/94) [1996] ECR I-2143. See for a more extensive overview, Tobler 2005, p. 28-31.

33 Dekker v. Stichting Vormingscentrum voor Jong Volwassenen (Case C-177/88), [1990] ECR I-3941; Webb v. EMO Air Cargo (Case C-32/93), [1994] ECR I-3567.

34 See for example McCrudden 2003, who observes that 'equality and non-discrimination is, arguably, in the course of being subsumed within a broader human rights discourse' (p. 7).

35 See for a discussion More 1999, p. 517-549.

36 Prechal 2004, p. 547.

37 Also Barbera 2002, who has argued that '(...) fundamental rights cannot [easily MG] be called into question by political or economic processes and [that] the courts are the "bastions" which defend these rights' (p. 83).

38 Quinn 2004, p. 9. Others have named it the substantive rights model. See Barbera 2002, p. 83 and with reference to the work and classification by G. Calabresi, 'I dirritti fondamentali in →

2.2. *Fostering the Ethical Cause for Equality*

In this section a number of developments will be considered which arguably foster the rights-based cause for EC equality law. First, it should be noted that in a number of well-known cases the ECJ has performed as a supranational constitutional adjudicator by recognising the fundamental rights nature of the principle of equality.[39] In *Schröder*[40] the ECJ even took the view that the fundamental rights rationale behind Article 141 EC trumped the economic and competitive goals pursued by that Article.[41] Secondly, the TEU contains a number of Articles relating to more general issues of human rights.[42] Mention should be made of Articles 6, 7 and 46(d) TEU as well as the Preamble to the TEU.[43] Furthermore, since the ToA, the EC Treaty makes specific mention of gender-equality in Articles 2 and 3(2) which have symbolically been placed under Part I of the Treaty entitled 'Principles'. Moreover, it should be noted that the ToA has meant a widening of the EC's competence in employment (Title VIII EC) and social policy (Title VI EC) matters. Both policy areas show clear links with the principle of equality. Article 125 EC (Title VIII) connects 'employment' with the objectives of Article 2 EC which include gender-equality. Article 137 EC (Title XI) states that

> '(...) the Community shall support and complement the activities of the Member States [in inter alia the area of; MG] equality between women and men with regard to labour market opportunities and treatment at work'.

With the adoption of the ToA, Article 141 EC has also been revised. Article 141(4) EC refers to 'ensuring equality in practice' which arguably boosts a substantive underlay to 'equality' to be achieved via the adoption of positive action measures and

quattro tipi di constituzione: quale è il modello americano'?, in: M. Bonazzi (ed), *La Constituzione statunitense* , (Il Mulino, 1988) , 232.

39 See in particular the following cases *Defrenne v. Sabena III* (Case 149/77) [1978] ECR 1365; *P v. S and Cornwall County Council* Case C-13/94 [1996] ECR I-2143. Fredman has argued that the inclusion of discrimination on grounds of trans-sexuality within the notion of 'sex discrimination' was not so much the result of a technically informed judicial exercise but rather marked a development of a 'much wider equality right' reflecting a dignity approach. See Fredman 2002, p. 72. Admittedly, however, the rights-based approach which characterised *P v. S* was not adopted in the later case of *Grant v. South-West Trains* (Case C-249/96)[1998] ECR I-621. In that case it was held that homosexuals could not derive equal treatment rights from EC *sex* equality law. Both cases will be discussed in further detail in Chapter 7.

40 Deutsche Telekom AG v. Lilli Schröder (Case C-50/96)[2000] ECR-I-743.

41 According to the ECJ, and with reference to earlier case law by the Court, '(...) it must be concluded that the economic aim pursued by Article 119 of the Treaty, namely the elimination of distortions of competition between undertakings established in different Member States, is secondary to the social aim pursued by the same provision, which constitutes the expression of a fundamental human right' (paragraph 57 of the judgment).

42 For a recent and more general discussion on human rights protection in the EU I refer to Young 2005, p. 219-240.

43 The preamble states *inter alia* that '[the Member States] [confirm] their attachment to the principles of liberty, democracy and respect for human rights and fundamental freedoms and of the rule of law'.

policies.[44] It is submitted that the introduction of Article 13 EC and the adoption of the RD and the EFD are *primus inter pares* in the process of constitutionalisation of equality. As one commentator has observed:

> 'the inclusion of Article 13 in the EC Treaty (...), and subsequently, the adoption of the two 2000 Directives, are vital elements in [the; MG] process of recognition that equality and non-discrimination are no longer matters related to market integration, despite the fact that there were a number of market-related factors behind the adoption of the directives (...)'.[45]

It should be noted that the Directives see the eradication of discrimination on the basis of personal characteristics. Therefore, discrimination in the areas of, e.g. the free movement of goods, or in the context of EC agricultural law which will not be considered, as this book takes as a starting-point a rights-based approach to equality and non-discrimination. Given their central importance, the RD and the EFD will be elaborated on in detail below. Another important development which should be mentioned in this section is the adoption of the EU Charter of Rights which, although non-binding, clearly denotes the constitutional and fundamental rights aspirations of the Union. Article 21(1) of the Charter provides that

> 'any discrimination based on any ground such as sex, race, colour, ethnic or social origin, genetic features, language, religion or belief, political or any other opinion, membership of a national minority, property, birth, disability, age or sexual orientation shall be prohibited'.

44 For further discussion on the implications of the ToA for gender equality law I refer to Tobler 1998, p. 5-12.

45 Prechal, 2004, p. 550. This vision has been shared by a number of other commentators. See, for example, Waddington 1999, who has observed that '(...) Article 13's inclusion in the Treaty was not primarily prompted by the desire to combat discrimination for economic reasons or to complement the single market. Instead it is part of a trend which is arguably presently reflected more in rhetoric than in reality: to bring Europe 'closer to its citizens'; Bell 2000a, who has noted that 'the theoretical underpinning of Article 13 seems to be a combination of guaranteeing fundamental rights and promoting the evolution of European citizenship' (p. 160); Flynn 1999, who has taken the view that 'Article 13 EC is one of several amendments to the EC and EU Treaties intended to give the protection of human rights a more secure foundation' (p. 1127). Others have, however, disagreed and have stressed the market-based causes for equality in the context of the RD and the EFD. See, for example, Sewandono 2001, who has observed that 'The Directives centralise equality and they are merely preoccupied with socio-economic law' (p. 219). Sewandono has contrasted this approach with the constitutionally inspired approach to equality in the NL; see also McInerney 2000, p. 322-323, cited by McCrudden 2003, p. 11. Yet others have taken a position which lies somewhere in between these two views. See, for example, Szyszczak 1999 who is of the opinion that 'Article 13 remains somewhat of an enigma. At one level it can be hailed as one of the new Constitutional provisions of the Treaty of Amsterdam. At another level, it is something of a disappointment (...) the wording of Article 13 EC limits Community competence to measures which will not prejudice other Treaty provisions and fall within the limits of the powers conferred by the Community' (p. 152).

Arguably, the clarity with which this Article is written stimulates synergies with Article 13 EC and the Directives and with Article 141 EC.[46] Moreover, and importantly, the principle of equality has received increased attention from the Community's institutions over the past years. This is *inter alia* reflected by the creation of special anti-discrimination networks, which at regular intervals report to the European Commission on developments in the anti-discrimination and equality frameworks at the municipal level.[47] This brings us to another point, namely the increased emphasis on the importance of monitoring human rights, including the right to equality and non-discrimination. Of particular importance in this context are the 2004 Commission proposals for the establishment of an EU Fundamental Rights Agency which seeks to extend the mandate of the existing European Monitoring Centre on Racism and Xenophobia (EUMC) based in Vienna, set up by the Union in 1997. In essence, the idea is that this Agency be endowed with the pro-active task of monitoring fundamental rights in the EU and its Member States.[48] In doing so, the Agency would clearly contribute to the ongoing debate on the constitutionalisation of rights in the EU.

46 Indeed, even if Article 21 of the Charter is not binding, strategic lawyers should not hesitate to invoke this Article in cases which arise in the context of Article 13 and 141 EC. Much depends however on the Court's willingness to employ the Charter as a dynamic, interpretative tool while considering anti-discrimination and equality cases which, doubtlessly, will continue to appear before it.

47 Within the framework of the Article 13 EC Action Programme, the Commission quickly established three networks (one for 'race', one for 'sexual orientation' and one for 'disability') of independent experts with a view to reinforcing the link between the Community and the Member States in the area of equality and non-discrimination and with the purpose of optimizing successful implementation of the Directives in the (then) 15 Member States. The various publications produced by the three ground-specific networks can be found at <http://europa.eu.int/comm/employment_social/fundamental_rights/public/pubst_en.htm#annual> (last visited on 15-04-06). Eventually, the three ground-specific networks were merged into a single network covering the 25 Member States of the Union. This single network regularly reports to the Commission of developments in national law with regard to the discrimination grounds covered by Article 13 EC, apart from gender which has its own, distinct, network (see <http://europa.eu.int/comm/employment_social/gender_equality/index_en.html> (last visited on 15-04-06). Mention should, moreover, be made of the European network of specialised bodies which has been set up in light of the requirement imposed upon the Member States by the RD (not the EFD) to create special bodies for the promotion of equal treatment (see <http://europa.eu.int/comm/employment_social/fundamental_rights/public/ pubst_en.htm#annual> (last visited on 15-04-06). With regard to fundamental rights more generally, an EU network on fundamental rights was created by the Commission in 2002 in response to a request by the Parliament to monitor the rights contained in the Charter both in the EU and its Member States. In its present shape it consists of 25 experts, who monitor the protection of fundamental rights across the Member States and by the Union whereby the EU Charter of Rights is taken as the point for departure. See for further information with regard to the last-mentioned point, De Schutter and Alston 2005a, p. 5-6.

48 For further discussion, I refer to Alston and de Schutter 2005.

2.3. *The Article 13 EC 'Acquis' and Novelties in EC Gender Equality Law*

2.3.1. Introductory Remarks

In the preceding section, I have outlined some developments which, it has been argued, mark a 'constitutionalisation' trend of equality in EU law. In this section, I will take a closer look at the Article 13 EC Directives, i.e. the RD and EFD. I will moreover look at the so-called Amended Equal Treatment Directive (AETD).49 Hereafter, I do not intend to make a fully-fledged analysis of every single provision of these Directives, given that this has been done elsewhere.[50] Nor do I intend to sketch the lobbying process,[51] by NGOs, nor the negotiation process,[52] by the political elite, which have led to the adoption of the Directives. Hence, the RD, EFD and AETD will be discussed hereafter to the extent necessary for a sound comprehension of the chapters to follow.

2.3.2. The RD, EFD and AETD: an Overview

2.3.2.1. The RD and the EFD

On the basis of Article 13 EC and notwithstanding the unanimity requirement contained within it, the RD was swiftly adopted on 29 June 2000.[53] The Directive has been characterised by one commentator as being 'one of the most significant pieces of social legislation recently adopted by the EU'.[54] Its importance is *inter alia* reflected in the Directive's broad material scope, which, not only, includes the areas of employment and vocational training, but also social protection, including social security and health care, social advantages, education, access to and supply of goods and services, including housing.[55] The Directive prohibits discrimination on grounds of

49 This refers to Council Directive 76/207/EEC as amended by Council Directive 2002/73/EC of 23 September 2002 *OJ* L 269/15, 23 September 2002.

50 A wealth of academic literature exists on the RD and the EFD and on Article 13 EC itself. See the following selected contributions: Bell 2000, p. 79-84; Bell 1999a, 5-23; Bell 2002; Fitzpatrick and Kilpatrick 2000, p. 416-423; Chopin and Niessen 2001; Guild 2000, p. 65-79; Hailbronner 2001, p. 254-259; Holtmaat 2001, p. 105-124; O'Hare 2001, p. 133-165; Rodrigues 2000, p. 279-284; Skidmore 2001, p. 126-132; Waddington 2000, p. 357-362; Waddington and Bell 2001, p. 587-611; Waddington and Bell 2003, p. 349-369; Whittle 2002, p. 303-326; Schiek 2002, p. 290-314 who has qualified the hierarchy in EC anti-discrimination law as constituting a 'multi-dimensional equality law' (see p. 308 of her Article). The AETD has *inter alia* been analysed by Masselot 2004, p. 93-104. Also, Equal Opportunities Review, 106 June 2002.

51 See Yu and Chopin 2001; Niessen 2001; Bell 2001a.

52 In respect of the RD, this process has been analysed by Tyson 2001, p. 199-229.

53 The speediness with which both the RD and EFD were adopted and the readiness of the governing political elite to afford the RD a very broad material scope can be explained in light of the political situation in Europe at the time and specifically in light of an increased popularity of the 'extreme right' (read: Joerg Haider's Freedom Party) in Austria.

54 Bell 2002a, p. 384.

55 See Article 3 RD, which determines the Directive's material scope of application. However, it follows from the text of Article 13 EC itself that the Community legislator may only act on the →

racial or ethnic origin in the aforementioned policy areas. It should be emphasised, however, that the ground 'nationality' is not covered.[56] The Directive defines discrimination as being one of the following: 'direct discrimination', 'indirect discrimination', 'harassment' and an 'instruction to discriminate' (Article 2 RD). The former two types are known, for they have been shaped already in the context of EC sex and nationality discrimination law. The latter two forms of discrimination are fresh in EC law. 'Harassment' especially reflects a vision of equality, which enshrines elements of the deontological justice model previously referred to. The different types of discrimination are each defined in subsection 2 of Article 2 RD.[57] In contrast, the Directive remains silent on the legal meaning of 'racial or ethnic origin' which means that the meaning of these notions will have to be interpreted by domestic courts and, ultimately, by the ECJ. Presumably, the courts, including the ECJ, will seek recourse to international and domestic interpretations of these concepts. If it does so, this will foster a 'cross-fertilisation' of legal interpretative standards. It should be highlighted that the RD offers protection from discrimination to all persons, who have been discriminated against on grounds of race or ethnic origin, and who reside legally[58] in the EU. In other words, the Directive does not make legal protection dependent upon the requirement of EU citizenship. The RD is modelled along the lines of a so-called 'closed model' of anti-discrimination law which (inter alia) implies that exceptions are listed exhaustively.[59] Provisions on remedies and enforcement

basis of Article 13 EC 'within the limits of the powers conferred by [the EC Treaty] upon the [European] Community.' Hence, instances of discrimination in the areas mentioned in Article 3 RD are covered by the Directive provided that the particular case at hand falls within the scope of EC law.

56 A much criticised Article 3(2) RD provides that the Directive does not cover instances of discrimination on grounds of nationality. The same Article moreover expressly regulates the Directive's inapplicability to provisions and conditions which relate to the entry into and residence of third country nationals (TNCs) and stateless persons on the territory of the Member States and to any treatment which arises from the legal status of these persons.

57 I shall not elaborate on these definitions at this juncture, given that they will be extensively dealt with in Parts II and IV of this book.

58 It should be noted that nothing in the RD and EFD requires *legal* residence. However, since one would have to find a situation in which the Directives apply in the first place, legal residence will arguably be a *de facto* requirement. After all, it will be difficult to imagine a situation in which an illegal immigrant without a work permit could avail him or herself of employment protection and anti-discrimination law standards. Perhaps the applicability of the law might be easier triggered in the context of areas outside the realm of employment (e.g. the area of health) covered by the RD.

59 Another feature of the 'closed' model is that the grounds of discrimination are explicitly and exhaustively mentioned in the legislative instrument concerned. Hence, a 'closed' model leaves considerably less judicial leeway to judicial bodies, compared with an 'open' model, which is characterised by an open-ended list of discrimination grounds and exceptions. In short, the principal actor in a 'closed' model is the legislator, whereas in an 'open' model much of the interpretative work is left to the courts and/or to semi-judicial enforcement bodies. In an open model, both direct and indirect discrimination is susceptible for a general justification defence. See Heringa 1999, p. 25-37. For a discussion of the advantages and disadvantages of both models, I refer to the following sources: Bowers and Moran 2002, p. 307-320; Vegter 2000, p. 118-125; Tobler 2001, p. 121-127; Barnard 1996, p. 70; Ellis 1998, p. 135-136.

are contained in Articles 7-12 RD. It is important to mention the right of associations to engage, either on behalf of, or in support of, the plaintiff and with the latter's approval in judicial and administrative proceedings (Article 7 RD). Moreover, Article 8 RD contains rules regarding the sharing of the burden of proof in anti-discrimination proceedings between the alleged victim and the alleged discriminator. Article 9 RD contains a prohibition against victimisation which seeks to ensure that persons who have complained about discrimination by, e.g. their employer, shall not as a consequence thereof be subjected to discrimination or adverse treatment. It follows from Article 10 RD that information on the guarantees contained within the RD shall be appropriately disseminated by the Member States. Moreover, an active role is set aside for the social partners with a view to fostering equal treatment (Article 11 RD). Lastly, Article 12 seeks to encourage the dialogue between the Member States, on the one hand, and NGOs, who are active in the fight against discrimination, on the other. Of prime relevance for the materialisation of the principle of equal treatment in daily life is Article 13 RD, which obliges the Member States to designate (a) special body(ies) for the promotion of equal treatment. Subsection 2 of this Article specifies that among the competencies of such a body are (i) the provision of independent assistance to victims of discrimination, (ii) conducting independent surveys concerning discrimination and (iii) publishing independent reports and making independent recommendations on any issue relating to such discrimination. It is submitted that in drawing up this provision, the EC legislator has felt inspired by existing domestic approaches. Indeed, both in Britain and in the Netherlands special equality bodies were already in place before the adoption of the Directive.[60] A number of 'Final Provisions' are contained in Articles 14-19 RD including the important requirement that sanctions must be 'effective, proportionate and dissuasive'.

Many things which have, so far, been said in relation to the RD apply *eo ipso* with respect to the EFD. Indeed, upon comparison, one can find many commonalities between the latter and the former. At the same time, one can find material differences. Hence, a number of provisions are merely characteristic for either one of the Directives.[61] In a well-reasoned article in the *Common Market Law Review*, Bell and Waddington explored the important question whether the diverging approaches in the Directives reflect principled causes, or whether these differences merely mirror a confusing legislative stance.[62] It should be noted that one of the factors which can influence the legislative approach to discrimination is the intrinsic nature of the different grounds of discrimination. In other words, the nature of a particular ground (e.g. sex) may call for a particular regulatory approach, which might diverge from the legal approach adopted with regard to another ground (e.g. disability). This point will be elaborated on throughout the book as a whole in the context of the 'cross-

60 Barnard 2001, p. 975. She has argued that Article 13 RD follows the model of the British Commission for Racial Equality.

61 Many commentators have paid attention to a perceived 'hierarchy' in the protective scope offered by Community anti-discrimination law for different grounds of discrimination. See, for example, Flynn 1999, p. 1127-1125.

62 Waddington & Bell, 2001, p. 587-611.

ground' comparison. At this juncture, I will focus upon factual differences and commonalities in the EFD, compared with the RD.

The EFD was adopted on 27 November 2000. It prohibits discrimination on the grounds of religion, belief, disability, age and sexual orientation (Articles 1 and 2 EFD). Once again, these notions are open for interpretation by the courts (and ECJ) which arguably fosters a cross-fertilisation of legal approaches across the EU. In contrast to the RD, the EFD's material scope is confined to employment (Article 3 EFD). Like the RD, the EFD enshrines prohibitions against direct and indirect discrimination, harassment and the instruction to discriminate (Article 2 EFD). In addition, Article 5 EFD imposes upon employers a duty to make reasonable accommodations for disabled persons. As will be clarified in Chapter 8, the 'Article 5 duty' reflects the substantive justice or 'difference' model of equality. In addition to the ones mentioned above in the context of the RD, the following exceptions are contained in the EFD. *Prima facie* indirect discrimination can be justified, either on the basis of an 'objective justification', or, if under domestic law, the employer is obliged to make reasonable accommodations in order to eliminate the disadvantages flowing from the application of a neutral 'provision', 'criterion', or 'practice'. The two-fold justification defence for indirect discrimination cases will be discussed in great detail in Chapter 3. A public security and health exception is found in Article 2(5) EFD, although a similar exception cannot be found in the RD. Article 2(3) EFD provides that the Directive is inapplicable to payments made by state schemes, including state social security and social protection schemes. Moreover, in relation to 'disability' and 'age', the Directive gives freedom to the Member States whether or not to apply the Directive to the armed forces. The genuine occupational requirements exception is contained in Article 4 EFD which also contains a 'religious-ethos' exception that can be invoked by religious employers. The latter exception seeks to strike a balance between the competing ideals of equality, on the one hand, and religious freedom, on the other. It will be discussed in depth in Chapter 6. It follows from Article 5 EFD that an employer will not be under a legal duty to make a reasonable accommodation for a disabled person, if doing so constitutes a 'disproportionate burden' for the employer. With regard to 'age', the Directive reflects an 'open model' of anti-discrimination law, given that according to Article 6 EFD both 'direct' and 'indirect' age discrimination can be justified.[63] This point will be considered in full detail in Chapter 9. It follows from Article 7(2) EFD that the prohibition of disability discrimination shall not prejudice the right of the Member States to adopt or to maintain provisions regarding health and safety at work, or measures seeking to promote their integration into the working environment. The provisions in the EFD on remedies and enforcement are contained in Articles 9-14 EFD. It is has previously been stated that in contrast to the RD, the EFD does not place the Member States under a legal duty to establish special equality bodies in the context of the grounds covered by the EFD. Lastly, Article 15 EFD contains a special positive action provision that applies to the police and to employment for teachers in Northern Ireland (NI). The insertion of

[63] See also *Mangold v. Helm* (Case C-144/04) of 22 November 2005 available at <www.europa.eu.int>. This case will be analysed in great depth in Chapter 9 concerning age discrimination.

this special provision arguably provides evidence for the Community's acceptance of elements of 'consociationalism' in the Northern Ireland context.[64] Articles 16-21 EFD contain a number of 'Final Provisions' equivalent to the ones found in Articles 14-19 RD.

2.3.2.2. Interim Observations

In the above, I have provided a factual overview of the provisions contained in the RD and the EFD. I have not attempted to analyse/rationalise or contextualise the various provisions referred to, given that the mere aim was to give a brief overview of the content of the Directives. Clearly, the constitutionalised character of the RD and the EFD is amongst other things reflected in the expanded list of discrimination grounds which are covered. Constitutionalisation of equality at the level of the EU moreover requires that the ECJ interpret the various concepts of discrimination contained in the Directives in a way that is in conformity with a fundamental rights philosophy. In particular, this implies that the Court should not easily accept market-based considerations as a justification for a breach of the principles of equality and non-discrimination. A legal analysis of many (although not all) of the provisions referred to above will be made in the chapters to follow. This will be done from the perspective of comparative law. Hereafter, I will proceed with a factual analysis of the AETD in the same way as has been done above with regard to the RD and the EFD.

2.3.2.3. The AETD

With the adoption of the RD and the EFD, the protective scope of EC sex discrimination law was lagging behind in comparison with that offered by the Article 13 Directives. Therefore, the EC gender-equality framework needed to be 'streamlined', in light of the RD and EFD, in order to minimise a divergence of legal standards. This streamlining exercise was realised by the Commission by the adoption[65] of Directive 2002/73, which has amended the old ETD.[66] It should be noted that Directive 2002/73 inserts into the (old) ETD a number of provisions which cannot be found in the RD and EFD. Directive 2002/73 only comprises 4 Articles, the first of which recasts the substantive guarantees contained in the (old) ETD.[67] Article 1 of the (amended)

64 With reference to the work by Arend Lijphart, McCrudden has defined 'consociationalism' as follows: '[c]onsociationalism is a term (...) to describe arrangements, utilized in several political systems with ethnic or other divisions, involving the sharing of power between segments of society joined together by a common citizenship but divided by ethnicity, language, religion, or other factors.' The issue of 'consociationalism' will not be addressed in more detail. For further discussion, the reader is referred to McCrudden 2006 (forthcoming) with further references.

65 On the basis of Article 141 EC rather than on the basis of Article 13 EC.

66 Directive 76/207/EEC on Equal Treatment for Men and Women as regards Access to Employment, Vocational Training and Promotion and Working Conditions, *OJ* 1976, L 39/40. See for a sound and recent analysis also Koukoulis-Spiliotopoulos 2005.

67 Articles 3 and 4 of Directive 2002/73 are of little importance in the present discussion. Article 3 provides that the Directive enters into force on the day of publication in the Official Journal and Article 4 provides that (as is known) the Directive is addressed to the Member States.

ETD[68] has been complemented with a positive obligation which is placed upon the Member States to 'mainstream' the principle of sex equality when formulating and implementing laws in the areas of employment, including promotion; vocational training; working conditions, and, social security. This 'mainstreaming' duty gives effect to Articles 2 and 3(2) EC. These Articles proclaim the principle of sex equality as a 'task' and an 'aim' of the Community and they impose a positive obligation upon the Community legislator to 'promote' sex equality in all of its activities.[69] The mantra of 'positive duties' and 'mainstreaming' will be touched on in Part III of this book. It should, however, be noted here that an equivalent duty is not applicable in the context of the RD and the EFD.[70] Article 2 AETD contains definitions of direct and indirect sex discrimination which parallel the ones contained in the Article 13 Directives. Moreover, Article 2 AETD contains definitions of 'harassment' and of 'sexual harassment'. Article 2(4) AETD contains a prohibition of 'instruction to discriminate', whereas Article 2(5) AETD imposes a proactive duty upon the Member States to encourage employers to take action to prevent sex discrimination from occurring at work. The GOR (genuine occupational requirement) exception is contained in Article 2(6) AETD, whereas Article 2(7) AETD contains an exception to the principle of sex equality in favour of the protection of women, particularly as regards pregnancy and maternity. The positive action exception is enshrined in Article 2(8) AETD. As will be illustrated in Chapter 5, this has been differently formulated than the positive action exceptions in the RD and the EFD. Article 3(1) a-d of the AETD streamlines the Directive's material scope with the one of the EFD (not, however, with the one of the RD which, as stated above, goes beyond employment).[71] Article 6 AETD places a duty upon the Member States to set in place judicial and/or administrative enforcement procedures, which shall be available to victims of sex discrimination even after the termination of the employment-relationship.[72] This Article moreover provides that compensation or reparation measures for a breach of the principle of sex equality shall be 'real', 'effective', 'dissuasive' and 'proportionate'. It follows from Article 6(3) AETD that associations are entitled to engage, either on behalf of, or in support of the complainant, and with the latter's approval, in judicial and/or administrative proceedings. A 'victimisation' clause is contained in Article 7 AETD. This seeks to prevent that persons receive adverse treatment (e.g. dismissal) by (e.g.)

68 I will hereafter refer to the AETD (Amended Equal Treatment Directive). This thus refers to Directive 76/207/EEC as amended by Directive 2002/73/EC.

69 See Recital 4 of the Preamble to Directive 2002/73.

70 Recitals 3 and 14 of the EFD and RD, respectively do however contain a positive duty to mainstream sex equality while implementing the principle of equal treatment on the grounds covered by the EFD and RD, especially also in light of the fact that women are often the victim of multiple, or 'intersectional' discrimination (e.g. discrimination of a black disabled woman). For a discussion on the 'multi-dimensionality' of the principle of equality (which goes beyond 'intersectionality'), I refer to Schiek 2005, notably p. 453-460.

71 With reference to Chapter 1, Council Directive 2004/113/EC of 13 December 2004 relates to equal treatment between men and women in the areas of access to and supply of goods and services. This Directive shall not be considered in further detail.

72 This provision implements the judgment by the ECJ in the case of *Coote v. Granada Hospitality Ltd* (Case C-185/97) [1998] ECR I-5199.

the employer as a result of having relied upon sex equality law against the employer. Like the RD, the AETD obliges the Member States to set up special equality bodies (Article 8a AETD). Moreover, Article 8(b) AETD seeks to promote the 'social dialogue' (i.e. the dialogue with the social partners) at the domestic level with a view to fostering sex equality. It furthermore seeks to encourage employers to promote equal treatment at work 'in a planned and systematic way' (Article 8(b) (3) AETD). What is more, Article 8(b)(4) AETD provides that employers should be encouraged to provide their employees, on a regular basis, with information on equal treatment between the sexes in the undertaking. This may include the provision of statistical data on the percentage of women and men at different levels of the organisation, as well as measures which could be taken to improve the situation in cooperation with the trade unions. It should be noted that this reflects a proactive approach in the quest for sex equality in practice. Finally, Article 8(d) AETD specifies that sanctions must be 'effective', 'proportionate' and 'dissuasive'.

It is interesting to note that in parallel with the approach adopted by the RD and the EFD, the notion of 'sex' is not defined by the AETD. The meaning of 'sex' has been subject to judicial interpretation by the ECJ. It follows from the Court's case law that 'sex' also embraces discrimination on grounds of gender-reassignment (i.e. discrimination against a trans-sexual),[73] however, not on grounds of sexual orientation[74]. This point will be illustrated in great detail in Chapter 7.

2.3.2.4. *Cross-Cutting Issues*

Before commencing with a general overview of the anti-discrimination and equality frameworks in the Netherlands and in England, the following points are worth mentioning. Firstly, the RD, the EFD and the AETD all apply symmetrically in the sense that they offer protection to persons belonging to the disadvantaged group, as well as to those in the advantaged group. For example, under the AETD a woman can claim an instance of discrimination relative to a man and *vice versa*.[75] However, as will be argued in Chapter 8, matters are less clear cut with regard to the ground 'disability' in the context of the EFD. Secondly, and as will be illustrated in the chapters to follow, whereas EC sex equality law has traditionally echoed 'formal equality', 'substantive equality' can be traced in selected provisions of the Directives. Moreover, notably with regard to 'sex', proactive approaches increasingly complement reactive strategies. This will be touched on in Chapter 5. Another matter worth pointing out is that the implementation period of the RD and the EFD lapsed on 19 July 2003 and on 2 December 2003,[76] respectively, although the EFD did allow the Member

73 *P v. S and Cornwall County Council* (Case C-13/94) [1996] ECR I-2143.

74 *Grant v. South-West Trains* (Case C-249/96) [1998] ECR I-621.

75 This can be contrasted with the asymmetrical framework underpinning the 1979 International Convention on the Elimination of All Forms of Discrimination against Women (CEDAW) whose protective guarantees are exclusively conferred upon women. For a recent analysis of the CEDAW in relation to EU gender discrimination law I refer to Holtmaat and Tobler 2005.

76 With the exception of 'disability' and 'age' with regard to which the Member States are allowed another 3 years from December 2003 (see Article 18 EFD).

States to opt for a maximum of three additional years to secure the effective implementation of the grounds 'age' and 'disability'. The AETD had to be implemented into domestic law on 5 October 2005. It is important to bear in mind that the Directives allow the Member States to go beyond what is strictly required.[77] Put differently, the Directives only set minimum standards. On the other hand, Member States are prohibited from reducing the existing levels of protection under the guise of transposition of the Directives. This follows from the so-called 'non-regression' clauses in the Directives.[78] Once a Directive has been transposed into domestic law individuals derive their rights from the national implementing provisions, unless the domestic legislature has failed to transpose the Directives correctly. If this is the case, an individual can directly rely on the provisions of the Directives (provided that they lend themselves as being 'directly applicable') in proceedings against the state.[79] This refers to the so-called 'vertical' direct effect of EC Directives. In contrast, Directives cannot be invoked in 'horizontal proceedings', i.e. in proceedings between, e.g. a private individual against a private employer,[80] although the recent decision by the ECJ in *Mangold v. Helm* did have the *de facto* effect that the Article 13 EC Framework Directive could be directly relied upon by Mr Mangold (a private actor) against Mr Helm (another private actor) in legal proceedings.[81] In any case, in 'horizontal proceedings' the national court is under a legal duty to interpret the case at hand in conformity with the spirit of the Directive,[82] even when the deadline for

77 Article 6(1) RD; Article 8(1) EFD; Article 8e(1) AETD.

78 Articles 6(2) RD; 8(2) EFD; 8e(2) AETD. It should, however, be noted that non-regression clauses have not been interpreted as being 'stand-still' clauses in the sense that they absolutely prohibit any lowering of the level of protection afforded by the law of the Member State at the time of implementation of the Directive. For legitimate grounds *other than the need to transpose a Directive into domestic law* the protective level granted by the law may be reduced. See in this respect the recent decision by the ECJ in *Mangold v. Helm* (Case C-144/04) of 22 November 2005 available at <www.europa.eu.int>, paragraphs 44-54 and notably the Opinion by Tizzano (AG), paragraphs 43-78.

79 *Van Duyn v. Home Office* (Case 41/74) [1974] ECR 1337.

80 According to settled case law by the Court a Directive, being formally addressed to Member States, 'cannot of itself impose obligations on an individual and cannot therefore be relied on as such against an individual'. See in particular *Marshall v. Southhampton & South-West Hampshire Area Health Authority (Teaching)* (Case 152/84) [1986] ECR 723 (paragraph 48); *Faccini Dori* (Case C-91/92) [1994] ECR I-3325 (paragraph 20); *Wells* (Case C-201/02) [2004] ECR I-723 (paragraph 56).

81 In *Mangold v. Helm* (Case C-144/04) of 22 November 2005 available at <www.europa.eu.int>, the ECJ seemingly *did* apply the EFD in a lawsuit between two private individuals, even when the implementation deadline had not yet expired. In *Mangold*, however, the Court simultaneously relied upon the general principle of non-discrimination law which, it opined, formed the source of the various prohibitions of discrimination contained in the Directive. See for a comment Schmidt 2005. See also the Editorial to the *Common Market Law Review* (43) 2006, p. 1-8. The ECJ's judgment in *Mangold* will be analysed in full in Chapter 9. In that chapter it will also be argued that *Mangold* does *not* warrant the general conclusion that Community Directives are directly effective in legal proceedings between individuals.

82 *Von Colson and Kamann v. Land Nordrhein-Westfalen* (Case 14/83) [1984] ECR 1891, paragraph 26 and, *Marleasing SA v. La Comercial Internacionale de Alimentacion SA* (Case 106/89) [1990] ECR I-4135. These cases concern the so-called 'indirect effect' of Directives. See more recently →

transposition of the Directive into domestic law has not yet expired.[83] On the basis of the well-known decisions by the ECJ in *Francovich*[84] and *Brasserie dû Pêcheur and Factortame III*[85] the State may under certain (by the ECJ established) conditions be held financially liable by an individual for failure to implement the Directive (correctly).

2.3.3. Interim Conclusions

In the above, an analysis has been made of the evolution of the RD, the EFD and the AETD. This has revealed a diverse picture. One important conclusion is that the Directives mark a progressive step in the fight against discrimination and the quest for equality on the covered grounds. Rather than 'market-integration' the prime rationale underpinning the Directives is a concern over human rights, although arguably, human rights will have to be balanced against the economic objectives of the EC. Another important conclusion is that the Directives clearly confer a heterogeneous level of protection for different grounds.[86] EC equality law can be visualised by a reverse pyramid: 'race' and 'ethnicity' are at the top of the pyramid, followed by 'sex' and subsequently by the remainder of the discrimination grounds. Thus, for instance, the wide material scope of the RD can be contrasted with the narrower scope of the EFD and the AETD, and, the open-ended possibility for justifying age discrimination can be opposed to the narrow scope for manoeuvre in, e.g. sexual orientation and race discrimination cases. In light of this hierarchy, it may be the case that the ECJ in future case law will adopt different standards of judicial scrutiny for different grounds of discrimination. If it does so, the ECJ will create its own judicial hierarchy amongst the grounds.[87] It will be particularly interesting to learn how the ECJ in future cases will interpret the provisions in the Directives including core

also *Pfeiffer* (joined Cases C-397/01 to C-403/01 [2004] ECR I-8835, paragraphs 113, 115, 116 and 118.

83 The ECJ in its recent decision in *Mangold v. Helm* (Case C-144/04) of 22 November 2005 available at <www.europa.eu.int> qualified the duty imposed upon domestic courts by EC law, namely to interpret national law in conformity with EC Directives, in more detail by holding that this duty exists even *before* the deadline for transposition of a Directive has lapsed. Tizzano (AG) had also endorsed this view (see paragraphs 115 and 120 of the Opinion of Advocate General Tizzano delivered on 30 June 2005 in *Mangold v. Helm* (Case C-144/04) (available at <www.europa.eu.int>). See moreover the Opinion by Kokott (AG) in *Konstantinos Adeneler and Others* (Case C-212/04) of 27 October 2005 (available at <http:// www.europa.eu.int>), paragraphs 43-54 and by Kokott (AG) in his (earlier) Opinion in *Nicole Wippel v. Peek & Cloppenburg GmbH & Co KG* (Case C-313/02) delivered on 18 May 2004, paragraphs 58-63.

84 *Francovich & Bonifaci v. Italy* (Cases C-6&9/90) [1991] ECR I-5357.

85 *Brasserie dû Pêcheur SA v. Germany,* and *R. v. Secretary of State for Transport, ex parte Factortame Ltd. And others* (Case C-46/93 and C-48/93) [1996] ECR I-1029. It should be noted that this case did, however, not concern the State's failure to implement a *Directive* but rather a breach by the State of EC primary law.

86 This has been one of the main points of criticism expressed by academic scholars as well as by lawyers and others who work in the areas of equality and non-discrimination. See the literature references in footnote 50 *supra;* also Parmar 2004, p. 131-154, p. 132.

87 See generally Gerards 2002.

notions such as, e.g. 'race', 'belief' and 'disability'.[88] Arguably, the Court will feel inspired by existing interpretative benchmarks flowing from international law (notably the ECHR)[89] and from the constitutional and/or legal traditions of the Member States. Moreover, the Court is likely to have regard to its own case law in the area of gender (as well as nationality) discrimination.[90] This would eventually lead to a cross-fertilisation of legal standards across different legal systems, as well as across different grounds of discrimination.

2.4. *Closing Remarks*

In the above, an analysis has been made of the principles of equality and non-discrimination in the context of EU law. This has been necessary in order to provide the necessary background information for the chapters to follow which will examine many of the issues referred to above in greater detail and from the perspective of comparative law. Hereafter, I will make a similar analysis in the context of Dutch (section 3) and English (section 4) law. It is to this that I will turn now.

3. Equality and Non-Discrimination: the Case of the Netherlands[91]

3.1. *The Legal Framework*

In the Netherlands, the principles of equality and non-discrimination are covered by various realms of the law. Important to mention are Constitutional law, specific statutory equal treatment Acts, employment law and criminal law.[92] Moreover, since the Dutch constitutional system adheres to a 'monist theory' of international law, the international equality guarantees automatically percolate into the domestic legal system.[93] Article 1 of the Constitution (last amended in 1983) contains a generic anti-discrimination and equality clause which reads as follows:

> 'All who are in the Netherlands shall be treated equal in equal circumstances. Discrimination on the grounds of religion, belief, political opinion, race, sex or any other ground shall be prohibited.'

Since Article 1 of the Constitution reflects the 'open model' of anti-discrimination law, it also (implicitly) covers the grounds 'disability' and 'age', as well as other, not explicitly mentioned, grounds. Article 1 of the Constitution reconciles the principles of equality, on the one hand, and non-discrimination, on the other. The Constitutional

88 While this book was finalised for publication, the ECJ gave judgment in the case of *Sonia Chacón Navas v. Eurest Colectividades SA,* Case C-13/05, 11 July 2006. In casu, the ECJ (*inter alia*) interpreted the concept of 'disability'. The case will be briefly touched on in Chapter 8.

89 European Convention on Human Rights.

90 The interaction between the Article 13 Directives and EU gender discrimination law has *inter alia* been analysed by Parmar 2004, p. 131-154 and by Schiek 2000, p. 239-258.

91 This part draws on Gijzen 2004.

92 Criminal law falls, however, outside the scope of this book.

93 This follows from Articles 93 and 94 of the Dutch Constitution (*Grondwet*).

equality guarantee has been interpreted as containing a right to both formal and substantive equality. Therefore, people are not only equal 'before' the law (*de iure* or formal equality), but they must also be equally treated 'by' the law (*de facto* or substantive equality).[94] Moreover, in a more modern fashion, Article 1 of the Constitution has been interpreted as containing a positive duty to respect the equal worth and dignity of all.[95] The second sentence contained in Article 1 of the Constitution concerns the prohibition against discrimination. It should be emphasised that in the specific context of Dutch equal treatment law, 'discrimination' (*discriminatie*) bears a highly pejorative connotation. This means that the notion of discrimination is strongly interlinked with the notion of 'disadvantage'.[96] Furthermore and related to the first point, the notion of discrimination echoes the tenets of 'group-justice', which can be contrasted with 'individual justice'. It follows that 'discrimination' is *not* a neutral term. It creates a link between the disadvantages suffered by an individual defined by 'race', 'sex', etc. on the one hand, with the disadvantage suffered by the group of persons to whom the individual belongs (e.g. black people, women), on the other. Put differently, 'discrimination' reflects 'asymmetry'. Holtmaat has explained the conceptual differences between the principles of equal treatment and non-discrimination as follows: (1) the principle of (both formal and substantive) equal treatment is *instrumental* to the fight against discrimination; (2) the principle of non-discrimination is a species of unequal treatment, but not every form of unequal treatment constitutes an act of discrimination.[97] In light of the foregoing, Dutch law has reserved the notion of discrimination for the areas of constitutional and criminal law. As will be explained, statutory equality law is premised upon the neutral concept of 'distinction' (*onderscheid*). This has not changed with the implementation of the Directives in Dutch law.

According to the classic doctrine of constitutional rights, Article 1 of the Constitution merely relates to 'vertical relations' (i.e. to disputes between an individual *v.* the state). With a view to extending the application of the constitutional equality guarantee to 'horizontal relations' (i.e. to disputes between private individuals), as well as in the light of EC law requirements, the government enacted a number of specific statutory equal treatment Acts (*gelijke behandelingswetten*). These are centred around the prohibition of making a 'distinction'. 'Distinction' is a neutral concept, in the sense that it disregards the disadvantaged position of the group to which the individual victim of discrimination belongs. Hence, 'distinction' reflects 'symmetry'. The aim of the prohibition of distinction (*verbod van onderscheid*) is securing justice at the level of individuals, rather than groups. The prohibition of *distinction* in Dutch

94 The terminology has been taken from Alkema, who has spoken of 'gelijkheid voor de wet' ('equality before the law') and 'gelijkheid door de wet' ('equality by the law'). See Alkema 2004, p. 54.
95 Hirsch Ballin 2003, p. 196-206.
96 Wentholt 1999, p. 90-91.
97 Holtmaat 2003, p. 1268. Holtmaat has fervently pleaded for drawing a stricter distinction by the law between 'unequal treatment' (which can be subjected to a relatively loose scrutiny test) and 'discrimination' (which must be subjected to a very strict scrutiny test).

law therefore parallels the prohibition of *discrimination* under EC law.[98] It is submitted that, in light of the particular meaning of 'discrimination' in Dutch law, it would be a breach of the Directives' non-regression clauses, if the notion of 'distinction' had been replaced by the asymmetrical notion of 'discrimination'.

In the context of this book a number of statutory equal treatment Acts will be of particular importance. First, mention is made of the 1994 General Equal Treatment Act (GETA).[99] This Act prohibits making a distinction on grounds of religion, belief, political opinion, race, sex, nationality, hetero-homosexual orientation and marital status. Given that the ground 'political opinion' is not covered by EC law, it will not be dealt with in the chapters to follow. 'Marital status' will only be dealt with insofar that discrimination on this ground constitutes indirect discrimination on grounds of sex or sexual orientation. The GETA's material scope covers *inter alia* the areas of employment, occupation and vocational training.[100] In light of the requirements imposed upon the Dutch legislator by the RD and EFD, the GETA was in need of being amended in various respects. These amendments have been made by the adoption of the 2004 'EC Implementation Act GETA'.[101]

98 Notwithstanding this, the Council of State ('Raad van State'), which is the highest advisor of the government in drafting new legislation, had advised the government to abandon the neutral concept of 'distinction' and to start using the more normative notion of discrimination. See: *'Advies van de Raad van State en nader Rapport'*, Tweede Kamer, 2001-2002, 28 169, B, p. 5-6. [Advisory Opinion of the Council of State, Second Chamber of Parliament, 2001-2002, 28 169, B, p. 5-6] and *'Implementatie van de richtlijnen inzake gelijke behandeling, Advies Raad van State en nader rapport'*, Tweede Kamer, 2001-2002, 28 187, A, p. 4-5. ['Implementation of the Directives on Equal Treatment, Advisory Opinion of the Council of State', Second Chamber of Parliament, 2001-2002, 28 187, A, p. 4-5]. The same advice had also been given by the Interdepartmental Commission European Law (ICER). See: ICER, *'Implementatie Richtlijnen op grond van Artikel 13 EG Verdrag, conclusie en aanbevelingen'*, 2001/54, p. 2. [ICER, 'Implementation of the Article 13 Directives, conclusions and recommendations', p. 2]. The government has however not followed this advice, whereby it has sought support from the opinion expressed by the Dutch Equal Treatment Commission (ETC). See: *Commentaar van de Commissie Gelijke Behandeling inzake de Implementatie van de Gemeenschappelijke Bepalingen van de EG-Kaderrichtlijn* (Richtlijn 2000/78/EG van 27 november 2000) en de EG Rassendiscriminatie Richtlijn (2000/43/EG van 29 juni 2000), p. 3. [Commentary by the Equal Treatment Commission on the Implementation of the Common Provisions of the EC Framework Directive (Directive 2000/78/EC of 27 November 2000) and the EC Racial Equality Directive (Directive 2000/43/EC of 29 June 2000), p. 3]. In the Commission's view, the usage of the notion 'discrimination' would wrongly suggest that an alleged perpetrator must have the intention to discriminate and to cause disadvantage. However, proof of intent is merely required in the context of criminal law.

99 *Algemene Wet Gelijke Behandeling* [General Equal Treatment Act] of 1994, *Stb.* [*Law Gazette*] 230.

100 The GETA moreover applies to the areas of the supply of goods and provision of services and to the entire field of education. Moreover, as far as the ground 'race' is concerned, the Act applies also in the areas of social protection, including social security and social advantages. The extension of the Act with the last-mentioned areas has been the result of a transposition of the RD into domestic law.

101 Wet van 21 februari 2004 tot wijziging van de Algemene Wet Gelijke Behandeling en enkele andere wetten ter uitvoering van Richtlijn 2 richtlijn 2000/43/EG en richtlijn 2000/78/EG (EG-Implementatiewet AWGB). [Act of 21 February 2004 regarding the amendment of the General Equal Treatment Act en some other Acts in order to implement Directive 2000/43/EC and Directive 2000/78/EC (EC Implementation Act GETA)]. The Dutch government has →

Secondly, mention should be made of the Acts on equal treatment on grounds of Disability and Chronic Disease (DETA),[102] and, the Act on equal treatment on grounds of Age (AETA).[103] Both of these Acts are the result of implementation of the EFD into domestic law. Both the DETA and the AETA apply to the area of employment, although the DETA will in future also apply to the area of transport.[104] It follows from the foregoing that 'disability' and 'age' have been regulated outside the general framework of the GETA. A separate legal regulation is partially also the case with 'sex'. The ground 'sex' is covered by the GETA but also by various other statutory Acts. Thus, sex equality law in employment is covered by the Act on Equal Treatment between Men and Women (AET w/m),[105] and, by Articles 646 and 647 of Book 7 of the Civil Code (*Burgerlijk Wetboek*). In order to implement the AETD, Dutch sex equality law has been in need of amendment. These amendments have, however, not yet been enforced. The legislative process with regard to the implementation of the AETD is still ongoing,[106] notwithstanding that the AETD should have been implemented into domestic law by 05-10-05. It should be noted that the AET w/m remains unaffected by the provisions of the GETA (which also covers 'sex') given that the former constitutes a *lex specialis vis-à-vis* the latter. *Grosso modo*, it can be said that sex discrimination in employment (including 'equal pay') is governed by the AET w/m, and by the above-mentioned Articles in the Civil Code, whereas the GETA covers instances of sex discrimination in other areas of social life (e.g. goods and services provision). It should be noted that the provisions in the Civil Code (logically)

deemed it desirable to extend many of the amendments that were legally required for the grounds covered both by the EFD/RD and the GETA to these discrimination grounds that are merely covered by the latter (i.e. political opinion, (sex), nationality and marital status). The EC Implementation Act GETA entered into force on 1 April 2004.

102 Act of 3 April 2003 concerning the establishment of the Act on equal treatment on the grounds of disability or chronic disease [*Wet gelijke behandeling op grond van handicap en chronische ziekte*] *Stb.* 2003, 206 [*Law Gazette* 2003, 206]. This Act will be referred to as the 'DETA' (Disability Equal Treatment Act). It entered into force on 1 December 2003 (except for Articles 7 and 8 which relate to public transport). It should be noted that the DETA has been partially amended and/or complemented by the EC Implementation Act (see footnote 101 *supra*) which entered into force on 1 April 2004.

103 Act of 17 December 2003, concerning the equal treatment on grounds of age in employment, occupation and vocational training [*Wet gelijke behandeling op grond van leeftijd*], *Stb.* 2004, 30 [*Law Gazette* 2004, 30]. This Act will be referred to as the 'AETA' (Age Equal Treatment Act). It entered into force on 1 May 2004.

104 See Articles 7 and 8 DETA.

105 Act on Equal Treatment between Men and Women [*Wet gelijke behandeling van mannen/vrouwen*], *Stb.* 1989, 168 [*Law Gazette* 1989, 168]. Together with Article 7:646 of the Civil Code (old Article 7A:1637ij of the Civil Code), this Act was adopted with a view to transposing the Netherlands' obligations under the (old) ETD, i.e. Directive 76/207. Initially, a separate Act existed on the principle of equal pay between men and women. This Act had been adopted in light of the obligations imposed upon the Dutch government by the 1975 EC Equal Pay Directive (Directive 75/117/EC on Equal Pay for Men and Women, *OJ* 1975, L 45/19). However, this Act was eventually integrated into the Act on Equal Treatment between Men and Women in 1989.

106 See *Parliamentary Documents II* 2004-2005, 30 237, no. 2 which is the Bill that seeks to amend existing sex equality law.

only refer to private employment, whereas the AET w/m covers both public and private employment, as well as the areas of vocational training, equal pay, the liberal profession, pension provision and membership of employers' organisations and trade unions. The government is presently considering the integration of the abovementioned Acts into a single Equal Treatment Act although this would merely entail a 'technical exercise' rather than a revision of existing equal treatment law.[107] Like EC law, Dutch equal treatment law foremost reflects the formal justice paradigm. Furthermore, like EC law, and with the exception of 'age', the legal framework is premised upon the closed model of anti-discrimination law. It is important to note that the GETA reflects a tentative reconciliation of diverse constitutional rights, e.g. the freedom of religion *v.* the right to equality and non-discrimination.[108] It will be explained in some of the chapters to follow, that a similar reconciliation exercise is echoed by the EFD.

3.2. *The Equal Treatment Commission*

Dutch equal treatment law falls (*inter alia*) within the jurisdiction of a quasi-judicial body, i.e. the Equal Treatment Commission (*Commissie Gelijke Behandeling*, hereafter, ETC). The ETC's functions are, on the one hand, quasi-judicial in kind and, on the other, preventive in character. Essentially, the Commission is a low threshold body that gives 'Opinions' (*Oordelen*) on the cases that come before it. Its main function is therefore to investigate alleged discriminatory treatment,[109] whereby it works independently.[110] Requests to the ETC must be made in writing. It follows from Article 12(2) GETA that such requests can be made by: (1) the alleged victim of a distinction; (2) the natural person or legal person or competent authority wishing to know whether (s)he/it acts in contravention of equal treatment law; (3) those concerned with the judgment of a dispute concerning an alleged unlawful differentiation (e.g. a judge in a civil or administrative procedure); (4) a works council or a committee

107 At the time of writing (May 2006) no bill had yet been proposed by the government to this effect. See, however, *Advies 2005-04 van de Commissie Gelijke Behandeling inzake het ontwerp-wetsvoorstel voor een Integratiewet* [Advice 2005-04 of the Equal Treatment Commission concerning the proposal for a bill for an Integration Act], available at <http://www.cgb.nl/_media/ ownloadables/advies%202005%2004.pdf>.

108 For a (practically oriented) discussion of the relationship between 'equality', on the one hand, and other (conflicting) constitutional rights, on the other, in the context of the closed model of Dutch equal treatment law, I refer to Goldschmidt and Hendriks 2003, p. 1277-1284.

109 In addition, the ETC performs a consultative function (e.g. to the government when drafting new laws in the areas of equality and non-discrimination). It moreover performs an informative and research function. The Commission disseminates information through equality newsletters, annual bulletins, its website (i.e. <www.cgb.nl>), etc.

110 It may be worth noting that the ETC's Chairman and Vice Chairman must have the same qualifications as those which are required for the profession of district judge (*rechterlijk ambtenaar*). Members of the Commission are appointed by the Minister of Justice with agreement of the Ministers of the *Interior, Social and Labour Affairs, Education and Science* and *Welfare/Health and Culture* (Article 16(3) GETA). By means of disciplinary measures, a Commission member may be dismissed by the Dutch Supreme Court in case that member seriously impedes the course of the law or, the trust that has been put in him/her. See also Gerards and Heringa 2003, p. 157.

which believes that a distinction has been made by the company or the civil service unit within which it has been appointed, and, (5) a legal person with full legal powers which, in accordance with its constitution or statutes, represents the interests of those whose protection is the objective of the equal treatment legislation (e.g. an anti-discrimination bureau). Moreover, the ETC may conduct an investigation through its own motion (Article 12(1) GETA). It therefore follows that it is not necessary for a complaint to be filed by an individual victim. In such cases where the Commission suspects systemic discriminatory patterns it is entitled to conduct an investigation through its own motion.[111] As the word implies, the ETC's Opinions are non-binding, but they are nonetheless morally authoritative and in many instances they are respected by the parties in the case at hand.[112] With respect to 'sanctions', the following can be said. According to Article 8(1) of the GETA, Article 11(1) and 11(2) of the AETA and Article 9(1) DETA, 'discriminatory dismissals' and 'victimisation dismissals'[113] are invalid (void) (*vernietigbaar*). This applies both with regard to public and private employment. Contractual provisions which are in conflict with the GETA, the AETA and the DETA, shall be null and void. This follows from Article 9, Article 13 and Article 11 of these Acts, respectively. Moreover, with regard to sanctions, Articles 13(2), 13(3) and 15 GETA are of importance. Sanctions under these Articles are imposed by the ETC (not by the courts). Under Article 13(2) GETA, the Commission may make 'recommendations' (*aanbevelingen*) when forwarding its findings to the party found guilty of unlawful distinction. Under Article 13(3) GETA, the Commission may also forward its findings in an Opinion to the Ministers concerned, and to organisations of employers, employees, professionals, public servants (consumers of goods and services) and to relevant consultative bodies. Under Article 15(1) GETA, the Commission may bring legal action with a view to obtaining a ruling that conduct contrary to the relevant equal treatment legislation is unlawful, requesting that such conduct be prohibited or eliciting an order that the consequences of such conduct be rectified.[114] This power must be regarded in light of the fact that the Commission's Opinions are non-binding. However, the Commission has so far never made use of this possibility. It should be emphasised that in proceedings before the ETC an alleged victim of discrimination cannot claim pecuniary damages, or the

111 Article 12(1) GETA used to provide that the ETC was only entitled to conduct an investigation on its own motion in the public sector, or in one or more sectors of society (e.g. the health sector). This restriction has, however, been repealed by an amendment to the GETA by the Act of 15 September 2005 *tot wijziging van de Algemene Wet Gelijke Behandeling en enkele andere wetten naar aanleiding van onderdelen van de evaluatie van de Algemene Wet Gelijke Behandeling, de Wet Gelijke Behandeling van mannen en vrouwen en Artikel 646 van Boek 7 van het Burgerlijk Wetboek (Evaluatiewet AWGB)*, in short: the Evaluation Act General Equal Treatment Act.

112 According to the Commission's annual report over the year 2005, the ETC's judgment was abided by in 73 percent of cases. The Equal Treatment Commission's annual reports can be downloaded from the Commission's website at <www.cgb.nl>. The foregoing explains why in practice binding litigation strategies are minimally used.

113 A victimisation dismissal refers to the dismissal of an employee by reason of the fact that the employee has brought legal proceedings against the employer under equal treatment law.

114 Unless the person affected by the alleged discriminatory conduct has made reservations (Article 15(2) of the General Equal Treatment Act.

invalidation of, e.g. a discriminatory dismissal and, thereupon, outstanding wages. The ETC cannot order a reinstatement in the job. This can only be done before the courts, which render binding judgments, in ordinary civil or administrative proceedings. Whilst the Court is not bound by the ETC's Opinion, the latter may of course increase the chance of a successful claim in ordinary court proceedings.[115] The courts, unlike the ETC, have also jurisdiction over Article 1 of the Constitution and, unlike the Commission, they have the power to refer preliminary questions to the ECJ within the framework of Article 234 EC Treaty. It follows that proceedings before the ETC have a low threshold character but, notwithstanding this, the ETC has been of prime importance to the effective functioning of Dutch equal treatment law.

4. Equality and Non-Discrimination: the Case of England[116]

In contrast with Dutch equal treatment law, English law is not characterised by a Constitutional equality guarantee.[117] Indeed, England does not have a written Constitution and the Constitutional equality guarantee is only mirrored in Dicey's perception of the rule of law which is *inter alia* characterised by the idea that:

> '[n]ot only that no man is above the law, but (what is a different thing) that here every man, whatever his rank or condition, is subject to the ordinary law of the realm and amenable to the jurisdiction of the ordinary tribunals. In England, the idea of legal equality, or of universal subjection of all classes to one law administered by the ordinary courts, has been pushed to its utmost limit.'[118]

This, however, does not confer rights upon English citizens, which may be invoked in anti-discrimination proceedings against public authorities, let alone against privately acting agents.[119] The Diceyan perception of equality reflects a vision of equality in terms of formal, not substantive, justice. The formal and comparative equality approach is strongly adhered to by the English legislator and courts. With the exception of English disability discrimination law, the statutory discrimination Acts apply symmetrically.

It should be highlighted that English anti-discrimination and equality law is primarily to be understood in a context of labour relations and employment law, rather than in the context of Constitutional law.[120] However, it is submitted that the

115 See Goldschmidt at <http://www.cgb.nl/media/downloadables/Booklet%20Dutch%20 Equal %20Treatment%20Commission.pdf> (last visited on 03-05-06).

116 For an eloquent analysis of the evolution of the principles of equality and non-discrimination in the context of English law, I also refer to McCrudden 2004b. In his contribution, McCrudden *inter alia* also analyses the development of the principles of equality and non-discrimination in English law prior to legislative intervention (see sections 11.11-11.18 of McCrudden's contribution).

117 See also Barnard, Deakin, Kilpatrick 2002, p. 129-130.

118 Dicey, An Introduction to the Study of the Law of the Constitution (10th ed. Macmillan, London, 1959, ed. E.C.S. Wade), p. 193, cited by the Rt Hon. Baroness of Richmond (2005), p. 574.

119 Barnard, Deaking, Kilpatrick 2002, p. 129.

120 Fredman 2003, p. 202.

1998 Human Rights Act (HRA), which transposes the rights and freedoms contained in the European Convention of Human Rights (ECHR) into domestic law,[121] increasingly replaces the private and economic dimension of equality with a focus upon human rights.[122] A similar trend has been discerned above in the context of EU equality law. It is submitted that the constitutionalisation of equality at the supranational level fosters similar trends at the domestic level. One might even argue that human rights attract more attention in the English legal context, precisely by reason of the UK lacking a Constitution.

Statutory anti-discrimination law in England has evolved over the decades in a piecemeal fashion, rather than as a result of a well-considered legal and political strategy. The various Statutory Acts and governmental Regulations must be understood, either as concrete legislative responses to social phenomena in the domestic context,[123] or, as instruments seeking to implement EC law. This partially explains the tremendous complexities and incoherencies that characterise the statutory anti-discrimination Acts and Regulations.[124] Thus, as Cohen has explained, the adoption of British race relations law in the 1960s was the response by law and policy-makers to the great influx of immigrants arriving from the former colonies (India, Pakistan, the West Indies) to the UK in the late 1950s and early 1960s with a view to taking up low-skilled employment in the textile branch.[125] In contrast, the adoption of anti-discrimination frameworks for 'religion' and 'sexual orientation' in 2003 is purely to be understood against the background of the need of implementing Article 13 EFD. Equal pay and sex discrimination law was adopted in the early 1970s without a single reference to supranational equality standards.[126] However, clearly, and notwithstanding its domestic roots, English sex equality law has received considerable 'top-down' influence from EC law throughout the decades. This also explains why domestic race and sex discrimination law have sometimes diverged, for the former has only received direct 'top down' influence from EC law since the adoption of the Article 13 RD. It should, however, be noted that in such instances where the courts have interpreted sex and race discrimination law in a consistent fashion, the stan-

121 English law, in contrast to Dutch law, adheres to a 'dualist' theory of international law. This means that international law does not *automatically* filter into domestic law. Hence the need for a separate statutory Act, which 'copies' and 'pastes' the human rights standards contained in the ECHR into domestic law.

122 See also Townshend Smith 2001, who has observed in this context '[...that there is an; MG] increasing shift from an economic inequality discourse to a human rights discourse' (p. 48).

123 McCrudden has moreover pointed out that legislative intervention in the realms of 'equality' and 'non-discrimination' was partly a reaction against the limited promise held by the Common Law in these areas. See McCrudden 2004b, p. 589.

124 Lord Lester of Herne Hill has observed the following in this context: 'Successive governments have refused to make the law user-friendly (...) preferring (...) to respond to each new judgment from Luxembourg with ad hoc subordinate legislation, patching the holes made in the statutes'. See Lord Lester of Lord Lester of Herne Hill QC 1997, p. 174.

125 Cohen 2005a, p. 1.

126 Millett 1987, p. 219: 'Shortly after accession [to the EC in 1973; MG], the English (...) law on sex equality was embodied in the Equal Pay Act 1970 and the Sex Discrimination Act 1975, which both came into force on 29 December 1975. They were adopted without any reference to the European Communities, whose law on the subject has developed in its own direction'.

dards flowing from EC sex discrimination law have 'cross-fertilised' into domestic race relations law. In other words, up until the adoption of the RD, race discrimination law has sometimes been influenced indirectly by supranational EC (sex equality) law. Lastly, the adoption of a disability discrimination framework must be perceived against the background of an effective lobbying campaign by disability rights activists in the early 1990s. Disability discrimination law has only started receiving top-down influence from EC law with the adoption of the EFD. In fact, as will be argued in Chapter 8, English disability discrimination law has influenced EC disability discrimination law contained in the EFD ('bottom-up' influence).

In the context of this book, the following Statutory Acts and governmental Regulations will be of central importance: the 1975 Sex Discrimination Act (SDA) as amended;[127] the 1976 Race Relations Act (RRA) as amended;[128] the 1995 Disability Discrimination Act (DDA) as amended;[129] the Religion and Belief Regulations (R&B Regulations)[130] and the Sexual Orientation Regulations (S.O. Regulations).[131] It should be noted that, unlike Statutory Acts of Parliament, governmental Regulations are, as the name suggests, adopted by the government which has the consequence that Regulations are less 'democratically' informed. What consequences this has for the implementation of EC law (in casu: Article 13 EFD) will become clear in the chapters to follow. It will, moreover, become clear that the DDA has a different conceptual framework than the SDA/RRA and the R&B and S.O. Regulations. Essentially, unlike any of the latter Acts/Regulations, the DDA applies asymmetrically. This means that it has been specifically drawn up with a view to protecting the rights of disabled persons, rather than non-disabled persons. This point will be clarified in great detail *inter alia* in Chapter 8. All of the aforementioned Acts/Regulations are (*inter alia*) applicable to the broad realms of employment and occupation.

The aforementioned Acts/governmental Regulations are subject to the interpretation by the courts whose case law is 'governed' by the rules of precedent.[132] Claims of discrimination in the context of employment are in first instance dealt with before the employment tribunals (ET) that are composed of a legally qualified Chair and by two lay members.[133] Although the Tribunal's findings are binding upon the parties concerned they do not constitute a binding precedent. If a party disagrees

127 The SDA has been amended by the Employment Equality (Sex Discrimination) Regulations 2005 (SI 2005/2467), with a view to transposing the AETD into domestic law.

128 The RRA has been amended by the Race Relations Act 1976 (Amendment) Regulations 2003 (SI 2003/1626), with a view to transposing the Article 13 RD into domestic law.

129 The DDA has been amended by the Disability Discrimination Act 1995 (Amendment) Regulations 2003 (SI 2003/1673), with a view to transposing the EFD, insofar as the ground 'disability' is concerned, into domestic law.

130 The Employment Equality (Religion or Belief) Regulations 2003, SI 2003, No. 1660. These Regulations have sought to implement the EFD for the grounds 'religion' and 'belief'.

131 The Employment Equality (Sexual Orientation) Regulations 2003, SI 2003, No. 1661. These have sought to implement the EFD for the ground of 'sexual orientation'.

132 Cooper 2004.

133 Cohen 2005a, p. 6. The need for more effective training of lay members of the ET and even of its Chair has been stressed in the Independent Review of the Enforcement of UK Anti-Discrimination Legislation (2000) carried out by Hepple, Coussey and Choudhury (p. 89-90).

with the judgment of the ET, it may appeal to the employment appeal tribunal (EAT) and, after that, to the Court of Appeal (CA). Leave may moreover be granted to the House of Lords (HL).

In the context of the SDA, the RRA and the DDA (but not the R&B Regulations and the S.O. Regulations) a number of equality bodies have been established, namely the 'Equal Opportunities Commission' (EOC), the Commission for Racial Equality (CRE) and the Disability Rights Commission (DRC), respectively. These Commissions are, however, not endowed with a quasi judicial mandate, as is the Dutch ETC (although they do have an investigation power). The EOC, CRE and DRC are funded by public money and they have the task of promoting equality and non-discrimination in their respective policy areas.[134] It should be mentioned that the equality Commissions have the right to provide legal assistance to victims of discrimination, including the right to represent them in judicial proceedings. It is worth pointing out that the Equality Act 2006,[135] which received Royal Assent on 16-02-06 but which has not yet entered into force, seeks to establish the 'Commission for Equality and Human Rights' which consequently entails a dissolution of the EOC, the CRE and the DRC.

5. Closing Remarks

The aim of this chapter was to provide the necessary background for the comparative law analysis to be carried out in the chapters to follow. It has *inter alia* been illustrated that in the context of EC equality and non-discrimination law, trends can be discerned towards a 'constitutionalisation' of equality at the supranational level. This has been contrasted with the economic rationale which dominated EC (sex and nationality) discrimination law at the inception of the integration project. Moreover the, for the purposes of this book, the most important aspects of the domestic equality law frameworks have been mapped. Whereas Dutch equal treatment law clearly reflects a constitutionalised principle of equality, English non-discrimination law has primarily taken shape in the context of labour relations and employment law. A number of substantive and theoretical aspects of both the EC, and the domestic legal frameworks will be considered in greater detail in the chapters to follow.

134 Cooper 2004.

135 This Act is available at <http://www.opsi.gov.uk/ACTS/acts2006/ukpga_20060003_en.pdf> (last visited on 04-05-06).

PART II

CONCEPTS OF DISCRIMINATION

Part II

CONCEPTS OF DISCRIMINATION

1. Presenting the Structure for Research

In present times, four different concepts of discrimination feature in the EC equality and non-discrimination *acquis*, namely (1) 'direct discrimination', (2) 'indirect discrimination', (3) 'harassment' and (4) the 'instruction to discriminate'.[1] In addition to these the EFD contains a duty imposed upon employers[2] to make reasonable accommodation for disabled people 'in order to guarantee compliance with the principle of equal treatment' (Article 5 EFD). Space and time have precluded the author from making an in-depth analysis of all of these concepts. The concept of reasonable accommodation will be submitted to a detailed analysis in Chapter 8 which deals with 'disability'. It will therefore not be discussed in the present Part II, given that strictly spoken EC law does not conceive 'reasonable accommodation' as a concept of discrimination.[3] In Part II a selection has been made to analyse the concepts of 'indirect discrimination' and 'harassment'. This will be done in, respec-

1 Article 2 RD; Article 2 EFD; Article 2 AETD. The 'instruction to discriminate' is mentioned here for purposes of completeness. It is contained in Article 2(2)(4) RD; Article 2(2)(4) EFD and Article 2(2)(4) AETD. These Articles specify that an instruction to discriminate against persons defined by a protected status (race, disability, sex, etc.) shall be deemed to be a form of discrimination for purposes of the Directives. A common example is the employer's instruction to a recruitment agency to merely recruit, e.g. white persons. Given that the concept of instruction to discriminate is self-explanatory it will be discussed in no more detail hereafter.

2 And others to whom the Directive is addressed within the context of employment.

3 This follows from the fact that this concept is not regulated in Article 2 EFD ('concepts of discrimination') but in a separate Article 5 EFD, which makes reference to the equal treatment principle but not to the principle of non-discrimination as such. In the Commission's original proposal for the EFD reasonable accommodation was regulated in the same Article as was direct discrimination, indirect discrimination and harassment. See Proposal for a Council Directive Establishing a General Framework for Equal Treatment in Employment and Occupation, 25.11.1999, COM (1999) 565 final. It will be argued in Chapter 8 that an employer's failure to make reasonable accommodation for disabled persons constitutes an autonomous form of discrimination which should not be conceived as either a form of direct or indirect discrimination nor as a form of so-called positive action. Positive action will be considered in Chapter 5.

tively, Chapters 3 and 4 hereafter. One of the reasons why 'indirect discrimination', rather than 'direct discrimination' was prioritised for detailed examination is that the former is far more elusive compared to the latter and is generally conceived as difficult to grasp. Furthermore, with reference to Chapter 1, the way in which 'indirect discrimination' has been regulated in the RD, the EFD and the AETD makes inroads into the theoretical premises underlying this concept. This is not the case with 'direct discrimination' which *inter alia* therefore makes it less appealing as a subject for detailed examination. This is all the more true, given that (as will be illustrated in Chapter 3) shifts in the theoretical rationales of the concept of indirect discrimination can be explained with reference to a cross-ground comparison. Notwithstanding that 'direct discrimination' shall not thoroughly be examined, it seems nonetheless useful to deal with this concept briefly, so as to provide a comprehensive analysis. This will be done in section 2 below. Furthermore, the concept of direct discrimination will be referred to at appropriate junctures in both Chapters 3 and 4. Prior to the adoption of the RD and the EFD 'indirect discrimination' (as well as 'direct discrimination') already featured EC sex and nationality discrimination law. However, (*inter alia*) as a result of the expansion of the EC equality law framework with new grounds the concept of indirect discrimination has undergone a number of conceptual changes. In Chapter 3 'indirect discrimination' will be analysed from a comparative law perspective which involves 'top down', 'bottom up', 'cross ground' and 'cross country' dimensions. In addition, I will illustrate this concept with reference to the theory of equality and non-discrimination. It will *inter alia* be shown that indirect discrimination parallels the comparative model of equality and non-discrimination, whereas at the same time this concept accords a substantive connotation to the equality principle.

In contrast to the concepts of direct and indirect discrimination, 'harassment' is a novel concept in Community equality and non-discrimination law. This is one reason why this concept was chosen to be examined in detail. In addition, 'harassment' is an interesting concept for analysis, given that it is to be conceived outside the classic framework of EC non-discrimination law. The latter is founded on the comparative model of justice, whereas 'harassment' accords a validated connotation to justice. By this I mean that establishing a case of harassment does not require the plaintiff to engage in a comparative exercise. In Chapter 4, I will analyse the concept of harassment within a theoretical context of equality and non-discrimination law. In addition, I will subject this concept of discrimination to a comparative law analysis, which will largely trigger a top-down and cross-country analysis, although the bottom-up and cross-ground dimensions will be referred to wherever appropriate. The analyses in Chapters 3 and 4 will be illustrated with reference to the discrimination grounds 'race', 'sex' and 'disability'. Other discrimination grounds will be considered in great deal in Part IV. At this juncture it is, however, necessary first to briefly expound upon the concept of direct discrimination. It is to this that I will now turn.

2. The Concept of Direct Discrimination

Anti-discrimination lawyers usually draw a distinction between the concepts of direct (sometimes called 'overt') and indirect ('covert') discrimination. An actor who discriminates directly explicitly utilises a forbidden ground (race, sex, disability, etc) in the decision-making process. For example, an employer who restricts certain employment-related advantages (e.g. a Christmas bonus) to e.g., white employees directly discriminates on grounds of race. Likewise, an employer who refuses to employ a pregnant job candidate makes himself guilty of direct sex discrimination, given that 'pregnancy' is inextricably linked to 'sex'.[4] The undercurrent of the legal prohibition of direct discrimination is the idea that considerations over race, sex, disability, etc. are illegitimate in the decision-making process and must therefore be ignored. Naturally, employers who are aware of anti-discrimination law and who wish to discriminate are not likely to do so directly but will search for a technique to achieve the same exclusionary effects without, however, referring directly to a protected ground. This is one of the reasons why it has been necessary to also prohibit indirect discrimination by law. This point will be discussed in further detail in Chapter 3.

The way 'direct discrimination' has been conceived by both supranational and domestic law reflects the comparative model of justice. Article 2(2)(a) of the RD specifies that 'direct discrimination shall be taken to occur where one person is treated less favourably than another is, has been or would be treated in a comparable situation on grounds of racial or ethnic origin'. Counterpart provisions are contained in Article 2(2)(a) EFD and in Article 2(2) first indent of the AETD with respect to the discrimination grounds covered by these instruments. It follows that in order to establish 'direct discrimination' the legislative framework requires the plaintiff to prove (1) 'less favourable treatment', (2) 'on a forbidden ground', (3) 'compared to a present/past/hypothetical comparator', (4) 'who is similarly situated as the plaintiff' (but for the forbidden ground). In other words, with reference to the example of the Christmas bonus above, a black worker who is denied this bonus must prove, not only, that this was on grounds of race. He will also have to prove that a white fellow worker, who is in the same circumstances as the plaintiff, is, was or would have been granted the bonus. In summary, the comparative model perceives the treatment meted out to 'A' relative to that meted out to 'B'.[5] For there to be no discrimination this treatment has to be 'consistent' and, therefore, the principle of direct

4 See *inter alia Dekker v. Stichting Vormingscentrum voor Jong Volwassenen* (Case C-177/88), [1990] ECR I-3941; *Webb v. EMO Air Cargo* (Case C-32/93), [1994] ECR I-3567. For further discussion of pregnancy-based discrimination in the context of EC law, I refer to Caraciollo and Masselot 2001.

5 Needless to say, the comparator requirement is an anathema in such situations where no relevant comparator can be found. It could be that in a segregated workforce certain jobs are exclusively performed by persons of one sex (e.g. cleaning jobs that are solely performed by females in a particular labour setting). An employer who treats his cleaners badly because they are women cannot be held responsible under anti-discrimination law in the absence of a male comparator who is, was or would have been treated more favourably. The 'comparative exercise' has moreover been particularly detrimental in cases of ground-related harassment. This point will be illustrated in detail in Chapter 4.

discrimination has been conceived in terms of 'consistency equality'.[6] The only exemption from the comparative model of justice which has been granted by EC law (i.e. by the ECJ's case law) so far, and therefore also by domestic law, concerns the example of pregnancy discrimination: since logically there is no relevant comparator to a pregnant woman, pregnancy-based discrimination constitutes direct sex discrimination *per se*.[7]

Creating a schism between 'direct' and 'indirect discrimination' is particularly pertinent when the legal framework is founded upon a 'closed model'[8] of anti-discrimination law.[9] This has twin reasons. Firstly, a 'closed model' of anti-discrimination law is characterised by a limited number of exceptions which are contained within the legislative instrument itself. With reference to Chapter 2, the EC and domestic legal frameworks largely[10] rest upon the 'closed model' and therefore they do not permit a *general* justification defence with respect to instances of direct discrimination. Once a plaintiff has proven the relevant legal requirements of 'direct discrimination' an instance of direct discrimination will be established, unless the alleged perpetrator successfully relies upon an exception contained within the legislative framework itself.[11] The situation is different with respect to indirect discrimination. As will be expounded upon in Chapter 3, indirect discrimination is open to a general 'objective justification' defence which can be relied upon by the alleged perpetrator and which is subject to interpretation by the courts. Therefore, once a plaintiff has proven the legal elements of indirect discrimination the courts will conclude a case of *prima facie* indirect discrimination. It is subsequently for the alleged discriminator to prove the element of 'objective justification'. Secondly, the 'closed model' of anti-discrimination law is defined by a limited number of anti-discrimination grounds. This means that *direct* discrimination on a given ground can only be established if this ground is explicitly protected by the legal framework. Gerards has referred to the example of 'working time'.[12] Let us imagine an employer who renders the availability of jobs dependent on a working-time requirement: jobs are only granted to those who are committed to working full-time. The applicable anti-discrimination law framework rests upon a 'closed model'. It prohibits discrimination on a number of grounds including 'sex', but excluding 'working time'. A dis-

6 Fredman 2002, p. 94. For a criticism to the comparative/consistency model of equality in relation to the concept of direct discrimination, I refer to Fredman 2002, p. 93-102.

7 Dekker v. Stichting Vormingscentrum voor Jong Volwassenen (Case C-177/88), [1990] ECR I-3941; Webb v. EMO Air Cargo (Case C-32/93), [1994] ECR I-3567.

8 See Chapter 2.

9 Gerards 2004a, p. 11. Also Heringa 2005, p. 1.

10 The EC and domestic anti-discrimination frameworks rest upon an 'open model' as far as the discrimination ground 'age' is concerned. As will be shown in greater detail in Chapter 9 both direct and indirect age discrimination are susceptible for a general justification defence. Another 'open' element in the EC and national legal frameworks concerns the 'objective justification' test for instances of *prima facie* indirect discrimination. This will be explained in the main-text hereafter and will be expounded upon in great detail in Chapter 3.

11 Exceptions in relation to direct discrimination will not be elaborated on at this juncture but will partially be dealt with in other sections of this book.

12 Gerards 2004a, p. 11.

advantaged female job applicant aims to challenge the employer's practice. She cannot, however, claim an instance of direct discrimination, given that 'working time' *in se* is not a forbidden ground. She will, therefore, have to take a sideways approach and challenge the employer's practice on the basis of indirect sex discrimination: given that the full-time working time requirement largely affects female applicants who, due to child-rearing responsibilities, tend to work part-time, the employer's practice *indirectly* discriminates on grounds of sex.[13] If, however, the legal framework was founded on an 'open model' the job applicant in casu would have had the opportunity to challenge the employer's practice on the basis of direct discrimination, given that the list of protected grounds would be open ended and would therefore also include the ground of 'working-time'. This would make her case stronger, given that unlike indirect discrimination, direct discrimination cannot be justified.

In the above a brief analysis has been provided of direct discrimination with a view to offering a more inclusive analysis of Part II. Direct discrimination will be embedded in the analysis in the two chapters to follow wherever this is apposite.

13 Unless the employer successfully invokes the objective justification defence. The example partially reveals the working in practice of the concept of indirect discrimination. This concept will, however, be dealt with in an in-depth fashion in Chapter 3.

Chapter 3

INDIRECT DISCRIMINATION

1. Introduction

Indirect discrimination, sometimes referred to as disparate or adverse impact discrimination,[1] stems from the equal application of neutral rules, practices, policies, etc. which causes a disproportionate disadvantage for a particular group of people defined by a forbidden ground and for which there is no objective justification.[2] Let us take the example of the employer who makes a job offer conditional upon a driving-licence requirement. Although this requirement is equally imposed upon all potential job candidates, it is likely to have a *particularly* disadvantageous effect upon certain disabled persons (e.g. persons with a visual impairment) who wish to be employed. Similarly, the employer who merely offers a job to those who can speak Dutch fluently is likely to indirectly discriminate against persons belonging to an ethnic minority designation. It goes without saying that the employer's language requirement operates to the advantage of the native population. What is more, the employer who merely offers a promotion to those who have been working in the enterprise for at least 10 consecutive years is likely to discriminate indirectly against female workers. This is so, for women are more likely than men to interrupt their professional lives for the sake of childcare and family responsibilities.[3] The fact that women rather than men tend to reconcile their professional lives with domestic duties also means that in practice many women work part-time.[4] Full-time working

1 Disparate or adverse impact discrimination is the terminology usually employed in U.S. law. In EC law and in the domestic laws of the Member States reference is commonly made to the notion of indirect discrimination. It is noted at the outset that the terms 'disparate impact discrimination' and 'adverse impact discrimination' imply the usage of statistical evidence in order to prove an instance of discrimination. This is, however, not implicit in the term 'indirect discrimination'. This point will be discussed in further detail in the analysis hereafter.

2 This is a general explanation of the concept of indirect discrimination. The legal definition of indirect discrimination will be expounded upon in Sections 3, 4 and 5 hereafter in the context of EC and domestic law.

3 For further discussion, I refer to Hervey and Shaw 1998.

4 See Fredman and Szyszczak 1992, p. 217-218, who have argued that one of the prime factors which causes discrimination of women is women's natural role as child bearers and rearers.

requirements therefore indirectly discriminate against female workers. In summary: although all of the aforementioned requirements are 'neutrally' applied to *all* (potential) employees, *in practice* they are more disadvantageous to members of a particular group (e.g. women) compared to members of a for the comparison relevant benchmark group (men).[5] The foregoing examples show that the concept of indirect discrimination is not concerned with the actor's motives behind the imposition of a neutral requirement but rather with the *effects* that such a requirement has *in practice* on those within a particular pool. Indeed, employers who discriminate indirectly are all too often not aware of this although sometimes an employer will act deliberately, precisely with a view to cloaking his intention to discriminate *directly*.[6] It follows therefore that indirect discrimination is devised to address those measures which are discriminatory in effect.[7] The prohibition by law of indirect discrimination firstly aims to *expose* the different socio-economic position of members of disadvantaged groups by decoding neutrally applied rules. It subsequently also aims to *accommodate* this different position in practice, for example, by obliging the employer to grant an employment benefit without distinction between part-time and full-time workers. Sometimes an employer will have valid reasons for the imposition of neutral requirements. Therefore the law does not prohibit indirect discrimination *per se* but permits employers to seek recourse to an 'objective justification' defence in order to vindicate their (at first sight) discriminatory conduct. For example, it will be far from reasonable to impose a native language requirement for the job of cleaner. However, the contrary can be true with respect to a teaching position. In other words, even if the application of a neutral requirement constitutes *prima facie* indirect discrimination it

5 In other words, in order to establish indirect discrimination is will not be necessary to prove that the vexed neutral requirement affects *exclusively* members of a particular group. The examples in the main text above refer to 'neutrally' applied requirements which are likely to affect members in the 'dominant' *and* in the 'disadvantaged' group. For example, a person without a leg impairment can equally be affected by a driving-licence requirement if he simply has never obtained such a licence. However, members of the disadvantaged group are *disproportionately* affected by the application of neutral requirements compared to members of the dominant group. In summary: the prohibition of indirect discrimination, like that of direct discrimination, is embedded within a 'comparative justice model'. However, whereas with direct discrimination the *entire* group of persons defined by a particular trait is excluded (e.g. a 'no blacks' requirement excludes the group of black persons for 100 percent), with indirect discrimination both members of the advantaged and disadvantaged group will be affected. However, members in the latter group will be far more affected compared to members in the former group. As stated, both direct and indirect discrimination reflect the comparative justice model. However, whereas with direct discrimination the comparison is to be drawn between individuals, 'indirect discrimination' calls for a comparison at the level of groups. This point will be further illustrated in the main text hereafter.

6 As stated in the preliminary issues to Part II one of the reasons why it has been necessary to prohibit indirect discrimination is to prevent employers from skirting around the prohibition of direct discrimination. In *Jenkins v. Kingsgate* (Case 96/80) [1981] ECR 911 (ECJ) the employer had purposely substituted a hitherto *directly* discriminating pay policy (women were paid less than men) by an indirectly discriminatory pay policy (part-time workers were accorded a lower wage than full-time workers) with the purpose of achieving the same result in practice. The *Jenkins* case will be expounded upon in more detail in section 3 hereafter.

7 Barnard 2000, p. 209.

may nonetheless be upheld by other overriding interests. These may include concerns over health and safety or legitimate business needs. As referred to in the preliminary issues to Part II the possibility for justification is one of the factors which distinguish indirect discrimination from direct discrimination in both EC and domestic law.

Up until this juncture the most important elements of indirect discrimination have been sketched. Hereafter, I will analyse this concept on the basis of a comparative law analysis. This covers an examination of the top-down, bottom-up, cross-ground and cross-country comparisons. As indicated earlier the analysis of 'indirect discrimination' will be exemplified with reference to the discrimination grounds race, sex and disability. The argument will proceed along the following stages. In section 2 hereafter I will first place the notion of indirect discrimination in its theoretical context. Various theoretical models of equality, on the one hand, will be bridged with the concept of indirect discrimination, on the other. In section 3, I will provide an analysis of indirect discrimination in EC law. The legal approaches to indirect discrimination adopted by English and Dutch law will be examined, respectively, in Sections 4 and 5. The domestic legal frameworks will be analysed in light of the requirements of supranational law. In section 6, I will offer an amalgamated analysis which reflects the top-down, bottom-up, cross-ground and cross-country analyses.

2. Theoretical Aspects of Indirect Discrimination

2.1. *Introduction*

Barnard and others have argued that the choice of which theoretical concepts of equality are translated into tangible provisions of law is one of the factors which account for the law's impact (which can be limited or great) on labour market structures.[8] Put differently, if the legal framework shows limited results in achieving the goals it seeks to pursue (e.g. combating discrimination, promoting diversity, preserving human dignity) this could *inter alia* be explained with reference to the theoretical framework underlying the law.[9] It follows that the theoretical foundations of the law function as a benchmark for its effectiveness. It is therefore important to gain some insight into these foundations.[10] Equality law may reflect divergent approaches to

8 Barnard, Deakin, Kilpatrick 2002, p. 146-147. The aforementioned authors have argued that the legislation in its present format, which hinges on a formal equality model, does little to address institutionalised forms of discrimination and occupational segregation. Also Loenen 1998, Chapter 2. In addition to explaining the law's successfulness in combating discrimination and achieving equality with reference to theoretical arguments, one should bear in mind the fact that the law by itself is inherently limited to realise major changes in societal structures (O'Leary 2000, p. 136 with further references). This is *a fortiori* true with respect to EC law given that the Community legislator is bound by the principle of attributed powers (Article 5 EC). See Hervey 2005, p. 318.

9 See also Fredman 2002, p. 92.

10 A number of scholars have argued that especially EU anti-discrimination and equality law is infused with a number of different theoretical models of equality. See notably McCrudden 2003 and 2003a. See also Bell 2003, who has referred to a 'patchwork of models' of equality that has become apparent in the context of EU equality law.

justice, including liberal, dignity, distributive and identity approaches.[11] Hereafter, I will link the concept of indirect discrimination to the theory of equality. Whilst doing so, I will pay attention to two common divides in equality and non-discrimination law, namely (1) the formal *v.* substantive equality divide and (2) the individual *v.* the group model of justice.[12]

2.2. *The Concept of Indirect Discrimination and the Formal v. the Substantive Equality Divide*

The legal prohibition of indirect discrimination reflects a recognition of the limits of the liberal or economic model of equality.[13] This model rests on the assumption that all are freely acting agents making independent individual choices. However, 'the economic model' [of equality; MG], writes Hepple, 'simply does not correspond to the real world in which individuals usually do not have a free choice, precisely because of differences in wealth, social class, gender, race and so on'.[14] Another voiced criticism is that the liberal model of equality strongly relies upon the (white) male norm as a starting-point for competition in the market.[15] Feminist legal writing argues that the liberal model is inherently limited in bringing about real changes in the lives of women.[16] The liberal model is in principle hostile to public intervention in the market, whereas feminists have argued that state intervention is an indispensable tool in the realisation of structural changes in existing inequalities for men and women.[17] According to a feminist vision of justice, such intervention ought to

11 See for in-depth discussions on each of these approaches the contributions by a number of authors in McCrudden 2004.

12 The question of whether anti-discrimination and equality law should offer legal protection to disadvantaged *groups* or rather to *individuals* has been fiercely debated in the U.S., particularly in the context of affirmative action. For example, in the case of *Adarand Constructors, INC. Petitioner v. Federico Pena, Secretary of Transportation, Et al.* 515 U.S. 200 (1995) [United States Supreme Court] it was explicitly held that '(…) the basic principle [is that] the Fifth and Fourteenth Amendments to the Constitution protect *persons*, not *groups* (italics MG) [per Justice O'Connor, who wrote the majority opinion for the Supreme Court]. In casu, it was held that '(…) all racial classifications [regardless of whether they are 'benign' or 'illegitimate'; MG], imposed by whatever federal, state, or local governmental actor, must be analyzed by a reviewing court under strict scrutiny' [per justice O'Connor]. Since U.S. equal treatment law falls outside the scope of this book this will not be discussed in further detail hereafter. The specific element of 'judicial review' in (*inter alia*) U.S. equal treatment law has been analysed in depth by Gerards 2005a, Chapter 5 (with further references).

13 Fredman 1997a, p. 287. Among the major advocates of the economic vision of equality are Posner and Epstein. See Posner 1989 and Epstein 1992.

14 Hepple 1997, p. 141.

15 Feminist scholars have strongly rejected the adherence to the male norm by the non-discrimination law framework with respect to 'sex'. See *inter alia*: MacKinnon 1991; Lacey 1987; Lacey 2004; Fredman 1996, p. 199-201. As Fredman writes: 'The first weakness of the equality principle is that because it is tied to a male norm, it is unable to achieve real structural change' (p. 199); Also Fredman 1992, p. 119 and Fredman 1994, p. 106. See also Fenwick and Hervey 1995, p. 443-450.

16 *Ibid.*

17 Lacey 1992, p. 106.

be directed at matters such as parental leave legislation, child care facilities, positive action, the gendered labour market, etc. The tenor of the feminist model is shared by proponents of Critical Race Theory (CRT) which equally seek to change power structures.[18]

The liberal vision of equality parallels the concept of formal equality.[19] Formal, or Aristotelian, equality requires that 'things (and persons) that are alike should be treated alike, while things that are unalike should be treated unalike in proportion to their unalikeness'.[20] The problem with formal equality is that, in practice, it has been taken to mean that all be accorded *the same* treatment regardless of the different starting positions of different people.[21] In other words, the principle of formal equality is insensitive to the fact that disadvantage is unevenly spread across society. Meting out *the same* treatment to, for example, a disabled person and a non-disabled person will often be disadvantageous to the former, given that a disabled person finds him (her) self in a *different* starting position compared with a non-disabled person. The same point could be applied with respect to members belonging to other disadvantaged groups. Formal equality has also been referred to as 'equality as consistency',[22] 'Arithmetic equality'[23] and 'liberal legalism'.[24] Formal equality underlies the legal prohibition of direct discrimination[25] which requires that one person be treated on an equal (i.e. consistent) footing with another person.

The formal equality model can be contrasted with the substantive model. The principle of substantive equality recognises the differences *in practice* between, for example, women *v.* men, persons in the ethnic majority pool *v.* persons in the ethnic minority pool and disabled *v.* non-disabled persons. Substantive equality recognises that genuine equality can only be achieved if decision-makers actively take account of the different socio-economic, cultural, or other position of people, rather than flushing out such differences from the decision-making process. *A fortiori* the substantive equality model argues that treating all persons in a consistent fashion merely leads to a perpetuation of inequality. The concept of indirect discrimination hinges on the model of substantive equality.[26] Gerards has expressed the link between substantive equality, on the one hand, and indirect discrimination, on the other, as follows: '[t]he concept of indirect inequality implies (...) recognition of the fact that formal

18 See Crenshaw, Gotanda, Peller and Thomas 1995, *Introduction.*

19 Fredman 2001, p. 23. Also, Hepple, Coussey and Choudhury 2000, p. 27.

20 Aristotle, *Ethica Nichomacea,* 1925 translated by Ross, p. 1131a-6, cited by Schiek 2002a, p. 150.

21 In other words, the clause 'while things that are unalike should be treated unalike in proportion to their unalikeness' has not generally been translated into the formal equality law framework.

22 Fredman 2002, p. 7.

23 Schiek, 2002a, p. 149-167.

24 Lacey 1992, p. 106.

25 The concept of direct discrimination has been discussed in brief in the preliminary issues to Part II.

26 See for a sound discussion on substantive equality in relation to the concept of indirect discrimination the contribution by Barnard and Hepple 2000, especially p. 567-576. See also McInerney 2003, p. 11: 'While a more formalistic, process-based perspective is evident in the definition of direct discrimination, a more expansive and contextualized perspective underpins the Directive's definition of indirect discrimination'. See moreover Loenen 1999, p. 199.

equality may sometimes result in substantive, factual inequality.'[27] The concept of indirect discrimination aims to dismantle the strategy of 'sameness of treatment' as a tool for achieving equality, given that it acknowledges that treating persons all the same is likely to reinforce inequality. It therefore aims to translate the different starting points of persons in today's competitive society into an enforceable right, namely the right not to be indirectly discriminated against on a forbidden ground. In summary: the concept of indirect discrimination endorses a view of equality which takes account of material differences between persons.

2.3. *The Concept of Indirect Discrimination and the Models of Individual and Group Justice*

2.3.1. Comparative Justice

As referred to in the preliminary issues to Part II the concept of direct discrimination is captured within a comparative model of justice. Whether a person has received unequal treatment has to be decided with reference to the kind of treatment that has been accorded to a similarly situated comparator. The fact that anti-discrimination law insists upon a comparative exercise has rightfully been criticised. As Prechal has argued

> '(...) non-discrimination is about situations where certain people are put at a disadvantage, because they have certain characteristics. It prohibits the use of certain traits as a criterion for different treatment. The relevance or irrelevance of the traits is sociologically and culturally determined (...) in principle [there is] no scope for the question whether (...) a white and a black man are comparable or not'.[28]

Furthermore, it is questionable whether it can be maintained that the relevant comparator is 'similarly situated' to the alleged victim (but for the forbidden ground). For example, the socio-economic position of black persons is so much different from that of white persons that both cannot fairly be compared. In the context of sex equality MacKinnon has argued that the comparison requirement forms the '*doctrinal guise of dominance*' and that as a result of it sex equality theory has been inadequate in addressing the substance of sex inequality.[29]

No less than direct discrimination is indirect discrimination fashioned along the lines of comparative justice. However, whereas direct discrimination requires that a comparison be drawn between two similarly situated individuals, indirect discrimination calls for a comparison at the level of groups.[30] In summary, whereas direct discrimination parallels the individual justice model, indirect discrimination

27 Gerards 2005a, p. 13.

28 Prechal 2004, p. 543-544. See also Gerards 2004b, p. 103-104 and footnote 18.

29 MacKinnon 1990-1991, p. 1296.

30 As will be illustrated in section 3 below, current EC indirect discrimination law marks a departure from the group-justice approach.

concurs with the group-justice model. Both models will respectively be discussed in sections 2.3.2 and 2.3.3 hereafter.

2.3.2. Individual Justice[31]

As its name suggests the individual justice model[32] aims to secure justice for the individual victim of discrimination, rather than for the group to which that individual belongs. The model therefore perceives the individual victim of discrimination outside the context of the group of which (s)he is a member.[33] According to this model, personal traits such as race, sex, disability, etc. should be entirely irrelevant factors in the decision-making process[34] which should be exclusively governed by the principles of individual merit, efficiency and individual autonomy.[35] The individual justice model harbours the principle of formal equality, referred to above, and reflects the tenets of liberal or market-based equality. As Quinn has put it 'the image at play is that of the unencumbered self'.[36] The law transposes the philosophy of individual justice by the prohibition of direct discrimination which, as earlier illustrated, requires a comparison of the equal treatment of individual *x* with that of individual *y*. The essential merit of the prohibition of direct discrimination is that it empowers individuals who might otherwise be discriminated against by reason of personal traits.

The fact that the individual justice model is not conscious of the unequal starting positions of persons within the dominant pool, on the one hand, compared to members of the oppressed group, on the other, has a number of consequences. Firstly, it brings with it that the legal framework which reflects individual justice applies symmetrically. This means that the law affords equal protection to, e.g. men and women, whites and blacks, disabled persons and non-disabled persons, notwithstanding that in reality women, black persons and disabled persons are the ones who are disadvantaged. As Hepple has argued, irregular patterns of disadvantage find their cause in history and they are preserved in current times due to unequal opportunities for disadvantaged groups to obtain education and training and to participate in the labour market.[37]

Secondly, given that the individual justice model adheres to the notion of formal equality it bears the risk of fostering assimilation and therefore inequality.[38] Assimilation means that the right to equality of those in the disadvantaged pool is

31 This model has *inter alia* been analysed by McCrudden 2001, p. 253-255.

32 Some have referred to [the] 'corrective justice' [model]. See Morris 1995, p. 204.

33 McCrudden 2001, p. 253-255 where he has analysed the essential elements of the individual and group justice models. Also McCrudden 2003, p. 14-15. See moreover Fredman 2005, p. 203-204.

34 McCrudden 2001, p. 253; McCrudden 2003, p. 14; McCrudden 2003a, p. 20-22; Fredman 2002a, p. iii, who has argued that the individual justice model seeks to create a 'colour blind' and 'gender neutral' world in which each individual can prosper in its own individual capacity.

35 See the illuminating analysis by Fredman 1997, p. 576-581.

36 Quinn 2004, p. 6.

37 Hepple 1990, p. 413-414.

38 Fredman 1996, p. 197.

adjusted to the standard which is adopted by those in the dominant pool. For example, a full-time working requirement rests upon a male dominated norm, given that men unlike women are likely to be full-time available for work.[39] Similarly, the absence of a lift in the work premises reflects the dominant standard of normality, given that the majority of workers can walk. In summary, although the individual justice model is aimed at meting out neutral (equal) treatment to all, the 'neutrality' of the treatment is in fact biased. This is so, given that the dominant standard is implicitly taken as a point for departure in the decision-making process.[40] Citing the words of Young,

> 'The strategy of assimilation aims to bring formerly excluded groups into the mainstream. So assimilation always implies coming into the game after it is already begun, after the rules and standards have already been set and having to prove oneself according to those rules and standards. In the assimilationist strategy, the privileged groups implicitly define the standards according to which all will be measured.'[41]

Thirdly, if the legal framework rests upon the individual justice model, this will have consequences too for the nature of legal proceedings. In essence, the model requires that for an instance of unequal treatment to be proven an individual harm will have to be established, which has been inflicted upon a discernible individual victim through the fault of an identifiable perpetrator.[42] Therefore, writes Quinn, 'the legal responsibility must never be ascribed to persons who bear no *personal* [italics MG] responsibility for the injustice complained of'.[43] Remedies are equally individualised in the sense that if harm can be established, a remedy will be afforded to the particular individual victim concerned without, however, providing legal redress to those who find themselves in a similar situation.

2.3.3. Group Justice[44]

Securing justice at the level of the individual is necessary, for it empowers persons and liberates them from discrimination and oppression. At the same time securing individual justice is not sufficient. One of the pitfalls of the individual justice model is that it fails to recognise the deeply embedded and structural nature of discrimination.[45] Often discrimination cannot be attributed to the acts of a single, individual

39 See in this context Hepple 1997, p. 144 (with reference to Whiteford) who has observed as follows: 'Existing employment and pension benefits are structured according to the expectations of the full-time worker in continuous employment from the age of 16 to that of (male) retirement.' Furthermore, the fact that part-time workers tend to be female workers is to be attributed to the shortage of paid paternity leave and adequate childcare facilities. See Fredman 2002, p. 115, who has argued that the introduction of a prohibition of indirect discrimination does not reverse the societal fact that most part-time employees are female.

40 MacKinnon 1987, p. 34.

41 Young 1990, p. 164.

42 Fredman 2005a, who has contrasted the individual complaints model with proactive strategies to achieve equality in practice; McCrudden 2001, p. 254.

43 Quinn 2004, p. 7.

44 This model has *inter alia* been examined by McCrudden 2001, p. 255-257.

45 Fredman 1996, p. 215-216.

perpetrator. In contrast, discrimination is deeply ingrained in the organisational setup of society. Somek, in the (rather different) context of a discussion on the European Economic Constitution has distinguished between what he has called the 'behavioural' and 'systemic' level of discrimination. The former can be traced back to individual conduct. The latter 'concerns the aggregate effect of actions that may be (legitimately) carried out by individual agents without the slightest discriminatory intent'.[46] The institutional nature of discrimination is acknowledged by the group-justice model which does not perceive victims of discrimination in a societal vacuum but against the contextual background of the group to which they belong.[47] 'The basic aim' [of group justice; MG], argues McCrudden, 'is the improvement of the relative position of particular groups (…)'.[48] This being so, the group justice model does recognise the fact that disadvantage is irregularly spread. Therefore, a legal framework which rests upon a group-justice approach to equality applies asymmetrically which means that it solely aims to protect *women, persons of ethnic minority designations, disabled persons* (etc.). The underlying rationale for the law's sensitivity to group disparity is a concern over redistribution, rather than discrimination.[49] Put differently, the aim of the group justice model is to secure that all persons regardless of colour, sex, etc. should get an equal[50] share in the distribution of goods, labour, wealth and the like, unless there exists an objective justification for unequal distribution.[51]

The undercurrent of the prohibition by law of indirect discrimination is also a redistribution rationale.[52] Indirect discrimination therefore parallels group justice.[53] As Schiek has argued,

46 Somek 2001, p. 180. See moreover Tobler 2003, p. 18, who has defined structural discrimination as follows: '[Structural discrimination] (…) connotes disadvantages flowing from a given society's organisation, deeply held views (sometimes even unconscious) prejudices and the like (…)'.

47 See *inter alia* Fredman 2001, p. 24.

48 McCrudden 2001, p. 255.

49 McCrudden 2001, p. 255. In a similar fashion Collins has argued that '(...) permitting claims for 'indirect discrimination' or 'disparate impact' serves the purpose of reducing institutional barriers to the achievement of a distributive goal such as more equality in results or fairer equality of opportunity'. See Collins 2003, p. 17. See moreover Michelman: '(…) the anti-discrimination principle is collectivist. It is a principle of distribution of goods among individuals, which can work as a mandate for redistribution' (Michelman 1986, p. 28). See, in contrast, Young 1990, who has argued that the need for taking account of group disparities and difference must be understood against the background of domination and oppression, rather than redistribution.

50 It should, however, be highlighted that what amounts to 'equal' is by itself object of academic debate. In other words, legal and philosophical minds differ on what are the exact parameters of equality. The principle of equality may, for example, be conceived in terms of 'equality of opportunities' or 'equality of outcomes'. Both notions will be discussed in Chapter 5 in the context of positive action.

51 This information was gained during a course organised by the Netherlands Research School of Women's Studies (NOV) coordinated by Professor Dr. Magda Michielsens and in which the author participated in March 2004.

52 Bamforth 1996, p. 59 with further references.

> '[indirect discrimination] transcends the formal and individualistic view of traditional equal treatment in favour of a substantive and collective view of equality while being sensitive to group disparity. However, the concept may be more or less group directed. The key is the standard for justification'.[54]

That indirect discrimination may be more or less group-oriented has also been argued by Morris: '[i]ndirect discrimination looks like a hybrid, combining the tort-like structure and individualised claims of direct discrimination with the group-based focus of positive discrimination'.[55] I will elaborate on this point in the discussions of indirect discrimination in the context of positive EC and domestic law hereafter. The group rationale of indirect discrimination becomes apparent from the fact that the prohibition of indirect discrimination is aimed at displaying structural patterns of discrimination which bear a disadvantageous impact upon *groups* of persons defined by a protected ground. If an indirectly discriminatory practice is successfully challenged in legal proceedings, this may have a beneficial effect on all the members of the group to which the individual plaintiff belongs.[56] Let us take the example of a part-time working female employee who brings proceedings against her employer by reason that the latter restricts participation in a pension scheme to full-time workers. If a court or tribunal decides that the employer's practice constitutes indirect sex discrimination this will not only be to the benefit of the individual plaintiff but indeed of all other part-time workers in the company. After all, the employer will be under a duty to extend participation in the scheme to all part-time working employees (both female and male).[57] Dismantling institutionalised forms of discrimination, as indirect discrimination aims to do, also bears the advantage of promoting diversity. After all, the different position of those who do not conform to the dominant norm is not only recognised by the law but is moreover aimed to be accommodated.[58] Therefore, although the law formulates the prohibition of indirect discrimination in a negative fashion ('you shall not') the concept nonetheless contributes to a positive vision of equality which strives for the accommodation and celebration of differ-

53 See for a different account Morris 1995, p. 199-228. In Morris' vision indirect discrimination finds its firmest basis in the 'individual oriented rationale' of the anti-discrimination principle. Morris' main thesis is that the underlying motivating values of the concept of indirect discrimination relate to the correction of wrongs done by individuals and that the concept fits best with a 'corrective justice' approach.

54 Schiek 2000, p. 244.

55 Morris 1995, p. 199.

56 Also Whittle 2002, p. 308.

57 On the other hand, the legal prohibition of indirect discrimination is a limited instrument, given that it does not change the societal fact *that* women and not men tend to work part-time due to domestic and family duties. As Fredman has argued outlawing indirect discrimination does not result in a 'reconfiguration of the norm itself'. See Fredman 2005, p. 203.

58 Fredman has in this context argued that 'by examining the impact of apparently neutral practices and criteria, indirect discrimination reveals the extent to which the dominant culture (...) is favoured'. See Fredman 2002, p. 109.

ence.[59] As such indirect discrimination contributes to the affirmation of the identity of various groups.[60]

3. Indirect Discrimination in EC Law

3.1. Introduction

According to one commentator, writing in 1998, '(…) indirect discrimination has been viewed as the greatest achievement of the ECJ in its corpus of sex equality in employment jurisprudence'.[61] Doubtlessly, the ECJ has played a pivotal role in the shaping of the concept of indirect discrimination. However, one must bear in mind that judicial activism in the context of EC law occurs at twin levels namely, that of the Luxembourg Court and that of the domestic courts. This duality is captured by Article 234 EC which governs the preliminary reference procedure which hinges on an idea of cooperation[62] between the ECJ, on the one hand, and the national judiciary, on the other. The importance of this procedure in the context of EC law cannot be over-emphasised.[63] Judicial shaping of the principle of non-discrimination, including the concept of indirect discrimination, largely depends therefore on the willingness of national courts to refer cases to the ECJ in the first place, and, on the willingness of the latter to subsequently provide detailed guidance to the referring court on how to interpret the concept of indirect discrimination in the concrete case at hand. In light of the foregoing, one commentator has characterised the relationship between the domestic courts and the ECJ as potentially 'fragile'.[64] Bearing these preliminary observations in mind, as well as the theoretical account of indirect discrimination provided in section 2 above, I will hereafter analyse this concept within the context of Community law. On the one hand, the analysis in the present section is functional to the top-down analysis in sections 4 and 5 hereafter. On the other hand, the analysis in this section takes account of cross-ground and bottom-up dimensions. It should be noted that the concept of indirect discrimination has up until now not been interpreted by the ECJ in the context of the RD and EFD. In contrast,

59 See Quinn 2004, p. 11.

60 This relatively recent vision of equality has *(inter alia)* been discerned by Fredman. She has explained that the central elements of this vision of equality are the following: (i) the view that the equality principle should not strive for 'neutrality' but should rather promote 'difference'; (ii) the view that a positive identity of the group is enriching rather than excluding and that consequently group identity ought to be visualised; (iii) the view that a mere negative prohibition of discrimination is not enough and that positive approaches are called for. See Fredman 2002a, p. 15.

61 Kilpatrick 1998, p. 141.

62 The principle of cooperation is enshrined in general terms in Article 10 EC Treaty. For a general overview of the development of this Article and the duties of national authorities including the national courts under this Article, I refer to Lang 2003-2004, p. 1904-1939.

63 O'Leary 2000, p. 179-183. For a comprehensive account of the judicial dialogue of the ECJ with the UK Courts in the area of sex equality law, I refer to Kilpatrick 1998, p. 121-147 and Kilpatrick 2001.

64 Szyszczak 2005.

given the EC's long-term engagement in sex equality law, the concept of indirect sex discrimination has been interpreted extensively by the Court. It is likely that the ECJ while dealing in future cases with indirect discrimination on the grounds protected by the RD and EFD (e.g. race and disability) will seek recourse to its established case law on indirect sex (and nationality) discrimination.[65] If the Court does so this will foster a cross-fertilisation of judicial interpretation across the different grounds of discrimination (cross-ground comparison). Alternatively, the ECJ may decide to adopt different tests of judicial scrutiny for different grounds depending on the Court's willingness to address a particular social harm. The analysis hereafter will proceed along the following stages. In section 3.2 hereafter, I will map the gradual shift from a case law approach to indirect discrimination, to a legislative stance. In doing so, the emphasis will be on the legislative stance whereby particular attention will be paid to the definitions of indirect discrimination in the RD, the EFD and the AETD. I will subsequently examine the legislative elements of proving a *prima facie* case of indirect discrimination (section 3.3). I will thereafter analyse the objective justification test of indirect discrimination (section 3.4) While analysing 'objective justification' it will become apparent that striving for non-discrimination and equality is often in tension with competing interests. Brief conclusions will be drawn in section 3.5.

3.2. *Indirect Discrimination: the Shift from a Case by Case Approach to a Legislative Framework*[66]

3.2.1. The Emergence of Indirect Discrimination in ECJ Case Law

It should be highlighted at the outset that in current times no definition of indirect discrimination is contained in primary EC law. Article 141(1) and 141(2) EC contain the principle of equal pay between women and men for equal work or work of equal value[67] but is short of a definition of (direct and indirect) discrimination.[68] Neither the 1975 Equal Pay Directive,[69] nor the 1976 Equal Treatment Directive[70] contain a

65 Also Parmar 2004.

66 The shift from a case law approach to indirect discrimination to a legislative framework has been extensively analysed by Tobler 2005, Part Two, under A and B. Tobler's analysis is all-inclusive in the sense that it goes far beyond the area of (sex) equality law.

67 Article 141(1) and 141(2) EC (i.e. old Article 119 EC) solely applies to 'pay'. The principle of equal treatment between women and men as regards working conditions is captured by the AETD. For further background reading, I refer to Watson 1995, p. 34-35 and Barnard 2000, Chapter 4.

68 Article 141 EC is a directly applicable provision which can be relied on by a private individual before a domestic court and which will set aside national law in case of conflict. See *Defrenne v. Sabena II*, (Case 43/75) [1976] ECR 455 (ECJ).

69 Directive 75/117/EC on Equal Pay for Men and Women, *OJ* 1975, L 45/19.

70 Directive 76/207/EEC on Equal Treatment for Men and Women as regards Access to Employment, Vocational Training and Promotion and Working Conditions, *OJ* 1976, L 39/40. This Directive has been amended by Directive 2002/73/EC which has resulted in the AETD. The latter does contain a definition of indirect discrimination. This definition will be elaborated on in the main text hereafter.

definition of indirect discrimination. The 1976 ETD merely provides that 'the principle of equal treatment shall mean that there shall be no discrimination whatsoever on grounds of sex either directly or indirectly (...)'.[71] It follows that initially the development of indirect discrimination was purely a matter for the ECJ in interaction with domestic courts (notably the English and the German Courts). It is worth observing that the United Kingdom was the first Member State to introduce a legal definition of indirect discrimination in the domestic anti-discrimination law framework.[72] It might be argued that judicial interaction between the ECJ and the national courts fosters the bottom-up shaping of Community law, given that the latter is moulded on the basis of a factual scenario that occurs at the municipal level which raises questions of the correct interpretation of Community sex equality law.

The evolution of indirect discrimination in EC law started off in the context of the free movement of workers.[73] In *Sotgiu*[74] the ECJ took the view that 'The rules regarding equality of treatment (...), forbid not only overt discrimination by reason of nationality, but also all covert forms of discrimination which, by the application of other criteria of differentiation, lead in fact to the same result'.[75]

In the 1981 case of *Jenkins v. Kingsgate*[76] the ECJ was invited by an English EAT to consider an instance of indirect sex discrimination in the context of pay. In casu, the employer, a manufacturer of women's fashion, accorded a 10% lower pay rate to part-time workers compared with full-time workers. The total amount of workers working in *Kingsgate's* factory in Harlow was 89 of whom 35 were male and 54 female. But for one,[77] all male employees were working full-time whereas of the female employees five worked part-time. Mrs Jenkins, a part-time working employee, claimed that by according her a lower hourly rate of pay compared with a full-time working man doing the same work the employer was acting in contravention of Article 119 (of the then called) EEC Treaty and the 1975 Equal Pay Directive. With its first three questions the referring court essentially wished to learn whether Article 119 of the EEC Treaty prohibited an employer from paying a higher rate of wages to full-time workers compared to part-time workers when the latter category embraces exclusively or predominantly women.[78] The ECJ replied to this question as follows:

> '(...)a difference in pay between full-time workers and part-time workers does not amount to discrimination prohibited by Article 119 of the Treaty unless it is in reality merely an

[71] Article 2(1) ETD.

[72] Tobler 2005, p. 95-96.

[73] See cases *Württembergische Milchverwertung-Südmilch AG v. Salvatore Ugliola* (Case 15/69) [1969] ECR 363 and Case *Sotgiu v. Deutsche Bundespost* (Case 152/73) [1974] ECR 153. Both cases have been discussed by Tobler 2005 at p. 104-107 and at p. 110-115, respectively.

[74] *Ibid.*

[75] Paragraph 11 of the judgment.

[76] J.P. *Jenkins v. Kingsgate (Clothing Productions) Ltd* (Case C-96/80) [1981] ECR 911. This case will be examined in further detail in section 3.4.3.2 henceforth whilst examining 'objective justification'.

[77] This single part-time working male employee concerned a worker who was recently retired and who was subsequently and exceptionally re-engaged to work part-time for 16 hours a week.

[78] See paragraph 9 of the ECJ's judgment which summarises the first three preliminary questions.

> indirect way of reducing the level of pay of part-time workers on the ground that that group of workers is composed exclusively or predominantly of women.'[79]

Although in *Jenkins* the ECJ erroneously focused upon the *intent* of the alleged discriminator[80] the case is commonly regarded as the basis upon which the Court thenceforth refined the concept of indirect sex discrimination.[81] As will be illustrated in later sections in many subsequent cases the Court rendered the contours of indirect discrimination more and more visible.

3.2.2. A Legislative Approach to Indirect Discrimination

The first legal definition of indirect discrimination was introduced into Community law by the 1997 Burden of Proof Directive[82] which is confined to the discrimination ground 'sex'. Article 2 of the Directive provides as follows:

> '(...) indirect discrimination shall exist where an apparently neutral provision, criterion or practice disadvantages a substantially higher proportion of the members of one sex unless that provision, criterion or practice is appropriate and necessary and can be justified by objective factors unrelated to sex'.

This definition reflects the group-justice model of discrimination discussed in section 2.3.3 above. In order to establish *prima facie* indirect discrimination, the definition requires proof that due to the application of the vexed neutral provision, criterion or practice 'a substantially higher proportion of the members of one sex' is disadvantaged (compared to the members of the opposite sex). It is therefore not sufficient to prove that the neutral treatment at issue constitutes a harm for the individual applicant. The latter will also be required to prove that the treatment at stake has a 'disparate impact' upon the group to which the individual plaintiff belongs. Given that the definition makes reference to proportions, the plaintiff will have to prove disparate impact by means of statistical evidence.

The definition of indirect discrimination in the Burden of Proof Directive uses the simple present tense of the verb 'to disadvantage' ('disadvantages'). By doing so, the definition requires proof of actual disadvantage to the exclusion of a hypothetical harm. As soon as an instance of *prima facie* indirect discrimination has been

79 Paragraph 15.

80 Paragraph 14 where it was held as follows: 'Where the hourly rate of pay differs according to whether the work is part-time or full-time it is for the national court to decide in each individual case whether, regard being had to the facts of the case, its history and the employer's intention, a pay policy such as that which is at issue in the main proceedings although represented as a difference based on working hours is or is not in reality discrimination based on the sex of the worker.'

81 See also the case of *Sabbatini* (Case 20/71) [1972] ECR 363, cited and commented upon by Tobler 2005, p. 107-110.

82 Council Directive 97/80/EC of 15 December 1997 on the Burden of Proof in Cases of Discrimination based on Sex, *OJ* 1998, L 14/6 (henceforth: Burden of Proof Directive).

made out by the plaintiff the definition permits the respondent to rely on a justifiability defence.

Since the adoption of the RD and the EFD new definitions of indirect discrimination (which apply with respect to the grounds covered by these Directives)[83] have been incorporated into Community equality law. Article 2(2)(b) of the EFD reads as follows:

> 'Indirect discrimination shall be taken to occur where an apparently neutral provision, criterion or practice would put persons having a particular religion or belief, a particular disability, a particular age, or a particular sexual orientation at a particular disadvantage compared with other persons unless:
> (i) that provision, criterion or practice is objectively justified by a legitimate aim and the means of achieving that aim are appropriate and necessary, or
> (ii) as regards persons with a particular disability, the employer or any person or organisation to whom this Directive applies, is obliged, under national legislation, to take appropriate measures in line with the principles contained in Article 5 [reasonable accommodation MG] in order to eliminate disadvantages entailed by such provision, criterion or practice.'

A counterpart provision is contained in Article 2(2)(b) RD. The latter logically lacks, however, the additional justification defence permitted by Article 2(2)(b) EFD with respect to the ground 'disability'. The justifiability question will not be dealt with in this section but will be separately considered in section 3.4 hereafter.

The definitions of indirect discrimination in the RD and the EFD mark a departure from the statistical evidence approach to indirect discrimination adopted by the Burden of Proof Directive. This is so, for these definitions are short of a reference to *proportions* and merely require that the neutral treatment on which the complaint is based would put persons defined by a protected ground 'at a particular disadvantage'. The usage of the conditional tense ('would put') in the definitions of indirect discrimination in the RD and EFD also means that *actual* disadvantage needs not be proven. The elements of proving a *prima facie* case of indirect discrimination will be studied in detail in section 3.3 henceforth. The relaxation[84] of the insistence by EC law of proving indirect discrimination by way of statistics can be explained by reference to the underlying values of different grounds of discrimination. The nature of the discrimination ground 'sex' brings with it that the collection of statistical data on, for example, the participation of women and men in paid labour is a rather insensitive and routine exercise in the Member States. In contrast, some Member States prohibit the collection of statistical data in relation to 'race' and 'ethnicity', either for privacy related reasons, or by reference to the argument that the collection of such statistics is a racist exercise *in se*.[85] The privacy argument is

83 Namely racial or ethnic origin (RD) and religion, belief, disability, age and sexual orientation (EFD).

84 As will be argued in section 3.3 below, the RD and the EFD (as well as the AETD) do, however, not fully depart from the statistical evidence approach.

85 Tyson 2001, p. 203. Also House of Lords Select Committee on the European Union, '*EU Proposals to Combat Discrimination*', HL Paper 65, Session 1999-2000, 9th Report, paragraph 83. It should be noted in this context that Recital 6 of the Preamble to the RD explicitly states that 'the European →

equally apparent with respect to 'sexual orientation'.[86] The discrimination ground 'disability' is very difficult to capture by statistical data by reason of the widely ranging forms of disability. What is more, 'disability' denotes shifting categories and therefore causes problems of 'demarcation', i.e. of defining who is 'in' and who is 'out'.[87] In other words, the nature of disability does not easily lend itself to being approached from the perspective of group-justice. This point will be illustrated in further detail in Chapter 8.

For the sake of legal consistency, rather than for ground-related reasons, the AETD launched a new definition of indirect sex discrimination which is parallel to the ones found in the RD and EFD.[88] What was stated earlier with respect to the definitions of indirect discrimination in the RD and EFD therefore also applies to the definition contained in the AETD. The latter does, however, not replace the definition of indirect sex discrimination contained in the Burden of Proof Directive. As indicated by Tobler, two legal definitions of indirect sex discrimination currently exist in Community law[89] and their respective applicability in a concrete case depends on the factual scenario at stake.[90] The area of social security is covered neither by the AETD, nor

Union rejects theories which attempt to determine the existence of separate human races. The use of the term 'racial origin' in this Directive does not imply an acceptance of such theories'.

86 As pointed out by de Schutter, the usage of statistical evidence prompts questions on the matter of personal data protection. See de Schutter 2003, section 1.3.1. See also the following study by the European Commission: *Comparative Study on the Collection of Data to measure the extent and impact of discrimination within the United States, Australia, the United Kingdom and the Netherlands*, August 2004.

87 Hendriks 2000; Whittle 2002, 309, who has argued that the reliance on statistical evidence with a view to proving disparate impact 'is inappropriate in the context of disability'.

88 Article 2(2) second indent of the AETD reads as follows: 'Indirect discrimination: where an apparently neutral provision, criterion or practice would put persons of one sex at a particular disadvantage compared with persons of the other sex, unless that provision, criterion or practice is objectively justified by a legitimate aim, and the means of achieving that aim are appropriate and necessary.'

89 Tobler 2005, p. 298-299.

90 The material scope of the AETD is defined by Article 3(1) of the Directive which reads as follows: 'Application of the principle of equal treatment means that there shall be no direct or indirect discrimination on the grounds of sex in the public or private sectors, including public bodies, in relation to: (a) conditions for access to employment, to self-employment or to occupation, including selection criteria and recruitment conditions, whatever the branch of activity and at all levels of the professional hierarchy, including promotion; (b) access to all types and to all levels of vocational guidance, vocational training, advanced vocational training and retraining, including practical work-experience; (c) employment and working-conditions, including dismissals, as well as pay as provided for in Directive 75/117/EEC; (d) membership of, and involvement in, an organisation of workers or employers, or any organisation whose members carry on a particular profession, including the benefits provided for by such organisations.' The material scope of the Burden of Proof Directive is defined in Article 3 of that Directive. Article 3(1) specifies that the Directive shall apply to (a) the situations covered by Article 119 (141) EC and by Directives 75/117/EEC [Equal Pay Directive; MG] and 76/207/EEC [Equal Treatment Directive; MG] and, insofar as discrimination based on sex is concerned, 92/85/EEC [Pregnancy Directive; MG] and Directive 96/34/EC [Parental Leave Directive; MG]; (b) to any civil or administrative procedure concerning the public or private sector which provides for means of redress under national law pursuant to the measures referred to under (a) with the exception of →

by the Burden of Proof Directive. Therefore, indirect discrimination on grounds of sex in this area remains regulated by the ECJ's case law approach.[91] It goes without saying that the foregoing unnecessarily compounds an already complicated area of the law.[92]

The discussion on the legislative definitions of indirect discrimination above can be briefly recapitulated as follows. The definitions of indirect discrimination in the Burden of Proof Directive, on the one hand, and the RD, EFD and AETD, on the other differ in two important respects. Firstly, whereas 'indirect discrimination' in the Burden of Proof Directive hinges on a group-justice approach, 'indirect discrimination' in the RD, EFD and AETD mirrors the model of individual justice. This is so, given that the individual plaintiff is not required by EC law to prove that the neutrally applied standard constitutes a disparate impact upon the group to which (s)he belongs. The moderation of the statistical evidence requirement has been explained with reference to the different nature of different grounds of discrimination. Secondly, whereas 'indirect discrimination' in the Burden of Proof Directive calls for proof of 'actual disadvantage', the counterpart definitions in the RD, EFD and AETD merely require proof of a hypothetical disadvantage. Hereafter, I will continue with a discussion on how to prove indirect discrimination. This discussion will be presented in light of the case law by the ECJ.

3.3. *Proving Indirect Discrimination*

3.3.1. The Partially Reversed Burden of Proof

De Schutter has argued that notably in the realm of anti-discrimination law the substantive rights, on the one hand, (e.g. the right not to be discriminated against directly or indirectly) and the procedural guarantees to enforce these rights, on the other, are 'inextricably linked'.[93] This means that the quality of the former is largely dependent on the quality of the latter.[94] 'This', writes de Schutter, is illustrated par-

out-of-court procedures of a voluntary nature or provided for in national law. According to Article 3(2) the Directive shall not apply to criminal procedures, unless otherwise provided by the Member States. See also Bosse 2000, p. 65; Fairclough 2001, p. 1126-1127.

91 Tobler 2005, p. 299.

92 Tobler 2005, p. 299. This was also acknowledged by the EC Commission which did a proposal for a so-called 'recasting Directive' with a view to simplifying, modernising and improving Community legislation in the area of equal treatment between the sexes in employment and occupation (see: Proposal for a Directive of the European Parliament and of the Council on the implementation of the principle of equal opportunities and equal treatment of men and women in matters of employment and occupation COM (2004) 279 available at<http://europa.eu.int /scadplus/leg/en/cha/c10940.htm>. As I write, this proposal has been transformed into a Community Directive. See: Directive 2006/54/EC of the European Parliament and of the Council of 5 July 2006 on the implementation of the principle of equal opportunities and equal treatment of men and women in matters of employment and occupation, *OJ* L 204/23. This Directive consolidates the provisions of the existing EC sex equality directives, including established case law by the ECJ, into a single text. See also Tobler 2005, p. 299 with further comments.

93 De Schutter 2003, p. 23.

94 *Ibid.*

ticularly clearly by the law governing proof'.[95] Proving discrimination often turns out to be a particularly difficult hurdle for the individual victim to overcome. In light of this EC law, starting off with the case law of the Court,[96] has introduced a 'sharing exercise' for proving an alleged instance of discrimination.[97] Eventually, this sharing exercise has been codified in the Burden of Proof Directive. Article 4 of the Directive states as follows:

> 'Member States shall take such measures as are necessary, (...), to ensure that, when persons who consider themselves wronged because the principle of equal treatment has not been applied to them establish, before a court (...), facts from which it may be presumed that there has been (direct or) indirect discrimination, it shall be for the respondent to prove that there has been no breach of the principle of equal treatment.'[98]

Equivalent provisions are currently also contained in the EFD (Article 10 and Recital 31 of the Preamble) and in the RD (Article 8 and Recital 21 of the Preamble). In essence, these provisions require the plaintiff to raise a presumption of (indirect) discrimination which can subsequently be rebutted by the respondent.[99] In summary, the above provisions enshrine a partially reversed burden of proof. Hereafter, I will consider what needs to be proven in order to establish a *prima facie* case of indirect discrimination. The employer's justifiability defence will henceforth be considered in section 3.4.

3.3.2. Indirect Discrimination, Statistical Evidence and Beyond

As stated in section 3.2.2 above, the definition of indirect discrimination in the Burden of Proof Directive interlocks with the group justice model. It was moreover illustrated that the legal definitions of indirect discrimination in the RD, EFD and AETD have mitigated the call for statistical evidence. In fact the approach adopted by the last three mentioned Directives does not reflect an unequivocal choice for either the group or individual justice approach.[100] Although the definitions themselves do not make reference to proportions the Preambular Recitals to the Directives provide

95 *Ibid.*

96 For example, *Bilka Kaufhaus GmbH v. Karin Weber von Hartz* (Case 170/84) [1986] ECR 1607 (paragraphs 30 and 31); *Kowalska v. Freie und Hansestadt Hamburg*; (Case C-33/89) [1990] ECR I-2591 (paragraph 16); *Enderby v. Frenchay Health Authority & the Secretary of State for Health* (Case C-127/92) [1993] ECR 5535 (paragraph 14).

97 See also *Handels- og Kontorfunktionaerernes Forbund I Danmark v. Dansk Arbejdsgiverforening acting on behalf of Danfoss* (Case 109/88) [1989] ECR 3199. This case concerned an employer's intellectually inaccessible payment system which therefore prevented female employees from understanding differences in pay compared with male colleagues. Against this background the ECJ decided that, in terms of legal evidence, the risk of adopting an intransparent payment system comes for the employer. It is for the latter to prove that the vexed payment scheme does not operate in a discriminatory fashion.

98 See moreover Recital 17 of the Preamble to the Burden of Proof Directive.

99 For a more extensive account, I refer to Ahtela 2005, p. 65-66.

100 This parallels a more general trend discerned by McCrudden namely, that EC anti-discrimination law as a whole lacks a coherent theoretical edifice. See McCrudden 2003a, p. 1-38.

evidence that the group-justice approach is not altogether departed from. Recital no. 10 of the AETD provides as follows:

> 'The appreciation of the facts from which it may be inferred that there has been (...) indirect discrimination is a matter for national judicial or other competent bodies, in accordance with rules of national law or practice. Such rules may provide in particular for indirect discrimination to be established by any means including on the basis of statistical evidence (...).'

In other words, statistical evidence could still be a legal requirement albeit not of EC law but of national law.[101] The same holds true for cases falling within the scope of the RD and the EFD. This, respectively, follows from Recitals 21 and 31 of these Directives.[102] In conclusion, it depends on national procedural law[103] rather than on EC law whether an instance of *prima facie* indirect discrimination must be proven on the basis of statistical data. The Directives themselves leave a discretionary choice to the Member States to opt for other methods of proof, including facts of common knowledge or qualitative (as opposed to quantitative) sociological research on the situation of disadvantaged groups.[104] Hereafter the question how to prove indirect discrimination will be considered against the background of the case law by the ECJ.

3.3.3. Disparate Impact

3.3.3.1. Introduction

In *Bilka Kaufhaus GmbH v. Karin Weber von Hartz*[105] a department store, *Bilka Kaufhaus*, excluded part-time workers from its occupational pension scheme. The ECJ in deciding on a number of preliminary questions referred by the German *Bundesarbeitsgericht* held amongst other things that:

> '(...) Article 119 of the EEC Treaty is infringed by a department store company which excludes part-time employees from its occupational pension scheme, where that exclusion affects a far greater number of women than men, [unless the undertaking shows that the exclusion is based on objectively justified factors unrelated to any discrimination on grounds of sex]'.[106]

101 Waddington and Bell 2001, p. 594; Ahtela 2005, p. 64-65.

102 These Recitals contain equivalent provisions to the one contained in Recital no. 10 of the AETD.

103 National procedural law must, however, comply with the principle of effective remedies. See, for example, *Johnston v. Chief Constable of the RUC* (Case 222/84) [1986] ECR 1651.

104 Schiek 2002, p. 296.

105 *Bilka Kaufhaus GmbH v. Karin Weber von Hartz* (Case 170/84) [1986] ECR 1607. This case will be discussed in further detail in section 3.4.4.2 hereafter in the context of objective justification.

106 Paragraph 31 of the judgment. The justifiability question will be analysed in section 3.4.4.2 hereafter.

This, or an equivalent, formulation has been voiced by the Court in many subsequent cases, both in the realm of employment and social security.[107] According to the above formula an applicant must establish that a 'far greater number of women than men' are affected by the contested neutral behaviour. This means that (s)he will have to prove 'disparate impact'. In casu, a male part-time worker employed by *Bilka Kaufhaus*, who is equally denied participation in the scheme, would not succeed in doing so, given that the great majority of part-time workers are women, not men.[108] The formulation expressed by the Court in *Bilka* requires that disparate impact is *actual* which follows from the usage of the simple present tense of the verb 'to affect' ('affects'). As we have seen this is currently no longer a requirement under the AETD, the RD and the EFD. With respect to the judicial appraisal of disparate impact a number of puzzling questions arise. Firstly, what is the correct pool for comparison? Secondly, can disparate impact be established by other means than statistics? Thirdly, what degree of disparity is required in order to establish disparate impact for purposes of the law? Clearly, as Freedland has indicated, the more disparity is required, the lesser an applicant is protected from indirect discrimination.[109] Hereafter these three questions will be studied in greater detail in sections 3.3.3.2, 3.3.3.3 and 3.3.3.4, respectively.

3.3.3.2. Identifying the Pool for Comparison

The question as to what is the correct pool for comparison in a particular case concerns the question of the relevant benchmark group with which the protected group (which has to be defined too) has to be compared. The complainant is by definition a member of the latter group. The benchmark group must be similarly situated as the protected group but for the 'sex', 'race', 'disability, etc. by which the protected group is defined. The identification of the pool for comparison equates to the question as to what are the relevant statistics to be employed in the case at hand.[110] Choosing the correct pool is vital, given that the outcome of the assessment as to whether or not there is 'disparate impact' may be radically different depending on the statistics employed.[111] For example, in order to prove that a particular neutral conduct dispro-

107 See, for example, *Nimz* (Case C-184/89) [1991] ECR I-297, paragraph 12; *Rinke* (Case 25/02) 2003] ECR I-2575 paragraph 33; *Kording* (Case 100/95) [1997] ECR I-5289, paragraph 18.

108 Given that Community sex discrimination law applies symmetrically men are not on principle excluded from lodging a complaint of sex discrimination. However, in order to prove disparate impact a male plaintiff complaining about indirect sex discrimination will have to show that a relatively large number of men compared to women is affected by the vexed neutral conduct.

109 Freedland 1994, p. 340 cited by Villiers and Woods 1997, p. 116, footnote 35.

110 Unless disparate impact is proven by other means than statistics. This will be considered in the passages to follow.

111 Fredman 2002, p. 109-110. This point has also been illustrated by Finlay in a discussion of the decision by the Australian Highcourt in the case of *Australian Iron and Steel PTY v. Banovic*, [1989] 168 CLR 165 FC 89/052. While analysing this case, Finlay pays special attention to the danger that the chosen pools themselves might be tainted with discriminatory practices that occurred in the past (Finlay 2003, p. 140-141).

portionately affects women compared to men, the employed statistics could concern the proportions of women and men who are working in the particular enterprise concerned, or in the domestic labour force, or in the EU labour force, or even worldwide. The ultimate decision on the correct pool for comparison lies with the domestic courts, rather than with the ECJ. The national courts delineate the appropriate pool for comparison on a case by case basis.

3.3.3.3. Legal Options for Establishing Disparate Impact

It follows from both the case law and academic commentary[112] that disparate impact can be distilled on the basis of various evidentiary mechanisms. Firstly, and as indicated at various junctures before, disparate impact can be proven in reliance on the conventional method of statistical data. This is the evidentiary mechanism provided for by the Burden of Proof Directive. It is also the approach which has generally been favoured by the Court in indirect sex discrimination cases.[113] In *Enderby*[114] for example, the applicants were speech therapists working for the UK National Health Service (NHS). The group of speech therapists was predominantly composed of women. Clinical psychologists and pharmacists who were working for the NHS were preponderantly male. They received more payment compared to speech therapists, although it was argued by the applicants that all three groups performed work of equal value. The ECJ *inter alia* held that

> '(...) where significant statistics disclose an appreciable difference in pay between two jobs of equal value, one of which is carried out almost exclusively by women and the other predominantly by men, Article 119 of the Treaty requires the employer to show that that difference is based on objective justified factors unrelated to any discrimination on grounds of sex'.

In *Enderby* the disadvantaged group was predominantly composed of women, whereas the advantaged group comprised chiefly men. It follows from the more recent case in *Jämställdhetsombudsmannen v. Örebro Läns Landsting*[116] that disparate impact can also be established where the statistics show that the disadvantaged group is

112 See, for example, Vick 2001, p. 7-8 with further references; Barnard and Hepple 1999, p. 405-407; De Schutter 2003, p. 24-26. De Schutter has essentially focused on the first two options to be outlined in the main text above.

113 De Schutter 2003, p. 24. Sometimes the ECJ has mitigated the statistical evidence requirement. In *Debra Allonby v. Accrington and Rossendale College et al* (Case C-256/01) [2004] ECR I- 9077 the ECJ held that '[in order to demonstrate disparate impact] a woman *may* (italics MG) rely on statistics' (paragraph 75 of the judgment).

114 *Enderby v. Frenchay Health Authority,* (Case C-127/92 [1993] ECR I-5535. See for an analysis of this case also Fredman 1994a, p. 37-41 and Ellis 1994.

115 Paragraph 19 of the judgment. See also paragraph 17 where the ECJ held that 'it is for the national court to assess whether it may take into account those statistics, that is to say, whether they cover enough individuals, whether they illustrate purely fortuitous or short-term phenomena, and whether, in general, they appear to be significant'.

116 *Jämställdhetsombudsmannen v. Örebro Läns Landsting* (Case C-236/98) [2000] ECR I-2189.

predominantly composed of females detached from the question whether the benchmark group is chiefly composed of men.[117]

It is clear that the comparison of the degree of disadvantage suffered by the protected group, compared to the reference group, implies the availability in the first place of such statistics. De Schutter has spoken of a 'paradox' where, on the one hand, the law requires statistical evidence to be forwarded in anti-discrimination proceedings and, on the other, data protection laws restrict the collection thereof exactly with a view to preventing discriminatory practices.[118] This paradox has been recognised by the legislative definitions of indirect discrimination in the RD and EFD.[119]

Secondly, the assessment of disparate impact could also occur by examining whether the vexed neutral behaviour is 'intrinsically liable' to result in disparate impact.[120] Put differently, under this approach it is not necessary to prove that the disparate impact is actual. Establishing a mere risk of disparate impact will be sufficient. This approach underlies the definitions of indirect discrimination in the RD, EFD and AETD. It reflects the approach adopted by the ECJ in the O'Flynn case, which has arisen in the context of the free movement of workers.[121] The case concerned an Irish father who resided in the United Kingdom as a former migrant worker. Mr O'Flynn had applied for a funeral grant with a view to burying his son in the Republic of Ireland. His application was, however, rejected. According to the applicable national rules a funeral grant is made only if the funeral takes place within the United Kingdom. The ECJ established first that a funeral payment constitutes a social advantage within the meaning of Article 7(1) of Regulation 1612/68[122] which must be enjoyed by migrant workers on an equal footing with national workers. It subsequently repeated its stance adopted in earlier case law, namely that Article 48 (currently 39) EC and Article 7 of Regulation 1612/68 'prohibit not only overt discrimination by reason of nationality but also all covert forms of discrimination which, by the application of other distinguishing criteria, lead in fact to the same result'.[123] The essence of the *O'Flynn* case lies in the stance taken thereafter by the ECJ, namely that rules such as the one at issue will be contrary to the free movement of workers, if they are 'intrinsically liable' of affecting a substantially higher proportion of migrant wor-

117 In paragraph 54 of the judgment the ECJ held that '(...) if a difference in pay between the two groups compared is found to exist, and if the available statistical data indicate that there is a substantially higher proportion of women than men in the disadvantaged group, Article 119 of the Treaty requires the employer to justify the difference by objective factors unrelated to any discrimination on grounds of sex'.

118 De Schutter 2003, p. 28.

119 With reference to section 3.2.2 above, the definition of indirect discrimination in the AETD does not reflect a recognition of this paradox but was merely inserted into the AETD for purposes of legal consistency.

120 Barnard and Hepple 1999, p. 406.

121 *O'Flynn v. Adjudication Officer,* (Case C-237/94) [1996] ECR I-2617.

122 Regulation (EEC) No. 1612/68 of the Council of 15 October 1986 on Freedom of Movement of Workers Within the Community as amended by Regulation 312/76, *OJ* Sp. Ed. 1968, No. 257/2, p. 475.

123 Paragraph 17.

kers.[124] *Ergo,* the ECJ considered it unnecessary that the contested rule has this effect *in practice:* a mere risk suffices to draw the legal conclusion on disparate impact. In deciding on whether or not a measure is intrinsically liable to have an indirectly discriminatory effect, courts and tribunals may take account of common knowledge facts in addition to statistical evidence.

In light of the foregoing the following point should be highlighted. As referred to above, the *O'Flynn* approach is reflected by the legal definitions of indirect discrimination in the RD, EFD and AETD. These definitions provide that an applicant must prove that 'a neutral provision, criterion or practice would put persons [defined by a protected ground] at a particular disadvantage compared with other persons.' Disadvantage need therefore not be actual. A more precise comparison with the approach to indirect discrimination in the Directive, on the one hand, and the one adopted by the Court in *O'Flynn,* on the other, nonetheless reveals that both approaches are not identical. Whereas in *O'Flynn* the Court did preserve a *group comparison* (namely 'migrant workers' *v.* 'non-migrant workers'),[125] the requirement of a group comparison appears absent in the legislative definitions of indirect discrimination. Waddington and Hendriks have argued that 'the Framework Directive (...) allows for a comparison of one individual with 'other persons'.[126] Although in the present author's view the reference to 'persons' (my italics) in the legal definitions of indirect discrimination excludes a comparison of one *single* individual with others, the aforementioned authors have rightly observed that the Directives depart from the group-justice model.[127] The Directives' definitions of indirect discrimination seemingly focus upon a harm suffered by persons defined by race, sex, disability, etc. quite separately from the question whether they are (also) members of a disadvantaged *group.*[128] The Directives' approach has been criticised for blurring the distinction between direct and indirect discrimination.[129] It could also be criticised for shattering the theoretical premises of the concept of indirect discrimination. Arguably, one could draw a dis-

124 See paragraphs 20 and 21 of the judgment where the Court held as follows: '(...) unless objectively justified and proportionate to its aim, a provision of national law must be regarded as indirectly discriminatory if it is intrinsically liable to affect migrant workers more than national workers and if there is a consequent risk that it will place the former at a particular disadvantage. It is not necessary in this respect to find that the provision in question does in practice affect a substantially higher proportion of migrant workers. It is sufficient that it is liable to have such an effect.'

125 See also House of Lords Select Committee on the European Union, '*EU Proposals to Combat Discrimination*', HL Paper 65, Session 1999-2000, 9th Report, paragraph 81 with reference to the oral evidence given by Mr Allen (QC), who has observed that '(...) the text in the Draft Directives misinterpreted O'Flynn in crucial respects'.

126 Waddington and Hendriks 2002. They have made this argument with reference to the EFD in the context of 'disability'.

127 Also Hepple and Barnard 2000, p. 568 who, with reference to the RD, have observed that 'literally interpreted, there will be discrimination if two or more individuals 'of a racial or ethnic origin' (presumably the same origin) suffer a particular disadvantage, even without evidence that the racial or ethnic group as such suffers from that disadvantage'.

128 This point has been taken from Hepple and Barnard 2000, p. 568-569. See also Hepple, Coussey and Choudhury 2000, p. 30 under point 2.30.

129 Barnard and Hepple 2000, p. 568-569.

tinction between the need for a departure from statistical evidence to prove disparate impact with reference to the underlying nature of different grounds of discrimination, on the one hand, and the group oriented nature of indirect discrimination, on the other. After all, as this section shows, proving disparate impact could occur on the basis of evidentiary means beyond statistics.

A third method for proving disparate impact is a 'rule of thumb' approach such as the 'four-fifths' rule used in the context of U.S. law.[130] This option has never been used by the ECJ in its case law. From the perspective of legal certainty this is an attractive option. However, the adoption of a 'rule of thumb' can lead to rigid approaches given that no or less account can be had of the specific circumstances in casu.[131]

A fourth and last approach concerns the 'considerably different impact approach'[132] which gives regard to both statistical evidence and to absolute numbers. Where appropriate it also takes into account facts of common knowledge, e.g. the fact that members of an ethnic minority designation have far more difficulties in complying with language requirements compared to the native population.

3.3.3.4. The Required Degree of Disparate Impact

In the case of *Seymour Smith and Perez*,[133] the ECJ took the view that statistical evidence indicating that 77.4% of men and 68.9% of women could comply with the contested neutral measure did not appear 'on the face of it' to show that a considerably smaller percentage of women than men was able to fulfil the contested requirement. *Seymour Smith* warrants further discussion, for it captures both the technical and conceptual essences of the appraisal of disparate impact in indirect discrimination cases.[134] The facts were as follows.

Ms Seymour-Smith and Ms Perez challenged a provision in the 1978 Employment Protection Act (EPA) according to which employees would only be protected from unlawful dismissal if, at the effective date of employment termination, they had worked for at least two years. The applicants challenged this two year qualifying rule for being indirectly discriminatory on grounds of sex, contrary to Article 119 EC and the 1976 ETD. They argued that the rule at issue disproportionately affects female workers in light of women's primary childcare and household responsibilities. The domestic court namely, the UK House of Lords,[135] referred a number of prelimi-

130 Barnard and Hepple 1999, p. 405.

131 Villiers and Woods 1997, p. 116.

132 Paragraph 60 of the ECJ's judgment in *The Queen v. Secretary of State for Employment, ex parte Nicole Seymour Smith and Laura Perez* (Case C-167/97) [1999] ECR I-623 to be discussed in the main text hereafter. See Barnard and Hepple 1999, p. 406.

133 *The Queen v. Secretary of State for Employment, ex parte Nicole Seymour Smith and Laura Perez* (Case C-167/97) [1999] ECR I-623. See also the case note by Moore 2000, p. 157-165.

134 Notwithstanding that the case has been criticised in academic circles for the limited amount of guidance offered by the ECJ to the referring court. See notably Barnard and Hepple 1999, p. 399-412. For a more mitigated stance, see O'Leary 2000, p. 164-165.

135 The claim of indirect discrimination was rejected in first instance by the divisional court ([1994] IRLR 448). It was subsequently upheld by the Court of Appeal ([1995] IRLR 464). It →

nary questions to the ECJ. For the purposes of the present discussion the third and fourth questions are of particular importance. With its fourth question the referring court wished to learn the relevant period in time at which the lawfulness of the contested neutral criterion has to be assessed. Is this the time when the vexed rule was adopted, or the time when the rule entered into force, or the time when the employee was dismissed? The question is important, given that the disparity of impact is not static but may change as time passes. The facts in Seymour Smith indicated that the disparity between women, who could/could not comply with the vexed rule, compared with men, who could/could not do so, had decreased over the years. In the ECJ's view the question referred concerns a question of fact which has to be determined by the national court. The ECJ nonetheless gave some guidance to the referring court by holding that where the authority that adopted the rule had allegedly acted *ultra vires*, the legality of the measure has in principle to be assessed at the time of its adoption. By contrast, where a national measure has been adopted unlawfully, and where it is subsequently applied to an individual situation, the legality of the measure has to be assessed at the time that it is applied. In such circumstances where regard is given to statistical evidence, the Court held that it may be appropriate to take account of statistics which were available when the contested rule was adopted, but also of statistics which are subsequently compiled and are likely to shed light on the question of disparate impact.[136] The ECJ's stance was thus ambiguous and the referring court was left with ample judicial freedom in deciding on the question in issue.

The third question which was referred was the most difficult one. By this question the Law Lords sought to ascertain the legal criteria for determining whether a neutrally applied measure has such a degree of disparate impact that it constitutes *prima facie* indirect discrimination as prohibited by EC law.

The ECJ took the following obscure view. The Court held that the available statistics must be compared in a 'positive' and 'negative' fashion. Hence, the proportions of men who *are* able to satisfy the two years qualifying rule must be compared with the proportions of women who are *also* able to do so. Furthermore, a comparison must be drawn between the proportions of men who *are not* able to comply with the contested rule, one the one hand, and the proportions of women who are *neither* able to do so.[137] The Court moreover held that it will not be sufficient to consider the number of affected persons since that is dependent on the number of working people in the Member State as a whole, as well as on the percentages of male and female employees in the Member State.[138] The ECJ then blurred its analysis by mingling[139] the 'considerably different impact approach'[140] and the 'statistically signi-

was ultimately brought before the House of Lords, which sought recourse to the preliminary reference procedure under Article 177 (currently 234) EC.

136 See paragraphs 42-50 and especially 46-50 of the judgment.

137 The ECJ's stance is, however, ambiguous with respect to this point. In its subsequent analysis *in Seymour-Smith* the Court seems to focus merely on the 'positive aspect' of the comparison.

138 Paragraph 59 of the judgment.

139 See Barnard and Hepple who have criticised the ECJ's stance for picking the cherries from the various options that are available for assessing disparate impact. Barnard and Hepple 1999, p. 407.

ficance approach'.[141] The Court stressed that any conclusions to be drawn from statistical evidence remains a matter for the national court.[142] The Court therefore declined to stipulate when one can legally speak of a 'considerable' or 'significant' impact. Put differently: the ECJ did not indicate when a percentage *x* compared to a percentage *y* bears a 'considerable' or 'significant' impact. The only guidance provided for was that in the ECJ's view *prima facie* indirect discrimination could also (my emphasis) be established, if the statistics revealed a 'lesser but persistent and relatively constant disparity over a long period'.[143] In *Seymour Smith* the Court therefore established two different tests for proving disparate impact: (1) either by showing a 'considerably disparity' at a particular point in time or (2) by showing a 'lesser' disparity which, however, is persistent and relatively constant over a longer time period. The Court also expressed its view on the quality of statistical evidence. Statistics must cover 'enough individuals', they must not illustrate 'purely fortuitous or short-term phenomena and they must in general 'appear to be significant'.[144] 'On the face of it', suggested the ECJ, does 77.4% of men who could comply as compared with 68.9% of women not support a conclusion of disparate impact.[145]

The above case shows that the appraisal of disparate impact and the appreciation of statistics largely remains a privilege of the domestic court.[146] As stated before, the approach adopted by the RD, the EFD and AETD departs from a statistical evidence approach in favour of a 'particular disadvantage' approach, whereby disadvantage need not be actual. In the absence of case law it is currently not clear, however, what exactly is meant by a 'particular disadvantage' and what degree of disparity distinguishes a 'particular disadvantage' from an ordinary 'disadvantage'.[147]

3.4. *Justifiability*

3.4.1. Objective Justification and Justification by way of Reasonable Accommodation

Once a *prima facie* case of indirect discrimination has been established, the law offers the alleged discriminator an escape route from liability by way of a justification defence. The assessment of justification is a matter of fact and falls ultimately within the judicial mandate of the domestic court. However, the Luxembourg Court has defined the parameters of the objective justification test in indirect discrimination cases.

140 Paragraph 60 of the judgment.
141 Paragraph 62 of the judgment.
142 Paragraph 61 of the judgment.
143 Paragraph 61 of the judgment.
144 Paragraph 62. See also *Enderby* (Case C-127/92) [1993] ECR I-5535, paragraph 17.
145 Paragraphs 63 and 64 of the judgment.
146 See O'Leary 2000, p. 165, who has argued that this reflects a correct stance in light of the limited role afforded to the ECJ in the context of a preliminary reference procedure. Furthermore, the domestic court will be best informed about the legal and factual details in casu.
147 Ahtela 2005, p. 64 who has posed the question as follows: 'How much more disadvantage does a particular disadvantage provide than just 'a disadvantage?'

These will become apparent in section 3.4.4 hereafter. With respect to justification, the RD, EFD and AETD provide as follows:

> 'Indirect discrimination shall be taken to occur where an apparently neutral provision, criterion or practice would put persons [defined by a forbidden ground; MG] at a particular disadvantage compared with other persons *unless that provision, criterion or practice is objectively justified by a legitimate aim and the means of achieving that aim are appropriate and necessary*.'[148]

The 'objective justification test' is a conventional element of 'indirect discrimination'. Less common, however, is the second justification defence introduced by the EFD with respect to indirect disability discrimination cases. Article 2(2)(b) under ii provides that:

> 'Indirect discrimination shall be taken to occur where an apparently neutral provision, criterion or practice would put persons having a particular disability at a particular disadvantage compared with other persons *unless as regards persons with a particular disability, the employer or any person or organisation to whom this Directive applies, is obliged, under national legislation, to take appropriate measures in line with the principles contained in Article 5 [reasonable accommodation; MG] in order to eliminate disadvantages entailed by such provision, criterion or practice*'.

The concept of reasonable accommodation will be extensively discussed in Chapter 8, both as regards its theoretical and legal premises. At this juncture, it suffices to say that due to the interplay between social attitudes, on the one hand, and a personal impairment (e.g. being blind) on the other, a disabled person is often prevented from participating in the labour market in the customary way. The paramount recognition by law of disability based difference is the legal obligation imposed upon employers[149] to make 'reasonable accommodation' for disabled persons. For example, a manual worker who has become disabled cannot simply be dismissed by the employer by reason that (s)he can no longer perform the job. The employer will have to consider the option of a reasonable accommodation, for example, by offering him/her a sedentary job. As the present chapter aims to show, the different position of disabled persons (as well as members of other disadvantaged groups) is also acknowledged by the prohibition of indirect discrimination. However, whereas the reasonable accommodation approach is aimed at mending the different position of disabled individuals on an *ad hoc* basis, the concept of indirect discrimination seeks to dismantle underlying power structures in a more structural manner.[150]

148 Article 2(2) (b) RD; Article 2(2) (b) EFD under (i); Article 2(2) second indent AETD.

149 And others to whom the EFD is addressed, e.g. training providers, trade unions, employers and professional organisations. See Article 3 EFD.

150 Waddington and Hendriks have expressed this as follows: '(…) an individual accommodation leaves unchallenged and unaffected the underlying discriminatory policy which resulted in the initial exclusion.' See Waddington and Hendriks 2002, p. 409. See also Whittle 2002, p. 310 who has observed as follows: '[o]ne of the effects of the 'second unless' clause [i.e., Article 2(2)(b) under ii EFD; MG] (…) is to remove any group benefits that may have otherwise accrued from a successful action [of indirect discrimination; MG].'

The insertion of a second escape route from liability for indirect disability discrimination in the Framework Directive prompts at least two questions. Firstly, what legal interpretation must be accorded to the clause contained in Article 2(2)(b) under ii EFD? Secondly, what were the motives behind the insertion of this additional defence? These two questions will be addressed, respectively, in sections 3.4.2 and 3.4.3 hereafter. In section 3.4.4 the conventional objective justification defence will be studied in detail in light of the ECJ's case law.

3.4.2. Interpreting Justification by way of Reasonable Accommodation (Article 2(2)(b) ii EFD)

Legal minds differ as to the correct interpretation of the second justifiability defence contained in Article 2(2)(b) under ii EFD. The present author agrees with the view expressed by Waddington and Bell namely, that Article 2(2)(b) under ii EFD constitutes a second modus of justification on top of the conventional 'objective justification' defence.[151] An employer will neither be held responsible for (*prima facie*) indirect disability discrimination, if he removes the *prima facie* indirectly discriminatory effect of a provision, criterion or practice by way of making a reasonable accommodation.[152] If, for example, an employer stipulates that animals are not allowed entry at the premises of work, this is likely to result in *prima facie* indirect discrimination against blind persons (who are accompanied by a guide dog). This (*prima facie*) indirectly discriminatory effect can, however, easily be removed by exempting blind persons from the applicable rule. By virtue of having made this reasonable accommodation, the employer does not commit an instance of indirect discrimination. A different interpretation of Article 2(2)(b) under ii EFD has, however, been advanced by Tobler. In her view, the second clause should be taken to mean that if the employer, on the basis of the legal duty to adjust provided by national law, makes a reasonable accommodation for disabled people such an accommodation cannot be challenged as being indirectly discriminatory by those people for whom a reasonable accommodation is not made.[153] Thus, quoting Tobler, '(...) the extra's that handicapped persons get by way of reasonable accommodation cannot be contested as being indirectly discrimi-

151 Waddington & Bell 2001, p. 594. The same view has moreover been adopted by Whittle 2002, p. 310-311. Bell and Waddington have, however, also pointed out that taking away *prima facie* indirect disability discrimination via reasonable accommodation risks affording a lower level of protection to disabled people compared to people belonging to other disadvantaged groups. This is so, for the adjustment may be merely minor rather than all-inclusive (p. 594).

152 In the absence of case law it is currently, however, not clear whether the conventional objective justification defence can ever be successful, if the possibility of reasonable accommodation has not been (fully) exhausted. See Tobler 2005, p. 294. The Select Committee on European Union (Fourth Report, 19 December 2000 paragraph 41) has with respect to this point observed as follows: 'We are uncertain whether an employee or employer would be able to turn to (i) [i.e. to 'objective justification; MG] where there has been a failure, either on the part of a Member State or employer, to meet the requirements of Article 5.' In summary: it is currently a hazy point whether the defences under (i) and (ii) of Article 2(2)b EFD are meant to be 'complementary or mutually exclusive'.

153 Tobler 2005, p. 293.

natory by those who do not get them'.[154] However, with greatest respect to Tobler, the present author finds it difficult to grasp how a 'reasonable accommodation', which is inherently not neutral, can be challenged at all for being *indirectly* discriminatory. Moreover, as will be argued in Chapter 8, the duty to make reasonable accommodations applies asymmetrically which means in any case that reasonable accommodations cannot be challenged by non-disabled persons *vis-à-vis* a disabled person.

3.4.3. The Motives behind the Insertion of Article 2(2)(b) ii EFD: 'Bottom-Up Influence'

It is argued that the insertion by the EC legislator of the second justification defence was induced by political circumstances, rather than by reasons of principle.[155] An analysis of the legislative history of the EFD supports the view that the introduction of the second escape clause was the result of 'bottom-up' pressure by the British delegation in the process of negotiation of the Directive.[156] The bottom-up comparison reveals that the second escape clause parallels the approach adopted by English (UK) disability discrimination law. It should be highlighted that the DDA 1995 falls short of a concept of indirect disability discrimination, both pre and post implementation of EC law.[157] The DDA's approach hinges upon the duty to make adjustments.[158] In its original proposal for the EFD the Commission had limited the possibility of justifying indirect discrimination to the conventional 'objective justification test'.[159] However, as a result of the British negotiation stance, Article 2(2)(b) under ii was added at a later stage. The European Council's working group on social questions in its report to the Committee of Permanent Representatives stated as follows:

> 'Afin de tenir compte d'un problème soulevé par la délégation brittanique qui souhaite que les tribunaux puissent évaluer les cas de discriminations indirecte au cas par cas et non pas en comparant l'effet d'une mesure apparemment neutre sur l'ensemble des personnes

154 Tobler 2005, p. 293. Tobler herself has, however, admitted that 'this interpretation is not readily apparent from the provision's wording'.

155 As explained in Chapter 1, the bulk of this book concerns a comparative *legal* analysis of selected issues in equal treatment law. However, given that the insertion of Article 2(2)(b) ii into the EFD has clearly been the result of 'bottom-up' influence which can solely be explained with reference to political factors, it seems appropriate to elaborate on these factors in some detail.

156 See also Tobler 2005, p. 293.

157 With reference to section 3.2.2 above, the approach adopted by English law arguably reflects the difficulties of 'demarcation' which are inherent to the ground disability and which render it difficult to adopt a group-based perspective to disability based disadvantage.

158 This is the legal terminology employed by the DDA. With reference to Chapter 8, this terminology is synonymous to the duty to make reasonable accommodations.

159 *Proposal for a Council Directive Establishing A General Framework for Equal Treatment in Employment and Occupation*, 25.11.1999, COM (1999) 565 final. Article 2 of the original proposal only referred to the conventional objective justification test which was formulated as follows '(...) unless that provision, criterion or practice is objectively justified by a legitimate aim and the means of achieving it are appropriate and necessary' (Article 2(2) under (b) of the Proposal).

> handicapées puisqu'il s'aggit nécessairement d'un ensemble hétérogène, la Présidence a proposé d'ajouter le texte suivant à la fin de l'Article 2, paragraphe 2, alinéa b.'[160]

La texte suivante' refers to Article 2(2)(b) under ii. The fourth House of Lords report on the EFD states that the UK government 'expressed considerable satisfaction' at the outcome of the possibility for a second justification clause.[161] In the government's view,

> 'the original text, (...), could have created a situation where an employer 'was not obliged to make an accommodation by adjusting a particular practice because it would cost too much but was still obliged in the end to end that practice because it would be deemed indirectly discriminatory'.[162]

This statement implies that, if realising an accommodation turns out to be too costly, the indirectly discriminatory conduct will remain intact. It moreover implies that the test for 'objective justification' is harder to meet than the 'undue hardship' test, which constitutes an exception from the duty to make adjustments.[163] The UK government's interpretation of the second justification clause has been that the Directive allows a discretionary choice to the Member States as to how to approach the question of justifiability of indirect discrimination. In the government's view, Member States

> '(...) may either, under Article 2(2) (b), outlaw indirect discrimination (unless objectively justified by a legitimate aim); or they may introduce national legislation providing for reasonable accommodation (...) in line with Article 5 [of the Directive].[164]

This interpretation obviously suits the UK government, given that the hitherto adopted approach, which is founded on the duty to adjust, can remain intact. However, it has *inter alia* been questioned by the House of Lords Select Committee whether the domestic approach as it currently stands is actually in conformity with the Directive.[165] It is argued that this question must be answered in the negative. The duty to make reasonable accommodation flows from Article 5 EFD, which is an autonomous Article that must be complied with in any case by the Member States, fully independent of their obligations under Article 2 EFD.[166] In other words, Article 5 cannot function as a substitute for the prohibition of indirect disability discrimina-

160 'As we would like to take into account an issue raised by the British delegation who wishes that courts should be able to evaluate indirect discrimination cases on a case by case basis and not by comparing the effect of an apparently neutral measure on the complete group of disabled persons as it concerns without doubt a very heterogenic group, the Presidency has therefore proposed to add the following text at the end of Article 2, paragraph 2, b' (unofficial translation by the author). See Dossier interinstitutionnel: 99/0225 (CNS) Rapport du Groupe 'Questions sociales' au Comité des Représentants permanents (1ière partie). Bruxelles, 29-09-2000 Limite Soc 307, JAI 98, p. 1-13, p. 2-3 (only available in French). It should be noted that the British view was supported by Portugal, Greece and Sweden.

161 Select Committee on European Union, Fourth Report, 19 December 2000, paragraph 39.

162 Select Committee on European Union, Fourth Report, 19 December 2000, paragraph 39.

163 The undue hardship test will be considered in detail in Chapter 8.

164 Select Committee on European Union, Fourth Report, 19 December 2000 paragraphs 40 and 41.

165 Select Committee on European Union, Fourth Report, 19 December 2000 paragraph 41.

166 See also Select Committee on European Union, Fourth Report, 19 December 2000 paragraph 41.

tion which is currently not covered by the DDA 1995. Case law will eventually have to unveil whether the stance adopted in English law is in conformity with EC law.

3.4.4. Objective Justification and the Case Law by the ECJ

3.4.4.1. Introductory Remarks

As referred to earlier, the decision on the objective justification defence ultimately lies with the domestic court, given that objective justification concerns a question of fact. However, the ECJ has held[167] that it may give judicial guidance to the national court on how to balance the principle of non-discrimination, on the one hand, with competing interests, on the other. In doing so, the ECJ's stance has sometimes been active, whilst it has been deferent at other times. Hereafter, the question of justifiability will be analysed with reference to the case law by the Court.

3.4.4.2. Private Employers, Indirect Discrimination and Objective Justification

As indicated before, in *Jenkins v. Kingsgate*[168] the seeds were sown for the recognition of the concept of indirect sex discrimination[169] in EC law including the possibility of justifying such discrimination by reasons unrelated to sex.[170] In casu, the employer (Kingsgate) had argued that the policy of paying different pay rates to part-time compared to full-time workers was solely rationalised by economic reasons, rather than by the (personal) characteristics of the worker or the quality of the work. The contested pay policy was motivated by the need: (a) to discourage absenteeism; (b) to ensure that the expensive machinery in the factory was optimally used and (c) to encourage greater productivity. It was argued on behalf of Mrs Jenkins that once it was shown that a given condition for obtaining equal pay for equal work, in casu: the full-time work requirement, disproportionately affected one sex, compared to the other, this would in principle constitute an infringement of the principle of equal treatment. This would only be otherwise, if the employer showed that the imposition of that condition was 'manifestly related to the services in question'.[171] In other words, Mrs Jenkins submitted that the question of justifiability fell to be interpreted restrictively.[172] In its assessment of the case at issue the ECJ held that

> '(...) the fact that part-time work is paid at an hourly rate lower than pay for full-time work does not amount per se to discrimination prohibited by Article 119 provided that the hourly rates are applied (...) without distinction based on sex. If there is no such distinc-

167 See, for example Freers and Speckmann (Case C-278/93) [1996] ECR I-1165, para. 24; The *Queen v. Secretary of State for Employment, ex parte Nicole Seymour Smith and Laura Perez* (Case C-167/ 97) [1999] ECR I-623, para. 68.

168 *Jenkins v. Kingsgate,* (Case 96/80) [1981] ECR 911. See for a discussion also Tobler 2005, p. 190-194.

169 Although in *Jenkins,* the Court did not *explicitly* refer to the concept of indirect discrimination.

170 Hervey 1991, p. 808.

171 This argument was made with reference to *Griggs v. Duke Power Co.,* (1971), 401, US 424. This case will be discussed in section 4 hereafter in the analysis of English indirect discrimination law.

172 See p. 917 of the judgment and the Opinion by Roemer (AG), p. 936.

> tion, therefore, the fact that work paid at time rates is remunerated at an hourly rate which varies according to the number of hours worked per week does not offend against the principle of equal pay (...) in so far as the difference in pay between part-time work and full-time work is attributable to factors which are objectively justified and are in no way related to any discrimination based on sex'.[173]

The Court subsequently indicated what these factors could include:

> '[S]uch may be the case, in particular, when by giving [lower rates to part-time workers, compared with full-time workers; MG] the employer is endeavouring, on economic grounds which may be objectively justified, to encourage full-time work irrespective of the sex of the worker.'[174]

It follows from the stance adopted by the ECJ that economic grounds may trump the principle of sex equality. However, simultaneously, the ECJ's analysis remains unclear as to *which* economic grounds may legitimately have this effect.[175] The Court itself did not indicate how to strike a balance between, on the one hand, the right of the group of female workers not to be discriminated against by the contested policy, and the employer's economic interests by maintaining this policy, on the other. The Court (somewhat indecisively) held that

> 'where the hourly rate of pay differs [between part-time and full-time workers; MG] it is for the national court to decide in each individual case whether, regard being had to the facts of the case, its history and the employer's intention, a pay policy such as that which is at issue in the main proceedings although represented as a difference based on weekly working hours is or is not in reality discrimination based on the sex of the worker'.[176]

Hence, it is for the national court to assess, on an *ad hoc* basis, whether the contested pay difference is grounded in the sex of a worker, or, whether it can be explained by objective factors. It would have been laudable, had the ECJ made a greater effort to indicate what (economic) grounds may 'qualify' as an objective factor. As referred to in section 3.2.1 above, the Court, what is more, plainly erred in law by holding that the employer's intention may be used as a yardstick in the assessment of objective justification.[177]

The justifiability question was further refined in the well-known case of *Bilka Kaufhaus* in the context of an equal pay claim.[178] The objective justification test as

[173] Paragraph 11 of the judgment.

[174] Paragraphs 10-12 of the judgment.

[175] Hervey 1991, p. 809 who has questioned whether the employer's economic benefits comprise (only) 'present savings due to the existing discriminatory situation' or (also) 'future costs of changing the present policy to a non-discriminatory policy'?

[176] Paragraph 14 of the judgment.

[177] As discussed in the introduction of this chapter indirect discrimination equates to 'effects discrimination' regardless of motive and intent. See moreover Ellis 1998, p. 113, who has observed that if only intentional indirect discrimination is unlawful under Article 119 EC '[this] would have drastically curtailed the efficacy of Article 119, since it is of the nature of indirect discrimination that it frequently occurs as a result of inadvertence'.

[178] *Bilka Kaufhaus GmbH v. Karin Weber von Hartz* (Case 170/84) [1986] ECR 1607.

designed by the ECJ in this case has functioned as a judicial template for assessing the justifiability of *prima facie* instances of indirect sex discrimination committed by a private employer.

In casu, part-time workers, in contrast to full-time workers, were excluded from participation in the employer's occupational pension scheme. Only those part-time workers who had been working full-time for a minimum of 15 years over a total period of 20 years were eligible to take part in the scheme. Ms Weber was employed by Bilka Kaufhaus initially on a full-time basis and later on a part-time basis. However, since she did not meet the 15 years full-time work requirement the employer (Bilka) refused to pay her an occupational pension. Ms Weber challenged the lawfulness of the scheme and claimed an infringement of Article 119 EC. She argued that the full-time work requirement placed women at a disadvantage compared with men, that women are likely to take up part-time employment in view of childcare and family responsibilities. In Bilka's view, the contested scheme was not tainted by reasons related to the sex of the workers but could be explained with reference to economic grounds. Bilka argued that, in order to ensure the availability of an adequate workforce at all times, it was necessary to promote full-time work over part-time work. Given that part-time workers generally refused to work in the late afternoons and on Saturdays, working on a part-time basis had to be discouraged. This was precisely the aim pursued by the vexed scheme. In Bilka's view, the scheme constituted a legitimate business need which, allegedly, was not illegal under Article 119 EC Treaty in light of *Jenkins*.

The referring court posed (*inter alia*) the following questions to the ECJ:

> (1) Are Bilka's justifications for its pay policy 'objectively justified economic grounds', as referred to in the Jenkins judgment, even though the interests of the department store sector do not require such a policy?[179]
> (2) Does Article 119 EC oblige the employer to organise its occupational pension scheme in such a way as to take account of the fact that women are prevented from complying with the requirements for obtaining an occupational pension due to childcare and family responsibilities?[180]

In replying to these questions the ECJ adopted the following stance. It started by indicating that the judicial mandate for deciding on justifiability is with the national court.[181] However, it thenceforth gave ample guidance to the domestic court on how to carry out this mandate. The Court established a three-stage test for the assessment of objective justification of *prima facie* indirect sex discrimination by private employers: (1) the objectives pursued by the contested conduct must correspond to a real need on the part of the undertaking;[182] (2) they must be appropriate with a view to achieving the objective in question and (3) they must be necessary to that end.[183] In brief, the first condition requires that the aim pursued is legitimate and is

179 Paragraphs 8 and 32 of the judgment. This was Preliminary Question 2(a).
180 Paragraph 8 and 38 of the judgment. This was Preliminary Question 2(b).
181 Paragraph 36 of the judgment.
182 This thus requires that the aim pursued must be a legitimate aim.
183 Paragraph 37 of the judgment.

not by itself discriminatory, whereas the second condition demands that the means employed to reach the ends pursued are suitable means, i.e. capable of reaching those ends. The third question concerns the question of proportionality. This has to be assessed by considering whether the aims pursued cannot be achieved with other, less intrusive or non-discriminatory means.[184] [185] If these factors are complied with, the fact that the contested measure disproportionately affects women, compared to men, will *not* be sufficient to constitute a breach of Article 119 EC.[186] The stricter the test of proportionality is applied, the more importance is given to the constitutional value of equality. In any case, a proportionality requirement obliges the domestic courts to pay due attention to the rights of those who are discriminated against, on the one hand, and the legitimate interests of the employer, on the other. Like in *Jenkins*, the Court accepted in *Bilka* that economic grounds ('a real need on the part of the undertaking') may constitute an 'objective justification'.

The question whether Article 119 EC obliges the employer to organise its occupational pension scheme in such a manner so as to take account of women's different social position, compared to men's (i.e. the second question referred to above) was answered by the Court in the negative. In the ECJ's view, the scope of Article 119 EC is confined to the question of pay discrimination and problems related to other conditions of work fall beyond its reach.[187] With this statement, the Court confirmed its adherence to formal, rather than substantive equality.

3.4.4.3. Statutory Legislation, Indirect Discrimination and Objective Justification

It has been observed in academic writing that, in practice, the three-stage test developed in *Bilka* is easier to comply with by the alleged discriminator in cases where not the employer's practice but statutory legislation has been the trigger for a claim of indirect discrimination.[188] The first case in which statutory legislation was at issue is the case of *Ingrid Rinner-Kühn v. FWW Spezial-Gebaudereinigung GmbH & Co.KG.*[189]

184 As indicated by Gerards, the ECJ has not interpreted 'necessity' as also embracing the question whether there exists a proportionate relationship between, on the one hand, the affected interests of the women concerned and, on the other, the interests of the employer in maintaining the disputed pay policy. See Gerards 2002, p. 238.

185 The *Bilka* test was also *inter alia* adopted in *Hill and Stapleton v. Revenue Commissioners and Department of Finance* (Case C-243/95) [1998] ECR I-3739 in which the test was strictly applied; *Enderby v. Frenchay Health Authority* (Case C-127/92) [1993] ECR I-5535. In *Enderby*, however, the ECJ seems to mitigate the third condition (i.e. the proportionality requirement). See with respect to this particular point, O'Leary 2000, p. 156-157 and paragraph 29 of the judgment in which the ECJ held that '(...) it is for the national court to determine if necessary by applying the principle of proportionality, whether and to what extent the shortage of candidates for a job and the need to attract them by higher pay constitutes an objectively economic ground for the difference in pay between the jobs in question'.

186 Paragraph 36 of the judgment.

187 Paragraph 41 of the judgment.

188 For example, O'Leary 2000, p. 137 and p. 181; Barnard and Hepple 1999, p. 411.

189 *Ingrid Rinner-Kühn v. FWW Spezial-Gebaudereinigung GmbH & Co.KG* (Case 171/88) [1989] ECR 2743. See also the case analysis by Shaw 1989, p. 428-434.

In casu, the ECJ availed itself of a strict necessity approach in the assessment of justification.

In *Rinner-Kühn,* the contested measure at issue was the German law on the continued payment of wages *(Lohnfortzahlungsgesetz).* This law stipulated that the employer was under a duty to continue to pay wages for a period of up to six weeks to any employee who, after the commencement of employment and beyond his fault, is incapable of working. Workers whose employment contract did not exceed 10 hours a week, or 45 hours a month, were, however, excluded from benefiting from that legislation. Ms Rinner-Kühn, who had been denied sick pay by her employer, claimed an instance of indirect sex discrimination in breach of Article 119 EC and the 1975 Equal Pay Directive. The German government contended that the vexed exclusion was justified given that workers who do not work more than 10 hours a week, or 45 hours a month, 'were not as integrated in, or as dependent on the undertaking' as other workers.[190] However, the ECJ repudiated this argument. In the Court's view such considerations 'are only generalisations of certain categories of workers' and cannot as such constitute objective justification.[191] The ECJ held:

> 'However, if the Member State can show that the means chosen meet a necessary aim of its social policy, and that they are suitable and requisite for attaining that aim, the mere fact that the provision affects a much greater number of female workers than male workers cannot be regarded as constituting an infringement of Article 119 [EC].[192]

It follows that social policy considerations may outweigh the principle of equality provided, however, that a stringent necessity test is complied with.

In subsequent equivalent cases, notably those cases which have arisen in the area of state social security law,[193] the ECJ's test has, however, thinned out.

In *Inge Nolte v. Landesversicherungsanstalt Hannover,*[194] national legislation excluded employees working less than 15 hours per week and receiving wages of up to 1/7 of the monthly reference amount, from the statutory old age insurance scheme. In casu, Mrs Nolte had been working as a cleaner in minor employment so as to combine work with child rearing responsibilities. Due to a severe illness she could no longer undertake regular paid work. She applied for a retirement and invalidity pension which was, however, rejected by the *Landesversicherungsanstalt* Hannover by reason that Mrs Nolte had been engaged in minor employment. The *Sozialgericht Hannover* stayed the proceedings and asked the ECJ whether the vexed exclusion

190 Paragraph 13 of the judgment.

191 Paragraph 14 of the judgment.

192 Paragraph 14 of the judgment. See, for example, also *De Weerd, neé Roks and Others* (Case C-343/92) [1994] ECR I-571, paragraphs 33 and 34 (Dutch social security legislation); *Kuratorium für Dialyse and Nierentransplantation e.V. v. Johanna Lewark* (Case C-457/93) [1996] ECR I-00243 (national legislation in the context of equal pay).

193 These cases are governed by Directive 79/7/EEC on Equal Treatment for Men and Women in matters of social security, *OJ* 1979, L6/24.

194 *Inge Nolte v. Landesversicherungsanstalt Hannover* (Case C-317/93) [1995] ECR I-4625.

was compatible with Article 4(1) of Directive 79/7/EEC,[195] if it affected considerably more women than men. The ECJ took the view that the Member States enjoy a wide margin of discretion in achieving the aims pursued by national social and employment policy. In casu, the German government argued that the vexed exclusion from the scheme of persons in minor employment corresponded to a structural principle of the German social security system. It was moreover argued that employees in minor employment were in great social demand and therefore, the supply of minor employment had to be encouraged. This aim was pursued by the vexed exclusion. It was argued by the government that compulsory insurance would not result in a substitution of minor employment by full-time or part-time employment, which was subject to compulsory insurance. To the contrary, it would lead to a rise of black employment and to 'circumventing devices'. Unlike in *Rinner Kühn,* the ECJ in *Nolte* granted a broad discretionary scope to the national court with respect to the question of justification. The ECJ held that

> '(...) social policy is a matter for the Member States (...) consequently, it is for the Member States to choose the measures capable of achieving the aim of their social and employment policy. In exercising that competence, the Member States have a broad margin of discretion (...) the social and employment policy aim relied on by the German government is objectively unrelated to any discrimination on grounds of sex and that, in exercising its competence, the national legislature was reasonably entitled to consider that the legislation in question was necessary in order to achieve that aim'.[196]

The above *dictum* erases some of the traces of the three-stage objective justification test applied in *Rinner Kühn* which set a high threshold for justification once *prima facie* indirect discrimination had been established. The key word in *Nolte* is 'reasonableness', rather than 'necessity'.[197] Other subsequent cases have confirmed the lowered threshold for justification in cases in which national legislation sparked off indirect discrimination proceedings.[198]

195 This Article provides as follows: 'the principle of equal treatment means that there shall be no discrimination whatsoever on grounds of sex either directly, or indirectly, by reference in particular to marital or family status, in particular as concerns: – the scope of the schemes and the conditions of access thereto; – the obligation to contribute (...)'.

196 Paragraphs 33 and 34 of the ECJ's judgment.

197 See also *Megner and Scheffel v. Innungskrankenkasse Vorderplatz* (Case C-444/93) [1995] ECR I-4741.

198 See, for example, *The Queen v. Secretary of State for Employment, ex parte Nicole Seymour Smith and Laura Perez* (Case C-167/97) [1999] ECR I-623 which, as referred to earlier, concerned employment legislation. In the *Seymour-Smith* case, the ECJ's stance was, however, stricter than the one adopted in *Nolte* and *Megner Scheffel.* Although it was held that '(...) in choosing the measures capable of achieving the aims of their social and employment policy, the Member States have a broad margin of discretion (...) [this] cannot however have the effect of frustrating the implementation of a fundamental principle of Community law such as that of equal pay for men and women' (paragraphs 74 and 75). However, like in *Nolte* and *Megner Scheffel,* the ECJ eventually held on to a 'reasonableness' standard, rather than to the stricter test adopted in *Rinner Kühn* and *Bilka.* See also Barnard and Hepple 1999, p. 410, who have observed that the ECJ in *Seymour-Smith,* '(...) seemed to vacillate between the Rinner-Kühn and Nolte/Megner test'.

In *Dr Helga Kutz-Bauer v. Freie und Hansestadt Hamburg*[199] questions were raised concerning the applicant's exclusion from a scheme of part-time work for older employees which was set up by a collective agreement and applied to the public service. The vexed provision stipulated that both male and female employees could benefit from the scheme up until the time when the person concerned became eligible for a full pension under the statutory old-age insurance scheme. Due to the different pensionable ages for women (60) and men (65)[200] this meant in practice, that for a period of 5 years after the age of 60 the chief beneficiaries of the scheme were male workers. The first Question referred to the ECJ was whether the vexed scheme was in breach of Articles 2(1) and 5(1) of the 1976 ETD. After establishing the applicable law in casu,[201] the ECJ held that the vexed provisions resulted in discrimination against female workers, compared with male workers.[202] They were therefore in principle in breach of EC law, unless the (*prima facie*) discriminatory treatment could be 'justified by objective factors unrelated to any discrimination based on sex'.[203] The ECJ instructed the national court by indicating that the latter, whilst assessing the justifiability question, had to proceed on the basis of the following questions: (1) the question as to the possibility of achieving by other means the aims pursued by the contested provisions ('necessity'); (2) the question whether the aims pursued appear to be unrelated to any discrimination based on sex ('legitimacy of the aim'); (3) the question whether those provisions are a capable means of advancing the aims pursued ('appropriateness').[204] Unlike in *Rinner Kühn,* the ECJ did not require that, for the aim to be legitimate, it must meet a 'necessary aim' of the Member State's social or employment policy. This relaxed stance appears to parallel the Court's view that Member States enjoy a 'broad margin of discretion' in matters of social policy.[205] The Court, however, warned that this margin was not without conditions. The German government argued that one of the aims pursued by the contested provisions was to encourage recruitment and reduce unemployment. The vexed rule at issue formed a maximum incentive to workers who are not yet eligible to retire to do so. This would

199 *Dr Helga Kutz-Bauer v. Freie und Hansestadt Hamburg* (Case C-187/00) [2003] ECR I-2741.

200 Laid down in the relevant paragraphs, in the version in force until 31-12-1999, contained in the German Social Code.

201 Tizzano [AG] had pleaded that the case at hand was governed by Directive 79/7/EEC on Equal Treatment for Men and Women in matters of social security, *OJ* 1979, L 6/24. The ECJ took the view that, given that the scheme of part-time work for older employees affected the exercise of the workers' occupation by an adjustment of their working time, the applicable law in casu was the 1976 ETD.

202 Given the clear-cut scenario, the ECJ decided this matter for itself without leaving this conclusion to be drawn by the national court and without bothering about statistical evidence or other possible means of evidence to establish disparate impact.

203 Paragraph 50 of the judgment with reference to *Rinner-Kühn v. FWW Spezial-Gebaudereinigung GmbH & Co.KG* (Case 171/88) [1989] ECR 2743, paragraph 12; *Lewark* (Case C-457/93) [1996] ECR I-243, paragraph 31; *Hill and Stapleton v. Revenue Commissioners and Department of Finance* (Case C-243/95) [1998] ECR I-3739, paragraph 34; *Jorgensen* (Case C-226/98) [2000] ECR I-2447, paragraph 29.

204 Paragraph 51 of the judgment.

205 Paragraph 55 of the judgment with reference to *R v. Secretary of State for Employment, ex parte Seymour Smith and Perez* (Case C-167/97) [1999] ECR 1999 I-00623, paragraph 74.

stimulate the inflow of unemployed workers into the labour market. In the ECJ's view, encouragement of recruitment and reduction of unemployment constitute legitimate aims of the State's social policy. However, the broad margin of discretion granted to the Member States in matters concerning social policy may not have the effect of thwarting a fundamental principle of Community law, such as the principle of sex equality.[206] The government also argued that, if a worker who had acquired the entitlement to a full rate pension was permitted to benefit from the scheme this would imply, not only that the post could not be allocated to an unemployed person, but also, that the additional costs entailed by this were to be borne by the state social security scheme.[207] With respect to the 'cost defence' the ECJ repeated its earlier case law to the effect that

> '(...) although budgetary considerations may underlie a Member State's choice of social policy (...) they do not in themselves constitute an aim pursed by that policy and cannot therefore justify discrimination against one of the sexes.'[208]

In summary: budgetary reasons *in se* cannot trump the principle of sex equality.[209] It was held that a decision to the contrary would mean that the scope and application of EC sex equality law *might vary in time and place according to the state of the public finances of the Member States.*[210] With respect to the element concerning the 'legitimacy' of the objective pursued and the element of 'appropriateness' the ECJ highlighted that

> '(...) mere generalisations concerning the capacity of a specific measure to encourage recruitment are not enough to show that the aim of the disputed provisions is unrelated to any discrimination based on sex or to provide evidence on the basis of which it could reasonably be considered that the means chosen are or could be suitable for achieving that aim'.[211]

The above case shows a relatively active Court in offering guidance to the domestic court on the matter of justification. Rather than holding on to a cushioned 'reasonableness' approach, the elements of a *legitimate aim*, *appropriateness* and *necessity* (although formulated in a different sequence) formed the basis of the justification test. It was furthermore explicitly stated that budgetary reasons cannot by themselves constitute objective justification.

206 Paragraph 57 of the judgment. See also *Erika Steinicke v. Bundesanstalt für Arbeit* (Case C-77/02) [2003] ECR I-9027, paragraph 63.

207 Paragraph 54 of the judgment.

208 Paragraph 59 of the judgment and in reference to *de Weerd and Others* (Case C-343/92) [1994] ECR I-571, paragraph 35.

209 See also *Erika Steinicke v. Bundesanstalt für Arbeit* (Case C-77/02) [2003] ECR I-9027, paragraph 66.

210 Paragraph 60 with reference to *de Weerd and Others* (Case C-343/92) [1994] ECR I-571, paragraph 36 and *Jorgensen* (Case C-226/98) [2000] ECR I-2447, paragraph 39.

211 Paragraph 58 of the judgment. See also *Erika Steinicke v. Bundesanstalt für Arbeit* (Case C-77/02) [2003] ECR I-9027, paragraph 64.

The last case to be discussed here is that of *Katharina Rinke v. Ärztekammer Hamburg*.[212] This case cuts across two intersectional areas of Community law namely, the free movement of doctors and the mutual recognition of their diplomas, on the one hand, and EC sex discrimination law, on the other. The latter was governed for purposes of the case at issue by the 1976 ETD. The former is regulated by Council Directive 93/16 EEC[213] and by Council Directive 86/457/EEC.[214] Frau Rinke was a doctor. The *Ärztekammer Hamburg* refused to issue her with a certificate of specific training in general medical practice and denied her the right to use the title of 'General Medical Practitioner'. The reason for this refusal was that Frau Rinke's medical training had taken place on a part-time, rather than on a full-time basis as required by the applicable law (i.e. the *Hamburgische Ärztegesetz*). Frau Rinke argued that the full-time training requirement constitutes a breach of EC sex discrimination law. She moreover argued that Article 5(1) of Directive 86/4, which merely contained a limited exception to the full-time training requirement, ought to be outweighed by the fundamental principle of non-discrimination. The Federal Administrative Court (*Bundesverwaltungsgericht*) dismissed Rinke's claim for indirect sex discrimination. In its view the application of the principle of *lex posterior derogat legi priori* inevitably led to the conclusion that the EC law regarding the free movement of doctors took precedence over the law contained in the ETD, which was earlier adopted. The Federal Constitutional Court (*Bundesverfassungsgericht*) dismissed that judgment on appeal and referred the case back for reconsideration to the *Bunderverwaltungsgericht*. The Constitutional Court held that the latter should have referred preliminary questions to the ECJ concerning the relationship between the two aforementioned (competing) areas of EC law. The following two Questions were subsequently referred to the ECJ:

> (1) Does the full-time training requirement contained in Directives 86/475/EEC and 93/16/EEC constitute an instance of indirect sex discrimination contrary to the ETD?
> (2) If so, (a) how is the incompatibility of the ETD with the former two Directives to be resolved? (b) Does the prohibition of indirect discrimination on grounds of sex constitute a basic unwritten right under Community Law that overrides any conflicting rule in secondary Community legislation?

The ECJ first considered Question 2. With reference to its case law in *Defrenne III*[215] and *P v. S*[216] the Court reiterated that the elimination of discrimination between men and women is a fundamental right and a general principle of Community law. With reference to Opinion 2/94[217] and *Grant*[218] the ECJ moreover affirmed that the respect

212 *Katharina Rinke v. Ärztekammer Hamburg* (Case C-25/02) [2003] ECR I-2575. See for a discussion also Szyszczak 2005.

213 Council Directive 93/116/EEC of 5 April 1993, *OJ* 1993, L 165, p. 1.

214 Council Directive 86/457/EEC of 15 September 1986 on specific training in general medical practice, *OJ* 1986, L 267, p. 26. This Directive has been incorporated into Directive 93/116 (*ibid*).

215 *Defrenne v. Sabena III* (Case 149/77) [1978] ECR 1365

216 *P v. S* (Case C-13/94) [1996] ECR I-2143.

217 Opinion 2/94 [1996] ECR I-1759.

218 *Grant* (Case C-249/96) [1998] ECR I-621.

for fundamental rights is a condition of the legality of Community acts.[219] The Court therefore held that a provision of an EC Directive that shows disrespect for the principle of sex equality is 'vitiated by illegality'.[220] It held that '(...) compliance with the prohibition of indirect discrimination on grounds of sex is a condition governing the legality of all measures adopted by Community institutions'.[221] By holding as it did, the ECJ implied that the fundamental right to equality may trump the guarantees contained in Council Directive 93/16[222] and, more generally, any other secondary legislation which makes an incursion into this principle. The ECJ then continued by an assessment of Question 1. Having established on the basis of statistical evidence that the full-time training requirement constituted disparate impact upon women, the Court thereupon analysed the question of justification. The Council and the Commission had argued that the overall objective pursued by the contested provisions was to ensure a high level of public health protection across the Community. Therefore, this interest, on the one hand, fell to be balanced against the right to sex equality, on the other. In Rinke's view the application of a full-time training requirement traversed the boundaries of necessity, given that such a requirement did not apply with respect to other medical specialisations. She argued that the objective pursued could be achieved with other, non-discriminatory, means.[223] Geelhoed (AG) affirmed Rinke's reasoning. In his view the Commission and Council had been unsuccessful in establishing 'objective justification'. His conclusion amounted to unlawful indirect sex discrimination. The ECJ decided differently. It held that the Community legislator enjoys a wide margin of discretion in pursuing the aim of a high level of health protection, although this should not obstruct a fundamental principle of EC law including the principle of non-discrimination between the sexes.[224] The Court adhered to a 'reasonableness approach':

> '(...) it was reasonable for the legislature to take the view that [the contested full-time training requirement; MG] enables doctors acquire the experience necessary, by following patients' pathological conditions as they may evolve over time, and to obtain sufficient experience in the various situations likely to arise more particularly in general medical practice.'[225]

In the Court's view, the necessity requirement was met and, in essence, public health interests took precedence over the principle of sex equality.

It is argued that the ECJ, by seeking recourse to a 'reasonableness' test on the basis of which it concluded that 'necessity' was complied with, adopted a conceptually muddled approach. The ECJ intermingled two different tests for judicial review, namely 'reasonableness' and 'objective justification'. The latter is a much stricter test which requires that the elements of legitimacy, appropriateness and necessity are

219 Paragraph 26 of the judgment.
220 Paragraph 27 of the judgment.
221 Paragraph 28 of the judgment.
222 Also Szyszczak 2005, p. 10.
223 Rinke's line of reasoning received support by the Swedish government which had submitted observations to the Court.
224 Paragraph 39.
225 Paragraph 40.

met. In contrast to the ECJ, the Advocate General did verify whether any non-discriminatory means could be employed to reach the pursued goals. As such it adopted a conceptually purer approach. Given that full-time training requirements were not applied with respect to other medical specialisations the ECJ's positive conclusion on necessity is questionable.

3.4.4.4. *Objective Justification: Balancing Rival Interests*

It follows from the case law above that analysing justification in indirect discrimination cases essentially involves a balancing exercise of the interests of different stake holders in a particular case. The ease with which 'equality' can be outweighed by other concerns depends on the strictness of the Court's scrutiny test. It moreover depends on the theoretical notion of equality underlying the legal framework. In the absence of case law, it is not sure whether the degree of judicial scrutiny will be different for different grounds of discrimination.[226] In the recent case of *Mangold v. Helm*,[227] which concerned an instance of age discrimination, the Court did extrapolate the objective justification test applied in *Bilka* to a case of *direct* age discrimination.[228] It should be highlighted that in EC law competing interests are evident at two distinct but inter-related levels. At macro level, the Court is required to act within the competing paradigms of 'market-integration' *v.* 'fundamental rights'.[229] It is argued that, given that the human rights rationale for equality has been invigorated in EC law, this should entail a tightened scrutiny exercise by the Court. At micro level, the ECJ must balance the rights of the victim of discrimination *v.* the interests of (e.g.) the employer. As the case law shows, a particular dilemma is posed where *equality* must be balanced against economic and cost efficiency considerations. In *Kutz Bauer* the ECJ held that 'budgetary reasons' and mere 'cost considerations' cannot lie at the heart of justification. Apparently, a difference therefore exists between 'economic grounds', on the one hand, and 'budgetary concerns', on the other.[230] Whereas the former may trump equality (*Jenkins, Bilka* and *Rinner Kühn*), the latter may not do so. In Tobler's view, 'economic grounds' is a broader notion than 'budgetary concerns'. She has argued that, although budgetary concerns cannot *in se* constitute an objective justification, they can nonetheless constitute one of more legitimate factors which

226 Parmar 2004, p. 147 has argued that '(...) it seems likely that the Court of Justice shall develop a common standard of 'objective justification' that proceeds from the base of gender equality jurisprudence'.

227 *Mangold v. Helm* (Case C-144/04) of 22 November 2005 available at <www.europa.eu.int>. See also the Opinion of Advocate General Tizzano delivered on 30 June 2005 in *Mangold v. Helm* (Case C-144/04). This Opinion is also available at <www.europa.eu.int>.

228 Article 6 EFD permits justification of both direct and indirect age discrimination. This Article therefore reflects an 'open' model of anti-discrimination law. *Mangold* will be analysed in great detail in Chapter 9.

229 O'Leary 2000, p. 135-183. O'Leary has *inter alia* examined the tensions between social and economic policy considerations. As she has emphasised, the Court '(...) [operates; MG] in an individual rights-based legal order largely of its own creation, yet one which is bound by avowed free market goals and aspirations' (p. 137-138).

230 Tobler 2005, p. 248-250.

the Member State can legitimately take into account. In other words, considerations of costs can be put into the balance, in addition to other factors. Ultimately, this may induce the Member State to opt for a particular social policy choice.[231]

3.5. Conclusions

The analysis of indirect discrimination in EC law has shown the following picture. It has been illustrated that the legislative definitions of indirect discrimination in EC law show a number of inconsistencies, both in terms of legislative drafting and with regard to legal theory. In current times two separate distinctive legislative definitions of indirect discrimination co-exist in EC sex discrimination law. The newly introduced definitions of indirect discrimination in the RD, EFD and AETD mark a shift from a group-justice model to the individual-justice model. With reference to the intrinsic nature of different grounds of discrimination the legislative framework has relaxed the call for statistical evidence in order to prove 'disparate impact'. However, this should not have infringed upon the group-oriented nature of indirect discrimination as a concept of law. The discussion has also shown that, in addition to 'objective justification', a second justification defence is contained in the Framework Directive which is merely applicable with respect to (*prima facie*) indirect disability discrimination. It has been argued that this second possibility of justifying indirect discrimination has been the result of bottom-up influence. Due to the absence of case law, the exact relationship between 'objective justification', on the one hand, and justification by way of reasonable accommodation, on the other, is currently, however, obscure. Towards the end of the analysis, 'objective justification' has been examined with reference to a selected number of cases. It has been argued that the constitutionalisation of equality in EC law should induce the Court to adhere to a strict judicial scrutiny exercise whilst balancing competing interests in indirect discrimination cases.

4. Indirect Discrimination in English Non-Discrimination Law: a Top-Down Analysis[232]

4.1. Introduction

In the previous sections the concept of indirect discrimination was analysed, both from a theoretical angle, and in the context of EC law. In section 4 it will be examined if and in what ways EC indirect discrimination law has made an impact upon English

231 Tobler 2005, p. 249.

232 The cross-ground comparison will not be dealt with in this section. For reasons that I will note in section 4.1 hereafter, the ground disability will be excluded from the discussion. The conceptual differences reflected by the legal approach to 'disability', on the one hand, and 'race' and 'sex', on the other, will become apparent in Chapter 8. Although both 'race' and 'sex' will be covered in the analysis hereafter, these two grounds have traditionally been dealt with *in pari materiae* by the courts, notwithstanding that 'sex', unlike 'race', has traditionally received influence from EC law. Only with respect to the matter of 'positive duties' have race and sex discrimination law shown major divergences. 'Positive duties' will, however, not be discussed here.

indirect discrimination law. This amounts to the top-down comparison. The analysis hereafter will be confined to the discrimination grounds of race and sex. As referred to earlier, the DDA 1995 is short of a prohibition of indirect discrimination. This has not altered with the implementation of the EFD in English law. As stated earlier, the English legal approach hinges upon the duty imposed upon employers to make reasonable adjustments for disabled persons with a view to accommodating the different position of disabled persons. The reasonable adjustment approach is conceptually different from the indirect discrimination approach and will be considered in Chapter 8 ('disability'). As discussed in Chapter 2, the RRA 1976 has been amended by the Race Relations Amendment Regulations[233] (henceforth: the Race discrimination Regulations) with a view to implementing the RD into domestic law. The SDA 1975 was amended in 2001 with a view to transposing the EC Burden of Proof Directive.[234] What is more, the SDA was amended again in 2005 so as to render domestic sex discrimination law in line with the requirements contained in the AETD. These amendments have occurred with the adoption of the Employment Equality (Sex Discrimination) Regulations[235] (hereafter: the Sex discrimination Regulations). The Race and Sex discrimination Regulations have *inter alia* introduced a revised definition of indirect discrimination into the RRA and SDA, respectively. Hereafter, the domestic approach to indirect discrimination will be analysed in light of EC law. One of the points I will make is that the transposition of the RD and the AETD by way of *Regulations*, rather than by way of a Statutory Act of Parliament, has vehemently shattered the internal coherence of the domestic anti-discrimination framework. This negative development especially comes to the forefront in the context of the RRA 1976 (as amended). The *modus operandi* hereafter will be as follows. In section 4.2, I will first provide some legal background information on 'indirect discrimination' in the context of English law. In section 4.3, I will delineate the borderlines between direct and indirect discrimination with reference to the case law by the House of Lords. Section 4.4 concerns the analysis of top-down influence. Regard will be given to the statutory provisions on indirect discrimination pre- and post-implementation of supranational law. Attention will moreover be paid to the case law on indirect discrimination prior to and after the implementation of EC law. It should be highlighted at the outset that the legal approach to indirect discrimination, both with regard to legislation and case law, is still valid in current times depending, however, on the area of social life at issue in the particular case at hand, and on the discrimination ground at stake. This point will be expounded upon in more detail in the analysis hereafter. Tentative conclusions will be drawn in section 4.5.

233 Race Relations Act 1976 *(Amendment) Regulations* 2003 (SI 2003/1626).

234 Sex Discrimination (*Indirect Discrimination and Burden of Proof Regulations*) 2001 (SI 2001/2260). These Regulations took force on 12 October 2001.

235 Employment Equality (*Sex Discrimination*) Regulations 2005 (SI 2005/2467).

4.2. *A Background Note to Indirect Discrimination in English Law*

When framing race and sex discrimination law in Britain in the late 1960s and 70s, 'indirect discrimination' received little attention from the lawmakers. Neither the 1965, nor the 1968 Race Relations Act, which were the statutory precedents of the 1976 RRA,[236] contained a prohibition of indirect discrimination. In the White Paper which preceded the RRA 1976 it was, however, acknowledged that

> '(...) the relevance of legislation to the less clear-cut, more complex situation of accumulated disadvantages and the effects of past discrimination may be less direct but is nonetheless real'. It was moreover acknowledged that '(...) one important weakness in the existing legislation is the narrowness of the definition of unlawful discrimination upon which it is based: the less favourable treatment of one person than of another on the ground of colour, race, or national or ethnic origins'.

Finally, it was recognised that '(...) it is insufficient for the law to deal only with overt discrimination. It should also prohibit practices which are fair in a formal sense but discriminatory in their operation and effect'.[237]

The aforementioned insights were gained by virtue of developments that had occurred in the context of American, rather than EC law.[238] Traditionally, American race discrimination law had predominantly focused upon sheer discrimination and prejudice. A shift in the legal approach was discernible in the late 1960s when the legal framework started focusing upon the institutional and structural causes of exclusion and discrimination.[239] This had a positive impact upon English race relations law which, since the early 1970s, has increasingly emphasised the institutional nature of disadvantage.[240] During the 60s (USA) and 70s (England), so-called 'aptitude tests' played an increasingly important role in the process of selection of candidates for employment. These tests constituted a complement to formal job qualifications and were often not related to the duties of the jobs at issue. Due to structural disadvantages suffered in the past such tests clearly had an exclusionary effect on members of disadvantaged groups.[241] The practice of selection of job candidates by means of aptitude tests was at issue in the seminal case of *Griggs v. Duke Power Co.*[242] In this case a unanimous US Supreme Court acknowledged for the first time that the aforementioned practice of selection for employment constituted un-

236 For further background information on these earlier Acts, I refer to McCrudden, Smith and Brown, Chapter 1. See also the seminal work by Lord Lester and Bindman 1972. In Part I of their book, Lester and Bindman sketch the background to the first Statutes governing English Race Relations Law. Also Hepple 1969, p. 248-257. For a sound background to English sex discrimination law, I refer to Fredman 1997a.

237 White Paper preceding the Race Relations Act 1976 Cmnd, 6234, 1775 London, HMSO.

238 Townshend-Smith 1997, p. 103; Lord Lester of Herne Hill 1997, p. 173. For further discussion of English indirect (race) discrimination law compared to the approach adopted by American law, I refer to Connolly 2002, p. 129-142.

239 McCrudden 1982, p. 305-306.

240 McCrudden 1982, p. 310 with further references.

241 McCrudden 1982, p. 308-309 and p. 315.

242 *Griggs v. Duke Power Co.* (1971), 401, US 424.

lawful indirect discrimination against black persons contrary to the 1964 Civil Rights Act. The facts in *Griggs* were as follows.

In casu, the employer used to conduct an overt policy of excluding black job applicants. This was subsequently substituted by a covert policy which pursued, however, the same exclusionary aim. The covert policy consisted of imposing a requirement on job candidates of having a high school qualification. In the absence of such a qualification, candidates were compelled to pass an intelligence test. Both the requirement of a high school qualification and the one of passing an intelligence test were fully detached from the jobs at issue which concerned unskilled work. Due to the structural disadvantages suffered by black persons in educational matters, the employer's covertly conducted policy had a disparate impact upon the group of black persons. The result was that the employer's work force almost entirely consisted of whites. The Supreme court held that equality [in terms of sameness; MG] of treatment could be discriminatory, if in practice fewer blacks than whites can comply with a particular requirement, unless the imposition of that requirement was necessary for the proper execution of the job at hand. In summary, 'business necessity' could set a proper limit on the prohibition of 'indirect discrimination'. With reference to the famous fable of the fox and the stork,[243] Chief Justice Burger articulated the concept of indirect discrimination as follows:

> 'Congress has now provided that tests or criteria for employment or promotion may not provide equality of opportunity merely in the sense of the fabled offer of milk to the stork and the fox. On the contrary, Congress has now required that the posture and condition of the jobseeker be taken into account. It has – to resort again to the fable – provided that the vessel in which the milk is proffered be one all seekers can use. The [United States Civil Rights; MG] Act proscribes not only overt discrimination but also practices that are fair in form, but discriminatory in operation'.[244]

The requirement that 'the vessel in which the milk is proffered be one all seekers can use' clearly denotes substantive justice, for it requires that material differences between persons (with reference to the aforementioned fable: the fox and the stork) be taken into account in the decision-making process. The Supreme Court moreover held that an employer's intention or motive constitutes no material factor in concluding an instance of (prima facie) indirect discrimination, as long as disparate impact is proven. As discussed in section 2, this is a correct point of view, for indirect discrimination is concerned with the disadvantageous effects in practice that stem from

243 The fable of the Fox and the Stork (by Jean de la Fontaine 1621-1695) concerns the following. The fox invited the stork to dinner and served soup in a very shallow dish. Whereas it was easy for the fox to drink the soup, the stork could only wet the end of her long bill in it and consequently left home without dinner. The stork took thereupon revenge by re-inviting the fox to dinner. She served dinner in a very long necked jar with a narrow mouth. This had the consequence that the fox could not enjoy his dinner and left home hungry. This small narrative entails an element of indirect discrimination: whereas dinner was served in the same manner to the fox and the stork alike, material differences between the two had as a consequence that either one of them could not enjoy dinner.

244 *Griggs v. Duke Power* (1971), 401, US 424, p. 431.

'neutral' conduct, rather than with what was in the mind of the alleged perpetrator. Although initially the White Paper preceding the 1975 SDA merely anticipated a legal prohibition of blunt instances of sex discrimination, the logic of *Griggs* was eventually transposed into the legal frameworks of the SDA and the RRA.[245]

In summary, the logic behind 'indirect discrimination' finds its roots in U.S. law. It subsequently made its presence felt in English law and from there it made an excursion towards the supranational level of the EC. It is worth noting at this juncture that the (English) applicant in *Jenkins* (a case earlier referred to) made explicit references to *Griggs* which doubtlessly has had an influence upon the judicial reasoning by the ECJ in the case at hand. Ultimately, 'indirect discrimination' became embedded within the domestic laws of all Member States. This is a clear example of cross-fertilisation. Since the insertion of indirect discrimination into English law *inter alia* proficiency requirements,[246] age bars,[247] the instruction to indirectly discriminate,[248] and dress and appearance requirements[249] have been challenged in legal proceedings.

4.3. *Demarcating the Borderlines between Direct and Indirect Discrimination: James v. Eastleigh Borough Council*

Before proceeding with the top-down comparison the borderline between *direct* and *indirect* discrimination deserves clarification. Gill and Monaghan have argued that 'one of the strengths of UK discrimination law is the clear distinction between direct and indirect discrimination'.[250] The main differences between both concepts have

245 McColgan 2000, p. 66-67.

246 See, for example, *Bayoomi v. British Railways Board* [1981] IRLR 431. In casu, the employer imposed a requirement upon trainee operators with British Rail to be proficient in six months. Training consisted of training on the job. The proficiency requirement was *inter alia* directed at job jargon and geography and disproportionately affected persons, including the applicant, who were born outside Britain. The Tribunal held that the vexed requirement amounted to indirect discrimination contrary to the RRA 1976. It could not be justified.

247 *Perera v. the Civil Service Commission* [1982] IRLR 147 (EAT); *Price v. The Civil Service Commission* [1978] 1 All ER 1228; *Rutherford and Bentley v. Secretary of State for Trade and Industry (no. 2)* 2004, IRLR 892 EWCA.

248 *Hussein v. Saints Complete House Furnishers,* [1979] IRLR 337. In casu, the employer informed the local employment agency that it did not wish to hire job applicants from the city centre as their unemployed friends assembled around the shop and perturbed customers. Thus, Mr Hussein was rejected for an interview because he lived in 'Liverpool 8'. The Employment Tribunal interpreted this 'policy' as a 'requirement' or 'condition', given that it amounted to the requirement that job applicants had to live outside certain City areas, if they wished to be considered for employment. It concluded unlawful indirect discrimination, given that 50% of those living in the city centre were black, compared to 2% in Merseyside as a whole.

249 See, for example, *Mandla v. Dowell Lee,* [1983] ICR 385, (HL) ('no Turban rule' which indirectly discriminated against Sikhs); *Kingston and Richmond Area Health Authority v. Kaur* [1981] ICR 631 (EAT) (requirement of 'no trousers' which constituted *prima facie* indirect discrimination against Sikh nurses which, in casu, could however be justified; *Panesar v. NESTlE Co. LTD* ICR [1980] 144 (CA) (requirement of 'no beards' in a chocolate factory was held to constitute *prima facie* indirect discrimination against Sikhs which, in casu, could however be justified (with reference to hygiene).

250 Gill and Monaghan 2003, p. 115.

already been explained in the preliminary observations to Part II. These will not be repeated at this juncture. What is worth pointing out, however, is that the 'clear distinction' between both concepts becomes less visible in cases where a race or sex-based criterion is at stake.[251] In *James v. Eastleigh Borough Council* [HL],[252] the distinguishing criterion was that of pensionable age. The facts in *James* were as follows.

Mr James and his wife visited the public swimming pool which was managed by Eastleigh Borough Council. Entrance was free for those having reached the state pensionable age, which was 60 for women and 65 for men. Hence, Mr James had to pay a 75p entrance fee, whereas his wife was offered free admission to the pool. In the view of the Court of Appeal (CA), a distinction must be drawn between sex discrimination, on the one hand, and a rule which merely referred to pensionable age, on the other. Given the different pensionable ages of women and men, the latter rule could amount to unlawful indirect sex discrimination. On appeal, a different view was taken by the House of Lords by a 3:2 majority. The House of Lords dealt with the case at hand on the basis of the statutory prohibition of *direct* sex discrimination, notwithstanding that the vexed policy did not make an explicit reference to 'sex'. The majority of the Law Lords held that pensionable age in Britain constituted a *gender-based criterion* i.e. a criterion which is *intrinsically* discriminatory between the sexes. According to Lord Bridge of Harwich,

> 'pensionable age cannot be regarded as a requirement or condition which is applied equally to persons of either sex precisely because it is by itself discriminatory between the sexes (...) the expression 'pensionable age' is no more than a convenient shorthand expression which refers to the age of 60 in a woman and to the age of 65 in a man'.[253]

The consequence of this view is that policies which are founded on a status-based criterion are not susceptible for 'objective justification'. In the present author's view, the majority of the Law Lords in *James* adopted a correct approach. It should be highlighted that the adoption of a gender-based criterion does not result in *disparate* impact on, for example, men. Disparate impact implies that men are *preponderantly* but not *exclusively* affected by a neutral criterion. A gender-based criterion, however, affects men exclusively. Indeed, in casu *all* men between 60-64 were affected by the respondent's admission policy. In light of this, gender-based criteria should be conceived in terms of direct discrimination.

The distinction between direct and indirect discrimination was blurred by the facts in *James* for yet another reason. As referred to earlier, direct discrimination often

251 Also Bindman 1992, p. 61.

252 *James v. Eastleigh Borough Council,* [1990] 2 All ER, 607. It should be noted that the facts in this case occurred outside the realm of employment. However, the legal effects of this case have had an impact on anti-discrimination law generally.

253 Per Lord Bridge of Harwich. An opposite view was taken by Lord Griffith and Lord Lowry. The former disagreed, for in his view the Council did not charge Mr James *because* he was a man: [the correct question should be] '(...) did the Council refuse to give free swimming because he was a man? To which I would answer No, they refused because he was not an old age pensioner and therefore could presumably afford to pay 75p to swim'. This view denies the potential of gender or race based criteria to amount to directly discriminatory acts.

occurs intentionally, whereas indirect discrimination is often unintentional.[254] In *James*, however, the respondent's admission policy was clearly not motivated by a malign intention to discriminate against men. Quite in contrast, it hinged on the benign intention to support those in need. To this effect, 'pensionable age' as a distinguishing criterion had merely been adopted for practical, administrative, reasons. The benevolent motive of the respondent (i.e. supporting those with fewer resources) did not preclude the majority of Law Lords from holding an instance of unlawful direct sex discrimination.[255] In summary, a perpetrator's intention is not a material factor for establishing a case of either direct,[256] or indirect discrimination.

4.4. *Top-Down Analysis*

4.4.1. Introduction

Hereafter, I will consider if, and in what respects, the regulation of indirect discrimination in the RRA 1976 and SDA 1975 has changed, post implementation of the RD and the AETD. In section 4.4.2 the legislative definitions of indirect discrimination will be subjected to a top-down comparison. In section 4.4.3 the same will be done with respect to the case law on this concept. The discussion will show that the transposition of the provisions on indirect discrimination in the RD has resulted in an intra-statutory twin-track approach which characterises the RRA 1976 in its amended format.[257] This unsatisfactory situation has been the result of implementation of the Directives by means of governmental Regulations. It will be argued that the aforementioned twin-track approach not only contravenes the principles of legal clarity and consistency, but also falls short of requirements of EC law. It moreover exacer-

254 However, as the facts in *Jenkins* (*Jenkins v. Kingsgate,* (Case 96/80) [1981] ECR 911) and *Griggs* (*Griggs v. Duke Power Co.,* (1971), 401, US 424) showed, indirect discrimination can also occur intentionally.

255 Lord Griffiths' dissenting judgment reflected disagreement with this view. He disagreed with the stance taken by the majority, namely that one must be entirely indifferent as to the question whether an instance of discrimination is rationalised by good or by bad motives. By taking into account the benevolent motive of Eastleigh Borough Council, Lord Griffiths adopted a substantive justice approach (see Fredman 2002, p. 105). Substantive justice, in contrast to formal justice, is not insensitive to the question whether an act of discrimination *furthers* or *prejudices* the interests of the disadvantaged group. The majority of the Law Lords pleaded, in contrast, for the application of the so-called 'but for' test. The application of this test means that the following question must be posed: 'Would Mr James have received the same treatment as his wife but for his sex?' If the answer to this question is positive, direct discrimination will be established. Application of the 'but for' test may result in rendering justice in a social vacuum, given that any benevolent motive is per definition carved out from the judicial analysis of direct discrimination.

256 This had already been held by the House of Lords in *R v. Birmingham City Council ex Parte EOC,* [1989] 1 All ER 769 (HL). In casu, it was unanimously held that 'the intention or motive of the defendant to discriminate, though it may be relevant so far as remedies are concerned (...) is not a necessary condition of liability; it is perfectly possible to envisage cases where the defendant had no such motive, and yet did in fact discriminate on the grounds of sex'.

257 See also Bell 2004, p. 467, who has referred to the 'corrosive effect' on the coherence of the RRA.

bates the judicial analysis in cases where intersectional discrimination is at stake. Brief conclusions will be drawn in section 4.4.4.

4.4.2. Legislative Definitions of Indirect Discrimination: a Dual Approach

4.4.2.1. Definitions of Indirect Discrimination in the RRA and SDA as Amended

Post implementation of the RD, the RRA 1976 as amended contains two distinct definitions of indirect discrimination in the area of employment. In contrast, only one definition of indirect sex discrimination features the SDA in its post-implementation format, at least insofar as the area of employment is concerned.[258] Pre-implementation of the RD, Section 1(1)(b) of the RRA 1976 defined indirect discrimination as follows:

> (1) A person discriminates against another in any circumstances relevant for the purposes of any provision of this Act if-
> (b) he applies to that other a requirement or condition which he applies or would apply equally to persons not of the same racial group as that other but-
> (i) which is such that the proportion of persons of the same racial group as that other who can comply with it is considerably smaller than the proportion of persons not of that racial group who can comply with it and
> (ii) which he cannot show to be justifiable irrespective of the colour, race, nationality or ethnic or national origins of the person to whom it is applied, and
> (iii) which is to the detriment of that other because he cannot comply with it.

An equivalent definition was contained in Section 1(1)(b) SDA 1975 pre-implementation of EC law.[259] With respect to the employment area only, the SDA's definition of indirect discrimination was in need of being amended with a view to implementing the EC Burden of Proof Directive. This occurred with the adoption of the 2001 Burden of Proof Regulations[260] which introduced a more flexible definition of indirect sex discrimination in employment.[261] The newly introduced definition was founded on a statistical evidence approach but it filled the so-called '*Perera* loophole'. This point will be expounded upon in detail hereafter. As a result of the implementation of the AETD, the definition of indirect discrimination as introduced by the Burden of Proof Regulations has ceased to exist. Section 1(2)(b) of the SDA, as amended by the (2005)

258 The pre-implementation definition of indirect sex discrimination has not been repealed and is currently still applicable outside the area of employment. It is contained in Section 1(1)(b) SDA.

259 This Section has not been repealed. It is still valid law for instances of indirect sex discrimination which occur outside the material scope of the AETD.

260 Sex Discrimination (Indirect Discrimination and Burden of Proof) Regulations 2001, (SI 2001/2260).

261 It provided as follows: '(...) a person discriminates against a woman if- (b) he applies to her a provision, criterion or practice which he applies or would apply equally to a man, but- (i) which is such that it would be to the detriment of a considerably larger proportion of women than of men, and (ii) which he cannot show to be justifiable irrespective of the sex of the person to whom it is applied, and (iii) which is to her detriment.' (Section 1(2) (b) SDA). It follows from Section 2(1) SDA that this provision equally applies to the treatment of men. The original definition (Section 1(1)(b) SDA) remained (and currently still remains) the applicable law with respect to areas outside employment.

Sex discrimination Regulations, provides that indirect sex[262] discrimination occurs where:

> 'a man applies to [a woman] a provision, criterion or practice which he applies or would apply equally to a man, but-
> (i) which puts or would put women at a particular disadvantage when compared with men,
> (ii) which puts her at that disadvantage, and
> (iii) which he cannot show to be a proportionate means of achieving a legitimate aim.'

An equivalent definition also features the RRA 1976, as amended by the (2003) Race discrimination Regulations. Section 1(1A) RRA 1976 as amended provides as follows:

> 'A person also discriminates against another if, in any circumstances relevant for the purposes of any provision referred to in subsection (1B), he applies to that other a provision, criterion or practice which he applies or would apply equally to persons not of the same race or ethnic or national origins as that other, but
> (i) which puts or would put persons of the same race or ethnic or national origins as that other at a particular disadvantage when compared with other persons,
> (ii) which puts that other at that disadvantage, and
> (iii) which he cannot show to be a proportionate means of achieving a legitimate aim'.

Unlike the definitions of indirect discrimination in the RD and the AETD, the definitions referred to above require that the plaintiff is actually put at a disadvantage. It therefore appears insufficient that the contested neutral standard poses a *risk* of disadvantage. Given that the English implementing provisions are narrower in this respect than their supranational equivalents, implementation has not occurred in conformity with EC law.

As emphasised earlier, the RRA 1976 currently contains two definitions of indirect discrimination in employment. The RRA in its post-implementation format is characterised by the following peculiar scenario. The definition 'old style' (i.e. the definition pre-implementation of the RD, referred to above) including the case law which has emerged from the interpretation of this definition, is still applicable in:

1. All cases (i.e. both inside and outside employment) in which 'colour' and 'nationality' are the grounds of discrimination at issue.
2. In cases which fall *outside* the scope of new Section 1(1)(b) RRA.[263] This Section essentially reflects the material scope of the RD.

262 The new definition also applies to the ground married status in the area of employment. See the amended definition in Section 3(1) of the SDA. The fact that this renewed definition only applies in employment follows from Section 1(3) SDA.

263 Section 1(1B) contains the following areas: (a) Part II ['employment'; MG]; (b) Sections 17-18D ['education'; MG]; (c) Section 19B ('functions of public authorities'; MG), insofar as they relate to: (i) any form of social security; (ii) health care; (iii) any other form of social protection; and (iv) any form of social advantage; (d) Sections 20-24 ('housing'; MG); (e) Sections 26A and 26B ('discrimination by and against barristers and advocates'; MG); (f) Sections 76 and 76 ZA; (g). →

With respect to the area of employment this means that, if discrimination occurs on grounds of *colour* and/or *nationality*, the judicial analysis will be informed by the definition of indirect discrimination 'old style', including any case law. In contrast, if the complaint of indirect discrimination is founded on *race* and/or *ethnic origin* and/or *national origin*, the definition of indirect discrimination 'new style' will be applicable.

4.4.2.2. *A Fragmented Framework*

The scenario sketched above reveals a particularly patchy framework of domestic race relations law, including indirect discrimination law. Clearly, the aim pursued by the RD, the AETD (and the EFD) was to bring about a set of common legal standards across the European landscapes.[264] However, paradoxically, transposition of the RD has resulted in a fragmentary legal framework of (indirect) race discrimination law at the *domestic* level. This raises a number of questions which will be discussed hereafter. Firstly, what were the underlying causes of the aforementioned scattered framework? Secondly, is this framework in conformity with EC law? Thirdly, what are the consequences of the statutory twin-track approach[265] for indirect discrimination proceedings?

With respect to the first question, it should be emphasised that the fragmentation was not caused by EC law *in se*, but by the modus of implementation chosen by the United Kingdom. As will become apparent hereafter, a diversity of standards is the price paid for speedy implementation of the Directives. Rather than via an Act of Parliament, the Directives were transposed via governmental Regulations.[266] This has as a consequence that implementation may not go beyond what is strictly required by EC law. Voluntary adoption of the European standard in areas which fall outside the scope of EC law is not permitted, given that Regulations have less democratic legitimacy than Parliamentary Acts. If Directives are implemented via Regulations, it will therefore be vital to discern which areas *are* and which *are not* governed by EC law, in casu, the RD. This leads us to the second question posed above.

Part IV ('instructions to discriminate', 'discriminatory advertising'; MG) insofar that this occurs with respect to the areas under (a)-(f). Thus, and perhaps superfluous, discrimination on grounds of *race* and/or *ethnic origin* and/or *national origin* which falls within the scope of any of the aforementioned policy areas is governed by the new definition of indirect discrimination inserted into the RRA post-transposition of EC law.

264 See also the Commission's Green Paper *Equality and Non-Discrimination in an Enlarged European Union* European Commission (Employment and Social Affairs), May 2004 p. 10: 'The adoption of Article 13 reflected the growing recognition of the need to develop a coherent and integrated approach towards the fight against discrimination'. For further analysis of the Green Paper, I refer to Waddington 2004, p. 367-373.

265 Others have referred to a 'patchwork framework' (Bell, 2004) and to 'regressive diversity' (Fitzpatrick, oral presentation at the London Conference '*Equal Protection- Working for a Single Equality Act*' 2003).

266 This has occurred on the basis of the 1972 European Communities Act.

The RD prohibits discrimination on grounds of 'race' and 'ethnic origin', notions which are not further defined.[267] Due to the absence of case law, EC law is currently unsettled as to the legal[268] meaning of race and ethnic origin.[269] The RRA has since its inception prohibited discrimination on grounds of 'colour', 'race', 'nationality', and 'ethnic or national origin'.[270] Whilst in the process of implementation of the RD, the UK government took the view that the notions of 'race' and 'ethnic origin' in the RD cover 'race', 'ethnic origin' and 'national' origin, to the exclusion, however, of 'colour' and 'nationality'. 'Nationality' has been excluded from the Directive's personal scope of application[271] and therefore the UK legislator's stance with respect to this ground is correct. It is argued, however, that the legislator falls short of its obligations under EC law by the exclusion of 'colour' from the post-implementation framework. This argument is supported by the fact that 'colour' is covered by the concept of 'race' as interpreted in the context of international human rights law.[272] In addition to the constitutional interpretations of 'race' and 'ethnic

267 Both notions must, however, be taken to be concepts of Community law, for otherwise legal protection from discrimination would be dependent on diverging interpretations of these concepts across the Member States. Therefore, the ultimate interpretation of 'race' and 'ethnic origin' is a matter for the Luxembourg Court.

268 The usage of race as a concept for purposes of the law must be distinguished from the argument made in social sciences literature, namely that human beings cannot be subdivided into different human 'races' in the absence of a scientific basis to this effect. See Rath 1991, Chapter 4. See in this context also Recital 6 of the RD which states that 'the European Union rejects theories which attempt to determine the existence of separate human races. The use of the term 'racial origin' in this Directive does not imply the acceptance of such theories'. The present author equally dissociates herself from such theories. The discussion of the legal meaning of 'race' does not warrant any opposite conclusion.

269 These notions have been defined in the context of domestic law. The seminal case in English law is that of *Mandla v. Lee* [1983] 2 AC 548; [1983] IRLR 209 (HL). In casu, the House of Lords held that for a group to constitute an 'ethnic group' for purposes of the RRA 1976 '(...) it [has to] regard itself and be regarded by others as a distinct community by virtue of certain characteristics (...)'. The House of Lords in *Mandla* indicated a number of decisive and a number of additional characteristics which determine whether or not a particular group constitutes an 'ethnic group'. The former include: (1) a long shared history of which the group was conscious as distinguishing it from other groups, and the memory of which it kept alive; (2) a cultural tradition of its own, including family and social customs and manners, often but not necessarily associated with religious observance. The latter include: (a) a common geographical origin or descent; (b) a common language; (c) a common literature; (d) a common religion; (e) being a minority or being an oppressed group or dominated group within a larger community. In practice, this has meant that Sikhs (*Mandla*), Jews (*Seide v. Gilette Industries* [1980] IRLR 427 (EAT) and Gypsies (*Commission for Racial Equality v. Dutton* [1989] 1 All ER 306 (CA) are covered by the RRA, in contrast to Rastafarians (*Dawkins v. Department of the Environment* [1993] IRLR 284 (CA). It is likely that the ECJ in future case law will have regard to national interpretations of 'race' and 'ethnic origin' which would amount to a form of bottom-up influence.

270 Section 3(1) of the Act.

271 Article 3(2) RD. It should be noted that the EC case law approach adopted in *O'Flynn* (a case earlier referred to) must, however, be applied to cases of nationality discrimination which fall inside the scope of Community law.

272 Article 1(1) CERD provides as follows: In this Convention the term 'racial discrimination' shall mean any distinction, exclusion, restriction or preference based on race, *colour* (italics →

origin' in the Member States ('bottom up influence') the ECJ is likely to have regard to the interpretation of these concepts in international law. If it is accepted that English implementation legislation falls short of Community law standards, the domestic courts will be under a legal duty to apply the guarantees contained in the RD to 'colour' discrimination cases too.[273]

The third question posed above concerns the consequences of the disrupted framework of the RRA for (*inter alia*) indirect discrimination proceedings. Leaving aside the argument made above namely, that the RRA as it currently stands is in breach of EC law, the following is stated. With a view to optimising legal protection from indirect discrimination, it becomes essential for lawyers to construct cases in a strategic manner. Lawyers will have to base complaints of race discrimination as much as possible on the grounds of race, ethnicity or national origin, given that discrimination on these grounds offers a wider scope of legal protection, compared to discrimination on grounds of race and/or nationality. Hereafter, I will illustrate this point in greater detail with reference to the case law concerning the interpretation of the statutory provisions of indirect discrimination. What is more, given the wider material scope of the RRA 1976 compared to the SDA 1975 (both as amended) strategic litigation becomes important in cases of 'intersectional discrimination',[274] such as for example (indirect) discrimination of a black women.[275] Although at the level of principle it is wrong to require a black female applicant to split up her identity in terms of race and gender, the current legal framework clearly imposes a challenge upon her to nevertheless do so.

4.4.3. Indirect Discrimination: Analysing the Case Law

4.4.3.1. Introduction

Hereafter, an analysis will be made of the case law concerning the concept of indirect discrimination. In the absence of case law on the definition of indirect discrimination post-implementation of EC law, the analysis will focus upon the judicial interpretation of indirect discrimination in its pre-implementation format. Perhaps superfluously, the law on indirect discrimination 'old style' is still valid with respect to colour (and nationality) discrimination cases in (*inter alia*) employment. It will be shown that the legislative concept of indirect discrimination in its pre-implementation format sets a

MG) descent or national or ethnic origin which has the purpose or effect of nullifying or impairing the recognition, enjoyment or exercise on an equal footing, of human rights and fundamental freedoms in the political economic, social, cultural or any other field of public law. It is worth noting that the approach adopted by Dutch law with respect to the interpretation of 'race' is identical to the approach adopted by the CERD. See Memorie van Toelichting [*Explanatory Memorandum*], II 1990-1991, 22 014, no. 3, p. 13; Also Dutch Supreme Court 15-06-1976, 551.

273 See generally Chapter 2 with reference to the relevant case law by the ECJ.

274 See for a discussion on 'intersectional discrimination', Hannett 2003; Crenshaw 1989.

275 If, for example, a black woman is discriminated against in an area which is not governed by sex discrimination law but which is covered by race discrimination law, it will be strategic to plea a case of race discrimination.

much more rigid standard of proof, compared with the equivalent definition post implementation of EC law. Before starting, it might be useful to briefly outline the legal elements of the definitions of indirect discrimination pre- and post-implementation. This will be done in section 4.4.3.2 hereafter.

4.4.3.2. Legal Constituents of Indirect Discrimination Pre- and Post-Implementation of EC Law

With reference to section 4.4.2.1 above, the constituent elements of the definition of indirect discrimination pre-implementation of EC law are the following: (1) application of a 'requirement' or 'condition'; (2) 'disparate impact' upon the group to which the plaintiff belongs; (3) a personal 'detriment'; (4) 'objective justification'. These elements have been interpreted in both indirect race and sex discrimination cases. The analysis of the case law hereafter will examine each of these elements with the exception of the third one, given that this has not been the source of legal controversy. The definition of indirect discrimination in its post-implementation format consists of the following legal limbs: (1) the neutral application of a 'provision, criterion or practice'; (2) which puts or would put persons defined by a forbidden ground at a 'particular disadvantage'; (3) compared with other persons; (4) proof that the plaintiff is put at an actual disadvantage; (5) objective justification.[276] The aforementioned elements will be brought into the discussion hereafter and will be contrasted (wherever appropriate) with the constituents of indirect discrimination 'old style'.

4.4.3.3. Requirement and Condition versus Provision/Criterion/Practice

The element of a 'requirement' or 'condition' has been interpreted to mean that the mere existence of a pattern of disadvantage is insufficient to establish indirect discrimination. In contrast, the applicant must be able to pin-point a concrete 'requirement' or 'condition' which has been the cause of disparate impact.[277] The legal meaning of 'requirement' and 'condition' has been considered in a number of cases. Initially, the courts preferred a liberal interpretation of these concepts over a verbatim approach. *Clarke v. Eley (IMI) Kynoch Ltd*[278] concerned an instance of alleged indirect sex discrimination.

In casu, the employer adopted a redundancy policy on the basis of which part-time workers were selected first. In the employer's view, this policy did not constitute a 'requirement' or 'condition' for the purposes of the SDA. In his view, a 'requirement' demands for action by the addressee. In the view of the employer, a 'condition' includes a qualification for holding a position but not a qualification for immunity from disadvantage. The EAT, per Mr Justice Brown-Wilkinson, refused to interpret

276 See also section 4.4.2.1 above where the statutory definition has been outlined in full.

277 Ellis 1994a, p. 573 has expressed it as follows: 'As a matter of UK law, it is therefore not enough to show simply that the ways things are organised in a particular enterprise works to the disadvantage of women [or racial minorities MG]; it is essential to be able to point to a particular hoop through which women [or racial minorities MG] are required to jump.'

278 *Clarke v. Ely (IMI) Kynoch Ltd*, [1982] IRLR 482 (EAT). See generally also McColgan 2005, p. 79.

the vexed notions in a limited way. The EAT held that a 'requirement' and 'condition' were to be understood as partly overlapping terms. It took the view that a 'condition' covers both a qualification for holding a position, a disqualification for continuing such a position, and a qualification for immunity from disadvantage. In the view of the EAT there is no valid distinction between a 'requirement', 'condition', 'test', and 'yardstick'. Importantly, with reference to the *Griggs* case (earlier discussed), the EAT emphasised the purpose of importing indirect discrimination into the RRA and SDA. Essentially, indirect discrimination was meant to eliminate those practices which have a disproportionate impact upon women and ethnic minorities in the absence of justification.

In *Hampson v. Department of Education and Science*,[279] the applicant was refused a qualified teacher status in England. She had, however, obtained a teacher qualification in Hong Kong but this was not considered comparable to the equivalent UK courses. The EAT, per Mr Justice Popple Well, established that the criteria for determining the comparability of courses, constituted a 'requirement' or 'condition'.[280]

The liberal approach in the aforementioned cases was overturned by a strict interpretation in subsequent case law in which it was held that a 'requirement' or 'condition' must amount to an 'absolute bar' or a 'must'. In *Perera v. Civil Service Commission (No. 2)*[281] the facts were as follows.

An advertisement for a post of legal assistant with the Civil Service stipulated that candidates with a good command of English, experience in the UK, of British nationality and of older age, would be at an advantage in the process of job-selection. The applicant, a Sri Lankan born, applied but was subsequently refused for the job. He started proceedings for unlawful indirect race discrimination. However, in the view of the EAT, none of the contested criteria constituted a 'requirement' or 'condition' which formed an absolute bar to the job. In essence, a 'mere' job *preference* is not a 'requirement' or 'condition' for purposes of the law. Although such a view clearly undermines the potential of indirect discrimination, it was nonetheless approved by the Court of Appeal which held that '(...) a brilliant man whose personal qualities made him suitable as a legal assistant might well have been sent forward (...) in spite of being, perhaps, below standard on his knowledge of English'.[282]

Perera creates a major legal lacuna, given that it grants freedom to employers to disguise critical job requirements as mere professional preferences.[283] This lacuna is known as the '*Perera* loophole', touched on earlier. Notwithstanding the foregoing,

279 *Hampson v. Department of Education and Science* [1988] IRLR 87 (EAT); [1989] IRLR 69 (CA); [1990] IRLR 302 (HL). The real importance of this case is, however, the issue of justification. This element will be discussed in section 4.4.3.5 hereafter.

280 The tribunal at first instance had taken the view that the criteria applied by the Secretary of State, constituted a test or a yardstick, rather than a requirement or condition.

281 *Perera v. Civil Service Commission & the Department of Customs & Excise* [1982] IRLR 147 (EAT); [1983] IRLR 166 (CA).

282 Per Stephenson LJ, p. 437-438. This stance has been heavily criticised in the literature. See, for example, Connolly 1996; McColgan 2000, p. 75-77 with further references; Williams 2003, p. 9-10.

283 See, for example, Williams 2003, p. 9-10.

the CA did not depart from its stance in *Perera* in the case of *Meer*.[284] It was held by Lord Justice Balcombe that

> 'had the case before us not been decided by Perera, as I believe it is, I accept that there are strong arguments (...) that the absolute bar construction of 'condition or requirement' may not be consistent with the object of the Act. But Perera is binding upon us (...); decisions of the Court of Appeal are binding and, unless they can properly be distinguished, do not disappear. I accept that there are arguments (...) which suggest that the law as stated by Perera, might need reform. But that is not a matter for this court to speculate on; it may be for Parliament'.[285]

Hence, despite acknowledgment of its own faulty reasoning in *Perera*, the CA felt bound by it and ruled that the unhappy situation created by *Perera* could merely be repaired by the Law Lords or by Parliament.

A conservative approach was also adopted by the EAT in *Brook* in the context of the SDA.[286]

In casu, a length of service requirement was applied as an important, although not exclusive, factor for redundancy. The female applicants *inter alia* claimed an instance of unlawful indirect sex discrimination. The EAT stated as follows:

> 'It is argued that the applicants were required to obtain a preset number of points to avoid redundancy and that this in itself was a condition. It seems to us that no-one could have told what the cut-off point would be in each particular trade until after the points had been calculated and there could not, in reality, be said to be any predetermined figure. A person who is rejected because he is not the best candidate on an amalgam of factors has not been subjected to any requirement or condition but he has simply failed to defeat his competitors. It is the position of the individual on the list which is the determining factor, not the amount of points scored. The cut-off is unknown until after the event.'[287]

Clearly, however, women have less of a chance to defeat their male competitors than *vice versa*, in light of women's childcare and family responsibilities. These are likely to affect their length of service with a particular employer. McColgan has therefore rightly insisted that the EAT's view in *Brooks* is 'flawed'.[288]

A more favourable approach was subsequently adopted by the CA in *Jones v. Manchester*.[289] In casu, the CA accepted that a specification in the respondent's job

284 *Meer v. Tower Hamlets LBC*, [1988] IRLR 399 (CA). The CA dismissed the applicant's appeal and leave to appeal to the House of Lords was refused. Both the tribunal and the EAT had taken the view that 'Tower Hamlets experience', which was one out of more criteria for long-listing, did not amount to an 'absolute bar'.

285 Paragraph 18 of the judgment. See with similar effect paragraph 24 of the CA's judgment where it was held by Lord Justice Dillon that 'it may well be that if Perera reflects the true state of the law there are reasons for altering the law, but that is not a matter for this court; still less it is for this court to draft an appropriate amendment'.

286 *Brook v. London Borough of Haringey* [1992] IRLR 478 (EAT). This case has also been discussed by McColgan 2005, p. 80.

287 Paragraph 91 of the judgment.

288 McColgan 2005, p. 82.

289 *Jones v. University of Manchester* [1993] IRLR 218 (CA).

advertisement which *inter alia* stipulated that the successful candidate would be a graduate and *preferably aged 27-35,* constituted a 'requirement' or 'condition' for purposes of the SDA.[290] A similar liberal stance was taken by the EAT in *Falkirk Council v. White*[291] with reference to Community sex discrimination law. The EAT explicitly held that

> '(...) if the (present) case turned upon whether or not the relevant factors to become a requirement or condition had to be an absolute bar to qualification for the post in question, we would not be inclined to follow the race discrimination cases, in particular, that of Perera'.[292]

It follows from the aforementioned two cases that the courts have been prepared to adopt a more relaxed stance with respect to sex discrimination cases, in view of supranational sex discrimination law standards. Since the ECJ's decision in *Enderby*[293] the outcome of *Perera* has no longer been valid law in cases which fell within the scope of EC law.[294] In *Enderby,* as discussed in section 3.3.3.3 above, the ECJ interpreted Article 119 EC in the context of a national pay structure which granted a chiefly female composed sector of the UK's NHS (namely: speech therapists) a lower rate of payment than a preponderantly male composed sector (namely: clinical psychologists and pharmacists), notwithstanding that the work performed by the respective sectors was of equal value. In the ECJ's view this by itself was enough to place the onus upon the employer to demonstrate that this did not amount to sex discrimination. The ECJ's decision in *Enderby* has also overruled *Brook.* This was explicitly stated by the CA in *Allonby.*[295] The *Perera* doctrine has been altogether departed from by the definition of indirect discrimination post implementation of EC law. The renewed definition of indirect discrimination merely requires proof of the existence of a 'provision', 'criterion' or 'practice' which covers both absolute bars and 'mere' job preferences.

4.4.3.4. Disparate Impact Versus a Particular Disadvantage

According to the original definition of indirect discrimination, a (proportional) comparison fell to be drawn between the persons of the group to which the plaintiff belongs who can comply with the vexed 'requirement' or 'condition', on the one hand, and the persons of a relevant benchmark group who can comply with it, on the other. 'Can comply' has been interpreted purposely: the applicant needs not prove a

290 The CA affirmed herewith the earlier decision by the EAT in *Manchester University v. Jones,* [1992] I.C.R. 52 (EAT).

291 *Falkirk Council v. White,* [1997] IRLR 560 (EAT).

292 Paragraph 6 of the judgment.

293 *Enderby v. Frenchay Health Authority,* (Case C-127/92 [1993] ECR I-5535, earlier discussed in the context of EC law.

294 See Connolly 1996, section 5.

295 *Allonby v. Accrington & Rossendale College and others* [2001] IRLR 364, paragraph 15 (per Sedley (LJ). This case will be discussed in section 4.4.3.5.

literal inability to comply. What matters is, that (s)he can in reasonableness not be expected to 'comply'.[296] Lord Fraser, in *Mandla v. Lee*, held as follows:

> 'It [i.e.'can comply'; MG] must in my opinion have been intended by Parliament to be read not as meaning 'can physically' as to indicate a theoretical possibility, but as meaning 'can in practice' or 'can consistently' with the customs and cultural conditions of the group.'[297]

The new definition of indirect discrimination does not require an applicant to prove that a particular *provision, criterion* or *practice* is to his (her) detriment because (s)he 'cannot comply with it'. The argument, for example, that women with full-time child rearing responsibilities 'can comply' with a full-time work requirement, if they make use of external child-care facilities, is therefore bound to fail. As discussed in earlier sections, the new definition of indirect discrimination infringes on the group dimension of justice, to the benefit of individual justice. Rather than establishing 'disparate impact', the plaintiff need merely prove that the vexed neutral provision (etc.) 'puts or would put women at a particular disadvantage compared with men' (or vice versa).[298] In the absence of case law, it is currently, however, unclear how many persons need to be adversely affected and what exactly is meant by a 'particular disadvantage'. Hereafter, I will examine existing case law with respect to 'disparate impact', the 'pool for comparison' and the usage of statistical evidence. This case law has arisen prior to the implementation of the RD and AETD. It will be illustrated that the English courts, in addition to statistical evidence, have accepted 'common knowledge facts' as a factor in proving disparate impact.[299]

London Underground[300] concerned the choice of the correct pool for comparison. Ms Edwards, a single-parent with a young child, was employed with London Underground as a train operator. The applicable work-roster enabled Ms Edwards to be at home in the mornings and evenings to look after her child. In order to save costs, the employer introduced in 1991 a flexible shift system which required that work started at 4.45 in the mornings including on Sundays. The applicant resigned thereupon from her job and claimed unlawful indirect sex discrimination. The Tribunal at first instance, concluded a *prima facie* indirect sex discrimination case, given that a considerable smaller proportion of female single parents, compared to male single parents, could comply with the new scheme. The EAT, on appeal, held that the Tribunal had chosen the wrong pool for comparison. It should have compared all female train operators, who were required to conform to the new scheme, with all male train operators who were equally required to do so. The Tribunal was wrong,

296 Bindman 1992, p. 59.

297 *Mandla v. Lee* [1983] 2 AC 548 (HL).

298 An equivalent requirement is contained in new Section 1(1A) of the RRA 1976 as amended.

299 See also *Allonby (appellant) v. Accrington & Rossendale College and others (respondents)* [2001] IRLR 364, paragraph 8, where the CA held that 'the employment tribunal was entitled to have in mind, as a matter of common knowledge in their field, that the substantial imbalance between men and women on hourly paid part-time contracts (...) reflected the national picture in the United Kingdom, where part-time work is overwhelmingly done by women'.

300 *London Underground Ltd (appellants) v. Edwards (Respondent)* [1995] IRLR 355 (EAT).

where it delineated the pool by reference to the exact factor (i.e. being a single parent) which had been the effective cause of the applicant's inability to comply.

In *Kidd*,[301] the EAT made clear that the identification of the pool is a question of fact for the first instance court to decide.[302] Hence, a decision on the pool may only be reversed by a higher court for reasons of 'irrationality'. *Kidd* appears, however, to have been over-ruled by the CA in *Allonby*.[303] In casu, Lord Justice Sedley sounded a 'strong note of caution' about the EAT's approach in *Kidd*. In his view,

> '(...) once the impugned requirement or condition has been defined there is likely to be only one pool which serves to test its effect. I would prefer to characterise the identification of the pool as a matter neither of discretion, nor of fact-finding, but of logic (...) Logic may on occasion be capable of producing more than one outcome, especially if two or more conditions are in issue. But the choice of pool is not at large.'[304]

The appraisal of disparate impact was at the centre-piece of the judicial analysis in *London Underground No. 2*.[305] It was questioned whether the imposition of the new rostering scheme was a condition 'with which a considerably smaller proportion of female than male train operators could comply?'.

At first instance, the Industrial Tribunal had given an affirmative answer to this question. The evidence showed, that 2,023 of the 2,023 male train drivers could comply with the new schedule, compared to 20 of the 21 female drivers. In percentages, this constitutes a 100% to 95.2% ratio. In the employer's view, and with reference to earlier cases, this ratio did not reflect disparate impact.[306] The EAT did, however, not agree: 'what is a considerably smaller proportion is a question of fact for the Industrial Tribunal. It would be a misuse of authority to take one proportion from one case and then use it as a yardstick or marker in another'.[307]

The employer moreover argued that the Tribunal had been wrong by also taking into account the absolute numbers of persons in the respective pools (which

301 *Kidd (appellant) v. DRG (UK) LTD (respondents)* [1985] IRLR 190 (EAT, per Mr Justice Wait).

302 In paragraph 20 of the judgment in *Kidd*, it was held as follows: 'The choice of an appropriate section of the population is in our judgment an issue of fact (or perhaps strictly a matter for discretion to be exercised in the course of discharging an exclusively fact-finding function (...).'

303 *Allonby (appellant) v. Accrington & Rossendale College and others (respondents)* [2001] IRLR 364. See also *University of Jones v. Manchester* [1992] IRLR 52 discussed by McColgan 2005, p. 86-87.

304 Paragraph 18 of the judgment (per Sedley (LJ). See moreover *Rutherford and Bentley (appellants) v. Secretary of State for Trade and Industry (respondent)* 2004 IRLR 892 EWCA Civ. 1186. In casu, it was *inter alia* held by the CA that the Tribunal at first instance had chosen the wrong pool for comparison. The correct pool was delineated by the CA prior to an assessment of disparate impact.

305 *London Underground Ltd v. Edwards (No. 2)* [1997] IRLR 157 (EAT). In casu, *London Underground* appealed against the earlier decision by the first instance Tribunal which had concluded an instance of indirect sex discrimination.

306 The employer supported its view with reference to the decision by the EAT in *Staffordshire County Council v. Black* [1995] IRLR 234 (EAT) (a ratio of 89.5% females: 97% males did not constitute a 'considerably smaller proportion') and the High Court's decision in *R v. Secretary of State v. Unison* [1996] IRLR 438 (a 4% disparity was likely to fall within the 'the minimis exception').

307 Paragraph 25 of the judgment.

were absolutely small in the female pool, compared to the male pool). The EAT disagreed once again: 'the absolute numbers of persons in the male and female pools will have a bearing, as will the nature of the employment (...)'.

The EAT was right in its view, given that the above percentages would show a much bigger discrepancy, had only one more woman been unable to comply with the scheme. Thus, the EAT recognised the value of absolute numbers as an aid for assessing the reliability of the statistics at hand.[308] The last matter for discussion concerns the following. In the employer's view, the general matter that women are more likely than men to be single parents looking after a child, should not be a factor to be considered in the assessment of disparate impact. The EAT rejected this argument too. A Tribunal may legitimately take account of the wider picture amongst the general population. It may (inter alia) do so, by paying attention to the possibility that where, in percentages, differences are minimal, some kind of generalisation exists at the workplace that the work concerned is typical 'men's work'. In casu, not a single man was affected by the vexed scheme. The importance of this last point is that the EAT accepted that, in the appraisal of disparate impact, factors other than statistical evidence may be taken into account. Ultimately, this view was affirmed by the Court of Appeal.[309]

Disparate impact was also at the heart of the legal analysis in *Seymour Smith*.[310] [311] After the case was remitted by the ECJ to the domestic level, the House of Lords was essentially concerned with (1) the legal test for assessing disparate impact; (2) the point in time at which this fell to be assessed; and (3) objective justification. The last point shall not be considered at this juncture. As referred to in section 3.3.3.4 above, the ECJ held that disparate impact could be demonstrated by (1) showing a considerable disparity at a particular point in time or (2) showing a lesser disparity which must be persistent and relatively constant over a longer period. It had moreover held, that choosing the right point in time is a matter for the national

308 Paragraph 25 of the judgment.

309 *London Underground v. Edwards (No 2)* [1998] IRLR 364 (CA).

310 Judgments- *Regina v. Secretary of State for Employment* (Original Appellant and Cross-Respondent) *Ex Parte Seymour Smith (A.P.) and Another* (Original Respondents and Cross-Appellants), [2000] 1 All ER 857 (HL). This case is also available at <http://www.parliament.the.stationery-office.co.uk/pa/ld199900/ldjudgmt/jd000217/se> (last visited on 15-04-06). The decision was taken by five Law Lords. Lord Slynn of Hadley and Lord Steyn (the latter concurring with the speech of the former) both found that the figures did not trigger a *prima facie* case of indirect sex discrimination. Lord Goff of Chievely, Lord Jauncey Tullichettle, and Lord Nicholls of Birkenhead (the former two concurring with the speech of Lord Nicholls) made a conclusion to the contrary (although, eventually, it was held that the *prima facie* case of indirect discrimination could be justified). The 3:2 majority once more illustrates that assessing disparate impact is a delicate matter which easily leads to diverging conclusions. The facts of the case have been discussed in section 3.3.3.4 above in the context of EC law and will not be repeated at this juncture. For a case comment, I also refer to Connolly 2000, p. 212-222.

311 See also the case of *Rutherford and Bentley (appellants) v. Secretary of State for Trade and Industry (respondent)* 2004 IRLR 892 EWCA Civ. 1186, in which the CA strongly relied on the ECJ's approach in *Seymour Smith*. In *Rutherford*, the CA *inter alia* held that, although both the percentages of the 'compliers' and 'non-compliers' in each group had to be compared, the emphasis must be on a comparison of the former.

court. Whereas the ECJ had availed itself of statistics of 1985, the HL considered the statistics of 1991 to be the correct ones. 1991 was the year in which the applicants were dismissed. The 1991 statistics revealed a 10:9 ratio of men *v.* women who qualified for protection from unlawful dismissal. Although at first sight, this ratio may not sustain an affirmative conclusion on the question of disparate impact, it was stressed that the disparity had been persistent and constant over the years. This conclusion fell within the remit for legal discretion granted by the ECJ to the domestic court.

The last case to be discussed here is that of *Coker and Osamor (appellants) v. Lord Chancellor and Lord Chancellor's Department (respondents).*[312] The facts were as follows.

In 1997, Gerry Hart (a white male) was appointed by Lord Irvine of Lairg (the Lord Chancellor, LC) as his special advisor. According to the relevant rules, special advisors to cabinet ministers need not be appointed on the basis of the principles of meritocracy and fair and open competition. The Lord Chancellor had therefore never advertised the post at issue and had merely looked for a suitable candidate within the circle of family and friends. Ms Coker and Ms Osamor both claimed unlawful direct and indirect sex discrimination ['old style'; MG]. Ms Osamor also claimed unlawful race discrimination ['old style'; MG]. Coker's direct sex discrimination claim was rejected by the first instance court as well as all claims by Osamor. Coker's indirect sex discrimination claim was, however, upheld. The Tribunal had taken the view that '(...) it was not justifiable to appoint someone you know where the reasonable need is to appoint someone on merit and it must be apparent that appointment on the basis of personal knowledge will result in a consideration of men rather then women'.

Essentially, 'being personally known to the LC' was conceived as a 'requirement' or 'condition' for job-selection which had a disparate impact on women. The EAT disagreed and decided in favour of the LC. It held that no relevant pool for comparison existed, given that the LC had always had in mind *one single person* only, to the exclusion of all others, be they women or men. As such, there could be no 'disparate' impact altogether. Upon appeal, this approach was affirmed by the CA:

> 'The test of indirect discrimination focuses on the effect that the requirement objected to has on the pool of potential candidates. It can only have a discriminatory effect (..) if a significant proportion of the pool are able to satisfy the requirement. Only in that situation will it be possible for the requirement to have a disproportionate effect on the men and the women, or the racial groups, which form the pool. Where the requirement excludes almost the entirety of the pool it cannot constitute indirect discrimination within the Statutes.'[313]
> For this reason, making an appointment from within a circle of family, friends or personal acquaintances is seldom likely to constitute indirect discrimination (...). The requirement of personal knowledge will exclude the vast proportion of the pool, be they men, women, white or another racial group.'[314]

312 *Coker and Osamor (appellants) v. Lord Chancellor and Lord Chancellor's Department (respondents),* [2001] IRLR 116 (EAT); [2002] IRLR 80 (CA). See also the case note by Morris 2003, p. 45-55.

313 Paragraph 38 of the judgment.

314 Paragraph 39 of the judgment.

The above line of reasoning could be criticised with reference to the following. Firstly, the wider object of the proceedings (which were backed up, both by the EOC[315] and by the CRE[316]), was to challenge the practice of 'closed job recruitment'. The practice of appointing employees from within a circle of family, friends and acquaintances is likely to create gender, or race-based, outcomes. Furthermore, and this was at the heart of Coker's claim, closed recruitment results in depriving a potential candidate from the opportunity in the first place to be considered for a post. Secondly, there is clearly a risk that the LC's appointment practice predominantly affected women and persons of a racial minority. The LC is a white man working in the higher ranks of political life in which, currently at least, white men are over-represented. The CA should have adopted a similar stance as that by the Tribunal at first instance. In doing so, it could arguably have relied on the ECJ's decision in *Jämställdhetsombudsmannen*,[317] where it was held that disparate impact can be established where the disadvantaged group is predominantly composed of females, detached from the gender-composition of the reference group. By deciding as it did, the CA in *Coker* sent off the wrong message which touches on the underlying philosophy of equality law. The CA was in error where it affirmed the legitimacy of a race and sex-biased selection process. Indeed, the LC himself had admitted that, had he considered his acquaintances as potential candidates, 'he would have considered more white men than women and those of African, Caribbean or Afro-Caribbean ethnic origin would have been in a very small minority'.[318] It is submitted that the CA's stance was *a fortiori* ill-founded in the context of high level political jobs. In such jobs, decisions are taken which affect society as a whole and the principle of 'equality as participation' requires that 'the full participation and inclusion of everyone in major social [and political MG] institutions is fundamental to social equality'.[319] Participatory equality seeks to address the under-representation of disadvantaged groups in important decision-making fora. However, the CA in *Coker*, took away much of the legal soil necessary for this principle to flourish in practice. Finally it should be noted that, since the definitions of indirect race and sex discrimination 'new style' essentially do away with the group-dimension of the concept, in favour of a more individualised approach, cases like *Coker* would arguably be approached differently in present times. Presumably, the requirement of being known to the LC constitutes a 'particular disadvantage' for women or ethnic minorities ('compared with other persons'). The truth of this submission would, however, have to be affirmed in future case law.

4.4.3.5. Objective Justification

The final constituent element to be assessed at this point concerns the test for objective justification. With reference to section 4.4.2.1 above, the definition of indirect

315 Equal Opportunities Commission.
316 Commission for Racial Equality.
317 *Jämställdhetsombudsmannen v. Örebro Läns Landsting* (Case C-236/98) [2000] ECR I-2189.
318 Paragraph 37 of the judgment.
319 Fredman 2002a, p. 16 with reference to Young 1990.

discrimination 'old style' contained in the RRA 1976 provides shallow guidance on the legal application of 'objective justification'. It merely stipulates that the employer's justification defence has to be 'irrespective of (...) colour, race, nationality or ethnic or national origin[s] (...)'. Similarly, the definition of indirect sex discrimination introduced into domestic law by the 2001 Burden of Proof Regulations[320] provides that justification has to be 'irrespective of (...) sex (...)'. The definitions of indirect discrimination 'new style', inserted into the RRA and SDA as a consequence of the implementation of, respectively, the RD and AETD, provide more detailed guidance. They specify that the *prima facie* indirectly discriminatory conduct must be a 'proportionate means of achieving a legitimate aim'.[321] Absent in this rubric is, it should be noted, the element of 'appropriateness' which features the justifiability defence in the RD (and EFD) and the AETD. Arguably, therefore, the UK legislator has introduced a laxer test for justification compared to EC law which means that implementation has unduly occurred. Up until present, 'objective justification' 'new style' has not been interpreted in the case law by the courts. The case law analysis of 'objective justification' hereafter is therefore (necessarily) confined to an analysis of 'objective justification' pre-implementation of EC law.

The touchstone of 'justifiability' in the *Griggs* case, earlier referred to, was that of 'business *necessity*'. This means that in order to justify the *prima facie* discriminatory conduct, the employer will have to prove that this 'conduct' (e.g. the application of a requirement, condition, practice, etc.) is *essential* for purposes of his business. If necessity forms part of the legal test of justification, this brings with it the fact that the judicial stance with respect to the assessment of the employer's defence is strict. As referred to earlier, the stricter the test for justification, the more importance is given to the intrinsic values of the principles of non-discrimination and equality. The philosophy underlying *Griggs* was reflected in the early case of *Steel v. Union of Post Office Workers*[322] which arose in the context of the SDA 1975. In casu, Phillips J distinguished the notion of 'necessity' from that of (mere) 'convenience'. Put differently, the suggestion was made in that case that justifiability requires some element of 'necessity'. By contrast, in *Panesar*[323] the (stringent) 'necessity' approach was substituted by a lenient 'reasonableness' test. In casu, the *Nestlé* company's chocolate factory at Hayes imposed a 'no beard' rule upon its workers with reference to hygiene. This resulted in *prima facie* indirect discrimination against (future) (orthodox) Sikh workers, including any applicant who wore an unshorn beard. The Industrial Tribunal at first instance held by unanimity

> '(...) that while beards were not in themselves the only potential cause, or even a major potential cause, of bacterial infection or contamination, the company was entitled to maintain a regulation against a well-recognised risk and the interests of the public and consumers of their products were served by taking all reasonable precautions to maintain

320 See section 4.4.2.1 above.

321 Section 1(2)(b) SDA as amended and Section 1(1A) RRA 1976 as amended. See section 4.4.2.1 above.

322 *Steel v. Union of Post Office Workers* [1977] IRLR 288 (EAT).

323 *Panesar v. NESTlE Co. LTD ICR* [1980] 144 (CA).

> the quality of their products and that on the facts of the case they had shown that the regulation against beards was justifiable'.

This view remained unaltered upon appeal. The CA, per Lord Denning M.R.[324] held that 'the industrial tribunal held that the rule about the wearing of beards was justifiable (...). It seems to me that that finding was essentially one of fact in the circumstances of the case, against which there is no appeal except on a point of law'.[325]

The 'reasonableness' standard also permeates the judicial analysis of justification in *Ojutiku and Oberoni v. Manpower Services Commission*.[326]

In casu, the two applicants were of West African origin. They wished to pursue a course in Management Studies but were denied a financial grant by the Manpower Services Commission (henceforth: MSC). Financial assistance was merely granted to those candidates who had experience in a post of commercial, administrative, professional or industrial responsibility. This rule was rationalised by the MSC by reference to the fact that the employment prospects of those without previous managerial experience would not be enhanced after having taken the diploma successfully. The parties in casu did not contend that the vexed rule resulted in *prima facie* indirect race discrimination, given that proportionately fewer black compared to white persons had the required experience. This fact was the result of earlier (direct) discrimination, for fewer blacks than whites were offered the opportunity of obtaining managerial experience in the first place. The judicial analysis centred around the question of justification. Both the ET and the EAT had decided in favour of the respondent and this view was eventually upheld by the CA. Eveleigh (LJ) refused to accept that 'it is essential, or at least that it is always essential, for the employer to prove that the requirement is necessary for the good of his business' thereby explicitly rejecting the EAT's approach in Steel.[327] He expressed the view that 'if a person produces reasons for doing something, which would be acceptable to right-thinking people as sound and tolerable reasons for so doing, then he has justified his conduct'.[328] Kerr (LJ) opined that the word 'justifiable' 'clearly applies a lower standard than the word 'necessary''[329] and that 'to justify' means 'advancing good grounds'.[330] This view is, however, opaque, given that it remained unclear to what extent the justifiability test bears a lower standard of scrutiny compared to a necessity test. Stephenson (LJ), with reference to *Steel*, took the view that

> '[w]hat Mr Justice Philipps there [i.e. in Steel; MG] said is valuable as rejecting justification by convenience and requiring the party applying the discriminatory condition to prove it to be justifiable in all the circumstances on balancing its discriminatory effect against the

324 Sir George Baker agreeing with the view expressed by Lord Denning (M.R.).

325 *Panesar v. NESTIE Co. LTD* ICR [1980] 144 (CA), p. 147.

326 *Ojutiku and Oberoni v. Manpower Services Commission*, [1982] IRLR 418 (CA).

327 Paragraph 20 of the judgment.

328 *Ibid.*

329 Paragraph 35 of the judgment.

330 Paragraph 37 of the judgment.

discriminator's need for it. But that need is that is reasonably (my underlining) needed by the party who applies the condition (...)'.[331]

The cases discussed thus far were decided prior to the ECJ's decision in *Bilka* which, legally viewed, merely bears an impact upon domestic indirect *sex* discrimination law.[332] However, the interpretation by the ECJ of EC sex discrimination law may cross-fertilise into domestic race relations law. This partly and indirectly occurred in the *Hampson*[333] case to be discussed immediately henceforth.

In *Hampson* the Court of Appeal adopted a more robust stance with respect to the justification question compared to the 'reasonableness' approach which featured the case law discussed above. *Hampson* was decided after the ECJ's decision in *Bilka*. Stephenson (LJ) criticised (with due respect) the judgments of Eveleigh (LJ) and Kerr (LJ) in *Ojutiku* for giving insufficient guidance on the question as to what test ought to be applied in the assessment of justification. In his view, the words 'justifiable' and 'to justify' connote a normative judgment which implies that the test has to be an objective one. It is therefore insufficient for an employer to establish that he considered his reasons adequate. Elaborating on the view aired by Stephenson (LJ) in *Ojutiku*, Balcombe (LJ) held that 'in my judgment 'justifiable' requires an objective balance between the discriminatory effect of the condition and the reasonable needs of the party who applies the condition'.[334] He supported this interpretation with reference to *Rainey v. Greater Glasgow Health Board*.[335] In that case, the House of Lords availed itself of the ECJ's decision in *Bilka* in the judicial assessment of the so-called 'material factor defence' in the context of an equal pay dispute.[336] Counsel for the appellant (in *Hampson*), however, argued that *Ojutiku* had been overruled by *Rainey*. By implication, therefore, the latter judgment cannot be employed in support of the former. The CA, however, disagreed. According to Balcombe (LJ) there is 'no significant difference between the test adopted by Lord Justice Stephenson in *Ojutiku*

331 Paragraph 54 of the judgment.

332 After all, at the material time the EC was not endowed with a legal competence to act in the area of race relations. See Hervey 1991, p. 822, especially footnote 54. The first case in which the *Bilka* test for justification was applied concerns the case of *Rainey v. Greater Glasgow Health Board* [1987] IRLR 26 which, however, did not concern justification for indirect discrimination but justification for a difference in pay between men and women under Section 1(3) of the Equal Pay Act. This case will be discussed in further detail in the main text to follow.

333 *Hampson v. Department of Education and Science* [1989] IRLR 69 (CA).

334 Paragraph 34 of the judgment. See also Nourse (LJ) in paragraph 55 of the judgment: '(...) the correct test is one which requires an objective balance to be struck between the discriminatory effect of the requirement or condition and the reasonable needs of the person who applies it. If, and only if, its discriminatory effect can be objectively justified by those needs will the requirement or condition be 'justifiable' (...).'

335 *Rainey v. Greater Glasgow Health Board* [1987] IRLR 26, referred to by Balcombe (LJ) in paragraph 35 of *Hampson*.

336 The material factors defence is enshrined in Section 1(3) of the Equal Pay Act which at the material time provided as follows: 'An equality clause shall not operate in relation to a variation between the women's contract and the man's contract if the employer proves that the variation is genuinely due to a material difference (other than the difference of sex) between her case and his.'

and that adopted by the House of Lords in *Rainey*' [which reflects the standard of justification applied by the ECJ in *Bilka*; MG].[337] This holding can be criticised: whereas in *Bilka* the ECJ adhered to a strict necessity test, the element of 'reasonableness' creeps into the equation in the CA's stance in *Hampson*.[338] Compliance with the 'necessity' element requires that the courts verify whether the goals pursued by the alleged perpetrator cannot be achieved with other (potentially less discriminatory) means. This question is, however, not encapsulated in a reasonableness defence. In summary, it appears that the CA in *Hampson* oscillated between, on the one hand, the lenient and obscure approaches adopted by Eveleigh (LJ) and Kerr (LJ) in *Ojutiku* (which it rejected) and the ECJ's rigorous approach in *Bilka*, on the other.

The *Hampson* test of justification was subsequently applied by the EAT in *London Underground*.[339] The Industrial Tribunal (to whom the case at been remitted by the EAT in *London Underground No. 1*)[340] had taken the view that justification in casu required a consideration of the needs of London Underground and their goal of saving money and be more efficient, on the one hand, *v.* the discriminatory effect this had on single parents looking after a child, including Ms Edwards, on the other. In assessing this, the Tribunal had reached the conclusion that London Underground

> 'could have easily, without losing the objectives of their plan and reorganisation, have accommodated the applicant who was a long-serving employee. They [London Underground] were aware of her particular difficulties quite early on and after the failure of the single parent link in September 1991, she had set out her misgivings and her difficulties in writing to management. They did not address themselves to these issues and therefore we find that they have not justified this act of discrimination'.[341]

This view was upheld by the EAT upon (the second) appeal.[342] In summary, the EAT affirmed that an imbalance existed between the discriminatory effect the newly introduced rostering scheme had on the applicant and others who were similarly situated, on the one hand, and the reasonable business needs of London Underground, on the other.

337 Paragraph 37 of the judgment. See for a criticism of this stance Hervey 1991, p. 822-823.

338 See also McColgan 2005, p. 105-106 where she has observed that 'the test established by the Court of Appeal in Hampson fell short of this [i.e., of a necessity approach; MG] replacing a requirement of business necessity with a demand for balance between the reasonable needs of the employer and the discriminatory impact of the requirements or conditions adopted'.

339 *London Underground LTD v. Edwards No. 2.* [1997] IRLR 157 (EAT). The facts of this case have been discussed in section 4.4.3.4 above.

340 *London Underground LTD v. Edwards* [1995] IRLR 355 (EAT). London Underground succeeded in its appeal to the EAT in respect of the question as to the correct pool for comparison and the case was remitted by the EAT to a freshly constituted Industrial Tribunal. Although the question regarding justification had been upheld by the EAT in *London Underground No. 1,* the newly constituted Industrial Tribunal nevertheless addressed the justification question afresh.

341 *London Underground LTD v. Edwards No. 2.* [1997] IRLR 157 (EAT), paragraph 30 where the EAT set out the stance taken by the Industrial Tribunal.

342 *London Underground LTD v. Edwards No. 2* [1997] IRLR 157 (EAT), paragraph 31.

The *Hampson* test was equally relied on by the CA in *Allonby*,[343] although in the latter case the element of 'necessity' was more apparent.

In casu, a college of further education terminated the employment contracts of all 341 part-time lecturers, 110 of whom were male and 231 of whom were female. The college subsequently retained their teaching services as subcontractors. This meant that those who were made redundant were re-engaged through an intermediary agency namely, ELS (Education Learning Services). The fact that part-time workers were no longer employees of the college but instead registered with the agency as self-employed persons, had the consequence that their income dropped and that they lost a series of employment benefits. Their status of self-employed persons also meant that part-time lecturers were no longer entitled to be a member of the occupational pension scheme for teachers contained in the TSS [Teachers' Superannuation Scheme]. The college rationalised its renewed policy with reference to a concern over costs and the need for obtaining a firmer budgetary control. By 1996 the College's financial burdens had heavily increased due to legislative changes requiring the treatment of part-time workers on a par with full-time workers in terms of benefits and notably, in terms of retirement pensions. The first instance tribunal considered the vexed policy justified:

> 'Whilst it appeared from the statistics (...) that the decision [to dismiss; MG] affected more women than men, the tribunal were reminded that any decision taken for sound business reasons would inevitably affect one group more than another group of people be they men, women, part-timers or other categories. Bearing these issues in mind, the tribunal concluded that the decision was justifiable and, whilst is may not have been the only solution to the college's problems or even one which would yield the desired results, it was taken after a proper analysis of the problems (...).'[344]

This line of reasoning was, however, rejected by the CA:

> 'What was required [in the assessment of justification; MG] was at the minimum a critical evaluation of whether the college's reasons demonstrated a real need to dismiss the applicant; if there was such a need, consideration of the seriousness of the disparate impact of the dismissal on women including the applicant; and an evaluation of whether the former were sufficient to outweigh the latter. There is no sign of this process in the tribunal's extended reasons. In particular, there is no recognition that if the aim of dismissal was itself discriminatory (as the applicant contended it was, since it was to deny part-time workers, a predominantly female group, benefits which Parliament had legis-

343 *Allonby v. Accrington & Rossendale College and others* [2001] IRLR 364. In this case, the CA referred a number of preliminary questions to the ECJ which, however, did not concern the justifiability question. See *Allonby v. Accrington & Rossendale College* (Case C-256/01) [2004] IRLR 224 (ECJ). In the main text above, I will merely analyse the CA's stance in *Allonby* insofar as the question of justification is concerned. For an in-depth analysis of the case at the level of the ECJ, I refer to Fredman 2004, p. 281-285.

344 See paragraph 20 of the CA's judgment in *Allonby* where the Tribunal's stance was recapitulated by Sedley (LJ).

> lated to give them) it could never afford justification [, for justification has to be irrespective of sex; MG].'[345]

It follows that in *Allonby* the CA adopted a rather strict stance with respect to the justifiability issue. It held that (1) the respondent must prove a *real need* to execute the vexed indirectly discriminatory policy and (2) that tribunals must carry out a due balancing exercise between the disparate impact the vexed policy has on a protected group *v.* the interests of the employer. The 'real need' requirement was interpreted to mean 'reasonably necessary'. The greater the disparity is, the more cogent must be the justification.[346]

In casu, the respondent had deliberately introduced the reformed labour arrangements with a view to circumventing equality and labour protection legislation which operated to the benefit of part-time workers and thus, women. This element had been ignored too in the tribunal's analysis. Given that the tribunal's analysis of justification had been deficient by reason of the foregoing points, the case was remitted to the tribunal for more explicit reconsideration.

The last case to be considered for the present purposes is the case of *Cross and others v. British Airways (plc)*.[347] In casu, the employer (British Airways) applied a retiring age of 55 to cabin crew employed after November 1971, whereas those who were employed before that date retained a retiring age of 60. This 'requirement or condition' resulted in disparate impact on a considerable larger proportion of women than men. Whilst dealing with the justifiability question, the first instance tribunal made explicit reference to the adjectives 'legitimate', 'appropriate' and '[reasonably] necessary'. It also gave regard to considerations of costs in the assessment of justification. The applicants argued in appeal before the EAT that considerations of cost cannot properly be a factor to be taken into account for purposes of justification. The EAT, with reference to established case law by the ECJ,[348] rejected this argument:

> 'It seems to us, as a matter of obvious common sense (and in accordance with the principle of the concept of proportionality) (...) that, albeit that, in the weighing exercise, costs justifications may often be valued less, particularly if the discrimination is substantial, obvious and even deliberate, economic justification such as the saving, or the non-expenditure, of costs (which must, for example, include the avoidance of loss) must be considered. It would, in our judgment, need clear reasoning and binding authority to prevent that occurring.'[349]

The EAT therefore reaffirmed the judicial stance taken by the first instance tribunal with respect to justification.

345 Paragraph 29 per Sedley (LJ). See with similar result the judgment by Gage (LJ) in paragraphs 63-72 of the judgment and Ward (LJ), paragraphs 84-85. The latter held that in cases such as the one at stake where the disparate impact was serious there is need of a 'cogent explanation of what the objective justification is' for the vexed redundancy policy (paragraph 85).

346 See also *Barry v. Midland Bank plc* [1999] IRLR 581 (HL), at 587 where this point was reaffirmed by Lord Nicholls.

347 *Cross and Others v. British Airways plc*, [2005] IRLR 423 (EAT).

348 Namely, *Jenkins* and *Bilka* both earlier referred to.

349 Paragraph 63 (per Mr Justice Burton (President) for the EAT).

4.4.4. Conclusions

The top-down comparison warrants the following conclusions. The analysis has shown that implementation of EC equality law by means of governmental regulations has resulted in a speckled framework of domestic anti-discrimination law. In the employment area, different statutory definitions of indirect discrimination feature domestic race relations law without adequate ground. It has been argued, with reference to international human rights law, that the current legal framework is not only obscure but moreover falls short of supranational law requirements. The exclusion of 'colour' from the implementation process reflects the wrong stance. The analysis has also illustrated that the restyled definition of indirect discrimination, introduced post-implementation of EC law, sets a much more favourable standard of proof compared to the definition 'old style'. The new definition has given short shrift to the '*Perera* loophole'. Currently, both absolute bars and job preferences can give rise to *prima facie* indirect discrimination. The new definition moreover departs from the 'group justice' approach which brings with it that disparate impact on a group of persons (defined by a forbidden ground) needs no longer be proven. Currently, a plaintiff is required to show that the vexed neutral conduct places persons defined by a protected ground '*at a particular disadvantage*' compared to other persons. Due to the lack of case law it is currently unclear what is meant by this phrase. A requirement of statistical evidence remains permitted in indirect discrimination proceedings. In carrying out a statistical data analysis, the English courts have given regard to both relative and absolute numbers, as well as to 'common knowledge facts'. It follows from recent case law that the choice of the pool for comparison is no longer exclusively a matter for the first instance court to decide. The new definition of indirect discrimination has also introduced a stringent justification test. By virtue of EC implemented law, 'objective justification' enshrines a *necessity* requirement which leaves no scope for a 'reasonableness' approach. Trends towards a stricter test of objective justification were already apparent from recent case law regarding justification 'old style'. The absence of the '*appropriateness*' requirement in the justifiability defence post implementation of EC law has been criticised. In order to comply with EC law, domestic courts have to assess 'justifiability' on the basis of three limbs namely, 'legitimacy', 'appropriateness' and 'necessity'.

5. Indirect Discrimination in Dutch Equal Treatment Law: a Top-Down Analysis

5.1. *Introduction*

Having examined 'indirect discrimination' in both EC and English law, I will hereafter present an analysis of this concept in the context of Dutch equal treatment law. The influence of supranational law upon domestic law will be highlighted in the discussion. Given that the underlying philosophy of indirect discrimination and its complexities have been spelt out in the analysis thus far, section 5 can be relatively short. In section 5.2 hereafter, I will first comment on the legislative definition of indirect distinction *(onderscheid)*[350] in the GETA, the DETA, the AET w/m and the relevant provisions in the Civil Code. I will subsequently examine in section 5.3 how this definition has been applied by the ETC (and the courts). Brief conclusions will be drawn in section 5.4.

5.2. *Legislative Definitions of Indirect Distinction*

Article 1(1) GETA provides as follows:

> 'In this Act and in the provisions founded thereon the following definitions shall apply:
> (a) Distinction: direct and indirect distinction, as well as the instruction to make a distinction;
> (b) Direct distinction: distinction between persons on grounds of [a protected ground; MG];
> (c) Indirect distinction: distinction on the ground of other qualities or acts than [a protected ground; MG] which results in direct distinction.'[351]

Article 2(1) GETA subsequently stipulates that

> 'the prohibition of distinction contained in this Act shall not apply with respect to indirect distinction which is objectively justified by a legitimate aim and provided that the means employed to achieve this aim are appropriate and necessary'.[352]

Unlike in English law, the Dutch DETA does enshrine a definition of indirect disability distinction. Therefore, Dutch disability equal treatment law hinges on both the duty to make reasonable accommodation and on the concept of indirect distinction. The latter notion is formulated in similar terms as the aforementioned definition of indirect distinction in the GETA.[353] The 'objective justification test' is enshrined in Article 3(2) DETA which contains similar language as Article 2(1) GETA.

350 The conceptual differences between the notions of discrimination (*discriminatie*) and distinction (*onderscheid*) have been explained in Chapter 2 and will not be repeated at this juncture.

351 The original Dutch text reads as follows: Artikel 1 (1) *'In deze wet en de daarop berustende bepalingen wordt verstaan onder: (a) onderscheid: direct en indirect onderscheid, alsmede de opdracht daartoe; (b) direct onderscheid: onderscheid tussen personen op grond van godsdienst, levensovertuiging; politieke gezindheid; ras, geslacht, nationaliteit; hetero- of homoseksuele gerichtheid of burgerlijke staat; (c) indirect onderscheid: onderscheid op grond van andere hoedanigheden of gedragingen dan die bedoeld in onderdeel b, dat direct onderscheid tot gevolg heeft.'* (The English language translation in the main text is by the author and unofficial).

352 The original language version of Article 2(1) GETA reads as follows: *'Het in deze wet neergelegde verbod van onderscheid geldt niet ten aanzien van indirect onderscheid indien dat onderscheid objectief gerechtvaardigd wordt door een legitiem doel en de middelen voor het bereiken van dat doel passend en noodzakelijk zijn.'* (The English language translation in the main text is by the author and unofficial). Article 2(1) GETA was amended by the EC Implementation Act GETA (see generally Chapter 2) in order to explicitly insert the elements of 'legitimacy', 'appropriateness' and 'necessity' into the legislative definition of 'objective justification'.

353 Article 1 DETA reads as follows: 'In this Act the following definitions shall apply: (a) distinction: direct and indirect distinction, as well as the instruction to make a distinction; (b) direct distinction: distinction between persons on the ground of an actual or an assumed disability or chronic disease; (c) indirect distinction: distinction on the ground of other qualities or acts →

Article 1 AET w/m[354] (which covers 'sex' in both private and public employment) provides that:

> 'In this Act distinction shall be taken to mean direct and indirect distinction, as well as the instruction to make a distinction.
> Direct distinction shall be taken to mean distinction between men and women.
> Indirect distinction shall be taken to mean distinction on grounds of other qualities than sex, such as for example marital status or family circumstances, which results in distinction on grounds of sex'. [355]

An identical definition of indirect sex distinction is contained in Article 7:646(5) of the Civil Code[356] which relates to private employment.[357] The 'objective justification' defence is contained in Article 6 AET w/m and in Article 7:646(10) of the Civil Code (post implementation of the AETD). Both of these Articles have been defined in identical terms as Articles 2(1) GETA and 3(1) DETA. Hence, the elements of 'legitimacy', 'appropriateness' and 'necessity' are explicitly contained in the legislative definition of 'objective justification'.

The aforementioned definitions of indirect distinction are far less comprehensive compared to the counterpart provisions in the RD, the EFD and the AETD. With reference to section 3.2.2 above, the Directives define (*prima facie*) indirect discrimination as follows: 'indirect discrimination shall be taken to occur where an apparently neutral provision, criterion or practice would put persons (...) at a particular disadvantage compared with other persons unless (...).' A comparison of the legislative approaches in EC and Dutch law warrants the following comments.[358] First, neither the definition of indirect discrimination in the Directives, nor that of indirect distinction in Dutch law, requires that the plaintiff suffer a personal detriment. Having suffered a personal detriment appears, however, to be a logical requirement, for otherwise an applicant would have little ground to lodge a complaint. It follows from established case law by the ETC that a personal detriment is one of the

than those meant by indent (b) which results in direct distinction (unofficial translation by the author).

354 Act on Equal Treatment between Men and Women [*Wet gelijke behandeling van mannen/vrouwen*], *Stb.* 1989, 168 [*Law Gazette* 1989, 168]. See generally Chapter 2. It should be highlighted that the AET w/m is currently being amended with a view to implementing the AETD into domestic law (see: *Parliamentary Documents* II, 2004-2005, 30 237, no. 2. See moreover *Parliamentary Documents* II, 2004-2005, 30 237, no. 3 (*Explanatory Memorandum*)). These amendments will not bear an impact on the legislative definition of indirect distinction.

355 This is the text of Article 1 AET w/m as proposed by the bill which implements the AETD into domestic law (see footnote 3 above). That part of Article 1 AET w/m which defines indirect distinction has not been amended as a result of implementation of the AETD.

356 This Article is currently too being amended in light of the requirements of the AETD (see also footnote 354 above). These amendments, however, will not have an impact on the definition of indirect distinction.

357 In Chapter 2 a general account has been given of the various statutory equal treatment Acts in Dutch law. In that chapter, I have also expounded on the relationship between the GETA, the AET w/m and Articles 7:646 and 7:647 of the Civil Code (all of which cover 'sex' and all of which cover 'employment'). This will not be repeated at this juncture.

358 The element of 'objective justification' will be dealt with in section 5.3.3 below.

legal conditions for establishing an instance of (indirect) distinction.[359] Logically, there must be a causal link between the personal detriment suffered by the applicant, on the one hand, and a forbidden ground, on the other.[360]

In Opinion 2001-143, the applicant worked as an executive secretary for the general director. She was informed by her employer that, for reasons of efficiency, she would be working in the future for one or two other (ordinary) directors. Although her payment and other conditions of employment would remain unaffected by this, the applicant claimed that the proposed change in her employment infringed her social status. In the Commission's view 'status is a subjective notion and a change in one's status does not automatically imply a detriment [for purposes of equal treatment law; MG]'.[361] Given that the applicant's conditions of employment would not be altered by the vexed transfer the ETC concluded the absence of a personal detriment. It held that 'given the absence of a personal detriment, the question of objective justification needs no longer be considered'.[362]

Secondly, the rubric 'provision, criterion or practice' contained in EC law, has been replaced in Dutch law by the (shallow) phrase 'other qualities or acts'.[363] The AET w/m and Article 7:646(5) of the Civil Code merely refer to 'other qualities' which results in an internal inconsistency in the legislative definitions of indirect distinction in domestic equal treatment law.

Thirdly, with reference to section 3.2.2 above, the definitions of indirect discrimination in the Directives refer to a 'particular disadvantage' which marks a departure from a statistical evidence analysis. The Directives (merely) anticipate a comparison between persons (defined by a protected status) who would be put at a 'particular disadvantage' by the vexed neutral conduct, on the one hand, and 'other persons', on the other. The usage of the verbal construction 'would put' brings with it that *actual* disadvantage needs not be proven. Proof of a *risk* of disadvantage is therefore sufficient. The Dutch definition of indirect distinction is less pronounced. It makes no reference to the rubric 'a particular disadvantage' but instead requires that the vexed neutral conduct *de facto results* in an act of direct distinction. The Dutch definition employs the present tense 'results' requiring therefore that *actual* disadvantage

359 Gerards 2003a, p. 80 and Gerards and Heringa, p. 43-44. It is submitted that, even if the detriment element was not contained in the ETC's case law, the Dutch definition would still be in conformity with EC law, given that the former would adopt a laxer standard than the latter which is allowed for by EC law. It follows from Article 6(1) RD, Article 8(1) EFD and Article 8 *sexies* AETD that the Directives merely contain *minimum* standards of protection and that the Member States may go beyond these by introducing more favourable measures of protection.

360 It does, however, follow from the Commission's case law that a forbidden ground needs not be the sole reason for the personal detriment suffered. In other words, a forbidden ground must be one of possibly more factors which has resulted in a personal detriment for the complainant. See, for example, Opinions 1995-15, 1995-47, 2003-41. See also Gerards and Heringa 2003, p. 44-45.

361 Paragraph 4.6. of Opinion 2001-143.

362 *'Aangezien er geen sprake is van benadeling, komt de Commissie niet toe aan de beantwoording van de vraag of the handelwijze van de wederpartij objectief gerechtvaardigd was'* (paragraph 4.6. of Opinion 2001-143).

363 See also Waaldijk 2004, p. 352.

needs to be proven. Given that this sets a more stringent standard than EC law, the Dutch definition falls short of supranational equality standards. However, as will be seen, the ETC does accept that a mere risk of disadvantage is sufficient for establishing disparate impact. The comparative exercise is only latently contained in the Dutch definition of indirect distinction in the sense that it makes reference to the notion of 'direct distinction'. The latter, in its turn, refers to a distinction 'between persons' or 'between women and men'. As will be illustrated below, the ETC tends to approach indirect distinction cases on the basis of a statistical evidence analysis which brings with it that the group dimension of equality remains preserved. As discussed in section 3.3.2, the insistence on advancing statistical evidence in order to prove *prima facie* indirect discrimination is not contrary to EC law. However, a statistical data analysis may be precluded in practice as a consequence of the intrinsic nature of the ground of discrimination at issue.

5.3. *Indirect Distinction: Analysing the Case Law*[364]

5.3.1. The Notion of 'Disparate Impact'

Rather than referring to the notion of 'disparate impact', the ETC's terminology equivalent to this notion is rather divergent. The Commission has held that (*prima facie*) indirect distinction occurs, if a distinction is made on other grounds than a protected ground with the effect that persons defined by a protected status 'are preponderantly affected' (*'in overwegende mate getroffen'*).[365] In other cases, it has taken the view that 'indirect distinction occurs, if the proportion of (e.g.) women [in a particular group, in casu: the group of part-time workers; MG] is substantially larger than that of men, with the effect that women 'are particularly [*'met name'*; MG] affected'.[366] Yet differently, the ETC has aired the view that indirect distinction occurs if the vexed neutral conduct 'would have a negative effect', in casu, for women (*'nadelig zou uitwerken voor vrouwen'*).[367] Alternatively, according to the Commission's case law, indirect distinction occurs where 'more persons' (*'meer personen'*) of one compared to another group are affected.[368] In all, the Commission's phraseology of 'disparate impact' is not only inconsistent but also appears to bear different degrees of disparity (e.g. *'more persons' compared* to *'preponderantly'*) in order to establish 'disparate impact'. The question as to the required degree of disparity in order to establish a (*prima facie*) instance of indirect discrimination will be discussed in more detail below.

364 Recent analyses have also been made by Gerards 2003a and by Waaldijk 2005.

365 For example, Opinion 1999-50, paragraph 4.6; Opinion 1997-04, paragraph 4.4. ('a preponderantly negative effect for persons of one sex'); Opinion 1997-45, paragraph 4.6.; Opinion 2005-187, paragraph 5.26.

366 Opinion 2000-60, paragraph 4.9.; Opinion 1998-151, paragraph 4.5.; Opinion 2001-83, paragraph 4.4.

367 Opinion 1998-119, paragraph 4.7.

368 Opinion 2005-153, paragraph 5.7.

5.3.2. Establishing Disparate Impact

In section 3.3.3.3 above, we saw that there are a number of legal options for establishing disparate impact. To recap, disparate impact can be established: (1) in reliance on a statistical data analysis; (2) on the basis of an '*intrinsically liable*' test (in conformity with *O'Flynn*); (3) by adopting a 'rule of thumb' approach; or (4) on the basis of a 'considerably different impact' approach, which in addition to relative numbers takes into account absolute numbers and/or facts of common knowledge. An analysis of the ETC's case law on indirect distinction reveals that the Commission avails itself of all of these options.

The legitimacy of the usage of statistical evidence in order to prove indirect discrimination was for the first time recognised by the Dutch Supreme Court in *Binderen-Kaya*.[369] The Supreme Court held that

> 'no rule of law prevents the judge from regarding numerical, statistical differences such as those in the case at hand as a sufficient motivation for a claim of discrimination, nor from deriving from such differences a strong presumption of discrimination, nor from – exclusively on grounds of that presumption – shifting the burden of proof to the alleged discriminator in order to show that the him reproached discrimination rests on legally justifiable grounds.'[370]

When the Commission adopts a statistical data approach to claims of indirect discrimination it must first delineate the apposite pool for comparison.

In Opinion 2005-144, the employer's regulations (*inter alia*) provided that an employee's personal contribution for a lease-car would be increased during the period of parental leave. It was moreover impossible for employees to temporarily renounce the usage of a lease-car for the period that parental leave was taken. The applicant claimed that the employer's rule operated to the disadvantage of female employees. The statistical evidence showed that in 2004, 4 out of 282 male employees (i.e. 1.4%) had taken parental leave, as compared to 4 out of 58 (i.e. 6.9%) female employees.[371] The Commission held that 'although these percentages indicate that proportionately more women compared to men are affected by the vexed rule, the total amount of employees who took parental leave in 2004 was that small that a coincidence cannot be ruled out'.[372]

In light of this, the Commission subsequently compared the numerical evidence that related to the proportions of men/women in the company, with equivalent

369 *Binderen-Kaya*, Hoge Raad [Dutch Supreme Court] 10 December 1982, *NJ* 1983, 87, also available at <www. rechtspraak.nl>.

370 *'Overigens verzet geen rechtsregel zich ertegen dat de rechter cijfermatige, statistische verschillen als de onderhavige aanmerkt als voldoende motivering van de stelling dat er gediscrimineerd is, noch dat hij aan dergelijke verschillen een (zwaarwegend) vermoeden voor discriminatie ontleent en enkel op grond van dat vermoeden op de van discriminatie betichte de last legt aan te tonen dat de hem verweten achterstelling berust op rechtens aanvaardbare gronden.'* (paragraph 4.1. of the Court's judgment; the translation in the main text above is by the author and unofficial).

371 Paragraph 5.21. of Opinion 2005-144.

372 Paragraph 5.22. of Opinion 2005-144.

statistical data at national level. In other words, in order to eliminate the chance that 'discrimination' was merely based on a coincidence, the Commission enlarged the pool for comparison. The statistical data at the national level revealed a similar picture as those at the company level namely, that significantly more women than men take parental leave. Hence, *prima facie* indirect sex discrimination was concluded.[373]

In order to eliminate the possibility that discrimination is merely coincidental, the Commission has also availed itself of the so-called 'chi-square' and 'correlation' tests.[374] Both tests are employed by statisticians to calculate whether there is a correlation between (e.g.) sex and (e.g.) differences in pay (*correlation test*) and whether this correlation is not merely coincidental (*chi-quare test*).[375] When the so-called 'φ-value', calculated on the basis of the correlation test, is higher than 0.20 the ETC accepts that there is a correlation between (e.g.) sex and differences in pay.[376] The Commission subsequently examines whether the established correlation does not rest on a mere coincidence. When the, on the basis of the chi-square test calculated, 'χ^2-value' is higher than 2.7, the Commission eliminates the possibility of a mere coincidence. Waaldijk has recently criticised the usage of both tests: 'The calculations that are involved (...) are thát complicated that hardly any applicant or respondent will be able in proceedings before the ETC to carry out these tests autonomously or to verify the outcomes thereof.'[377]

In establishing disparate impact on the basis of a statistical data analysis, the ETC makes use of relative numbers, given that absolute numbers show a biased picture. The Commission tends to explain this with reference to the following example.[378]

A company employs 10 women and 1000 men. 9 women and 9 men work part-time. If 'working-time' is used as a distinguishing criterion, 9 women and 9 men will be affected. However, relatively viewed, 9 out of 10 women will be affected (i.e. 90%) as opposed to 9 out of 1000 men (i.e. 0,9%).

The definitions of indirect discrimination in the EC Directives merely refer to a '*particular* disadvantage'. With reference to section 3.3.3.4 above, it is currently obscure what degree of disparity is required by EC law for a disadvantage to amount to a '*particular* disadvantage'. In *Seymour Smith* (discussed earlier in section 3.3.3.4) the ECJ merely held that 'disparate impact' can be proven (1) either by showing a 'considerable disparity' at a particular point in time, or (2) by showing a 'lesser disparity' which is, however, persistent and relatively constant over a longer time

373 See also Opinion 2000-60 in which the Commission adopted the same approach (see paragraph 4.9. of that Opinion). See moreover Gerards 2003, p. 81, who has argued that the Commission takes, in principle, the smallest possible pool for comparison as a point for departure, unless this results in an unrepresentative statistical analysis.

374 For example, Opinion 2002-161 and Opinion 2006-98. See also Waaldijk 2005, p. 152-155.

375 See Opinion 2006-98, paragraph 3.21. Opinion 2002-161, paragraph 3.4.

376 See Opinion 2006-98, paragraph 3.21.

377 Waaldijk 2005, p. 154: *'Beide toetsen hebben een groot nadeel: de berekeningen die gemaakt moeten worden zijn zó ingewikkeld dat vrijwel geen verzoeker of wederpartij by the CGB die zelfstandig zal kunnen uitvoeren of controleren.'*

378 See, for example, Opinion 1998-119, paragraph 4.7.; Opinion 1997-04, paragraph 4.5.; Opinion 1998-151, paragraph 4.5. Also Gerards 2003a, p. 81 with reference to the ETC's case law.

period. This case was, however, decided prior to the adoption of the RD, EFD and AETD and therefore sheds no light on the interpretation of the rubric 'a *particular* disadvantage'.

In making a statistical data analysis the ETC has sometimes used a 'rule of thumb' in the assessment as to whether the *degree* of disparity is sufficient in order to establish *prima facie* indirect discrimination. A rule of thumb is a more accessible alternative to the usage of the already mentioned correlation and chi-square tests. The Commission has held that, if the vexed neutral criterion affects group *x* 1.5times more than the relevant reference group (group *y*), *prima facie* indirect discrimination will be established.[379]

In Opinion 1997-45, the statistical data that related to the applicant's job level indicated that members of the disadvantaged group were 1.2 times more affected by the vexed neutral rule compared to members of the relevant reference group. The Commission held that this is insufficient to establish disparate impact. The Commission thereupon considered whether the equivalent statistics perceived in relation to the workforce as a whole, as well as in relation to the national level, showed a different picture. However, the statistics gathered in relation to all of the aforementioned pools for comparison remained below the detriment factor of 1.5 and therefore, *prima facie* indirect discrimination could not be established.

That the choice for a particular pool for comparison bears an impact on the outcome of a statistical data analysis clearly follows from Opinion 2001-83.

In casu, the Commission equally used a detriment factor of 1.5 as a rule of thumb in its analysis of disparate impact. A comparison of the statistical data which related to the job sector as whole (in casu: the mental health sector) showed a detriment factor of 1.3 which was too small to establish *prima facie* indirect discrimination. In contrast, the equivalent statistics perceived in relation to the employer's workforce, showed a detriment factor of 3.2. This was far above the minimum detriment factor (of 1.5) and therefore provided clear evidence of *prima facie* indirect discrimination. However, given the great numerical differences depending on which pool for comparison was chosen in the case at hand, the ETC stayed legal proceedings pending the outcome of statistical expert advice.

The Commission has also accepted facts of common knowledge as a means to be taken into account in the assessment of disparate impact. However, as Gerards has indicated, common knowledge facts seldom constitute an autonomous source of evidence.[380]

In Opinion 2003-91, the respondent's salary scheme used a future employee's last received salary as a criterion for the determination of his or her starting salary. The contested scheme gave no regard to earlier paid or unpaid job experience. The applicant, who had interrupted her teaching career in the 1970s in order to look after her children, claimed an instance of indirect sex discrimination. The Commission accepted as a fact of common knowledge that in the past more women than men interrupted their careers in order to be able to look after their children. As a result, those

379 Gerards 2003a, p. 83; Waaldijk 2005, p. 152.

380 Gerards 2003a, p. 82, with reference to the ETC's case law.

who re-entered the labour market (read: women) were paid less compared to those who had remained in continuous employment (notably men). This constituted *prima facie* indirect sex discrimination which, in casu, could not be objectively justified.

In Opinion 2005-187, the Commission employed an 'intrinsically liable' test in order to establish disparate impact. In that case, 'disability' was the discrimination ground at issue.

In casu, the employer offered his employees the possibility of joining an additional and private disability insurance scheme.[381] The scheme's terms and conditions *inter alia* stipulated that those who became unable to work due to a disease which already existed at the moment when the employee concerned joined the scheme, would not be entitled to an insurance payment. The disabled applicant claimed that both her employer and the insurance company committed an instance of unlawful disability distinction. With reference to earlier case law, the ETC held that the vexed exclusionary criterion did not result in direct disability discrimination, given that the notions of 'disease' and 'inability to work' are not synonymous to 'disability' and 'chronic disease'.[382] However, held the Commission,

> 'the criterion used by the insurance company has undeniable the result that those who join the scheme and who have a disability or chronic disease have more chance of becoming disadvantaged [compared to non-disabled persons; MG]. The effect of the by the insurance company employed exclusionary clause is that insured persons who at the time when they joined the scheme had a disability or chronic disease, as opposed to insured persons without a disability or chronic disease, bear the risk during the entire duration of the scheme that the insurance company will not grant an insurance payment in case a person's inability to work is connected with a disability or chronic disease.[383]

In light of the foregoing, the Commission concluded an instance of *prima facie* indirect disability discrimination which could not be objectively justified.

The ETC's analysis in the above case correlates with the approach to indirect discrimination adopted by the Directives. The Commission accepted that actual disadvantage needs not be proven and that a risk of disadvantage sufficed for the establishment of disparate impact. No statistical data analysis was carried out. Like in *O'flynn*, where the vexed rule was intrinsically liable to affect a substantially higher proportion of migrant compared to non-migrant workers, the contested exclusionary

381 The Commission regards this as being a condition of employment which is covered by the material scope of the DETA. See paragraph 5.2. of Opinion 2005-187.

382 See paragraph 5.11 of Opinion 2005-187. Also Opinion 2004-145 and 2005-77.

383 Paragraph 5.26 of Opinion 2005-187 (*'Het criterium dat de verzekeraar hanteert, heeft echter onmiskenbaar tot gevolg dat verzekeringnemers die bij aanvang van de verzekering een handicap of chronische ziekte hebben, meer kans hebben om hierdoor te worden benadeeld [dan zij die op dat moment geen handicap of chronische ziekte hebben; MG]. Het effect van de door de verzekeraar gehanteerde uitsluitingsclausule is dat verzekerden die ten tijde van het afsluiten van de arbeidsongeschiktheidsverzekering een handicap of chronische ziekte hebben, anders dan verzekerden zonder handicap of chronische ziekte, gedurende de gehele looptijd van de verzekering het risico lopen dat de verzekeraar niet tot uitkering overgaat in geval een op enig moment intredende arbeidsongeschiktheid verband houdt met de handicap of chronische ziekte.'*). The English language translation in the main-text is by the author and unofficial).

clause in Opinion 2005-187 was intrinsically liable for preponderantly affecting disabled persons. As referred to in the discussion of indirect discrimination in EC law, a departure from a statistical data analysis corresponds with the intrinsic nature of disability as a ground of discrimination.

The ETC has also denounced a statistical evidence approach in such cases where the usage of a particular neutral criterion *self evidently* results in disparate impact. Thus, for example, in Opinion 2005-153 the respondent (a recruitment agency) imposed on future employees the requirement that they speak Dutch without accent. The Commission, without more, simply stated that such a requirement affects more persons who are not of Dutch descent compared to those who are. It thereupon concluded *prima facie* indirect race discrimination.[384]

The Commission adopted a similar approach in Opinion 2002-122. In casu, the applicant had been refused twice for a job with the respondent. The applicant had a dark skin colour and frizzy hair. The reason why he had been refused the jobs was by reason of his hairstyle. During his first job interview, the applicant wore an afro hairstyle, whereas on the second occasion he wore his hair in flat braids. The Commission simply considered that the applicant's frizzy hair determines the choice of his hairstyle. It thereupon immediately concluded *prima facie* indirect race discrimination.[385]

5.3.3. Objective Justification

As referred to in section 5.1 above, 'the prohibition of distinction shall not apply with respect to indirect discrimination which is objectively justified by a legitimate aim and provided that the means employed to achieve this aim are appropriate and necessary'. This legislative formulation closely follows the ECJ's test of objective justification designed in the earlier discussed cases of *Bilka*[386] and *Rinner-Kühn*.[387] The Commission interprets the objective justification test as follows:

> 'Whether [*prima facie* indirect distinction; MG] is objectively justified has to be assessed in the light of an assessment of the goal pursued by the distinction and the means employed in order to achieve this goal. The goal must be legitimate, in the sense of being sufficiently weighty, that is to say it must respond to a real need. A legitimate goal moreover requires that is free of a discriminatory purpose. The means employed must be appropriate and necessary. A means will be appropriate, if it is suitable to reach the goal pursued. A means will be necessary, if the goal pursued cannot be reached with a means which does not

384 See also Opinion 2004-143.

385 One could argue that in casu the employer committed an instance of direct race distinction, given that the applicant's afro hairstyle was intrinsically linked up to his race.

386 *Bilka Kaufhaus GmbH v. Karin Weber von Hartz* (Case 170/84) [1986] ECR 1607.

387 *Ingrid Rinner-Kühn v. FWW Spezial-Gebaudereinigung GmbH & Co.KG* (Case 171/88) [1989] ECR 2743.

result in a distinction, or which is less objectionable, and the means employed must stand in a proportionate relationship with the goal pursued.'[388]

It follows that the Commission's stance with respect to justification is strict. With respect to the legitimacy of the aim, the Commission has taken the view that, if the aim is to comply with a statutory obligation, it will not be subject to scrutiny by the Commission.[389] When a respondent fails to indicate what goals are pursued by a vexed neutral conduct, objective justification is bound to fail.[390] With respect to 'language requirement' cases, the Commission has taken the view that a phone interview is not an appropriate means for assessing whether a future employee has a good command of (e.g.) the Dutch language.[391] In line with the ECJ's case law, the Commission has also held that pure budgetary objectives cannot constitute an objective justification.[392] An exclusion which is definite, whereas it could have been restricted in time, has been held to breach the principle of proportionality.[393]

5.4. *Conclusions*

The analysis of Dutch indirect discrimination law in light of EC law prompts the following conclusions. A comparison of the legislative definitions of indirect discrimination (distinction) in Dutch and EC law has shown that the Dutch definition uses far less elaborate language. Although a personal detriment requirement is not contained in the definition, this is nonetheless a legal constituent as follows from the ETC's case law. The Dutch definition seems to require proof of actual disadvantage but the Commission's case law indicates that a risk of disadvantage is sufficient to establish *prima facie* indirect distinction. It has been illustrated that the Commission avails itself of a number of different methods for establishing 'disparate impact'. When carrying out a statistical data analysis, it has sometimes availed itself of a 'correlation' and 'chi-square' test in order to establish 'disparate impact'. At other times, it has simply used a rule of thumb, in the sense that disparate impact will only be established if group x is affected at least 1.5. more compared to group y. In addition to statistics (i.e. relative numbers), the Commission sometimes backs its analysis with reference to common knowledge facts. In cases in which statistics are not readily available (e.g.

388 *'Of in een concreet geval sprake is van een objectieve rechtvaardiging moet worden nagegaan aan de hand van een beoordeling van het doel van het onderscheid en het middel dat ter bereiking van dit doel is ingezet. Het doel dient legitiem te zijn, in de zin van voldoende zwaarwegend dan wel te beantwoorden aan een werkelijke behoefte. Een legitiem doel vereist voorts dat er geen sprake is van een discriminerend oogmerk. Het middel dat wordt gehanteerd moet passend en noodzakelijk zijn. Een middel is passend indien het geschikt is om het doel te bereiken. Het middel is noodzakelijk indien het doel niet kan worden bereikt met een middel dat niet leidt tot onderscheid, althans minder bezwaarlijk is, en het middel in een evenredige verhouding staat tot het doel.'* See, for example, Opinion 2003-91, paragraph 6.10; Opinion 2005-187, paragraph 5.28; Opinion 2005-21, paragraph 5.15; Opinion 2005-154, paragraph 5.13; Opinion 2005-153, paragraph 5.9; Opinion 2004-143, paragraph 5.9.

389 Opinion 2005-187, paragraph 5.31.

390 For example, Opinion 2006-98, paragraph 3.25.

391 For example, Opinion 2005-154, paragraph 5.14.

392 For example, Opinion 2005-144, paragraph 5.26; Opinion 2002-161, paragraph 4.8.

393 See Opinion 2005-187.

disability distinction cases), the Commission has used an 'intrinsically liable test' which corresponds with the ECJ's test in *O'Flynn* (and with the approach to indirect discrimination in the RD, EFD and AETD). If the distinguishing criterion self-evidently results in disparate impact, the Commission readily concludes *prima facie* indirect distinction. The approach adopted in Dutch law with respect to 'objective justification' correlates with the ECJ's approach in *Bilka* and *Rinner Kühn*. The Commission adopts a strict stance by requiring that justification will only be upheld if the requirements of legitimacy, appropriateness and necessity are met.

6. Conclusions and Cross-Country Comparison

In this chapter, the concept of indirect discrimination has been looked at through the prism of comparative law. In addition, this concept has been examined from the perspective of legal theory. It has been argued that indirect discrimination correlates with a substantive model of equality, although it remains embedded in the comparative justice model. From the perspective of theory, indirect discrimination clearly reflects a group connotation to justice, notwithstanding that the group dimension has been moderated in positive equality law. Indirect discrimination aims to dismantle institutionalised patterns of disadvantage, as well as to redistribute resources from the advantaged to the disadvantaged group. The concept moreover strives for diversity and as such contributes to the affirmation of group identity.

After an analysis of legal theory, indirect discrimination has been examined in the context of EC, English and Dutch law. The analysis has shown that the group connotation to justice has vanished in the restyled definitions of indirect discrimination in the RD, the EFD and the AETD. This contrasts with the (group oriented) approach to indirect sex discrimination adopted by the EC Burden of Proof Directive. Two conclusions could be drawn from this. First, in present times, no consistent theoretical model underlies the concept of indirect discrimination in EC law. Secondly, the legislative definitions of indirect discrimination in the RD, EFD and AETD erode on the theoretical foundations of the concept itself. The cross-ground comparison has revealed that the different nature of different grounds means that a statistical data approach to indirect discrimination is not always appropriate. Therefore, the legislative definitions of indirect discrimination in the Article 13 EC Directives (and the AETD) hinge on the approach adopted by the ECJ in migrant worker cases. However, the fact that a statistical evidence analysis will not always be apposite, depending on what ground indirect discrimination has occurred, should not have infringed on the group justice rationale itself. After all, as the analysis has shown, 'disparate impact' can be proven by other means than statistics.

EC indirect discrimination law as it currently stands contains two justification defences, one of which merely applies with respect to 'disability'. This second defence has been the result of bottom-up influence and reflects the 'duty to make adjustments' approach which features UK disability discrimination law. The relationship between the objective justification test, on the one hand, and justification by means of making a reasonable accommodation, on the other, is currently unclear and needs to be interpreted by the ECJ in future case law.

The analysis of indirect discrimination in English law, perceived in light of supranational requirements, prompts the following conclusions. First, a clear example of 'cross-fertilisation' was highlighted where English indirect discrimination law has been decisively influenced by U.S. law which subsequently (indirectly) influenced EC law. The latter, in its turn, has shaped indirect discrimination law in all EC Member States. Secondly, due to the modus of implementing EC into domestic law, English (indirect) discrimination law is currently characterised by fragmentation. The exclusion of 'colour' from the scope of EC implemented law has been argued to be in contravention of supranational requirements. Furthermore, the statutory twin-track approach which marks English race relations law results in diverse standards of legal protection depending on the ground at stake in an indirect discrimination complaint. The so-called *Perera* loophole has not ceased to exist with respect to 'colour'. This is a particularly unsatisfactory situation and streamlining is therefore required. Parallel to the approach adopted in the Article 13 Directives and the AETD, the definitions of indirect discrimination 'new style' contravene the group oriented nature of 'indirect discrimination'. At the same time, a statistical evidence approach to 'disparate impact' remains permitted. This is so, for EC law grants a discretionary choice to the Member States with respect to the rules on how to establish *prima facie* indirect discrimination. In carrying out a statistical data analysis, the English courts have given regard to relative and absolute numbers and recent case law indicates that the delineation of the correct pool is a matter of logic, rather than of fact finding. With respect to 'justifiability' it has been argued that EC law leaves no scope for a reasonableness approach but requires a review of the elements of legitimacy, appropriateness and necessity.

Unlike in English anti-discrimination law, the legislative definitions of indirect discrimination in Dutch law are the same with respect to all grounds of discrimination.[394] No discrimination ground has been singled out from the implementation process (neither these grounds which are not covered by the Directives). This constitutes an example of voluntary application of European law. What is more, unlike the DDA 1995, the Dutch DETA contains a prohibition of indirect disability discrimination law. The approach adopted by the ETC to alleged instances of indirect disability discrimination is in line with the migrant workers model of indirect discrimination which has informed the approach adopted in the RD, the EFD and AETD. In indirect disability discrimination cases, the ETC has not relied on a statistical data analysis but has instead followed the ECJ's approach to 'disparate impact' in the *O'flynn* case. By doing so, the Commission appears to acknowledge that 'disability' cannot easily be captured by statistical data given the fluid and heterogeneous character of this ground. By contrast, notably in indirect sex discrimination cases, the Commission has analysed 'disparate impact' on the basis of a statistical evidence analysis. In deciding on the question of 'disparate impact', the ETC avails itself of diverging methods of proof, including the mathematically oriented 'correlation' and 'chi-square' tests, a rule of thumb, an intrinsically liable approach and facts of

394 Although Dutch age discrimination law renders no distinction between 'direct distinction' and 'indirect distinction'. This point will be considered in Chapter 9.

common knowledge. Facts of common knowledge have also been accepted by the English courts as a means of evidence in indirect discrimination proceedings.

A reasonableness approach has never informed the Commission's stance with respect to objective justification. The Commission acts on the basis of the *Bilka* and *Rinner-Kühn* tests which reflects a correct stance in light of supranational law.

Chapter 4

HARASSMENT

1. Introduction

Empirical research has shown that many women, homosexuals and persons belonging to an ethnic minority designation are victims of harassment at work.[1] The effects of harassment are multiple. Acts of harassment (may) affect the victim's psychological and physical good health and moreover his or her economic performance.[2] In this chapter the concept of harassment will be examined from a comparative perspective which will essentially trigger a top-down and cross-country analysis. To a limited extent reference will be made to the cross-ground comparison and to bottom-up influence. Like in Chapter 3 a selection has been made to illustrate the analysis in this chapter with reference to the discrimination grounds 'race', 'sex' and 'disability'. The analysis will be confined to harassment as a concept in equality and non-discrimination law. Hence bullying and other acts of harassment which cannot be linked to the equality paradigm fall outside the scope of this chapter. Therefore harassment as a concept of criminal law, tort law or general employment law will not be expounded upon. This chapter therefore offers a limited picture which, it is argued, is justifiable in light of the subject-matter of this book as a whole.[3] The discussion will be presented as follows. Section 2 as documented below aims to build a bridge between various theoretical notions and models of equality, on the one hand, and harassment, on the other. Section 3 is concerned with an examination of harassment in EC law. That analysis will be of assistance to the top-down analyses carried out in sections 4 (England) and 5 (the Netherlands). Finally, section 6 seeks to tie

1 Houghton Jones, *Sexual Harassment*, London Cavendish Publishing 1995 and Fredman *Women and the Law* Oxford Clarendon Press 1997, p. 320-330, cited by Hepple, Coussey and Choudhury 2000, p. 39 in footnote 99. Also Driessen-Reilly and Driessen 2003, p. 493.

2 Bakirci 1998, p. 3 and p. 7 under A; Dine and Whatt 1995, p. 343, who have stressed the long and devastating effects of harassment.

3 For a discussion of alternative causes of action, I refer to *Note* 1979-1980, p. 155. In that contribution actions in tort law (particularly assault, battery and intentional infliction of severe emotional distress) and actions for breach of contract are addressed.

matters together in an amalgamated analysis which at the same time allows for reflection on the cross-country comparison.

2. Theoretical Reflections

2.1. *Harassment as a Matter of Equality and Non-Discrimination*

The conceptualisation of 'harassment' as a non-discrimination matter has clearly been inspired by American law.[4] 'In the American conception', write Friedman and Whitman, 'harassment is a form of discrimination, a way of tormenting members of minority and other disadvantaged groups seeking upward social mobility through work'.[5] The approach of conceiving (sexual) harassment as a form of discrimination and as challengeable through law has since the mid-1970s found strong support from (radical) feminists, notably MacKinnon.[6] MacKinnon argues:

> 'Sexual harassment, the event, was not invented by feminists; the perpetrators did that with no help from us. Sexual harassment, the legal claim- the idea that the law should see it the way its victims see it, is definitively a feminist invention. Feminists first took women's experience seriously enough to uncover this problem and conceptualize it and pursue it legally.'[7]

Others too have argued that harassment ought to be seen as a form of discrimination. In Curtin's view, for example, harassment of women occurs in a segregated labour market which is characterised by gender-specific roles for women and for men and which is the result of the fact that, compared with men, women are accorded an inferior status.[8] Curtin has indicated that the discriminatory treatment is two-fold. Discrimination occurs not only through the employer's retaliation against a woman's refusal to condone the employer's sexual demands. It also occurs because such demands are imposed at all.[9] Van Maarsseveen has equally underscored the approach of perceiving (sexual) harassment as a form of discrimination: 'discrimina-

4 See, for example, Curtin 1984, p. 422-425; Defeis 2004, p. 86; Schultz 2001-2002, p. 425; Bakirci 1998, p. 5; Sperling 1996, p. 242-246. It should be noted that in US harassment law the focus has been on sexual harassment and racial harassment to the exclusion of harassment of members belonging to other disadvantaged groups and of workers in general. For further (explanatory) comments on this I refer to Friedman and Whitman 2003, p. 241-274.

5 Friedman and Whitman 2003, p. 241.

6 MacKinnon 1987, p. 103.

7 MacKinnon 1987, p. 103; Bakirci 1998, p. 5 and footnote 25.

8 Curtin 1984, p. 421 ('(...)ongewenste intimiteiten komen voor in een arbeidsproces dat zich kenmerkt door geslachtsrolverdeling en een lagere status van vrouwen houdt dat in stand'). See also Bakirci 1998, p. 3, where she has observed that '[Sexual harassment] reflects the patriarchal relations between men and women and the subordinate position which women tend to have in the hierarchy at work'.

9 Curtin 1984, p. 425, 'de discriminatie bestaat niet alleen uit de vergelding voor het niet ingaan op sexueel gerichte eisen, maar ook uit het feit dat deze sexueel gerichte eisen űberhaupt worden gesteld'. Curtin's observation relates to 'quid pro quo' harassment cases. This notion will be explained in section 2.4 to follow.

tion [of women; MG] in social and economic life is underpinned by 'cultural discrimination' of women [which manifests itself; MG] by the denial in the public sphere of value-differentiations between the sexes and the monopoly of male values.[10]

Friedman and Whitman have contrasted the American approach to harassment with that adopted in Continental law.[11] They have argued that '[i]n effect, there are now two paradigms for harassment law in the Western World: an American anti-discrimination paradigm and a Continental dignity paradigm'.[12] Hence, the former perceives harassment as a form of discrimination, whereas the latter sees it as an infringement upon a person's dignity.[13] In addition, the aforementioned authors have argued that, whereas the American approach is concerned with harassment understood as discriminatory treatment of particular groups (women, racial minorities), the Continental (European) model is concerned with the preservation of the dignity of employees in general.[14] Despite these perceived opposite approaches Friedman and Whitman have argued that both models should not be 'mutually exclusive'. Nonetheless, they have argued, the Continental experience itself submits that a reconciliation of both models may be a difficult exercise.[15]

At this juncture the following can be said. Firstly, and as shall be seen, in England, harassment law has traditionally been conceived in the context of discrimination and this therefore accords with the American model referred to by Friedman and Whitman. To a lesser extent this holds equally true for the Netherlands. However, as will become clear, Dutch harassment law is also rationalised by concerns over health and safety which indeed is one of the by Whitman and Friedman outlined characteristics of the Continental European model.[16] Secondly, the present author agrees with Whitman and Friedman that the 'harassment as discrimination model' and the 'harassment as dignity model' can co-exist in harmony. As will be illustrated, with the adoption of the RD, the EFD and the AETD[17] harassment has been introduced into the realm of EC equality and non-discrimination law. Contemporary EC equality places a stress upon both dignity and discrimination and as such it bridges both models. In section 3 hereafter this point will be illustrated on the basis of the legal provisions on harassment in EC law. In the passages immediately to follow it will be clarified that the reconciliation of both models is facilitated by an expansion of the theoretical premises which may underpin the equality principle *in abstracto*. Firstly, as *inter alia* Fredman has argued,

10 Van Maarsseveen 1990, p. 988.

11 Friedman and Whitman 2003, p. 241-274. The Continental countries examined in their study are Germany, France and Sweden.

12 Friedman and Whitman 2003, p. 243.

13 The meaning of the values of equality and dignity have been discussed by Feldman 2002 in the context of English and international human rights law. See Feldman 2002, Chapter 3.

14 Friedman and Whitman 2003, p. 242.

15 Friedman and Whitman 2003, p. 243.

16 Friedman and Whitman 2003, p. 245, where they have observed that 'European sexual harassment law (...) moreover (...) became very much law of the terms and conditions of employment'.

17 With reference to Chapter 2, the AETD refers to Council Directive 76/207/EEC as amended by Council Directive 2002/73/EC of 23 September 2002 *OJ* L 269/15, 23 September 2002.

showing equal respect for the dignity and worth of all persons is one of the underlying premises of the principle of equality itself.[18] Secondly, the participative goal of equality has been accentuated in recent theoretical accounts of the equality principle.[19] Arguably, harassment can also be appreciated in the context of the 'equality as participation' model. Hereafter, both theoretical visions of equality shall be further examined in the context of ground-related harassment.[20]

2.2. *Harassment, Equality and Dignity*

The equality as dignity model or 'moral equality model'[21] underpins the theoretical work on sexual harassment which was instigated by early (radical) feminist legal doctrine.[22] Essentially this doctrine conceives harassment from the perspective of gender-power relations and dominance whereby man's abuse of women's sexuality is heavily emphasised. In essence, in (early) feminist legal doctrine sexuality is the key word in the theorisation of sex related harassment.[23] The abuse of women's sexuality could be regarded as an attack on a woman's human dignity, integrity and worth.[24] It moreover undermines a woman's professionalism at work given that she

18 Fredman 2002a, p. 13.

19 *Inter alia* Fredman 2002a, p. 16 and McCrudden 2003, p. 31. Fredman has characterised the participation model of equality as a new concept of equality. See Fredman 2002a, p. 10.

20 It should be noted that the theoretical comments on the social reality of harassment have focused upon the discrimination ground sex. To a large extent, however, it appears that these comments can be extrapolated to other grounds of discrimination without insurmountable conceptual problems.

21 The model which analyses equality in close connection with human dignity has also been referred to as the 'moral equality model'. The moral equality model has been the reaction to the idea believed in until the 18th century, namely that there exists a natural human hierarchy. Moral equality thus advocates the principle that all human beings must be afforded the same freedom and must be treated with equal dignity and respect. This information was gained during a course organised by the Netherlands Research School of Women's Studies (NOV) coordinated by Professor Dr. Magda Michielsens and in which the author participated in March 2004.

22 Especially, MacKinnon, *Only Words,* Harvard University Press 1993, p. 60, cited by Bacik 2003, p. 175-176; MacKinnon, *Toward a Feminist Theory of the State* 137 (1989), cited by Schultz 2000-2001, p. 418, footnote 6; MacKinnon, *Sexual harassment of Working Women – A Case of Sex Discrimination* (1979), cited by Franke 1998, p. 1246 footnote 5. Although the women's movement has emphasised equal dignity and worth in the combat against sexual harassment of women by men it has also focused upon equal opportunities (or even results equality) between the sexes and upon realising greater social justice at work.

23 Obviously feminist legal doctrine has not been concerned with harassment of members of other disadvantaged groups (ethnic minorities, disabled persons *etc.*). *A fortiori*, it has not been concerned with acts of harassment inflicted upon men. Bakirci has indicated that men, who have been the victim of harassment, generally have a 'special vulnerability'. She has *inter alia* mentioned the examples of young men, men who have just taken up employment, homosexuals and men from ethnic minorities (Bakirci 1998, p. 4). Arguably, in these cases it will be very difficult to discern whether the act of harassment was inflicted on grounds of sex or on grounds of another status such as ethnicity or homosexuality.

24 Schultz 2000-2001, p. 426. She herself has, however, favoured a different conceptualisation of harassment. This will be explained in section 2.3 hereafter.

is portrayed as a sexual object rather than as a human being who is just like a man doing her job.

The link between equality and dignity has been encouraged by a (re)conceptualisation of the principle of equality with the aim of taking it beyond formal equality. Hence, equality entails more. Fredman has emphasised that modern interpretations of equality surpass the (early) ideals of 'equality as consistency' and 'equal opportunities' which fit in well with the comparative justice model.[25] Fredman has emphasised four new visions of equality, including one which stresses the equal respect for the dignity and worth of all.[26] Thus, writes Fredman, '(...) in the field of harassment, the stress on dignity has facilitated a transformation of direct discrimination from a principle based entirely on consistency, to one embedded in substantive values'.[27] It should be noted that such a vision corresponds with the 'deontological justice model'[28] which accords a validated connotation to justice.[29] This model can be contrasted with the 'comparative model',[30] which accentuates that a disadvantage is to be measured relative to the disadvantage suffered by a relevant comparator. The importance of dignity in the equality discourse has also been emphasised by Holtmaat, with reference to the work by Dworkin. Holtmaat has shown herself a proponent of a vision of equality which stresses the intrinsic connection between equality, human dignity and individual autonomy.[31] Hirsch Ballin supports a similar view where he has stated that '(...) the duty to treat [people; MG] equally [must be understood as; MG] respecting the personal dignity of every human being equally'.[32] The perception of equality within a model of human dignity has moreover been advanced by Bacik.[33] The present author agrees with the aforementioned authors that highlighting human dignity in the debate of equality is vital, for it fosters the moral, rather than, e.g. the economic cause for equality. Furthermore, a dignity approach to 'harassment', as a concept of non-discrimination law, abolishes the need for drawing a comparison with a relevant equivalent which is similarly situated. This point will be discussed in further detail in the passages to follow.

By way of interim conclusion the following can be said. The concept of harassment in positive equality law is in the first place underpinned by a theoretical vision

25 See Chapter 2.

26 Fredman 2002a, p. 13. Other, modern, visions of equality distinguished by Fredman are: 'equality as a means to break the cycle of disadvantage'; 'equality as a means to affirm community identities'; 'equality as a means to foster participation'. See also Fredman 2002, p. 120-121. The equality as participation paradigm will be considered in the main text hereafter.

27 Fredman 2002, p. 120.

28 Quinn 2004, p. 10 and Chapter 2 of this book.

29 Quinn 2004, p. 10.

30 Quinn 2004, p. 10 and Chapter 2 of this book.

31 Holtmaat 2004, p. 1 with reference to R. Dworkin, *Taking Rights Seriously*, London: Dukworth 1977, p. 272-273.

32 Hirsch Ballin 2003, p. 197. See also Lord Lester of Herne Hill 1997, p. 168, where he has *inter alia* discussed what ideas and concerns were underpinning the introduction of law with a view to promoting equality. Lord Lester has stressed that all are morally equal because of a 'common humanity'.

33 Bacik 2003, p. 168 and p. 170-171.

of equality which seeks to foster the equal respect for everybody's dignity and worth. It follows from this that one of the objectives pursued by the regulation of harassment is to prevent a person's dignity from being violated. As such harassment law (*inter alia*) seeks to prohibit the disparaging, belittling, degrading, stereotypical and/or hostile treatment often meted out by those in the dominant pool *vis-à-vis* those in the disadvantaged pool (e.g. women, ethnic minorities and disabled persons).

2.3. *Harassment, Equality, Exclusion and Participation*

Hepple, Coussey and Choudhury have observed that '[harassment is a means; MG] to intimidate and shut out [members belonging to disadvantaged *groups; MG]* as well as [to undermine] their dignity and right to private life'.[34] Van Maarsseveen has voiced a similar concern: 'unwanted intimacies are notably a means by which women are kept as outsiders at work'.[35] It follows that harassment could arguably be conceived too in the context of 'equality as participation'. This model has *inter alia* been designed by both Fredman and McCrudden in their theoretical work on the equality principle more generally.[36] 'The 'participative model' of equality, writes McCrudden, (…) addresses the need for all, including those previously excluded, to have a voice in public affairs especially in the daily decisions of those who shape their life chances'.[37] Although McCrudden seems to place an emphasis on participation in public affairs, Fredman has taken a broader perspective by holding that '[p]articipation extends across many levels, whether in the workforce, the political arena, the health service, or education'.[38] The key word in the participation model of equality is *inclusion* of those who were formerly excluded.

The effect of exclusion arising from harassment is central to Schultz's theoretical work on sex-harassment. Schultz has thoroughly criticised the (mere) conceptualisation of sex-harassment from the perspectives of equal worth and dignity.[39] She has labelled the sexuality and dignity model designed by radical feminists as the 'sexual desire-dominance paradigm'.[40] Essentially, writes Schultz, 'Within that paradigm, a male supervisor's sexual advances on a less powerful, female subordinate represent the quintessential form of harassment'.[41] Schultz has subsequently

34 Hepple, Coussey and Choudhury 2000, p. 39.

35 Van Maarsseveen 1990, p. 988 (*'Opgedrongen intimiteiten zijn in het bijzonder een middel waarmede vrouwen in de positie van buitenstaanders in de werkomgeving worden gehouden.'*).

36 It is therefore certainly not confined to the narrower context of harassment and equality.

37 McCrudden 2003a, p. 31.

38 Fredman 2002a, p. 16.

39 Although Schultz has not argued that such a conceptualisation is wholly flawed she has criticised it for being a 'reductionist and potentially dangerous' approach: 'Now, it's not that I don't believe sexual advances can ever infringe on interests we might think of as dignitarian in nature; of course they can. But to legally equate sexual advances toward women with inherent violations of women's dignity strikes me as a reductionist, potentially dangerous move that feminists should evaluate very carefully.' Schultz 2000-2001, p. 426-427.

40 Schultz 1997-1998, p. 1692-1710.

41 Schultz 1997-1998, p. 1686.

outlined a number of problems which, in her view, are intrinsic to this paradigm. Firstly, she has criticised it for being 'top down'[42] in nature: the sexual desire-dominance paradigm assumes that sex harassment is inflicted by those who enjoy more power than others, hence, by those in the higher rankings of an employment organisation (men) upon those in lower jobs (women) (i.e. 'vertical harassment'). However, as she has argued, sex harassment often occurs by male colleague co-workers who are in the same ranking of employment as their female victims (i.e. 'horizontal harassment'). Secondly, she has condemned this paradigm for its single focus upon the sexual nature of a particular conduct whereas 'much of the time harassment assumes a form that has little or nothing to do with sexuality but everything with gender'.[43] Thirdly, in Schultz's view, the sexual desire-dominance paradigm obscures the nature of harassment as a 'set of social relations' which reflects the institutionalised, i.e. the structural nature of inequality at work.[44] Schultz has argued that by focusing upon the sexual advances or assaults by malicious men working in the higher echelons upon women the paradigm stresses the misconduct of male individuals thereby, however, neglecting the wider concepts of a pattern of unequal treatment.[45] Schultz has emphasised the link between harassment, on the one hand, and a 'larger system of workplace gender inequality that relegates women to inferior jobs', on the other.[46] A final criticism upheld by Schultz is that the premise of the law lies upon the sexual desire-dominance paradigm giving importance to whether or not the harassing acts complained of were 'unwelcome'. As such, harassment law that focuses on sexual misconduct '(...) invites inquiry into the sexual history and sexual self-presentation of the person who was harassed'.[47]

42 Schultz 2000-2001, p. 418-419.

43 Schultz 1997-1998, p. 1687. This prompts the question as to the difference between 'sex' and 'gender'. 'Sex' refers to biological differences between men and women, such as differences related to pregnancy or the different biological features between women and men. In contrast, 'gender' refers to the socially or culturally constructed differences between women and men (e.g. the perception that women are more caring than men or that men are braver than women). In short, sex differences reflect a biological truth, whereas gender differences are socially constructed. For example, laws which grant paid parental leave to women in fact amount to gender rather than to sex discrimination. MacKinnon has disagreed with this distinction and has argued that sex and gender can be used interchangeably: 'Since I [MacKinnon] think that the importance of biology to the condition of women is the social meaning attributed to it, biology is (with emphasis) its social meaning for purposes of analyzing the inequality of the sexes, a political condition. I therefore tend to use sex and gender relatively interchangeably.' (MacKinnon 1987, p. 263, footnote 5).

44 See also Abrams, who has taken the view that sexual harassment is wrong, for it effectively helps to 'preserve male control and entrench masculine norms in the workplace' (K. Abrams, The New Jurisprudence of Sexual Harassment, 83 *Cornell Law Review* 1169 (1998) cited by Franke 1998, p. 1246).

45 Schultz 2000-2001, p. 424. Schultz has expressed herself as follows: 'The sexual model (...) encourages people to think of harassment as a form of behavioral misconduct in which individual bad actors engage, rather than as a set of social relations that are embedded in a larger context of structural inequality in the workplace'.

46 Schultz 2000-2001, p. 426.

47 Schultz 2000-2001, p. 427. A theoretical model which places the emphasis on exclusion rather than on dignity and sexuality would make such an inquiry redundant. Under such a model →

With a view to overcoming all of these disadvantages Schultz has advocated an alternative model for explaining sex-harassment at work which emphasises the effects of *exclusion*. She has labelled this the 'competence-centered paradigm'.[48] It essentially expounds an understanding of harassment as a tool used by men to secure the fact that certain prestigious jobs and work competence remain the ultimate terrain of 'masculinity', to the exclusion of female workers (or 'lesser men').[49] In summary, in this paradigm the focus shifts from sexuality to exclusion. In Schultz's view sex harassment is a prime tool to accomplish female exclusion and to preserve typical masculine and typical feminine work-roles: '(...) harassment is not driven by a need for sexual domination but by a desire to preserve favoured lines of work as masculine'.[50] Perceived in this way harassment law contributes to an attack on the gendered labour market, which is characterised by a high percentage of women in unskilled and thus low paid jobs and a high percentage of men in jobs where (political) decisions are taken.

It is submitted that, although Schultz has never referred to the 'equality as participation model' Schultz's 'competence-centered paradigm' amalgamates well with this model. The participation model is, however, wider in scope and its application goes beyond the realm of harassment so as to include acts of more general discrimination. Schultz's paradigm could arguably be regarded as a subset of the equality as participation model. As has been seen both the former and the latter focus upon exclusion, or positively formulated, upon the need for fostering inclusion.

2.4. *Dignity and Participation: Mutually Exclusive Paradigms?*

In the present author's view the above outlined theoretical models should be used in a complementary, rather than exclusionary fashion by legislators, judges and policy-makers, whilst addressing the social harm of ground-related harassment. Depending on the form of harassment at stake, one or the other paradigm may be more or less pertinent. (Early) feminist analysis which has centralised the notions of dignity and sexuality is still at a premium in so-called *quid pro quo* harassment cases. These concern the classical act of harassment which is (often) vertically inflicted by

argues Schultz, '(...) it would make no sense to ask whether someone had welcomed being subjected to an environment that interfered with their ability to pursue their work. 'Did the harasee welcome being driven out of her job?' (Schultz 2000-2001, p. 427).

48 Schultz 1997-1998, p. 1755. Alternatively, she has also referred to it as the 'work-centered model' (Schultz 2000-2001, p. 420).

49 Schultz 1997-1998, p. 1755 where she has observed that 'contrary to the assumption of the cultural-radical feminist tradition that inspired the development of harassment law, men's desire to exploit or dominate women sexually may not be the exclusive, or even the primary, motivation for harassing women at work. Instead, a drive to maintain the most highly rewarded forms of work as domains of masculine competence underlies many, if not most, forms of sex-based harassment on the job'.

50 Schultz 1997-1998, p. 1690.

male workers in power upon female workers.[51] *Quid pro quo* harassment is a form of harassment whereby the alleged victim condones or is induced to condone certain sexual acts, or acts of a sexual nature, by the harasser (e.g. a male chef) in return for a certain reward or profit such as being promoted.[52] This being so, *quid pro quo* harassment is of less relevance to harassment which is related to (e.g.) 'race' or 'disability'. This point will be discussed further in section 3.2.2 hereafter. The present author takes the view that Schultz's conceived approach constitutes a sound theoretical basis in which to account for hostile work environment harassment. This can be both sexual and non-sexual in kind and can be horizontally or vertically inflicted upon women as well as upon members of other disadvantaged groups. It lacks, however, a *quid pro quo* element. Hostile work environment harassment may consist of physical or verbal (sexual) hostilities which create a hostile environment at work. This has not only an effect upon the victim's dignity but it is likely to have exclusionary effects too. As such it parallels the participation model outlined above.

Having considered harassment from a theoretical perspective I will hereafter consider this concept in the context of Community and domestic law.

3. Harassment in EC Law

3.1. Historical Development of the Concept of Harassment

Prior to the adoption of the RD, the EFD and the AETD harassment had only been a matter of non-binding soft law.[53] The 1976 ETD[54] remained silent on the matter of harassment. The relevant soft-law provisions merely concerned the harmful effects of *sexual harassment* to the exclusion of other forms of ground-related harassment. By way of Resolution the European Parliament (EP) in 1986 requested the adoption of a Directive which prohibited sexual harassment.[55] In 1987 the Commission published a report on sexual harassment written by Rubenstein.[56] In 1990 the Council

51 Bakirci 1998, p. 5: 'Most commentators accept the view that quid pro quo harassment cannot be performed by so-called co-workers since they are not in a position to affect the job status of each other'.

52 Holtmaat 2004a, p. 101.

53 As indicated by McCrudden soft law is a 'hybrid' between legislation and litigation: 'This hybrid is legislation, of a type, but legislation devised as much to influence national court and ECJ interpretations of existing legal provisions as to influence Member States to adopt new legal provisions or new practices.' See McCrudden 1993, p. 362 with reference to Wellens and Borchardt, 'Soft Law in European Community Law', 14 *European Law Review* (1989), 276.

54 Directive 76/207/EEC on Equal Treatment for Men and Women as regards Access to Employment, Vocational Training and Promotion and Working Conditions, *OJ* 1976, L 39/40. See generally Chapter 2.

55 Resolution of 11 June 1986 of the European Parliament on violence against women, *OJ* 14/07/1986 C 176, p. 1, cited by Masselot 2004, p. 97.

56 Rubenstein 1987, cited by McCrudden 1993, p. 363. It was the Commission itself which had commissioned the drawing up of this report.

adopted a Resolution on the protection of the dignity of women and men at work[57] whereas the Commission, in 1991, adopted a Recommendation for the Member States accompanied by a Code of Practice for employers.[58] The invitation by the Commission to the European Social Partners to negotiate an agreement on an EC policy aimed at combating work related sexual harassment was not accepted.[59]

In the Code of Practice sexual harassment was defined as follows: 'sexual harassment means unwanted conduct of a sexual nature, or other conduct based on sex affecting the dignity of women and men at work. This can include unwelcome physical, verbal or non-verbal conduct'.[60] As will be illustrated, the new definition of sexual harassment is partly based on this definition.[61] It is explicitly stated in the Code that 'the essential characteristic of sexual harassment is that it is unwanted by the recipient, that it is for each individual to determine what behaviour is acceptable to them and that they regard as offensive'.[62] This reflects a subjective test for the establishment of sexual harassment.[63]

Rubenstein has suggested that sexual harassment could have been litigated under the 1976 ETD[64], however, this has never occurred. An argument which supports Rubenstein's view is that the Code of Practice in Article 3 explicitly states that 'conduct of a sexual nature or other [conduct; MG] based on sex affecting the dignity of women and men at work may be contrary to the principle of equal treatment within the meaning of Articles 3, 4, and 5 of Council Directive 76/207/EEC (...)'.

Although the legal status of the Code of Practice is non-binding soft law it has served as a construal tool for courts and tribunals at the domestic legal level. For example, in the English case of *Insitu Cleaning CO LTD and another v. HEADS*[65], which will be discussed in further detail in section 4 hereafter, the EAT decided that a sufficiently serious one incident act can also constitute an act of 'sexual harassment'. This judicial stance accords with Article 2 of the Code of Practice to which reference was made by the EAT. Article 2 of the Code of Practice reads as follows: 'sexual attention becomes sexual harassment if it is persisted in once it has been made clear that it is regarded by the recipient as offensive, although one incident of harassment may constitute sexual harassment if sufficiently serious'.

At present ground-related harassment is a matter of binding Community law. In the analysis of harassment in the context of the RD, the EFD and the AETD

57 Council Resolution of 29 May 1990 on the protection of the dignity of women and men at work, *OJ* C 157/3 of 27 June 1990. See moreover Masselot 2004, p. 97; McCrudden 1993, p. 364; Driessen-Reilly and Driessen 2003, p. 494.

58 Commission Recommendation 92/131/EEC of 27 November 1991 on the protection of the dignity of women and men at work, *OJ* L 49 of 24 February 1992.

59 Driessen-Reilly and Driessen 2003, p. 494, with further references. Also Masselot 2004, p. 97 and footnote 26.

60 Article 2 of the Code of Practice.

61 EOR 2002, p. 22-25.

62 Article 2 of the Code of Practice.

63 Bacik 2003, p. 167.

64 Bacik 2003, p. 167, with reference to Rubenstein, 'Sexual harassment: European Commission Recommendation and Code of Practice', *Industrial Law Journal* (1992), p. 70.

65 *Insitu Cleaning CO LTD and another v. HEADS* [1995] IRLR 4 (EAT).

hereafter, it will be illustrated that 'harassment' is conceived by the Directives as a form of discrimination denoting substantive rather than comparative justice.

3.2. *Harassment in the RD, EFD and AETD*

3.2.1. Introduction

The insertion of tailor-made Articles on ground-related harassment into the RD, the EFD and the ETD reflects a clear step forward in the legal protection from this social harm. With the adoption of the Directives, ground-related harassment has for the first time ever become a matter of binding EC equality law. Hereafter, an analysis will be made first of harassment as a concept of discrimination contained in the RD and the EFD (section 3.2.2). I will subsequently examine harassment in the context of the AETD (section 3.2.3). It will be shown that the approach to harassment adopted by the AETD differs in various respects from that adopted by the RD and the EFD.

3.2.2. The Concept of Harassment in the RD and the EFD

3.2.2.1. Defining Harassment

Article 2(3) of the RD reads as follows:

> 'Harassment shall be deemed to be a form of discrimination within the meaning of paragraph 1, when an unwanted conduct related to racial or ethnic origin takes place with the purpose or effect of violating the dignity of a person and of creating an intimidating, hostile, degrading, humiliating or offensive environment. In this context, the concept of harassment may be defined in accordance with the national laws and practice of the Member States.'

An identical definition is contained in Article 2(3) EFD for the grounds covered by that Directive, including disability. Neither the RD nor the EFD refer to harassment in the preambular Recitals. The above definition of harassment prompts the following two comments. Firstly, Article 2(3) of the RD and Article 2(3) of the EFD unequivocally state that harassment shall be deemed to be a form of discrimination in the circumstances defined by these Articles. This approach avoids many of the problems that have occurred, particularly in the context of English non-discrimination law, which has traditionally dealt with harassment-claims on the premises of 'comparative justice'. The approach to harassment adopted by the RD and the EFD (and the AETD) departs from the model of comparative justice. A perpetrator, for example, a white chef is therefore prevented from arguing that the alleged acts of harassment do not constitute race related harassment, given that a white (equivalent) worker would have been subjected to exactly the same harassing treatment.[66] Such an argument clearly sounds absurd, however, it has been victorious in the context of

[66] In the context of sex related harassment this defence has been named by MacKinnon the 'bisexual defence'. See MacKinnon 1987, p. 107-108 and footnote 9 at p. 252.

English anti-discrimination law. This will be seen in section 4 hereafter. The just-mentioned example shows that harassment is ill-placed in the comparative justice paradigm.

Secondly, Article 2(3) of the Directives relates to hostile work environment-harassment not to *quid pro quo* harassment. Both notions of harassment have been touched on earlier in the analysis. Hostile work environment-harassment concerns the inflicting of demeaning or degrading acts upon a person defined by (e.g.) race or disability which results in a deteriorated and prejudiced work environment. In contrast to *quid pro quo* harassment it is not a form of harassment which 'conditions'[67] the victim's employment on the acceptance of the perpetrator's demands. In *quid pro quo* harassment cases the victim tends to be female, the perpetrator male, and the latter's demands are sexual in kind.[68] It should be noted that the very nature of *quid pro quo* harassment states that it is of no relevance in pure race and disability harassment cases[69] (cross-ground comparison). Put differently, the underlying values of these grounds of discrimination do not lend themselves well for *quid pro quo* scenarios. Although the discrimination ground sexual orientation is not covered in this chapter the following is worth pointing out. Sexual orientation is a ground covered by the EFD and the omission of *quid pro quo* harassment in Article 2(3) of the Framework Directive constitutes a particular loss for the protection of gays and lesbians. In contrast to the other grounds covered by the RD and EFD a person's sexual orientation can easily trigger a quid pro quo scenario. It remains to be seen whether such a scenario can be effectively challenged in accordance with the law as it currently stands.[70]

3.2.2.2. Establishing a Case of Ground-Related Harassment

What conditions must be fulfilled before ground-related harassment can be established on the basis of Article 2(3) of the RD and of the EFD? These are four-fold: (1) the harassing conduct on which the complaint is based must be 'unwanted'; (2) the conduct must be related to a forbidden ground; (3) the conduct must have had the purpose or the effect of violating the dignity of the alleged victim; (4) the conduct must have had the purpose or the effect of creating an intimidating, hostile, degrading, humiliating or offensive environment. These requirements in conjunction set a high threshold for establishing a claim of harassment. This reflects a fair approach, given that harassment is prohibited *per se*, which means that once established, a claim of harassment cannot be justified. With respect to the first condition (proof of 'unwanted' conduct') the question arises *who* decides whether a certain conduct is 'unwanted'? Must the interpretation of the adjective 'unwanted' occur on the basis of an

67 *Note* 1979-1980, p. 155.

68 Hence, the principle of *symmetry* (see Chapter 2) uneasily fits with this reality.

69 *Quid pro quo* acts of harassment may, however, be inflicted upon for example a black woman or a disabled woman. In such cases different protected statuses 'interact' and various 'patterns of domination intersect'. For further discussion the reader is referred to Fredman 1997a, p. 330-334.

70 Also Bell and Waddington 2001, p. 595-596.

objective or a subjective test? Put differently, should the courts decide on whether or not the conduct at stake amounts to 'unwanted conduct', or should the individual perception of the victim be decisive? In the context of sex related harassment the Code of Practice clearly favours a subjective approach: 'The essential characteristic of sexual harassment is that it is unwanted conduct by the recipient, that it is for each individual to determine what behaviour is acceptable to them and what they regard as offensive' (Article 2). Compared to Article 2 of the Code of Practice, the definition of harassment in the RD and the EFD is less pronounced on the subjectivity or objectivity of the legal test. It is submitted that a purely subjective test tilts the balance of probability that harassment has taken place too much in favour of the alleged victim. This is particularly the case in light of the fact that harassment cannot be justified. The present author therefore favours a mixed subjective and objective test. The question as to whether a particular conduct was 'unwanted' should largely be answered on the basis of the subjective feelings of the victim. However, whether this has led to a violation of the person's dignity and to the creation of a hostile work-environment should ultimately be for the courts to decide on the basis of the concrete facts of the case at hand.

The Definition in Article 2(3) of the Directives requires the establishment of a causal link between the complaint of acts of harassment, on the one hand, and a protected status, on the other. Bullying or mobbing which cannot be connected with a forbidden ground is therefore not covered.[71] Hence, the Directives grant a limited form of protection from harassment at work. This is the result of the need to fit harassment within the straight-jacket of equality law, notwithstanding that the theoretical premises of the law presently go beyond the comparative justice model. The requirement that the reprehensible conduct must be related to a prohibited ground is ample to cover the situation of 'associated harassment', i.e. harassment of a person by reason of her association with, e.g. a black or a disabled person. It follows from the third and fourth conditions that *both* the violation of the harassed person's dignity *and* the creation of a hostile work environment must be proven. This means that a high burden of proof is placed upon the alleged victim of harassment. It should, however, be noted that the alleged victim needs not prove a malicious intent on the part of the alleged perpetrator. This follows from the rubric 'purpose *or effect*' (emphasis MG) in the third and fourth conditions referred to above. It will be illustrated hereafter that the AETD, with respect to '*sexual harassment*' (*not* 'sex-based harassment') places a lower evidentiary burden upon an alleged victim, compared with the provisions on harassment in the RD and EFD.

3.2.2.3. Establishing Ground-Related Harassment 'in accordance with the National Laws and Practice of the Member States'

The definition of harassment in the RD and EFD provides that '(...) the concept of harassment may be defined in accordance with the national laws and practice of the Member States'. As will be seen hereafter, a counterpart provision is not contained

71 Also Driessen-Reilly and Driessen 2003, p. 497.

in the AETD. The provision just referred to brings with it that matters related to harassment which have not been regulated in Community law remain entirely within the policy discretion of the Member States. An example of this concerns the matter of liability for ground-related harassment.[72] The Directives remain silent on the question whether an employer can be held liable for acts inflicted by a worker upon another worker (vicarious liability), or whether the employer can be held legally responsible for harassing acts meted out to an employee by a third party, for example, a student, a client or a patient. In this context the following is worth noting with respect to the personal applicability of the Directives.[73] It remains unclear from the text of the RD and the EFD to whom the prohibition of discrimination, including harassment, is addressed. For instance, if a colleague worker harasses an employee at the workplace, may only the formal employer be held liable or also (and/or alternatively) the individual perpetrator him(her)self? Article 3(1) of the EFD provides as follows:

> 'Within the limits of the areas of competence conferred on the Community, this Directive shall apply to *all persons* [italics MG] as regards both the public and private sectors, including public bodies, in relation to [employment and vocational training; MG].'[74]

A counterpart provision is found in Article 3(1) of the RD.[75] In a different modus, Article 3 of the AETD provides that 'application of the principle of equal treatment means that there shall be no (...) discrimination on the grounds of sex in the public or private sectors, including public bodies, in relation to (...).[76] It is argued that the phrase 'all persons' in the RD and the EFD is ample to cover the following in the context of employment: employers, employees and third persons. A similar conclusion has been drawn by Whittle and Holtmaat.[77] For the sake of legal consistency, the present author suggests that Article 3 of the AETD be interpreted in an analogous fashion. In practice the aforementioned interpretation of the personal applicability of the Directives means that an alleged victim of harassment may directly litigate against the individual perpetrator. If domestic non-discrimination law prevents a victim from doing so[78] it can be seriously questioned whether this is in conformity with EC law.

As will be illustrated below, in English law the employer's liability for acts of 'third persons' has led to controversial perspectives and radically different views

72 See also Bell and Waddington 2001, p. 595.

73 This passage draws on Gijzen 2004, section 3.1.3.

74 After the rubric 'in relation to' a number of employment-related areas are listed in paragraphs (a)-(d).

75 After the rubric 'in relation to' a number of areas of social life are listed in paragraphs (a)-(f). These include employment but also go beyond that. See generally Chapter 2.

76 After the rubric 'in relation to' a number of areas of employment are listed in paragraphs (a)-(d).

77 Whittle 2002, p. 316; Holtmaat 2004a, p. 97 and footnote 47.

78 Dutch equal treatment law appears to be exclusively directed to employers and to other organisations but not to employees and third persons. This point will be discussed in more detail in section 5 hereafter.

have been aired on the matter by the EAT, on the one hand, and the House of Lords, on the other. It follows that *inter alia* questions of liability remain to be addressed at the domestic level. However, in doing so, the Member States must comply with the principle that sanctions are effective, proportionate and dissuasive.[79] Moreover, it will be argued in section 4 hereafter, that the regulation of liability for harassment should reflect the fact that in EC law harassment is conceived as an independent, rather than as a comparative, wrong. At this juncture, the regulation of 'harassment' in the RD and the EFD, on the one hand, will be contrasted with the approach to 'harassment' adopted by the AETD, on the other.

3.2.3. Harassment in the AETD

3.2.3.1. Defining Sexual Harassment and Sex-Based Harassment

Like the RD and EFD the AETD also creates a link between harassment and discrimination. This already begins in the Preamble. Thus, Recital 8 of the Preamble to the AETD reads as follows:

> 'Harassment related to the sex of a person and sexual harassment is contrary to the principle of equal treatment between women and men; it is therefore appropriate to define such concepts and prohibit such forms of discrimination. To this end it must be emphasised that these forms of discrimination occur not only in the workplace, but also in the context of access to employment and vocational training, during employment and occupation.'

Recital 9 subsequently provides that:

> 'In this context, employers and those responsible for vocational training should be encouraged to take measures to combat all forms of sexual discrimination and in particular, to take preventive measures against harassment and sexual harassment in the workplace.'

It should be noted that the definition of harassment in the AETD differs in a number of respects from that contained in the RD and the EFD. Particularly important is that the AETD draws a distinction between sexual harassment, on the one hand, and harassment (based on sex),[80] on the other by incorporating two different definitions.[81] The definition of sex-based harassment is contained in Article 2(2) third indent of the AETD. It provides as follows:

[79] Article 15 RD and Article 17 EFD. See moreover Recital 26 RD and Recital 35 EFD. See for a detailed analysis of this principle in the context of Community non-discrimination law, Tobler 2005a, Part I.

[80] Hereafter: sex-based harassment.

[81] See also EOR 2002, p. 22. The same distinction has been drawn in the Code of Practice for employers referred to above in section 3.1.

> '[Sex-based; MG] harassment: where an unwanted conduct related to the sex of a person occurs with the purpose or effect of violating the dignity of a person, and of creating an intimidating, hostile, degrading, humiliating or offensive environment.'

The definition of sexual harassment is found in Article 2(2) fourth indent of the AETD:

> 'Sexual harassment: where any form of unwanted verbal, non-verbal or physical conduct of a sexual nature occurs, with the purpose or effect of violating the dignity of a person, in particular when creating an intimidating, hostile, degrading, humiliating or offensive environment.'

Like with the RD and the EFD harassment is deemed to be discrimination. To this effect Article 2(3) of the AETD provides as follows:

> 'Harassment and sexual harassment within the meaning of this Directive shall be deemed to be discrimination on the grounds of sex and therefore prohibited.
> A person's rejection of, or submission to, such conduct may not be used as a basis for a decision affecting that person.'

The last sentence of Article 2(3) AETD explicitly regulates *quid pro quo* harassment. As has been explained earlier, this form of harassment is of less relevance to the grounds contained in the RD and the EFD, with the exception of 'sexual orientation'. The above legal provisions warrant a number of comments.

Firstly, and importantly, what would or could be the difference in practice between sex-based harassment and sexual harassment? In fact the distinction between the two is not very clear[82] but the following is suggested. The keyword in 'sexual harassment' is *sexuality*. It refers to acts which in fact amount to sexual conduct. This may include touching a woman's body or making comments about it (whether verbally or in writing); staring at a woman's breasts; leering at her; *quid pro quo* harassment, etc. The theoretical analysis of harassment designed by feminist legal doctrine is particularly apt to account for sexual harassment.

It is submitted that the central tenet of 'sex-based harassment' is not sexuality but *gender*. Thus, acts of sex-based harassment arguably find their root in (by a male dominated society) perceived social and cultural differences between 'the masculine' and 'the female'. An example of sex-based harassment is a female manager who is badgered by her male colleague managers regarding her leadership-skills. In this example, harassment is not so much triggered by the woman's sexuality but rather by an idea that men have better management skills than women. As analysed before, sex-based harassment has been theoretically approached by Schultz on the basis of the 'competence centered paradigm'.

The above differences are not merely a matter of semantics or solely theoretical in kind. Indeed, upon comparison of Articles 2(2) third indent ('sex based harassment') and 2(2) fourth indent ('sexual harassment') of the AETD it becomes clear that the former is more difficult to prove than the latter. In contrast to alleged

82 See also Masselot 2004, p. 98, who has observed that 'in practice (...) it is not always easy to differentiate between sexual harassment and general harassment related to sex'.

victims of sex-based harassment, a victim of sexual harassment is not required to prove *both* that her dignity has been violated *and* that the acts on which the complaint is based have had the effect of creating an intimidating, etc. environment. In contrast, the definition of sexual harassment specifies that the creation of a hostile work environment *reinforces* the alleged victim's claim that her dignity has been infringed upon and that she thus has been subjected to sexual harassment. However, that the work environment was soiled needs not *cumulatively* be proven.

A second matter which is worth observing concerns the following. Only the definition of sexual harassment specifies that the conduct on which the complaint is based can be *verbal, non-verbal* or *physical* in kind (in addition to the requirement that it must be 'sexual' in nature). In contrast the definition of sex-based harassment in the AETD, and the definitions of harassment found in the RD and the EFD, do not specify in further detail what forms of conduct are captured by the notion of 'unwanted conduct'. This could be interpreted to mean that *only* sexual harassment could occur on the basis of both active behaviour (verbal and physical conduct) and passive behaviour. One could argue that, in contrast, establishing a case of sex-based or other ground-related harassment requires *active* behaviour. The reasoning would thus be that had the EC legislator intended that 'unwanted conduct' in the definitions of sex-based harassment in the AETD, and other ground-related harassment in the RD and EFD, included *both* active *and* passive conduct, it would have inserted the adjectives *verba', non-verbal* or *physical* into these definitions too.[83] It is argued that domestic courts and the ECJ should not follow this line of reasoning. The notion of 'unwanted conduct' should be interpreted broadly and resolutely, so as to cover both active and passive forms of behaviour. An employer who turns a blind eye to harassment in the workplace and remains passive in terminating it should not escape from liability under EC harassment law.

3.2.3.2. Establishing Sex-Based and Sexual Harassment 'in accordance with the National Laws and Practice of the Member States'

In contrast with the definitions of harassment in Article 2(3) of the RD and Article 2(3) of the EFD, the definitions of sex-based harassment and sexual harassment in the AETD do not specify that '(...) the concept of harassment may be defined in accordance with the national laws and practice of the Member States'. It has already been argued that this provision *inter alia* implies that the liability for harassment remains within the discretionary scope of the Member States provided that effective, proportionate and dissuasive sanctions are guaranteed by national procedural law. It should, however, be noted that Article 2(5) AETD specifies that the

> 'Member States shall encourage, in accordance with national law, collective agreements or practice, employers and those responsible for access to vocational training to take measures to prevent all forms of discrimination on grounds of sex, in particular harassment and sexual harassment at the workplace'.

83 Driessen-Reilly and Driessen 2003, p. 496-497.

Arguably, this provision, in conjunction with Recital 9 of the AETD (referred to in section 3.2.3.1 above), places a greater legal duty upon the Member States to adequately regulate the matter of liability of the employer for omitting to prevent harassment from occurring.

In the present author's view it would have been better had the EC legislator inserted a number of benchmarks into the Directives themselves with regard to the liability question. Amongst these could have been an obligation for the employer to state explicitly that acts of (ground-related) harassment are contrary to the policy of the enterprise. The Directives could, moreover, have placed a duty upon the employer to set up an internal complaints mechanism which could be used by alleged victims of harassment in the workplace. The ECJ should feel encouraged to formulate legal yardsticks which qualify the question of liability for ground-related harassment in employment. The ECJ could do so in reliance upon Article 15 RD, Article 17 EFD and Article 6(2) AETD (which require that sanctions shall be proportionate, effective and dissuasive) and in reliance upon Article 2(5) AETD in conjunction with Recital 9 in the Preamble of the AETD.

3.3. *Closing Remarks*

In section 3, the concept of harassment has been analysed in the context of EC law. Whereas prior to the adoption of the RD, the EFD and the AETD ground-related harassment was merely regulated by Community soft-law provisions, it currently forms part of binding EC equality law. The analysis has shown that with respect to 'harassment', Community law deviates from the traditionally adopted comparative justice model to the benefit of a freestanding approach which conceives 'equality' in a more substantive fashion. This conceived approach bears a mandatory impact upon the regulation of harassment in domestic anti-discrimination law. The 'Europeanisation' of English and Dutch non-discrimination and harassment law will, respectively, be considered in Sections 4 and 5 hereafter.

4. Harassment in English Non-Discrimination Law: a Top-Down Analysis

4.1. *Introduction*

The objective of section 4 is to analyse the top-down influence exercised by Community law upon the approach adopted in English anti-discrimination law to ground-related[84] harassment.[85] This involves a comparison of the legal approach adopted pre-implementation of the RD, the EFD and the AETD, with the one post-

[84] This excludes an analysis of harassment in criminal law and tort law. Consequently, the 1997 Protection from Harassment Act (PHA) which prohibits harassment both as a tort and as a criminal act will not be discussed.

[85] An analysis of harassment in English law has *inter alia* also been made by Palmer, Gill *et al.*, 2002, Chapter 28 and by McColgan 2005, p. 55-63.

transposition of the Directives. The analysis to follow is moreover functional to the cross-country comparison which will be drawn in section 6. The analysis hereafter will be presented according to the following stages. In section 4.2, an overview will be given first of the types of conduct which may amount to harassment. This will be done in light of the case law rendered by the domestic courts. In section 4.3, the statutory test of harassment will be subjected to a top-down comparison. This involves a comparison of the statutory test for establishing a case of ground-related harassment pre- and post-transposition of the Directives. In section 4.4, the domestic approach to liability for ground-related harassment will be examined in light of Community law. It will be seen that notwithstanding that the Directives remain silent on the matter of liability, Community law nonetheless bears an impact upon the liability question. Tentative conclusions will be drawn in section 4.4.

4.2. *What Type of Conduct May Amount to Harassment?*

Acts of harassment can take a variety of forms. Harassment may be verbal (e.g. 'jokes'), written (e.g. displays) or physical (e.g. slapping a female's bottom). Harassment may be addressed to an identifiable other or it may be 'environmental'; it may be explicit, or subtle.[86] For example, if a disabled worker is persistently ignored by his fellow workers, this may amount to harassment. The distinction between *quid pro quo* harassment and hostile work environment harassment has been explained already in the analysis of EC harassment law. *Quid pro quo* harassment was at stake in *Driskel v. Peninsula Business Services LTD and others.*[87] In casu, Mrs Driskel had scheduled an interview with the head of her department for a promotion. One day before the interview, the employer had allegedly recommended to Mrs Driskel that, if she wanted to be successful, she should wear a short skirt and a see-through blouse showing plenty of cleavage. After the interview Mrs Driskel brought an internal complaint of sexual harassment which was, however, rejected. The Tribunal at first instance dismissed the applicant's complaints of sex discrimination (and unfair dismissal). In deciding on the sex discrimination complaint the Tribunal examined each incident of alleged sexual harassment *in se*. The EAT disagreed with this approach. It was *inter alia* stressed that in deciding on sexual harassment regard must be had to the *totality of successive incidents*. The EAT concluded a case of unlawful sex discrimination.[88]

86 Equal Opportunities Commission, 'types of harassment' at <www.eoc-law.org.uk> (last visited on 01-05-06).

87 *Driskel v. Peninsula Business Services LTD and others* [2000] IRLR 151 (EAT), paragraph 12. See also the unreported case of *Quereshi v. Victoria University of Manchester*, 21 June 1996, EAT/484/95 to which the EAT referred in paragraph 3 of its judgment in *Driskel*. In *Quereshi* the EAT had warned already that '(...) there is a tendency (..) where many evidentiary incidents or items are introduced, to be carried away by them and to treat each of the allegations, incidents or items as if they were themselves the subject of a complaint'.

88 The case shall be discussed in further detail in the passages to follow.

The approach adopted by the EAT in *Driskel* reaffirms the earlier stance taken by the EAT in the case of *Reed and Bull Information Systems Ttd v. Stedman.*[89] In that case the EAT had held already that in cases where a series of incidents occur Tribunals and courts should refrain from analysing each of these incidents in isolation, as if each of them were by themselves the object of the claim at hand. This view was based upon the approach adopted by the USA Federal Appeal Court in *USA v. Gail Knapp* where it was held as follows:

> 'Under the totality of circumstances analysis, the district court [the fact finding tribunal] should not carve the work environment into a series of incidents and then measure the harm occurring in each episode. Instead, the trier of each act must keep in mind that 'each successive episode has its predecessors, that the impact of the separate incidents may accumulate, and that the work environment created may exceed the sum of that individual episodes.'[90]

In other words where harassment consists of multiple incidents, 'ad hoc assessments' are to be avoided, for such assessments bear a risk that the impact of the totality of successive incidents at stake is overlooked. After all, the impact of each of the incidents assessed *in se* might be insignificant.

Hostile work environment harassment can either be specifically directed to a single person or it can soil the work environment as a whole, thus, without the reprehensible conduct being specifically targeted at an 'identifiable other'.[91] An example of the former type of harassment occurred in *Insitu Cleaning Co LTD and another v. HEADS.*[92] In casu, Mr Brown, who was the son of two of the four company's directors and himself a manager with the firm, said to Mrs Heads 'Hiya big tits'. The remark was made in the presence of a director and another employee. Mrs Head was found to have been a victim of unlawful sex discrimination, contrary to the SDA 1975. This case is *inter alia* important for the following reason. In *Insitu* the EAT established that, in addition to reprehensible acts of ground-related harassment which are persisted in after the alleged victim has made it clear that she regards such acts as objectionable, a sufficiently serious single incident act of harassment may also amount to an act of harassment under the Statutes.[93] To this effect, the following was held:

89 *Reed and Bull Information Systems Ltd v. Stedman* [1999] IRLR 300 (EAT).

90 *USA v. Gail Knapp* [1992] 955 Federal Reported, 2nd series at p. 546, cited by the EAT in *Reed and Bull Information Systems Ltd v. Stedman* (referred to in footnote 89 above), paragraph 28. See also the unreported case of *Quereshi v. Victoria University of Manchester*, 21 June 1996, EAT/484/95.

91 Bell 2004, p. 471.

92 *Insitu Cleaning Co Ltd and another v. HEADS* [1995] IRLR 4 (EAT).

93 In the earlier case of *Bracebridge Engineering Ltd v. Darby* [1990] IRLR 3 (EAT) it was held by the EAT that a single incident act of sexual harassment may constitute a detriment for the purposes of the SDA (see Article 6(2)(b) SDA) provided that it was sufficiently serious (see paragraph 6 of the *Insitu* case referred to above). In the earlier case of *Wadman v. Carpenter Farrer Partnership* [1993] IRLR 374 (EAT), cited by McColgan 1995, p. 182, the EAT had taken the opposite view: 'harassment indicates a degree of repetition rather than a single act' (p. 377).

'Whether a single act of verbal sexual harassment is sufficient to found a complaint is also a question of fact and degree. It seems to be the argument that because the Code [of Practice; MG][94] refers to 'unwanted conduct' it cannot be said that a single act can ever amount to harassment because until done and rejected it cannot be said that the conduct is 'unwanted'. We regard this argument as specious. If it were correct it would mean that a men was always entitled to argue that every act of harassment was different from the first and that he was testing to see if it was unwanted: in other words it would amount to a licence for harassment'.[95]

In the EAT's view the term 'unwanted' is essentially the same as 'unwelcome' or 'uninvited'.

As referred to earlier, hostile work environment may be anonymous in the sense that it need not be directed specifically at an individual.[96] In *Garbett and Others v. Sierotko*[97] female employees were covertly videoed in the toilets. Although the employees were ignorant of this fact the conduct was nonetheless held to amount to sexual harassment.[98] Anonymous hostile work environment harassment was also at stake in *Stewart v. Cleveland Guest Engineering Ltd.*[99] In this case, male workers displayed pictures of (half) naked women in the manufacturing area. Essentially, Ms Stewart's claims of sexual harassment were rejected both by the ET and by the EAT.

94 See section 3.1 above. As observed already the Code of Practice has sometimes functioned as a tool employed by the national courts in the interpretation of domestic harassment law.

95 Paragraph 11 of the judgment.

96 See also Bacik 2003, p. 155.

97 *Garbett and Others v. Sierotko*, 2406815/97 (ET) available at <www.eoc-law.org.uk>.

98 The ET's approach in *Garbett* deviates from the CA's initially adopted stance in *De Souza v. Automobile Association* [1986] IRLR 103 (CA). The question in that case was whether Ms *De Souza*, who had overheard a racial remark about herself, had suffered a 'detriment' for establishing direct race discrimination under the RRA 1976. The CA took the view that where the alleged discriminator did not intend and ought not to have reasonably anticipated that the (alleged) victim would become aware of words or acts subsequently complained of, such words or acts cannot amount to a 'detriment' for purposes of the Statute. See also Palmer, Gill *et al.* 2002, p. 796.
The approach adopted by the ET in *Garbett* is, however, in line with the stance adopted by the CA in *Garry v. London Borough of Ealing* [2001] IRLR, 681 (CA). In that case the CA rejected the stance adopted by the EAT which was essentially founded upon the adage that 'ignorance is bliss'. In casu the legal question was whether the persisting investigations into Mrs Garry for ethnic-related reasons and of which she had not been aware for most of the time, amounted to a detriment for purposes of the RRA. The EAT had taken the view that, given that Mrs Garry had been unaware of the investigations into her she could not have suffered 'less favourable treatment' for purposes of the RRA 1976. However, the CA correctly considered Mrs Garry's detriment as being 'obvious': the serious and lengthy investigations known to senior Council Officers had been detrimental to her, given that the attitude of these Officers to Mrs Garry and to her work was important both in the context of her present and future employment. The fact that Mrs Garry had been unaware of the investigations into her could not provide a defence for the employer if, after careful legal consideration, the treatment meted out to Mrs Garry had been held to constitute a detriment for purposes of the Statute. In deciding as it did the CA departed from its earlier stance in *De Souza v. Automobile Association* [1986] IRLR 103 (CA). For a further commentary on the *Garry* case, I refer to Moon 2001, p. 20-21.

99 *Stewart v. Cleveland Guest Engineering Ltd* [1994] IRLR 440 (EAT).

Hereafter the *Stewart* case will be discussed in further detail. It will become clear that the preposterous outcome of this case was due to a strict application by the courts of formal (comparative) equality.

In the above it has been illustrated what types of conduct may amount to harassment. In order to establish harassment legally, all elements of the statutory test will have to be proven. In section 4.3 hereafter this test will be expounded upon, both pre- and post-implementation of the RD, the EFD and the AETD.

4.3. *The Statutory Test for Establishing a Case of Ground-Related Harassment: a Top-Down Comparison*

4.3.1. Introduction

Hereafter, the statutory test for establishing a case of ground-related harassment will be examined upon both pre- and post-implementation of the RD, the EFD and the AETD. It should be emphasised at the outset that, with reference to Chapter 3,[100] the regulatory framework of harassment in its post-implementation format is characterised by fragmentation. This has been the consequence of the modus of implementation of EC law, which has occurred by means of governmental Regulations, rather than by the adoption of statutory Acts of Parliament. The consequences of this modus of implementation of supranational law have been illustrated in detail in Chapter 3 and need not be repeated at this juncture.[101] It is, however, called to mind that the pre-implementation approach is currently still highly significant. In the context of employment, the pre-implementation approach is valid law with respect to colour and nationality harassment cases. In section 4.3.2 hereafter, I will examine the statutory test of harassment pre-implementation of EC law. Regard will be given to both the statutory provisions and to the interpretation of these provisions by the courts. In section 4.3.3 the statutory test of harassment will be analysed in its post-implementation format. In section 4.3.4 both approaches will be compared in a brief amalgamated analysis.

4.3.2. Harassment Pre-Implementation of EC Law: a Direct Discrimination Approach

4.3.2.1. Introduction

Prior to the adoption of the Sex Discrimination Regulations 2005,[102] the Race Discrimination Regulations 2003[103] and the Disability Discrimination Regulations 2003,[104]

[100] Chapter 3, section 4.4.2.

[101] Chapter 3, section 4.4.2.

[102] *Employment Equality (Sex Discrimination) Regulations* 2005 (SI 2005/2467) which have transposed the AETD into domestic law. See generally Chapter 2.

[103] *Race Relations Act 1976 (Amendment) Regulations* 2003 (SI 2003/1626) which have transposed the RD into domestic law. See generally Chapter 2.

there was no explicit statutory provision on harassment in the SDA, the RRA and the DDA. Hence, write Hepple and others, in its pre-implementation format '(...) [the] UK law on discriminatory harassment [was] a judicial gloss on the Statutes'.[105] Pre-implementation, all claims of ground-related harassment were dependent upon proving a case of direct discrimination. The 'harassment as direct discrimination approach' has essentially been developed by the courts. As will be seen, fitting harassment into the legal straight-jacket of direct discrimination has been problematic and has at times resulted in fallacious legal reasoning.

As stated, the pre-implementation approach requires that harassment be construed as a case of direct discrimination. *Ergo*, the statutory elements of direct discrimination must be proven by the alleged victim. At this point it should be noted that the statutory test for establishing an instance of direct discrimination under the SDA and RRA, on the one hand, and the DDA, on the other, is fundamentally different.[106] Pre-implementation of the EFD the concept of direct discrimination did as such not exist in the DDA. Instead, the Act merely adopted a 'less favourable treatment' approach which could be justified. It is not the aim of this chapter to analyse all the legal intricacies of direct discrimination. Direct discrimination will be discussed henceforth in relation to harassment. Therefore, the DDA's approach to direct discrimination will not be considered in the analysis to follow. This can be justified with reference to the following. To the best knowledge of the author, no disability-related harassment cases have arisen under the DDA in its pre-implementation context. Currently, disability-related harassment cases are governed by the DDA 1995 as amended (post-implementation of the EFD). The post-implementation approach to harassment will be discussed in section 4.3.3 hereafter. The RRA and SDA (but not the DDA) have traditionally been regarded by the courts *in pari materiae*: precedents established in the context of the former Act have been applied in sex discrimination cases and *vice versa*. Sex-related harassment cases which have been decided by the courts on the basis of the pre-implementation approach are of prime importance to legal reasoning *currently* still to be adopted in harassment cases which arise under the RRA and which are *not* governed by the law post-implementation of the RD.

104 *Disability Discrimination Act 1995 (Amendment) Regulations 2003* (SI 2003/1673) which have transposed the EFD (insofar as the ground disability is concerned) into domestic law. See generally Chapter 2.

105 Hepple, Coussey and Choudhury 2000, p. 39.

106 See the important case of *Clark v. Novacold Ltd* [1999] IRLR 318 (CA). In that case the CA stressed the different nature of the SDA/RRA, on the one hand, and the DDA, on the other: 'Contrary to what might be reasonably assumed, the exercise of interpretation is not facilitated by familiarity with pre-existing legislation prohibiting discrimination in the field of employment (and elsewhere) on the grounds of sex (Sex Discrimination Act 1975) and race (Race Discrimination Act 1976). Indeed, it may be positively misleading to approach the 1995 Act with assumptions and concepts familiar from experience of the workings of the 1975 Act and the 1976 Act.' (paragraph 30 of the judgment).

4.3.2.2. *Conceptualising Harassment as Direct Discrimination: the Statutory Elements*

In order to establish a case of harassment in terms of direct discrimination the plaintiff will need to prove the following: (1) 'less favourable treatment'; (2) on grounds of a forbidden ground; and (3) which constitutes a 'detriment' for him or her.[107] It follows that like in EC law mere bullying is not covered. Instead the reprehensible treatment on which the complaint is based must be linked to a forbidden ground.[108] A motive or intention to discriminate does not play a determining role in establishing direct discrimination, and therefore harassment.[109] In the *Driskel* case referred to above, the EAT did not accept as a defence that the sexually provocative remark was 'flippant' and ought not be taken seriously:

> 'It is irrelevant that he [the head of department] never expected her to turn up for the interview in a sexually provocative dress – what is relevant is that by this remark (flippant or not) he was undermining her dignity as a woman when, as a heterosexual, he would never similarly have treated a man.'[110]

107 Section 1(1)(a) RRA in conjunction with Section 3(4) RRA. Section 1(1)(a) RRA provides as follows: 'A person discriminates against another in any circumstances relevant for the purposes of any provision of this Act if – (a) on racial grounds he treats that other less favourably than he treats or would treat other persons'. Section 3(4) RRA reads as follows: 'A comparison of the case of a person of a particular racial group with that of a person not of that group under Section 1(1) (…) must be such that the relevant circumstances in the one case are the same, or not materially different, in the other'. The equivalent Sections in the SDA are Section 1(1) SDA in conjunction with Section 5(3) SDA. The 'detriment' element is contained in Section 4(2)(c) RRA. The equivalent Section in the SDA is Section 6(2)(b) SDA.

108 See in this respect also the following observation by Dine and Watt 1995, p. 349: 'Where a discrimination claim is made, there must be some real connection between the gender of the harassee and the action of the perpetrator; for the SDA 1975 prohibits discrimination on the grounds of sex rather than bad treatment simpliciter'. See also *Zafar v. Glasgow City Council* [1998] IRLR 36 (HL). In casu, the House of Lords unanimously took the view that the applicant, a UK citizen of Indian origin, had not been discriminated against under the RRA 1976. According to the House of Lords, the fact that the applicant had been treated in a way well below the standards of a 'reasonable employer' did not shed light on the question whether he had been treated less favourably on grounds of race: '…the conduct of a hypothetical reasonable employer is irrelevant. The alleged discriminator may or may not be a reasonable employer. If he is not a reasonable employer, he might well have treated another employee in just the same unsatisfactory way as he treated the complainant, in which case he would not have treated the complainant 'less favourably' for the purposes of the Act of 1976' (paragraph 11, per Lord Brown Wilkinson).

109 *James v. Eastleigh Borough Council*, [1990] 2 All ER, 607 (HL).

110 Paragraph 14 of the judgment by the EAT in *Driskel v. Peninsula Business Services LTD and others* [2000] IRLR 151 (EAT). See also *Reed and Bull Information Systems Ltd v. Stedman* [1999] IRLR 300 (EAT) where it was held that 'Motive and intention of the alleged discriminator is not an essential ingredient [for establishing harassment], as in any other direct discrimination case, although it will often be a relevant factor to take into account. Lack of intent is not a defence'. (paragraph 25 of the judgment).

In the context of employment, harassment claims have hinged upon the claim of a 'detriment' under Section 4(2)(c) RRA (Section 6(2)(b) SDA). These Sections stipulate in essence, that an employer is prohibited from discriminating against an employee by dismissing him or her, or by subjecting him or her to any other 'detriment' (including therefore, 'harassment'). It follows from *Thomas v. Robinson* (discussed immediately hereafter) that, although in practice the 'less favourable treatment' requirement often overlaps with the detriment requirement, both requirements must nonetheless be distinguished. In other words, a person can be treated 'less favourably' and yet, she may suffer no detriment.[111] This can be illustrated with reference to *Thomas v. Robinson*.[112] In casu, the facts were as follows.

Ms Robinson who was English and of black Afro-Caribbean origin had been subjected to harassing language by her colleague worker, Miss Thomas, who was white. Miss Thomas had asked Ms Robinson where her parents lived to which the latter had replied that her parents had recently returned to the Caribbean. Miss Thomas then thereupon said: 'they [Caribbean people] come over here and scrounge off the system then go back'. Although the offensive language had not succinctly been directed at Ms Robinson, it could clearly be interpreted as being directed at her parents. As a result of another work-related incident, Ms Robinson was dismissed for misconduct, whereas Miss Thomas was given an oral warning in respect of the racially abusive language indicated above. Ms Robinson lodged a complaint of race discrimination against the employer and against Miss Thomas. In legal proceedings before the Employment Tribunal Ms Robinson made it clear that she had been deeply offended by the racially abusive language. The Tribunal had thereupon prevented counsel for the respondent from cross-examining Ms Robinson on the effects the remarks had had upon her. In the Tribunal's view all racial abuse constitutes 'detrimental' treatment and thus an instance of harassment can immediately be established. Upon appeal, the EAT, however, considered this reasoning to be an error in law. It upheld the fact that 'harassment' involves two legal elements. The first is the targeting of the person being harassed. The second is that as a consequence of this the individual victim has suffered a detriment. In the EAT's view '[t]here are some work environments in which (undesirable though it may be) racial abuse is given and taken in good part by members of different ethnic groups. In such cases the mere making of a racist remark could not be regarded as a detriment'.[113]

Hence, the distinctness of both requirements was stressed, although the EAT did acknowledge that establishment of the second element will usually be extremely easy. By simply assuming the second element the ET had, however, erred in law

111 The notion of 'detriment' has been interpreted broadly. In *Shamoon v. Chief Constable of the Royal Ulter Constabulary* [2003] IRLR 285 (HL) it was, for example, held that the establishment of a detriment does not require demonstration of some physical or economic consequence. It was moreover held that in deciding on the detriment requirement it must be questioned whether a reasonable worker would or might take the view that in all circumstances it was to the detriment of the complainant (per Lord Hope of Craighead]. See moreover *De Souza v. Automobile Association* [1986] IRLR 103 (CA).

112 *Thomas v. Robinson* [2003] IRLR 7 (EAT, per Mr Judge J R Reid QC).

113 Paragraph 27 of the judgment.

and therefore the case was remitted to a differently constituted ET. In deciding as it did, the EAT had taken into consideration the fact that Ms Robinson and Miss Thomas were on friendly terms after the incident.

It follows from the *Robinson* case above that it is vital for an applicant to indicate the detrimental impact an act of harassment (or discrimination more generally) has had on him or her. Apparently, detriment cannot simply be assumed, although caution should be exercised by the courts that an alleged victim's claim is not readily dismissed with reference to 'over-sensitiveness' (on the part of the latter).

4.3.2.3. Conceiving Harassment as Direct Discrimination: the Comparative Exercise

As stated above in section 4.3.2.2 the plaintiff will have to show that he has been treated 'less favourably' by the alleged perpetrator than the latter treats (or would treat) other persons in the same circumstances (Section 3(4) RRA and Section 5(3) SDA). In other words, the statutory discrimination Acts do not prohibit sex- or race-based treatment as such but only treatment of that kind which is discriminatory.[114] A strict, grammatical, interpretation of these provisions brings with it that an employer who, for example, harasses a white and black employee indistinctly is freed from liability. In other words, the statutory provisions place great emphasis upon a 'comparative exercise'. This is the regrettable result of the application of formal, consistency, equality which permits *both* treating persons equally badly *and* treating them equally well. As such, formal equality pursues 'equality' as an end in itself whereby it remains insensitive to the substantive contents of a given treatment.[115]

The strict application of formal equality resulted in fallacious legal reasoning by the first instance Tribunal in *Porcelli*.

Ms Porcelli, a female laboratory technician, was subjected to a course of abusive, indecent and tormenting treatment by two male colleagues. This also included unwanted physical contact and intimidation. The facts of the case show that the treatment complained of was plainly sexual in nature. The Tribunal at first instance nonetheless drew the staggering conclusion that Ms Porcelli had not been discriminated against on grounds of sex: any disliked male co-worker would have been subjected to equally odious (albeit different) treatment as Ms Porcelli's. Hence, it could not be ascertained that the treatment was carried out 'less favourably on grounds of sex'. No sex discrimination was therefore established. Upon appeal, the EAT decided in favour of Ms Porcelli upon which the employer cross-appealed to the (Scottish) Court of Session.[116] Rather than a grammatical approach, Lord President Emslie for the Court held on to a deliberate interpretation of the relevant provisions in the SDA: '(…) 'sexual harassment' [is] a particularly degrading and unacceptable form of treatment which it must be taken to have been the intention of Parliament to

114 McColgan 1995, p. 182.

115 Holtmaat 2004, p. 8, who has observed that 'the evil which [formal equality legislation] aims to combat is the inequality as such of a given treatment, rather than the substantive contents of such treatment' (*'Het kwaad dat met [formele gelijkebehandelingswetgeving] wordt bestreden is de ongelijkheid van de behandeling als zodanig, niet de inhoud van de behandeling'*).

116 *Strathclyde Regional Council v. Porcelli* [1986] IRLR 134 (Court of Session).

restrain'.[117] The Court of Session in *Porcelli* developed the principle that where the form of the harassment is sexual, that of itself established 'less favourable treatment' on grounds of sex. Lord President Emslie's message was that, regardless of 'equality of overall unpleasantness',[118] repulsive treatment which is meted out by a perpetrator because of the fact that the victim is a woman materially differs from unpleasant treatment inflicted on a male worker, who is equally disliked. In President Emslie's view the sexual harassment complained of '(…) was plainly adopted against Mrs Porcelli because she was a woman. It was a particular kind of weapon, based upon the sex of the victim, which (…) would not have been used against an equally disliked man'.[119] It was properly held by Lord Grieve that the offensive remarks which were subject to the complaint '(…) were examples of the use by [the perpetrators] of a 'sexual sword' and were of a sufficiently material nature to be to the respondent's detriment'.[120]

In summary, in *Porcelli* the view was taken that in cases where the incidents of abuse are gender or race specific there is no need for a comparison. In other words, in such cases the required causal link between a person's sex and the less favourable treatment received as a result thereof is *ipso facto* established.[121] What is vital is that the plaintiff's gender (or race) constitutes *the reason* for the harassing acts by the perpetrator.[122]

In the present author's view, the approach adopted by the CS was doubtlessly correct, both on principle and for legal reasons. Ms Porcelli's dignity as a woman had clearly been violated; she had moreover suffered a detriment and therefore, on principle, it should be quite irrelevant how a man would have been treated 'in similar circumstances'.[123] Upon legal analysis the outcome in Porcelli is proper too.

117 Paragraph 10 of the judgment.

118 Paragraph 10 of the judgment.

119 Paragraph 9 of the judgment.

120 Paragraph 32 of the judgment.

121 This approach is in line with the later decision by the House of Lords in *James v. Eastleigh Borough Council,* [1990] 2 All ER, 607 (HL) which has already been discussed in Chapter 3. In *James* 'pensionable age' was used as the distinguishing criterion which itself was 'gender-based' given the different statutory pensionable ages for women (60) and men (65). The Law Lords employed the so-called 'but for' test in order to establish whether sex discrimination had occurred. Under this test sex discrimination is established, once the conclusion has been drawn that the treatment on which the complaint is based would not have been meted out to the alleged victim *'but for'* the fact that he was a man (or, as the case might be, a woman). See in this context McColgan 1995, p. 183, who has observed that 'Even had the Court of Sessions not reached its decision in Porcelli, the same effect would have resulted from the decision of the House of Lords in *James v. Eastleigh Borough Council*'. The 'but for' test has most recently been affirmed in *R v. Immigration Officer at Prague Airport & Anor ex parte ERRC and others* [2004] UKHL, cited by Cohen 2005, p. 14.

122 See also *British Telecommunications Plc v. Williams,* 1997 IRLR 668, where it was held by Morison J that 'it would be no defence to a complaint of sexual harassment that a person of the other sex would have been similarly so treated'. This case has been cited from De Marco 2004, p. 31. See moreover McColgan 2005, p. 60.

123 See also Gerards 2004b, p. 106: 'In cases of harassment it is simply the [offensive] act and the therefrom resulting infringement of a person's dignity which is considered reprehensible. Therefore harassment is prohibited.' (*'Bij intimidatie zijn het eenvoudigweg het handelen en de* →

Applying a 'but for' test to the case at hand leads to the conclusion that Ms Porcelli had been a victim of direct sex discrimination indeed.[124] The relevant question to be posed under this test is the following: *Would Ms Porcelli have received the same treatment as would have been meted out to a man 'but for' her sex*? An affirmative answer is inescapable: Ms Porcelli would not have been subjected to the particular (sexually tainted) treatment complained of had she been a man.[125] Indeed, it can be legitimately questioned whether a man could find himself at all in 'similar circumstances'? It is difficult to contemplate who is the relevant male equivalent in sexual harassment cases. As referred to earlier, feminist doctrine has emphasised the causal link between sexually harassing acts, on the one hand, and women's subordinate position in society, which is male-dominated,[126] on the other. In McKinnon's view, for example, *only women* and not men can be the victim of sexual harassment, where evil finds its source in women's lower and secondary status in society.[127] In other words, women's ascribed secondary status makes it that they are much easier (if not the sole) victims of sexual harassment, than men. In this sense, sexual harassment cases could be paralleled with pregnancy-discrimination cases, which equally lack a relevant counterpart with which a pregnant woman could be compared.[128]

In contrast to the common sense approach adopted by the Court of Session in *Porcelli*, the strict application of formal equality resulted in a senseless outcome reached by the EAT in the *Stewart* case[129], earlier referred to. This case concerns anonymous hostile work environment harassment.

Ms Stewart worked as an inspector with Cleveland Guest, an engineering business. She took offence to the display of pictures of (half) naked women put up by male colleague workers in the manufacturing area. She reported her feelings of distress to management, which showed itself to be unprepared to undertake action to remove the displays. In their view, the pictures were not embarrassing nor abusive. Ms Stewart felt compelled to stay away from work and she had become depressed, partially too, due to the reaction of some of her colleague workers after she had complained about the pictures. Ms Stewart *inter alia* lodged a complaint of unlawful sex discrimination under the SDA. In agreement with the view which had been

aantasting van de persoonlijke waardigheid die daaruit voortvloeit, die laakbaar worden geacht. Daarom wordt intimidatie verboden.').

124 See McColgan 1995, p. 183. See also footnote 120 above where the 'but for' test has been explained in the context of the *James* case.

125 In U.S. case law this has become known as the 'sex-plus'-argument: the contested acts are only inflicted upon women because they are women and not upon men. A woman is merely required to prove that the acts were inflicted upon her because she was a woman which obviates the need for a comparison with a male equivalent. See Curtin 1984, p. 426.

126 The (in society) institutionalised male dominance or power is captured by the feminist notion of 'patriarchism'.

127 MacKinnon 1979, p. 174-175.

128 This has indeed been recognised by the ECJ and thereupon by the domestic courts. In pregnancy cases a substantive equality approach has been adopted: see *Dekker v. Stichting Vormingscentrum voor Jong Volwassenen* (Case C-177/88), [1990] ECR I-3941; *Webb v. EMO Air Cargo* (Case C-32/93), [1994] ECR I-3567.

129 *Stewart v. Cleveland Guest Engineering Ltd* [1994] IRLR 440 (EAT, per Mr Justice Mummery).

taken by the ET, the EAT was also of the opinion that the applicant had not been a victim of sexual harassment discrimination: since the pictures were displayed 'neutrally' they could be equally offensive to a man. On this point, the EAT recalled the decision by the ET which was as follows: 'A man might well find this sort of display as offensive as the applicant did... We are driven to the conclusion that the nature of the treatment by way of display of the pictures would have been the same to men and women.'[130]

In the present author's view, the ET and the EAT by deciding as they did appear to have wholly missed the point.[131] It is argued that pin-up pictures of naked women at the work place have, to say the least, a different detrimental impact upon women's dignity than men's.[132] This was also argued by counsel for the appellant:

> 'A man's objection to such a display would be based on other grounds (e.g. moral grounds) not on the ground of his sex. As the pictures depicted women, and not men, a man, even one who objected to the pictures, would not have found the pictures offensive in the same way as Miss Stewart did. The display was not in an environment where men were in the minority, nor in an environment where men, as opposed to women, were subjected to suggestive remarks.'[133]

Hence, men might find sexually tainted pictures offensive on a more general, neutral level. In contrast, (most) women object to such pictures, for they inherently undermine women's dignity and equal worth. Such pictures foster an image of women as sexual objects, rather than professional co-workers of equal status. They transmit the idea that women at work are ultimately appreciated for sexual, rather than for professional reasons. In other words, such pictures are not gender neutral whatsoever but they clearly have a gendered sexual impact. This point was, however, entirely overlooked by the courts whilst deciding on the *Stewart* case. Lastly, even if it were accepted that (some) men find such pictures equally objectionable, this very fact would not diminish the negative effect such pictures have upon (most) women's dignity.[134]

In the aforementioned case of *Insitu Cleaning*[135] (arisen after *Stewart*) the EAT did take into account the gendered impact of the treatment that was subject to the complaint. The employer had argued that the remark 'hiya big tits' was not sex-related, and that it consequently did not pass the statutory test of sexual harassment discrimination. In the employer's view, a similar remark could have been inflicted upon a man, for instance, with reference to his beard or balding head. The EAT

130 See paragraph 20 of the judgment where reference was made to the decision by the ET in first instance.

131 See for major criticism also Bacik 2003, p. 155. Bacik discusses the *Stewart* case in light of relevant U.S. law and in light of academic doctrine. Also McColgan 1995, p. 184-186.

132 See McColgan 1995, p. 185: 'The issue is, in reality, that the display of nude pictures simply does not affect men in the same way as it affects women (....) exposure to pictures of nude women can never amount to the same kind of injury for a man as it can for a woman.'

133 Paragraph 27 of the judgment.

134 Hepple, Coussey, Choudhury 2000, p. 39.

135 *Insitu Cleaning CO LTD and another v. HEADS* [1995] IRLR 4 (EAT).

rightly considered this argument 'absurd': 'A remark by a man about a woman's breasts cannot sensibly be equated with a remark by a woman about a bald head or a beard. One is sexual the other is not'.[136] It goes without saying that any other conclusion would have been a delusion.

Race-specific, environmental, harassment was at stake in *Chief Constable of the Kent Constabulary v. Kufeji*.[137]

In casu, a white police officer subjected a black Constable to racial harassment by sending him, and the other white colleagues, a holiday postcard from South Africa. The card showed a picture of bare breasted black African women and an offensive and degrading comment, insinuating prostitution, was written on the back of the card. The combination of picture and text rendered the card a race specific communication: it would and did hurt differently the feelings of a black than of a white person. In such circumstances, the EAT stated, the need for a comparison does not become automatically redundant. However, the elements of 'less favourable treatment on grounds of race' become implied by the facts of the case at hand.[138] It is this approach which could and should have been applied in the Stewart case discussed above.

With reference to the above cases, the following interim conclusion could be drawn. The above case law shows that two forms of harassment cases[139] exist: (1) cases in which the repugnant treatment is considered by the court as *race or gender specific*. In such cases the need for a comparison is obviated (*Porcelli, Insitu, Kufeji*), and, (2) cases in which the harassing acts are (sometimes wrongly) not considered as being race or gender-specific and which call for a comparative exercise. The adoption of a comparative exercise risks, however, illogical legal outcomes (*Stewart*). However, since the House of Lords dictum in the Pearce case, the distinction between these two types of harassment cases is no longer valid. It is to this case that I turn now.

4.3.2.4. The House of Lords' Judgment in Pearce

The unanimous decision by the House of Lords in *Macdonald v. Advocate General for Scotland/ Pearce v. Governing Body of Mayfield School*[140] undermines the common sense approach adopted by the Court of Session in *Porcelli*. *Pearce* concerned a female teacher who was 'emotionally compelled' to abandon her teaching job after a sustained, venomous, anti-lesbian and abusive campaign by her pupils.[141] The pupils

136 Paragraph 9 of the judgment.

137 *Chief Constable of the Kent Constabulary v. Kufeji EAT 1135 00 (unreported)* available from Industrial Relations Law Bulletin 669, July 2001. An extract could also be found at <http://www.eoc-law.org.uk>.

138 The same approach was moreover taken in the later case of *Thomas v. Robinson* [2003] IRLR 7 (EAT). The case has been discussed above (see section 4.3.2.2) in the context of the detriment requirement. Since the language used was race-specific the applicant was not required to prove that a person of another racial group would have been treated differently.

139 See Palmer, Gill *et al.* 2002, p. 793 *et. seq.*

140 *Macdonald (Appellant) v. Advocate General for Scotland (Respondent) and Pearce (Appellant) v. Governing Body of Mayfield School (Respondents)* [2003] UKHL 34 (judgment of 19 June 2003).

141 At the material time sexual orientation discrimination was not yet prohibited in English law. As will be seen in great detail in Chapter 7 sexual orientation discrimination has only been →

inter alia shouted at her words like 'lesbian', 'lemon', 'lezzie'; 'lesbian shit' and 'pussy'. Moreover, in her presence, the children made comments about the smell of fish and cat food and Ms Pearce at one occasion found an opened tin of cat food in the pocket of her coat. On behalf of Ms Pearce, and with reference to *Porcelli*, the argument was made that, given that the children's campaign of verbal abuse referred to Ms Pearce's lesbian orientation, and given that any of the maligning terms used by the pupils were applicable only to a woman (and not to a man) the incidents of abuse were 'gender specific' and thus, amounting *ipso facto* to discrimination on grounds of sex. This line of reasoning was decisively rejected by the Law Lords: circumventing the comparative exercise was not permitted in their view. It was made crystal-clear that a comparison is required in all discrimination law cases, including those concerning harassment. Lord Rodger of Earlsferry held that:

> '(...) on no view is the decision [in Porcelli] authority for holding that sex discrimination in the form of sexual harassment can be established without using a male comparator. In so far as the reasoning in later decisions proceeds on the basis that Porcelli is authority for such a proposition, it is misconceived (...).'[142]

With similar effect, Lord Nicolls held as follows:

> 'In some cases [with reference to *Porcelli* and *British Telecommunications Plc v. Williams*; MG] (...) it has been suggested that if the form (with emphasis) of the harassment is sexual, that of itself constitutes less favourable treatment on the ground of sex. When the gender of the victim dictates the form of the harassment, that of itself, it is said, indicates the reason for the harassment, namely it is on the ground of the sex of the victim. Degrading treatment of this nature differs materially from unpleasant treatment inflicted on an equally disliked male colleague, regardless of equality of overall unpleasantness [with reference to *Porcelli*; MG]. Because the form of the harassment is gender specific, there is no need to look for a male comparator. It would be no defence to a complaint of sexual harassment that a person of the opposite sex would have been similarly treated [with reference to *British Telecommunications Plc v. Williams*; MG] (...) I respectfully think some of these observations go too far. They cannot be reconciled with the language or the scheme of the statute. The fact that the harassment is gender specific in form cannot be regarded as of itself establishing conclusively that the reason for the harassment is gender based: 'on the ground of her sex'. It will certainly point in that direction. But this does not dispense with the need for the tribunal of fact to be satisfied that the reason why the victim was being harassed was her sex (...).'[143]

prohibited in English law since 2003. This being the case, Ms Pearce could merely challenge the case on the basis of sex discrimination law. However, since 'sexual orientation', rather than 'sex' constituted the reason for the harassing acts complained of her case was bound to fail. This element of the case shall be discussed further in Chapter 7. At this juncture the focus is merely upon that part of the case which concerns the issue of the 'comparative exercise'.

142 Paragraph 188 of the judgment.

143 Paragraphs 16 and 17 of the judgment.

The requirement of a comparator was most recently (in 2004) upheld by the EAT in *Brumfitt v. Ministry of Defence*[144] in which the EAT adopted the view that

> 'the fact that a man uses offensive words of a sexual nature in conversation with a woman does not constitute discrimination unless it can be shown or inferred that this was less favourable treatment than the man would have meted out to another man in a comparable situation.'[145]

It is worth observing that in *Brumfitt* counsel for the applicant had argued that the AETD which contains a freestanding prohibition of sexual harassment could already form the subject of a complaint under the (unamended) 1976 ETD. In light of this counsel for the applicant invited the EAT to refer a preliminary question to the ECJ on the correct interpretation of the SDA in light of the 1976 ETD *and* Directive 2002/73/EC (which aims to amend the former). However, this argument was decisively rejected by the court essentially by reason of the fact that the Member States are not required to give effect to Directive 2002/73/EC until October 2005. In current times the stance adopted by the EAT with respect to the application of EC equality Directives (in casu: Directive 2002/73/EC) prior to the expiry of the implementation deadline can be criticised with reference to the *Mangold* judgment recently decided by the ECJ.[146] As referenced in Chapter 2, the ECJ decided in *Mangold* that the national court is under a legal duty to interpret domestic law in conformity with the spirit of a Community Directive even when the deadline for transposition of the Directive has not yet expired.

It will be illustrated hereafter that by virtue of EC implemented law, the comparator requirement insisted on by the Law Lords in Pearce and by the EAT in *Brumfitt* has been overtaken by a much more favourable, flexible and common sense approach to harassment. However, as stated, *Pearce* remains the applicable authority for those cases of harassment which were carved out from the implementation process and which have been highlighted at the outset of the analysis (see section 4.3.1 above).

4.3.3. Harassment Post-Implementation of EC Law

4.3.3.1. Harassment: a Freestanding Approach

Post-implementation of EC law, the law on harassment has been liberated from the rigidities inherent to the comparative model of discrimination. Post-implementation, harassment has become an independent ground of complaint. Harassment remains regulated within the discrimination law framework, however, as referred to earlier in the context of EC law, this framework has been reconceived with the effect that the comparative model has made room for a 'dignity and participation approach'.

144 *Brumfit v. (1) Ministry of Defence (2) Sergeant JJ Fitzpatrick* Appeal No. UK EAT/1004/MAA.
145 Paragraph 18 of the judgment by the EAT.
146 *Mangold v. Helm* (Case C-144/04) of 22 November 2005 available at <www.europa.eu.int>.

The latter correlates with the 'deontological justice model'[147] which diminishes the importance of the comparative exercise to the benefit of substantive justice.

Regulation 5 of the Race Discrimination Regulations 2003 complements Section 3 of the RRA 1976 with a new Section 3A which reads as follows:

> 'Harassment
> 3A.- (1) A person subjects another to harassment in any circumstances relevant for the purposes of any provision referred to in Section 1(1B) where, on grounds of race or ethnic or national origins, he engages in unwanted conduct which has the purpose or effect of-
>
> (a) violating that other person's dignity, or
> (b) creating an intimidating, hostile, degrading, humiliating or offensive environment for him.
> (2) Conduct shall be regarded as having the effect specified in paragraph a or b of subsection (1) only if, having regard to all the circumstances, including in particular the perception of that other person, it should reasonably be considered of having that effect.'

In the employment area, newly adopted Section 3A is thus merely applicable in respect of the grounds 'race', and/or 'ethnic origin' and/or 'national origin' (to the exclusion therefore of 'colour' and 'nationality').

A counterpart provision has been inserted into the DDA 1995 by the Disability Discrimination Regulations 2003. A new Section 3B of the DDA 1995 as amended currently provides as follows:

> 'Harassment
> (1) For the purposes of this Part, a person subjects a disabled person to harassment where, for a reason which relates to the disabled person's disability, he engages in unwanted conduct which has the purpose of effect of-
> (a) violating the disabled person's dignity, or
> (b) creating an intimidating, hostile, degrading, humiliating or offensive environment for him.
> (2) Conduct shall be regarded as having the effect referred to in paragraph (a) or (b) of subsection 1 only if, having regard to all the circumstances, including in particular the perception of the disabled person, it should reasonably be considered as having that effect.' [148]

This provision may merely be relied upon by persons who qualify as a 'disabled person' for purposes of the Statute.[149]

Regulation 5 of the Sex Discrimination Regulations 2005 inserts a new Section 4A into the SDA. It provides as follows:

147 Quinn 2004, p. 9. See also Chapter 2.

148 It should be noted that that counterpart provisions also exist in relation to the grounds sexual orientation and religion and belief. See Regulation 5 of the S.O. Regulations (The Employment Equality (Sexual Orientation) Regulations 2003, SI 2003, No. 1661) and Regulation 5 of the R&B Regulations (The Employment Equality (Religion or Belief) Regulations 2003, SI 2003, No. 1660).

149 The meaning of a 'disabled person' for purposes of the DDA 1995 (as amended) will be discussed in detail in Chapter 8.

'4A.- (1) For the purposes of this Act, a person subjects a woman to harassment if-
(a) on the ground of her sex, he engages in unwanted conduct that has the purpose or effect-
(i) of violating her dignity, or
(ii) of creating an intimidating, hostile, degrading, humiliating or offensive environment for her,

[sex-based harassment; MG]
(b) he engages in any form of unwanted verbal, non-verbal or physical conduct of a sexual nature that has the purpose or effect
(i) of violating her dignity, or
(ii) of creating an intimidating, hostile, degrading, humiliating or offensive environment for her, or

[sexual harassment; MG]
(c) on the ground of her rejection of or submission to unwanted conduct of a kind mentioned in paragraph (a) or (b), he treats her less favourably than he would treat her had she not rejected, or submitted to, the conduct.

[quid pro quo harassment; MG]
(2) Conduct shall be regarded as having the effect mentioned in sub-paragraph (i) or (ii) of subsection (1)(a) or (b) only if, having regard to all the circumstances, including in particular the perception of the woman, it should reasonably be considered having that effect.
(...)
(5) Subsection (1) is to be read as applying equally to the harassment of men, and for that purpose shall have effect with such modifications as are requisite.
(...)'

These definitions demonstrate that harassment has become a free-standing form of discrimination and thus the House of Lords *dictum* in *Pearce* (explicitly requiring a comparison) has been trumped by obligations placed upon the government by EC law. With respect to the aforementioned definitions, the following can be stated. Firstly, in contrast to the Directives, English law imposes alternative, not cumulative, conditions: the reprehensible conduct must *either* have the purpose or effect of violating the victim's dignity *or* of creating a hostile work environment. Imposing cumulative conditions would breach the 'non-regression' clauses contained in the Directives. These stipulate that implementation of the Directives may not result in a reduced level of protection compared with the hitherto existing one, which merely required that one of both conditions be proven.[150] Secondly, the definitions of harassment in the SDA and RRA (not DDA) provide that the harassing conduct must be 'on grounds of' (rather than 'related to', as is required by the Directives) a protected ground. McColgan has taken the view that the 'on grounds of' formulation '*is tainted by the comparator-driven approach*' and that it would be a wrong implementation of the Directives, if this approach remained embedded within the analysis of

150 *Consultation Document, Towards Equality and Diversity, implementing the Employment and Race Directives* 2001, p. 24.

harassment.[151] This is clearly true, given that the Directives specify that harassment 'related to' a forbidden ground is *deemed* to be a form of discrimination thus reflecting a dignity model of equality. McColgan has furthermore warned that the 'on grounds of' approach may leave possible cavities in legal protection from ground-related harassment. As follows from Lord Nicolls' speech in the *Pearce* case, the fact that the treatment complained of is ground-specific does not warrant the *a priori* conclusion that (therefore) the treatment is 'on grounds of' sex (or race). Hence, in 'ground-specific' harassment cases, proof is still required that, either the reason for the treatment is the person's sex (or race), or, that it was sexual in nature.[152] The Directives' 'related to' formulation appears to set a wider and more flexible standard which has to be adhered to by the courts whilst rendering judgments on complaints of harassment. After all, domestic courts are under a legal duty to ensure the full effectiveness of Community law.[153] Thirdly, in conformity with EC law, *quid pro quo* harassment has merely been regulated for the ground sex (Section 4A (1) under (c)). This reflects a logical approach in light of the very nature of this ground for discrimination. This point has been explained already in the context of EC law above.

4.3.3.2. *An Objective or Subjective Test for Establishing Harassment?*

A last comment before proceeding with the issue of liability concerns the objectivity or subjectivity of the test for establishing harassment. The definitions of harassment referred to above stipulate that

> 'conduct shall be regarded as having the effect (...) [of violating the person's dignity or of creating a hostile working environment; MG] only if, having regard to all the circumstances, including in particular the perception of that other person, it should reasonably be considered of having that effect'.

The law requires thus that both the individual perception of the victim and that of a 'reasonable person' be taken into account, which renders the test both objective and subjective.[154] This concurs with the pre-implementation approach adopted in the *Driskel* case,[155] referred to earlier in the analysis. In *Driskel* the EAT held that

> 'the ultimate judgment, sexual harassment or no, reflects an objective assessment by the Tribunal of all the facts. That said, amongst the factors to be considered are the applicant's

151 McColgan 2005, p. 58. See also Clarke 2006, p. 167-169, who has warned that the 'on grounds of' formulation bears the danger that the freestanding approach to harassment in EC law 'becomes meaningless, and [that] the comparator is reintroduced' (p. 168).

152 McColgan 2005, p. 58.

153 See Chapter 2 with references to the relevant case law by the ECJ.

154 The 'reasonable person's standard' has been criticised in the (feminist) literature which has strived for the adoption of a 'reasonable women's standard'. There is an alleged discrepancy between the perceptions of men and women in deciding on whether a given conduct amounts to sex-based or sexual harassment. For further reading on this matter the author refers to Blumenthal 1998 and Ehrenreich 1990.

155 *Driskel v. Peninsula Business Services LTD and others* [2000] IRLR 151 (EAT).

subjective perception of that which is the subject of complaint and the understanding, motive and intention of the alleged discriminator'.[156]

It is, however, emphasised that although the perpetrator's intent might be one of more factors to be taken into account by the courts whilst assessing the act of harassment complained of, lack of intent on the part of the perpetrator is not a defence.

In the present author's view the mixed objective/subjective test reflects a proper approach, *a fortiori* in light of the fact that harassment cannot be justified. The subjective view of the victim has been prioritised in the test given that the latter's perception must *'in particular'* be taken into account. It therefore appears that the objective element of the test foremost plays a role in carving out liability for harassment in such cases where the victim's reaction to the acts complained of could 'reasonably' be said to be over-sensitive.

4.3.4. The Pre- and Post-Implementation Approaches to 'Harassment' Compared

It follows from the above analysis that post-implementation of EC law, the direct discrimination approach to harassment, which requires a comparison of the treatment to which the alleged victim was subjected with the treatment to which an appropriate comparator was or would have been subjected, has been replaced by an autonomous wrong which does not require a comparator, although it does require a link between harassment, on the one hand, and a forbidden ground, on the other. It has also been shown that the post-implementation approach does not apply across the board. The harassment as 'direct discrimination' approach is still valid law with respect to claims of harassment on grounds of colour and/or nationality in (*inter alia*) employment. This unsatisfactory approach has been the result of the modus of implementation of EC law. Post-implementation of the Directives, the comparative approach to harassment is still latently represented in the 'on grounds of' formulation adopted by the relevant Sections in the RRA and SDA. This formulation should have been repealed and replaced by a requirement that the harassing acts which form the subject of the complaint are 'related to' a protected status. It is for the domestic courts to ensure that the comparator element is not relaunched and that domestic harassment and non-discrimination law is interpreted in light of Community law.

[156] Paragraph 12 of the judgment. See also *Reed and Bull Information Systems Ltd v. Stedman* [1999] IRLR 300 (EAT), in paragraph 28 where it was held as follows:'Because it is for each individual to determine what they find unwelcome or offensive, there may be cases where there is a gap between what a Tribunal would regard as acceptable and what the individual in question was prepared to tolerate. It does not follow that because the Tribunal would not have regarded the acts complained of as unacceptable, the complaint must be dismissed.'

4.4. *Liability for Harassment*

4.4.1. Forms of Liability

The question arises as to who can be held liable for work-related harassment? Liability can either be direct or vicarious. Vicarious liability refers to the employer's liability for acts done by his employees. Vicarious liability is regulated in Section 41 SDA, Section 32 RRA and Section 58 DDA (all as amended).

Direct liability refers, in the first place, to the employer's liability for his own acts. It stems from Sections 6(2)(b) SDA, 4(2)(c) RRA and 4(2)(d) DDA. As referred to earlier, these Sections in the anti-discrimination Acts make it unlawful for the employer to discriminate against an employee by subjecting him or her to a 'detriment', including harassing treatment. Secondly, direct liability covers the situation whereby the employer is not personally held liable for his own acts but for harassing treatment meted out to a worker by a third person. A third person is somebody other than the employer himself and other than an employee. Examples are: customers, clients, pupils, patients, etc. Liability of an employer for the acts done by a third person has been dealt with in the landmark case of *Burton v. de Vere Hotels*,[157] in which the EAT took a welcome and deliberate approach to the matters at stake. The *Burton* decision has, however, been overruled by the Law Lords in the *Pearce* case earlier referred to. Both decisions shall be examined hereafter in the context of direct liability.

Hereafter, vicarious liability and direct liability will be examined in sections 4.4.2 and 4.4.3, respectively. In the discussion of vicarious liability in section 4.4.2 hereafter, I will moreover analyse the question whether an employee himself can be held liable for acts of harassment which (s)he has inflicted upon another worker (in addition to the employer's vicarious liability for the acts of the harassing worker). Although EC law does not contain concrete rules with respect to the issue of liability, a top-down analysis will be made wherever appropriate.

4.4.2. Vicarious Liability: the Employer's Liability for Acts Done by His Employees

Both the SDA, the RRA and the DDA enshrine a section which renders the employer vicariously liable for acts done by his employees.

Section 41 of the SDA 1975 reads as follows:

> (1) Anything done by a person in the course of his employment shall be treated for the purposes of this Act as done by his employer as well as by him., whether or not it was done with the employer's knowledge or approval.
> (3) In proceedings brought under this Act against any person in respect of an act alleged to have been done by an employee of his it shall be a defence for that person to prove that he took such steps as were reasonably practicable to prevent the employee

157 *Burton & Rhule v. de Vere Hotels Ltd*, 1996 IRLR 596.

> from doing that act, or from doing in the course of his employment acts of that description.

Counterpart provisions are contained in Section 32 of the RRA and in Section 58 of the DDA. It follows from the statutory provisions that employers are granted a dual defence in cases where they are held vicariously liable for their employees' acts:

> (1) The employer may argue that the acts complained of were committed by the employee outside the course of employment (Section 41(1) SDA; Section 32(1) RRA and Section 58(1) DDA, all as amended).
> (2) The employer may (in addition or alternatively to the first defence) rely on the so-called 'reasonable steps defence' (Section 41(3) SDA; Section 32(3) RRA; Section 58(5) DDA, all as amended).

Both defences shall be examined hereafter in light of the relevant case law.

4.4.2.1. The 'Outside the Course of Employment' Defence

This defence was the object of the decision by the CA in the case of *Tower Boot Co Ltd v. Jones*.[158] The case concerned racial harassment of a young 16 year old man of mixed race by his colleagues. The abuse was of a severe verbal and physical kind and included amongst other things the burning of Mr Jones' arm with a hot screw-driver. Until the decision by the CA in *Tower Boot* the (narrowly applied) rules for vicarious liability in general tort law had simply been extrapolated to the realm of non-discrimination law.[159] Under the Common Law on tort the employer's vicarious liability is only established if '[the acts on which the complaint is based; MG] are so connected with acts which he [the employer] has authorised that they may rightly be regarded as modes - although improper modes - of doing them'.[160] This rule was applied by the EAT in *Tower Boot* with the astounding effect that the employer was freed from liability. The EAT's approach was rightfully rejected by the CA on appeal. The latter adopted a broad and resolute approach to the issue of vicarious liability in the context of the statutory anti-discrimination Acts.[161] Per Waite LJ it was held as follows:

> 'It would have been particularly wrong to allow racial harassment on the scale that was suffered by the employee in this case at the hands of his workmates - treatment that was wounding both emotionally and physically - to slip through the net of employer responsibility by applying to it a common law principle evolved in another area of the law to deal with vicarious responsibility for wrongdoing of a wholly different kind. To

158 *Tower Boot Co Ltd v. Jones* 1995 IRLR 529 (EAT); [1997] ICR 254 (CA).

159 Buckley 1997, p. 159.

160 *Irving and Anor v. The Post Office* [1987] IRLR 289, cited by McColgan 2005, p. 237. See also Buckley 1997.

161 See for a comment Monaghan and Javaid 1997, p. 350-352.

> do so do so would seriously undermine the statutory scheme of the discrimination Acts and flout the purposes which they were passed to achieve.'[162]

In deciding as it did, the CA set a high threshold for employers to prove that their employees acted outside the course of employment. Conduct outside work-hours, or off the work-premises, may be 'in the course of employment' depending on the facts of the case at hand. The decision on this is a matter of fact which is therefore ultimately to be decided by the Tribunal. Although *Tower Boot* warrants the conclusion that the defence by the employer is not readily accepted, it was successfully invoked in the case of *Sidhu v. Aerospace Composite Technology Ltd.*[163] In casu, Mr Sidhu and his wife became victims of violent and racial insults inflicted upon them by a new employee, Mr White. The incidents took place at a family day out organised by the employer. Mr Sidhu commenced legal proceedings against his employer *inter alia* for racial discrimination. At first instance, the ET rejected Mr Sidhu's complaint of race discrimination. It held that the employer was not vicariously liable for the aggressive conduct of Mr White, given that the incidents occurred 'outside the scope of Mr Sidhu's and Mr White's employment'. Upon appeal, the EAT decided in favour of Mr Sidhu.[164] In its view, the first instance Tribunal had applied the wrong statutory test when it equated the 'scope' of employment to the rubric 'in the course of' employment. The latter rubric is the statutory language contained in Section 32(1) RRA. The employer appealed to the CA, which held that the first instance Tribunal did not misapply the test for vicarious liability in casu, even though they erroneously interpreted the 'scope' of employment and the 'course' of employment as synonymous.

4.4.2.2. The Reasonable Steps Defence

An employer will neither be legally liable for the acts of his employees, if he successfully relies on the so-called 'reasonable steps defence'. The first case to be mentioned in this context is that of *Canniffe v. East Riding CC,*[165] which provides guidance to employers as to what they must do in order to prevent from being held vicariously liable for the acts of their employees.[166]

Ms Caniffe had been the victim of a serious sexual assault by a colleague worker in the course of her employment. The ET at first instance had exonerated the employer from vicarious liability by reason of the fact that the employer had in place a personal harassment policy and disciplinary and grievance procedures. The Tribunal had taken the view that the acts on which the complaint was based were *that* severe that in any case they could not have been prevented by the employer from occurring. Upon appeal, counsel for the appellant argued correctly that the Tribunal's line of

162 See the conclusion on page 265 of the judgment.

163 *Sidhu v. Aerospace Composite Technology Ltd* [2000] IRLR 602, CA (per Lord Justice Peter Gibson).

164 See *Sidhu v. Aerospace Composite Technology Ltd* [1999] IRLR 683 (EAT).

165 *Canniffe v. East Riding* CC [2000] IRLR 555 (EAT).

166 See also Roberts 2001, p. 389 *et seq.*

reasoning was aberrant, given that it appeared to imply that, the more serious the alleged acts were, the more easily an employer was freed from liability. The EAT adopted a more favourable approach. The EAT gave importance to the fact that the appellant had complained of the sexual incidents to a senior colleague worker. Therefore the EAT held that the employer should have been aware of the serious nature of the alleged acts. The EAT held that, regardless of the question whether further steps *could* or *could not* have prevented the facts from occurring, Tribunals should adopt the following *two-stage test* in deciding on the 'reasonable steps defence': (1) they must examine what, if any, preventive steps were taken by the employer; (2) they must consider what further (additional) steps could have been taken by the employer and which were reasonably practicable. The first instance Tribunal erred in law by failing to consider these questions. The case was remitted to the ET.

In the case of *Balgobin and Francis v. London Borough of Tower Hamlets*,[167] the employer did have no knowledge about the malicious conduct inflicted upon the applicants.

Mrs Balgobin and Mrs Francis were working as cleaners in the canteen of a hostel managed by the respondents. They were allegedly sexually harassed by Mr Clarke in the period of June-October 1985. In October 1985 they complained of the malicious acts to management, who initiated an inquiry into the events. However, given that the truth of the allegations could not be established the applicants and the alleged perpetrator continued working in the same working area. The Tribunal of first instance decided upon the evidence before it that the acts of harassment had indeed occurred in the time period referred to by the applicants, but that management could not be held vicariously liable by reason of its successful reliance upon the 'reasonable steps defence' (Section 41(3) SDA). It was *inter alia* this finding which was challenged by the applicants upon appeal.[168] The majority of the EAT held that the Tribunal's legal finding had not been perverse: the alleged acts of harassment had not been made known to management, the employer had in place adequate and sound staff supervision and it had made known its equal opportunities policy to its employees. The EAT concluded that it was rather hard to imagine how the employer

167 *Balgobin and Francis (appellants) v. London Borough of Tower Hamlets (respondents)* [1987] IRLR 401 (EAT).

168 The applicants had furthermore challenged the Tribunal's finding that having to work with Mr Clarke in the period of November-January in what were termed 'intolerable conditions' did not constitute direct sex discrimination. Counsel for the applicants had argued that by exposing the female applicants to the risk of sexual harassment by Mr Clarke they were treated less favourably than a man would have been treated, given that Mr Clarke would not have sexually harassed a man. However, the EAT disagreed: the women were required to continue working with Mr Clarke *not* because they were women but because they were employees and therefore, the treatment complained of had not been 'on grounds of sex'. Moreover, the employers were not treating the applicants less favourably than they would have treated a man, given that a man to whom homosexual advances had been made by Mr Clarke would have been dealt with in precisely the same manner. The present author objects to this formalistic line of reasoning, given that the consequences of the ladies having to work with the alleged perpetrator were clearly detrimental to them *because they were women* and not men.

in practical terms could have reasonably prevented the acts of sexual harassment from occurring.

It follows from the aforementioned two cases, that the severity of the acts at issue as well as the employer's awareness of the harassing acts complained of, are factors to be taken into account in the assessment of a 'reasonable steps defence'.[169]

In *Home Office v. Coyne*[170] the facts were as follows.

Ms Coyne was employed by the Home Office as an instructional officer at Halloway Prison. Although it was Mr Julian who was Ms Coyne's line manager, on a day-to-day basis she was under the supervision of Mr Brown. Ms Coyne was the victim of sexually tainted gestures made to her by a Mr Smith who was a seconded employee of the local education authority. Mr Smith had made an apology to the applicant for the gestures complained of but Mr Brown had subsequently reacted furiously on this: in his view, the facts complained of were a direct consequence of the applicant's poor relationship with her fellow workers. The applicant then formally complained to her line manager (Mr Julian) both of the incidents as such and of Mr Brown's reaction to them. She did so in July 1990. Nothing was, however, done with her complaint, and to the contrary, in September 1990 she received the lowest possible rating on her appraisal report by her line manager and in March 1991 the applicant's employment was terminated. The applicant's complaint had been neglected by the Home Office for nearly two years. Eventually, the conclusion was drawn by the respondents that it had been the victim's own fault that she had been subjected to acts of sexual harassment.

The ET in the first instance had concluded unlawful direct sex discrimination by the way in which Ms Coyne's complaint had been dealt with. In the Tribunal's view

> 'there is no material difference between a failure to prevent harassment occurring and a failure to deal properly with a complaint of sexual harassment, since the natural consequence of a failure to deal with a complaint will be a risk of continuation of the same conduct'.[171]

The Tribunal had taken into account the fact that the acts complained of had entirely been treated by management as having been the applicant's own fault. Her complaint had furthermore been neglected for nearly two years and the eventual investigation into her complaint had been biased. This view was subsequently affirmed by the EAT. However, astoundingly and due to a strict application of formal equality, the CA disagreed: since Ms Coyne had been unable to prove that a man in similar circumstances would have received more favourable treatment than she had received, direct sex discrimination could not be established. Moreover, management's allegation that the incidents complained of had merely been her own fault could not be causally

169 Roberts 2001, p. 388.

170 *Home Office v. Coyne* [2000] IRLR 838 (CA) (Lord Justice Morritt, Lord Justice Sedley, Sir Christopher Slade; majority decision (Lord Justice Sedly dissenting).

171 Paragraph 57 of the decision by the Tribunal, referred to in paragraph 9 of the judgment by the CA [2000] IRLR 838.

connected with the applicant's sex. Rather, the majority took the view that this allegation was made by reason of the applicant's poor relationship with her fellow worker.

Home Office v. Coyne shows once again that an employer who treats a female employee equally badly as the relevant male equivalent does not infringe the genesis of the SDA. It would have been laudable had the majority of the Court followed the sensible legal approach adopted by the minority member. In Sedley LJ's view, the assumption that Ms Coyne herself was to blame for the incidents complained of rests upon a *stereotypical assumption* that a female victim has in a way asked herself for the sexual harassment to be meted out to her by a male perpetrator. In his view it is a 'tenable conclusion that, but for the fact that she was a woman, Ms Coyne would not have found her complaint being neglected on the explicit assumption that she had only herself to blame for her difficulties'.[172]

4.4.2.3. *The Worker's Personal Liability for Harassment*

Apart from holding the employer vicariously liable for harassing acts committed by an employee upon a fellow worker, the latter may also hold the individual perpetrator him or herself liable under the Statutes. This approach is in conformity with EC law. As referenced earlier, the Directives' personal scope of applicability arguably extends to employers, employees and third parties.

The Statutory approach to personal liability is slightly puzzling. Personal liability of the perpetrator cannot be established unless the employer is also liable for the acts complained of, or, would have been liable had he not successfully invoked the reasonable steps defence. Once the employer's liability has been established, the relevant Statutory Sections (Section 42 of the SDA; Section 33 of the RRA and Section 57 of the DDA, all as amended) extend liability to those who have consciously aided in the commission of the unlawful act(s) in issue. For example, as illustrated above, Section 41 of the SDA regulates the employer's vicarious liability for acts done by his employees. Section 42(1) SDA subsequently provides as follows:

> 'A person who knowingly aids another person to do an act made unlawful by this Act shall be treated for the purposes of this Act as himself doing an unlawful act of the like description.'

In summary, this person is regarded by the law as committing these acts herself.

Further, Section 42(2) SDA stipulates as follows:

> 'For the purposes of subsection (1) an employee (…) for whose act the employer (…) is liable under Section 41 (or would be so liable but for Section 41(3) [the latter Section containing the reasonable steps defence; MG] shall be deemed to aid the doing of the act by the employer (…).'

172 Paragraph 22 of the judgment.

It thus follows that for acts of harassment inflicted by one worker upon another worker both the individual perpetrator and the employer can be held liable by the victim of harassment. However, if the employer successfully relies upon the reasonable steps defence, it will only be the colleague worker who can be held liable. Matters can be illustrated with reference to *AM (appellant) v. (1) WC and (2) SPV (respondents)*.[173] In casu, the EAT confirmed the applicability of the SDA to both the employer and the individual colleague perpetrator. The facts were as follows.

AM was a female police constable who complained of sexual harassment meted out to her by another individual police officer. She complained of sex discrimination, both against the police force, and against her individual perpetrator. The Employment Tribunal had taken the view that the SDA did not apply between colleagues *inter se*: although an individual police officer has rights under the Act, (s)he did not have a burden, for (s)he could not be personally held liable under the Act. This view was, however, rejected by the EAT:

> 'Section 41 [SDA] is there to protect the employer from liability for acts committed by their staff outside the scope of their employment, and to give the employer a special defence. Section 42 [SDA], which is the partner to Section 41, makes the employee liable even where the special defence exists. Thus, without Section 41, there would be no vicarious liability and an employer, such as a company, would never be liable. Equally, without Section 41, a police constable would effectively be unprotected from unlawful discrimination since it would be rare indeed that the Chief Constable or the police authority would have committed the acts complained of. The argument on behalf of the second respondent [i.e. the alleged personal perpetrator; MG] that he cannot be held liable under Section 42 because he cannot aid and abet his own acts of discrimination, betrays a misunderstanding of the way the Act works. The correct interpretation [of Section 42] is that liability arises where the employee aids and abets his employer's vicarious liability. The structure of the Act is to place responsibility for unlawful discrimination in the workplace upon the employer (Section 6(2)). (…) Since employers normally act through their servants and agents, Section 41 defines the circumstances in which the activities of persons on behalf of the employer will create liability. Section 42 makes the employee personally liable, as well as the employer.'[174]

4.4.3. The Employer's Direct Liability for Acts Committed by Third Parties

What if the acts complained of have not been committed by the employer nor by an employee? Can the employer be held personally liable for acts committed by a 'third party' under Section 6(2)(b) SDA (discrimination by subjecting an employee to a 'detriment') in conjunction with Articles 1(1)(a) SDA ('direct discrimination') and 5(3) SDA (similarly situated comparator-requirement)?[175] The seminal case in respect of third-party liability is the case of *Burton and Rhule v. de Vere Hotels*.[176] It should be noted immediately that the (for the victim) advantageous reasoning by the

173 *(Appellant) v. (1) WC and (2) SPV (respondents)* [1999] IRLR 410 (EAT, per Mr Justice Morison).
174 Paragraph 22 of the judgment.
175 The equivalent Sections in the RRA 1976 are Section 4(2)(c) RRA (in conjunction with Section 1(1)(a) RRA and Section 3(4) RRA).
176 *Burton and Rhule v. de Vere Hotels* [1996] IRLR 596 (EAT).

EAT in *Burton* has been fully subverted by the House of Lords' decision in *Pearce*, a judgment earlier referred to[177] and which will be further elaborated on hereafter.

In *Burton and Rhule* two young black waitresses were the object of racist and sexist conduct inflicted upon them by Bernard Manning. Manning was an entertainer and guest speaker at a social gathering of gentlemen in the Penine Hotel Derby. The case was brought on the basis of the RRA. The ET at first instance, adopting a *verbatim* approach, decided that the employer (the hotel) could not be held liable for the acts complained of, given that it could not be said that it was the hotel that had *subjected* the waitresses to a detriment (i.e. the harassing treatment complained of).[178] The EAT rejected this text-based approach and favoured a teleological interpretation of the relevant wordings in the RRA. It decided that the employer was liable for the harassing acts by Manning. It held that '*subjecting*' also means '*controlling*': an employer does 'subject' an employee to a detriment, when he causes or allows that detriment to happen in such circumstances where the employer can control whether or not that detriment happens. In summary: in the view of the EAT, the employer's direct liability could be established by the latter's failure to prevent the harassing treatment in issue from occurring. In the present author's view the EAT's line of reasoning reflects a correct approach. A judicial line of reasoning with the opposite effect fails to afford adequate protection from harassment inflicted upon workers by third parties. Moreover, as indicated by the EAT, the employer will only be held directly liable in such scenarios where the employer could *control* the detriment from occurring. In the case at hand, the hotel could have better supervised Bernard Manning's speech and it could and should have withdrawn the waitresses from their duties once the situation became seriously insulting. Furthermore, the assistant managers in charge of the social gathering could and should have been instructed more properly.

Notwithstanding the foregoing arguments, the EAT's *dictum* in *Burton and Rhule* has been overturned by the House of Lords in *Pearce* (a judgment rendered pre-implementation of the Directives). The facts in *Pearce* have been explained in section 4.3.2.4 above. Ms Pearce argued, on the basis of *Burton and Rhule*, that the school was directly liable under the SDA 1975 for the harassing acts meted out to her by the pupils.[179] In her view, the school could and should have adopted measures to protect her from harassment. Ms Pearce's reasoning was decisively rejected by the Law Lords, who considered the EAT's reasoning in *Burton and Rhule* 'defective' [per Lord Rodger of Earlsferry, with reference to the opinion by Lord Scott of Foscote]

177 See section 4.3.2.4.

178 See the Statutory wordings in Section 4(2)(c) RRA: 'It is unlawful for a person, in the case of a person employed by him at an establishment in Great Britain, to discriminate against that employee by dismissing him, or subjecting [emphasis added] him to any other detriment.'

179 In *Pearce*, the issue of 'liability' was the third ground of appeal. In theory the liability question needed no further judicial consideration, given that the rejection by the HL of the first and second grounds of appeal meant that Ms Pearce had failed to establish a case of unlawful sex discrimination. Obviously, the respondent could not be held liable unless sex discrimination had been established. Notwithstanding the foregoing, the HL did elaborate on the matter of liability.

and 'unsatisfactory' [per Lord Nicholls of Birkenhead]. The latter held, whilst analysing *Burton and Rhule*, that

> 'the hotel's failure to plan ahead properly may have fallen short of the standards of good employment practice, but it was not racial discrimination'. It was furthermore emphasised that 'had the factual position been otherwise, and had the employer permitted exposure of the black waitresses to racist remarks by a third party when it would not have treated white employees similarly in a corresponding situation, *this* (italics MG) would have been a case of direct racial discrimination' (...). In such circumstances the employer would be liable without it being necessary, or appropriate, to have recourse to 'good employment practice'.[180]

In summary: given that the school could neither be held vicariously liable under Section 41(1) SDA, nor for its own acts under Section 6(2)(b) SDA (in conjunction with Sections 1(1)(a) and 5(3) SDA) and, given that the school had *not* failed to protect Ms Pearce *by reason that she was female* (the school would have equally failed to protect a male gay teacher) no liability could be established.

The reasoning adopted by the Law Lords in *Pearce* brings to the forefront the constraints of the 'comparative model' of non-discrimination law. The Law Lords applied the non-discrimination principle in a legal vacuum, without paying attention to its wider purposes. Incontestably, the House of Lords' decision in *Pearce* was decisively influenced by the importance given by the Law Lords to the 'comparative exercise': direct liability can only be established if the plaintiff (e.g. a female worker) can prove that the employer failed to protect her from harassing treatment meted out to her by a third party, whereas the employer had or would have protected a similarly situated comparator (i.e. a male worker). At this juncture, the following should be highlighted. It has been illustrated in earlier sections that EC law has introduced a freestanding wrong of harassment, which brings with it that the 'comparative exercise' needs no longer be carried out. However, the departure from the comparative exercise in order to establish 'harassment', has not had an impact upon the establishment of the employer's direct liability for harassing acts meted out by third parties, to employees and which the employer could have controlled.

The last matter worth observing, concerns the following. As discussed in prior sections the definitions of harassment post-implementation of EC law stipulate that the alleged perpetrator 'engages' in conduct which has the purpose or effect of violating the alleged victim's dignity or of creating a hostile work environment. 'To engage' ought to be amply interpreted by the courts with a view to covering also the passive toleration of harassing treatment (at stake in *Burton and Rhule* and *Pearce*). As stated before, the definition of sexual harassment in EC law covers both active and passive conduct. Therefore, the domestic courts have to interpret the verb 'to engage' in an analogous fashion, at least in sexual harassment cases. For the sake of legal clarity and consistency and in order to guarantee a broad legal protection from acts of harassment the same approach should be adopted in respect of harassment related to other grounds.

180 Paragraphs 35 and 36 of the judgment.

4.4.4. Interim Conclusions

In section 4.4, domestic law governing the liability for harassment has been analysed in light of EC law. An employer can escape from vicarious liability for the acts of his employees if, either the harassing acts on which the complaint is based occurred outside the course of employment, or if the employer successfully invokes the 'reasonable steps defence'. Hence, although EC law is short of a justification defence in respect of 'harassment', this does not affect the possibility granted to the employer by domestic law, namely to escape from vicarious liability. In addition to the (formal) employer, the victim of harassment at work can hold the individual perpetrator himself liable for the odious conduct complained of. It has been argued that this reflects a correct stance, in light of the personal applicability of the RD, the EFD and the AETD. Lastly, the employer's direct liability for failure to control the harassing acts inflicted upon a worker by a third party has been analysed. In *Pearce,* a unanimous House of Lords emphasised the need for a comparison in order to establish the employer's direct liability for acts of third parties. This is still valid law, notwithstanding that EC law currently conceives 'harassment' *in se* as an independent wrong.

5. Harassment in Dutch Equal Treatment Law: a Top-Down Analysis

5.1. Introduction

Having analysed harassment in the context of EC and English law, it will be examined henceforth how this concept has been regulated in Dutch law. As will be seen, the Dutch approach to work-related harassment reflects a twin concern: (1) a *health and safety concern* which stems from the idea that employees must be protected from work-related hazards which could harm their psychic state of mind, including (sexual) harassment; (2) a concern over *equality* (which initially focused upon equality between men and women in a context of sexual harassment). These two distinct rationales explain why, in the Netherlands, the regulation of harassment at work has been achieved at two separate levels. First, harassment is regulated in the 1998 Act on Working Conditions (henceforth: AWC).[181] Although broadly spoken the undercurrent of this Act is a health and safety rationale, the Act also mirrors a concern over equality between women and men. The equality rationale is, however, without

181 *Wet van 18 maart 1999 houdende bepalingen ter verbetering van de Arbeidsomstandigheden (Arbeidsomstandighedenwet 1998), Stb.* 1999, 184 [Act on Working Conditions 1998, *Law Gazette* 1999, 184]. This is the Act in its amended format. It should be noted that the provisions on sexual harassment, agression and violence at work were inserted in 1994 into the Act. See: *Wet van 29 juni 1994 tot wijziging van de Arbeidsomstandighedenwet in verband met seksuele intimidatie en agressie en geweld, Stb. 1994, 586* [Act of 29 June 1994 amending the Act on Working Conditions with respect to sexual harassment and agression and violence, *Law Gazette* 1994, 586]. The 1998 AWC entailed a renumbering of the Articles within it. The present analysis refers to the number of the Articles of the 1998 Act. It entered into force on 1 November 1999 (Besluit van 25 oktober 1999, *Stb.* 1999, 450 [governmental decree of 25 October 1999, *Law Gazette* 1999, 450].

doubt most clearly embedded within Dutch equal treatment legislation (*gelijke behandelingswetgeving*). Pre-implementation of EC law the ETC[182] interpreted this legislation creatively with the aim of bringing ground-related harassment under the wings of the prohibition of 'direct distinction' (*direct onderscheid*).[183] In this respect the stance adopted by the ETC is therefore the same as that adopted by the English courts. It is worth noting that legal requirements and judicial interpretations, which are adopted in the context of the AWC, may cross-fertilise into the realm of equal treatment law, and *vice versa*. This will be illustrated in the passages to follow. Furthermore, the law stemming from the AWC and from equal treatment law bears an impact upon claims of harassment which emerge within the context of general employment law and tort law.

In the analysis to follow, I will examine the concept of harassment both in the context of the AWC and in the context of equal treatment law. Given the subject matter of this book the emphasis will, however, be on the latter. The analysis will be presented as follows. Harassment in the AWC will be analysed in section 5.2 hereafter. Given that the implementation of the RD, the EFD and the AETD has not had an impact upon the regulation of harassment by this Act, section 5.2 will not ingrain the top-down comparison. In section 5.3, harassment will be discussed as a matter of equal treatment law. Given that this chapter as a whole has been confined to a consideration of harassment in relation to 'race', 'sex' and 'disability', the analysis in section 5.3 involves an examination of the following Statutory Acts:[184] the GETA[185] (which *inter alia* covers 'race'); the AET w/m[186] (which covers the ground 'sex' in both private and public employment), a number of Articles in the Civil Code (which relates to 'sex' in private employment) and the DETA[187] ('disability'). In section 5.3. the legal approach to harassment pre-implementation of the Directives

182 Equal Treatment Commission. See generally Chapter 2.

183 With reference to Chapter 2 Statutory Dutch equal treatment law is centred around the concept of 'distinction' (*onderscheid*), rather than 'discrimination' (*discriminatie*).

184 In Chapter 2 a general account has been given of the various statutory equal treatment Acts in Dutch law. In that Chapter, I have also expounded upon the relationship between the GETA, the AET w/m and Articles 7:646 and 7:647 of the Civil Code (all of which cover 'sex' and all of which cover 'employment'). This will not be repeated at this juncture.

185 *Algemene Wet Gelijke Behandeling* [General Equal Treatment Act] of 1994, *Stb.* [*Law Gazette*] 230. See generally Chapter 2.

186 Act on Equal Treatment between Men and Women [*Wet gelijke behandeling van mannen/vrouwen*] *Stb.* 1989, 168 [*Law Gazette* 1989, 168]. See generally Chapter 2. It should be highlighted that the AET w/m is currently being amended with a view to implementing the AETD into domestic law. These amendments have not yet entered into force. The legislative process with regard to the implementation of the AETD is still ongoing, notwithstanding that the AETD should have been implemented into domestic law by 05-10-05. What will be said hereafter is based upon the bill which aims to amend the AET w/m and Article 7:646 and Article 7:647 of the Civil Code with a view to implementing the AETD into Dutch law. See *Parliamentary Documents* II, 2004-2005, 30 237, no. 2. See also *Parliamentary Documents* II, 2004-2005, 30 237, no. 3 (*Explanatory Memorandum*).

187 Act of 3 April 2003 concerning the establishment of the Act on equal treatment on the grounds of disability or chronic disease [*Wet gelijke behandeling op grond van handicap en chronische ziekte*] *Stb.* 2003, 206 [*Law Gazette* 2003, 206]. See generally Chapter 2.

will be compared with the approach post-implementation of EC law. Tentative conclusions will be drawn in section 5.4.

5.2. *The Regulation of Harassment in the Act on Working Conditions*

5.2.1. The AWC and Harassment

The AWC is an instrument of public law. The insertion into the Act in 1994 of provisions regarding sexual harassment, aggression and violence at work was stimulated by the relevant provisions of EC soft-law.[188] Geers has succinctly explained the importance of the AWC for combating harassment at work with reference to the following factors. First, the AWC for the first time enshrines legal definitions of sexual harassment, aggression and violence at the workplace. Secondly, the Act explicitly compels employers to conduct a specific policy with a view to preventing sexual harassment, aggression and violence at the workplace. Thirdly, and as earlier touched on, the regulation of harassment, aggression and violence at work by the AWC has had an important cross-fertilisation effect upon a number of so-called 'open norms'[189] in private employment law.[190] These notably include the undefined norm that an employer must act as a 'good employer' (Article 7:611 Civil Code '*goed werkgeversschap*'), and, the employer's 'general duty of care' (*algemene zorgverplichting*) towards his employees (Article 7:658 Civil Code).[191] In summary, the standards set in the AWC in relation to harassment and sexual harassment at work function as a construal benchmark for the civil courts whilst deciding harassment cases on the basis of 'open norms' contained in private employment law. In a case decided by the Cantonal court[192] in Harderwijk[193] it was explicitly held that Article 7:658 of the Civil Code ('the employer's duty of care') brings with it, the concept that the employer must abide by the norms enshrined within the AWC. It was held that by virtue of Article 7:658 of the Civil Code, perceived in light of the AWC, the employer is under a duty to protect his employees from becoming a victim of sexual abuse and harassment in the workplace. In the case at hand the employer had failed to respect this duty. He was then held liable, both for material and immaterial damage suffered by the applicant.[194] The ETC in its non-binding case law has equally referred to the employer's obligations under the AWC.[195]

188 Geers 1996, p. 157. EC soft law provisions on harassment have been dealt with in section 3.1 above.

189 These norms are 'open' in the sense that they are subject to judicial application and interpretation by the courts in concrete cases that come before them. These norms have therefore not been interpreted *ex ante* by the legislator.

190 Geers 2003, p. 184; Geers 2003a, p. 36. Holtmaat has also emphasised these three functions of the AWC in the context of harassment. See Holtmaat 2004a, p. 90-91.

191 Geers 2003, p. 184; Geers 2003a, p. 36.

192 The cantonal court (*kantongerecht*) is the first instance court in labour law disputes.

193 Kantongerecht Harderwijk, 25 April 2001, no. 119618 854/00, *JAR* 2001, 118.

194 The compensation for immaterial damage in the case at hand was rather high (+/- €14.000). In the court's view this was justified with reference to the following factors: (1) the longevity of the sexual abusive acts which had lasted for two and a half years; (2) the fact that the →

As referred to earlier, the AWC primarily reflects a concern over health and safety. However, it nonetheless follows from the *travaux préparatoires* to this Act that a concern over gender-inequality has been the driving force behind the insertion of a definition of 'sexual harassment' into the Act. The relevant passage in the Parliamentary History states the following:

> 'A starting point for the government's policy has been that men and women must be able to perform on an equal basis. In order to guarantee that (female) employees are not systematically restricted, sexual harassment in the workplace must be prevented from occurring.'[196]

The health and safety rationale does, however, underlie the provisions on 'aggression' and 'violence' in the workplace.

5.2.2. Defining Sexual Harassment, Aggression and Violence

Sexual harassment is defined in Article 1(1)(e) AWC. The definition includes both *quid pro quo* harassment and hostile work environment harassment. It reads as follows:

> Sexual harassment: unwanted sexual approaches, requests for sexual favours or other, verbal, non verbal or physical conduct which at the same time embraces one of the following matters:
> (1) A person's subjection to such behaviour is either explicitly or implicitly used as a condition for recruitment; [quid pro quo harassment; MG]
> (2) A person's subjection to or rejection of such behaviour is used as a basis for decisions regarding that person's employment; [quid pro quo harassment; MG]
> (3) Such behaviour has the purpose of affecting a person's performance at work and/or, of creating an intimidating, hostile or unpleasant work environment, or, [such behaviour has] the effect that a person's employment performance is affected and/or, that an intimidating, hostile or unpleasant work environment is created.[197] [hostile work environment harassment; MG]

respondent had abused his capacity of employer; (3) the fact that the applicant's private life had been intruded upon, even at times when she was ill; (4) the fact that, as a consequence of the sexually abusive acts, the applicant was forced to quit her job by reason of her inability to deal with male colleague workers. The fact that the respondent's financial situation was not prosperous was not accepted by the court as a sound reason which could lead to a reduced liability for damages.

195 See e.g. Opinion 2004-170 (paragraph 5.7.).

196 *'Uitgangspunt voor het beleid van de overheid is dat vrouwen en mannen in arbeidssituaties op gelijkwaardige wijze moeten kunnen functioneren. Om er zorg voor te dragen dat de mogelijkheden van (vrouwelijke) werknemers niet systematisch beperkt worden, dient seksuele intimidatie op de werkplek niet voor te komen'* (*Explanatory Memorandum*, II, 1992-1993, 23 326, no. 3, p. 4).

197 The original Dutch text reads as follows: *'seksuele intimidatie: ongewenste seksuele toenadering, verzoeken om seksuele gunsten or ander verbaal, non-verbaal or fysiek gedrag waarbij tevens sprake is van een van de volgende punten: (1) onderwerping aan dergelijk gedrag wordt hetzij explicitiet hetzij impliciet gehanteerd als voorwaarde voor de tewerkstelling van een persoon; (2) onderwerping aan of afwijzing van dergelijk gedrag door een persoon wordt gebruikt als basis voor beslissingen die het werk van deze persoon raken; (3) dergelijk gedrag heeft het doel de werkprestaties van een persoon aan te* →

It should be highlighted that the implementation of the AETD into Dutch law has not led to a revision of the above definition. This has meant that the definition of sexual harassment in the AWC differs from the one contained in the AET w/m. The definitions of sexual harassment and sex-based harassment in the latter Act aim to transpose the relevant provisions of the AETD. Sexual harassment and sex-based harassment in the AET w/m will be expounded upon in sections 5.3.2.1 and 5.3.2.2 hereafter. For current purposes it suffices to say that it would have been better had the legislator streamlined the definitions of sexual harassment in the various statutory Acts concerned.[198]

The definition of sexual harassment in Article 1(1) under 'e' AWC makes it clear that the conduct must be 'unwanted' which inserts an element of subjectivity into the test for establishing sexual harassment.[199] The definition is broad: it *inter alia* covers comments with a double, sexual, meaning, unnecessary touching, leering, pin-up displays at the workplace, but also, sexual assault and rape.[200]

Verrijn Stuart has characterised the insertion of sexual harassment in the AWC as 'immoral' given that the overall genesis of this Act reflects a concern over health and safety,[201] rather than an ethical cause. Hence, the Act is primarily focused upon the regulation of work-related hazards. However, as discussed above, the ethical cause for equality has underpinned the sexual harassment provisions in the Act. Moreover, a commonality between a 'dignity approach' to harassment, on the one hand, and a 'health and safety approach', on the other, could arguably be found in the fact that both approaches seek to foster equality of opportunity at the work-place. From a pragmatic point of view it is certainly desirable that sexual harassment is regulated both in the AWC and in equal treatment legislation, given that in current times these two realms of the law adopt a different strategy to combating (sexual) harassment at work. Whereas the AWC aims to combat sexual harassment at work in a preventive manner, equal treatment legislation is more reactive in kind. A combination of preventive and reactive strategies offers the most inclusive legal approach to the problem of sexual harassment at work.

tasten en/of een intimiderende, vijandige, of onaangename werkomgeving te creeëren, dan wel heeft tot gevolg dat de werkprestaties van een persoon worden aangetast en/of een intimiderende, vijandige of onaangename werkomgeving wordt gecreëerd'.

198 See in this context the Advisory Opinion to the legislator by the Dutch Council of State (*Raad van State*) which is the highest advisor to the government in regard to legislation, *Wijziging van de Wet Gelijke Behandeling van mannen en vrouwen en het Burgerlijk Wetboek ter uitvoering van Richtlijn 2002/73/EG*, Advies Raad van State en Nader Rapport, II 2004-2005, 30 237, no. 4, p. 4-5 [Amendment of the Act on Equal Treatment between men and women and the Civil Code with a view to implementing Directive 2002/73/EC, Advisory Opinion of the Council of State, II 2004-2005, 30 237, no. 4, p. 4-5]. The Council of State questioned whether the government had intended to leave intact different definitions of sexual harassment in the AWC, on the one hand, and in the AET w/m, on the other and if not it advised the government to streamline both definitions.

199 Also Konijn 1995, p. 36.

200 Memorie van Toelichting [*Explanatory Memorandum*] *II* 1992-1993, 23 326, no. 3, p. 2.

201 Verrijn Stuart 1990, p. 2 (*'Seksuele intimidatie als arbeidsrisico in de Arbowet opnemen vind ik haast immoreel'*).

'Aggression' and 'violence' are captured by Article 1(1)(f) AWC. These notions are defined as follows: 'occurrences where an employee is physically or psychologically harassed, threatened or attacked under such circumstances which are within the course of employment'.[202] Although aggression and violence need not be ground-related, given that these notions also relate to mobbing more generally, they can be linked to a forbidden ground. In other words, aggression and violence at the workplace can be targeted at workers defined by a protected status. In this way ground-related harassment other than sexual harassment is also covered by the Act.

5.2.3. The Employer's Obligations under the AWC

The employer's duty to conduct a specific policy with a view to preventing sexual harassment, aggression and violence at the workplace is regulated in Article 4(2) AWC. This Article reads as follows: 'the employer conducts, within the general policy on working conditions, a policy with regard to the protection of employees against sexual harassment and against aggression and violence'.[203] This policy must address (sexual) harassment and violence between employees *inter se*, as well as between the employer, on the one hand, and employees, on the other.[204] In addition to this the employer is under a duty to protect his employees from (sexual) harassment by 'third parties', and *vice versa*.[205] Some scholars have argued that the employer's policy prescribed by Article 4(2) AWC should also address the protection of employees from discrimination more generally.[206] This would encourage employers to combat discrimination in a structural manner, i.e. on the basis of a consistent policy.[207] Under Article 5 AWC the employer is furthermore under a duty to carry out a risk assessment of the hazards which may occur in the workplace. In this context the employer must also pay attention to the risk of (sexual) harassment.

The last note concerns the matter of enforcement.[208] It should be highlighted that the AWC does not provide for a control mechanism via which a victim of (sexual) harassment can claim damages for acts done by the employer, a colleague worker or a 'third party'. Damages can merely be claimed on the basis of an action under private employment law or tort law. The issue of liability will be expounded upon in further detail in section 5.3.2.3 hereafter. The employer's duties under the AWC can be enforced via administrative sanctions which may be imposed upon the employer (and employees)[209] by the employment inspectorate (*arbeidsinspectie*). Sanctions

202 *'Agressie en geweld: voorvallen waarbij een werknemer psychisch of fysiek wordt lastiggevallen, bedreigd of aangevallen onder omstandigheden die rechtstreeks verband houden met het verrichten van arbeid'* (Article 1(1)(f) AWC).

203 *'De werkgever voert, binnen het algemene arbeidsomstandighedenbeleid, een beleid met betrekking tot het beschermen van werknemers tegen seksuele intimidatie en tegen agressie en geweld.'*

204 Memorie van Toelichting [*Explanatory Memorandum*] II 1992-1993, 23 326, no. 3, p. 10.

205 Geers 2003, p. 185 and Article 10 AWC.

206 Houtzager and Bochhah, 2004, p. 276-277.

207 Houtzager and Bochhah, 2004, p. 276-277.

208 For a more detailed account, I refer to Geers 2003, p. 187-192 and Geers 2003a, p. 35-36. This section largely draws on these two contributions. See also Chapters 5 and 7 of the AWC.

209 Although this has not often happened in practice. See Geers 2003, p. 192.

may include an administrative fee (*bestuurlijke boete*, Article 33 AWC). Moreover, the employment inspectorate can demand that the employer abide by his obligations under Article 4(2) AWC. In doing so the inspectorate can give mandatory instructions to the employer as to what measures will need to be adopted with a view to rendering Article 4(2) AWC effective in practice. Lastly, criminal law may play a role in the enforcement of the employer's obligations under the AWC. This element will, however, not be considered in more detail, given that criminal law falls outside the scope of this book.

5.3. *Harassment as a Matter of Equal Treatment Law*

5.3.1. Harassment Pre-Implementation of EC Law

5.3.1.1. The Statutory Framework

Prior to the implementation of the RD, the EFD and the AETD harassment and sexual harassment were not defined as an independent form of discrimination in Dutch equal treatment law. As in English law this lacuna was circumvented by the ETC which has dealt with harassment on the basis of the statutory prohibition of direct distinction. More specifically, the Commission has approached claims of harassment on the basis of direct distinction *with respect to the conditions of employment.* With regard to the discrimination ground 'sex' in public employment this was prohibited by Article 1 in conjunction with Article 1a AET w/m (this is currently: Article 1 in conjunction with Article 1B(1) of the AET w/m (as amended in light of Directive 2002/73/EC)[210]); with respect to 'sex' in private employment it was and currently still is prohibited by Article 7:646(1) Civil Code. Direct distinction on grounds of race with respect to the conditions of employment was prohibited by Article 1 GETA in conjunction with Article 5(1)(d) GETA (which post-implementation of the RD has become Article 5(1)(e) GETA). Since pre-implementation of the EFD discrimination on grounds of disability was not at all covered by statutory equal treatment law (but solely by Article 1 Constitution) a discussion of harassment in relation to this ground becomes redundant (at least insofar as the legal situation pre-implementation of EC law is concerned).

Whilst dealing with claims of harassment under the respective equal treatment Acts the Commission has not felt constrained by the fact that the government, whilst adopting the GETA in the early 1990s, had explicitly indicated that it did not wish to include a prohibition of sexual harassment within the Act.[211] As will be seen

210 The implementation of the AETD into Dutch law has not yet been finalised. All what will be said hereafter in the main text will be based on the bill which aims to amend the AET w/m and the relevant Articles in the Civil Code in order to implement the AETD into Dutch law. See *Parliamentary Documents* II, 2004-2005, 30 237, no. 2.

211 *Parliamentary Documents* I 1988-1989, 19 908 no. 5b, p. 7, cited by Holtmaat 1999a, p. 25. Asscher-Vonk and Wentholt 1994, p. 125. Nothing was mentioned on racial harassment or other ground-related harassment. This can be explained by the fact that it has been the women's movement which as from the 1970s onwards has stimulated discussions on sexual →

below the ETC has successfully stretched the limits of the law with the explicit aim of rendering (sexual) harassment actionable under equal treatment law.

5.3.1.2. *The Case Law by the ETC*

With a view to bringing harassment under the scope of equal treatment legislation the ETC has adopted a broad and purposive approach to the notion of employment conditions (*arbeidsvoorwaarden*). According to the Commission's case law the notion of 'employment conditions' also covers 'working conditions' (*arbeidsomstandigheden*).[212] It should be noted that pre-implementation of EC law the latter notion was not *explicitly* covered by the relevant Statutory Acts which has changed post-implementation of the RD and AETD (see new Article 5(1)(f) of the GETA and new Article 1B(1) of the AET w/m). In other words, since the implementation of the Directives equal treatment law in the Netherlands has contained an independent prohibition of distinction with respect to 'working conditions' (*arbeidsomstandigheden*).

It follows from the Commission's case law that the right to equality with respect to conditions of employment, including thus working conditions, encapsulates a person's right to be freed from ground-related harassment at work.[213] Unlike in English law where, as has been illustrated, the comparative exercise has been a major stumbling block for applicants claiming an instance of ground-related harassment, the ETC has given little importance to this exercise. In general, it appears that the Continental legal tradition gives much more space for a teleological interpretation of the law, whereas the English legal tradition tends to favour a grammatical interpretation of the law.

Like in English and EC law, intention is no material factor for establishing a case of direct distinction, including harassment.[214] Furthermore, as is the case with English and EC law, harassment has to be ground-related for it to be actionable under domestic equal treatment law.[215]

It also follows from the Commission's case law that the notion of employment conditions covers the right of an employee to develop him or herself at work and to

harassment in political and legal circles. A similar development did not occur with respect to the other discrimination grounds. See Holtmaat 1999, p. 13.

212 See, for example, Opinion 1999-72.

213 See, for example Opinions 1996-88; 1997-82; 1997-91; 2001-131; 2003-138. Also Asscher-Vonk and Monster 2002, p. 164.

214 See, for example, paragraph 4.8. of Opinion 1996-23 in which the ETC held as follows: 'Under the GETA unequal treatment is deemed prohibited regardless of the intention of the person who treats another person unequally' [*'In de AWGB wordt een ongelijke behandeling verboden geacht ongeacht de intentie van degene die een ander ongelijk behandelt'*]. See moreover Opinion 2001-88.

215 For example, in Opinion 2005-65 (which has arisen post-implementation of EC law) the Commission acknowledged that the contested conduct by the respondent had been unprofessional but it did nonetheless not amount to an act of act of disability-based harassment, given the absence of a link between the applicant's disability, on the one hand, and the respondent's conduct, on the other (paragraph 5.7. of the Opinion).

gain experience.[216] In all, like under the AWC, the employer has a duty under equal treatment law to strive for a discrimination and harassment free workplace. This duty also entails the duty placed on the employer to have in place an adequate complaints mechanism which functions well in practice and which is followed with 'due diligence'.[217] Preferably such a procedure ensures the availability of independent and professional people who deal with complaints lodged by victims of work-related harassment.[218] Furthermore, an effective complaints mechanism requires that both parties are adequately heard and that confidentiality is secured. It moreover requires that both the victim and the perpetrator are adequately informed about the conclusions of the procedure and about the measures which are intended to be taken.[219]

The Commission's case law moreover indicates that an alleged victim of harassment is supposed to inform the employer that (s)he felt harassed (*kenbaarheidsvereiste*).[220] If (s)he fails to do so, the employer may defend himself against liability by stating that he was unaware of the (alleged) acts of harassment. With reference to section 4.4.2.2, this was successfully done by the employer in the case of *Balgobin and Francis v. London Borough Tower Hamlets*,[221] in the context of English law. The requirement that the victim should notify the employer about the acts of harassment should, however, be assessed with care. A victim might feel barred from doing so by fear of retaliation of by a concern of upsetting the atmosphere at work. Moreover, she might feel prevented from notification due to the difference in power-relations which might exist between the victim and the perpetrator. In light of the aforementioned concerns, the ETC has taken the view that complaints of harassment can also be notified to third parties including the occupational health and safety service (*Arbeidsomstandighedendienst*).[222]

5.3.2. Harassment Post-Implementation of EC Law

5.3.2.1. Harassment: a Freestanding Form of Distinction

Post-implementation of the RD, the EFD and the AETD a freestanding provision on (sexual) harassment is contained in the GETA, the AET w/m, Article 7:646 of the Civil Code and the DETA.[223] It should be highlighted that, although the law as it currently stands contains an autonomous prohibition of harassment, the pre-implementation

216 Opinions 1997-07; 1997-122; 2001-131 and Houtzager and Bochhah 2004, p. 274.

217 Asscher-Vonk and Monster 2002, p. 165; Opinion 1999-48, commented upon by Holtmaat 1999a.

218 Holtmaat 1999a; Geers 2003, p. 194; Judgment by the Cantonal Court of Alkmaar of 19 October 1998 *JAR* 1998, 191 cited by Holtmaat 1999a; Opinion 2004-82.

219 See, for example, Opinions 2004-82 and 2004-170.

220 Opinion 1999-1.

221 *Balgobin and Francis (appellants) v. London Borough of Tower Hamlets (respondents)* [1987] IRLR 401 (EAT).

222 Occupational Health and Safety Services are agencies responsible for the enforcement of the Act on Working Conditions. They, *inter alia*, advice on working conditions and health and safety standards. See Opinion 2004-170.

223 A freestanding prohibition of harassment is moreover contained in the Act on Equal Treatment on grounds of Age (AETA). See Article 2 AETA.

approach to harassment has not ceased to exist. It follows from the post-implementation case law that, if 'harassment' cannot be established, the ETC may subsequently analyse whether the respondent has taken insufficient care in guaranteeing a discrimination free work environment. In Opinion 2005-65 the ETC explicitly held as follows:

> '[i]f a case of harassment cannot be made out, the Commission [subsequently] assesses whether the applicant can submit facts which support a presumption that the respondent has fallen short of his duty of care to realise a discrimination free [in case: educational] environment'.[224]

In casu, the applicant had failed to make out a case of disability-related harassment. He, however, succeeded in raising the presumption that the respondent had fallen short of its duty to secure a discrimination free educational environment. The ETC thence concluded a case of unlawful distinction on grounds of disability, but *not* a case of disability-related harassment. In summary: the pre-implementation approach to harassment discussed in section 5.3.1.2 above has not lost its relevance in the post-implementation context.

5.3.2.2. *Explaining the Statutory Provisions on 'Harassment' and 'Sexual Harassment'*

Harassment which is related to the grounds contained in the GETA (including 'race') is prohibited by a new Article 1A of the Act which reads as follows:

> (1) The prohibition of distinction laid down in this Act shall also include a prohibition of harassment.
> (2) Harassment as referred to in the first subsection shall mean conduct related to the characteristics or behaviour, as referred to in Article 1 under 'b' [i.e., the grounds covered by the Act including 'race'; MG], and, which has the purpose or effect of violating the dignity of a person and of creating an intimidating, hostile, degrading, humiliating or offensive environment.
> (3) Article 2, Article 5 subsections 2-6, Article 6a subsection 2 and Article 7 subsections 2 and 3 shall not apply to the prohibition of harassment contained in this Act [these Articles contain exceptions to the central prohibition of distinction; harassment is, however, prohibited *per se*; MG].

An equivalent legal provision is contained in Article 1A of the DETA. The definitions of harassment in the GETA and the DETA prompt the following comments. In line with the RD and EFD the definitions of harassment in the GETA and the DETA have been confined to 'hostile work environment harassment' to the exclusion of '*quid pro quo* harassment'. The statutory way of drafting makes it clear that harassment is considered by the law to be a form of 'distinction'. It would nonetheless have been conceptually purer had the government inserted the concept of harassment in Article 1 of the GETA and in Article 1 of the DETA.[225] Both of these Articles

224 Opinion 2005-65. See moreover Opinion 2004-170.
225 See ETC Advice 2001/03 available at <www.cgb.nl>, p. 3.

define the meaning of the concept of distinction. Thus, Article 1(a) of the GETA provides as follows: 'For the purposes of this Act (...) the following definitions shall apply: (a) distinction: direct and indirect distinction as well as the instruction to make a distinction (...).' An equivalent provision is contained in Article 1(1) DETA.

The definitions of harassment in the GETA and the DETA do not refer to the adjective 'unwanted' before the word 'conduct', as the RD and the EFD do. Since, however, the absence of this adjective merely amplifies the definitional scope of harassment and furthermore alleviates the burden of proving an instance of harassment, the government has acted in conformity with the requirements of the Directives.[226]

It follows from the definition above that the contested conduct must *both* have the purpose or effect of violating the dignity of a person and of creating a hostile work environment.[227] It follows from the Commission's case law that whether or not this is the case must be assessed on the basis of an objective test.[228] Thus, for example, in Opinion 2005-65 the Commission stated that 'it must concern conduct of which it can be objectively established that it does or may have this effect' (i.e. the effect of violating a person's dignity and of creating a hostile work environment).[229] Although the ETC advised the government to opt for alternative conditions this advice has not been taken on.[230] In light of this the ETC has set a high threshold for making out a case of ground-related harassment:

> '(t)he legislator has had in mind that harassment constitutes a qualified and severe form of discrimination (the ETC does not use the word 'distinction' here!), that severe that it cannot be justified. Hence, if a case of harassment is to be established, strict and

226 Waaldijk 2004, p. 354. See in this context also *Parliamentary Documents*, II, 2002-2003, 28 770, no. A, p. 14-15 and *Parliamentary Documents*, II, 2004-2005, 30 237, no. 4, p. 2. The Council of State had shown itself proponent of inserting the adjective 'unwanted' into the definitions of harassment and sexual harassment, given that such an approach would streamline the Dutch definitions of this concept with the definitions contained in Community law. The government has, however, not followed this advice.

227 It should be noted that in the ETC's case law rendered pre-implementation of the RD and EFD, establishing a case of ground-related harassment occurred on the basis of alternative conditions. The introduction of cumulative conditions has been criticised for being in breach of the Directives' non-regression clauses. See Houtzager and Bochhah 2004, p. 274. However, as was argued before, if an applicant cannot establish a case of ground-related *harassment*, the ETC is free to (subsequently) analyse (in line with the pre-implementation approach to harassment) whether the respondent has taken sufficient care in guaranteeing a discrimination free workplace.

228 See, for example, Opinion 2005-65 paragraph 5.5. 'it must concern conduct of which is can be objectively established that it does or may have this effect' (i.e. the effect of violating a person's dignity and of creating a hostile work environment). (*'Het moet hierbij gaan om gedrag waarvan objectief kan worden vastgesteld dat het dit effect heeft of kan hebben').*

229 *'Het moet hierbij gaan om gedrag waarvan objectief kan worden vastgesteld dat het dit effect heeft of kan hebben'* (paragraph 5.5. of the Commission's Opinion).

230 See ETC Advice 2001/03 available at <www.cgb.nl>.

> cumulative requirements must be met. A mere insult or humiliation is insufficient for presupposing a case of harassment'.[231]

Similarly, in Opinion 2004-170 the Commission took the view that

> '(...) [it cannot be established] whether the by the applicants alleged discriminatory remarks have indeed been made, given that the parties in the case at hand give contradictory comments on this alleged fact and given the absence of other facts which could support the applicants allegations (...) in light of this the Commission concludes that the applicants (...) have failed to make out a case of unlawful distinction (i.e. harassment)'.[232]

Post-implementation of the AETD provisions on sex-based harassment and on sexual harassment currently feature in new Article 1A of the AET w/m. This reads as follows:

> (1) The prohibition of direct distinction in this Act includes a prohibition of harassment and a prohibition of sexual harassment.
> (2) Harassment referred to in subsection 1 means: conduct which is related to the sex of a person and which has the purpose or effect of violating a person's dignity and of creating an intimidating, hostile, degrading, humiliating or offensive environment.
> (3) Sexual harassment referred to in subsection 1 means: any form of verbal, non-verbal or physical conduct of a sexual nature, which has the purpose or effect of violating the dignity of a person, in particular when creating an intimidating, hostile, degrading, humiliating or offensive environment.'
> (4) It shall be unlawful to disadvantage a person by reason by reason of the fact that she has rejected the conduct referred to in subsections 2 and 3 or has passively underwent it.
> (5) Articles 3(2), 4(2) and 5(1) and 5(2) [of this Act] shall not be applicable to the prohibition of harassment and sexual harassment referred to in subsection 1 above.

Counterpart provisions are currently also contained in, respectively, Articles 7:646 (6), 7:646(7), 7:646(8), 7:646(9) and 7:646(13) of the Civil Code.

With respect to the above definition the following comments can be made. The AET w/m and Article 7:646 Civil Code conceive 'harassment' and 'sexual harassment' as forms of *direct distinction*, rather than as forms of *distinction* (as the GETA and the DETA do). It is not clear what legal effect this different conceptualisation has in practice, given that under none of the aforementioned Acts 'harassment' and 'sexual harassment' can be justified. It is neither clear why a different stance has

231 *'De wetgever heeft bedoeld met het verbod van intimidatie aan te geven dat het een gekwalificeerde en zware vorn van discriminatie is, zo ernstig dat daarvoor geen enkele rechtvaardiging bestaat. Daarom moet, wil er sprake zijn van intimidatie, aan zware en cumulatieve eisen zijn voldaan. Enkele belediging of vernedering is onvoldoende om intimidatie aan te nemen'* (See Opinion 2005-65, paragraph 5.9.). The Commission's case law indicates more generally that merely stating that an act of distinction has occurred is insufficient for making out a case of distinction (e.g. Opinion 2003-75).

232 Opinion 2004-170 *'De Commissie kan niet vaststellen of de door verzoekers gestelde discriminatoire opmerkingen inderdaad zijn gemaakt, nu partijen elkaar tegenspreken en er geen andere feiten zijn aangevoerd ter onderbouwing van deze stelling (...) Derhalve concludeert the Commissie dat met de (...) argumenten van verzoekers geen feiten zijn aangevoerd die onderscheid [i.e., intimidatie] kunnen doen vermoeden'* (paragraph 5.11).

been adopted at all. Given that the AETD conceives harassment as a *sui generis* form of unequal treatment, the Dutch approach is conceptually wrong.

It follows from Article 1A(5) AET w/m that harassment cannot be justified. The same point applies with respect to Article 7:646 of the Civil Code.

The definitions of harassment and sexual harassment are nearly synonymous with the ones contained in the AETD, except for the fact that the term 'unwanted' has been omitted from the Dutch definitions. As argued before in relation to the definitions of harassment in the GETA and the DETA, this omission is not in breach of EC law. In line with the AETD, sex-based harassment in Article 1A(2) AET w/m requires proof of cumulative conditions, whereas sexual harassment in Article 1A(3) AET w/m only requires proof of a violation of the alleged victim's dignity. The allegation by a plaintiff that her (his) dignity has been infringed upon can be reinforced by proving that the alleged reprehensible acts have had the effect of creating an intimidating, hostile, degrading, humiliating or offensive environment. This approach is likewise adopted by the AETD.

5.3.2.3. Liability for Harassment[233]

It does not follow from the provisions in the above mentioned Acts to whom the prohibition of distinction, including harassment and sexual harassment, is addressed.[234] Although the material scope of the GETA, the DETA, the AET w/m and Article 7:646 Civil Code is readily apparent, the Acts remain silent on the matter of personal applicability. The fact that the aforementioned Acts apply to the area of employment, broadly defined, sheds no light upon the question *who*, the employer, colleague workers or third parties acting within the employment context, can be held liable for acts of harassment. This question was explicitly raised in the Parliamentary discussions on the implementation of the Directives. It clearly follows from these discussions that the government has not intended to render the equal treatment Acts applicable in relationships between colleagues inter se, let alone in relationships with 'third parties'.[235] The government has defended this stance by noting that between colleagues *inter se* there is no contract or relationship of authority. However,

233 This section draws on Gijzen 2004, section 3.1.3.

234 Cremers-Hartman 1999, p. 33.

235 See *Parliamentary Documents* II 2002-2003, 28 770, no. 5, p. 28 ('[The GETA] is not applicable to the relationship between colleagues. A colleague worker has got no authority over the victim of unequal treatment and he or she is not legally involved in the employment contract.)' *[Artikel 5 heeft geen betrekking op de relatie tussen werknemers onderling. Een collega-werknemer staat niet in een gezagsrelatie ten opzichte van het slachtoffer van ongelijke behandeling en is niet in juridische zin betrokken bij de arbeidsovereenkomst.]'*. See, moreover, *Memorie van Toelichting* [*Explanatory Memorandum*] *II* 2001-2002, 28 170, no. 3, p. 3-4 and *Parliamentary Documents* II 2001-2002, 28 170, no. 5, p. 28. The latter two *Parliamentary Documents* concern the AETA (Act on Equal Treatment on grounds of Age). The provisions on harassment contained in the AETA are, however, identical to the ones contained in the GETA and the DETA. There is therefore no reason to assume that the government's submissions which were made in the context of the provisions on 'harassment' in the AETA do not also apply to 'harassment' contained in the GETA and the DETA. See also Gerards and Heringa 2003, p. 18.

it was indicated by the government that employees, who in the name of their employer exercise authority over their fellow workers, *are* addressees of the central norm. *De facto*, it was argued, such an employee functions in the capacity of employer.[236]

In the analysis of harassment in EC law above it was argued that the Directives are sufficiently wide in scope so as to cover acts of the employer, colleagues and third parties, acting within a context of employment. In light of this it appears to the present author that the inapplicability of Dutch equal treatment law to unlawful distinctions committed by colleagues and by third parties is unduly restrictive and therefore in breach of EC law. The purported inapplicability of the Dutch Acts in relationships between colleagues *inter se* appears particularly problematic in the context of work-related (sexual) harassment.[237] In its current format and in light of the Parliamentary comments the law prevents an alleged victim of harassment from holding a colleague or a third party him or herself liable for the contested acts. The only way to do this is by seeking recourse to the general provisions of employment law or tort law in the Dutch Civil Code.[238] In its (pre-implementation) Opinion 2004-11, the ETC *inter alia* ruled upon the applicant's complaint of racial harassment by a colleague worker. The Commission considered that '(...) the employer's duty to refrain from distinction in employment also includes the duty to supervise that those who are under his authority refrain from and are protected against discrimination'.[239] An employer's failure to do so results, in principle, in an act of distinction by the employer.[240] Depending on the circumstances of the case at hand, the employer may, however, escape from vicarious liability, if he has abided by his duty of care.[241] In other words, although the statutory equal treatment Acts do not contain a 'reasonable steps defence', this defence appears to have been incorporated in the Commission's case law. It follows from the Commission's case law that in such cases in which the employer did have in place an adequately functioning anti-harassment policy, a case of direct distinction with respect to the conditions of employment will

236 *Memorie van Toelichting* [*Explanatory Memorandum*] *II* 2001-2002, 28 170, no. 3, p. 19. This was observed by the government in relation to the prohibition of harassment contained in the AETA (i.e. Act on Equal Treatment on grounds of Age) which is, however, identically formulated as the counterpart prohibitions of harassment in the GETA and the DETA.

237 Waaldijk 2004, p. 355, who has observed that '[o]nly rarely it will be the formal employer who harasses an employee. In most instances of harassment, it is carried out by a boss or colleague, or even by a client, or by a group of colleagues or clients'. It should, however, be highlighted that a 'boss' *is* an addressee of the prohibition of harassment, given that a boss exercises authority over other employees in name of the formal employer.

238 This was explicitly stated by the government in the Parliamentary discussions regarding the EC Implementation Act GETA (referred to in a general fashion in Chapter 2): 'An employer can hold an employee who has harassed another employee liable under Article 7:611 of the Civil Code which contains an obligation for the employee to act and behave as a good employee. An employee can hold his or her co-employee liable under the general provisions of tort law'. *[Een werkgever kan een werknemer die zich jegens een andere werknemer schuldig maakt aan intimidatie aanspreken op het goed werknemersschap ex artikel 7:611 BW. Een werknemer kan tegen een collega-werknemer ageren in het kader van een onrechtmatige daadsactie']*.

239 Paragraph 5.8. of Opinion 2004-11.

240 See also, for example, opinion 2004/08 in the context of the grounds race and religion.

241 Also Waaldijk 2004a, p. 69.

not be established in the first place.[242] It is likely that the Commission will adopt a similar stance with respect to cases of harassment which arise in the post-implementation context.

The employer's liability for harassing acts by a third party was at stake in Opinion 97-82. The case concerned racial harassment of a nurse by a patient. The Commission repeated its stance that the employer is under a legal duty to prevent from occurring acts of harassment done by persons under his supervision. The Commission took the view that, although the alleged harassing acts were not done by a colleague worker, but by a third party, this did not circumscribe the employer's duty of care.

It follows from the Commission's case law that under Dutch equal treatment law the person exercising authority may be held responsible for acts of distinction, including harassment, committed by employees as well as by third parties. However, the practical effect of this is rather limited. It should be emphasised that the Commission's case law is non-binding, although it can still be valuable in terms of recognition of the complaint and in terms of emotional satisfaction. Moreover, the Commission may not impose pecuniary or other sanctions upon a perpetrator other than making recommendations to the parties concerned. Any compensation for (pecuniary) damages must be claimed on the basis of general employment law, administrative law or tort law. However, the ordinary courts are not bound by the Commission's Opinion in a case. Against this background it is seriously doubted whether the range of sanctions available under Dutch equal treatment law are in conformity with the Directives' requirements that sanctions be 'effective', 'proportionate' and 'dissuasive'.[243]

Beyond the scope of Dutch equal treatment legislation the following is essential to take account of. The employer may be held vicariously liable for harassing acts committed by colleague workers under general private employment law. The relevant Articles upon which a claim can be based are: *(1)* the good employer's practice (*goed werkgeversschap*, Article 7:611 of the Civil Code); *(2)* the employer's general duty of care (i.e. the employer's liability for damages suffered by an employee in the performance of job-related duties regulated in Article 7:658 of the Civil Code). Both of these Articles are directed at the employer's liability for acts done by the employer himself, or by others over whom the employer has control. It is disputed in legal circles whether Article 7:658 of the Civil Code can form the legal basis for claims which concern mere psychological damage, rather than physical damage.[244] It is submitted that damage resulting from discriminatory treatment and harassment is most often of a psychological kind. Although the Dutch Supreme Court has given no decisive answer the lower courts have been prepared to accept Article 7:658 of

242 See, for example, Opinion 1997-122.

243 Also Asscher-Vonk 1999, p. 301-319.

244 Geers 2003, p. 188 with further references to the literature on this question. Also Vegter 2001, p. 134. With regard to Article 7:611 of the Civil Code the Supreme Court has decided that this Article may be relied upon to claim compensation for damages of a mere psychological kind. See HR 11 juli 1993, *NJ* 1993 667 (*Nuts/Hofman*), cited by Geers 2003, p. 188, footnote 12.

the Civil Code as a basis for financial compensation of psychological damage resulting from sexually harassing acts.[245]

6. Conclusions and Cross-Country Comparison

In this chapter, the concepts of harassment and sexual harassment have been examined from the perspective of comparative law. Furthermore, 'harassment' and 'sexual harassment' have been analysed in the context of legal theory. With reference to Friedman and Whitman, it has been illustrated that, whereas American law has traditionally conceived harassment as a form of discrimination, the continental legal tradition has emphasised the element of dignity in the discourse on harassment. It has been argued that the approach to harassment adopted by contemporary EC equality law reconciles the paradigms of 'discrimination' and 'dignity', by stretching the underlying values of the principle of equality itself. Notably in the realm of harassment, the principle of equality accords a validated, rather than a comparative, connotation to justice, given that 'harassment' has been defined as an autonomous form of discrimination. It has been illustrated that 'harassment' fits well with a 'dignity model' of equality, which has traditionally inspired the feminist discourse on sexual harassment. Furthermore, as argued, the concept of harassment correlates with the 'equality as participation' model. This argument has been inspired by Schultz's theoretical work on harassment and sexual harassment. Rather than 'dignity' and 'sexuality', Schultz has emphasised the effects of exclusion arising from harassment.

The analysis of harassment in positive EC law has shown that 'harassment' and 'sexual harassment' have, for the first time, become regulated in binding Community law. The legal establishment of harassment and sexual harassment is liberated from the requirement of drawing a comparison with a similarly situated legal equivalent. This constitutes a quantum leap forward in the protection by anti-discrimination law from this social evil. Harassment needs to be ground-related in order to be actionable under EC law which means that mere mobbing is not covered. Unlike direct and indirect discrimination, 'harassment' is prohibited *per se* and therefore strict conditions have to be met before a case of harassment can be established. The analysis of harassment in the AETD has, however, shown that a lower evidentiary burden is placed on the plaintiff who claims an instance of *sexual* harassment. Furthermore, it has been shown that, whereas hostile work environment harassment is regulated by EC law with respect to all grounds of discrimination, *quid pro quo* harassment is solely regulated with respect to 'sex'. With the exception of 'sexual orientation', *quid pro quo* harassment is not relevant in relation to other discrimination grounds which, by nature, do not lend themselves for *quid pro quo* 'scenario's'. The RD and the EFD remain silent on the issue of liability for harassment. The matter of liability remains therefore a matter for the Member States to decide on. However, the latter will have

245 Vegter 2001, p. 134-135 with reference to the following cases: Rb Rotterdam [Rotterdam District Court] 30 september 1999, *JAR* 1999, 230. Pres. Rb Amsterdam [President of Rotterdam District Court] 22 februari 2001, *Rechtspraak Nemesis* 2001, 1319. Kantongerecht [Cantonal Court] Harderwijk 25 april 2001, JAR 2001, 118.

to comply with the requirement that sanctions are effective, proportionate and dissuasive. It has moreover been argued that the AETD, compared to the RD and the EFD, places a duty upon the Member States to take preventive measures against harassment and sexual harassment at the workplace.

The autonomous approach to harassment and sexual harassment adopted by EC equality law has had an impact upon the legal approach adopted by the domestic legal frameworks. This is particularly true with respect to English law. In its pre-implementation format, the approach to harassment adopted by English law was governed by a 'direct discrimination' and 'detriment' approach, which placed great emphasis upon the comparative exercise. Although the lower courts adopted a common sense approach to harassment by holding that, in such cases where the harassing act at issue is *race or gender specific,* the need for a comparative exercise becomes redundant. This line of reasoning has eventually been undermined by the Law Lords' unanimous decision in *Pearce.* It has been shown that *Pearce* is no longer the applicable authority with respect to instances of harassment that fall within the scope of EC implemented law. Post-implementation of EC law, the need for a comparative exercise has been abolished and harassment is conceived as an independent form of discrimination. However, as the discussion has shown, with respect to these areas which fall outside the scope of EC implemented law, the pre-implementation approach to harassment remains valid law. With respect to the matter of liability for harassment, the discussion of English law has shown that liability may either be vicarious or direct. Moreover, a colleague worker, who has meted out harassing treatment to another worker, can be held personally liable for the reprehensible conduct complained of. This, it has been argued, is in line with the spirit of Community law. The analysis of the employer's direct liability for harassing acts inflicted upon employees by third parties has shown once again the pivotal role played by the legal comparison. This role has not been diminished post implementation of EC law, notwithstanding that the latter conceptualises harassment as an autonomous form of discrimination. In summary, establishing an employer's direct liability for acts of third parties remains founded on the direct discrimination and detriment approach which calls for a comparative exercise.

In Dutch law, the regulation of harassment at work embeds both a health and safety rationale, and a concern over equality. The regulation of harassment and sexual harassment by the AWC has not received top-down influence by EC law with the result that the legal definitions of sexual harassment in the AWC, on the one hand, and the AET w/m, on the other, have not been streamlined. Similar to the approach adopted in the context of English statutory anti-discrimination law, pre-implementation of EC law, the Dutch ETC has analysed claims of harassment on the basis of direct distinction (*direct onderscheid*). However, whereas in English law the judicial line of reasoning has often been frustrated by the need for drawing a legal comparison with a similarly situated comparator, this has not been the case in Dutch law. The Dutch equal treatment Acts *inter alia* prohibit direct distinction with respect to the conditions of employment. This has been interpreted by the Commission as covering the right of an employee to be protected from ground-related harassment. The Commission's case law indicates that a victim of harassment should inform the employer about the (alleged) acts of harassment, for the latter can otherwise defend himself against liability by asserting that he was unaware of the alleged harassing conduct. The same has been held by the courts in the context of English law. In the post-implementation context, harassment has become a *sui generis* form of distinction, although the pre-implementation approach has not ceased to exist. In line with EC law, Dutch law requires that cumulative conditions be proven in order to establish harassment, with the exception, however, of sexual harassment. English law, in contrast, merely requires proof of alternative conditions with respect to all forms of harassment, a stance which has been necessitated by the non-regression clauses in the Directives.

Lastly, the matter of liability has been considered in the context of Dutch law. It has been argued that the asserted inapplicability of Dutch equal treatment law to acts of discrimination, including harassment, between colleague workers *inter se*, falls short of supranational equality law. It follows from the ETC's case law that an employer can be held responsible for the acts of harassment meted out by his employees to other employees, as well as for acts of harassment by third persons. If, however, an employer has acquitted himself of his duty of care and has in place a properly functioning anti-harassment policy, a case of distinction will not be established. In this way a 'reasonable steps defence' seems to have been incorporated into the ETC's case law. Notwithstanding that the ETC has held that an employer can be held liable for acts of employees and third parties, the analysis has emphasised that this holding has little practical effects. It has been highlighted that the ETC cannot impose pecuniary or other binding sanctions upon a perpetrator. Pecuniary damages can only be claimed before an ordinary court on the basis of general employment law, tort law or administrative law. In light of this it can hardly be maintained that Dutch equal treatment law provides for sanctions which are 'effective' and 'dissuasive'.

PART III

PROACTIVE STRATEGIES

Part III

PROACTIVE STRATEGIES[1]

In the foregoing Part II, two concepts which present themselves generally in the areas of equality and non-discrimination were analysed on the basis of a top-down, cross-country, cross-ground and bottom-up comparison wherever this was appropriate. In Chapter 5 hereafter, I will proceed with an analysis of 'positive action' on the basis of a multi-facetted comparison. Seeking greater equality for members of disadvantaged groups can be achieved by 'reactive' strategies and by 'proactive' strategies. The reactive strategy reflects a non-discrimination approach: the law prohibits, e.g. direct and indirect discrimination on the basis of certain protected grounds (race, sex, religion, etc.) and in a limited number of areas of social life (employment, social security, the provision of goods and services, etc.). The reactive strategy has also been termed the 'negative obligations' approach.[2] Reactive strategies are sought to be materialised by means of 'hard law' measures[3] (rather than with 'soft law' measures), which can be enforced by individual victims against individual perpetrators before the courts. In light of this, Fredman has spoken of the 'complaints-led model' which seeks to enforce individual rights.[4] In contrast, proactive strategies seek to ameliorate the disadvantaged position of out-groups by means of 'positive obligations' and positive strategies.[5] At least two distinct modes of proactive approaches

1 In writing this Part, I have benefited from the seminars on European Employment and Equality Law (by Freedland, McCrudden, Davies and Costello) in which I participated during a research visit at the University of Oxford in 2005.

2 See Hervey 2005, p. 316.

3 In the context of the EU Shaw has spoken of the so-called 'Monnet' or 'Community' method of achieving the objectives set by the Union. Shaw has highlighted 2 characteristics of this method: (1) the pivotal role of *legislation* in seeking to pursue the Union's objectives, and, (2) the 'institutional configuration' as foreseen by the Rome Treaty for the adoption of legislation with defined roles for the Commission, the Council of Ministers and the Parliament. See Shaw 2004, p. 268. The 'Monnet Method' has also been characteristic for the evolution of EC equality and non-discrimination law, although it has been complemented with proactive strategies since the entering into force of the ToA. This will be elaborated on in the main text above.

4 Fredman 2005a, p. 369.

5 Hervey 2005, p. 317.

can be discerned namely, (1) a strategy of 'mainstreaming' and a (2) 'positive action' strategy.[6] Mainstreaming has been defined as follows:

> '[Mainstreaming is] the integration of equal opportunities principles, strategies and practices into the every day work of Government and other public bodies from the outset, involving 'every day' policy actors in addition to equality specialists. In other words, it entails rethinking mainstream provision to accommodate gender, race, disability and other dimensions of discrimination and disadvantage, including class, sexuality and religion.'[7]

Hence, mainstreaming is conceived of as a strategy seeking to influence policy processes and seeking to guarantee certain outcomes. Moreover, it is pre-eminently a strategy which is aimed at raising consciousness in daily decision-making processes. Since the entering into force of the ToA, *gender*-mainstreaming[8] has been a legal requirement under EC law. This follows from Article 3(2) EC which provides as follows: 'In all the activities referred to in this Article [including employment; MG], the Community shall aim to eliminate inequalities, and to promote equality, between women and men.'

Due to constraints of time and space, the strategy of mainstreaming will not be analysed in further detail hereafter.[9] In the analysis to follow, I will solely focus upon the secondly mentioned proactive strategy, namely positive action. In contrast with 'mainstreaming', 'positive action' must be reconciled with the (reactively oriented) non-discrimination paradigm. This required reconciliation is caused by the principle of formal equality, which largely features both EC and domestic non-discrimination law.[10] This will be examined in great depth in Chapter 5 to follow. There is yet another important difference between 'mainstreaming' and 'positive action' which is worth pointing out: unlike *(gender)* mainstreaming, positive action is not legally required by EC law. However, as will be explained, if the Member States avail themselves of positive action strategies, they will have to act within the legal parameters set by EC law. The legal parameters within which positive action must remain will be discussed hereafter from the perspective of comparative law. It is to this analysis that I will turn now.

6 It is worth observing that English law is characterised by a third modus of proactive strategies namely, the 'positive duties approach'. The RRAA (Race Relations Amendment Act) 2000, the DDA 2005 and the proposed Equality Act 2006 impose a positive duty upon public sector authorities to promote equality. For further discussion on the positive duties approach in English law as well as its historical background, I refer to the following contributions: Hill 2001; O'Cinneide 2005; O'Cinneide 2005a.

7 See Shaw 2004, p. 255, footnote 1 with reference to the website of the UK Equal Opportunities Commission.

8 No equivalent provisions are contained in the EC Treaty with respect to the other discrimination grounds contained in Article 13 EC.

9 The reader is referred to the following academic commentaries: Fredman 2005a, p. 369-397; Shaw 2004, p. 255-312; Bell 2001, p. 20-34 (who has analysed mainstreaming of equality in the specific context of EU asylum law); Beveridge, Nott and Stephen 2000, p. 136-154; Veldman 1999; Rees 1998.

10 With the exception of the DDA 1995 in the context of English non-discrimination law. Moreover, the concept of indirect discrimination analysed in Chapter 3 reflects a substantive interpretation of the principle of equality.

Chapter 5

POSITIVE ACTION

1. Introduction

What is meant by positive action? It is suggested that a broad definition of positive action could be the following: positive action is a temporary proactive strategy which seeks to further *de facto* or genuine equality for disadvantaged groups such as, women, racial minorities, disabled persons, etc. This definition reflects a wide interpretation of what may fall within the scope of positive action measures. It will be seen below that such measures can indeed be very diverse in form and nature. It is important to stress that because of its proactive and positive nature, positive action has to be contrasted with more conventional strategies, notably the prohibition of discrimination by law, which are reactive. Reactive strategies (which may nevertheless be infused with a substantive justice rationale)[1] were discussed in Part II.

In this chapter I will analyse the concept of positive action from a comparative law perspective. This means that this concept will be subjected to a top-down, cross-ground and cross-country analysis.[2] The top-down analysis sheds light on the question if, and to what extent, domestic positive action law has received top-down pressure from EC law. As will be seen, EC positive action law flows from both hard and soft law measures. Moreover, and importantly, EC positive action law with regard to sex has been interpreted in the case law of the ECJ. The cross-ground comparison seeks to examine what lessons could be learned from positive action

1 Thus, as was illustrated in Chapter 3, the prohibition by law of indirect discrimination is premised upon the theoretical concept of substantive justice. Moreover, as we saw in Chapter 4, harassment as it is currently defined in EC and domestic law is premised upon deontological justice (rather than comparative justice) which echoes concerns over substantive justice. See for further analysis, Chapters 3 and 4.

2 In this chapter, I will not discuss positive action in the context of international law Treaties, notably the UN Convention on the Elimination of All Forms of Discrimination Against Women (CEDAW Convention, 1979) and the UN Convention on the Elimination of All Forms of Racial Discrimination (CERD Convention, 1965). For an extensive analysis of so-called 'temporary measures' in the context of (Article 4 of) the CEDAW, I refer to the excellent contributions in Boerefijn, Coomans, Goldschmidt, Holtmaat and Wolleswinkel (eds.) 2003.

law in the field of sex, for other grounds, e.g. race or disability. It is to be noted that EC law has traditionally regulated the adoption of positive action measures in the field of sex equality law. However, positive action measures for the other grounds of discrimination, contained in Article 13 EC, have only been regulated since the adoption of the RD and the EFD in 2000. The foregoing helps explain why all existing ECJ case law on positive action concerns the discrimination ground of sex. The cross-country comparison will reveal possible differences in the approaches adopted in England and in the Netherlands with respect to positive action. Such differences may exist even post-implementation of EC law. Indeed, as will be seen, EC law does not place Member States under a legal obligation to enact positive action measures but rather sets the outer limits to such measures. This means that a great deal of legislative discretion in this area has been left to the Member States. Therefore, the cross-country comparison is likely to reveal divergences in the legal approaches embedded in English[3] and Dutch law. Only if relevant, I will make reference to bottom-up influence in the discussion to follow. Bottom-up influence refers to the (possible) influence of national approaches and practices upon the shaping of EC law. The discussion to follow will be presented as follows. In section 2, I will first outline different forms of positive action and the different purposes which positive action measures seek to pursue. In section 3, I will subsequently link the concept of positive action to a number of theoretical issues concerning equality and non-discrimination as principles of normative justice. In section 4, positive action will be discussed in the context of EC law. This discussion will also be functional to the top-down analysis to be carried out in sections 5 and 6. Section 5 will analyse positive action in the context of English non-discrimination law, whereas section 6 will examine positive action in the context of Dutch equal treatment law. In the analysis of positive action in EC and domestic law, I will establish links with the theoretical issues considered in section 3. Overall conclusions will be drawn in section 7.

2. Positive Action: Forms and Purposes

2.1. Forms of Positive Action

What does positive action encompass? In 1986 McCrudden wrote in an article in the Industrial Law Journal that '(...) almost all that has been written about [positive action; MG] (…) concentrates not on its content, but on the techniques and methods (…) by which it may be encouraged or required'.[4] Having examined a wide range of academic commentaries on positive action in the context of EC and domestic law, it appears that in present times McCrudden's observation can be mitigated. Academic commentary nowadays tends to focus upon the theoretical foundations of positive

3 It should be noted that this chapter does not cover an analysis of positive action measures in the context of Northern Ireland. An empirical analysis of Northern Irish law on affirmative action has been made by McCrudden, Ford and Heath 2004 to which the reader is referred.

4 McCrudden 1986, p. 220.

action and upon the scope granted by the law for the adoption of such measures.[5] Despite this (partially) renewed focus it nonetheless remains important to know what types of positive action measures exist because the diverse measures tend to be infused with different theoretical conceptualisations of equality and justice. Positive action might embrace a wide range of measures, policies and practices all of which to a greater or lesser degree shatter the paradigms of the individual libertarian model of justice.[6] McCrudden has distinguished five types of action which *might* (his emphasis) be embraced by the notion of positive action.[7] Firstly, writes McCrudden, positive action may be directed at those measures which are aimed at 'eradicating [present and future; MG] discrimination'. They are a necessary complement to the 'negative' non-discrimination approach, which is most clearly embedded within the prohibition of direct discrimination on a forbidden ground.[8] Measures falling within this category show only slight tensions with the ideas underlying formal justice given that they are merely responsive to past (and present) disadvantages suffered by minority groups without, however, permitting preferential treatment. Such measures might also be called 'positive supporting measures'. An example is open advertising to counteract discrimination nourished by 'word of mouth hiring'. Secondly, positive action includes 'facially neutral but purposefully inclusionary policies'. The aim of such policies is to ensure a greater proportional representation of members of the disadvantaged group through the application of *prima facie* neutral criteria. Such

5 See for example the work by Fredman 1997; Young 1990, Chapter 7; Caruso 2002; Burrows and Robison 2006. This partially renewed focus can *inter alia* be explained by the fact that in the context of Community law a number of important judgments on positive action for women have come before the ECJ. The outcome of these judgments have had an impact upon the legal scope for positive action measures at the level of the Member States. Moreover, the Court's outcome in these decisions tells us much about the underlying theoretical foundations of the principle of equality in the context of Community sex discrimination law. EC positive action law will extensively be dealt with in section 4.

6 Fredman 1997, p. 575-600. The central tenets of the individual libertarian model of justice have been discussed in Chapter 3 in the context of indirect discrimination. In section 3 hereafter, I will elaborate further on theoretical models of equality and justice in relation to the concept of positive action.

7 McCrudden 1986, p. 223-225. Also Costello 2003, 178-180. See for a different classification Connolly 2004, p. 571.

8 Costello has moreover argued that such measures acknowledge the limits of the individual enforcement approach. The individual enforcement approach grants individual persons a right to non-discrimination on certain forbidden grounds of discrimination. This model tends to outlaw discrimination in a limited number of areas of social life. If an individual's right to non-discrimination has been infringed by a discernible perpetrator who has committed a 'fault', the right-holder will be entitled to bring a claim before a court. The individual enforcement approach thus reflects a 'fault-based approach'. See Costello 2003, p. 178. The fault based approach has traditionally characterised EC and domestic non-discrimination law. It can be contrasted with 'fourth generation equality rights' which support a positive duties and mainstreaming approach. Fourth generation equality law recognises that acts of discrimination are often institutionalised which means, that the acts as such and the individual perpetrator who commits these acts cannot always easily be discerned. Positive duties and mainstreaming strategies have *inter alia* been analysed by the following: Fredman 2001a; O'cinneide 2005a; Beveridge, Nott and Stephen (2000); Shaw 2005 and Veldman 1999.

measures do not overtly use a person's group-membership as a criterion for eligibility for training, employment, etc., but the effect in practice of such measures is that persons who can comply with the neutrally applied criterion overwhelmingly belong to the disadvantaged group. Strictly spoken, from the view point of formal justice, such measures constitute indirect discrimination against people belonging to the majority group.[9] Examples of such measures are the following: the condition of living in a particular geographical area in order to obtain a training position; preference afforded by the employer to those who have been long-term unemployed; preference for part-time workers; taking into account a person's capabilities and experience which have been acquired by carrying out family work or caring tasks. As stated, the formal justice doctrine functions as a watchdog for such measures which infringe on the moral foundations of formal equality. If the law was premised upon substantive justice, it would prescribe that the objective justification test for indirect discrimination should allow for the application of 'neutral criteria' whose underlying purpose is the furtherance of substantive justice.[10] In the context of English law, the EAT has, however, rejected such an approach. In *Greater Manchester Police Authority v. Lea*[11] it was held that indirectly discriminatory practices by employers could not be justified on the basis that the goals pursued by the contested measures served laudable social aims (in the case at hand: helping the unemployed).[12] In the third place, McCrudden has mentioned 'outreach programmes'. These are programmes or measures which quite actively promote and encourage members belonging to minority groups to apply for jobs and training. Such measures guarantee a fairly representative pool of applicants for new jobs perceived, for example, in light of the population in a given geographical area.[13] Some of the contested measures in the *Badeck*[14] case, to be examined in section 4 hereafter, belong to this category. Outreach measures can be distinguished from the first and second mentioned measures in that they openly and consciously use a person's group membership as a material factor in the decision-making process. Outreach measures support the principle of equality of opportunity but not genuine substantive equality. Such measures are aimed at equalising the 'starting points' without, however, providing guarantees for equality of outcome.[15] Once the starting points have been equalised, the principle of formal equality governs the remainder of the decision-making process. The reservation of a certain percentage of places for women in training programmes is a common example of an outreach measure. Since outreach measures merely seek to equalise 'starting points',[16] they are necessarily taken prior to the actual recruitment

9 For this reason, Townshend-Smith has termed such measures 'indirect discrimination in reverse'. See Townshend Smith 1989, p. 227.

10 Hepple 1990, p. 415.

11 *Greater Manchester Police Authority v. Lea* [1990] IRLR 372 (EAT).

12 See for further discussion McColgan 2005, p. 140-141.

13 Hepple 1990, p. 414.

14 *Badeck & Others v. Hessische Ministerpraesident and Landesanwalt beim Staatsgerichtshof des Landes Hessen* Case C-158/97 [2000] ECR I-1875.

15 Fredman 2000, p. 175.

16 It should be noted that outreach measures stand in parallel with the equal opportunities paradigm in the sense that such measures are aimed at bringing about equal opportunities →

process or prior to a decision regarding the promotion of an employee.[17] Fourthly, positive action entails 'preferential treatment in employment'. Preferential treatment may be underpinned by, either the philosophy of equality of opportunity, or by the philosophy of equality of outcome. If the formal principle of equality is taken as a starting point, measures which echo 'equality of opportunity' will be regarded as less controversial than measures which aim at equality of outcome. This is so because the principle of equality of opportunity preserves, more than the principle of equality of outcome, the principle of 'meritocracy'[18] (i.e. the principle that the 'best' person should be given a particular opportunity, e.g. a job, a promotion, etc), which is one of the elements of the formal justice paradigm. Both approaches have in common that they consciously use status-based criteria (race, sex, disability, etc.) in the decision-making process. The difference is, however, that, whereas in the equality of opportunities approach such criteria are advantageous, they are instrumental (or functional) to an equality of outcome approach. Let me briefly elaborate on this point hereafter.

Preferential treatment infused with an equal opportunities approach

If preferential treatment is infused with an equal opportunities approach, it will show sympathy for the so-called 'merit tie-break principle'. In merit tie-break situations being of, e.g. a particular sex or race, or being disabled, is advantageous but not conditional in the decision-making process. Once it is clear that a number of persons are equally competent for the job at hand, the tie-break principle permits the employer to treat a person belonging to a disadvantaged group more favourably.[19] The principle of merit is, however, preserved, for the tie-break principle insists that all persons who are eligible for the job are equally qualified. In summary, the application of the tie-break principle is preferred over throwing a dice or tossing a coin.

Preferential treatment embedded within an equality of outcome (or results) model

If, however, preferential treatment is embedded within an equality of outcome (or results) model, such kind of treatment will be far more controversial. This is so, for such measures overthrow the central tenets of formal equality including the principle of merit, the principle of symmetry and the principle of individual justice. It is recalled from other junctures in this book that symmetry requires that persons of the dominant group (e.g. men) are no less protected than persons of the disadvantaged group (e.g. women). The principle of individual justice seeks to guarantee justice at the level of individuals, rather than at the level of groups.[20] Preferential treatment

before the actual competition for jobs starts. However, at the level of *training* such measures amount to preferential treatment and thus, at that level, they appear to parallel with the equality of outcome paradigm. This is so, for such measures *guarantee* that a certain percentage of women fill the available training places.

17 Costello 2003, p. 179.

18 For an in depth discussion of the concept of 'merit', I refer to McCrudden 1998.

19 Hepple 1990, p. 415.

20 The individual and group justice models were explained in Chapter 3 in the context of indirect discrimination.

which is based on the equality of outcome or results paradigm is tantamount to so-called 'reverse discrimination'.[21] Reverse discrimination accords the ultimate victory to a person's group-membership, rather than to 'merit', given that it permits preferential treatment of less qualified candidates belonging to an out-group (e.g. employment quotas for disabled people).

The commonality between the two forms of preferential treatment outlined above is that both afford more favourable treatment to members belonging to an out-group at the level of employment (including recruitment, promotion or, as the case might be, dismissal), although the intensity of 'more favourable treatment' differs for both forms of preferential treatment. In sharp contrast, outreach measures and programmes are necessarily to be taken prior to a decision on employment.

A fifth and last form of positive action distinguished by McCrudden is the 'redefinition of merit'. This type of positive action alters the qualifications necessary for the job. Suddenly, a person's gender, race, disability, etc. may become a relevant job criterion. This type of positive action underpins the genuine occupational requirement exception (GOR) to the principle of non-discrimination.[22] For example, being a woman could be a relevant job-criterion for the function of counsellor to women who have been the victims of rape. In this example, a woman may show more empathy for the needs of the care receivers. The GOR exception is a clear-cut example. More generally, decision-makers should constantly be wary of biases and stereotypes permeating the notion of merit.[23]

The foregoing discussion has shown that the scope of positive action is arguably very wide. Important to bear in mind, however, is that positive action measures are

21 Preferential treatment in this sense is sometimes wrongly referred to as 'positive discrimination'. Bossuyt has convincingly argued that the notion of positive discrimination' is a contradiction in terms. The concept of discrimination is pejorative in the sense that is refers to arbitrary, illegitimate, irrational, biased or unjust distinctions between persons or groups of persons. This being so, discrimination can never be logically reconciled with the adjective 'positive'. Once the distinction is no longer arbitrary, illegitimate, irrational etc., it can no longer be said to constitute discrimination. See Bossuyt 1998, p. 243 and Bossuyt 2002, p. 1-2.

22 This will be discussed extensively in Chapter 6 in the context of 'religion' and 'belief'.

23 Many have criticised the usage of 'merit' (defined as 'best technically competent') in decision-making processes. Young, who has referred to the 'myth of merit' has argued that merit is never objective, nor unbiased with regard to personal attributes (Young 1990, p. 202). Fredman has also argued that merit cannot be defined in the abstract, for prejudicial assumptions may well infiltrate into the appraisal of merit itself. She has argued that the application of 'merit' operates to the advantage of men. If, for example, women's informal work-experiences are a priori neglected in the definition of merit, the application of this principle will work to the benefit of men (Fredman 2000, p. 174 and Fredman 1997a, p. 381). In other words, the usage of 'merit' criteria may trigger instances of indirect discrimination. A similar criticism has been voiced by Hepple, who has argued that the usage of merit cannot guarantee 'equality of opportunity', if this principle is uncritically applied to those who never have had a chance to acquire 'merit' in the first place (Hepple 1990, p. 411). See moreover Schiek 2000a, p. 256 who has observed that '(...) finding that a woman is equally qualified often disguises the fact that her superior qualifications are not acknowledged in a gendered employment surrounding'.

meant to be temporary, which brings with it the fact that their legitimacy fades when the hitherto disadvantageous group can no longer be said to be in a socially disadvantageous position. Inter alia in this respect, we must distinguish positive action from the notion of reasonable accommodation,[24] which is not featured by temporal limits. Hereafter, I will not deal with all of the different forms of positive action mentioned above. I will foremost deal with outreach measures and with preferential treatment at the level of employment. Where appropriate, I will also touch on measures seeking to redefine merit.

2.2. *What Purposes Do Positive Action Measures Pursue?*[25]

2.2.1. Introductory Remarks

Positive action in the form of preferential treatment is defined by Bossuyt as follows:

> 'Affirmative action [which in his view is synonymous with positive action MG] is a coherent packet of measures, of a temporary character, aimed specifically at correcting the position of members of a target group in one or more respects of their social life, in order to obtain effective equality.'[26]

Thus, positive action is about correcting institutionalised imbalances which are caused, not only due to past disadvantage but also, and no less important, by current and future biases and prejudices.[27] As seen above, once the imbalance has been corrected, the legitimacy for positive action declines.[28] The question arises what are the purposes pursued by positive action measures and policies? It should be noted that the question of purposes must conceptually be distinguished from the question of (moral) justification of positive action, although both questions are clearly interrelated. After all, if the purposes of positive action measures are legitimate, it will be

24 This notion will be extensively discussed in Chapter 8 in the context of 'disability' (see sections 3.2.4 and 4.5. of Chapter 8).

25 This part draws to a large extent on Bossuyt 2002, under II.

26 Bossuyt 2002, p. 3.

27 Young, p. 194. The 'forward-looking justification' (to be contrasted with the 'backward-looking justification') has also been emphasised by Duppert 2005.

28 One of the most difficult, preliminary, questions in the positive action debate is *which groups* find themselves in a 'sufficiently' socially imbalanced position so as to legitimately benefit from positive action measures and policies? This question is often decided by the national legislator (Bossuyt 2002, p. 3). As will be seen later on in the analysis, although EC law permits the usage of positive action measures for a wide range of disadvantaged groups, it is ultimately for the Member States to decide whether or not to adopt positive action measures and for which groups. In deciding on whether or not a group finds itself in a disadvantaged position statistics are a crucial factor. However, in certain jurisdictions it is not permitted to gain statistics on matters regarding 'race' and 'ethnicity'. See Tyson 2001, p. 203. Also McCrudden 2003, footnote 71. Moreover, in light of the fluid and heterogeneous character of 'disability' (to be examined in detail in Chapter 8) it is very difficult to capture the degree of disadvantage suffered by disabled persons by statistical data. The same holds true with regard to 'sexual orientation' (to be discussed extensively in Chapter 7) which, in addition, entails the risk of breaching privacy rights.

easier to justify their adoption.[29] Justification of positive action measures will be considered in section 3 from the perspective of legal theory, and in Sections 4 to 6 in the context of EC and domestic law. Hereafter, I will elaborate on the various purposes which may be pursued by positive action measures in light of a number of wider rationales which lie at the root of positive action.

2.2.2. Positive Action: Rationales and Purposes

An analysis of the relevant literature reveals that the overarching rationales which underlie positive action measures and policies can be classified along four separate strands: (1) bringing about a fairer distribution of resources (e.g. jobs, housing, training-places etc.);[30] (2) achieving greater participation of disadvantaged groups in decision-making processes; (3) enhancing effectiveness; and (4) combating oppression and dominance.[31] As is often the case with classifications, the lines between them are not rigid but fluid instead. Hereafter, I will examine a number of purposes of positive action measures. The various purposes will be linked with the wider rationales referred to under 1-4 above.

Perhaps the most cited purpose of positive action is to redress historical or past disadvantage.[32] Positive action measures function as a counter-mechanism to restore these. One should, however, add a (perhaps) more pressing purpose served by the ideology of affirmative action namely, addressing *current* biases, stereotypes and prejudices in decision-making processes.[33] The purposes of redressing past and current (and future) disadvantage neatly fit with the first-mentioned rationale above (i.e. 'redistribution'). After all, by granting preferential treatment to those who have suffered past disadvantage, jobs, training-positions and the like are re-allocated from the advantaged to the disadvantaged group. The just-mentioned purposes moreover interlock with the fourth rationale mentioned above (i.e. 'combating oppression and domination') which has particularly been stressed by Young.[34] Secondly, positive action measures may pursue the objective of counteracting and unmasking

29 However, as the analysis of the ECJ's case law on positive action will reveal, justification requires more than merely that the aims pursued by positive action are legitimate.

30 See Caruso, who has argued that positive action ought not to be conceptualised as an exception to the principles of non-discrimination and equality but as one of many strategies which seek to re-allocate resources from the advantaged to the disadvantaged group. See Caruso 2002, p. 2 and under II.

31 Notably Young 1990.

32 For example, Boxill 1984, p. 148-167 cited by Young 1990, p. 194. See also Bossuyt 2002, p. 5 who has mentioned this as the first theoretical basis permitting for positive action. Also Gerards 2005b, p. 631-632 (with further references).

33 Young 1990, p. 194 and Duppert 2005 who has especially emphasised the 'forward-looking justification' of positive action.

34 Young 1990. In general Young, favours to conceptualise equality along the lines of 'oppression' rather than 'redistribution'. See Young 1990, Chapter 1. She has argued at p. 195 that '[affirmative action] (..) becomes one of many group-conscious policies instrumental in undermining oppression'.

'structural' or 'institutionalised' forms of discrimination.[35] For example, if an employer affords preferential treatment to women in the allocation of childcare facilities with a view to attracting more female workers, this may help overcome gender-divisions in the family. This purpose also concurs with the redistribution rationale: the positive action measures help redistribute jobs from men to women. It moreover interlocks with the second and fourth rationales mentioned above (i.e. 'participation' and 'combating oppression and domination', respectively).

Thirdly, positive action measures and policies may seek to pursue the goals of inclusion and diversity.[36] Naturally, this fits with the *participation rationale* mentioned above. In Young's view, '[e]quality refers not primarily to the distribution of social goods, though distributions are certainly entailed by social equality. It refers primarily to the full participation and inclusion of everyone in society's major institutions (...)'.[37] It is submitted that the 'participation rationale' is for its turn ingrained with notions of 'fairness' and 'effectiveness'. Young has convincingly argued that 'justice' requires the inclusion and participation of as many groups as possible within a given decision-making process.[38] Not only does this mirror a fairer representation of interests, it also safeguards the opportunity for as many as possible to exercise their talents.[39] The 'participation rationale' reflects concerns over effectiveness in the sense that it transmits the idea that, the fairer the representation of disadvantaged groups in the decision-making process, the more effective decisions are taken. It is submitted that, if members of the excluded group occupy seminal positions in socio-

35 Bossuyt 2002, p. 15.

36 Bossuyt 2002, p. 6, where he has referred to the creation of diversity and proportional group representation as a conceptual basis permitting positive action. See also Quinn 2004, p. 11 where he has observed as follows: '(...) there is a congruence between the end (if not always the means) of positive action and non-discrimination and it is this congruence that allows both to co-exist. It is precisely because non-discrimination is a tool for the achievement of diversity that it can sit well with (...) positive action measures.' See also Gerards 2005b, p. 634-638, who in this context has referred to 'descriptieve representatie' ['descriptive representation'] i.e., to '(...)[the] representation of socially relevant groups in certain functions or institutions'. *('(...)[de] vertegenwoordiging van maatschappelijke relevante groepen in bepaalde functies of instellingen.'* (translation; MG], (p. 634-635). As Gerards has stressed, the 'descriptive representation' rationale for positive action measures has *not* been acknowledged in the ECJ's case law (to be discussed in section 4.3 hereafter). This can be contrasted with the modus of legal reasoning by the UN Human Rights Committee in the case of *Jacobs v. Belgium* (CCPR/C/81/D/943/2000) in which this rationale *was* recognised. For further commentary on the aforementioned case *in se*, as well as in relation to EC law, I refer to Gerards 2005b.

37 Young 1990, p. 173. Young has made this argument within a discussion on the politics of difference. However, she also seems to regard participation as the primary goal of affirmative action (see p. 198). Others have argued that equality has little to do with the idea of distribution. Somek, for example, has argued as follows: 'Equality is not a rule of distributive justice in the sense that its point is to determine what kind of treatment people are entitled to in virtue of some 'natural dimension', such as need, effort, well-being and so on. (...) equality is not an elementary distributive principle (...).' See Somek 2001, p. 175. He has argued that equality is purely to be conceived of as a comparative right. That equality entails more has been and will be illustrated at various junctures in this book. See, for example, Chapters 3, 4 and 8.

38 Young 1990, p. 173.

39 See McCrudden 2003a, p. 31 *et seq.* where has explained the model of 'equality as participation'.

political and economic life, the interests of all excluded groups will be better served. Fourthly, some have regarded positive action as a necessary tool to optimise economic efficiency within the free market.[40] On this vision the operation of the free-market is allegedly hampered by irrational assumptions and bias related to a person's race, sex, etc. This fourth purpose of positive action could be linked with the third strand mentioned above (i.e. 'enhancing effectiveness').

It is once again stressed that even if we all agreed on the legitimacy of the above purposes, the usage of positive action would not necessarily be lawful. As Rubenfeld has observed in the context of race relations law, '[t]he ultimate question is whether whites' equal protection rights are violated when the government purposefully acts to assist blacks and other minorities by granting them special opportunities'.[41] Whether or not the answer to this question is affirmative is largely dependent on which theoretical model underpins the legal framework on equality. Put differently, whether positive action can be justified is dependent upon one's vision of moral justice and, related to that, on one's opinion as to how 'equality' must be conceptualised. In the section to follow, I will examine how positive action interlocks with various theoretical models of equality and justice.

3. Positive Action and Theoretical Issues of Equality

3.1. 'Equality': a Multiply-Edged Principle

Having shed light upon various forms of positive action measures, and upon different objectives that may be pursued by such measures, I will henceforth look at positive action in light of theoretical issues of equality. In other parts of this book we saw that concepts that present themselves generally in the realms of equality and non-discrimination are infused with divergent notions of equality. For example, in Chapter 3, it was illustrated that the concept of indirect discrimination is premised upon a 'group-justice model',[42] whereas direct discrimination mirrors the tenets of the 'individual justice model'.[43] Moreover, and related to the first point, indirect discrimination is more concerned with substantive equality, whereas direct discrimination fits well with formal equality. Further, in Chapter 4 we saw that harassment is analysed at best from the perspectives of 'equality as dignity' and 'equality as participation' and that this concept is ill placed in a comparative justice paradigm.

40 Bossuyt, p. 6 in reference to the economist Samuelson (1970).

41 Rubenfeld 1997, p. 429 in the context of U.S. law. The question posed by Rubenfeld can easily be extrapolated to other grounds of discrimination such as sex, disability, etc.

42 Although it is acknowledged that indirect discrimination in positive law has increasingly become infused with elements of individual justice. This was also illustrated in Chapter 3.

43 Both models have been discussed *in abstracto* in Chapter 3, sections 2.4.1 (individual justice model) and 2.4.2 (group justice model). The central tenets of these models will thus not be repeated in this Chapter. The fact that indirect and direct discrimination are underpinned by different models of justice can be explained in light of the different forms of discrimination which indirect and direct discrimination seek to combat. Hence, indirect discrimination is aimed at tackling institutional discrimination whereas direct discrimination seeks to address 'blunt' forms of discrimination. This has also been discussed in Chapter 3.

The notions of symmetry and asymmetry have already been referred to in Chapters 2 and 3. It was explained that, whereas the former requires that members of the advantaged group receive as much protection by the law as members of the disadvantaged group, the principle of asymmetry portrays equality within the social, political and economic reality of the day. It is recalled that if the legal framework applies asymmetrically, it will only grant protection from discrimination to members of the disadvantaged group. One of the consequences of this is that positive action is not a vexed issue, for it is accepted that the law's aim is to further *de facto* equality for members of out-groups. This point will be elaborated upon in more detail in the context of English positive action law in section 5 to follow.

One of the basic conclusions which can be drawn from the theoretical analysis in the previous chapters is that the equality principle is multiply-edged and that it may take on different shapes, in different contexts.[44] The different shapes of equality ought to be perceived in light of diverging ideologies of justice. For example, a liberal ideology of justice favours the concept of formal equality, which fits within the individual justice paradigm. Formal equality calls for sameness of treatment and thus for a 'like for like comparison'. It seeks to secure justice at the level of individual persons, rather than groups, and it requires a symmetrical application of the law. Its aim is not to protect members of out-groups, but rather to secure the principle of non-discrimination on grounds of 'race', 'sex', 'disability', etc. It correlates with 'liberalism', for the latter valorises personal autonomy and (therefore) rejects a too high degree of state-intervention in the market.[45] The liberal doctrine of equality can be contrasted with feminist legal doctrine. This has analysed the principle of sex-equality through the prisms of group-justice and asymmetry. Its aim is not to achieve the eradication of discrimination on grounds of sex, but rather *de facto* equality for women. In contrast, feminist legal doctrine has analysed the principle of sex-equality from a group-perspective seeking to achieve greater equality for women.[46] Yet others have perceived equality in terms of 'difference'. The notions of equality and difference have inter alia been linked by Young in her analysis of 'identity politics'.[47]

The foregoing has shown that different ideologies of justice cling to different ideals of equality. Equality may for example be expressed in terms of 'sameness' ('procedural', 'formal' or 'de iure' equality), of 'equal opportunities' (i.e. seeking to equalise 'starting points') or, 'equal outcomes or results' (i.e. an ideal of equality which seeks to achieve a material result, e.g. a guarantee that 30% of University professors in the Netherlands will be female). The notions of 'equality of opportunity' and 'equality of results or outcome' will be pertinent in the discussion to follow in section 3.2. In that section the concept of positive action will be linked to theoretical issues of equality. It will be illustrated that the various theoretical premises of equality can, *grosso modo*, be categorised along two material axes: formal *v.* substantive equality.

44 See notably also McCrudden 2003, p. 10-17.

45 Fredman 1997; Fredman 2000a; Lacey 1987, p. 411-421; Lacey 1992, p. 106 where she has referred to the notion of 'liberal legalism'.

46 Feminist legal doctrine has been analysed in Chapter 4 in the context of harassment. See also Lacey 1987, p. 411-421 and Lacey 1992.

47 Young 1990, especially Chapter 6.

Whereas formal equality stresses the sameness of treatment, substantive equality emphasises material differences calling for difference of treatment. The relationship between positive action, formal v. substantive equality, and, the notions of 'equality of opportunity' and 'equality of outcome', will be further elaborated on in the upcoming section.

3.2. *Positive Action and the Theory of Equality*

In contrast to so-called 'first generation'[48] equality rights which essentially require that status-based criteria (race, sex, etc.) are ignored in the decision-making process, positive action measures consciously embrace a person's race, sex, disability, etc. as a factor to be taken into account in the re-allocation of jobs, status, wealth, benefits, etc. Thus, writes Fredman, positive action is 'inherently controversial'.[49] Or, in Mancini's words, positive action requires law and policy-makers to 'penetrate into the province of substantive equality'.[50] As will become clear, the controversy of positive action depends on one's vision of social and moral justice. Positive action is especially feared by advocates of liberalism, who argue in favour of a formal equality framework seeking to bring about equality at the levels of individuals and in a symmetrical fashion.[51] If we perceive the concept of positive action in light of the theory on equality a diffuse picture emerges. With regard to the question as to whether positive action is justifiable, we can distinguish between two diametrically opposed schools namely, 'formalists' and 'substantivists'. A hybrid between these two extremes is formed by those who cling to an 'equality of opportunities' approach.[52] Advocates of the latter approach might *either* cling to a notion of equality of opportunity that is foremost infused with the principle of formal equality, *or*, with the principle of substantive equality.[53] Hereafter, I will consider the three approaches in more detail.

1. Formalists argue that, given that positive action measures consciously use status-based criteria in decision-making processes, they are intrinsically bound to infringe the principle of (formal) equality. After all, they argue, the principle of equality requires that justice is realised at the level of an individual regardless of the question whether that individual is a member of an out-group. They take as a starting point the fact that all individuals who possess the required 'merit' for (e.g.) the job should compete equally for that job, regardless of whether they are male/female, black/ white, etc. They also argue that this principle should not get interfered with by the State, for this would hamper the principle of individual autonomy and the develop-

48 See Fredman 2002a, section 2.1 where she explains 'early ideals' of equality law.

49 Fredman 1997, p. 575. In a similar fashion Costello has observed that 'few issues in equality law are as controversial as positive action'. (Costello 2003, p. 177).

50 Mancini 2000, p. 150.

51 Also Young 1990, p. 195. See in a more general fashion also Mulder 1999, p. 66 (in reference to the work by Alexy).

52 Fredman 1997a, p. 383-385 where she has distinguished between these three 'analytical models'.

53 See Fredman 1997a, p. 383-385.

ment of one's self regardless of a personal status or trait.[54] One of the problems with formal equality is that it perceives acts of discrimination which *downgrade* the interests of the disadvantaged group as being morally equivalent to acts of discrimination which *further* these interests.[55] It is submitted that this equation is senseless.[56] Feldman has argued that from a moral perspective the principle of equal treatment does not *per se* require the distribution of *identical* benefits and burdens to all. This is only needed in the scenario where two persons find themselves in morally identical positions. In Feldman's view, moral equality involves taking account of inequalities with a view to giving effect to the principle of equal treatment at a 'higher level of abstraction'.[57] Indeed, illustrates Feldman, what sense would it make to distribute treatment for sickness equally between those who are ill and those who are well?[58] It is submitted that imparting identical treatment in a societal vacuum thwarts the full potential of equality as a principle for bringing about greater justice and social change. This is so, for the 'sameness-model' of equality fosters the preservation of the dominant norm which, for its turn, feeds assimilation.[59] Given that formal equality calls for sameness of treatment without taking account of the different social and economic position of disadvantaged groups, it appears to reinforce inequalities, rather than doing away with them.[60] It follows from the foregoing that, for a fair interpretation of equality and justice, it should matter whether differential treatment is used as a strategy to meet the different needs of those who are differently situated. Simply meting out the same treatment to all, neglects the reality that different groups have different needs and find themselves at different starting points. In light of the foregoing it is argued that a strict formal equality model should not underpin anti-discrimination law.

2. Substantivists argue that formal equality effectively holds back substantive (or, *de facto*) equality. How can it sensibly be maintained that formal equality can do away with matters such as a gendered workforce or a labour market which is centred

54 See Fredman 2002, p. 126-128 and Fredman 1997a, p. 383-384.

55 Rubenfeld 1997, p. 444.

56 Dworkin has argued that 'the difference between a general racial classification that causes further disadvantage to those who have suffered from prejudice and a classification framed to help them is morally significant'. See Dworkin 1985, p. 314.

57 Feldman 2002, p. 137.

58 *Ibid.*

59 Fredman 2002a, p. 4, who has spoken of 'conformist pressures'. That sameness equality fosters assimilation has *inter alia* been illustrated in Chapters 3 (indirect discrimination) and 4 (harassment) and will furthermore become apparent from the analyses in Chapters 6 (religion and belief), 7 (sexual orientation) and 8 (disability).

60 In the context of U.S. equality law, which for purposes of analysis can be extrapolated to the discussion at hand, the matter has strikingly been expressed by Fish: 'Blacks have not simply been treated unfairly; they have been subjected first to decades of slavery, and then to decades of second-class citizenship; widespread legalized discrimination, economic persecution, education deprivation, and cultural stigmatization ... When the deck is stacked against you in more ways then you can ever count, it is small consolation to hear that you are now free to enter the game and take your chances.' See S. Fish, *Reverse Racism or how the Pot got to call the Kettle Black,* Atlantic Monthly November 1993 at 128, 130, cited by Rubenfeld 1997, p. 444 in footnote 66.

around the white and able-bodied norm? Once one has been convinced of the inherent limits of formal equality, and, once the insight has been gained that formal equality does little more than guarantee procedural equality, the support for positive action measures becomes so much easier.[61] Those who cling to a substantive vision of justice promote going beyond procedural justice. They argue that equality should not be regarded as an end *in se*. By contrast, it should be conceived of as being functional to an end. The end could for example be bringing about equality of opportunity, or, equality of outcome (but not merely procedural equality). It follows that substantivists perceive positive action measures as measures which are *functional* to the equality ideal, rather than being a narrowly defined exception to this ideal.

So far, we have seen that pure formalists reject the lawfulness of positive action measures altogether. They argue that a liberal conception of equality should be the starting point in the decision-making process. At a minimum, formalists argue that positive action is an irregularity or an aberration of the formal justice model, which should be interpreted strictly. In contrast, those who regard the principle of substantive equality as the highest ideal argue that the principle of equality of outcome or results ought to be the guiding principle in the decision-making process. Therefore, they regard a strategy of 'reverse discrimination' as unproblematic. They argue that, for the sake of *de facto* equality, the principle of merit may have to be trumped by status-based criteria such as race, sex, etc. As previously stated, a hybrid between 'formalism' and 'substantivism' is formed by the equality of opportunities model of justice.[62]

3. Advocates of the equal opportunities model argue that 'unequal'[63] treatment is allowed for with a view to equalising unequal starting positions of, e.g. women *v.* men and blacks *v.* whites.[64] Once equal chances have been created the principles of competitiveness and formal equality awake. It is submitted that it is hard, if not impossible, to determine when starting points have been equalised. This is *a fortiori* true, if the group to whose benefit positive action measures are adopted is heterogeneous in kind, such as the group of disabled persons. Rawls has argued that the equal opportunities paradigm constitutes an illustration of an imperfect form of procedural (or formal; MG) justice.[65] The reason for this is, that the principle of equality of opportunity seeks to realise procedural equality *with a view to* achieving a certain preferred outcome, but at the same time, it does not have the potential to *secure* this outcome. In other words, although equality of opportunity is *meant to be functional* to bring about greater justice for disadvantaged groups, it cannot be said with certainty that greater justice will truly be achieved *in effect*.

The discussion so far has taught us about different forms of positive action, about the various purposes which may be pursued by positive action and about

61 See Fredman 1997 and Fredman 1997a, p. 383-385.

62 Fredman 1997, p. 579 and Fredman 1997a, p. 384-385.

63 i.e. 'unequal' from the perspective of formal equality.

64 See Fredman 2002, p. 14 where she has used the metaphor of competitors in a race. Also Fredman 1997, p. 579.

65 This point has been taken from Hepple 1990, p. 412 with reference to Rawls.

different theoretical stances on the lawfulness, or not, of positive action measures. I will now proceed with a discussion of positive action law in the context of EC law. At appropriate junctures I will establish links with the issues raised in sections 2 and 3.

4. Positive Action and EC law

4.1. *Introduction*

The aim of this section is to make an analysis of positive action in the context of EC law. This analysis will be instrumental to the top-down analysis to be made in sections 5 (England) and 6 (The Netherlands) hereafter. The core question underpinning the passages to follow is what scope EC law offers for the adoption of positive action measures for women, racial minorities, religious and sexual minorities, disabled persons and the elderly? This question will be examined on the basis of a discussion of the relevant legislative framework (section 4.2) which, for present purposes, will be largely confined to hard-law measures[66] and, on the basis of the ECJ's case law on positive action (section 4.3). It should be noted that up until now, the Court's case law on positive action has been limited to the ground of sex. No case law has yet occurred for the other grounds of discrimination covered by Article 13 EC. In light of this, it remains currently unclear whether the permissible scope for the adoption of positive action measures granted by the ECJ will differ for different grounds of discrimination (cross-ground comparison). It is submitted that the answer to this question will be dependent upon the social context in which positive action measures are adopted and upon the degree of disadvantage suffered by a particular out-group in a particular period in time.[67] It should be noted that the degree of disadvantage suffered by an out-group is usually measured on the basis of statistical evidence.[68] By means of statistics we can for example measure the percentage of black persons working in the employer's workforce v. the percentage of black persons in the labour force of a particular geographical area (e.g. the City of London). If there is a great discrepancy between these percentages, it could be concluded that black persons find themselves in a disadvantaged position. However, as argued in Chapter 3 ('indirect discrimination'), not every ground of discrimination lends itself to being captured by statistical data. This is notably true with regard to disability and sexual orientation whose intrinsic nature[69] prevents these grounds from being 'poured' into statistical evidence. It will therefore be interesting to learn how the ECJ

66 For a discussion of positive action and EC soft-law, notably the EU Charter of Rights, I refer to Costello 2003a, p. 122-128. For a general discussion of the principle of equality in the context of the EU Charter of Rights, I refer to Bell 2003, p. 91-110.

67 See also Parmar 2004, p. 151.

68 In this respect positive action shows commonalities with the principle of indirect discrimination (discussed in Chapter 3).

69 The underlying values and intrinsic nature of different grounds of discrimination will be discussed in much detail in Chapters 6-10. The intrinsic nature of sexual orientation will be discussed in section 2 of Chapter 7; the underlying values of 'disability' will be studied in section 2.2 of Chapter 8.

will analyse positive action measures for, e.g. disabled persons or sexual minorities in future case law.

The extension of the list of grounds bears an impact upon positive action law in yet another respect. One could argue that the introduction by Article 13 EC of new grounds of discrimination may bear an impact upon the legal limits of positive action in the context of gender, given that women are likely to having to compete with other disadvantaged groups in the allocation of jobs, training-positions, places on employees' representative bodies, etc. The question may for example arise whether in a merit tie-break situation, a non-disabled woman ought to be given preference over a disabled or a black man. It is worth observing in this context that the Community legislator has taken the view that the different discrimination grounds in Article 13 EC stand on an equal footing.[70] However, in concrete cases that may come before it the Court might have to make a choice of one ground above another depending on the particular facts of the case at hand.

It should be emphasised that EC law itself does not impose an obligation upon the Member States to adopt positive action measures for disadvantaged groups. Hence, if at all, the adoption of such measures is by definition instigated by the Member States.[71] However, if the Member States adopt positive action measures, such measures will have to be in conformity with EC law and notably, as will become clear, with the principle of proportionality (top-down influence). Moreover, the fact that EC law does not compel the Member States to adopt positive action measures means that national approaches are likely to be different in different Member States (cross-country comparison).[72] As will become clear from the ECJ's case law, notably Germany[73] has been an active Member State in the area of positive action for women. This, for its turn, has resulted in a number of cases before the ECJ in which the Court has defined the contours of the lawfulness of positive action in EC law.[74] In light of the foregoing, it could be argued that the ECJ's case law on positive

70 See Recital 5 of the Community Action programme to combat discrimination 2000 *OJ* L 303/23. However, as seen in Chapter 2 this point of view has been widely contested in academic literature.

71 I am grateful to Dr. Cathryn Costello for this point.

72 This will be considered in sections 5 and 6.

73 Although the active stance by Germany in the realm of positive action is limited to public (not private) employment. See Schiek 2000a, p. 254.

74 McCrudden 2004a, p. xi-xxxii, p. xiii. Costello has observed in a more general fashion that 'the process of norm articulation in the EU is characterised by a tight nexus between legal and political fora and a highly institutionalised and politicised interlocution between the Court and those who plead before it and national judges who refer questions to it'. (See Costello 2003, p. 116 with reference to Sciarra 2001). As will be seen, 7 cases have so far been decided on by the ECJ on positive action. 4 of these cases have arisen in the German legal context, 1 in the Swedish legal context, 1 in the Dutch legal context and 1 in the French legal context. It is submitted that the reason why English law has not given rise to positive action cases before the ECJ is because English law is largely premised upon the symmetry principle. This principle works to the advantage of men and forms a legal barrier to the adoption of positive action measures for women with a view to achieving substantive equality. This point will be taken further in the analysis of English positive action law in section 5 to follow.

action has been 'bottom up' inspired. Hereafter, this case law as well as the legislative framework will be considered in detail. It is to this that I will turn now.

4.2. *Mapping the Legislative Framework – a Chronological Overview of Existing Law*

Given the role of the equality principle as 'market unifier' in the early decades of Community law[75] positive action in EC law was necessarily confined to the area of gender discrimination in employment. Old Article 119 EC (now Article 141 EC) regarding the principle of equal pay between the sexes mentioned, however, nothing about positive action.[76] Positive action for women and men was for the first time voiced in Community law by the 1976 ETD.[77] Article 2(4), in conjunction with Article 2(1) ETD, opened the gates for positive action measures for women (and men) in the areas of employment and vocational training. Article 2(1) reads as follows:

> 2(1) 'For the purposes of the following provisions, the principle of equal treatment shall mean that there shall be no discrimination whatsoever on grounds of sex either directly or indirectly by reference in particular to marital or family status (...).'

In addition, Article 2(4) subsequently provides that:

> 2(4) 'This Directive shall be without prejudice to measures to promote equal opportunity for men and women, in particular by removing existing inequalities which affect women's opportunities in the areas referred to in Article 1(1).'

In line with the formal equality approach, Article 2(4) ETD perceives positive action measures as *exceptions* to the central prohibition of discrimination in Article 2(1).[78] Moreover, the wording of Article 2(4) ETD suggests that positive action ought not to go beyond an equal opportunities approach and thus 'results equality' is prohibited. In 1984 the Council of Ministers adopted a Community soft law measure on the promotion of positive action for women. This took the shape of a Council Recommendation[79] which overtly stated the limits of the formal equality model and which emphasised the structural nature of gender discrimination.[80] It has been argued in

75 More 1999, p. 517-553. See generally Chapter 2.

76 Also Tobler 2002, p. 4.

77 Directive *76/207/EEC* on Equal Treatment for Men and Women as regards Access to Employment, Vocational Training and Promotion and Working Conditions, *OJ* 1976, L 39/40. It has (*inter alia*) been seen in Chapter 2 that the 1976 ETD has been amended by Directive 2002/73/EC of 23 September 2002, *OJ* 2002, L 269/15. Later on in this section, it will be illustrated that these amendments have also had an impact upon the issue of positive action.

78 See for further discussion also Tobler 2002, p. 12 with further references.

79 Recommendation 84/635/EEC of 13 December 1984.

80 Recital 3 of the Recommendation reads as follows: 'Existing legal provisions on equal treatment, which are designed to afford rights to individuals, are inadequate for the elimination of all existing inequalities unless parallel action is taken by governments, both sides of industry and other bodies concerned, to counteract the prejudicial effects on women in employment which arise from social attitudes, behaviour and structures.'

Chapter 2 that since the Treaty of Amsterdam the principle of equality as a fundamental right has gained momentum in political circles.[81] Articles 2 and 3(2) of the EC Treaty clearly indicate that equality calls for more than a negative prohibition of discrimination. Article 2 EC provides that 'the Community shall have as its task (...) to promote (...) equality between men and women.', whereas Article 3 EC stipulates that [the Community shall; MG] 'in all the activities referred to in this Article (...) aim to eliminate inequalities and to promote equality between men and women'.[82]

Since the ToA the personal and material scope for the adoption (by the Member States) of positive action measures has become widened. The ToA inserted a new Article 141(4) into the EC Treaty.[83] This Article seems to have mitigated the character of positive action as an aberration of formal equality where it provides that:

> '[w]ith a view to ensuring full equality in practice [italics MG] between men and women in working life, the principle of equal treatment shall not prevent any member state from maintaining or adopting measures providing for *specific advantages* [italics MG] in order to make it easier for the under-represented sex to pursue a vocational activity or to prevent or compensate for disadvantages in professional careers'.

The combination of Articles 2, 3(2) and 141(4) EC arguably boosts a substantive analysis by the ECJ of cases concerning positive action.[84] A generous interpretation of Article 141(4) EC would seem to allow for preferential treatment of women in merit tie-break situations (i.e. where the male and female candidates are equally qualified) even without a 'savings clause'.[85] However, as will be explained hereafter, such a

81 See Chapter 2, section 2. In that section I have sketched the history of equality in the context of EC law. It is recalled that up until Amsterdam the fundamental rights nature of gender equality had primarily been stressed by the Court.

82 See for further discussion Koukoulis-Spiliotopoulos, 2001, p. 24. See also the preliminary issues to Part III.

83 Being an Article of primary law, Article 141(4) EC has taken precedence over Article 2(4) ETD. This also follows from the case law by the Court to be discussed in later on in the analysis. At present, this point has lost much of its relevance, for Article 2(4) EFD has been amended by the AETD in light of Article 141(4) EC. This will become clear hereafter.

84 This has been argued by Koukoulis-Spiliotoupoulos 2001, p. 59-61. After comparison of Article 141(4) EC with Article 2(4) ETD she has concluded that the former inclines to 'results equality'. See also M. Sargeant (ed.) *Discrimination Law* (2004), p. 39, cited by Burrows and Robison (2006), p. 28, who has argued that Article 141(EC) 'now incorporates the principle of positive discrimination'. The present author agrees with the view that Article 141(4) EC is more oriented towards substantive justice than Article 2(4) ETD, however, she doubts that this Article allows for 'reverse discrimination' or positive discrimination at the level of employment (rather than e.g. training). This point will be dealt with in more detail in the analysis of the ECJ's case law on positive action in section 4.3 hereafter. It should be noted that the fact that Article 141(4) EC speaks of the 'under-represented sex' (which denotes of symmetry) reflects 'formal equality'. However, Declaration No. 28 to the Amsterdam Treaty makes it clear that positive action measures adopted on the basis of Article 141(4) EC should be aimed at improving the socio-economic position of women (rather than men).

85 *Unconditional* priority for the female candidate in merit tie-break situations in decision-making processes at the level of employment has not been permitted by the ECJ. This point will be illustrated in greater detail in the analysis of the ECJ's case law on positive action to be discussed hereafter.

generous interpretation has not hitherto been a feature of the ECJ's case law on positive action for women.

The Treaty of Amsterdam has also facilitated positive action beyond the realm of gender equality. It has been seen already that both the RD (Article 5) and the EFD (Article 7(1)) allow the Member States to adopt positive action measures with respect to the discrimination grounds contained in the Directives. Article 7(1) EFD reads as follows:

> 'With a view to ensuring full equality in practice, the principle of equal treatment shall not prevent any Member State from maintaining or adopting specific measures to prevent or compensate for disadvantages linked to any of the grounds referred to in Article 1.[86]

Upon comparison, it follows that the wording of Article 7(1) EFD and 5 RD differs in certain respects from the provision in Article 141(4) EC. Firstly, Article 141(4) EC specifically refers to full equality in practice in *working life and professional careers.* This has been interpreted by some as an argument pro *results equality* at the level of employment, rather than merely at the level of training.[87] Secondly, whereas the relevant Articles in the Article 13 Directives speak of 'specific measures' which may be adopted in favour of out-groups, Article 141(4) EC refers to providing 'specific advantages' to members of the under-represented sex (women). Given the lack of case law it remains currently unclear whether this difference in terminology will denote any material difference in a legal assessment as to the (un)lawfulness of positive action measures for women compared with other disadvantaged groups.[88] With reference to the 'non-regression' clauses[89] contained in the EFD and the RD,[90] Costello has argued that positive action measures adopted at the national level in favour of out-groups, which fall within the Directives' scope, and which are premised upon a strategy of 'reverse discrimination', or, of 'automatic' preferential treatment in merit

86 A similar provision is contained in Article 5 RD.

87 See Koukoulis-Spiliotoupoulos 2001, p. 59-61 and Sargeant 2004, p. 39 cited by Burrows and Robison 2006, p. 28. As will be seen, results equality at the level of training has been allowed for by the ECJ in the *Badeck* case which will be discussed in section 4.3 hereafter.

88 Bell and Waddington (2001) have argued that the wording of Articles 7(1) EFD and 5(1) RD have been stricter formulated compared with the wording of Article 141(4) EC.

89 See Chapter 2. The 'non regression' clauses provide that the Member States main introduce or maintain provisions which are more favourable to the protection of the principle of equal treatment than those laid down in the Directives. They moreover prevent the Member States from reducing existing levels of protection against discrimination in the areas which are covered by the Directives' scope. See Article 8 EFD and Recital 28 EFD and Article 6 RD and Recital 25 RD.

90 This argument is less pertinent with regard to 'sex'. It should be noted that Directive 73/2002/EC also contains a 'non-regression' clause, however, the legal scope for manoeuvre for the Member States in respect of positive action for women has been defined by the ECJ in its case law prior to the entering into force of the AETD. In other words, even before the adoption of the AETD the Court had made clear that results equality for women at the level of employment was disallowed for under EC law.

tie-break situations at the level of employment,[91] may not be struck down by the ECJ on the ground that such measures traverse the boundaries of the principles of formal equality or equal opportunities.[92] Indeed, if at the national level, 'justice' has been explained in terms of 'substantive justice',[93] reverse discrimination and, permitting automatic priority in merit tie-break situations, will mirror a *higher* level of equality, compared with the principle of equality which is confined to equalising starting points. Future case law must tell whether the Court will accept this argument. If it does, this will bring with it that diverging legal standards may be set for the lawfulness of positive action measures for different grounds, and, for different Member States. On the other hand, it seems unlikely that the Court will adopt a radically different stance in respect of positive action in the context of, e.g. 'race', 'disability', 'religion', etc. compared with 'gender', although the Court might do so, if there is evidence of a great degree of disadvantage of ethnic or religious minorities, or disabled persons, in a particular sector of social life.[94]

The last amendment to the legislative framework on positive action in the realm of gender has been brought about by an amendment to the ETD by Directive 2002/73/EC.[95] Article 2(8) of the AETD allows for positive action measures within the meaning of Article 141(4) EC. It reads as follows: 'Member States may maintain or adopt measures within the meaning of Article 141(4) of the Treaty with a view to ensuring full equality in practice between men and women'. This provision denotes substantive justice, for it refers to equality *in practice* and for it establishes a link with Article 141(4) EC which speaks of 'specific advantages'.

In the above, an analysis has been made of the EC legislative framework on positive action. Whereas this framework initially inclined to equal opportunities equality infused with the philosophy of formal equality, since Amsterdam, more room has been given for the achievement of substantive equality. Hereafter, this point will be further examined in light of the ECJ's case law on positive action in the context of gender.

91 As will be seen in section 4.3, in its case law on gender positive action measures, the ECJ has not permitted 'reverse discrimination' in the sense of giving a job to a woman, even if she is less competent than her male competitor. At the level of employment, the Court has neither allowed for granting *automatic* priority to female candidates in 'merit-tie break situations', i.e. in situations where a woman and a man are equally competent for the job.

92 Costello 2003, p. 199.

93 It will be seen that this is, for example, the case with the DDA 1995 as amended which has been specifically designed to further the rights of disabled persons. In contrast with the SDA and RRA, the DDA therefore applies asymmetrically which mirrors 'substantive equality'. However, and only after the possibility of making a reasonable accommodation has been considered, the DDA does not require employers to hire persons who do not possess the requested merit for the job. This means that the DDA 1995 does not permit for 'reverse discrimination'. See for further discussion Chapter 8.

94 In such cases the proportionality test is likely to be differently applied by the Court. The proportionality test will be further elaborated on in section 4.3 to follow in the context of a discussion of the Court's case law. See also Parmar 2004, p. 150-151.

95 Directive 2002/73/EC of 23 September 2002, *OJ* 2002, L 269/15. See Chapter 2, section 2.3.2.3.

4.3. *Positive Action in the Case Law of the Court*

4.3.1. From Kalanke to Briheche

Although the ECJ's case law on positive action for women has been limited to seven cases only[96], it has led to a wealth of academic commentary.[97] In this section I will present the main principles which have flowed from the Court's case law and which bear a decisive impact upon the permissible scope for positive action measures adopted by the Member States ('top down influence').

What principles can be deduced from the ECJ's case law on positive action for women? It follows from the first positive action case that came before the Court *(i.e, Kalanke)*[98] that a national rule to the effect that, where equally qualified men and women are candidates for the same promotion, in sectors where there are fewer women than men at the level of the relevant post, women must automatically be given priority, constitutes discrimination on grounds of sex contrary to Community law.[99] Hence, the relevant German law was held to traverse the boundaries of the exception contained in Article 2(4) EFD given that, in the Court's view, it went beyond the principle of equality of opportunity, which was substituted for by results equality.[100] The Court thus adopted a cautious stance in *Kalanke* which clearly reflects the tenets of the model of formal equality.

As follows from *Marshall*[101] the scenario will become different, if the national legislation contains a so-called 'savings clause' which might tilt the balance in favour of a male candidate. In *Marshall* the contested rule of the Beamtengesetz of the Land Nord Rhein Westphalia provided as follows:

> 'Where, in the sector of the authority responsible for promotion, there are fewer women than men in the particular higher grade post in the career bracket, women are to be given priority for promotion in the event of equal suitability, competence and professional performance, unless reasons specific to an individual candidate tilt the balance in his favour.'[102]

96 *Kalanke v. Freie Hansestadt Bremen* (Case C-450/93) [1995] ECR I-3051; *Marschall v. Land Nordrhein-Westfalen* (Case C-409/95) [1997] ECR I-6363; *Badeck v. Hessischer Ministerprasident* (Case C-158/97) [2000] ECR I-1875; *Abrahammson and Anderson v. Fogelqfist* (Case C-407/98) [2000] ECR I-5539; *Schnorbus* (Case C-79/99) [2000] ECR I-10997. *Lommers v. Minister van Landbouw, Natuurbeheer en Visserij* (Case C-476/99) [2002] ECR I-2891; *Briheche v. Ministre de l'Intérieur, Ministre de l'Education and Ministre de la Justice* (Case C-319/03) [2004] ECR 0000.

97 See, for example, Schiek 2000a; Tobler 2002a; Clayton 1998; Zuleeg 1999; Fredman 2000; Szyszczak 1996; Küchhold 2001; Nummhauser-Henning 2001; Barnard and T. Hervey, 1998; Fenwick 1998, p. 507-516. Veldman 1999; Veldman 1998; Prechal 1996; Loenen 2002.

98 See footnote 95 above. *Kalanke* concerned the 1990 Bremen Law on Equal Treatment for Men and Women in the Public Service (1990 '*Landesgleichstellungsgesetz*'). It concerned a decision by the employer.

99 Paragraph 16 of the judgment.

100 See paragraphs 22 and 23 of the judgment.

101 Cited above in footnote 95. Like *Kalanke, Marshall* also concerned the decision by the employer.

102 See paragraph 3 of the judgment.

The Court was asked whether this provision did, or did not, overstep the limits of the Article 2(4) ETD exception. The ECJ held that

> '(...) a national rule in terms of which, subject to the application of a savings-clause, female candidates for promotion who are equally as qualified as the male candidates are to be treated preferentially in sectors where they are under-represented may fall within the scope of Article 2(4) ETD if such a rule may counteract the prejudicial effects on female candidates of the attitudes and behaviour described above [i.e. stereotypical behaviour concerning the role and capacities of women in working life; MG] and thus reduce actual instances of inequality which may exist in the real world'.[103]

It follows from the foregoing that although women may under Community law not be given *automatic* preference over their male competitors, the Court nevertheless paved the way for a more substantive justice approach.

Concerns over substantive justice are also reflected in *Badeck*[104] which concerns the third German positive action case which appeared before the Court.[105] Different from *Kalanke and Marshall*, *Badeck* did not concern a decision by an employer which was challenged in judicial proceedings, but concerned instead a review of legality (*Normenkontrolverfahren*) of the contested German law.[106] In *Badeck* five different forms of positive action were subjected to legal scrutiny by the Court. The first and main positive action measure contained in the relevant law stipulated that in sectors of the public service where women are underrepresented, they are to be given priority, where male and female candidates are equally qualified, and where that proves necessary for complying with the binding targets in the women's advancement plan, and provided that no reasons of greater legal weight are opposed. In deciding on the question whether such a measure falls within the ambit of the Article 2(4) ETD exception,[107] the Court paid particular attention to the nature of all five measures at stake which in conjunction were termed 'flexible results quota' (*flexible Ergebnisquote*). *Flexible Ergebnisquote* are featured by the following: (i) the binding targets of the quota are not defined uniformly across all sectors and departments concerned but the particularities of these sectors and departments constitute a decisive factor for fixing the binding targets; (ii) the contested measures do not *a priori* require that where the male and female candidate are equally qualified the outcome of each selection

103 See paragraph 31 of the judgment.

104 Cited above in footnote 95.

105 The relationship between *Kalanke*, *Marshall* and *Badeck* has been analysed in an excellent fashion by Schiek 2000a.

106 The German law which was at stake was the Law of the Land of Hesse on equal rights for women and men and the removal of discrimination against women in the public administration (*Hessisches Gesetz über die Gleichberechtigung von Frauen und Männern und zum Abbau von Diskrimienierungen von Frauen in der Offentlichen Verwaltung*, of 21 December 1993 and which is valid for 13 years). See Also Schiek 2000a, p. 252-253.

107 It is to be noted that the question referred to the ECJ by the domestic Court related to the compatibility of the measures with Articles 2(1) and 2(4) of the ETD. In the Court's view Article 141(4) EC will therefore only be of relevance to the outcome of the case at hand, if the Court concludes that Article 2 ETD precludes national legislation such as that in issue in the case at hand (see paragraphs 13 and 14 of the judgment).

procedure must necessarily be in favour of a female candidate.[108] In sum, the contested measures (with the exception of the 'strict' quota system in training places)[109] secured that a person's sex did never *automatically* constitute a *decisive* factor in the outcome of a given decision-making process.[110] In light of this the Court had no problems to re-affirm its stance in *Marshall* where it held that the contested measures fall within the scope of the Article 2(4) ETD exception 'provided that the rule guarantees that candidates are the subject of an objective assessment which takes account of the specific personal situations of all candidates'.[111] It is worth noting that the contested German legislation provided that in the assessment of a candidate's suitability and capability (i.e. in assessing 'merit') a number of positive and negative factors fell to be taken into account. Thus, capabilities and experience which have been acquired by carrying out family work fell to be taken into account insofar as they are of importance for the suitability, performance and capability of candidates, whereas seniority, age and the date of the last promotion only constituted relevant factors, insofar as they bear an impact in this respect (i.e. in respect of the candidate's 'suitability', 'performance' and 'capability'). Not to be taken into account in the assessment procedure of candidates were the family status or income of the partner. Lastly, part-time work, leave and delays in completing training as a result of looking after children or dependents in need of care must not bear a negative impact upon a candidate's assessment.[112] It should be noted that these factors belong to what McCrudden has termed 'facially neutral but purposefully inclusionary policies'[113], a fact which was also recognised by the ECJ: '[s]uch criteria, although formulated in terms which are neutral as regards sex and thus capable of benefiting men too, in general favour women'.[114] The court has arguably precluded such measures from being challenged by men on the basis of ('reverse') indirect discrimination by holding that such measures '(..) are manifestly intended to lead to an equality which is substantive rather than formal, by reducing the inequalities which may occur in practice in social life'.[115] Hence, rather than staying within a formal paradigm of justice, the Court clearly made an excursion to the realm of substantive justice.

The second positive action measure challenged in *Badeck* concerned a national rule which stipulated that the binding targets of the women's advancement plan for temporary posts in the academic service and for academic assistants must provide for a minimum percentage of women which is at least equal to the percentage of women among graduates, holders of higher degrees and students in the relevant subject area. The applicants had argued that such a rule falls outside the ambit of Article 2(4) ETD, for it aims at achieving a defined result as to the percentages of

108 See paragraph 28 of the judgment.
109 This will be discussed in the main text to follow.
110 Paragraph 29 of the judgment.
111 See paragraph 38 of the judgment.
112 See paragraph 31 of the judgment.
113 See section 2 above.
114 See paragraph 32 of the judgment.
115 See paragraph 32 of the judgment. However, this cannot be said with certainty because the legitimacy of these factors were not challenged in *Badeck*. See Also Tobler 2002a, p. 368.

women and men in each discipline. However, the Court held that the measure was compatible with Community law because the contested rule did not breach the principle of merit and did not fix an absolute ceiling in favour of women, but rather one which was fixed with reference to the number of persons who have received appropriate training. As such an *actual fact* was used as a quantitative criterion for giving priority to women.[116]

The Court in *Badeck* furthermore approved of a *strict* quota-system in training places: a rule applicable in the public service according to which at least half of the training positions are to be allocated to women is not in contravention of Community law, unless the State has a monopoly of training.[117] Hence, reverse discrimination at the level of training is in principle not prohibited by EC law, for it fosters equality of opportunity at the level of competition for jobs. A fourth rule in *Badeck* which was subjected to judicial analysis concerned a rule which *guaranteed* that where male and female candidates were equally qualified for the job, women were called for an interview in sectors where they were under-represented. In the Court's view such a measure also falls within the permissible limits of Community law: '(…) the provision at issue (...) does not imply an attempt to achieve a final result – appointment or promotion – but affords women who are qualified additional opportunities to facilitate their entry into working life and their career'.[118] Hence, such measures do not amount to results equality. Fifthly and lastly, the ECJ in *Badeck* also permitted a national rule relating to the composition of employees' representative and supervisory bodies which recommended that half of the places on these bodies be allocated to women. In deciding as it did, the Court paid great attention to the fact that the rule at stake was not mandatory in kind but had the nature of a non-binding recommendation.

It clearly follows from *Badeck* that the ECJ has moved beyond the formal equality framework in favour of substantive justice. The Court's stance in *Badeck* dovetails with the developments in the legislative framework which, as illustrated before, has been infused with concerns over substantive justice since the ToA. However, it must be stressed that, although in *Badeck* the Court did not disapprove of preferential treatment measures for women (e.g. preferential treatment for women in public sector employment, provided that the 'merit principle' is preserved and 'no reasons of greater legal weight are opposed'; preferential treatment with regard to training places (whereby it is, however, not fully clear whether or not the 'merit principle' must remain intact); preferential treatment with regard to calls for an interview, provided that the 'merit principle' remains unaffected) these measures did not concern decisions as to whom *employment* was to be given. At the level of employment, no *automatic* priority may be given, and the 'merit principle' must unconditionally be complied with. That 'reverse discrimination' is *not* permissible at the level of employment clearly follows from the *Abrahammson* case[119] which concerned Swedish legislation. According to the relevant Swedish rules a candidate for a University chair belonging to the

116 See paragraph 42 of the judgment.

117 Meaning that male candidates cannot avail themselves of training in the private sector.

118 Paragraph 60 of the judgment.

119 Cited above in footnote 95.

underrepresented sex and who *possesses* sufficient qualifications, must be given priority over a candidate of the opposite sex who would otherwise have been chosen unless the difference between the candidates' qualifications is so great that such application would give rise to a breach of the requirement of objectivity in the making of appointments.[120] The Court contrasted the vexed rule in *Abrahammson* with the national legislation analysed by it in the cases of *Kalanke, Marshall* and *Badeck* and stressed that, in contrast with the latter three cases, the rule in *Abrahammson* infringed the principle of merit.[121] Given that the relevant Swedish rules permitted *automatic* preference to be given to female candidates even where the merits of the selected candidate were inferior to those of a candidate belonging to the opposite sex, such measures did not fall within the ambit of the Article 2(4) ETD exception.[122] The Court subsequently went on to consider whether the measures could be justified under Article 141(4) EC and quickly concluded as follows:

> '(...) even though Article 141(4) EC allows the Member States to maintain or adopt measures providing for special advantages intended to prevent or compensate for disadvantages in professional careers in order to ensure full equality for men and women in professional life, it cannot be inferred from this that it allows a selection method of the kind at issue in the main proceedings which appears, on any view, to be disproportionate to the aim pursued.'[123]

The importance of the principle of proportionality in the assessment of the lawfulness of national positive action measures has also and most recently been stressed by the Court in the *Briheche* case to be discussed later on in the analysis.

The contested rule in the *Schorbus* case[124] concerned in fact a 'facially neutral but purposefully inclusionary policy' which operated to the advantage of men and which for that reason cannot truly be conceptualised as a positive action measure. The contested rules provided that where a decision, concerning the admission of applicants to practical legal training, was required because the number of applicants exceeds the number of training places, an applicant who has completed military service is to be immediately admitted to the training, whereas the admission of other applicants (both male and female) may be deferred by up to 12 months. In the Court's view such a rule has to be analysed on the basis of indirect sex discrimination, rather than direct sex discrimination notwithstanding that no single woman could ever be a beneficiary of the preferential rules.[125] The referring court had moreover asked whether justification of the vexed provisions on the basis of Article 2(4) ETD is precluded because they resulted in preferential admission for men, although the vexed rules were not targeted at men as such. The ECJ held that Community law

120 Swedish law on equality (*Jämställdhetslagen*) 1991: 433 and Swedish Regulation on Universities (*Högskoleförordningen*) 1993:100.

121 Paragraph 45 of the judgment.

122 See paragraph 53 of the judgment.

123 See paragraph 55 of the judgment.

124 Cited above in footnote 95.

125 This being the case, the present author agrees with Tobler that the Court's analysis of indirect discrimination is not truly convincing. See Tobler 2002a, p. 370.

'does not preclude national provisions such as those in issue (...), insofar as such provisions are justified by objective reasons and prompted solely by a desire to counterbalance to some extent the delay resulting from the completion of compulsory military or civilian service'.[126]

It remains, however, obscure whether the ECJ's answer must be conceptualised within the framework of objective justification of indirect discrimination, or, within the parameters of positive action in the context of Article 2(4) ETD.[127]

Lommers[128] concerned a Dutch positive action measure according to which subsidised nursery facilities were in principle only to be allocated to female workers working at the Dutch Ministry of Agriculture, whereas male workers would only be eligible under the subsidised nursery scheme in the case of an emergency to be determined by the Director. The rationale behind the vexed measure was to tackle the under representation of women in the Ministry and to reduce *de facto* inequality of women. In respect of the question by Mr Lommers – who had been refused a subsidised nursery place for his yet unborn child – whether the vexed rule constituted an infringement of Article 2(1) and 2(4) ETD, the ECJ held as follows:

'(...) Article 2(1) and (4) of the Directive does not preclude a scheme set up by a Ministry to tackle extensive under representation of women within it under which, in a context of a proven insufficiency of proper, affordable care facilities, a limited number of subsidised nursery places made available by the Ministry to its staff is reserved for female officials alone whilst male officials may have access only in cases of emergency, to be determined by the employer. That is so, however, only in so far (...) as the said exception in favour of male officials is construed as allowing those of them who take care of their children by themselves to have access to that nursery places scheme on the same conditions as female officials.'

In reaching this conclusion the Court had paid due attention to the following. It had stressed that like in *Badeck* the vexed measures in *Lommers* reflected a 'restricted concept of equality of opportunity'[129] in the sense that preferential treatment had not been meted out in a decision-making process determining to whom a *job* should be given, but rather with regard to working conditions designed to facilitate women's careers.[130] The Court had furthermore emphasised the role of the principle of proportionality in assessing the lawfulness of the measure concerned. Proportionality 'requires that derogations must remain within the limits of what is appropriate and necessary in order to achieve the aim in view and that the principle of equal treatment be reconciled as far as possible with the requirements of the aim thus pursued'.[131] If the aim of bringing about equality of opportunity between the sexes could still be

126 Paragraph 47 of the judgment.

127 Tobler 2002a, p. 370.

128 Cited above in footnote 95. See for a case note also *Equal Opportunities Review* no. 105, May 2002. See also Veldman 2001.

129 See paragraphs 33 and 38 of the judgment.

130 In *Badeck* the relevant measures sought to accord automatic preferential treatment to women in respect of training-places.

131 Paragraph 39 of the judgment.

achieved if nursery places were allocated to *both* women and men working for the Ministry, the exclusion of men would result in an infringement of this principle. This was the more so, given that a rule such as the one in issue might help to reinforce a traditional division of roles between men and women in the family.[132] Hence the Court's stress on the fact that in the case at hand there was an insufficiency of supply of nursery places, which meant that only a limited number of such places were altogether available. Moreover, it was held that a total exclusion of male officials from the advantageous measure would traverse the boundaries of proportionality, for it would not be reconcilable with the principle of equal treatment. However, given that the vexed rule contained an emergency clause for male officials, and given that it had been indicated by the Ministry that male officials who were single child-rearers should have access to the beneficiary scheme, proportionality was complied with in the case at hand.

The importance of proportionality was also evident in the last case on positive action which has come before the Court so far. *Briheche*[133] concerned a French rule which set an age limit of 45 years old for obtaining access to public-sector employment. However, this age limit did not apply to the following categories of persons: mothers with three or more children, widows who have not remarried, divorced women who have not remarried, legally separated women and unmarried women with at least one dependent child.[134] Furthermore, unmarried men with at least one dependent child who are obliged to work were added to the list.[135] Serge Briheche was a 48 year old widower who had not remarried and who looked after one dependent child. On the basis of the applicable rules, he had been refused access to public-sector employment. According to Article 3(1) ETD 'there shall be no discrimination whatsoever on grounds of sex in the conditions, including selection criteria, for access to all jobs or posts, whatever the sector or branch of activity, and to all levels of the occupational hierarchy'. The question was whether the vexed measure could nevertheless be justified under Article 2(4) ETD? The ECJ reiterated its earlier case law in *Kalanke, Badeck* and *Lommers* and emphasised that with regard to access to employment, a positive action measure may not automatically grant priority to female candidates. Moreover, it recalled from *Lommers* that positive action measures may not overstep the limits imposed by the principle of proportionality. Furthermore, and importantly, it was explicitly held that the rationale behind Article 2(4) ETD was to further substantive, not formal equality.[136] In light of the automatic nature of the measure which a priori excluded all widowers who have not remarried, the vexed rule fell outside the ambit of the Article 2(4) exception. The next question which arose was whether the rule could nonetheless be captured by the Article 141(4) EC ex-

132 Paragraph 41 of the judgment.

133 Cited above in footnote 95.

134 JORF of 8 July 1979.

135 JORF of 19 May 2001, p. 7320.

136 Paragraph 25 of the judgment: 'The aim of that provision [i.e., Article 2(4) ETD] is to achieve substantive, rather than formal, equality by reducing de facto inequalities which may arise in society and, thus, in accordance with Article 141(4) EC, to prevent or compensate for disadvantages in the professional career of the persons concerned.'

ception? Like in *Ambrahammson* the Court readily held that this question fell to be answered in the negative:

> 'Irrespective of whether positive action which is not allowed under Article 2(4) of the Directive could perhaps be allowed under Article 141(4) EC, it is sufficient to state that the latter provision cannot permit the Member States to adopt conditions for obtaining access to public-sector employment of the kind in question in the main proceedings which prove in any event to be disproportionate to the aim pursued.'[137]

It follows that the automatic nature of the measure breached the principle of proportionality, both in the context of Article 2(4) ETD and 141(4) EC.

4.3.2. Conclusions

The analysis of the ECJ's case law on positive action in the context of gender warrants the following conclusions. It has been discussed that, at the level of employment and promotion, EC law permits women to be given priority over men provided that women are equally qualified as their male competitors, and, provided that males are not *automatically* excluded from the decision-making process. It has also been seen that the degree of judicial scrutiny adopted by the ECJ in its assessment of the permissibility of 'positive action' has been less strict with regard to measures that are taken *prior* to the decision as to whom employment or a promotion must be given, compared with equivalent measures at the level of employment. Thus, the Court has allowed for automatic preferential treatment of women in respect of the allocation of training places, unless men cannot avail themselves of equivalent training possibilities elsewhere (e.g. in the private sector). Furthermore, the ECJ has not struck down preferential treatment measures in favour of women in respect of the decision as to who a job interview is to be given, provided that women are under-represented in the particular sector concerned. What is more, the ECJ has allowed for a (non-binding) recommendation seeking to secure that employees' representative and supervisory bodies are 50% composed of women. In addition, the Court has not thwarted measures which seek to achieve a proportionate representation of women in academia perceived in relation to the proportion of women among graduates, holders of higher degrees and students in the relevant discipline. Moreover, the Court has permitted preferential treatment of women in the allocation of childcare facilities, provided that males are not automatically excluded, and provided that 'proportionality' is complied with. The importance of 'proportionality' in the assessment of 'positive action' has been reaffirmed by the Court in *Briheche.* The analysis of the case law has also shown that the Court allows for positive action in the form of 'facially neutral but purposefully inclusionary policies'. Such policies are arguably precluded from being challenged in legal proceedings on the basis of 'reverse' indirect discrimination, although it seems that matters are less clear-cut in cases where such policies operate to the benefit of *men*, rather than women.

[137] Paragraph 31 of the judgment.

5. Positive Action in English Law

5.1. *Introduction*

Having analysed positive action in the context of EC law, I will henceforth examine the possibilities for positive action offered by the SDA 1975, the RRA 1976 and the DDA 1995 (all as amended), and by the R&B and S.O. Regulations.[138] With reference to McCrudden's classification of positive action measures the following types of measures will be discussed below: 'outreach measures', 'preferential treatment' and 'measures redefining merit'. The discussion of domestic positive action law will be subjected to a top-down comparison, which seeks to discern the (possible) influence of EC law upon domestic law in the subject area concerned. With reference to Chapter 2, the SDA 1975 and the RRA 1976 adopt a symmetrical approach. This holds equally true for the R&B Regulations and the S.O. Regulations. In contrast, the DDA 1995 is underpinned by asymmetry. In other words, the SDA and RRA are respectively aimed at eradicating discrimination on grounds of sex and race, rather than discrimination against women and disadvantaged ethnic groups. Likewise, the Regulations seek to outlaw discrimination on grounds of religion and belief, and sexual orientation. Differently, the purpose of the DDA 1995 is to tackle discrimination against disabled persons, rather than persons who have received discriminatory treatment on the ground of *not* being disabled.[139] These conceptual differences bear an important impact upon the lawfulness of positive action measures under the DDA, on the one hand, and the SDA/RRA/R&B and S.O. Regulations, on the other. Hereafter, I will make three distinct analyses of positive action law. In section 5.2, I will first consider the limits of permissible positive action under English sex and race discrimination law. In sction 5.3, positive action will be examined in the context of the R&B and S.O. Regulations. Positive action for disabled persons will be discussed in section 5.4. In section 5.5 analytical comments will be made with regard to the top-down and cross-ground comparisons. It will *inter alia* be seen that the SDA and RRA leave far less room for positive action compared with EC (gender) positive action law. This cannot, however, be said with respect to domestic law which permits positive action in favour of sexual and religious minorities. As will be seen, the relevant provisions in the S.O. and R&B Regulations appear to reflect the more flexible EC law approach. Most sympathetic to positive action is the DDA. Because of its asymmetrical framework the DDA regards positive action as wholly unproblematic. It will be argued that the domestic legislator has missed a window of oppor-

138 The Employment Equality (Religion or Belief) Regulations 2003, SI 2003, No. 1660 and the Employment Equality (Sexual Orientation) Regulations 2003, SI 2003, No. 1661. These Regulations have implemented the Article 13 EC EFD in respect of, respectively, the grounds 'religion' and 'belief', and 'sexual orientation'. Both sets of Regulations will be subjected to a detailed analysis in, respectively, Chapters 6 and 7. In this chapter, I will merely concentrate on 'positive action' in the context of the statutory Acts and Instruments referred to in the main text above.

139 This point will be elaborated in further detail in Chapter 8. See also Lacey 1992, p. 104 and Slater 2002, p. 13.

tunity for relaxing the unduly complex provisions on positive action which currently feature in English race and sex discrimination law.

5.2. *Positive Action: 'Race' and 'Sex'*

5.2.1. Introduction

In the case of *London Borough of Lambeth v. CRE*[140] Malcombe (LJ) for the Court of Appeal reaffirmed a stark reliance by the RRA 1976 upon the negative orientation of English Race Relations Law by holding that

> '(...) I am wholly unpersuaded that one of the two main purposes of the Act is to promote positive action to benefit racial groups. The purpose of the Act, as stated in its long title, is 'to make fresh provision with respect to discrimination on racial grounds and relations between people of different racial groups', and the substance of the operative parts (I-IV) of the Act is to render acts of racial discrimination unlawful'.[141]

The nature of the SDA must be understood in an identical fashion, given that the SDA and RRA have largely been treated in parallel both by the legislator and by the courts. In the present context, the negatively and symmetrically oriented approach of the law implies that both English sex and race discrimination law are unsympathetic to ideas about positive action and, notably, about preferential treatment at the level of employment. This is the case notwithstanding that the law insists that the principle of merit is left intact.[142] It will be seen hereafter that upon comparison, English race and sex discrimination law leave far less scope for positive action than EC law.[143] As we have seen in the previous section, EC positive action law is foremost instilled with an equality of opportunities rationale, although results equality has been allowed for by the ECJ regarding decisions unrelated to whom a job should be awarded. The application of the principle of equality of opportunity by the ECJ has meant that in merit tie-break situations a job or promotion may be given to a woman, provided that the merit principle is preserved and that an *automatic* preference for the female candidate is disallowed for.[144] Rather than 'equality of

140 *London Borough of Lambeth v. CRE* [1990] IRLR 231 (CA per Lord Justice Malcombe).

141 Paragraph 17 of the judgment.

142 'The "symmetrical" approach', writes McColgan, 'to discrimination adopted by the SDA [and] RRA (...) has the effect that much of what could be defined as "positive ['reverse' MG] discrimination" amounts to direct discrimination and is, therefore, unlawful.' See McColgan 2000, p. 138.

143 It is noted that English non-discrimination law is also much more hostile to positive action in comparison with U.S. law. U.S. law falls outside the scope of this book. Why positive action has been received with much more sympathy in the American legal forum has *inter alia* been clarified by Atkins and Hoggett 1984, cited by Richard Townshend Smith 1989, p. 228 (footnote 8).

144 Although it is acknowledged that this constitutes preferential treatment, it is not a form of preferential treatment that is infused with an equality of outcome rationale. Thus, this form of preferential treatment reflects an equality of opportunity rationale: merit is clearly preserved and a savings clause guarantees that the balance may tilt in favour of the male candidate. See also section 2.1 above.

opportunity', the key principle for positive action in the context of the SDA and RRA is 'symmetry'.[145] As we saw already, symmetry mirrors formal equality and thus adheres to an ideology of what Lacey has called 'liberal legalism'.[146] The comparison between EC and domestic law will be taken further in section 5.5 hereafter in the analysis of the top-down comparison. I will now first consider what kind of positive action measures are permissible under the SDA and RRA. The positive action provisions in the SDA and RRA are extremely complex, however, an analysis reveals that various different types of measures may lawfully be taken. Some of these measures fall within the realm of employment (section 5.2.2 hereafter), whereas others are designed to address 'power relations' in decision-making processes (section 5.3.3 hereafter). It is to a discussion of these various measures that I will turn now.

5.2.2. Positive Action Measures in the Realm of Employment

Broadly speaking, the SDA and RRA allow for the following types of positive action measures in the area of employment:

1. Measures which are designed to equip members of out-groups (women, ethnic minorities) with the necessary skills with a view to enabling them to compete on equal terms for jobs.[147] These measures will hereafter be referred to as *status (gender/race)-conscious training measures*. Along the lines of McCrudden's classification of positive action measures these measures belong to the group of outreach measures.
2. Measures designed to encourage members of a disadvantaged group to apply for a job. These measures will be referred to as *'job encouragement measures'*.[148] They too belong to the category of outreach measures.[149]

It is to be stressed that the measures under 1 and 2 are necessarily taken *prior* to an employment decision. Hence, they disallow for preferential treatment in decisions regarding access to employment, promotion and dismissal. Preferential treatment, with and without the preservation of the principle of merit,[150] in the allocation of

145 See also Fredman 2002, p. 130 *et seq.* and Fredman 1997a, p. 383 *et seq.*

146 Lacey 1992.

147 See Connolly 2004, p. 574.

148 See Connolly 2004, p. 574.

149 McCrudden has explicitly mentioned this in his typology of positive action measures: '[o]utreach programmes are designed to attract qualified candidates from the previously underrepresented group. They do so in two ways: first, by bringing employment opportunities to the attention of members of the group who might not previously have been aware of them and encouraging them to take up the opportunity to apply when otherwise they might not; second, by providing members of the underrepresented group without the necessary skills or qualifications with training the better to equip them for competing when they do apply.' See McCrudden 1986, p. 224. See also McColgan 2000, p. 141.

150 Thus, preferential treatment in merit tie-break situations is not permitted under the Acts ('merit' is preserved), let alone preferential treatment in such cases in which a male candidate is better qualified for the job than his female competitor. The last situation amounts to 'reverse' →

jobs or with regard to promotion or redundancy is *never* permitted under the SDA and RRA. Hence, although for example a *Marshall* scenario has passed the legal test under EC positive action law, this would not be the case under the SDA and RRA. This does not mean that domestic law is in contravention of EC law, for the latter merely leaves an *option* to the Member States to adopt positive action measures for out-groups.

3. *Genuine Occupational Requirements.* A particular job or position may be restricted to persons of either gender or to a person of a particular racial or ethnic group where being a man or a woman, or, belonging to a specific ethnic group constitutes a genuine occupational qualification for the job or the position concerned. Along the lines of McCrudden's classification of measures, the genuine occupational requirements exception constitutes a measure which 'redefines merit'. Conceptually speaking, the above exception is not really rationalised by concerns over balancing 'under representation', bringing about diversity or, seeking to realise equality of opportunity. Hence, this exception is not truly about positive action. In fact, and as will become clear, this exception is rationalised by concerns over privacy and personal inter-relationships.[151] This exception is nonetheless discussed in section 5 for - as a matter of fact - it has been treated by the judiciary in the context of positive action law.
4. *A variety of other measures.* In the area of employment the SDA and RRA furthermore allow for a number of measures which are not positive action measures in the conventional meaning of the work but which, for purposes of inclusiveness, will briefly be touched on in the analysis to follow.

The measures under 1-4 will be considered in greater detail hereafter. The measures under 1 and 2 will be analysed in conjunction with each other, given that this is also done by the statutory provisions themselves. This will be done in section 5.2.2.1. The measures under 3 and 4 will be separately examined in sections 5.2.2.2 and 5.2.2.3, respectively.

5.2.2.1. Outreach Measures: Status-Conscious Training Measures and Job Encouragement Measures

Status-conscious training measures and job encouragement measures are captured by Sections 47 and 48 of the SDA and by Sections 37 and 38 of the RRA. These Sections allow for such measures to be taken by certain actors (e.g. by employers) and under certain, carefully defined, circumstances. Given that the provisions in the SDA differ in certain respects from their counterpart provisions in the RRA, I will hereafter deal firstly with positive action measures in the gender context (I), and, subsequently in the context of race relations law (II).

discrimination or results equality which, at the level of employment, is neither allowed for by EC law.

151 Fredman 1997a, p. 385.

I. Sections 47 and 48 SDA

In analysing Sections 47 and 48 of the SDA I will firstly deal with gender-conscious training measures and, secondly, with job encouragement measures.

1. *Gender-conscious training measures*

Gender-conscious training measures, such as for example special management courses for female employees only, may be adopted both on the basis of Section 47 and Section 48 of the SDA. However, depending on what Section is relied on, the actors who may adopt such measures differ, as well as the circumstances under which such measures may lawfully be taken. In line with the principle of symmetry, Sections 47 and 48 are formulated in gender-neutral terms which means that in theory, training may also be restricted to male candidates only. However, *de facto*, Sections 47 and 48 of the Act tend to operate in favour of women. The rationale behind gender-conscious training measures is to redress the under representation of women in the job market as a whole and, more specifically, in higher level jobs. In other words, such measures seek to bring about a level playing field of competition between women and men in the quest for jobs. Undeniably, training is of prime importance to tackle segregated job markets, the gender pay gap as well as the low employment status of women.[152] It will, however, be seen that Sections 47-48 SDA and 37-38 RRA permit far less in terms of 'positive action', compared with what is allowed for under EC law.

Subsection 3 of Section 47 SDA furthermore recognises the disadvantaged position of women in the realm of work due to women's disproportionate share in dealing with domestic or family affairs,[153] as a result of which they are under represented or, for that matter, over represented in low level jobs. Section 47(3) SDA is once again formulated in gender-neutral terms which means that training could be confined to both males and females who return to paid employment. The symmetrical way of drafting the law echoes a refusal by the legislator to acknowledge in explicit terms women's preponderant role in domestic and child-rearing tasks. However, in reality, Section 47(3) nevertheless tends to work in favour of women.

As stated, the objective pursued by both Sections 47 and 48 SDA is to equip women for the race in the competition for jobs through raising knowledge and imparting skills.[154] It follows that these Sections do not contain a guarantee that women's representation in the labour market or in higher level jobs will indeed increase after

152 Sacks 1992, p. 357.

153 See Connolly who has observed that the two possible 'triggers' of positive action provisions in the SDA and the RRA are those of 'under representation' (which can apply to both the RRA and the SDA) and 'domestic responsibilities' (which is logically confined to the SDA). Connolly 2004, p. 575.

154 It is, however, to be noted that the dichotomy 'women' (disadvantaged) *v.* 'men' (advantaged) is not always straightforward. It is hard to point out whether in the competition for jobs a white woman is better off than a black man. In other words: different 'statuses' may intersect, a fact which is of particular importance in the context of positive action law. See for an analysis of intersectional discrimination Hannett 2003. Also Lacey 1992, p. 110 who has in this context spoken of the 'differentiated nature of social oppression'.

having participated in a gender-conscious training scheme.[155] Hence, meritocracy is by all means preserved. In addition, all positive action measures permitted by the statutory Act are merely optional and do not *have to* be taken by the relevant actors under these Sections.

The next question which arises is *who* may provide for gender-conscious training under Sections 47 and 48 SDA and *to whom*? The original language version of Section 47 SDA provided that only a number of (by the Department of Employment) 'designated training bodies' could be actors under that Section.[156] The 1986 amendments to the SDA have, however, widened the group of potential actors, so as to include 'any person' including thus employers. Therefore, employers may provide for gender-conscious training schemes under Section 47 SDA, either on their own initiative or in collaboration with a local authority.[157] However, it must be noted that according to Section 47(4) SDA training under Section 47 may only be provided to individuals who are not employees, apprentices or job applicants. In light of this it is unlikely that employers will indeed act under Section 47 SDA and thus the principal actors under Section 47 are training providers. The widening of the scope of actors under Section 47 SDA has meant that it partially overlaps with Section 48 SDA. On the basis of Section 48 SDA employers, trade unions, employers' organisations or other professional organisations may provide for gender-conscious training schemes to existing employees.

Gender-conscious training measures may only be taken in the context of Section 47 or 48 SDA if certain by the law defined conditions are fulfilled. In the context of Section 47(3) SDA it must 'reasonably appear to [the actor; MG] that [women; MG] are in special need of training by reason of the period for which they have been discharging domestic or family responsibilities (…)'. Hence, under Section 47(3) SDA 'under representation' needs not be proven. Positive action measures taken on the basis of this Section can become manifest either, by limiting training courses to female participants only, or by the way in which candidates for such courses are selected. If Section 47(3) SDA did not exist, men could claim an instance of unlawful ('reverse') indirect discrimination. After all, if training is limited to those who have been taking care of children or domestic or family responsibilities this will usually work to the advantage of women. It follows that Section 47(3) SDA must be conceptualised as what McCrudden has termed 'facially neutral but purposefully inclusionary policies'.[158] An example of a measure which could be adopted on the basis of Section 47(3) is a course in IT skills in order to update women's knowledge in this respect. Except for Section 47(3) SDA, the qualifying condition for measures to be taken in the context of both Sections 47 and 48 SDA is that of 'under representation'. The way in which this concept is applied in Section 47 SDA differs however from that in Section 48 SDA. In Section 47 SDA 'under representation' is assessed, either by reference to the

155 See Fredman 2002, p. 135: 'A woman who has participated in a women's only training scheme declared lawful by the Act stands no better chance of being offered the employment for which she has been trained than anyone else.'

156 See Bindman 1985, p. 1169.

157 IDS Employment Law Handbook, 1998 p. 52.

158 See section 2.1 above. See also Burrows and Robison 2006, p. 36-37.

numbers of persons doing particular work in Great Britain as a whole, or within a particular geographical area in Great Britain. Either no women at all perform the particular work, or the number of women performing it is comparatively small. As Burrows and Robison have argued 'only a relatively narrow range of courses and initiatives will in fact fall within [this] definition'.[159] 'Under representation' is to be assessed by looking at the preceding 12 months. In contrast, what matters under Section 48 SDA is that women in the preceding 12 months were either not represented at all in a particular work in the employer's enterprise, or that the number of female workers doing that work was 'comparatively small', a notion which has however never been determined by the judiciary. Under the same circumstances, trade unions and employers' organisations may lawfully afford gender-conscious training to female members of the organisation, with a view to helping them to hold any kind of post in the organisation.

2. *Job Encouragement Measures*

As noted, the second type of measure which may lawfully be taken under Sections 47 and 48 SDA constitutes what I have labelled 'job encouragement measures'.[160] What has been said above with regard to 'gender-conscious training measures' in terms of who may act and under what conditions applies *eo ipso* to 'job encouragement measures'.[161] Job encouragement measures share the same objective as the one pursued by gender-conscious training measures namely, creating equal opportunities for women and men which, it is hoped, but not guaranteed, will increase female representation. The strategy for achieving this objective is, however, different. Job encouragement measures aim to promote women to take advantage of opportunities for doing particular work (or for holding a particular post in an organisation). Examples of job encouragement measures are: job advertising in the women's press and a provision in a job advertisement text that 'women are particularly encouraged to apply'.[162] The boundaries of 'job encouragement measures' are, however, overstepped once males are excluded from applying for jobs, or from holding particular posts.[163] For example, a measure stipulating that women are called to an interview first provided they are 'under represented (*viz.* the *Badeck* case discussed above) goes beyond the mandate of 'job encouragement'. This is *a fortiori* the case with respect to measures providing that a job should be given to a female candidate under the conditions mapped by the ECJ in *Marshall*, *Abrahammson* and *Badeck* (all discussed above). The limited ambit of 'job encouragement measures' has also been affirmed in domestic case law. Thus, in the case of *Jones v. Chief Constable of Northamptonshire*

159 Burrows and Robison 2006, p. 36.

160 Or, in the context of organisations acting under Section 48, 'measures which encourage women to take advantage of opportunities for holding posts, for example executive posts, in such an organisation (e.g. a trade union)'.

161 With the exception of what was mentioned in relation to Section 47(3) SDA.

162 See for a more practical account of what kind of positive action measures have been taken in the English context, I refer to Sacks 1992, p. 357-385.

163 This is only different for jobs with regard to which a person's sex constitutes a 'genuine occupational requirement'.

Police,[164] Section 48 of the SDA did not grant a defence to a claim of sex discrimination instituted by a male police officer whose application was rejected with a view to addressing women's under representation in a particular branch of the police force. Similarly, in *Acas v. Taylor*[165] EAT held that a decision by the Employment Tribunal that a promotion policy was conducted to the advantage of female and to the disadvantage of male applicants, constituted an unlawful instance of sex discrimination against men.[166] A similar outcome has been voiced in the context of the RRA in the (unreported) case of *Hughes v. London Borough of Hackney*.[167] In that case, the London Borough of Hackney had advertised for two posts for gardening apprentices (which entailed 'learning on the job'). In view of the (benign) motive to redress 'under representation' in the recruitment and training opportunities of persons belonging to racial and ethnic minority groups, the job advertisement included the following provision:

> 'Blacks and ethnic minorities are heavily under-represented in the Parks and Open Spaces Services. Where such conditions exist, the RRA [Section 38; MG] allows an employer to establish extra training opportunities specifically for those groups. We would therefore warmly welcome applications from black and ethnic minority people for the two apprenticeships'.

Essentially, however, the white job applicants were informed by the personnel officer that the available jobs were only open to those belonging to a racial minority group. In interpreting the limits of Section 38 RRA it was firmly held by the tribunal that this Section does not allow for the restriction of jobs to ethnic minority groups. Neither had the respondent succeeded in proving the alleged 'under representation'. Hence, the applicant's claim of unlawful racial discrimination was upheld.

II. Sections 37 and 38 of the RRA

Basically, Sections 37 and 38 RRA must be understood in exactly the same spirit as has been explained above in much detail in the context of Sections 47 and 48 SDA. Thus, Sections 37 and 38 RRA also allow for the provision of 'race-conscious' training measures and for job encouragement for members belonging to a certain racial or ethnic group in respect of particular work where these members are 'under represented'. Similarly, like under Section 48 of the SDA, trade unions/employers' organisations/ other professional organisations may encourage membership among racial groups which are 'under represented' within the organisation. However, the way in which the key notion of 'under representation' is assessed in the context of the RRA differs

164 *Jones v. Chief Constable of Northamptonshire Police*, ET case no. 1201171/98 (EOR DCLD 41). See http://www.eoc-law.org.uk where this summary of the case was taken from.

165 Acas v. Taylor (EAT 788/97).

166 Outside the realm of employment the most pertinent illustration of the illegality of results-based measures is the case *Jepson v. the Labour Party* [1996] IRLR 116. This case will be discussed later on in the analysis.

167 *Hughes v. London Borough of Hackney* (IT, unreported case, *viz.* 7 EOR 27 1986). This case has also been discussed in Richard Townshend Smith 1989, p. 230-231.

slightly from that in the context of sex discrimination law. A comparison between Section 47 SDA and 37 RRA reveals that under the former (and as discussed above) the object of comparison is the number of women compared with the number of men. Under the latter, proportions rather than numbers must be compared. Thus, the proportion of, e.g. Indian people working in particular employment x in Great Britain would be compared with the proportion of Indian people among the population in Great Britain. Moreover, and logically, no equivalent to Section 47(3) SDA (women in need of training due to women's role in child-rearing) exists in Section 37 RRA. If one compares Sections 48 SDA and 38 RRA, one finds the following differences. As seen above, the former is about comparing numbers rather than proportions. Moreover, under representation in the context of Section 38 RRA is assessed by looking at one of the following: 1) either, no persons of that particular racial group are working in a particular job in the employer's enterprise; 2) or, the proportion of persons of that particular racial group doing a particular work in the employer's enterprise is small in comparison with the proportion of persons of that group among the entire workforce (in the enterprise); 3) or, (…) among the population of the employer's (conventional) recruitment area.

So far, an analysis has been made of two types of 'outreach measures' permitted by the SDA and RRA in the context of employment namely, 'gender/race-conscious training measures' and 'job (or post)-encouragement measures'. These measures constitute the core of 'positive action' found in the statutes. The just-mentioned measures may be adopted by training institutions, employers, trade unions, employers' organisations and other professional organisations, as the case might be. Notwithstanding that the just-mentioned measures are aimed at creating a level playing field of competition in the labour market between women/men, and the ethnic minority/ethnic majority, their legal ambit is defined by 'symmetry', rather than by 'equality of opportunity'. This clearly follows from the (limited number of) cases which have reached the courts and which, without a single exception, have been interpreted unduly restrictively. With the exception of Article 47(3) SDA, Sections 47/48 SDA and 37/38 RRA require proof of 'under representation'. However, how to prove 'under representation' is uncertain, because different statutory Sections impose different legal conditions and, because 'under representation' has not been interpreted in the case law of the courts.

5.2.2.2. *Measures Redefining 'Merit': the Genuine Occupational Requirement Exception*

As stated earlier, intrinsically perceived, the genuine occupational requirement (GOR) exception is not infused with the rationales underpinning positive action namely, seeking to bring about a fairer representation of members belonging to an out-group, although in practice it might have this effect. In a broader sense the GOR exception could, however, be perceived within the positive action paradigm as a measure which redefines merit.[168] Although a person's sex or race should on many (perhaps most)

168 See also Dworkin 1985, p. 299.

occasions not be taken into account in a given decision-making process, a person's gender or race sometimes constitutes a genuine occupational qualification for the job. The GOR exception is contained in Section 5(2) under 'd' of the RRA 1976.[169] This Section will permit the imposition of a GOR, if it is rationalised by a concern over 'authenticity' (e.g. the black actor) or by a concern over 'privacy and personal inter-relationships' which to a limited extent also covers legitimate cultural needs.[170] Although, as stated above, a broad conceptualisation of positive action may include the GOR as a form of positive action, the English courts have stressed that it has to be conceptualised as an exception to what otherwise would amount to discrimination rather than as a proviso under the guise of which positive action measures could be taken. The leading case on the matter is that of *London Borough of Lambeth v. CRE* decided by the Court of Appeal.[171] In the case at hand, the London Borough of Lambeth had advertised two jobs at managerial level within their housing benefits department. Given that over half of the tenants with whom the department dealt with were of Afro Caribbean or Asian ethnic origin the Council had taken the decision that the posts were to be confined to Afro Caribbean and Asian applicants. This was rationalised by the Council's desire to hire candidates having a particular empathy with claimants for housing benefits who are of black origin. The tribunal had taken the view that the GOR did not apply to the facts at hand given that the posts concerned were primarily of a managerial kind. As such they could not legitimately be understood as involving 'personal service provision' (in the sense of Section 5(2) indent 'd' RRA). This view was subsequently endorsed by Lord Justice Balcombe for the Court of Appeal whereby he explicitly repeated that the RRA should in no circumstances be understood as an instrument for the promotion of positive action to the benefit of racial groups.[172]

5.2.2.3. Other Statutory Provisions and Alternative Measures

In the above sections, mention has been made of positive action provisions in the context of the SDA and RRA in the employment realm. But for the existence of these provisions the 'discriminatory' instances which are the result of the adoption of these measures are allowed for by the statutory framework. In the context of race relations law brief mention is made at this juncture of two additional provisions. Section 35 of the RRA provides that

169 The equivalent provision in the gender context is enshrined in Section 7(2) under 'e' of the SDA.

170 Fredman 1997a, p. 388 and Palmer, Gill *et al.* 2002, p. 341.

171 London Borough of Lambeth v. CRE [1990] ICR 768 (CA).

172 See paragraph 17 of the judgment. See also EAT in *Tottenham Green Under Fives' Centre v. Marshall,* [1989] IRLR 148 and *Tottenham Green Under Fives' Centre v. Marshall (No 2)* [1991] IRLR 162. In this case the EAT took the view that in the construction of Section 5 RRA, Tribunals must carry out a 'delicate balancing exercise, bearing in mind the need to guard against discrimination and the desirability of promoting racial integration. It is important not to give Section 5 too wide a construction, which would enable it to provide an excuse or cloak for undesirable discrimination. On the other hand, where genuine attempts are being made to integrate ethnic groups into society, too narrow a construction might stifle such initiatives'.

> 'nothing [in the RRA] shall render unlawful any act done in affording persons of a particular racial group access to facilities or services to meet the special needs of persons of that group in regard to their education, training or welfare, or any ancillary benefits'.

This provision thus allows for example language training schemes which are expressly targeted at immigrants. Moreover, on the basis of Section 36 RRA discrimination is also allowed with regard to the education or training of persons who are not ordinarily resident in Great Britain, where it reasonably appears to the person affording such education and training, that these persons would not remain in Great Britain after the training period.[173] It is by reason of the symmetry principle that all measures discussed up until this point have been in need of being explicitly addressed by the statutes themselves. If these provisions did not exist, alleged victims of discrimination caused by the enactment of positive action measures could lodge a complaint of discriminatory treatment before a court. It should be noted, however, that other strategies could be employed with a view to addressing under representation of disadvantaged groups in the realm of work which do not shatter the paradigms of formal equality. Such measures notably include the provision of affordable childcare facilities so as to encourage women to take up paid employment, giving men a right to paid paternity leave, flexible rules in respect of career breaks, etc. Such measures form an aid to restoring the gender-divisions in the family without being discriminatory in nature. Hepple has moreover mentioned the possibility of so-called 'contract compliance' which he has defined as '(...) the procedure by which a purchasing body seeks to satisfy itself that firms with whom it contracts are fair employers'.[174] In the assessment of 'fairness', an important factor should be the existence in practice of a sound equal opportunities policy.[175]

Up until this juncture, I have examined positive action measures in the context of 'race' and 'sex' in employment. In the section to follow, I will look at positive action measures for women outside employment. These provisions seek to counteract power structures in decision-making processes. It should be noted that similar provisions do not exist in respect of race as a ground of discrimination. The discussion will therefore be confined to the relevant provisions in the SDA.

5.2.3. Positive Action Measures Seeking to Address Power Structures in Decision-Making Processes[176]

Fredman has observed that the symmetry principle constitutes a prime obstacle to strategies seeking to redress the serious under representation of women in the higher

173 Connolly 2004, p. 578, who has mentioned the example of language schools.

174 Hepple 2001, p. 1384/9.

175 In the present legal, political and social context, the strategy of contract compliance is not received with sympathy (in contrast to e.g. the situation in the US). For a further discussion of the effectiveness of the strategy of contract compliance and of its evolution in the British context I refer to Hepple 2001, section 1.6, p. 1384/9 and to Fredman 1997a p. 388 *et seq.*

176 Although, admittedly, this section extends the scope of employment (the area with which this book is primarily concerned) it seems nonetheless legitimate to address this issue, given its importance in the area of positive action law and measures.

echelons of the decision-making process most notably in Parliament.[177] Since its inception, the SDA (in Section 49 of the Act) has served the purpose of improving women's representation in trade unions, employers' organisations or other professional organisations. Section 49 of the Act clearly depicts substantive justice by providing as follows:

> (1) If an organisation to which section 12 applies [i.e. a trade union or equivalent organisation; MG] comprises a body the membership of which is wholly or mainly elected, nothing in Section 12 [this Section contains the prohibition of sex discrimination by such bodies; MG] shall render unlawful a provision which ensures that a minimum number of persons of one sex are members of the body –
> (a) by reserving seats on the body for persons of that sex, or
> (b) by making extra seats on the body available (by election or co-option or otherwise) for persons of that sex on occasions when the number of persons of that sex in the other seats is below the minimum, where in the opinion of the organisation the provision is in the circumstances needed to secure a reasonable lower limit to the number of members of that sex serving on the body; and nothing in [the SDA; MG] shall render unlawful any act done in order to give effect to such a provision.
> (2) This Section shall not be taken as making lawful
> (a) discrimination in the arrangements for determining the persons entitled to vote in an election of members of the body, or otherwise to choose the persons to serve on the body, or
> (b) discrimination in any arrangements concerning membership of the organisation itself.

In short, this Section entitles trade unions, employers' organisations and other professional organisations to reserve a minimum number of seats for women on elected bodies for such organisations, with the purpose of counter-balancing 'under representation'. It is recalled that the ECJ in *Badeck* was not opposed to such measures, although, it should be noted that in *Badeck* the vexed measure amounted to a *non-binding recommendation*.

Hence, in respect of Section 49 SDA a substantive vision of justice clearly creeps into the analysis of the Act's provisions on positive action.

The second domain which must be mentioned in the present context concerns Parliament. In the 1996 case of *Jepson and Dyas-Elliott (applicants) v. The Labour Party and Others (respondents)*[178] the Industrial Tribunal gave its view on the Labour Party's strategy to increase the number of women MPs.[179] Indeed, the situation of a vast under representation of women in the British Parliament was highly worrying. The

177 Fredman 2002, p. 131.

178 *Jepson and Dyas-Elliott (applicants) v. The Labour Party and Others (respondents)* [1996] IRLR 116.

179 The fact that matters such as that in stake in *Jepson* have been dealt with by an Industrial Tribunal has rightfully been criticised in legal circles. The issues at stake were (and are) of great Constitutional importance and an Industrial Tribunal simply lacks the necessary knowledge and expertise to deal with the matter at stake. The matters at stake in *Jepson* should have been taken outside the realm of the law dealing with employment and non-discrimination and should instead have been dealt with in the context of English public law. This would have prompted a judicial review exercise carried out by a competent court in light of eloquent principles of English public law. This criticism has been expressed by Fredman 1997a, p. 387 and is fully underscored by the present author.

strategy consisted of allowing for women-only shortlists for the selection of Labour MPs in certain designated constituencies. Mr Jepson was not considered for selection as a Parliamentary candidate in constituencies *x* and *y*, for those constituencies were required to have all-women shortlists. In a highly unsatisfactory decision the Tribunal took the view that Labour's practice constituted direct discrimination against men given that 'but for' his sex Mr Jepson had not been considered for selection.[180] Hence, in the Tribunal's view it was beyond doubt that Mr Jepson had been a victim of unlawful direct sex discrimination. Fredman has rightfully criticised the adoption by the tribunal of a 'but for' test in the case at hand, in light of the constitutional character of *Jepson*.[181] The present author shares this criticism, for ensuring a fair representation of women,[182] who make up more than half of the population, is called for in democratic society based upon the rule of law.

In 2002 it was the legislator, rather than a judicial forum, which has eventually recognised the need for a substantive application of the principle of equality as the only means towards a fairer representation of women in British Parliament. All-women shortlists, as well as other measures whose aim is to tackle inequality in the numbers of males and females elected as representatives of a political party, have since 2002 been permitted by Section 42 of the SDA. This Section was added to the Act by the Sex Discrimination (Election Candidates) Act 2002. Section 42 thus stipulates as follows:

> (1) Nothing in [the SDA MG] shall –
> (a) be construed as affecting arrangements to which this Section applies, or (b) render unlawful anything done in accordance with such arrangements.
> (2) This Section applies to arrangements made by a registered political party which –
> (a) regulate the selection of the party's candidates in a relevant election, and (b) are adopted for the purpose of reducing inequality in the numbers of men and women elected, as candidates of the party, to be members of the body concerned.
> (3) the following elections are relevant elections for the purposes of this Section –
> (a) Parliamentary elections;
> (b) Elections to the European Parliament;
> (c) Elections to the Scottish Parliament;
> (d) Elections to the National Assembly for Wales;
> (e) Local government elections …

It is observed that Section 42 of the Act will expire at the end of 2015 unless it is renewed by statutory law. This reminds us of the fact that in order to be legitimate positive action measures must be of a temporary nature.

180 The adoption of the 'but for' test is the conventional way for dealing with direct discrimination claims in the context of the SDA and the RRA. See the seminal case by the House of Lords in *James v. Eastleigh Borough Council* [1990] 2 AC 751 (HL) discussed in Chapter 3.

181 Fredman 1997a.

182 As well as of members of other disadvantaged groups.

5.3. *Positive Action: Religion, Belief and Sexual Orientation*

In contrast to positive action measures with respect to the grounds 'race' and 'sex', the positive action measures adopted in the context of 'religion', 'belief' and 'sexual orientation' reflect a more flexible approach. Essentially, the relevant provisions in the Regulations (i.e. Regulations 25(1) and 26(1) of the R&B and S.O. Regulations, respectively) allow the employer and other persons (e.g. training providers) to afford preferential treatment to members of minority religions, or to (e.g.) gay persons, with regard to access to training or encouragement for doing particular work, where it 'reasonably appears' to the person adopting the positive action measure that it 'prevents or compensates for disadvantages'. Regulations 25(2) and 26(2) of the R&B and S.O. Regulations, respectively, permit trade unions to grant preferential treatment to out-groups defined by religion/belief, or sexual orientation, in terms of making training places for posts or encouragement to apply for posts only available to the members of the religious or sexual minority group to whom the positive action measure or policy is targeted. This may be done, once again, where it 'reasonably appears' to the person adopting the positive action measure that it 'prevents or compensates for disadvantages'.[183]

A number of matters should be pointed out. First, it ought to be emphasised that the Regulations are confined to training and job encouragement measures. Therefore, they do not permit granting preferential treatment to, e.g. a Muslim or gay job applicant in 'merit tie-break' situations (on the same conditions as the ECJ has formulated in the *Marshall* case). Moreover, as referred to above in the context of sex and race, job encouragement measures may not go so far as to exclude members of the majority group from applying for jobs, for this would be tantamount to 'results equality'. Secondly, the crucial difference between the positive action provisions in the R&B and S.O. Regulations on the one hand, and similar provisions in the SDA/RRA is that under the Regulations the employer (or other actor) needs not prove 'under representation' in order to justify positive action. In contrast, the employer is merely required to show that it reasonably appeared to him that the vexed measures prevent or compensate for disadvantages. In sum: positive action measures for religious and sexual minorities pass more easily the legal test than similar measures adopted in favour of women or ethnic minorities.[184] In this context it should be observed that proving the 'under representation' of sexual minorities would anyhow be a particularly difficult, if not impossible exercise, in light of the intrinsic nature of this ground of discrimination. As will be explained in Chapter 7, 'sexual orientation' is a fluid notion in the sense that a person's sexual orientation need not be static. Moreover, collecting statistical data about sexual orientation is likely to show tensions with concerns over privacy which, as will be analysed in Chapter 7, are closely linked with the ground sexual orientation.

183 See also de Marco 2004, section 6.3.

184 See also Burrows and Robison 2006, p. 40.

5.4. *Positive Action under the DDA 1995 – Asymmetry Rules*

Having considered positive action within the symmetrical straight-jackets of the SDA and RRA, and within the context of the R&B and S.O. Regulations, I will now turn to a very brief discussion of positive action in the context of the 1995 DDA. The reason why the discussion will be brief is a simple one. Unlike the SDA and RRA, the DDA reflects *asymmetry*. Hence, the Act has been specifically designed to foster the rights of *disabled people* and having a disability is thus a material condition in order to rely on the provisions contained in the Act.[185] Given the asymmetrical application of the provisions of the DDA 1995 positive action measures for disabled people are not a vexed issue. After all, a non-disabled person cannot lodge a complaint under the Act for having been the victim of discrimination as a result of preferential treatment meted out to a disabled person. Hence, it is perfectly permissible for an employer to advertise for employment which is only open to disabled people, although the employer is under no obligation to hire persons who do not have the requested merit for the job concerned. As will be argued in Chapter 8, merit has, however, to be assessed *after* the possibilities for making a reasonable adjustment have been considered. The foregoing shows that in light of the radically different conceptual framework underpinning the DDA, compared with the SDA and RRA, the insertion of a positive action exception in the context of disability discrimination law has not been necessary.

5.5. *Top-Down and Cross-Ground Comparison*

In this section, the above analysis of English positive action law will be looked at from a 'top-down' and 'cross-ground' perspective. This prompts the following conclusions. The provisions concerning 'gender- and race-conscious training measures' and 'job encouragement measures' found in the SDA and RRA have been framed in a particularly inaccessible manner, which makes it difficult for employers to understand these provisions in the first place. In addition, the adoption of these measures is not legally required, although doing so would not be barred by EC positive action law. Moreover, Sections 47/48 SDA and 37/38 RRA are inoperative at the level of employment. As such, they permit much less compared with what is allowed for under EC law. The situation has become exacerbated by a restrictive interpretation and application of the law by the courts. It is clear that outreach measures under English race and sex discrimination law have only a limited capacity to reach the objective pursued namely, bringing about a fairer representation of women and persons belonging to ethnic minority groups in the realm of work. By rigidly preserving 'symmetry' and by disallowing preferential treatment in merit tie-break situations (analogous to the ECJ's approach in *Marshall* and *Badeck*) the underlying purposes of the provisions are largely undermined. In order to achieve the objectives pursued by the relevant Sections in the SDA and RRA, the legal framework would

185 A detailed discussion on 'asymmetry' in the context of English disability discrimination law will be presented in Chapter 8 ('disability').

have to be reconceived and re-interpreted in a more teleological fashion. This should be done by taking EC positive action law as a starting point. It must be stressed that a window of opportunity to do so was given by the need for transposing the RD and AETD into domestic law. This opportunity has, however, not been exploited.

Not only do the complexities and rigidities which feature in English positive action law for women and racial minorities not dovetail with the more flexible approach in EC law, they neither correspond with the positive action provisions in the R&B and S.O. Regulations. It is argued that the divergences in the permissible scope for positive action in the SDA/RRA, on the one hand, and the Regulations, on the other, cannot be rationalised on the basis of the intrinsic nature of the discrimination grounds concerned. Although the ground 'sexual orientation' cannot easily be captured by statistical data by reason of its fluid character, and in view of concerns over privacy rights,[186] this should not have prevented the domestic legislator from relaxing the positive action provisions in the context of 'gender' and 'race'. Arguably, the divergent approaches to positive action in the context of the latter two grounds, compared with 'sexual orientation' and 'religion' must be comprehended against the background of a *de minimis* approach adopted by the British legislator whilst implementing the RD, EFD and AETD. Given that the positive action provisions in the SDA and RRA do not fall short of EC law, the legislator has apparently deemed it unnecessary to alter these provisions. The discussion of positive action in English law has ended with the ground of disability. It has been illustrated that positive action measures for disabled persons are not at all contested in the context of domestic law, given the asymmetrical framework of the DDA. It is, however, currently not clear, in the absence of ECJ case law on the matter, whether *automatically* granting a job to a disabled person, provided that she is equally qualified as her non-disabled competitor, will be in conformity with EC law. As argued in section 4.2 above, this will largely depend on the interpretation by the ECJ of the 'non-regression clause' contained in the EFD.

6. Positive Action in Dutch Law

6.1. Introduction

In section 5 above, English positive action law has been considered from a 'top-down' and 'cross-ground' perspective. An analogous analysis will be made hereafter with respect to Dutch law. It will be argued that with regard to those grounds of discrimination for which positive action has been allowed by the domestic legal framework, Dutch law has fully consumed the legal scope granted by the ECJ for the adoption of such measures. However, for other grounds of discrimination, Dutch law does not permit positive action *at all*, notwithstanding that doing so is not precluded by EC law. Hereafter, I will first consider the applicable legal framework governing positive action in the Netherlands (section 6.2). I will subsequently

186 See Chapter 7.

analyse the case law on positive action by the ETC (section 6.3) Brief conclusions will be drawn in section 6.4.

6.2. *Legislative Framework*

In the Netherlands positive action measures may only be adopted in the context of the discrimination grounds 'sex', 'race' and 'disability', to the exclusion of any other ground.[187] In other words, although EC law permits positive action for religious minorities, sexual minorities and the elderly (or young people), this is not allowed for under domestic law. It should be noted that the expansion, or not, of the legal possibility for positive action for grounds other than 'sex', 'race' and 'disability' has explicitly been addressed by the Dutch government.[188] Contrary to the advice given to the government by the ETC, the former deemed such an expansion undesirable, by reason of the (alleged) absence of a 'structurally disadvantaged position' of (*inter alia*) sexual minorities, religious minorities and the elderly (or young people).[189] The ETC moreover advised the government that the positive action provisions in Dutch equal treatment law should be defined in a symmetrical fashion, implying that the possibility for positive action should not be limited to women, members of an ethnic minority and disabled persons, but should be extended to men, members of the ethnic majority and non-disabled persons.[190] This advice has not been followed by the government, and rightfully so, for such an approach would not correlate with the wider rationales underlying positive action earlier discussed. The Dutch approach, like the English and EC law approach, does, however, reflect 'symmetry' in the sense that positive action measures in favour of minority members may be

187 See also Opinion 2006-61 in which the ETC affirmed the *a priori* unlawfulness of positive action measures in respect of (*inter alia*) 'age' and 'sexual orientation'. Positive action in respect of the grounds 'religion' and 'belief' was not at stake in Opinion 2006-61 but is neither allowed in Dutch law.

188 See *Parliamentary Documents* II, 2004-2005, 28 770, no. 11, p. 1-29.

189 It should be noted that the ETC agreed with the government that currently only women, members of (certain) ethnic minorities and disabled persons find themselves in a structurally disadvantaged position. Nonetheless, the ETC has deemed it desirable to extend the possibility for positive action beyond 'sex', 'race' and 'disability' mainly for the sake of legal consistency and legal transparency. See Advice of the Equal Treatment Commission on the positive action exception in equal treatment legislation, 2004. This advice is available at <www.cgb.nl>.

190 *Ibid*, Section 6. It should be noted that one of the reasons referred to by the ETC in order to support its preference for a 'symmetrically' defined positive action exception was EC law itself. In the Commission's view, Article 141(4) EC as well as the relevant provisions in the RD, EFD and AETD have all been symmetrically defined. However, this view can be contested, at least with respect to the grounds 'sex' and 'disability'. As indicated in footnote 83 above, Declaration No. 28 to the Amsterdam Treaty makes it explicitly clear that positive action measures adopted on the basis of Article 141(4) EC should be aimed at improving the socio-economic position of women (rather than men). Moreover, as will be argued in Chapter 8, it is far from clear whether the EFD applies in a symmetrical fashion insofar as the ground disability is concerned. If it does not, it would arguably be a breach of EC law, if the Dutch government changed the positive action provision in the DETA, so as to also cover 'non-disabled persons'.

challenged by members of the majority group. It will be illustrated that in Dutch law the principle of 'symmetry' has not been interpreted as strictly as it has been in the context of the English RRA and SDA. If positive action measures are adopted, they will have to be in conformity with the relevant requirements stemming from *both* Dutch *and* EC law (top-down influence). These requirements will be dealt with hereafter in a discussion of the case law of the ETC.

Positive action measures for women can be adopted on the basis of Article 5(1) of the AET w/m[191] and Article 7:646 (4) of the Civil Code.[192] These provisions have been amended in minor respects with a view to implementing Article 2(8) of the AETD.[193] Article 5(1) AET w/m in its amended format provides as follows:

> '[The prohibition of distinction between women and men in the material areas covered by the Act shall not apply MG] if the distinction is aimed at placing women in a privileged position with a view to eliminating de facto disadvantages, or, with a view to reducing these and, provided that the distinction stands in a proportionate relationship with the aim(s) pursued.'[194]

An equivalent provision as the one found in Article 5(1) AET w/m is contained in Article 7:646(4) Civil Code. Article 7:646(1) Civil Code prohibits the employer from making distinctions between men and women with regard to the commencement of an employment relationship; the provision of training to the employee; the employment conditions and working conditions; promotion and the termination of the employment relationship. This Article is merely directed at private employment. The AET w/m in contrast covers both private and public employment. Moreover, it *inter alia* also covers the areas of vocational training and equal pay, the liberal profession, pension provision and membership of employer organisations and trade unions. Hence, the Act has a much broader material scope than Article 7:646(1) Civil Code and the former and the latter only partially overlap. Article 3(1) of the AET w/m prohibits from making distinctions between men and women with regard to the offering of employment; with regard to procedures leading to the filling of vacancies and with respect to employment mediation (Article 3(1) AET w/m). Furthermore, it follows from Article 3(2) of the Act that if an employer conducts a positive action policy, he will have to state this explicitly in the advertisement for employment.

191 Act on Equal Treatment for Women and Men. See generally Chapter 2.

192 See generally Chapter 2. It is to be noted that the discrimination ground sex is also covered by the GETA. However, *grosso modo* it could be maintained that the GETA is only applicable to sex discrimination outside the context of employment. The reason for this is because the AET w/m is a *lex specialis vis-à-vis* the GETA (See Article 4 of the GETA).

193 These amendments have not yet entered into force. The legislative process with regard to the implementation of the AETD is still ongoing, notwithstanding that the AETD should have been implemented into domestic law by 05-10-05. What will be said hereafter is based upon the Bill implementing the AETD. See *Parliamentary Documents* II, 2004-2005, 30 237, no. 2.

194 In its pre-implementation format Article 5(1) AET w/m referred to de facto 'inequalities', rather than *de facto* 'disadvantages'. This amendment has been made because Article 2(8) AETD refers to Article 141(4) EC which speaks of disadvantages, not inequalities. However, this is only a minor amendment which is not likely to affect the legal scope for positive action measures for women.

Moreover, the advertisement must expressly state that both women and men are eligible for the job on offer (Articles 3(3) and 3(4) of the Act). As will be seen, in positive action cases which have come before the ETC the Commission usually distinguishes between the question whether the employment advertisement is in conformity with equal treatment law (1), and, whether the employer's positive action policy meets the legal requirements (2).[195]

The exception for positive action in the context of 'race' is contained in Article 2(3) GETA as amended.[196] It provides as follows:

> 'The prohibition of distinction in this Act shall not apply if the distinction concerns a specific measure which has the aim of placing (…) persons belonging to a particular ethnic or cultural minority group in a privileged position in order to eliminate or reduce de facto disadvantages in relation to the discrimination ground race (..) and the distinction is reasonably proportionate to the aim pursued.'

A counterpart provision is contained in the DETA[197] 2003 with respect to the grounds 'disability' and 'chronic disease'. It should be noted that whilst Dutch law explicitly enshrines a proportionality requirement, this is not contained in the relevant provisions of the RD, the EFD and the AETD. However, as seen before, that positive action measures must comply with the principle of proportionality explicitly follows from the ECJ's case law in *Lommers* and *Briheche.*

Before proceeding with a discussion of the (non-binding) case law of the ETC the following matter is worth paying attention to. In 1998 the Act on the Promotion of Labour Participation of Ethnic Minorities (*Wet Stimulering Arbeidsdeelname Minderheden: Wet SAMEN*)[198] entered into force. This Act gave effect to the Netherlands' obligations under the United Nations CERD Convention.[199] It obliged employers to strive for a proportional representation of ethnic minorities in the employer's workforce. This meant that the percentage of ethnic minority workers in the employer's total workforce was approximately equivalent to the percentage of members of an ethnic minority in the regional labour force taking the merit principle into account. The Act SAMEN expired, however, on 31 December 2003 and has not been renewed. It will only be discussed henceforth, in the context of case law which has arisen when the Act was still in force. This case law reveals that legal standards stemming from international non-discrimination and equality law potentially show tensions with similar standards stemming from EC law.

195 See for example Opinion 2004-173.

196 General Equal Treatment Act. In order to comply with the requirements stemming from the RD and EFD the GETA has been amended by the EC Implementation Act GETA. This has been explained in Chapter 2. It should be noted that in the Parliamentary discussions on the EC Implementation Act, it was proposed to *eradicate* the possibility provided for by the law to enact positive action measures for women and racial minorities. However, this proposal has not received majority support.

197 Disability Equal Treatment Act. See Chapter 2.

198 *Staatsblad* 1998, 241 [*Law Gazette* 1998, 241].

199 International Convention on the Elimination of All Forms of Racial Discrimination, available at <http://www/ohchr.org/english/law/cerd.htm>.

6.3. *Case Law of the ETC*

6.3.1. 'Sex' and 'Race': Divergence or Convergence in Positive Action Law?

In its assessment of the lawfulness, or not, of positive action measures the ETC has largely acted in line with the approach adopted by the ECJ.[200] Up until now, the Commission has only rendered Opinions on positive action in the context of 'sex' and 'race', to the exclusion of 'disability'. The ETC has explicitly held that in reviewing positive action measures in the context of 'race', it will adopt, as much as possible, the legal principles which it applies in the context of 'sex'.[201] This has meant that the case law by the ECJ, discussed earlier in the analysis, has had (and arguably continues to have) a 'cross-fertilisation' effect upon Dutch positive action law in the context of 'race'.[202] It should, however, be noted that in the context of Dutch law, divergences between positive action law in the context of 'sex', on the one hand, and 'race', on the other, have occurred as a result of different legal contexts.[203] In the period of 1998-2003, when the Act SAMEN was in force, positive action measures for 'race' had to be in conformity with international law (i.e. the CERD), rather than with EC law. It follows from Opinions 1999-31 and 1999-32 that the Act SAMEN, perceived in light of the CERD, called for results equality for members belonging to certain ethnic minority groups through the reservation of jobs. Had the Dutch government decided to renew the Act SAMEN, there would arguably have been a clear tension between, on the one hand, the Netherlands' obligations under international law *v.* its obligations under EC law. After all, and as seen before, the ECJ has struck down measures seeking to achieve results equality for women at the level of employment. It is unlikely, that the Court will reach a different conclusion with respect to positive action provisions in the RD, although this might depend on the degree of 'under representation' of the various groups, defined by race, sex, etc. concerned.

6.3.2. The Legal Parameters of Positive Action

What are the legal parameters in positive action cases? Like the ECJ, the ETC adopts a stricter test of judicial review in cases concerning positive action at the levels of employment and promotion than in counterpart cases which regard the *pre*-employ-

200 See section 4.3 above.

201 See Opinion 2004-36, paragraph 4.6. See notably also Opinion 1999-31, paragraph 4.4.

202 Vice versa, future ECJ case law on positive action measures for racial minorities may have an effect upon domestic law on positive action in the context of 'sex', unless the ECJ will adopt different legal approaches for different grounds of discrimination. This might depend upon the degree of under representation of the various groups defined by 'race', 'sex', etc. See in this context Parmar 2004, p. 150, who has observed that '[o]ne might argue that complexities of different kinds of discrimination merit different types of positive action programmes, adjusted to the particular social context within which the protected group finds itself'.

203 See Opinion 2004-36, paragraph 4.6. and Opinions 99-31 and 99-32 in which the ETC has stressed that the outcome of a particular case at hand is largely dependent on the legal and social context in which positive action measures are enacted.

ment context. This will become clear hereafter. It follows from the case law[204] that positive action measures at the level of employment and promotion must meet the following requirements:

1. The disadvantaged position of the group of persons for whose benefit positive action is taken must be proven;
2. Per type of employment and per level of employment, it has to be determined with which intensity positive action measures must be adopted in order to eliminate or reduce the disadvantages;
3. The job advertisement must state that a positive action policy is applicable;[205]
4. The policy must guarantee that all candidates are subjected to an objective assessment and that no automatic priority is given to a woman or to a person belonging to an ethnic minority group;[206]
5. The principle of proportionality must be complied with.

It should be noted that the second condition has not always been stated explicitly by the ETC.[207] However, it is submitted that the appropriate intensity of positive action measures is closely connected with the principle of proportionality which must be interpreted in light of the concrete circumstances of the case at hand.[208] Although this has not been listed as a separate condition above, it is clear from the ETC's (and ECJ's) case law that the principle of merit must remain intact.[209] The next question is how the Commission has applied and interpreted the above criteria in concrete cases? The Commission's case law indicates that the 'relative disadvantaged position' of, for example, women must not only be determined per type and level of employment, but must moreover be assessed against the background of the total potential supply of women/members of an ethnic minority group in the labour market.[210] Thus, for example, in Opinion 1994-04 the employer had rationalised its preference for a female candidate for the job of personnel manager on the basis that management functions tend to be executed by men. The employer had indicated that at meetings, conferences and the like there were usually hundreds of men present and only a few women. In the Commission's view, such a line of reasoning is insufficient for proving the disadvantaged position of women.

204 See, for example, Opinions 2004-173; 1999-31; 2003-01; 2004-10; 2004-36.

205 In the context of 'sex' this conditions stems directly from Article 3(2) AET w/m. A counterpart provision is however not contained in the GETA.

206 This condition has been explicitly imposed by the ETC since the ECJ's judgments in *Kalanke* and *Marshall*. In earlier case law this condition had not explicitly been imposed. See e.g. Opinion 1995-35, notably paragraph 4.4.

207 For example Opinion 2004-36.

208 This submission has been explicitly supported by the ETC. See Opinion 1995-35 in which the Commission explicitly held that the question as to the desired intensity or form of positive action entails an assessment of the necessity and appropriateness of the positive action measure or policy at stake. See paragraph 4.6. of Opinion 1995-35.

209 That merit must remain unaffected is encapsulated by the requirement that all candidates must be subjected to an objective assessment. See for example Opinion 2004-36, paragraph 4.13.

210 For example Opinions 1994-04 and 2004-173 and 2004-36.

It should also be noted that the disadvantaged position of the group is usually proven on the basis of statistical evidence.[211] However, in the context of 'race' and during the period that the Act SAMEN was in force, the Commission has sometimes accepted that in the absence of statistical data, regard may be given to common knowledge facts to prove the relative disadvantaged position of the group in whose favour positive action measures are taken.[212]

In line with the ECJ's case law the Commission has held that results equality at the level of employment goes beyond the parameters of lawful positive action measures and policies. In Opinion 2004-173 the employer had advertised for the job of head of the personnel department. The employer formed part of the Amsterdam City Council. The contested job advertisement explicitly stated that the job would be reserved for a female candidate.[213] The employer's works council doubted whether this was in conformity with sex equality law and sought an Opinion from the ETC in this regard. In respect of the first condition, it had been proven by the employer that women were in a disadvantaged position: statistical evidence showed that the percentage of women working for the employer was 14% whereas the percentage of women in the geographical labour force (i.e. in the City of Amsterdam) was 46%. However, and quite obviously, the employer did not meet the requirement that all candidates have to be subjected to an objective assessment, given that men were *a priori* excluded from being considered for the job. Hence, the positive action measure was in contravention of the AET w/m. The following is worth mentioning. By way of *obiter dictum* the ETC held that the employer's positive action measure necessarily also excluded all male ethnic minority candidates as well as disabled male candidates. It is submitted that, if positive action is permitted by the law for ethnic minorities and disabled persons, this will have an impact upon the legal limits for positive action measures for women. Indeed, and although this has not been stated explicitly by the ECJ in *Marshall*, being 'disabled' or (e.g.) 'black' is arguably one of the factors which may tilt the balance in favour of a male candidate in cases where the female and male candidates are equally qualified (i.e. merit tie-break scenarios). After having considered that the employer's positive action measure went beyond the applicable legal requirements, the ETC considered separately whether the offer

211 E.g., in Opinion 2004-36 the disadvantaged position of persons belonging to an ethnic minority group was proven on the basis of a 5:16.9 ratio. Thus, whereas 5% of the employees in the employer's workforce was member of an ethnic minority group this could be contrasted with 16.9% of ethnic minority members in the geographical labour force as a whole. On the basis of this statistical evidence the disadvantaged position of the group could be made out. The disadvantaged position of women was also proven in the case at hand: 32% of the employer's workforce were women. In the employer's executive service 21.1% were women and in the higher salary scales (scales 8 and higher) of the executive service 5.9% were women. In contrast, in the relevant geographical area 43.9% of the relevant labour force was female and of higher educated women 43.3%.

212 See Opinions 1999-31 and 1999-32 (positive action in the context of 'race').

213 This can be contrasted with Opinion 1997-70 where the employer had expressly indicated its preference for a male candidate. The Commission logically had to conclude that a positive action policy in favour of men is not allowed for. It sustained its Opinion *inter alia* in reference to the Parliamentary history to the AET w/m which explicitly stated that positive action measures and policies are meant to be adopted to the benefit of women.

for employment had been in line with the requirements stemming from the AET w/m. Given that the employment advertisement had been explicitly addressed to women and given that it failed to mention the applicability of a positive action policy, it constituted a breach of Articles 3(3) and 3(2) of the AET w/m respectively.

In line with ECJ case law, the ETC has interpreted the principle of proportionality as meaning that there must be a proportionate relationship between the application of a positive action measure, on the one hand, and the degree of disadvantage suffered by the protected group, on the other. This formulation seems to imply a necessity requirement demanding that the reduction/elimination of disadvantage could not be achieved with other (less discriminatory) means. This also dovetails with the earlier Opinions by the Commission in which the Commission has solely held that per type and level of employment it must be determined which intensity of positive action is required.[214] The Commission has held that the contested measure should have the potential effect that disadvantages are in fact reduced or eliminated.[215] This amounts to the requirement of appropriateness: the vexed measure must be a suitable or appropriate means to actually reduce/eliminate disadvantage.

On the basis of the five legal requirements with which a positive action measure or policy has to comply the Commission's case law shows that the following measures are in principle lawful under Dutch equal treatment law:

a. Giving priority to a female candidate or to a candidate who belongs to an ethnic minority group, provided that merit remains unaffected and that men, or persons who belong to the ethnic majority group, are not *a priori* excluded from the selection-making process.[216]
b. Giving priority in the first selection round to women, whereas men will only be invited in a later round if there was not a suitable female candidate available.[217]
c. The ETC has moreover held that, if a positive action policy is adopted by a 'third party' (e.g. an employment or recruitment agency acting on the employer's behalf), it will adopt a less strict judicial scrutiny test. It follows from Opinion 2003-01 that a recruitment agency may, in principle, assume that the employer's positive action policy is conducted within the permissible limits of the law. However, if there are facts from which it can be deduced that the contrary is true, the recruitment agency will have a duty under equal treatment law to inform the employer about this.

So far, I have considered the semi-judicial stance adopted by the ETC in respect of positive action at the level of employment. Hereafter, I will briefly consider the Commission's approach with respect to positive action measures outside the employment context with regard to which it has taken a less rigid stance similar to the one adopted by the ECJ in comparable cases. In Opinion 2005-225 the facts were as follows.

214 E.g., Opinion 1995-35.
215 See for example Opinion 2004-36, paragraph 4.17.
216 Opinion 2004-36; Opinion 2004-10.
217 Opinion 1995-35. It should be noted that this is an Opinion rendered prior to the availability of ECJ case law.

The applicant was female and on social security. The respondent was an organisation for public welfare. The latter offered a range of training courses some of which were only accessible to Turkish and Moroccan women. Other courses were also accessible to other people, including the applicant, however, for a higher fee. The applicant claimed an instance of unlawful distinction on grounds of race. With regard to the respondent's practice of only offering training courses to Turkish and Moroccan women the ETC considered as follows. It first indicated that no statistical evidence was required to prove the disadvantaged position of Turkish and Moroccan women, for this was a 'fact of common knowledge'. The Commission subsequently dismissed the applicant's allegation that she too, found herself in a disadvantaged position by holding that '[t]he disadvantaged position of Turkish and Moroccan women is (…) not primarily determined by their financial position but rather by their position in the Netherlands and by their specific cultural and social background position'.[218] It subsequently assessed the contested measures in light of the principle of proportionality which entails an assessment of 'appropriateness' and 'necessity'. The respondent had argued that by adopting the contested measures, it intended to break the social isolation of the target-groups, and to reduce their disadvantaged position in Dutch society. The Commission considered that offering tailor-made courses which sought to meet the particular needs of the target group was an appropriate means to reach this aim. The respondent had moreover argued that by offering these courses in the language of the target group it sought to promote the participation of members of the target group. This would moreover be encouraged if the group of participants was limited to persons of the same cultural background. The aim of promoting participation could in the respondent's view not be achieved by alternative means. The applicant had, however, argued that the overall aim of fostering the integration of Turkish and Moroccan women in Dutch society could be better achieved by permitting others too, to participate in the contested courses. The ETC agreed with the respondent's arguments, insofar as it concerned these types of courses which were specifically designed to meet the special needs of Turkish and Moroccan women. However, in respect of courses (e.g. a general computer course) which did not primarily aim at meeting the special needs of the target groups, the proportionality principle had not been met which meant that direct race distinction had occurred. The Commission stressed that, whether or not 'proportionality' has been met, depends on the specific goal which is pursued by a particular training course. The ETC concluded that the GETA does not prevent reserving certain training courses for Turkish and Moroccan women where these courses are aimed at the creation of *equal opportunities* for members of ethnic minority groups.

The Commission subsequently questioned whether the respondent had made an unlawful distinction on grounds of race by charging different fees depending on the ethnic origin of the participants. Given that it followed from the facts of the case that the difference in fees was a direct result of the conditions imposed upon the respondent by local government, which subsidised the respondent's training courses, the applicant's claim was not admissible in respect of this aspect of her claim. Had

218 Paragraph 5.14 of Opinion 2005-225.

the applicant litigated against the local government, her claim would have been admissible. In this context it is worth noting that, prior to the implementation of the RD, the GETA's scope did not extend to unilaterally adopted governmental acts (e.g. giving a subsidy). However, with respect to 'race' this has changed post-implementation of EC law. This is so, for the RD requires equal treatment on grounds of race in the area of social security and advantages, which includes a subsidy such as this in the case at hand.

The above case shows that with regard to positive action measures outside the realm of work the Commission has accepted a 'non-statistical' evidence approach with respect to proving 'structural disadvantage'. It has not done so in similar cases within employment, unless doing so was be required by mandatory provisions of international law.

6.4. *Top-Down and Cross-Ground Comparison*

Perceiving the analysis of Dutch positive action law from a 'top-down' and 'cross-ground' perspective reveals the following picture. The Dutch approach is in line with the ECJ's case law on positive action in the context of gender, both within and outside the realm of work. This means that the law is underpinned by an 'equality of opportunities' paradigm and that results equality has not been disallowed at the level of training. Interestingly, the case law by the Luxembourg Court has had (and arguably will continue to have) a 'cross-fertilisation' effect upon domestic positive action law in the context of 'race', although sometimes, this effect has been thwarted by requirements imposed upon the government by international law. This has meant that during the period that the Act SAMEN was in force, results equality at the level of employment has occasionally been permitted. Whether a similar 'cross-fertilisation effect' will also occur with regard to 'disability' is currently unclear, in the absence of case law by the ETC on positive action measures for disabled persons. The discussion has also made clear that in present times Dutch law solely allows for positive action in favour of 'women', 'ethnic minorities' and 'disabled persons'. The refusal to expand the list with other minority groups has been rationalised by the government, *not* by reference to the different logics underpinning different grounds of discrimination, but by the (alleged) fact that other minority groups cannot be said to find themselves in a 'structurally disadvantaged position'. Regardless of whether this is true or not, it would have been desirable had the government extended the possibility of positive action to all grounds captured by Dutch equal treatment law. Such an approach would correspond better with the applicable legislative approach in EC law.

7. Conclusions and Cross-Country Comparison

In this chapter 'positive action' has been analysed through the prism of comparative law. This has essentially entailed an examination of positive action from a 'top-down', 'cross-ground' and 'cross-country' perspective. At the outset of this chapter, different types of positive action have been outlined, as well as the over-riding purposes which may be pursued by such measures. Subsequently, an analysis has been made of positive action in relation to diverse theoretical notions of equality. It has been argued that whether or not positive action is a vexed issue largely depends on one's vision of what the principle of equality should strive for. In EC law, positive action legislation and case law in the context of 'sex' has been infused by a 'restricted principle of equality of opportunity'. As a consequence of this, the Luxembourg Court has disapproved of 'results equality' at the level of employment and promotion. However, a more relaxed stance has been adopted by the ECJ with regard to positive action measures taken prior to the decision as to whom a job or promotion should be given. In the absence of case law by the ECJ, it is currently unclear whether or not the Court will extrapolate its legal approach to positive action measures in the context of 'sex', to the other grounds of discrimination. Different legal stances might be called for, depending on the degree of disadvantage suffered by different groups, and, arguably, depending on the Court's interpretation of the 'non-regression' clauses in the RD and the EFD. Moreover, the expansion of the groups to whose benefit positive action may be adopted arguably bears an impact upon the legal analysis of positive action measures for women in future case law. This may be so, for women will have to compete with other minority groups in the quest for jobs, training-positions, places at representative boards, etc. After the analysis of positive action in the context of EC law, positive action has been considered in English law. It has become clear that the scope for positive action in English law differs for different grounds of discrimination. Thus, whereas positive action law in the context of 'race' and 'sex' is governed by the principle of 'symmetry', the definitions of positive action in the R&B and S.O. Regulations reflect a more flexible approach. It has been argued that these different approaches cannot, however, be rationalised on the basis of a 'cross ground' comparison. In light of this, it has been argued that the provisions on positive action in the RRA and SDA should be revised whereby EC law ought to be taken as a template for a reconceived framework. The most relaxed approach with respect to positive action is adopted by English disability discrimination law. In light of the asymmetrical framework underpinning the DDA, positive action measures for disabled persons is uncontroversial, at least from a legal perspective. Whether the English approach is in conformity with the approach in EC law remains to be seen, although the 'non-regression' provisions in the Framework warrant an affirmative answer. Lastly, positive action has been considered in the context of Dutch law. It has been seen that Dutch positive action law has been confined to 'sex', 'race' and 'disability'. In this regard it is stricter in scope than English positive action law which may apply to all discrimination grounds contained in Article 13 EC. However, in a different respect, Dutch law is broader in scope than English law, for the former adheres to the paradigm of 'equality of opportunity', analogous to EC law. The analysis of Dutch positive action law has also illustrated that the ECJ's case law on positive action for women, had cross-fertilised into the legal analysis by the ETC of positive action measures for ethnic minorities. However, for a limited period of time, such an effect was sometimes blocked by legal obligations imposed upon the Dutch government by international law. Whether 'cross fertilisation' will also occur in respect of positive action measures for disabled persons cannot be said, given the absence of relevant case law by the Dutch ETC.

PART IV

STRETCHING THE SCOPE OF NON-DISCRIMINATION AND EQUALITY LAW

Part IV

STRETCHING THE SCOPE OF NON-DISCRIMINATION AND EQUALITY LAW

1. Presenting the Structure for Research

In Part II (Chapters 3 and 4) two concepts that present themselves generally in the areas of equal treatment law were analysed on the basis of a top-down, cross-country, cross-ground and bottom-up comparison, wherever this was appropriate. In Part III (Chapter 5) positive action, a proactive strategy that seeks to further factual equality for disadvantaged groups, was examined on the basis of the multi-layered comparison. In this Part, i.e. Chapters 6-9, I will look at the expansion of the scope of anti-discrimination law, both in the EC and domestic legal context. Although it is widely accepted that 'race'[1] and 'sex' should be 'morally irrelevant',[2] or indeed, relevant[3] grounds in the decision-making process, it has only comparatively recently been acknowledged that the list should be complemented with other statuses such as 'religion' and 'belief', 'sexual orientation', 'disability' and 'age'. In EC law the legal mandate for this was given with the adoption of Article 13 EC by the ToA.[4] Concretely, employment-related discrimination on grounds of religion and belief,

1 The EU appears to be an exception. As is known, race discrimination has only become a matter of EU law with the adoption of Article 13 EC by the ToA and the subsequent adoption of the RD. See generally Chapter 2.

2 See Feldman 1993, p. 136: 'The outlawing of certain types of discrimination is justified on the basis of the single premise, that there are certain criteria for treating people differently which will never be regarded as morally relevant, or which are relevant in an admissible way only in a restricted range of situations which can be defined by law. It appears that what is morally irrelevant changes over time.'

3 It is recognised by the principle of substantive equality that a 'blind eye approach' is (often) counterproductive in the fight against discrimination and the search for equality. Especially the ground *disability* and (to a lesser extent) *religion and belief, sex,* and *age* must often actively be taken into account if greater 'equality' is to be achieved. Hence, whereas these statuses may be irrelevant in some cases, they could be highly relevant in others. It is recognised by a substantive vision of justice that the principle of equality may as much be violated by treating equal cases unequally, as by treating unequal cases unequally.

4 See Chapter 2.

sexual orientation, disability and age has been prohibited in EC law since 2000 when the EFD was adopted.

The application of the comparative exercise in the present Part calls for the examination of a number of concrete issues. The starting point for each of the chapters to follow has been the following question: *With which discrimination ground(s) was the domestic legal framework in need of being expanded in light of requirements imposed upon the Member States by EC law and how have these grounds been regulated by the legal framework?* As will be seen, the transposition of the EFD into English law has resulted in the coverage by the statutory framework of prohibitions of discrimination on grounds of religion and belief, and sexual orientation in employment. These three grounds of discrimination have been prohibited by the Dutch GETA since 1994 and, already before that year, by Article 1 of the Dutch Constitution. Therefore, it will be interesting to analyse the new legal frameworks in English law, in light of existing approaches and practices in the Netherlands. Dutch law, for its turn, has been enriched with anti-discrimination frameworks for the grounds disability[5] and age[6] post-implementation of the EFD. 'Age' will also have to be introduced into English law. As I write, this has not yet been achieved but it will be in the foreseeable future.[7] In contrast, 'disability' has been covered by the English anti-discrimination framework since 1995. This being the case, it will be interesting to analyse the Dutch DETA in light of existing approaches and practices in English disability discrimination law. It follows from the foregoing that both English and Dutch non-discrimination law already covered 'sex' and 'race' as grounds of discrimination, prior to the transposition of the AETD and RD, respectively. Although the existing legal frameworks for 'race' and 'sex' had to be amended in various respects in order to be in conformity with the requirements stemming from EC law, and with reference to Chapter 1, I will not make a separate analysis hereafter of the legal frameworks concerning these two grounds of discrimination.

Part IV will be presented as follows. In Chapters 6 and 7, I will analyse, respectively, discrimination on grounds of religion and belief, and, sexual orientation on the basis of the multi-layered comparative exercise referred to above. Moreover, and

5 It should, however, be noted that already prior to the adoption of the EFD there had been a long-standing social and political discussion, including a legislative proposal, on the principle of equal treatment with respect to disability in the context of employment. Hence, the 'top-down' influence exercised by EC law on national law has not been 'unqualified' in the area of Dutch equal treatment law. This point will be addressed in more detail in Chapter 8.

6 Although prior to the adoption of the EFD there had already been two legislative proposals on age discrimination in the employment area. Therefore, EC law has not exercised an 'absolute' top-down influence on Dutch age discrimination law. This point will be elaborated upon in Chapter 9.

7 It should be noted that Article 18 of the EFD provides that implementation of the Directive should have been achieved by 2 December 2003. However, Article 18 of the Directive also provides that the Member States may have an additional period of 3 years from December 2003 onwards to transpose the Directive insofar as 'age' and 'disability' are concerned. The UK has availed itself of this extended deadline. The Age Regulations, which aim to implement the Framework Directive with respect to the ground age do not take effect until 1 October 2006. The final version of the Regulations has only recently been published and is available at <http://www.opsi.gov.uk/si/si2006/uksi_20061031_en.pdf>.

for reasons to be explained hereafter, I will take account of the law stemming from the European Convention on Human Rights (ECHR). It will be argued that the case law by the European Court of Human Rights (ECtHR, or the 'Strasbourg Court') is likely to serve as an interpretative instrument for the ECJ, and for the domestic courts, whilst interpreting religious and sexual orientation discrimination in the context of EC and domestic law, respectively. In Chapters 8 and 9, I will analyse, respectively, disability and age discrimination law from a comparative perspective. In contrast to Chapters 6 and 7, I will not make an excursion into the law stemming from the ECHR in Chapters 8 and 9. The reasons for this will become apparent hereafter.

2. The Role of the European Convention on Human Rights

2.1. Introduction

Before proceeding with the substantive analyses in Chapters 6-9 an important point must be clarified. This concerns the question as to why in Chapters 6 and 7 to follow account will be made of the law stemming from the European Convention on Human Rights (ECHR, or 'Strasbourg Convention'), whereas this has and will not be done in any other chapter of this book. How can this be rationalised? In Chapter 1 it was stated that this book is concerned with a comparative analysis of the legal systems of the EU, England and the Netherlands. As explained above, the starting point in Chapters 6 and 7 to follow will be to analyse the extension of the scope of English statutory anti-discrimination law with prohibitions of discrimination on grounds of religion and belief, and sexual orientation (in employment). These frameworks will be viewed in light of supranational law. Moreover, account will be made of legal approaches and practices in Dutch law. Upon further consideration it, however, appeared that a complete omission of the law stemming from the Strasbourg Convention on issues concerning the grounds religion and belief and sexual orientation and/or discrimination on these grounds, would result in an unduly restrictive analysis. It is submitted that Strasbourg Convention law may have an (arguably) large impact upon the interpretation by the ECJ of the provisions contained in the Framework Directive.[8] At the same time it is acknowledged that the judicial role of the ECtHR is different from that of the ECJ. This may explain why the ECJ's stance in future cases regarding (e.g.) religious and belief and sexual orientation discrimination might nonetheless diverge from that of the Strasbourg Court in comparable cases. I will come back to this point in the passages to follow.

The law stemming from the Strasbourg Convention may also serve as an interpretative tool for the (English) domestic courts in proceedings on the R&B Regulations,[9] and the S.O. Regulations[10] which, respectively, transpose the religion and belief and sexual orientation provisions contained in the EFD into domestic law. The adoption of these Regulations has largely occurred in a legal void, *inter alia* due

8 See generally the analysis by de Schutter 2005.

9 The Employment Equality (Religion or Belief) Regulations 2003, SI 2003, No. 1660.

10 The Employment Equality (Sexual Orientation) Regulations 2003, SI 2003, No. 1661.

to the fact that their enactment has not been the result of a profound Parliamentary debate. Indeed, with reference to Chapter 2, Regulations, in contrast to statutory Acts of Parliament, are less democratically informed. As will be explained below, the Strasbourg legal framework is of direct legal value to the judicial interpretation of these Regulations.[11]

The present author points out that the impact of Strasbourg Convention law has traditionally been more pertinent to (discrimination) issues regarding the grounds religion and belief and sexual orientation, compared with disability (Chapter 8) and age (Chapter 9). How can this be explained? The answer begs an explanation of the following two questions, the first of which is a preliminary one:

1. In what ways do English[12] domestic law and EU law on the one hand, interconnect with Strasbourg Convention law on the other?
2. Why are (or have) the legal ties with Strasbourg (been) stronger in the context of the grounds religion and belief and sexual orientation, compared with disability and age?

These two questions will be answered hereafter in sections 3 and 4, respectively. They will be referred to as the 'first' and 'second' question. However, before doing so, I will first outline in brief the relevant provisions of the Convention and the Protocols attached to it, which bear an impact upon issues regarding religion and belief and sexual orientation, and upon discrimination on these two grounds.[13] It is to these matters that we will turn immediately hereafter.

2.2. *The Relevant Convention Framework*

Henceforth, a concise account will be given of the relevant Convention framework in the context of issues regarding religion and belief and sexual orientation and regarding discrimination on these two grounds. Matters will be elaborated upon in Chapters 6 and 7 to follow insofar that doing so is required for a sound understanding of the issues at stake.

The right to religious freedom is contained in Article 9 of the Convention[14] and in Article 2 of Protocol no. 1 attached to it (education). Sexual orientation claims have been premised upon Article 8 of the Convention which secures the right to private life. Lastly, the non-discrimination clause is contained in Article 14 of the Convention which reads as follows:

11 Oliver 2004, p. 11.
12 The emphasis is on English, rather than on Dutch law, given that English (and EC) law form the starting point for analysis in Chapters 6 and 7.
13 These provisions will be further dealt with in Chapters 6 and 7 to follow.
14 See for an in-depth account of the right to freedom of religion in the context of the ECHR *inter alia* the following: Martinez-Torron 2001, p. 185-204; Also, and with an emphasis upon the contemporary and historical context of Article 9 of the Convention, Evans 1997; also Van Dijk, van Hoof en Heringa 1998, p. 541-557.

> 'The enjoyment of the rights and freedoms set forth in the Convention will be secured without any discrimination on any ground such as sex, race, colour, language, religion, political or other opinion, national or social origin, association with a national minority, property, birth or other status.'[15]

The ECtHR has traditionally attached a formal meaning[16] to Article 14 of the Convention. However in the *Thlimmenos* case (2000)[17] the Court has complemented the formal interpretation of Article 14 of the Convention with a substantive approach to equality.

The applicant in that case, Mr Iakovos Thlimmenos, was a Jehovah's witness who had been convicted in the past for insubordination for his refusal to enlist in the army and for his refusal to wear the military uniform. Some years later he was also refused from being appointed as a chartered accountant by reason of his past criminal record. In essence, the applicant's claim was directed at a failure by the relevant authorities to make a distinction as between, on the one hand, those persons who had been convicted for refusing to serve in the armed forces on religious grounds, and, persons who had been convicted of other serious crimes, on the other. The ECtHR adopted the following point of view:

> 'The Court has so far considered that the right under Article 14 not to be discriminated against in the enjoyment of the rights guaranteed under the Convention is violated when States treat differently persons in analogous situations without providing an objective and reasonable justification (...). However, the Court considers that this is not the only facet of the prohibitions of discrimination in Article 14. The right not to be discriminated against in the enjoyment of the rights guaranteed under the Convention is also violated when States without an objective and reasonable justification fail to treat differently persons whose situations are significantly different.'

This is a laudable *dictum*, for it leaves no further doubt that Article 14 of the Convention reflects both a formal and substantive notion of equality.

It follows from the drafting style of Article 14 that this provision is not a free-standing equality provision but that it was merely intended to confer an 'ancillary'

15 For an excellent analysis of the application of Article 14 of the Convention by the Strasbourg Court, I refer to Gerards 2004a.

16 See for example the ECtHR in *Dahlab v. Switzerland* [2001] ECHR 42393/98 (ECtHR): '(...) Article 14 affords protection against different treatment, without an objective and reasonable justification, of persons in similar situations'. This constitutes a reiteration of earlier case law to which the Court referred namely, *Observer and Guardian v. the United Kingdom,* 26 November 1991, Series A no. 216, p. 36, paragraph 73 and *The Sunday Times v. the United Kingdom (No. 1)*, 26 April 1979, Series A no. 30, p. 43, paragraph 70.

17 Case of *Thlimmenos v. Greece* 34369/97, 6 April 2000 (ECtHR), available at <www.echr.coe.int/echr>, paragraph 44. See for a similar formulation by the ECJ in the context of EC law *Gillespie v. Northern Health and Social Services Board,* (Case C-342/93), [1996] ECR I-475, paragraph 16 where the ECJ has held that '[i]t is well settled that discrimination involves the application of different rules to comparable situations or the application of the same rule to different situations' (with reference to *Finanzamt Köln-Altstadt v. Schumacker* (Case C-279/93) [1995] ECR I-225, paragraph 30).

right to equality.[18] As will be explained in further detail hereafter, before the entry into force of Protocol no. 12, the principle of non-discrimination secured in Article 14 could only be relied on in combination with one or more other substantive rights contained within the Convention. Hence, Article 14 constitutes a supplement to all the substantive rights contained in the Convention in that it requires that these rights be secured and interpreted without discrimination.[19] Article 14 is, however, autonomous in the sense that the Strasbourg Court has not required that the substantive Convention provision(s) must be *breached* before an applicant can effectively rely on Article 14 ECHR.[20] Another feature of Article 14 is that it is premised upon an 'open model' of discrimination law. In contrast with the EFD and with both English and Dutch law (except for Article 1 of the Dutch Constitution) the list of grounds of discrimination in this Article is 'open ended' (as follows from the 'such as'-formulation).

The ancillary nature of the principle of non-discrimination under ECHR law has ceased to exist with the entry into force of Protocol no. 12 on 1 of April 2005. Article 1 of the Protocol provides as follows:

> The enjoyment of any right set forth by law will be secured without discrimination on any ground such as sex, race, colour, language, religion, political or other opinion, national or social origin, association with a national minority, property, birth or other status.
> No one will be discriminated against by any public authority or any ground such as those mentioned in paragraph 1.

It follows from this formulation that it is no longer necessary for an applicant to establish a connection with the principle of non-discrimination on the one hand, and a substantive Convention provision, on the other.[21] In practice this means that the Court's jurisdiction has been extended to cover all non-discrimination complaints in vertical relations, i.e. in relations between an individual and the state, regardless of whether they simultaneously fall within the scope of any other Convention right. Hence, at present the Court has for example also jurisdiction in discrimination complaints in the context of public employment or public service provision.[22] Certain important limitations remain nonetheless apparent. Firstly, it is to be stressed that

18 It has been argued by Alkema and Rop in the context of a theoretical discussion of the principle of equality that 'the major advantage of this [ancillary; MG] approach is that the material content of the equality principle is co-determined by the substantive right to which it is attached in the concrete context [of the case at hand; MG]' ['het grote voordeel van deze benadering is dat de inhoud van de gelijkheidsnorm mede bepaald wordt door het materiële recht waaraan hij in de concrete context wordt gekoppeld']. Alkema and Rop 2002, p. 35.

19 De Schutter 2005, p. 20.

20 See *Thlimmenos v. Greece* 34369/97, 6 April 2000 (ECtHR), available at <www.echr.coe.int/echr>, paragraph 40 with reference to *Inze v. Austria* judgment of 28 October 1987, Series A No. 126, p. 17, paragraph 36. See moreover Heringa 2005, p. 1-3 with further references to the case law by the ECtHR.

21 It should, however, be noted that paragraph 33 of the Explanatory Report provides that both Article 1 of the Protocol and Article 14 of the Convention remain in existence. Article 14 ECHR will not be abolished or amended. It will eventually be for the ECtHR to determine the exact relationship between these two Articles. I am grateful to dr. Jakob van der Velde for this point.

22 Also Heringa 2005, p. 26.

not all Parties States to the Convention have signed or ratified Protocol No. 12. For example, whereas the Netherlands has done so[23], the UK has not shown any intention to do so.[24] This means that the accessory character of Article 14 of the Convention has not been eliminated across the board. Secondly, the Protocol adopts a rather cautious approach with respect to the doctrine of 'positive obligations'. In the present context, the doctrine of positive obligations concerns the question to what extent Article 1 of Protocol No. 12 imposes a positive duty (obligation) upon the state authorities to prevent acts of discrimination from occurring in horizontal relationships, i.e. relationships between two or more private individuals?[25] The same question can moreover be posed in the context of remedies: to what extent is the state under a positive obligation to remedy instances of discrimination between two or more privately acting agents?[26] The Explanatory Report to Protocol No. 12 is clear on the matter: '(...) the prime objective of Article 1 is to embody a negative obligation for the Parties: the obligation not to discriminate against individuals'.[27] It further states that '[Article 1 of Protocol No. 12] is not intended to impose a general positive obligation on the Parties to take measures or remedy all instances of discrimination in relations between private persons'.[28] It concludes by indicating that '(...) the extent of any positive obligations flowing from Article 1 is likely to be limited'.[29] It thus follows that the impact of Article 1 of Protocol No. 12 in horizontal relations, including thus relations between a private employer and an employee, is likely to be minimal (unless, of course, a State that is Party to the Convention decides itself to accord horizontal applicability to the 12th Protocol).

Like the Convention itself, the Protocol is directly addressed to public authorities (which embraces all branches of the *trias politica*) and only indirectly namely, via a *de minimis* positive obligations duty, to privately acting agents.[30] In summary, analogous to the Convention, the Protocol has been principally designed to ensure that the rights of citizens are not encroached by acts of public authorities in such ways that would be incompatible with the rights and freedoms sought to protect.

It follows from the above that prior to the entry into force of Protocol No. 12 complaints of religious and sexual orientation discrimination were to be based, res-

23 *Trb.* 2001, 18, Rijkswet van 13 Mei 2004, *Stb.* 2004, 302 and <http://conventions.coe.int>.

24 See for a critique on the UK government for its failure to sign and ratify Protocol No. 12, Fredman 2002b.

25 See Protocol No. 12 to the Convention for the protection of human rights and fundamental freedoms, EVRM R & C, aanvulling 18, 11-2000, *Explanatory Report*, no. 24.

26 See Protocol No. 12 to the Convention for the protection of human rights and fundamental freedoms, EVRM R & C, aanvulling 18, 11-2000, *Explanatory Report*, no. 24.

27 Protocol No. 12 to the Convention for the protection of human rights and fundamental freedoms, EVRM R & C, aanvulling 18, 11-2000, *Explanatory Report*, no. 24.

28 Protocol No. 12 to the Convention for the protection of human rights and fundamental freedoms, EVRM R & C, aanvulling 18, 11-2000, *Explanatory Report*, no. 25.

29 Protocol No. 12 to the Convention for the protection of human rights and fundamental freedoms, EVRM R & C, aanvulling 18, 11-2000, *Explanatory Report*, no. 27.

30 See de Schutter 2005, p. 25, where he has explained that under the positive obligations doctrine the States Parties to the Convention and/or the Protocol may have to adopt measures to outlaw discriminatory acts by private actors if a failure to do so effectively bereaves persons from the enjoyment of protected rights.

pectively, upon Article 9 in conjunction with Article 14 ECHR, and upon Article 8 in conjunction with Article 14 ECHR. This is still the legal scenario for applicants who are citizens of a State that has not signed up to Protocol No. 12, such as the UK. A point worth noting concerns the following. The need for providing a connection of Article 9 or 8 of the Convention with Article 14 ECHR has not meant that the Strasbourg Court has actually always analysed the Article 14 aspects of the claim at hand.[31] Indeed, and as will be seen in Chapters 6 and 7 to follow, the Court has sometimes deemed it redundant to make a separate examination of the complaint regarding Article 14. The reason for this is that the Court has already examined the Article 14 aspects of the claim at hand in its assessment of the alleged violation of the substantive Convention provision.[32]

In Chapters 6 and 7 to follow relevant case law by the ECtHR will be referred to, wherever this is deemed appropriate to clarify the relevant matters in issue. As the respective chapters will show in greater detail, the Strasbourg Court treats 'religion' and 'belief' as 'semi-suspect'[33] grounds of discrimination and sexual orientation as a 'suspect' ground of discrimination. This is in contrast, for example, with disability which is not regarded as a 'suspect' ground. If a ground of discrimination is seen as 'suspect', this means in practice that the Strasbourg Court adopts a comparatively strict scrutiny test. Whether or not a ground is considered as 'suspect' is *inter alia* dictated by its intrinsic nature.[34] The diverse character of the various grounds of discrimination will be discussed throughout Chapters 6-9 to follow. Important to stress at this juncture is the following. If, analogous to the approach by the ECtHR, the ECJ and the domestic court adopt a different scrutiny test for the different

31 See generally Gerards 2004a, who has observed as follows: '[An] important consequence of the accessory character of Article 14 is the fact that the Court almost never gives an actual, substantive assessment of a discrimination complaint. In the large majority of cases, the complaint concerns unequal treatment with respect to the exercise of a right or freedom protected by the Convention. As the Court always starts its examination of a complaint with the assessment of the alleged violation of the substantive Convention provisions, it will often consider certain aspects of the difference in treatment in that context. In those cases, the Court almost always concludes that separate examination of the Article 14 complaint is superfluous or otherwise unnecessary' (p. 9). Also Heringa 2005, p. 3. However, sometimes the Court does begin with a consideration of Article 14 in combination with the substantive Convention Right and does it consider a separate consideration of the alleged breach of the substantive right a redundant exercise. See for an example *Salgueiro da Silva Mouta v. Portugal* EHRC 2000, 16 (Article 14 in conjunction with Article 8 ECHR), with a case comment by Gerards 2003.

32 In addition to this reason, Heringa (with reference to the relevant case law) has discerned yet two more reasons why the ECtHR is generally not inclined to consider separately the issues regarding Article 14 of the Convention: (1) a separate consideration of Article 14 is of no extra juridical benefit to the complainant, given that the Court has decided positively on the applicant's allegation that a substantive Convention provision has been infringed; (2) a separate consideration of Article 14 is deemed unnecessary in such cases where the Article 14 dimension only constitutes a minor part of the complaint as a whole. In other words, Article 14 is not considered if it does not constitute a fundamental aspect of the case at hand. See Heringa 2005, p. 3-5.

33 The adjective 'suspect' is not employed by the ECtHR itself but is commonly employed in American law and doctrine.

34 Gerards 2004a, p. 23-24.

discrimination grounds, the hierarchy between the grounds is felt not only at the legislative level (e.g. the protective scope of EC race discrimination legislation differs from that of sex discrimination law and discrimination law concerning the other grounds protected by Article 13 EC)[35], but also at the judicial level. Hence, writes de Schutter, '(…) the level of scrutiny exercised by the [ECtHR] will vary according to a largely implicit and evolving, but nevertheless identifiable, hierarchy of prohibited grounds of discrimination (…)'.[36]

In the above the relevant Convention framework has been sketched in the context of the grounds religion and belief and sexual orientation. The 'first' and 'second' questions referred to above have not yet been answered. It is to these questions that we will turn immediately below.

2.3. *Explaining the 'First Question'*

Hereafter, it will be explained how EU law and English law, on the one hand, connect with ECHR law, on the other.

The EU and the ECHR

The link between EU and ECHR law is effectively established by the recognition that respect for fundamental human rights is a general principle which the Union must abide by. This has not only been established in the case law of the ECJ;[37] it moreover follows from the text of the EU Treaty itself,[38] and, importantly (although non-binding), the significance of fundamental rights protection is prominently mirrored by the European Union's Charter of Fundamental Rights.[39] Very concretely, the connection Brussels/Luxembourg and Strasbourg is affirmed by Recitals 1 and 2 of the EFD and RD respectively. These Recitals are identical to each other and they provide as follows:

35 See Chapter 2.

36 De Schutter 2005, p. 5.

37 See e.g. Opinion 2/94 by the ECJ regarding the Community's accession to the ECHR [1996] ECR- I-1759. See in particular also the Court's first cases in which it expressed that fundamental rights inherently belong to Community law *Stauder v. City of Ulm* (Case 29/96) 1969 ECR 419, 425; *Internationale Handelsgesellschaft* (Case 11/70), 1970 ECR 1125; *Nold, Kohlen und Baustoff-grosshandlung v. Commission of the European Communities* (Case 4-73) ECR 1974, p. 00491).

38 Article 6 of the TEU reads as follows:
(1) 'The Union is founded on the principles of liberty, democracy, respect for human rights and fundamental freedoms, and the rule of law, principles which are common to the Member States.
(2) The Union will respect fundamental rights, as guaranteed by the European Convention for the Protection of Human Rights and Fundamental Freedoms signed in Rome on 4 November 1950 and as they result from the constitutional traditions common to the Member States, as general principles of Community law.
(3) (…)
(4) (…).'

39 For a recent and in depth discussion of the relationship in dealing with human and fundamental rights between the Luxembourg and Strasbourg Courts, I refer to Wetzel 2002-2003, p. 2823-2862.

> 'In accordance with Article 6 of the Treaty on European Union, the European Union is founded on the principles of liberty, democracy, respect for human rights and fundamental freedoms, and the rule of law, principles which are common to all Member States and it respects fundamental rights, as guaranteed by the European Convention for the Protection of Human Rights and Fundamental Freedoms and as they result from the constitutional traditions common to the Member States as general principles of Community law.'

In brief, it follows that in deciding cases the ECJ is required to show respect for Strasbourg Convention law, notwithstanding that the ECJ is not under an obligation to follow *verbatim* the Strasbourg Court's stance in a concrete case.[40] This last point can also be explained with reference to the different genesis and judicial role of the Strasbourg Court compared with that of the ECJ. The former is not concerned with imposing 'uniform solutions'.[41] Rather, the judicial role of the Strasbourg Court is confined to an assessment whether a State Party to the Convention has breached one (or more) right(s) and/or freedom(s) secured by the Convention in the concrete case before it.[42] The degree of judicial restraint or judicial activism in assessing this question differs from case to case. It largely depends on the 'margin of appreciation' accorded (by the Court) to the state in the concrete case at hand. According to established case law by the ECtHR, the Contracting States have a certain 'margin of appreciation' in assessing the necessity for interference with a Convention right, although this margin is subject to 'European supervision'.[43] Essentially, this European supervision is less vigorous in such cases where the state enjoys a wide margin of appreciation; conversely, it is more profound in cases where the state's margin of appreciation is limited. Gerards has indicated on the basis of existing case law a number of factors which determine the 'margin of appreciation'.[44] She has discerned the following: (1) the existence of a European consensus (or common standards)[45] on the contested issues at stake; (2) the fact that in the Court's view the national authorities are 'better placed' to decide how best to discharge their obligations under the Convention; (3) the character and weight of the aims pursued; (4) the context of the contested measure; (5) the character and importance of the affected right; and (6) the character of the infringement. It is noted that the first factor requires a comparative

40 This may also work the other way round. See the following observation by the Schutter: '(...) the adoption in 2000 within the European Community of the 'Race' and Framework Directives have influenced both the European Court of Human Rights in its interpretation of Article 14 ECHR and the European Committee of Social Right' (de Schutter 2005, p. 38).

41 See the dissenting Opinion of Judge Tulkens in the case of *Leyla Sahin v. Turkey*, 44774/98, 10 November 2005 (ECtHR GC) available at <www.echr.coe.int/echr>: 'The Court's jurisdiction is, of course, subsidiary and its role is not to impose uniform solutions (...)'. Reference was made to the judgment of the Court in *Cha'are Shalom Ve Tsedek v. France*, judgment of 27 June 2000, paragraph 84.

42 Heringa 1999a, p. 1.

43 See, for example, *Kokkinakis v. Greece*, 14307/88 [1993] ECHR 20 (25 May 1993) (ECtHR), paragraph 47; *Leyla Sahin v. Turkey*, 44774/98, 10 November 2005 (ECtHR GC) available at <www.echr.coe.int/echr>, paragraph 110.

44 Gerards 2004a, section 4.1.2.

45 Heringa 2005, p. 2.

analysis of different legal approaches adopted by the various States Parties to the Convention in regard to a given subject matter.[46] Indeed, as will be seen, in so-called 'headscarf cases' the ECtHR has availed itself of a comparative law analysis in order to decide on the complaints at stake. For present purposes it is not necessary to elaborate on each of the factors mentioned above.[47] It is, however, necessary to stress the importance of the doctrine of the margin of appreciation in the context of the application and interpretation of Convention rights.

The judicial mandate of the ECJ is different from that of the ECtHR sketched above. The Luxembourg Court is concerned with 'guaranteeing a unique interpretation (and application) of Community Law'.[48] A keyword in Community law is uniformity and the supranational character of the EC as a whole effectively contributes to a convergence of legal standards across the Member States. Hence, the doctrine of the margin of appreciation is not applicable in the context of supranational EC law, although the ECJ may afford the Member States a certain margin of discretion. This is also supported by Article 6(3) TEU which states that '[t]he Union will respect the national identities of its Member States'.

In light of the different genesis of EC law compared with Convention law, and, in light of the different roles of the Strasbourg Court and the ECJ in securing ECHR and EC law respectively, national diversity is much more at a premium in the context of Convention law compared with Community law. This must be borne in mind in the analyses in Chapters 6 and 7 to follow.

In the above I explained in what ways EU law and ECHR law interconnect. This interconnection means that the ECJ in its future case law on the EFD (and RD) will be likely to take account of the legal approach adopted by the Strasbourg Court in comparable cases. On the other hand, it has been explained that the nature of EU/ EC law fundamentally differs from that of ECHR law. This applies *eo ipso* to the judicial mandate of the ECJ compared with that of the Strasbourg Court. These differences do not necessarily mean that the judicial stance of both Courts should always diverge. They however do constitute an explanatory factor why the ECJ's approach in future case law *might* differ from that adopted by the ECtHR in comparable cases.

English law and the ECHR

The connection between English law and Strasbourg law is realised via the 1998 Human Rights Act (HRA) which came into force on 2 October 2000. The HRA essentially transplants the content of the Convention into domestic law. In contrast with the Netherlands, which adheres to a monist theory of international law,[49] England adheres to a dualist theory which in practice means that international (human rights) standards do not automatically infiltrate into the domestic legal system. Hence the need for the adoption of a separate statutory Act (in casu: the HRA). The HRA thus constitutes the legal device which secures that UK courts and other public

46 Also Heringa 2005, p. 2.

47 The reader is referred to the analysis by Gerards 2004a.

48 Heringa 2005, p. 1.

49 See Chapter 2.

authorities[50] show due respect for Convention rights and freedoms, both in private and public law proceedings.[51] In light of the fact that this book is confined to the realm of employment, and given that the EFD is limited to employment, the following must be paid attention to. The HRA can only be directly relied on by employees working for the public sector (Section 6(1) HRA). In other words, only in vertical legal relationships can an individual invoke the HRA forthrightly. It follows that private sector employees cannot directly invoke the fundamental rights enshrined within the HRA. They can however invoke them indirectly. Put differently, the Act is not entirely bereaved of substance in horizontal legal relationships. On the basis of Sections 3 and 6 of the HRA 1998 courts and tribunals are under a duty to inter-

50 It should be noted that the HRA has been designed in a unique fashion; the principle of *Parliamentary sovereignty,* which is pivotal in English constitutional doctrine and theory, has remained unchallenged and unaffected. The HRA does not permit the judiciary to strike down Acts of Parliament even not where they ostentatiously violate the guarantees contained within it. If a provision of primary legislation falls short of the rights and freedoms contained in the HRA the Courts (i.e. the HL; the Judicial Committee of the Privy Council; the Court-Martial Appeal Court; in Scotland, the High Court of Justiciary sitting otherwise than as a trial court of the Court of Session; in England and Wales or Northern Ireland, the High court or the Court of Appeal) may in such cases only render a judicial declaration of incompatibility (Section 4 HRA). It is at this point that the domestic remedies available to the individual litigant have been entirely 'consumed'. The applicant, by way of *ultimum remedium,* may then seek recourse to the Strasbourg Court itself. The Court's judgment is binding upon the State party to the legal proceedings and its judgment is transmitted to the Committee of Ministers which shall supervise the execution of the Court's judgment. Matters could be illustrated with reference to the case of *Bellinger v. Bellinger* [2003] 2 AC 467 (HL). The facts were as follows. In the case at hand, the House of Lords dismissed an application concerning the right of a transsexual to marry with a person of the sex opposite to the transsexual person's 'psychological' sex. The Law Lords held that English law does not legally recognise a person's reassigned sex. The House of Lords, however, made a declaration of incompatibility (which it *may* (not must) do so on the basis of Section 4(2) HRA 1998) in the sense that it declared Section 11(c) of the Matrimonial Causes Act 1973 incompatible with the ECHR (Articles 8 (private life) and 12 (right to marry) of the Convention). The House of Lords could thus not *strike down* the relevant provisions of the Matrimonial Causes Act. A judicial declaration of incompatibility puts, however, pressure upon the UK government to enact new legislation with a view to eliminating the perceived incompatibility of national law with Convention law. See generally Lord Lester 2004, p. 259-260; See also the appendix to Lord Steyn's opinion in the case of *Ghaidan v. Godin Mendoza* [2004] UKHL 30, in which he has listed a (wide) number of cases in English law in which a declaration of incompatibility has been made under Section 4 of the HRA 1998.

51 Prior to the adoption of the HRA and in view of the UK's adherence to a dualist theory of international law, the Convention did not automatically form part and parcel of domestic law. This had the practical implication that individuals claiming an infringement of their human rights by (an) act(s) of (a) public authority(ies) could not invoke the Convention in proceedings before the national courts. Hence, the only legal route open to an applicant was to exhaust all national legal remedies and to challenge subsequently the case before the Strasbourg Court itself.

pret domestic law, 'so far as it is possible to do so', in accordance with Convention rights and freedoms.[52] Hence, Section 3(1) HRA and 6(1) HRA provide as follows:

> 3(1) HRA
> 'So far as it is possible to do so, primary legislation and subordinate legislation must be read and given effect in a way which is compatible with Convention rights.'
>
> 6(1) HRA
> 'It is unlawful for a public authority [including courts and tribunals; MG] to act in a way which is incompatible with a Convention right.'

Lord Lester has expressed it as follows:

> 'As part of [the Act's; MG] object and purpose, it enables the courts to breathe new life into fossilized Statutes by applying the dynamic values and standards prescribed by the HRA. In the absence of a clear and unequivocal legislative intention to the contrary, the rights it declares and protects must, where possible, prevail over latent or apparent inconsistencies in future as well as existing legislation.'[53]

Hence, the obligation of 'Convention conform interpretation'[54] applies both to public and private litigation alike. The legal scenario has succinctly been phrased by Loveland: 'HRA litigation in which the substance of the relationship between the parties turns on the interpretation of statutory provisions is always vertical in nature irrespective of the identity of the parties [public or private; MG].'[55] The reason for this is that it was the State itself that drafted the challenged legislation at stake in a given case. To sum up, a private individual can indirectly rely upon the HRA both in public and private law proceedings, for (s)he can argue that another piece of primary or secondary legislation (for example, the R&B Regulations and the Sexual Orientation Regulations) are to be interpreted in such a fashion that it shows sympathy for the spirit of Convention law.[56] The judicial method of Convention conform

52 The interpretative judicial exercise must not, however, result in what Lord Bingham has called 'judicial vandalism' which is to be distinguished from 'judicial interpretation'. In other words, Convention conform interpretation of domestic law must not pertinently be in conflict with the expressed words contained in that law. See *R (Anderson) v. Secretary of State for the Home Department* [2003] 1 AC 837. See also Lord Steyn in the same case: 'Section 3(1) is not available where the suggested interpretation is contrary to express statutory words or is by implication necessarily contradicted by the statute' (paragraph 59 of the judgment).

53 Lord Lester 2004, p. 260.

54 This rubric is used to reflect the analogy with the obligation imposed upon domestic courts by EC law to construct national law in such a manner so as to interpret it in accordance with EC Directives (see Chapter 2). This analogy has been noted by Bamforth 1999.

55 I. Loveland, 'Making it up as they go along? The Court of Appeal on same sex spouses and succession rights to tenancies', 2003 PL 222, at 231-232 cited by and taken from Wintemute 2003a, p. 623 and footnote 14.

56 In addition, suggests Wintemute, in the absence of an existing Statute or subordinate legislation an individual is not barred from arguing that a 'positive obligation' rests upon the government to enact legislation which for example prohibits sexual orientation discrimination in the private sector. See Wintemute 2000, p. 617.

interpretation can outstandingly be illustrated with reference to the (to English constitutional lawyers) well-known case of *Ghaidan v. Godin Mendoza*.[57] In that case, their Lordships (with the exception of Lord Millett, who dissented) clearly departed from a verbatim interpretation of domestic law (namely, of the Rent Act 1977).[58] The facts were as follows. Mr Ghaidan was a homosexual who had been living in a stable and monogamous relationship with his partner, Mr Hugh Wallwyn-James. After the death of the latter, Mr Ghaidan claimed the possession of the flat. The legal analysis by the Law Lords was focused upon the correct legal interpretation of a number of provisions contained in the 1977 Rent Act. These read as follows:

> '[t]he surviving spouse (if any) of the original tenant, if residing in the dwelling house immediately before the death of the original tenant, will after the death be the statutory tenant if and so long as he or she occupies the dwelling-house as his or her residence.
> [f]or the purposes of this paragraph, a person who was living with the original tenant as his or her wife or husband will be treated as the spouse of the original tenant. (...).'

On a customary reading of these provisions one could legitimately conclude that a heterosexual person, who survived on the death of his partner, may become a statutory tenant by succession whereas this right is not accorded to the partner of a homosexual person. However, the majority of the House of Lords were of the opinion that 'a person who was living with the original tenant as his or her wife or husband' must be judicially construed, so as to embrace both unmarried opposite and same-sex partners, for any other conclusion would be contrary to Articles 8 and 14 of the ECHR.[59] Hence, by application of Section 3 HRA,[60] the HL could legitimately extrapolate the right of unmarried couples to succeed a surviving partner to the rented home (where they had been living together) to homosexual partners. *Ghaidan* forms

57 *Ghaidan (appellant) v. Godin-Mendoza (FC) (respondent)* [2004] UKHL 30 (4-1, Lord Millett dissenting). See for a commentary also the Rt Hon. Baroness of Richmond 2005, p. 580-583; also Mead 2005, p. 459-467, who has discussed the judgment in light of the question regarding the retrospective effect of the HRA in private party litigation.

58 This can be contrasted with the case of *x v. y* [2003] IRLR 561 (EAT). In that case the applicant had been dismissed for 'gross misconduct' consisting of him having been engaged in consensual sexual activity with another (to him unknown) man in a public lavatory. He claimed unfair dismissal but the tribunal in first instance rejected the argument that his dismissal had been in breach of Articles 8 and 14 ECHR. The applicant thereupon appealed. EAT however (rightfully) held that they were '(...) not persuaded that transitory sexual encounters between consenting male adults in public lavatories fall within the right to respect for private life enshrined in Article 8(1) of the Convention' (see paragraph 41 of the judgment). Hence, Article 14 ECHR had been improperly engaged in the case at hand. And even if it were properly engaged, the dismissal could nonetheless not be seen as having been discriminatory, for the applicant's sexual orientation had not been a material factor in the employer's decision to dismiss him. The test of fairness in Section 98(4) of the Employment Rights Act could thus be carried out on the basis of 'ordinary dismissal law' (perceived outside the context of the Convention).

59 Notably also in light of the judgment by the ECtHR in *Karner v. Austria* EHRC 2003, 83. *Karner* will be discussed in detail in Chapter 7.

60 Rather than by application of Section 6 HRA.

moreover a clear illustration of the applicability of the HRA in private party litigation which thereupon becomes 'publicly infused'.[61]

It is to be stressed that the judicial obligation of 'Strasbourg conform interpretation' has only existed since 2000 when the HRA entered into force.[62] Hence, no such obligation existed whatsoever in the mid-1970s when English sex and race discrimination law was adopted. As stated in Chapter 2 sex discrimination law has largely evolved under the wings of EC law, whereas race discrimination law has developed comparatively independently. With regard to English disability discrimination law judicial reference was sought to the American with Disabilities Act (ADA), rather than to Strasbourg Convention law. Indeed, hardly any case law exists under the Convention which touches on disability issues certainly not in the context of employment.[63]

In the above it has been explained which legal mechanisms trigger and demand respect for the rights and freedoms contained in the ECHR, both in the context of the EU/EC and England. It will now be pronounced why the application of Convention law has, *de facto*, been more pertinent in the areas of religious and sexual orientation discrimination compared with discrimination on grounds of (e.g.) disability and age. This constitutes the 'second question' referred to above.

2.4. *Explaining the 'Second Question'*

It follows that Article 9 in conjunction with 14 ECHR secures the right to be free from religious discrimination in the areas to which the Convention applies. Thus, for instance in *Thlimmenos v. Greece*.[64] a case to be discussed in further detail hereafter, the aforementioned Articles were successfully married. A similar marriage has occurred in the context of sexual orientation discrimination (Articles 8 and 14 of the Convention).[65] These will be discussed in further detail in Chapter 7. Why is it that the ties with Strasbourg have tended to be stronger in the context of 'religion and belief' and 'sexual orientation' compared with the other grounds of discrimination, such as for example 'disability' and 'age'? The answer lies in the fact that the establishment of a connection between Article 14 ECHR and a 'sister right or freedom' has turned out to be a much more straightforward exercise in cases regarding so-called 'choice grounds' (including religion and belief and sexual orientation) compared with 'non-choice grounds' (including disability and age). Full academic credentials in reaching this conclusion are to be given to Wintemute, who has designed a sophisticated theory on the 'size of the 'gap' left by Article 14 of the Convention in com-

61 Mead 2005, p. 460.

62 See with regard to the retrospective effect of the HRA 1998, Mead 2005.

63 For a discussion of the HRA 1998 and the rights of disabled people, I refer to the following contributions: Lawson 2005, p. 135-154; de Schutter 2005a.

64 Case of of *Thlimmenos v. Greece* 34369/97, 6 April 2000 (ECtHR), available at <www.echr.coe.int/echr>.

65 E.g. *Salgueiro da Silva Mouta v. Portugal* EHRC 2000, 16. In *Salgueiro* it was accepted for the first time by the Court that discrimination on grounds of sexual orientation was in breach of Article 14 ECHR. See also Gerards in her case comment to *Salgueiro da Silva Mouta v. Portugal* EHRC 2000, 16.

bating discrimination and inequality.[66] For present purposes it is not necessary to examine Wintemute's theory in full. However, it is important to stress one of the constituents of his theory namely, that choice-grounds fall more easily than non-choice grounds within the ambit of a substantive Convention provision.[67] As Wintemute has put it:

> '[non-choice grounds] are grounds with respect to which no choice is realistically possible, and which are therefore not reflected in any other Convention right protecting a freedom to choose: the Convention contains no right to 'freedom of biological sex', 'freedom of race', 'freedom of disability' or 'freedom of age', such rights being largely non-sensical (except for transsexual individuals in the case of biological sex).'[68]

Indeed, and as will be seen in Chapters 6 and 7, the case law that has arisen under the Convention (logically) underpins this.[69] The foregoing explains the availability of ECtHR cases on religious and sexual orientation discrimination complaints and the unavailability of similar cases in the context of disability and age. Indeed, the few employment-related cases which have arisen under the Convention regard the grounds religion and belief and sexual orientation.

66 Wintemute has called his theory the 'two access routes theory' of the Article 14's 'within the ambit' principle. See Wintemute 2004.

67 Wintemute 2004, p. 366-382; Wintemute 2004a, p. 484-499. In the latter contribution Wintemute essentially stresses the importance of Protocol No. 12 for 'non choice grounds'. See further Wintemute (2000).

68 Wintemute 2004, p. 373, whereby he has acknowledged that Article 8 ECHR includes sexual orientation and gender-identity but, that it is nonetheless not very likely that the right to private life would cover sex (apart from gender-reassignment), race, disability and age. The author has moreover recognised that certain choices linked to non-choice grounds (whereby he *inter alia* mentions the example of pregnancy, abortion or medical treatment) could come within the scope of a material Convention right. See for these acknowledgements and further comments footnote 23 of Wintemute's Article.

69 For example, in respect of disability the *Botta*-case illustrates the Strasbourg Court's reluctance of linking 'disability' with Article 8 ECHR (*Botta v. Italy* (24 February 1998) Reports and Decisions of the ECtHR 1998-I, No 66 412). The case concerned a complaint by Mr Botta who was physically disabled. The complaint regarded the Italian State's failure to take measures in order to remedy omissions on the part of private bathing establishments and which omissions prevented disabled persons from having access to the beach and the sea. Hence, Mr Botta did not complain about actions by the Italian State but, conversely, about the omission by the authorities to undertake action against private bathing establishments ('positive obligations doctrine'). The Strasbourg Court held that Article 8 ECHR can only be successfully invoked if there is a direct and immediate link between the measures sought by the applicant and the applicant's private life. In the case at hand, the Court concluded that this link could not be established. Consequently, Article 8 was inapplicable. It was held that '(…) the right asserted by Mr Botta, namely the right to gain access to the beach and the sea at a place distant from his normal place of residence during his holidays, concerns interpersonal relations of such broad and indeterminate scope that there can be no conceivable direct link between the measures the State was urged to take in order to make good the omissions of the private bathing establishments and the applicant's private life'. In light of the inapplicability of Article 8 of the Convention in the case at hand, Article 14 ECHR can as a logical result not be invoked either. For further discussion the reader is referred to the analysis by de Schutter 2005a, p. 35-63.

In light of this the ECHR dimension will be exempted from the scope of Chapters 8 and 9 to follow. It is acknowledged that in light of Protocol No. 12 cases on disability and age are likely to appear more easily before the Strasbourg Court given that a connection with a 'sister right or freedom' is no longer required. Thus, writes Wintemute,

> '[w]hen deciding on the scope of a constitutional prohibition of discrimination, there is no principled basis for distinguishing between (...) 'choice grounds' that can be easily linked to particular Convention rights ([such as inter alia] religion [and] sexual orientation) and 'non-choice grounds' that generally cannot be so linked (sex, race, disability age). Protocol No. 12 would eliminate the effective hierarchy whereby (...) Art. 14 provides general protection in relation to 'choice grounds' but not 'non choice grounds'.[70]

In essence thus, Protocol No. 12 fills the judicial lacuna created by Article 14 ECHR and especially for what has been referred to as 'non choice grounds'. However, at the time of writing no cases regarding Protocol No. 12 have appeared before the Strasbourg Court.

In addition to the argument made above concerning the theory by Wintemute, I submit that the *material contents* of the rights protected by the ECHR also provide an explanation for the second question posed above. Thus, Article 9 ECHR protects the right to freedom of religion. As will be explained in Chapter 6 hereafter, the right to non-discrimination on grounds of religion or belief falls within this wider right. It follows that religious discrimination cases can easily appear before the ECtHR. Indeed, and as referenced earlier, the ECtHR has sometimes dealt with the non-discrimination complaint on the basis of Article 9, without considering it necessary to make a separate analysis under Article 14 of the Convention. Similarly, Article 8 ECHR protects the right to private life. As will be explained in Chapter 7, the ground 'sexual orientation' is closely related to matters concerning 'privacy'.

2.5. *Strasbourg Convention Law and Employment Law*

Before proceeding with the substantive analysis in Chapter 6, the following point must be paid attention to. As explained, the EFD is limited to employment and vocational training. This applies *eo ipso* to the English R&B and S.O. Regulations. The ECHR has, however, not often been invoked in discrimination cases in the context of employment. Indeed, the dependent character of Article 14 of the Convention has prevented this. As Gerards writes, 'the Court is particularly limited in the examination of distinctions that infringe social and economic rights, as the Court only rarely finds that these rights fall under the scope of the Convention'.[71] In other words, since the Convention does, for example, not contain a right to work, or other employment-related rights, it has been difficult to trigger the realm of work in the

70 Wintemute 2004a, p. 485.

71 Gerards 2004a, p. 8. Also de Schutter 2005, p. 5.

context of Article 14 of the Convention. Despite this, the realm of work was at stake in a number of cases, including for example *Thlimmenos* (earlier referred to).[72]

The applicant was a Jehovah's Witness, who was convicted in 1983 for his refusal to serve in the armed forces. This refusal was by reason of the applicant's religious beliefs. In 1988 the applicant sat a public exam for the appointment of 12 chartered accountants. Albeit being the second best candidate, the relevant authorities nonetheless refused to appoint him by reason of his past conviction under criminal law. The applicant essentially complained of the fact that the applicable domestic law, which excluded persons who had been convicted of a serious crime from being appointed for the position of chartered accountant, did not make a distinction as between those persons who (like the applicant) had been convicted as a result of their religious beliefs, on the one hand, and persons who had been convicted for a serious crime for other reasons, on the other. The applicant alleged that the failure by the government to make a material distinction between these 'incomparable' categories of convicted persons amounted to a breach of Article 14 in conjunction with Article 9 ECHR. The government in its turn contended (*inter alia*) that Article 14 ECHR did not apply, for the facts of the case did not fall within the scope of Article 9 ECHR. With regard to the question as to the applicability of Article 14 in conjunction with Article 9 the Court considered as follows.

> (Paragraph 42) 'In essence, the applicant's argument amounts to saying that he is discriminated against in the exercise of his freedom of religion, as guaranteed by Article 9 of the Convention, in that he was treated like any other person convicted of a serious crime although his own conviction resulted from the very exercise of this freedom. Seen in this perspective, the Court accepts that the 'set of facts' complained of by the applicant- his being treated as a person of a serious crime for the purposes of an appointment to a chartered accountant's post despite the fact that the offence for which he had been convicted was prompted by his religious beliefs- 'falls within the ambit of a Convention provision, namely Article 9'.

The Court did thereupon consider that it was not necessary to address the question as to whether the facts of the case did constitute a violation of Article 9 by itself. Rather, it went on to hold that the facts of the case did constitute an interference with Article 14 ECHR in conjunction with Article 9 given that Article 14 not only captures formal but also substantive equality (i.e. the failure to treat different cases differently, as had occurred in the case at hand). This aspect of the case was considered earlier in the analysis. *Thlimmenos* shows that public employment is covered by the scope of the Convention.[73] This can also be illustrated with reference to the cases of

72 Case of of *Thlimmenos v. Greece* 34369/97, 6 April 2000 (ECtHR), available at <www.echr.coe.int/echr>.

73 See moreover Wintemute 2004, p. 371: '(…) the statement, "the Convention does not apply to employment discrimination" struck[s] me as too broad, because it seem[s] to me that discrimination in access to public employment based on religion ("no Jews need apply for civil service jobs") must be a violation of Article 14 combined with Article 9.' This argument can easily be extrapolated to the ground sexual orientation ('no homosexuals need apply for civil service jobs').

Smith and Grady and *Lustig Prean*[74] (the so-called 'armed forces cases'), decided on by the Strasbourg Court on the basis of Article 8 ECHR. These cases concerned a blanket ban by the UK authorities on lesbians and gays serving in the armed forces. Most recently, in *Sidabras*,[75] the Court accepted that inequality of treatment with regard to access to employment in the private sector falls within the scope of Article 14 in conjunction with Article 8 ECHR. In casu, the applicable Lithuanian law imposed a ban on former employees of the KGB on applying for jobs in the public sector[76] and in various branches of the private sector. In analyzing the question whether the facts complained of fell within the scope of Article 8 ECHR the Court held as follows: 'The ban (...) affected their ability to develop relationships with the outside world to a very significant degree and has created serious difficulties for them in terms of earning their living, with obvious repercussions on the enjoyment of their private lives.'

It thereupon concluded the applicability of Article 8 in the case at hand. Hence, on the basis of this case it can be concluded that also private employment law has been brought under the scope of the Convention. In addition, it should be observed that relevant cases decided on by the ECtHR *outside* the employment realm, may nonetheless bear a legal impact upon comparable cases arising in the context of the EFD and/or national law and which occur *within* employment.

2.6. *Closing Remarks*

The above analysis has explained why reference to Strasbourg Convention Law is particularly relevant in the context of Chapters 6 and 7 to follow. It has been argued that Strasbourg Convention law on complaints regarding the grounds religion and belief and sexual orientation and, particularly, regarding acts of discrimination on these grounds is of interpretative value both for the ECJ and for the domestic courts. The links between Strasbourg on the one hand, and EC/EU and domestic law, on the other have also been clarified. At the same time the different role of the Strasbourg Court and the ECJ (as well as the domestic courts) has been highlighted. The present author has acknowledged that with the adoption of Protocol No. 12 the ECHR becomes increasingly relevant for discrimination complaints on all discrimination grounds. After all, such complaints need no longer fall within the ambit of another substantive Convention right. However, as stated, no case law on Article 1 of Protocol No. 12 is currently available.

74 *Smith* and *Grady v. the United Kingdom*, 33985/96 and 33986/96, 27 September 1999 (available at <http://www.echr.coe.int/echr> (Article 8 ECHR; no separate examination under Article 14 in conjunction with Article 8 ECHR); *Lustig-Prean* and *Beckett v. the United Kingdom*, 31417/96 and 32377/96, 27 December 1999 available at <http://www.echr.coe.int/echr> (Article 8 ECHR; no separate examination under Article 14 in conjunction with Article 8 ECHR).

75 *Sidabras and Dziautas v. Lithuania*, EHRC, 2004, 90 (with a case comment by Gerards).

76 The applicants' complaints under Article 8 taken alone or in conjunction with Article 14 ECHR was, however, not directed at their inability to find employment in the *public* sector (see paragraphs 36 and 37 of the judgment).

RELIGION AND BELIEF

1. Introduction

EC law has only granted effective protection from religious discrimination since the adoption of the EFD in 2000. Similarly, prior to December 2003, nothing was palpable when raising the matter of religious discrimination in employment in the context of English non-discrimination law. In contrast to grounds such as race, sex and disability, an employer could overtly discriminate on grounds of religion and belief.[1] This was the case notwithstanding the rapid emergence of a 'religious pluralism' across the European landscapes.[2] In English law, victims of religious nation at work could only bring anti-discrimination law proceedings, if an alleged religiously inspired act of discrimination could (also) be presented as an issue of race, ethnicity, ethnic origin or colour and could thus be litigated under the wings of race relations law. The situation in English law has, however, changed profoundly with the adoption in 2003 of the R&B (*Religion and Belief*) Regulations).[3]

In this chapter religious discrimination law will be examined from a multiply edged comparative law perspective. In section 2 hereafter, I will first make a number of theoretical comments on religion and belief as grounds of discrimination. This will be instrumental to the 'cross-ground' comparison to be drawn in Chapter 10. I will subsequently analyse EC religious discrimination law on the basis of a comparative approach (section 3). In section 4, the R&B Regulations will be analysed in light of the relevant requirements in the EFD. Tentative conclusions will be drawn in section 5. Wherever appropriate, the analysis hereafter will be embedded with relevant elements of religious discrimination law in the Netherlands. Given that

1 It may be worth noting that in Northern Irish law, the 1998 Fair Employment and Treatment Order (FETO) prohibits discrimination on grounds of religion and belief (as well as political opinion). See McColgan 2001, p. 215-216; Hepple and Choudhury 2001, p. 1-3.

2 Bell 2003a, p. 49-68. Labuschagne 1999, p. 133, who has drawn a similar conclusion in the context of Dutch law.

3 The Employment Equality (Religion or Belief) Regulations 2003, SI 2003, No. 1660. The Regulations apply to England, Wales and Scotland to the exclusion, however, of Northern Ireland (Part I, Regulation 1(2)).

Dutch law has prohibited discrimination on grounds of religion and belief since 1994, the Dutch approach may set an interpretative benchmark for the ECJ whilst interpreting the EFD. At the same time, however, it must be born in mind that issues of religion and the law cannot be perceived outside the specific historical and cultural context which is different from one Member State to another. As will be argued, different historical and cultural traditions across the Member States could thwart the cross-fertilisation of legal approaches in the area under review, notably in disputes over religion which have occurred in public life (e.g. in the context of public employment). The analysis of Dutch experiences and practices triggers the question regarding 'bottom-up' influence, as well as the 'cross-country' comparison. In this chapter, and for reasons that I noted at the outset of Part IV, I will moreover give regard to the relevant case law by the Strasbourg Court, which is likely to serve as an interpretative instrument both for the ECJ and for the domestic courts. Before proceeding, the following ought to be explained. Although firmly intertwined, a distinction should be made between, on the one hand, the right to be free from discrimination on grounds of religion and belief, and, the wider right to religious freedom, on the other. 'Non-discrimination', writes Evans, is simply a tool to assist the realisation of religious liberty [and tolerance; MG]; a means, not and end'.[4] In this chapter the emphasis will be on the non-discrimination aspect of the freedom of religion, although the right to freedom of religion will be triggered particularly in the context of Strasbourg Convention law.

2. The Intrinsic Values of 'Religion' and 'Belief'

In this section, I will reflect on religion and belief as grounds of discrimination from a more theoretical angle. What could be said on the intrinsic logic of these grounds and what equality ideal should be adhered to by the non-discrimination framework in the context of religion and belief? The existence of adequate legal[5] protection from religious discrimination is important by reason of the following. As Malik writes, with reference to the theory on the 'politics of recognition',[6] '(...) a person's iden-

4 An in depth analysis of the relationship between 'religious liberty', which centralises the 'free exercise' of religion *v.* 'religious equality', which calls for 'non-discrimination' has been made by Evans 1999, p. 119-131.

5 Although it is acknowledged that a mere legal approach is insufficient. See in this respect the following observation by Curtin and Geurts in the context of racism and the law: '(...) we acknowledge that action against racism and xenophobia will only be effective where it is embedded in a wider range of policies inter alia aiming to improve economic conditions which are seen as potentially aggravating factors.' (Curtin and Geurts 1996, p. 150). This observation can easily be extrapolated to the area of religious discrimination. See also Gearty 1999, p. 332 (footnote 27), who has underscored the view by Curtin and Geurts.

6 See notably the work by Young 1990. The theory on the politics of recognition prioritises the positive identification of a person in relation to the *group* to which (s)he belongs. See also Bickenbach 1999, p. 103, who has defined identity politics as follows: '(...) identity politics seizes on a form of human difference that, historically, has marginalised people (skin colour, gender, religious belief) and seeks through political action to infuse that difference with positive value so as to create self-affirming pride and group identification.'

tification with a group characteristic [such as 'religion'; MG] may be an important component of his or her well-being'.[7] Bijsterveld has voiced it as follows:

> 'It is important to realise that religion refers to more than just an individual having a particular set of opinions or the expression of such opinions in a liturgical context, however important these aspects are (...) religion has social, educational, communicative and institutional dimensions as well'.[8]

In other words, religion, or the absence thereof, transcends an individual's inner circle and has a potentially huge impact upon intra-community relations. This brings with it that religion cannot be explained in terms of a simple preference.[9] Religion and belief are about processes of thought and they often form part of a wider intra-community system. In light of this, Schiek has categorised 'religion'[10] within the group of grounds that reflect a 'chosen lifestyle', which can be distinguished from the group of grounds that can be traced back to a 'biological footing' ('sex', 'age' and, partly, 'disability') or that exist as 'mere ascriptions' ('race', 'gender' (not 'sex') and, partly, 'disability').[11] Like sexual orientation, religion and belief are 'choice-grounds' rather than reflecting 'immutability' (like, e.g. race and sex). Accordingly, religion and belief (and sexual orientation) allow for a *distinction* to be drawn between the so-called *forum internum* (i.e. the right to *have* a religion/belief/sexual orientation) and the *forum externum* (i.e. the right to *act* in accordance with that religion/belief/sexual orientation). A similar distinction cannot be drawn with respect to immutable grounds.

It follows from the foregoing that religion and belief can be vital marks of *identity*, both at the level of the individual believer, and at the level of the group to which (s)he belongs. In light of this, the role of the principles of equality and non-discrimination should be to foster diversity, rather than sameness. Fredman has argued that, in the context of the grounds religion and belief, the function of the equality principle should be to ensure that all religious groups are equally capable of manifesting their religious identity, whether alone or in community with others.[12] Securing the right to equality in the context of religion, argues Fredman, presupposes the *a priori* acceptance of a religious pluralism in society.[13] The 'equality in diversity' paradigm acts as a counterforce to so-called 'assimilation strategies'. If we perceive discrimination on grounds of religion as an attack on religious diversity, the approach to be adopted by the law ought to reflect substantive equality. Substantive equality is the most promising ideal to unravel religious discrimination and bias at work, for

7 Malik 2000, p. 129. Also Labuschagne 1999, p. 133; Also Fredman 2002a, p. 20.
8 Van Bijsterveld 2001, p. 304-305.
9 Hence, the argument that religion and belief should not be considered 'suspect' grounds of discrimination, because disadvantageous treatment on these grounds can allegedly be avoided in view of an element of 'choice', has to be rejected.
10 Together with sexual orientation, ethnicity (not ethnic origin), sexual orientation and political conviction.
11 Schiek 2002, p. 290-314.
12 Fredman 2002a, p. 19-20.
13 Fredman 2002a, p. 19-20.

it calls for some form of accommodation and positive understanding, rather than for a 'blind eye' approach insisting upon consistency and assimilation. However, and not least with a view to fostering the social acceptability of the accommodation of religious difference, the employer's interest in an efficient operation of his business must not altogether be neglected by the legal framework. Therefore, the interests of the religious worker must be adequately balanced against those of the employer. However, in doing so, it is vital to bear in mind the constitutional and human rights character of issues touching on religion and belief. In light of a discerned shift in EU law, from 'economic equality' to a principle of equality based on moral values[14], a strict scrutiny test ought to be adhered to by the ECJ and the domestic courts whilst carrying out that balancing exercise.[15] This point will be further dealt with below. It will also be illustrated how the Strasbourg Court has dealt with conflicting interests in cases regarding religious discrimination.

What more can be said on the intrinsic nature of 'religion' and 'belief'? Unlike 'race' and 'sex', and like, for example, 'sexual orientation', a person's religion or belief might be either kept visible or invisible. Further, unlike, for example, sexual orientation, which hardly ever constitutes a relevant factor in the (employer's) decision-making process, religion and belief are criteria which must not *a priori* be cleansed from the decision-making process. At times, a person's religion and belief might bear an impact upon her job performance or upon her availability for work at conventional days and hours. In this respect religion shows commonalities with 'sex'.[16]

3. Discrimination on Grounds of Religion and Belief in EC Law: an Analysis in light of Dutch and ECHR Law

3.1. Introduction

Since the adoption of the Article 13 Framework Directive discrimination on grounds of religion and belief has been prohibited in the broad area of employment. Prior to the adoption of Article 13 EC the matter of religious discrimination had occurred only once in the context of Community law. In the case of *Prais v. Council*,[17] a staff case, it was held by the ECJ that the right to be free from discrimination on grounds of religion is a fundamental right secured by Community law. The coverage of 'religion' and 'belief' by the EFD, rather than the RD, has meant a conceptual and practical

14 See Chapter 2.

15 It is worth noting that in the first judgment which has arisen in the context of the Article 13 EFD the ECJ has indeed adopted a strict scrutiny test in the context of (direct) age discrimination. See *Mangold v. Helm* (Case C-144/04) of 22 November 2005 available at <www.europa.eu.int>. This case will be extensively commented upon in Chapter 9.

16 Notably in light of the need to accommodate a woman's pregnancy. See in this respect Council Directive 92/85/EEC of 19 October 1992, on the introduction of measures to encourage improvements in the health and safety at work of pregnant workers and workers who have recently given birth or are breastfeeding, *OJ* L 348 of 28 November 1992 ('the Pregnant Workers Directive'). See Bell and Waddington 2003, p. 360-361.

17 *Vivien Prais v. Council of the European Communities*, (130/75) [1976] ECR 1589.

separation of these two grounds, on the one hand, and race and ethnicity, on the other. Initially, however, in 1998, the Starting Line Group[18] had launched a proposal for a Community Directive covering both race and ethnicity and religion and belief. The coverage of the just-mentioned grounds within a single legal framework would have reflected a more realistic approach, for race, ethnicity, religion and belief are closely interlaced. Taking the example of discrimination of a black Muslim, it will be very difficult to discern whether discrimination has occurred on grounds of race *or* religion. The insertion of religion and belief into the EFD has also meant that religious discrimination is only prohibited in employment, whereas race discrimination is prohibited in a wide range of areas of social life.[19]

What are the types of conflicts which tend to arouse judicial controversy in a debate on religious dispute regulation in public and private sector employment? At least five distinct controversies can be highlighted:

Firstly, and most generally, controversy is likely to arise over the meaning of 'religion' and 'belief' and over the question *who*, the legislator, the individual believer, the employer, or, the courts, should ultimately interpret these notions. The meaning of 'religion' and 'belief' will be considered in section 3.2 below in light of relevant Dutch law and Strasbourg Convention law.

Secondly, controversy may also arise over the imposition by employers of dress-code regulations. Employees who abide by the religious tenets of minority faiths are often precluded from wearing attire at work, which is in conformity with their religious belief. May, for example, an employer lawfully refuse to hire a Muslim woman wishing to wear a headscarf, or, a Sikh man who wants to wear a turban? Will the answer be different in the context of public employment, compared with private employment? What is the role of 'secularism' in this debate? Is the employer under a legal duty to accommodate religious difference in the workplace?

Thirdly, burgeoning discussions can arise out of disagreement between a religious employee and his employer over the reconciliation of working-time, on the one hand, and religious worship, on the other. Is an employer under a legal obligation to permit an employee to take time off from work for the sake of abiding by religious rituals (including praying)?[20] Does the principle of non-discrimination on grounds of religion require an employer to provide a religious employee with adequate facilities, such as praying rooms?[21]

Fourthly, disagreement can arise between a religious worker and an employer over the refusal by the former to carry out certain duties of the job. For example,

18 This is an informal network of some 400 non-governmental organisations, semi-official organisations, trade unions, churches, independent experts and academics in the EU, who are active in the area of combating racism and xenophobia and have lobbied for the adoption of legal measures by the EC to combat racism and xenophobia. See also Yu and Chopin 2001, p. 5-6, notably footnote 1.

19 See Chapter 2.

20 Cumper 1996, p. 227. See also Opinions 1997-23 and 1999-49 by the Dutch ETC. See also *Stedman v. UK* (1997) 23 EHRR 168 (CD) and *Ahmad v. UK* (1981) 4 EHRR 126 (CD) which will be discussed later on in the analysis.

21 See, for example, Opinion 2000-51 of the Dutch ETC.

may the director of a hospital lawfully refuse to employ a person for the job of nurse, if she refuses to help with carrying out an abortion?

Fifthly, the rights of religious employers can clash with the rights of a(n) (future) employee not to be discriminated against on the basis of a protected ground. May a Roman Catholic School for example lawfully refuse to employ a homosexual teacher?

Many of the above disputes are concrete manifestations of institutionalised, or systematic, patterns of discrimination. We saw in Chapters 3 and 4 that, e.g. in the context of gender, discrimination often comes to the surface given that the male norm is taken as a point for departure in the organisation of the labour market. Similarly, in the context of religion, instances of discrimination are rooted in the dominant Christian norm.[22] As Fredman has observed, many practices which find their source in Christianity, e.g. the working week, the weekly day of rest, annual holidays, dressing requirements, etc. remain unchallenged, for they are presented under the guise of 'secularism' and a perceived 'neutrality'.[23] Similar concerns have been voiced by Fahlbeck:

> 'Civic adherence to these Christian patterns does in a way reflect Christian ethnocentricity. However, we are here faced with civic arrangements that no longer express Christian values per se but simply a way of organising temporal matters of a mundane character'.[24]

In other words, 'neutrality' means in practice that elements of Christianity, rather than other religions, are preserved.[25] Clearly, the above controversies are not easily resolved. Settling the above disputes by law calls for a careful balancing of interests of all the relevant parties to the dispute.

3.2. *The Meaning of 'Religion' and 'Belief'*

The EFD remains silent on the meaning of 'religion' and 'belief'.[26] The absence of a definition in the legislative framework means in practice that it will be for the national courts, and ultimately for the ECJ, to interpret the meaning of these notions. In doing so, domestic courts and the ECJ are likely to use existing case law by the Strasbourg

22 See also Cumper 1996, p. 205-241, who has mapped the history of Christian bias.

23 Fredman 2002a, p. 19.

24 Fahlbeck 2004, p. 52. See also Hepple and Choudhury 2001, p. 38: '(…) our society is structured around basic Christian assumptions and therefore already accommodates the needs of Christians (…) in a multi-faith society, the needs of individuals with different religious faiths should be met.'

25 Various legal scholars in the Netherlands have made interesting analyses of the impact of deeply entrenched Christian values, which underlie the set-up of today's society, upon the interpretation of openly defined legal norms (e.g. 'reasonableness') in general private law and contract law. An examination of these analyses goes beyond the scope of this book. The interested reader is referred to the following contributions: Rutten 2003, p. 21-28; Mulder 1999, p. 338; Smits 2000, p. 290.

26 It is submitted that as a matter of political reality the unanimity requirement contained in Article 13 EC prevented a common conclusion by the Member States on the legal meaning of these two notions.

court as an interpretative benchmark.[27] The right to religious freedom in Article 9 of the ECHR has been interpreted by the ECtHR as comprising both the right to *have* a belief (i.e. the *'forum internum'*) and the right to *manifest* a belief (i.e. the *'forum externum'*), for example, through worship, teaching, practice and observance. It will be seen below that a similar approach has been adopted in Dutch law. Article 9(1) ECHR protects the *forum internum*, as well as the *forum externum*.[28] The former has been phrased in absolute terms, which means that this right is unqualified. The *forum externum* is subject to limitations that are contained in Article 9(2) of the Convention.[29] The right to *manifest* one's religion or belief is not unconditional and thus 'derogable' with a view to the protection of other, competing, interests.[30] The Strasbourg Court has interpreted Article 9 of the Convention as protecting both those who believe, and those who do not belief. Put differently, Article 9 ECHR protects the freedom *of* religion and the freedom *from* religion.[31] The leading case in the present context is the case of *Kokkinakis v. Greece*.[32] The applicant, Mr Kokkinakis, who was a Jehovah's Witness, complained before the Court of his conviction for proselytism by the Greek authorities. The Court gave the following interpretation of Article 9 of the Convention:

> 'As enshrined in Article 9, freedom of thought, conscience and religion is one of the foundations of a 'democratic society' within the meaning of the Convention. It is, in its religious dimension, one of the most vital elements that go to make up the identity of believers and their conception of life, but it is also a precious asset for atheists, agnostics, sceptics and the unconcerned. The pluralism indissociable from a democratic society, which has been clearly won over the centuries, depends on it (...).'[33]

In *Arrowsmith v. UK*[34] the Court held that pacifism is covered by Article 9 of the Convention. The case law shows that the legal threshold set by Article 9(1) of the Convention is comparatively low.

27 See also Vickers 2004, p. 181 *et seq*.

28 Article 9(1) ECHR provides as follows: 'Everyone has the right to freedom of thought, conscience and religion; this right includes freedom to change his religion or belief, and freedom, either alone or in community with others and in public or private, to manifest his religion or belief, in worship, teaching, practice and observance.'

29 Article 9(2) ECHR provides as follows: 'Freedom to manifest one's religion or belief shall be subject only to such limitations as are prescribed by law and are necessary in a democratic society in the interests of public safety, for the protection of public order, health or morals, or the protection of the rights and freedoms of others.'

30 See, for example, the Commission's decision in *Ahmad v. UK* (1981) 4 EHRR 126 (CD) in which it was held as follows: '(...) the freedom of religion, as guaranteed by Article 9, is not absolute, but subject to the limitations set out in Article 9(2). Moreover, it may, as regards the modality of a particular religious manifestation, be influenced by the situation of the person claiming that freedom.' For a discussion, I also refer to Fahlbeck 2004, p. 27-64, especially p. 29-30.

31 Fahlbeck 2004, p. 36.

32 *Kokkinakis v. Greece*, 14307/88 [1993] ECHR 20 (25 May 1993) (ECtHR).

33 Paragraph 31 of the judgment. See also the Court's judgment in the case of *Buscarini and others v. San Marino*, 24645/94 [1999] ECHR 7 (18 February 1999) (ECtHR), paragraph 34.

34 *Arrowsmith v. UK*, 7050/75, [1978] (12 October 1978) 19 DR 5 (CD)

The legal approach in the Netherlands is similar to the one adopted by the Strasbourg Court.[35] This is not surprising, because the Netherlands adhere to a monist theory of international law which means that international legal standards automatically form part and parcel of Dutch law. The freedom of religion is contained in Article 6 of the Constitution which protects both the *forum internum* and the *forum externum*. The right not to be discriminated against on grounds of religion and belief is secured by Article 1 of the Constitution and by the GETA.[36] Neither instrument defines the meaning of religion (*godsdienst*) and belief (*levensovertuiging*). The ETC has explicitly held that the right not to be discriminated against on grounds of religion and belief covers both the right to *have* and to *manifest* one's belief.[37] The Commission has interpreted the notion of religion as being a 'conviction about life whereby a supreme being stands central'.[38] However, according to the ETC's case law, such a 'supreme being' is lacking in the notion of belief which concerns a 'coherent perception about life' such as humanism[39] or anthroposophy.[40] A 'coherent perception about life' does, however, not cover the expression of a set of opinions about the organisation of society, e.g. the opinion that society is best organised on the basis of a *laissez-faire* approach. Hence, the ETC has held that 'belief' means 'a conviction consisting of a more or less coherent framework of ideas and which concerns fundamental view-points about the human existence'.[41] The ETC has also considered it relevant that such ideas are not only individually believed in, but that they are shared with others.[42] On the other hand, it is not necessary that all who adhere to a particular religion interpret that religion in a universal fashion. For example, that not all Muslims pray five times a day, does not reduce the protective scope of the law for those who do so.[43] The same principle applies to the protection of Muslim girls wishing to wear the headscarf.[44] In Dutch equal treatment law an applicant needs not prove his (or her) religion or belief and both notions have been interpreted by the ETC in a liberal fashion. This reflects a correct stance for, it is

35 For example, Opinion 2003-114.

36 The GETA prohibits making a distinction (*onderscheid*) rather than discrimination (*discriminatie*) on grounds of religion and belief. The difference between these two notions was explained in detail in Chapter 2.

37 For example, Opinions 1997-46; 2004-112; 2004-148. Dutch equal treatment law must in this respect be perceived in light of Article 6 of the Dutch Constitution as well as in light of the ECHR given that the Netherlands adhere to a monist theory of international law. The approach that religious freedom comprises both a *forum internum* and a *forum externum* is moreover reflected in the Parliamentary History to Dutch Equal Treatment law and Article 6 of the Constitution. See *Parliamentary Documents* II, 1990/1991, 22 014, no. 5, p. 39-40; Parliamentary History II 1975/1976, 13 872, no. 3, p. 29; *Parliamentary Documents* II 1990/1991, 22 014 no. 3, p. 3.

38 Opinion 2003-114.

39 See also *Parliamentary Documents* II, 1983-1984, 16 635, no. 4.

40 The ETC decided this with reference to a case decided by the Highest Administrative Court. See ARRvS, 07-04-1983, AB 1983, 430.

41 See Opinion 2003-114.

42 See e.g. Opinions 97-15 and 2005-28.

43 See e.g. Opinions 1997-23 and 2004-148.

44 See e.g. Opinion 1995-31.

submitted, judicial bodies ought to adopt a 'hands off' approach in deciding on what exactly falls within the ambit of 'religion' and 'belief'. If they do not, they will risk becoming entangled in complicated questions of religion which fall outside the scope of their judicial mandate.[45] Hence, judicial bodies must respect the *forum internum* as much as possible. However, sometimes it will be necessary to set a judicial boundary to the *forum internum*. This can be illustrated with reference to the *Satans Church* case[46] decided by the Dutch Supreme Court in the context of Dutch criminal law.

The applicant was a sex club which, however, maintained to be a religious sect adhering to the Church of Satan. In the applicant's view, and with reference to the relevant Sections in the Criminal Code, the State authorities were not entitled to access the premises on which the 'religious activities' took place. The Supreme Court held that the legislator must in principle refrain from interpreting the notion of religion but this must not be taken to mean that criminal acts can lawfully be committed under the guise of religion. The facts of the case revealed that the 'religious' activities of the applicant were not distinguishable whatsoever from the activities in an ordinary sex club and thus the applicant's claim was correctly rejected.

Whereas judicial bodies should show judicial restraint in respect of the *forum internum*, they should perform an active role with regard to the *forum externum*. The reason for this is that the manifestation of a person's belief may bear a negative impact upon the rights of others. This point will be taken further in the passages to follow.

3.3. *Concepts of Discrimination and the Resolution of Religious Disputes*

3.3.1. Introduction

In section 3.1 above, a number of controversies were highlighted which tend to arise in the context of religion and work. In this section, a legal analysis will be made of the second, third and fourth types of dispute which, respectively, concerned disputes over dress code regulations, controversies over requests for time off from work,

45 See in this context the case of *Gereformeerde Kerk Hasselt* decided by the Dutch Supreme Court (HR 15-02-1957 *NJ* 1957/201). In this case, the Supreme Court held as follows: 'The principles of full freedom of religion and of equality before the law of all religious groups which (...) [apply in the Netherlands] bring with them, that the civil courts may not be partial with regard to different interpretations by these groups on the meaning of religion and the way in which religion should be manifested, and, especially (....), the civil courts may not make their judgments on a point of law dependent on their in interpretation of religious doctrines, with regard to which disagreement exists as to their correctness, their incorrectness or their importance.'[unofficial translation; MG]. (The original text reads as follows: *[De Hoge Raad oordeelde dat de] 'beginselen van volkomen vrijheid van geloof en gelijkheid voor den Staat van alle godsdienstige gezindten, welke ten onzent gelden (...) meebrengen, dat de burgerlijke rechter geen partij mag kiezen in op het terrein dier gezindten rijzende geschillen omtrent geloof en belijdenis en met name ook niet (...) zijn uitspraak omtrent enig rechtspunt afhankelijk mag stellen van zijn oordeel met betrekking tot theologische leerstellingen, omtrent welker juistheid, onjuistheid of gewicht aldaar verdeeldheid bestaat).'* For a further in depth comment on the question *if* and *to what degree* the judiciary should give a judgment on whether particular acts fall or do not fall within the scope of 'religion' or 'belief', I refer to de Winter 1996.

46 HR 31 October 1986, *NJ* 1987 173. See also, HR 13 April 1960 *NJ* 1960 436 (*AOW Predikant*).

and, disagreement over an employee's refusal to perform certain duties attached to a post. More concretely, it will be questioned whether the various prohibitions of discrimination contained in the EFD effectively contribute to resolve these disputes. Given the absence of relevant case law by the ECJ, it will be examined how the aforementioned types of conflicts have been approached by the Strasbourg court and by the Dutch ETC or, as the case may be, by the Dutch courts. If the Luxembourg court feels inspired by legal approaches and practices adopted by the ECtHR, or, by the constitutional traditions of the Member States, a cross-fertilisation of norms between legal systems will occur. In the analysis to follow, attention will also be paid to the fact that the approach adopted by the law in the resolution of religious conflicts may be different, depending on whether conflicts have arisen between two private individuals, or, between a private individual and the State. As noted by Fahlbeck, in private party disputes, the values of 'state neutrality' and 'secularism' are not at a premium, whereas these principles may have a decisive impact upon the resolution of religious conflicts that have arisen in the context of public life.[47] Furthermore, the different 'social fabric' of different States bears an impact upon the stance adopted by judicial bodies in settling religious disputes.[48]

As we know,[49] the EFD prohibits (*inter alia*) direct and indirect discrimination. Moreover, the Directive imposes a duty on the employer to make reasonable accommodations for disabled persons. The concept of reasonable accommodation is referred to, given that it could be of relevance in the context of religious discrimination law. This point will be clarified in further detail in the analysis below. Hereafter, the aim will not be to examine the intricacies of the just-mentioned concepts *in se*. This was or will be done at other junctures.[50] The objective of this section is to illustrate how the various concepts of discrimination can be employed in the resolution of religious disputes at work. Of course, the nature and the theoretical premises of the various prohibitions of discrimination remain unaltered in the context of religious discrimination law. By contrast, the legal questions that occur in practice which prompt the usage of the diverse prohibitions of discrimination tend to vary depending on the discrimination ground(s) at stake. For example, whereas indirect discrimination in the context of sex has frequently been employed with a view to challenging full-time work requirements, indirect discrimination in the context of religion is an appropriate tool for challenging dress-code regulations.[51] It will become apparent that the prohibitions of discrimination in the EFD arguably play an important role,

47 Fahlbeck 2004, p. 53.

48 Fahlbeck 2004, p. 39.

49 See Chapters 2 and 3.

50 'Direct discrimination' was discussed at the outset of Part II. 'Indirect discrimination' was extensively analysed in Chapter 3. In that Chapter, indirect discrimination was moreover contrasted with direct discrimination at several junctures. 'Harassment' was examined in Chapter 4. 'Reasonable accommodation' will be examined in Chapter 8 in the context of disability discrimination law. The prohibition of the instruction to discriminate is self-explanatory. It covers, for example, the scenario where an employer instructs a recruitment agency not to employ Muslims.

51 From a conceptual point of view, dress-code rules could also be challenged on the basis of direct discrimination. This point will be elaborated on in the passages to follow in the main text.

not only in eradicating religious discrimination at work, but also in fostering pluralism and religious diversity.

3.3.2. The Concept of Direct Discrimination

The prohibition of direct discrimination[52] is enshrined in Article 2(2) 'a' of the EFD. It will be taken to occur 'where one person is treated less favourably than another is, has been or would be treated in a comparable situation, on any of the grounds referred to in Article 1 [including religion and belief; MG]'. In other words, the legal prohibition of direct discrimination calls for an actual, a past or a hypothetical comparison[53] of a religious person with a non-religious person (or with a person who adheres to a different religion or belief) and who finds herself in an otherwise similar situation. As was explained at the outset of Part II, 'direct discrimination' mirrors 'consistency' equality and its objective is to eradicate blunt instances of discrimination. Direct discrimination can be established too, if the discriminatory act occurs on the basis of a falsely assumed characteristic. It moreover covers 'associated discrimination'. Hence, an employee who is dismissed by reason of the fact that his spouse is a member of the Church of Scientology is protected by the prohibition of direct discrimination on grounds of religion and belief.[54] Direct discrimination is also an important tool in addressing stereotypical views about a person's religion or belief. Given that the EFD is modelled along the lines of the closed model of anti-discrimination law, direct discrimination can only be justified on the basis of a limited number of exceptions contained in the Directive. Exceptions will be dealt with separately in section 3.4 hereafter.

3.3.3. Indirect Discrimination and Reasonable Accommodation

More than 'direct discrimination', the concept of indirect discrimination is a particularly powerful tool to accommodate diverse religious needs and traditions. Given that 'indirect discrimination' goes beyond 'consistency' strategies, it reflects substantive, not formal equality. The legal prohibition of indirect discrimination is particularly pertinent in the context of religion and belief, given that the Framework Directive does not oblige employers to make reasonable accommodations for those who adhere to a particular religion. Thüsing has criticised the Directive for

52 See also Part II under (ii).

53 The possibility for using a hypothetical comparator in discrimination cases had been denied by the ECJ in the context of EC sex discrimination law. In *MacCarthys Ltd. v. Smith Advel* (Case 129/80) [1980] ECR 1275, the Court has held has follows: 'It follows that, in cases of actual discrimination falling within the scope of the direct application of Article 119 [EC; MG], comparisons are confined to parallels which may be drawn on the basis of concrete appraisals of the work *actually* [italics MG] performed by employees of different sex within the same establishment or service.'

54 Unless, of course, the ECJ decides that the Church of Scientology is not covered by the notion of religion or belief. See in this respect Thüsing 2003, p. 199 where he refers to a number of cases by the German and the English courts in which Scientology was not accepted as a religion. He has contrasted this with legal approaches in French and U.S. law.

'(...)[making way; MG] for formal equal treatment rather than accommodation or effective equalisation, as there is no duty of consideration and adaptation with regard to religious belief comparable with Article 5 [EFD; MG] concerning disability'. He has moreover argued that '(...) most cases of conflict arising from an employee's religious persuasion are not caused by examples of rare unequal treatment, but rather by equal treatment with inequitable consequences'.[55]

He has eventually concluded that the Directive's approach to religious discrimination is 'surprisingly cautious'.[56] A similar argument has been voiced by Hepple and Choudhury.[57] In their view, the most effective protection from discrimination on grounds of religion and belief would be achieved if the prohibition of indirect discrimination and the duty to make reasonable accommodation were merged.[58] They have indicated that this can be effectuated by a rephrasing of the 'objective justification test' for indirect discrimination cases. As we saw in Chapter 3, 'objective justification' consists of the elements of 'legitimacy', 'appropriateness' and 'necessity'.[59] Hepple and Choudhury have proposed to reformulate the test of objective justification for *prima facie* cases of indirect religious discrimination in the following manner:

'a provision, criterion or practice should not be regarded as appropriate and necessary in the case of indirect discrimination which disadvantages (...) persons of a religious group unless the needs of that group cannot be reasonably accommodated without causing undue hardship on the person responsible for accommodating those needs, having regard to factors such as financial and other costs and health and safety requirements'.

The 'merged' legal approach favoured by the aforementioned authors essentially requires employers to consider, in reasonableness, the possibility of making an accommodation, with a view to adjusting religious difference. If an employer omits making a reasonable accommodation in cases where he could do so, the objective justification test for indirect discrimination will be bound to fail. The present author agrees with the above scholars that merging the concepts of indirect discrimination and reasonable accommodation would be an effective means to combat the institutionalised causes of religious discrimination at work. On the other hand, case law in the Netherlands shows that indirect discrimination is a powerful tool by itself to foster religious pluralism at the workplace although, admittedly, in the Netherlands religious diversity is also promoted by the prevailing tradition of multiculturalism. Arguably, the test of objective justification as it has been interpreted by the ECJ in indirect discrimination cases leaves sufficient room for the balancing of conflicting

55 Thüsing 2003, p. 200.

56 Thüsing 2003, p. 201.

57 Hepple and Choudhury, 2001. Also Fredman 1999, who has argued that religious discrimination law could borrow from disability laws, like the English DDA, by imposing duties of reasonable adjustments. The duty to adjust does not require conformity, but diversity and change. Also, Bolger 2003, p. 372-374.

58 This approach has moreover been recommended by the Independent Review of UK anti-discrimination law. See Hepple, Choudhury and Coussey, 2000.

59 See Chapter 3. It is recalled that this is the objective justification test, which the ECJ has established in the context of indirect sex discrimination law.

interests in religious discrimination cases. It is worth emphasising that a *prima facie* discriminatory treatment will only be justifiable, if the 'necessity requirement' is complied with. This means that *prima facie* disadvantageous treatment will only be lawful, if the objective pursued by the vexed treatment cannot be achieved by an alternative, *i.e.* by less or non-discriminatory, means.[60] One could argue that the judicial analysis of whether the necessity requirement is complied with could involve the examination of whether reasonable accommodation can be made. After all, making a reasonable accommodation could be an 'alternative means' to the vexed (*prima facie*) indirectly discriminatory conduct. In summary, a reasonable accommodation requirement could be classified under the 'necessity' requirement in the context of 'objective justification' of *prima facie* indirect discrimination.[61]

De Schutter has suggested that, whilst carrying out the balancing exercise in an indirect religious discrimination case, courts may take into account the following factors: (1) the centrality of a particular religious manifestation (e.g. praying) to the religion or belief in question; (2) the burden imposed upon the employer for making an exception to the applicable rules in order to accommodate diverse religious needs; (3) the question whether the religious employee has voluntarily accepted certain rules which restrict his (or her) right to manifest his (her) belief, implying a waiver of the right not to be discriminated against on grounds of religion or belief.[62] In addition, the balancing exercise is arguably highly influenced by existing national traditions, given that the significance of religion in daily life is different in one country, compared to another. Moreover, the outcome of the balancing-exercise is influenced by whether or not a religious dispute arises in the realm of public life, or between privately acting individuals. These and related matters will be examined in further detail hereafter whilst discussing relevant case law in the context of Dutch law (under 3.3.3) and ECHR law (under 3.3.4).

3.3.4. Resolving Religious Conflicts at Work: the Case of the Netherlands

Hereafter, it will be analysed how the ETC, and as the case may be, courts in the Netherlands, have approached religious conflicts in the area of employment. The analysis will examine: (1) disputes concerning dress regulations with an emphasis on Muslim headscarf cases; (2) time off from work cases; (3) disputes over the employee's refusal to perform certain job-related duties for religious reasons. Whilst analysing the case law, it must be born in mind that the social climate in the Netherlands is characterised by tolerance and by a recognition of a diversity of the populace.[63] This is important, for it provides the relevant legal and social context in which the interpretation by the (semi)judiciary of religious conflicts must be appreciated. The Dutch approach may form a source of inspiration for the ECJ in comparable cases

60 See generally also Chapter 3.
61 I am grateful to Professor Janneke Gerards for this point.
62 De Schutter 2005, p. 47.
63 I am grateful to Professor Dagmar Schiek for this point.

that may arise in the context of the EFD, although this is less likely to be the case in Muslim headscarf for reasons that I will note below.

3.3.4.1. Disputes over Religious Dress

Disputes over the wearing of the Muslim headscarf at work, or in schools, have sometimes been approached by the ETC on the basis of direct distinction and, at other times, on the basis of indirect distinction.[64] In Opinions 1995-31 and 1996-16 the ETC took the view that a direct and blunt reference to the Muslim headscarf is tantamount to a direct reference to her religion. In other words, given that the headscarf is intrinsically linked to Islam, a distinction on grounds of wearing the headscarf is interpreted as a short-hand for discrimination against Muslims. Although the analysis of direct distinction reflects *in se* a pure way of legal reasoning, it bears the practical disadvantage that it precludes the ETC from carrying out a balancing exercise of all interests at stake. After all, the GETA, like the EFD, is framed on the basis of the closed model of anti-discrimination law.[65] For this reason, the ETC has shifted its legal analysis from 'direct' to 'indirect' discrimination. Reasons of health and safety have been accepted as constituting an objective justification for *prima facie* indirect distinction cases[66] on grounds of religion, depending, however, on the facts of the case at hand. Opinion 1997-24 concerned the dismissal of a Sikh employee. *In casu*, the ETC did not accept the employer's argument that the applicant's small dagger (worn by the Sikh community for religious reasons) constituted a threat to the safety at work. In contrast with health and safety rationales, the ETC has rejected arguments relating to the employee's 'good appearance' and 'representation' at work with which a headscarf or other religious headgear would allegedly be in tension.[67] A particularly interesting case was at stake in Opinion 2003-53. The facts were as follows:

The applicant was a lawyer who had applied for the position of legal clerk in the courtroom. She was refused the job by reason of her Muslim headscarf. The respondent, a District Court in the Netherlands, argued that this prohibition was necessary with a view to preserving the values of the absolute independence and impartiality of the judiciary. In the applicant's view, the contested dress code rules constituted an infringement of the non-discrimination principle and her right to religious freedom. The ETC concluded a case of indirect distinction on grounds of religion, which could not be objectively justified. Although the Commission agreed with the respondent that the aims of impartiality and judicial independence were legitimate aims for the purposes of 'objective justification', it held that the 'necessity' requirement was not complied with. In the Commission's view, there was in the first place no real need for the respondent to impose the vexed dress-code regulations. In taking

64 Hence, headscarf disputes have been approached by the ETC as a matter of discrimination, rather than as a matter of religious freedom. The reason for this is that the ETC does not have jurisdiction on Article 6 of the Constitution, which secures freedom of religion. The Commission's semi-judicial mandate is thus confined to an interpretation of the GETA.

65 See Chapter 2.

66 Opinions 97-149 and 99-106.

67 Opinion 96-109.

this view, the ETC referred to evidence, which indicated that judges sometimes perform their judicial tasks without wearing the official garments. Moreover, in the ETC's view, the requirement of 'proportionality' was not met, for the vexed regulations had the effect of excluding all Muslim women who wear the scarf from performing the job of clerk in the court room. The ETC also considered that the scarf did not necessarily preclude the woman concerned from wearing the official uniform at the same time. The Commission moreover held that, in contrast with judges, clerks in the courtroom are not endowed with the classic task of administering justice.

The judicial outcome in the above case is not surprising in light of the stance taken by the ETC in earlier cases. In these cases teachers were prohibited from wearing the Muslim headscarf in public schools.[68] In public school cases, the ETC has taken the view that wearing the Muslim headscarf does not *in se* preclude Muslim teachers from having an 'open attitude' towards all religious and ideological values represented in society. Such an open attitude is *required* in the Netherlands by the 'neutral' character of public schools.[69] It follows from the ETC's case law that the Muslim headscarf can in principle not be prohibited by private employers, nor in public schools and neither in the courtroom. The Commission's point of view is essentially based on a reconfigured interpretation of the principle of 'secularism'. Traditionally, 'secularism' has been interpreted as meaning the *eradication* of religion from public life. It will be seen, in the context of Strasbourg Convention law hereafter, that this meaning of 'secularism' is strongly adhered to by States such as Turkey and Switzerland (and France)[70]. These states are in favour of a *laïcité approach* which secures that religion is reduced to a purely private issue. At the outset, it was highlighted that the social fabric in the Netherlands is featured by multiculturalism. This largely explains why the ETC has not endorsed the principle of secularism in the classic *(laïcité)* sense. Rather, the ETC has taken the view that the notions of secularism and neutrality in their traditional meaning cannot trump the right of Muslim women not to be discriminated against on grounds of religion. According to the reconfigured meaning of 'secularism', 'pluralism' is a *conditio sine qua non* for 'neutrality'. Zoontjens has in this context spoken of 'negative neutrality' and 'positive neutrality'. Whereas the former calls for a strict separation of religion and the public sphere, the latter requires that equal space be granted to persons of all religious groups in the realm of public life, including public employment. In academic circles this approach has *inter alia* been defended by Loenen, who has labelled it the 'pluralist inclusiveness'

68 In Opinions 99-18 and 99-103 the Commission dealt with such kind of cases on the basis of the legal prohibition of 'direct distinction'.

69 This has recently been affirmed by the government in its memorandum entitled 'Human rights in a pluriform society' (*Regeringsnota 'Grondrechten in een pluriforme samenleving'*), *Parliamentary Documents* II, 2003-2004, 29 614, no. 2, p. 16-17.

70 There has been no case law rendered by the Strasbourg Court with regard to the headscarf in a French legal context. However, the headscarf has been a particularly contentious issue in France which – with reference to the principle of secularism – adopted in 2004 a law banning the Islamic headscarves and other religious symbols from French state schools. See *Loi no. 2004-228 du 15 mars 2004 encadrant en application du principe de laicité, le port the signes ou de tenues manifestant ane appartenance religieuse dans les écoles, collèges et lycées publics.* This law came into effect on 2 September 2004.

approach.[71] The positive neutrality approach is, however, not uncontroversial. In the present author's view, this approach should in principle be adopted in the context of both private and public employment. The positive neutrality approach fosters religious pluralism and parallels with the prevailing social and cultural traditions in the Netherlands.[72] It enables religious employees to exercise their constitutionally protected rights to freedom of religion and non-discrimination. However, positive neutrality should not have governed religious disputes in the context of the courtroom. As Cliteur has rightfully argued, in the courtroom even the *semblance* of partiality should be avoided and therefore, the argument that the Muslim headscarf *may* be impartial, cannot be decisive.[73] It is in this respect that the courtroom fundamentally differs from the classroom in democratic society.

The positive neutrality approach has not been adopted by the ETC in so-called niquab cases. The Muslim niquab fully covers a woman's head and face apart from her eyes. In Opinion 2003-40, the applicants were prohibited by the respondent, a vocational training institution, from wearing the niquab at school. After having established a *prima facie* case of indirect distinction on grounds of religion, the ETC subsequently analysed the question of justifiability. The respondent indicated that the contested prohibition pursued a three-fold aim, namely (1) fostering intra pupil communication; (2) enabling itself to establish every pupil's identity; (3) compliance with the applicable law according to which the school's education must fit in with wider societal needs and according to which pupils needed to be prepared for a job in social life. In the ETC's view, these were all legitimate aims and the vexed prohibition was an appropriate and necessary means for achieving these.

3.3.4.2. Time Off from Work Cases

In the *Sugarfeast* case,[74] decided by the Dutch Supreme Court, the Muslim applicant requested a day off from work in order to celebrate the Islamic Sugarfeast. The applicant had been refused by her employer to take the requested time off. In spite of this, she did not appear at work and as a consequence of this, she was summarily dismissed. The question arose as to whether the right to religious freedom, secured by Article 6 of the Constitution and by Article 9 ECHR,[75] brings with it that an applicant's request for time off from work in order to celebrate a religious feast must in principle be respected by the employer. The Supreme Court answered this question in the affirmative.[76] In the Court's view, in circumstances such as these in the case at hand, an employee's presence at work cannot in reasonableness be required, provided

71 Loenen 2001, p. 586.
72 This point is emphasised, for the adoption of the 'positive neutrality approach' would be ill-fitted in other States in Europe whose socio-cultural and historical traditions have developed quite differently. This point will be taken further in the analysis to follow.
73 Cliteur 2002, p. 97.
74 HR 30 Maart 1984 *NJ* 1985, 350.
75 It should be noted that the GETA only entered into force in 1994. This Act could therefore not be relied upon.
76 Also Opinion 1999-49 of the ETC.

that the request was made in time and well-reasoned. In summary, according to *Sugarfeast,* the employer is in principle required to allow a religious employee a day off from work in order to celebrate a religious feast, unless this would (seriously) obstruct the continuation of the work process.

The case is interesting, not only as to its material outcome, but also in view of the fact that constitutional and human rights guarantees percolated a lawsuit between private individuals. In other words, the right to freedom of religion, protected by the Constitution and by international human rights law, effectively 'coloured' open norms of private employment law, such as the notions of 'reasonableness' and 'urgent reasons' for dismissal. It will be seen in the analysis hereafter that the approach adopted by the Dutch Supreme Court differs from the one adopted by the ECtHR (and the Commission) and the English courts in comparable cases. Arguably, as far as English law is concerned, this may be explained with reference to the lack of a written Constitution in English law and the pivotal role of the freedom of contract.[77] The Dutch ETC has adopted a similar stance to the one adopted by the Supreme Court in the *Sugarfeast* case. For example, in Opinion 99-49, the Commission took the view that the employer's request that all employees were to be present at work on a Friday afternoon constitutes unlawful indirect religious distinction, given the need for (some) Muslim workers to visit the Mosque on Friday afternoons. Hence, via the concept of indirect distinction the different needs of Muslim workers were effectively accommodated. This case can, however, be contrasted with the outcome in Opinion 97-23. In that case, the ETC held that the employer's interest in the continuity of the production process may trump the right of the employee to pray at work, depending on the particular circumstances of the case at hand.

3.3.4.3. The Employee's Refusal to Perform Certain Duties of the Job

Religious disputes at work have also arisen out of a refusal by an employee to carry out certain duties attached to the job, or, by an insistence on the part of the employer that the job is performed under certain conditions imposed by the employer. In Opinion 2005-31, the ETC was asked to give its opinion on the following.

The applicant was a trainee nurse and the respondent a hospital. For reasons related to her religion the applicant refused to comply with the requirement that she be vaccinated against Hepatitis B. The respondent consequently refused to enter into an employment relationship. The question was whether the respondent's vaccination policy resulted in an unlawful distinction on grounds of religion. The ETC first established that the refusal to comply with the vexed vaccination policy was covered by 'religion' as a protected ground.[78] In line with earlier authorities, it thereupon analysed the complaint on the basis of the legal prohibition of indirect distinction.[79] The

77 This point will be considered in further detail in section 4.3 to follow.

78 See also, for example, Opinion 2000-13, in which the Commission held that the refusal by a (trainee) nurse to cooperate in carrying out an abortion, or in carrying out euthanasia, may be perceived as a direct expression of the applicant's religion or belief.

79 See Opinions 2003-09 and 2003-10 which, respectively, concerned the refusal by a nurse, and a nurse to be, to get vaccinated against Hepatitis B. In contrast with the case discussed in the →

Commission concluded a *prima facie* instance of indirect distinction, given that the vexed policy disproportionately affected those who for religious reasons could not comply with it. It then went on with a consideration of 'justifiability'. Accordingly, it considered (1) whether the respondent's aim was legitimate, whether it corresponded with a real need, and whether it was free from any discriminatory purpose; (2) whether the means chosen to reach the objectives pursued were appropriate; (3) whether the necessity requirement was met. The latter demands that the objective(s) pursued cannot be reached with other, non- or less discriminatory, means (i.e. 'subsidiarity'), and that the means chosen stand in a proportionate relationship to the objective(s) pursued (i.e. 'proportionality').[80]

The aims pursued by the respondent were three-fold: (a) to protect the applicant from getting infected with Hepatitis B; (b) to protect patients from getting similarly so infected; (c) to avoid financial liability for infection of patients and/or personnel. According to the ETC, all of these aims were legitimate aims and the contested requirement was an appropriate means for achieving these. However, the vexed requirement did not pass the necessity test. The ETC considered it of importance that Dutch law does not impose vaccination obligations upon hospitals. Hence, argued the Commission, 'the legislator and medical experts apparently considered individual interests and objections more important than striving for maximum prevention'. On the basis of medical expert evidence the Commission drew the conclusion that the first and second mentioned aims could be pursued by alternative means (namely by periodical check-ups) which would not be in tension with the applicant's religion. Given that already employed staff were allowed to use the alternative methods, if they objected against vaccination, the Commission concluded that these means were, albeit not an optimal, an adequate alternative to vaccination. All in all, it was concluded that the extra degree of protection, which would be achieved with the respondent's vaccination requirement, was outweighed by the applicant's right to equal treatment. In respect of the respondent's aim to minimise financial liability, the Commission repeated its case law that financial considerations cannot by themselves constitute an objective justification. Moreover, it emphasised that the respondent was not obliged to offer a further degree of protection to patients than was required under national law. However, if it did decide to go further than that, it would have to act within the limits of the law, including equal treatment law.

The case law discussed above shows that the Dutch ETC adopts a strict scrutiny test in its assessment of cases of (*prima facie*) religious discrimination. The objective justification test designed by the ECJ in its case law on indirect sex discrimination has been extrapolated by the Commission to cases concerning indirect religious discrimination. It is argued that, in the context of private employment, the ECJ should adopt the same strict judicial stance. However, the cogency of this reasoning cannot easily be extrapolated to the much more sensitive and complex context of public

main text, the respondents in Opinions 2003-09 and 2003-10 were nursing homes, rather than a hospital. The hospital in Opinion 2005-31 had argued that the risk of infection is higher in a hospital than in a nursing home.

80 Paragraph 5.6. of Opinion 2005-31.

employment (or the public sphere more generally), given the highly divergent and long-standing traditions across Europe on the meaning of 'secularism'. This point will be elaborated on in further detail below in the context of a discussion of relevant case law arisen under the Strasbourg Convention.

3.3.5. Headscarf Cases before the Strasbourg Court

As will be illustrated below, the principled judicial stance adopted by the Dutch ETC in Muslim headscarf cases is very much different from the judicial way of reasoning by the Strasbourg Court in comparable cases. These divergent judicial approaches can be explained with reference to the different legal mandates of the Dutch ETC (and Dutch courts), on the one hand, and the Strasbourg Court, on the other. Neither the Dutch ETC/courts, nor the Strasbourg Court operate in a judicial vacuum and their respective judicial roles must be perceived in context. Thus, whereas the ETC and the Dutch courts apply and interpret Dutch equal treatment law in the context of a tradition of multiculturalism and tolerance, the Strasbourg Court has the task of determining whether a State Party to the Convention has violated a Convention right or freedom. In doing so, the ECtHR may not disregard the absence or the existence of a 'common ground' across the different States Parties to the Convention with regard to, for example, the proper role of religion in the public sphere. Depending on the existence or not of a European consensus on this and related matters, the ECtHR may grant a wider, or narrower, margin of appreciation to the State involved in judicial proceedings. The Strasbourg Court renders its case law pretty much on a case by case basis, whereby due attention is paid to the particular circumstances of the case at hand.[81] Especially when complicated questions are at stake, such as the question over the proper relationship between the State and the Church in a democratic society, the Court has shown a great degree of judicial restraint. In cases concerning the Muslim headscarf, the Court has attached great importance to the role of religion in public life in the particular State involved in judicial proceedings. Thus, writes Fahlbeck, '(…) at least to some extent, the Convention allows countries to fashion their response to religion and religious manifestations according to their basic notions of what constitutes a democratic society'.[82] In other words, the ECtHR has acknowledged that religious traditions in the States Parties to the Convention fundamentally differ from one another. This point is vital to bear in mind in the discussion of the case law hereafter. The most recent case on the Muslim headscarf is that of *Leyla Sahin v. Turkey* rendered by the Grand Chamber (GC) in 2005.[83] The applicant was a female Turkish student who enrolled at the Faculty of Medicine at Istanbul University. For religious reasons she felt compelled to wear the scarf. As a result of this she was denied access to university examinations and lectures. In 2004, the ECtHR's Fourth Section had unanimously held that the ban on headscarves by

81 Fahlbeck 2004, p. 53.

82 Fahlbeck 2004, p. 33.

83 *Leyla Sahin v. Turkey*, 44774/98, 10 November 2005 (ECtHR GC) available at <www.echr.coe.int/echr>. The ECtHR (Fourth Section) rendered its judgment in the case of *Leyla Sahin v. Turkey*, 44774/98, 29 June 2004 (ECtHR) available at <www.echr.coe.int/echr>.

institutions of higher education did not constitute a violation of Article 9 ECHR.[84] The case was subsequently referred to the GC. By 16 votes to 1 the Court held that there had been no violation of Article 9 of the Convention and of Article 2 of Protocol No. 1.[85] It held unanimously that Articles 8 and 10 had not been breached and that there had been no violation of Article 14 of the Convention. In respect of the Article 9 claim the Court considered as follows. It first held that the ban on headscarves in universities constituted an interference with Article 9 of the Convention which was, however, prescribed by law and which pursued the legitimate aims of protecting the rights and freedoms of others and of protecting public order. It clearly followed from the facts of the case, and notably from the historical circumstances, that the principle of secularism, which in Turkey has constitutional status, was the paramount rationale underpinning the contested ban. Moreover, the ban was premised upon the principle of gender equality. The legal analysis focused on the question whether the ban was 'necessary in democratic society'? With reference to established case law the Court *inter alia* clarified that Article 9 does not protect every act that is inspired by a person's religion or belief.[86] On the basis of earlier authorities, it was moreover held that the State's duty of neutrality and impartiality is not compatible with any power, vested on the part of the State, to assess the legitimacy of religious beliefs or the particular ways in which those are expressed.[87] Moreover, in the Court's view, the State has a duty to ensure mutual tolerance between opposing groups.[88] The Court subsequently emphasised the impossibility of discerning throughout Europe a uniform perception as to the proper role of religion in society.[89] Hence, held the Court,

> '(...) the meaning or impact of the public expression of a religious belief will differ according to time and context [and] [r]ules in this sphere will consequently vary from one

84 In the Court's view no separate issues had arisen under Articles 8 and 10 of the Convention (protecting, respectively, the right to private life and the right to freedom of expression), Article 14 taken together with Article 9 ECHR, and Article 2 of Protocol No. 1 to the Convention (protecting the right to education).

85 With a concurring opinion of judges Rozakis and Vajic and a dissenting opinion of judge Tulkens. Judges Rozakis and Vajic disagreed with the approach adopted by the majority, namely that a separate analysis of Article 2 Protocol No. 1 was called for. Judge Tulkens' dissenting opinion will be considered in the main text above.

86 Paragraph 105 of the judgment with reference to earlier case law in *Kalac v. Turkey*, [1997], 01 July 1997, Reports of Judgments and Decisions 1997-IV, p. 1209, paragraph 27; *Arrowsmith v. UK*, 7050/75, [1978] (12 October 1978) 19 DR 5 (CD); *C v. the United Kingdom*, 10358/83, 15 December 1983 DR 37, 142 (CD); *Tepeli and Others v. Turkey*, 31876/96, 11 September 2001.

87 Paragraph 107 of the judgment with reference to *Manoussakis and Others v. Greece*, 26 September 1996, *Reports 1996 IV*,1365, paragraph 47; *Hassan and Tsaouch v. Bulgaria*, 30985/96 ECHR 2000-XI, paragraph 78 (GC); *Refah Partisi and Others v. Turkey*, nos. 41340/98, 41342/98, 41343/98, 41344/98 ECHR 2003 II, paragraph 91 (GC).

88 Paragraph 107 of the judgment with reference to *United Communist Party of Turkey and Others v. Turkey*, 30 January 1998, *Reports* 1998-I, paragraph 57 and *Serif v. Greece*, no. 38178/97, ECHR 1999-IX, paragraph 53.

89 Paragraph 109 of the judgment with reference to its earlier judgment in *Otto Preminger Institut v. Austria*, 20 September 1994, Series A, no. 295-A, p. 19, paragraph 50.

> country to another according to national traditions and the requirements imposed by the need to protect the rights and freedoms of others and to maintain public order'.[90]

Interestingly, this conclusion was reached after a detailed comparative law analysis of the various traditions across Europe regarding the proper place of the Islamic headscarf in State education.[91] In light of the absence of a 'common ground' a comparatively wide margin of appreciation was afforded to the Turkish State. This being the case, the Court's assessment was limited to a marginal 'European supervision' as to whether the measures taken at the domestic level 'were justified in principle and proportionate'. Hence, no strict scrutiny test was carried out in the case at hand which illustrates that 'religion' is not always regarded a 'suspect' ground of discrimination.[92] In the Court's view, upholding the principle of secularism may be regarded as necessary to protect the democratic system in Turkey.[93] In other words, upholding this principle by way of banning the Muslim headscarf from public life did not transcend the legal boundaries of Article 9 of the Convention. In deciding so, much attention was paid to the specific historical background against which this principle was to be understood in the particular case of Turkey.[94] Moreover, attention was paid by the Court to the existence of extremist political movements in Turkey which, it was stated, 'seek to impose on society as a whole their religious symbols and conception of a society founded on religious precepts'.[95] This, I submit, is a particularly dangerous modus of reasoning, for it insinuates that the individual applicant herself held fundamentalist views whereas nothing in the case upheld such a conclusion.[96]

With regard to the principle of gender equality, with which the Islamic headscarf was allegedly in tension, the Court referred to the (shallow) legal analysis adopted by the Court in its 2004 judgment in the same case. It was thus repeated that the principle of gender equality is one of the key principles underpinning the Con-

90 Paragraph 109 of the judgment with reference to *Dahlab v. Switzerland* [2001] ECHR 42393/98 (ECtHR) (decision on admissibility) and *Wingrove v. the United Kingdom*, 25 November 1996, *Reports* 1996-V, p. 1957, paragraph 57.

91 The comparative law analysis was made in paragraphs 55-65 of the judgment. The Court looked at the situation in Turkey, Azerbaijan, Albania, France, Belgium, Austria, Germany, the Netherlands, Spain, Sweden, Switzerland, the UK, Finland, Czech Republic, Greece, Hungary, Poland and Slovakia. With regard to the last four mentioned countries, it concluded that the Islamic headscarf did not yet appear to have given rise to any detailed legal debate.

92 This can, however, be contrasted with the Court's strict scrutiny test in *Hoffman*, ECHR 23 June 1993, Series A, Vol. 255-C (ECtHR) in which it held that '(...) a distinction based essentially on a difference in religion alone is not acceptable' (paragraph 36) and cited and commented upon by Gerards 2004a, p. 55.

93 Paragraph 114 of the judgment.

94 See paragraphs 30-35 of the judgment. On the basis of the historical analysis it was *inter alia* emphasised that the Turkish Republic (founded in 1923) was founded on the premise that the State must be secular (*laik*), which brings with it that the public sphere and the religious sphere must clearly be separated.

95 See paragraph 115 of the judgment.

96 See also the dissenting Opinion by Jugde Tulkens, paragraph 10, who rightfully criticised the majority on this point. Also Verhey 2004, p. 753.

vention. For obscure and thus unconvincing reasons the Court considered the Muslim headscarf incompatible with the principle of gender equality[97] notwithstanding the absence of any evidence that the applicant was wearing the scarf against her own free will. This point was also stressed by Judge Tulkens' dissenting Opinion, in which she *inter alia* held that

> '(...) wearing the headscarf has no single meaning; it is a practice that is engaged in for a variety of reasons. It does not necessarily symbolise the submission of women to men and there are those who maintain that, in certain cases, it can even be a means of emancipating women'.[98]

It appears to the present author that prohibiting a Muslim woman from wearing the headscarf in the absence of any evidence that she is *forced* to do so (and would thus merely serve the (fundamentalist/patriarchal) ends of others) constitutes an infringement upon her identity as a *Muslim woman*.[99] A similar stance has *inter alia* also been defended by Alibhai-Brown who has opined as follows: 'What critics of Islam fail to understand is that when they see a young woman in a hijab [Muslim headscarf; MG] she may have chosen the garment as a mark of her defiant political identity and also as a way of regaining control over her body'.[100] A headscarf ban constitutes a breach with a chosen life style and fosters patterns of assimilation. Moreover, as observed by Judge Tulkins,

> '(...) by accepting the applicant's exclusion from the University in the name of secularism and equality, the majority have accepted her exclusion from precisely the type of liberated environment in which the true meaning of these values can take shape and develop'.[101]

In other words, banning the scarf bears the danger of leaving a backlash effect on the principle of gender equality, for it entails the risks that women become excluded from mainstream education and jobs.[102] In all, Judge Tulkens' dissenting opinion is not only convincing but also reflects a nuanced approach to the sensitive issues at stake.

But for the dissenting judge, the Strasbourg Court in *Leyla Sahin* took the view that Article 9 ECHR had not been breached. A similar conclusion was reached in respect of the complaint under Article 2 of Protocol No. 12, which secures the right

97 See also the earlier case *Dahlab v. Switzerland* [2001] ECHR 42393/98 (ECtHR). This case will be discussed in the main text to follow.

98 See paragraph 11 of her dissenting Opinion.

99 See also Marshall 2006, p. 459, who in this context has emphasised the equality in difference paradigm: '(..) upholding a form of equality that acknowledges differences amongst people, including their cultural identity and religious beliefs, rather than insisting they somehow be the same, is also a conception of equality: indeed some would say a more meaningful one.'

100 Y. Alibhai-Brown(2000), WHO do WE THINK we ARE?, p. 246 cited by Baroness Hale of Richmond in the case of R (on the application of Begum (by her litigation friend, Rahman (Respondent) v. Headteacher and Governors of Denbigh High School (Appellants) [2006] UKHL 15 of 22 March 2006, paragraph 94 of the judgment.

101 Paragraph 19 of her dissenting opinion.

102 See also Marshall 2006, p. 460, who has argued that the consequences and impact of a headscarf ban on women's life in practice must at least be examined before rendering a judgment.

to education. In the view of the GC, the analysis of the case with respect to the right to education could not be divorced from the conclusion reached by the Court in respect of the Article 9 ECHR claim. It was moreover held that Article 14, either alone or taken together with Article 9 of the Convention, had not been breached: '(…) the reasons which led the Court to conclude that there has been no violation of Article 9 of the Convention (…) incontestably also apply to the complaint under Article 14 (…).'

The GC's judgment in *Leyla Sahin* comes as no surprise. In *Karaduman v. Turkey*[103] (a Commission decision) a Turkish student was informed by Ankara University that a degree certificate would only be issued to her, if she submitted a photograph of herself without wearing the headscarf. In the Commission's view the applicant's rights under Article 9 ECHR had not been interfered with:

> 'By choosing to pursue her higher education in a secular university a student submits to those university rules, which may make the freedom of students to manifest their religion subject to restrictions as to place and manner intended to ensure harmonious existence between students of different beliefs.'

The Court equally decided against the applicant in the case of *Dahlab v. Switzerland.*[104] In that case the applicant was a primary school teacher who had converted to Islam and who began wearing the headscarf in a Swiss public school. In the Court's view the vexed prohibition was compatible with Article 9 of the Convention largely with reference to the principles of secularism (which in Switzerland has constitutional force) and gender equality. In the Court's view the Islamic headscarf is 'hard to square' with the latter principle. In deciding as it did, particular attention was paid to the young age of the children (they were between 4-8 years old) which allegedly inferred that they were easily influenced. Hence, said the Court, '(…) it appears difficult to reconcile the wearing of an Islamic headscarf with the message of tolerance, respect for others and, above all, equality and non-discrimination that all teachers in a democratic society must convey to their pupils'.[105]

This is a very bold and negative statement from which the Court clearly should have refrained. As argued above, wearing the Islamic headscarf is engaged in for wide-ranging reasons, which may include a genuine desire for emancipation of Muslim women. Secondly, banning the scarf, rather than wearing it, appears to be in conflict with 'the message of tolerance' and 'respect for others', for it denies Muslim women, who *choose* to be veiled the right to religious difference and to their own chosen identity. As emphasised by judge Tulkens' dissenting Opinion in *Leyla Sahin,* 'what is lacking in [the debate on the Muslim headscarf; MG] is the opinion of women, both those who wear the headscarf and those who choose not to'.[106]

It should be stressed that cases equivalent to the one in *Leyla Sahin* can in present times also come before the ECJ in the context of the preliminary reference procedure contained in Article 234 EC. Domestic courts might ask the ECJ whether

103 *Karaduman v. Turkey*, 16278/90, [1993] (3 May 1993) 74 DR 93 (CD)
104 *Dahlab v. Switzerland* [2001] ECHR 42393/98 (ECtHR) (decision on admissibility).
105 See p. 15 of the Court's decision in *Dahlab.*
106 Paragraph 11 of Judge Tulkens' dissenting Opinion in *Leyla Sahin.*

it is, for example, lawful under Community law to prohibit students and/or lecturers from wearing a headscarf in universities, given that the EFD's material scope of application covers employment and vocational training, including university education.[107] In light of the diverse traditions in the Member States with regard to the question regarding the proper relationship between religion and the public sphere, it will be highly interesting to learn how the Luxembourg Court, being a supranational (constitutional) adjudicator, will deal with these and comparable religious disputes. It is improbable that the ECJ will adopt a radically different stance from the one adopted by the Strasbourg Court in equivalent cases, notwithstanding the different judicial mandates of both courts. It can be expected that the Luxembourg Court will address headscarf disputes on the premise of an indirect discrimination analysis allowing itself to examine the justifiability defence. Where disputes over the Islamic headscarf (or other visible religious dress) arise in the context of the public sphere, the Court should adopt a deferent stance leaving a considerable degree of judicial discretion to the national court in the context of assessing 'objective justification'. The Court should do so, notwithstanding its own established case law that the principle of non-discrimination is a general principle of Community law. Most recently, in *Mangold* the Court has reaffirmed this principle in the context of the EFD and the discrimination ground 'age',[108] whereby it explicitly referred to the fact that the principle of equal treatment is secured 'in various international instruments and in the constitutional traditions common to the Member States'.[109] In the *Mangold* case the ECJ adopted a strict proportionality test in its assessment of the lawfulness or not of an instance of discrimination on grounds of age.[110] It has been argued that the Court in *Mangold* gave a 'much sharper contour' to the principle of non-discrimination and that the Court's reasoning in that case 'could clearly apply to the other characteristics listed in Article 13 EC Treaty'.[111] The present author in principle agrees with these viewpoints, however, she does not do so in respect of headscarf disputes in public settings. As the discussion of the case law has clearly shown, there is certainly no common ground across Europe as to the befitting role of religion in public life. It is submitted that any judicial assessment on this role cannot and should not disregard the views prevailing within the Community as a whole. These views are rooted in historical and cultural legacies which are much better appreciated at the domestic level than at the remote level of the Luxembourg Court.

107 The Directive does, however, not apply to primary education and to regular secondary education. See also the following two cases by the ECJ: *Blaizot* (Case 24/86) [1988] ECR 379 and *Gravier* (Case 293/83) [1985] ECR 593.

108 *Mangold v. Helm* (Case C-144/04) of 22 November 2005 available at <http://www.europa.eu.int> paragraphs 74 and 75 of the judgment.

109 Paragraph 74 of the judgment.

110 Paragraph 65 of the judgment. Although the aim pursued by the contested discrimination in *Mangold* was legitimate, the act of discrimination did nonetheless not pass the Court's strictly applied proportionality test. It should be noted that in *Mangold* direct discrimination on grounds of age was at stake. As will be seen in Chapter 9, unlike direct discrimination on other grounds, direct discrimination on grounds of age is susceptible for objective justification.

111 European Anti-Discrimination Law Review, April 2006, p. 46.

3.3.6. Interim Conclusions

In this section an analysis was made of the concepts of direct and indirect discrimination, and reasonable accommodation. This was done with reference to religiously inspired conflicts in the private and public sphere. Given the absence of relevant case law by the ECJ, an excursion was made into Dutch law, as well as into Strasbourg Convention law. Both excursions shed light upon the way in which the various prohibitions of discrimination in the Directive could be employed in the resolution of religious disputes by the ECJ. The discussion illustrated that in the Netherlands the legal prohibitions of direct and indirect discrimination have turned out to be effective means in fostering religious pluralism at work and in schools. The Dutch approach might form a source of inspiration for the ECJ. At the same time, the supranational adjudicator should not disregard divergent socio cultural and historical traditions in the Member States. That States easily differ in their interpretation of 'secularism' became apparent from the discussion of the case law by the ECtHR, whose approach was contrasted with the judicial approach to comparable matters in Dutch law. Divergent judicial stances were explained on the basis of different judicial mandates and in light of different socio-cultural and historical contexts. The principle of 'secularism' surmises that the thorniest religious disputes tend to arise in the context of public life. It has been argued that the ECJ, if called upon to give its legal assessment on religious discrimination issues in public life, notably, ought to adopt a great degree of judicial self-restraint. The Court should act on the basis of subsidiarity and should not for itself determine what the apposite place of religion is in the public sphere of different Member States.

3.4. *Exceptions*

3.4.1. Introduction

Balancing conflicting rights is not a straightforward exercise. The Community legislator has done part of the balancing exercise by inserting a number of lawful exceptions into the EFD. Henceforth, I will discuss two of these exceptions which are of particular importance in the context of the present chapter. These are the exceptions found in Articles 4(1) and 4(2) of the Framework Directive.[112] So far, the ECJ has not given any judgments on the interpretation and application of these Articles. As will become clear, notably Article 4(2) of the Framework Directive is difficult to grasp. Hereafter, it will be argued that judicial interpretations in the Netherlands could set an interpretative benchmark for the ECJ in cases concerning this particular exception in EC religious discrimination law.

112 In this section, I will neither discuss the objective justification exception for cases of indirect discrimination, nor the positive action exception. 'Indirect discrimination', including 'objective justification', was extensively discussed in Chapter 3. 'Positive action' was examined in depth in Chapter 5. I will neither discuss the Article 2(5) EFD exception which concerns an exception for public security and health and the rights and freedoms of others.

3.4.2. Article 4(1) EFD

Article 4(1) of the Directive contains an exception to the prohibition of discrimination on all grounds covered by the Directive, namely religion, belief, sexual orientation, age and disability. It reads as follows:

> '[Notwithstanding the prohibitions of direct and indirect discrimination on any of the grounds covered by the Directive; MG] Member States may provide that a difference of treatment which is based on a characteristic related to any of the grounds referred to in Article 1 shall not constitute discrimination where, by reason of the nature of the particular activities concerned or the context in which they are carried out, such a characteristic constitutes a genuine and determining occupational requirement, provided that the objective is legitimate and the requirement is proportionate.'

The Article 4(1) EFD exception can be relied upon by any employer, including religious employers. In order to rely successfully on this exception, an employer is required to comply with the following three conditions:

1. the difference of treatment must find its basis in a genuine and determining, i.e. 'decisive' occupational requirement. Whether a requirement is 'genuine' and 'determining' has to be assessed on the basis of the particular occupational activities concerned and by looking at the context in which these activities are carried out;
2. the objective(s) pursued by the difference in treatment must be legitimate;
3. the principle of proportionality must be complied with.

It is argued that the combination of 'genuine' and 'determining' in the first condition above, in conjunction with the second and the third conditions, renders the exception in Article 4(1) of the Directive particularly narrow.[113] This exception requires proof of a very tight connection between the work to be performed, on the one hand, and the imposition of a (religious) job requirement, on the other.[114] According to the ECJ, observance of the principle of proportionality requires 'every derogation from an individual right to reconcile, so far as is possible, the requirements of the principle of equal treatment with those of the aims pursued'.[115] In other words, 'proportionality' clearly reduces the permissible scope for making exceptions. Examples which

113 This follows also from Consideration 23 of the EFD which reads as follows: '[Whereas] in very limited circumstances, a difference of treatment may be justified where a characteristic related to religion or belief, disability, age or sexual orientation constitutes a genuine and determining occupational requirement, when the objective is legitimate and the requirement is proportionate. Such circumstances should be included in the information provided by the Member States to the Commission.'

114 See also Vickers 2003, who has drawn the same conclusion in the context of the English implementing legislation.

115 See, for example, *Lommers v. Minister van Landbouw, Natuurbeheer en Visserij* (Case C-476/99) [2002] ECR I-2891, paragraph 39 (in the context of gender equality) and *Mangold v. Helm* (Case C-144/04) of 22 November 2005 available at <www.europa.eu.int>, paragraph 65 (in the context of age equality).

are presumably covered by the exception in Article 4(1) EFD are the function of priests, rabbis and imams.

3.4.3. Article 4(2) EFD

A much more controversial exception is found in Article 4(2) EFD, which provides as follows:

> 'Member States may maintain national legislation in force at the date of adoption of this Directive or provide for future legislation incorporating national practices existing at the date of the adoption of this Directive pursuant to which, in the case of occupational activities within churches and other public or private organisations the ethos of which is based on religion or belief, a difference of treatment based on a person's religion or belief shall not constitute discrimination where, by reason of the nature of these activities or of the context in which they are carried out, a person's religion or belief constitute a genuine, legitimate and justified occupational requirement, having regard to the organisation's ethos. This difference of treatment (...) should not justify discrimination on another ground.
> Provided that its provisions are otherwise complied with, this Directive shall thus not prejudice the right of churches and other public or private organisations, the ethos of which is based on religion or belief, acting in conformity with national constitutions and laws, to require individuals working for them to act in good faith and with loyalty to the organisation's ethos'.

Basically, Article 4(2) EFD maps the legal circumstances in which a religious employer may impose a job requirement upon his employees or future employees. The exception transmits a 'balancing exercise' in the sense that it seeks to weigh the right of religious employers to exercise their freedom of religion, on the one hand, and the right of others not to be discriminated against on a protected ground (e.g. sex, or sexual orientation), on the other.[116] Article 4(2) EFD uses, however, convoluted language and it gives rise to a number of outstanding questions that are likely to be the object of judicial interpretation in future case law by the domestic courts and by the ECJ. These questions will be examined in sections 3.4.3.1-3.4.3.3 hereafter, whereby references will be made to legal approaches and practices in Dutch equal treatment law.

3.4.3.1. The Meaning of 'Religious Ethos'

Unlike Article 4(1) of the Directive, Article 4(2) EFD can only be relied on by employers who act on the basis of a particular religious ethos ('religious employers'). This includes Churches, religious schools, religious hospitals, religious charity organisations, etc. The fact that religious employers can only invoke the exception prompts the following questions: (1) what is meant by 'religious ethos'? (2) Who must determine the meaning of this notion (e.g. the courts, the employer, the State)? (3) Who must determine whether a(n) (future) employee complies with the employer's

116 See in this context also Recital no. 24 of the EFD which reflects the same legal balancing exercise. For a comprehensive account of 'conflicting rights' in the context of the freedom of religion in international human rights law, I refer to Mullaly 1996, p. 480-506.

religious ethos and how must this be done? The Directive remains silent on all of these issues. Therefore, a short excursion will be made hereafter into comparable Dutch law.

Whether or not an institution is founded upon religious or ideological principles is decided on by the Dutch ETC on a case by case basis.[117] According to the ETC, it is primarily for the religious institution itself to establish its religious ethos.[118] The Commission's task is to assess this objectively by having regard to the institution's statutes, and, to what the institution does *in practice* to materialise its founding principles.[119] The ETC moreover verifies whether the institution conducts a consequent policy in order to safeguard its religious or ideological identity.[120] In addition, the ETC insists upon the establishment of a logical link between, on the one hand, the imposition of the contested job requirement, and the institution's religious founding principles, on the other. In Opinion 2003-145, the facts were as follows.

The applicant worked as a photographer for the respondent, a publishing house, which intended to dismiss him. The reason for this was that the applicant was no longer a member of a religious community that considered the Bible and the 3 Forms of Unity as the foundations of its faith. It was not contested by either party that the respondent's intention to dismiss the applicant was by reason of the latter's belief. Moreover, both parties agreed that the intended dismissal constituted a form of (*prima facie*) direct distinction. However, the respondent argued that the intended dismissal could be justified on the basis of Article 5(2) 'a' GETA which permits a religious institution to impose requirements which, having regard to the institution's purpose, are necessary for carrying out the duties attached to a post.[121] The ETC took the view that it was primarily for the institution itself to establish its founding principles as well as its purpose. Moreover, it was in principle for the institution itself to decide what consequences its religious ethos has for the imposition of job requirements. The institution's point of view on this was (merely) subjected to a 'marginal reasonableness test', which meant that the ETC reviewed whether the institution acted with 'reasonableness'.[122] This deferent approach can be explained by the fact that, like Article 4(2) EFD, the equivalent exception in Dutch law seeks to balance two constitutional rights, namely the right to non-discrimination *v.* the right to freedom of religion. In assessing 'reasonableness' the ETC had regard to the institution's Statutes. In addition, the ETC stressed the need for a logical link between the institution's aim to abide by its religious principles, on the one hand, and the

117 *Parliamentary Documents* II, 1990-1991, 22 014, no. 10, p. 21.

118 E.g. Opinion 1999-38 and *Explanatory Memorandum* to the GETA, II, 1990-1991, 22 014, no. 3, p. 18.

119 This follows also from the relevant *Parliamentary Documents* which indicate that, in determining whether or not an institution is founded upon religious or ideological founding principles regard may be had to: the religious employer's 'course of behaviour', statutes, publications and other sources. See *Parliamentary Documents* 1991-1992, no. 10, p. 22.

120 See also *Parliamentary Documents* 1991-1992, no. 10, p. 22 and Gerards and Heringa 2003, p. 105.

121 It should be noted that Article 4(2) EFD seems not to require a nexus between the imposition of the religious requirement, on the one hand, and the performance of the job, on the other.

122 See also *Parliamentary Documents* II, 1990-1991, 22 014, no. 5, p. 51, to which the ETC referred.

imposition of the contested job requirement, on the other.[123] Whether such a link exists must be assessed on the basis of the concrete circumstances of the case at hand.[124] The imposed job requirement must be premised upon a 'consistent and fixed policy' which has to reflect the institution's purpose and its ideological founding principles.[125] It is for the institution to show that this is the case. In the case at hand all these conditions were met. Hence, the relevant exception in the GETA could successfully be relied on.[126]

3.4.3.2. A Genuine, Legitimate and Justified Occupational Requirement

Article 4(2) EFD provides that the occupational requirement which is imposed by a religious employer upon e.g. a job applicant (or an existing employee) must be 'genuine', legitimate' and 'justified'. Unlike Article 4(1) EFD, Article 4(2) of the Directive does not require that the imposition of a job requirement has to be 'determining' for the performance of a particular job. Some scholars have taken the view that the usage of different adjectives in paragraphs 1 and 2 of Article 4(2) EFD, does not reflect a material difference. Hence, writes Thüsing, 'what is genuine, legitimate and justified (Article 4, paragraph 2) is also genuine and determining (Article 4, paragraph 1) and *vice versa*'.[127] One could, however, argue that a 'determining' job requirement is one which is *decisive* in order to effectively perform the job at stake. In practice, this would mean that the scope, granted by the law, to an employer for the imposition of job requirements gets reduced. Simply put: it could be argued that an employer acting under Article 4(2) EFD can more easily discriminate against his employees, than an employer acting under Article 4(1) EFD.[128] It should be noted that unlike Article 4(1) EFD, Article 4(2) of the Directive does not contain a proportionality requirement. It is, however, submitted that *this* difference in legal drafting does not reflect a material difference between both Articles, given that 'proportionality' is a general principle of Community law that should *always* be complied with. Hence, Article 4(2) EFD may arguably not be relied on by, e.g. a Christian hospital which requires its cleaners to be Christian (given that the 'means/end' equation would be disrupted).[129]

At this juncture, it is worth noting that the Dutch GETA (also) contains an exception to the prohibition of distinction which does *not* require the existence of a decisive link between, on the one hand, effective job performance, and the im-

123 See also *Parliamentary Documents* II, 1990-1991, 22 014, no. 5, p. 51, to which the ETC referred.

124 See also *Parliamentary Documents* II, 1990-1991, 22 014, no. 10, p. 21, to which the ETC referred.

125 See also *Parliamentary Documents* II, 1990-1991, 22 014, no. 10, p. 22, to which the ETC referred.

126 See moreover Opinions 1996-118; 1997-25; 1997-105; 1997-138; 1997-147; 1998-38; 2000-64; 2000-67.

127 Thüsing 2003, p. 202.

128 See also House of Lords, *Select Committee on European Union*, Fourth Report, 19 December 2000, available at <http://www.parliament.the-stationery-office.co.uk>.

129 As will be seen immediately below, a similar stance has been taken by the ETC in the context of comparable Dutch law.

position of a religious job requirement, on the other.[130] This exception is contained in Article 5(2)(c) GETA.[131] It provides as follows:

> '[The prohibition of distinction is without prejudice to] the freedom of a private educational establishment to impose requirements on the occupancy of a post which, in view if the establishment's purpose, are necessary for it to live up to its founding principles, although such requirements may not lead to a distinction on the sole grounds of political opinion, race, sex, nationality, heterosexual or homosexual orientation or civil status.'[132]

The above exception embeds the reconciliation of the principle of non-discrimination, on the one hand, and the freedom of religion and of education, on the other.[133] It follows that denominational schools in the Netherlands may impose religious requirements upon their staff which do *not* need to be functional to the effective performance of the job, but which are nonetheless necessary for the school in order to abide by its religious ethos.[134] The Commission's case law[135] shows that the exception in Article 5(2)(c) GETA is approached in the following manner:

1. The institution concerned must be a private educational establishment (i.e. a denominational school).
2. The vexed job requirement must be necessary for the realisation of the establishment's religious founding principles. This means that there must be a direct

130 See also *Explanatory Memorandum* to the GETA, II, 1990-1991, 22 014, no. 3, p. 8 and 17.

131 This must be contrasted with the exception in Article 5(2)(a) GETA which does insist upon a link between the imposed religious requirements and job performance. Article 5(2)(a) GETA can be relied on by institutions which are founded on religious or ideological founding principles. However, Article 5(2)(c) GETA has been reserved for private educational establishments (i.e. denominational schools). It should be noted that Article 7(2) GETA moreover contains an exception, equivalent to the one found in Article 5(2)(c) GETA, but which applies in the context of education (rather than employment). Therefore, Article 7(2) GETA applies in cases regarding the entrance of pupils to denominational schools.

132 In contrast to Article 4(2) EFD, which can be relied on by all religious employers, Article 5(2)(c) GETA can only be relied on by private educational establishments (i.e. by denominational schools).

133 Freedom of education is protected by Article 23 of the Dutch Constitution. It *inter alia* secures the freedom of private individuals to establish denominational schools and to receive financial funding from the state for that purpose, and, the right to permeate an ideological or a religious vision in the education offered by the school (See Zoontjens 2003, p. 59-60). It follows from the Parliamentary history to the GETA that freedom of education also entails the right of denominational schools to impose requirements upon a person's conduct outside the premises of the school (See *Explanatory Memorandum* to the GETA, II, 1990-1991, 22 014, no. 3), provided that the legal conditions set by Article 5(2)(c) are met. These conditions will be discussed in the main text to follow. Article 23 of the Constitution also provides that public schools, in contrast to private denominational schools, must have due respect for everybody's religion. The way 'neutrality' has been conceived of in the social and legal context in the Netherlands has been outlined earlier on in the analysis.

134 Also *Parliamentary Documents* to the GETA, 1991-1992, 22 014, no. 5, p. 83 and *Explanatory Memorandum* to the GETA, II, 1990-1991, 22 014, no. 3, p. 18.

135 See, for example, Opinions 2001-09, 2003-145; 2004-168 and 2005-222.

and logical link between the difference in treatment, on the one hand, the institution's religious ethos, on the other. For example, in Opinion 2005-102, a Protestant Christian School imposed a religious requirement upon the applicant, a non-practising Muslim, who had applied for the job of roster-maker. In the ETC's view the 'direct and logical link' between the school's religious ethos, on the one hand, and the imposition of the religious requirement, on the other, could not be established. In assessing this, the ETC avails itself of a 'marginal reasonableness test'.[136]

3. The institution must conduct a consequent policy for the preservation of its religious or ideological identity. This policy must not only exist in form but also in practice.
4. Due regard must be had to the concrete circumstances of the case at hand.
5. The so-called 'sole ground construction' may not be violated. This requirement will be addressed in more detail towards the end of the analysis.

The way in which the Dutch ETC has approached the Article 5(2)(c) GETA exception could arguably operate as an interpretative framework for the interpretation by the ECJ of Article 4(2) EFD, notwithstanding that the latter may be relied on by all religious employers, whereas Article 5(2)(c) GETA can only be invoked by denominational schools (see condition no. 1 referred to above). However, in line with earlier case law in the context of gender[137] and, recently, age,[138] the ECJ is likely to go beyond the adoption of a 'reasonableness test' in favour of a (stricter) 'necessity test' requiring that the imposition of a religious job requirement does not go beyond what is 'appropriate' and 'necessary' in order to attain the (legitimate) objective pursued.

3.4.3.3. The 'Sole Ground Construction' and Conflicting Rights

It is clear from the discussion so far, that Article 4(2) EFD seeks to reconcile freedom of religion, on the one hand, and the principle of non-discrimination, on the other. The same holds true for Articles 5(2)(a) and 5(2)(c) of the Dutch GETA. One of the most thorny questions which may have to be settled by the ECJ, in future case law, is whether a religious employer may lawfully discriminate against an employee, on the basis of the latter's sex, or sexual orientation (or on any other by the EFD forbidden ground).[139] It may be worth noting that this question led to burgeoning dis-

136 See also *Parliamentary Documents* 1991-1992, 22 014, no. 10, p. 23-24. See moreover Opinion 2001-09 in which the ETC explicitly held that it is not its task to intensively review the decision of the opposing party but, in contrast, that its task is merely to review whether the opposing party has reached a reasonable decision (see paragraph 4.6. of the Opinion). A similar view has been taken by the Commission in Opinion 2000-64 (paragraph 4.7.) and in Opinion 1998-38 (paragraph 4.6.) and in Opinion 1997-147 (paragraph 4.6.).

137 See e.g. *Lommers v. Minister van Landbouw, Natuurbeheer en Visserij* (Case C-476/99) [2002] ECR I-2891, paragraph 39.

138 *Mangold v. Helm* (Case C-144/04) of 22 November 2005 available at <www.europa.eu.int>, paragraph 65.

139 It is acknowledged that 'sex' is not covered by the EFD, however, a teleological interpretation of Article 4(2) EFD which stipulates that the difference of treatment should not justify dis- →

cussions in the Dutch Parliament at the beginning of the 1990s when the GETA went through its Parliamentary passage. The wording of Article 4(2) EFD show a rather ambiguous stance with respect to the question just posed. On the one hand, a major restriction appears to be set by Article 4(2) EFD upon the employer's freedom to impose religious requirements, where it provides that '[the difference in treatment (...)] should not justify a discrimination on another ground (apart from religion/ belief)'. This clause seems to support a negative answer to the question posed above, although it is not clear what legal meaning must be attached to the fact that the Directive here uses the verb 'should', whereas at two other junctions in the same Article is employs the verb 'shall'. An affirmative answer to the just-posed question might, on the other hand, be deduced by the ending clause in Article 4(2) EFD which stipulates as follows:

> 'Provided that its provisions are otherwise complied with, this Directive shall [underlining; MG] thus not prejudice the right of churches and other public or private organisations, the ethos of which is based on religion or belief, acting in conformity with national constitutions and laws, to require individuals working for them to act in good faith and with loyalty to the organisation's ethos.'

This is the so-called 'loyalty clause' of Article 4(2) EFD which appears to be in tension with the other requirement, namely that no discrimination should occur on another forbidden ground. Above all, the loyalty clause seems to support the right of, e.g. a Catholic school to refuse to hire a homosexual teacher. In all, Article 4(2) EFD reflects a muddled approach which is arguably the result of a negotiation compromise by the Member States in the process of adoption of the Directive. Arguably, the clause that religious requirements should not justify discrimination on another ground, has been the result of 'bottom up' influence by the Netherlands' government, given that a nearly identical clause is contained in the GETA. According to both Articles 5(2)(a) and 5(2)(c) GETA, the imposition of a religious requirement by, respectively, religious institutions and denominational schools, 'may not result in a distinction on the sole ground of political opinion, race, sex, nationality, heterosexual or homosexual orientation or marital status'. Among Dutch non-discrimination lawyers, this clause is known as the 'sole ground construction' (*enkele feit constructie*). It is contended that the requirement in the EFD that no discrimination should occur on another covered ground, *in conjunction with* the 'loyalty clause' equates to the Dutch 'sole ground construction'. The latter is therefore worth exploring in greater detail. In the context of Dutch equal treatment law, the 'sole ground construction' has been interpreted as meaning that forbidden grounds, other than 'religion' and 'belief' may never constitute an autonomous ('sole') ground for a difference of treatment meted out by a religious employer or by a denominational school. It should, however, be noted that this rule does not apply to the internal affairs of churches (or of other communities/associations of a spiritual nature), nor to the office of minister of

crimination 'on another ground' should secure that 'sex' is also included. The same applies to 'race', which is, however, less likely to be a reason for discriminatory treatment by a religious employer.

religion, for these are altogether exempted from the GETA's scope (Article 3 GETA). It was explicitly stated in the Parliamentary discussions on the GETA that *being homosexual* cannot *in se* form the reason for a difference in treatment by a religious employer/school.[140] Indeed, the aim pursued by the sole ground construction is to eliminate the possibility that *as a matter of fact* a person is discriminated against on grounds of, e.g. sexual orientation *under the guise of* the legal escape-route offered to religious organisations by Articles 5(2)(a) and (c) GETA. However, although sexual orientation cannot *in se* form a ground for a difference in treatment by religious entities, the situation will become different if regard is had to 'concomitant conduct'.[141] This is conduct from which it can be deduced that the person (e.g. a job candidate) concerned *de facto* rejects the religious founding principles of the employer with the effect that his/her functioning in the institution is effectively hampered.[142] It should, however, be emphasised that the ETC has held that 'cohabitation' with a same sex partner *without more* cannot be regarded as constituting 'concomitant conduct'.[143] This is a logical and correct approach. As will be seen in Chapter 7, the right to be free from discrimination on grounds of sexual orientation covers the *forum internum* (i.e. being homosexual) and the *forum externum* (i.e. the right to manifest this, e.g. by cohabitating with a same-sex partner). It follows that homosexual cohabitation cannot *by itself* justify a difference in treatment meted out to a homosexual person by a religious employer. Moreover, if e.g. a religious school *a priori* refuses a homosexual job-applicant, without enabling the latter to express his viewpoints on how to reconcile his homosexuality with the school's religious ethos, this will be tantamount to direct discrimination on grounds of sexual orientation.[144]

Against the background of what was stated before with respect to the 'sole ground construction' in the Dutch GETA, the following comments can be made in respect of Article 4(2) EFD. It is submitted that the tensions which are apparent in the wording of Article 4(2) EFD could be resolved, if the ECJ interprets this exception in the same way as this has been done by the ETC in the context of Dutch law. This would mean that religious employers acting on the basis of Article 4(2) EFD may only discriminate against, e.g. a homosexual person, if the latter has shown express conduct from which it can be concluded that he/she rejects the religious ethos of the

140 *Parliamentary Documents* 1992-1993, I, 22 014 no. 212 c, p. 10-11.

141 *Parliamentary Documents* 1991-1992, II, no. 3, *Explanatory Memorandum*, p. 18-19. Also *Parliamentary Documents* 1990-91, II, 22 014, no. 5, p. 49. See moreover Opinion 1999-38 by the ETC and Gerards and Heringa 2003, p. 105.

142 *Parliamentary Documents* I, 22 014, no. 48a, p. 12. The following example was given in the Parliamentary comments on the GETA. A denominational school has advertised for a teaching position in social studies. Job candidate *x* is homosexual and cohabitates with his same-sex partner. According to the Parliamentary history, the school may legitimately expect the prospective teacher to elaborate on the concept of marriage in his teaching. If *x* refuses to do so, the school may lawfully refuse him for the job. In essence, the reason for the refusal is the candidate's resistance to elaborate on 'marriage', rather than his sexual orientation *in se*. The refusal by *x* to elaborate on marriage constitutes 'concomitant conduct'.

143 Opinion 1999-38.

144 Opinion 1999-38.

employer.[145] This line of reasoning is also supported by observations made by the UK government in a discussion on the scope and the meaning of Article 4(2) EFD. The UK government has suggested that the restriction contained in Article 4(2) EFD, namely that religious requirements may not result in discrimination on another forbidden ground, regards a person's identity, whereas the loyalty clause relates to a person's conduct.[146] However, and as stressed by the Dutch ETC, 'conduct' should go beyond the 'normal' conduct which is inherent to homosexuality, e.g. same-sex cohabitation. By way of conclusion the following could be said. It has been argued that the way in which the 'sole ground construction' has been interpreted in the context of Dutch equal treatment law effectively and fairly balances the right to freedom of religion of religious entities, on the one hand, and the right of others not to be discriminated against on a forbidden ground, on the other. It has been argued that the 'sole ground construction' is latent in the wording of Article 4(2) EFD. In its interpretation of this Article, the ECJ may want to use the Dutch interpretation as a template for judicial reasoning. If the Court does so, the Dutch legal approach will cross-fertilise into the laws of the other Member States. On the other hand, the ECJ might decide to adopt a 'hands-off' (or 'subsidiarity') approach in respect of the judicial interpretation of the Article 4(2) EFD exception and leave the matter for the Member States to decide. The Court might feel induced to do so, in light of diverging approaches across the Member States on how to reconcile freedom of religion with other conflicting rights.

4. Discrimination on Grounds of Religion in English Law: a Comparative Analysis

4.1. *Introduction*

Hereafter, the influence of EC religious discrimination law on English law will be examined (top-down comparison). The EFD's requirements in relation to the grounds religion and belief have been transposed into English law by the R&B Regulations[147] which entered into force on 2 December 2003. The Regulations prohibit discrimination on grounds of religion and belief in the area of employment.[148] The Regulations were adopted on the basis of the 1972 European Communities Act. They constitute

145 It should be noted that requirements which are imposed by, e.g. Churches upon candidates for the function of priest, will have to be based upon the Article 4(1) exception, given that such requirements are 'determining' for the performance of the job concerned.

146 House of Lords, Select Committee on European Union – Fourth Report- 19 December 2000 available at <http://www.parliament.the-stationery-office.co.uk>.

147 See footnote 3 above.

148 It should be noted that the Equality Act 2006, which received Royal Assent on 16-02-06 (but which has not yet entered into force), introduces provisions on religion and belief in relation to the provision of goods, services, facilities, premises and education (See Part II of the Act). As will be illustrated in the main text to follow, the Equality Act 2006 also makes partial amendments to the R&B Regulations. The Equality Act 2006 moreover places a duty upon public sector authorities not to discriminate whilst carrying out their public functions. See also Choudhury 2006, p. 13-17.

one of the modifications to the existing legal framework as required by supranational law.[149] At the outset of this chapter it was noted that prior to the adoption of the R&B Regulations, discrimination on grounds of religion and belief in employment could only be tackled on the basis of the Statutory anti-discrimination framework, if an alleged act of religious discrimination *simultaneously* constituted an act of race or ethnicity discrimination as prohibited by the RRA 1976.[150] Unfortunately, the legal assessment of whether a given religious group also constitutes an ethnic group for purposes of the RRA 1976 has been featured by staunch technicalities. The adoption of a technical legal approach turned out to be detrimental to any teleological interpretation of Statute and has led to arbitrary outcomes. In essence, due to a strict interpretation of the law it has been established in a number of cases that Jews[151] and Sikhs[152] are ethnic groups for purposes of the RRA 1976 to the exclusion, however, of Rastafarians[153] and Muslims.[154] The outcome in these cases shows the drawbacks of an anti-discrimination framework which lacks a coherent legal strategy and which prohibits from discrimination on a limited number of grounds across separate Statutes. It may be worth noting that the Dutch ETC has accepted that discrimination against Rastafarians might in certain circumstances also constitute race discrimination (in addition to discrimination on grounds of religion).[155] Moreover, in Opinion 1998-57 the ETC held that a claim of differential treatment of Muslims can be lodged both on the ground of religion and on the ground of race, depending on the facts of the case at hand.[156] It follows that legal minds may easily differ on whether or not a legal claim can be shoe-horned into already forbidden grounds.[157]

It is clear that the need for bringing religious discrimination disputes within the framework of race relations law has ceased to exist with the adoption of the R&B Regulations. The general structure underpinning the Regulations parallels the one of sex and race discrimination law. As was emphasised in the preliminary issues to Part IV the Regulations must be perceived within the wider context of the ECHR and the 1998 HRA. Hence, whilst interpreting the R&B Regulations, courts and tribunals must pay due attention to any relevant jurisprudence which has emerged on the basis of European human rights law.[158] For the purposes of this chapter the

149 For a general discussion of the modifications to the existing domestic anti-discrimination framework in light of the RD and the EFD, I refer to Bell 2004, p. 465-477.

150 The need for a religious discrimination Act in British law was already considered in the seventies. See, for example, J.A. Robilliard, 'Should Parliament Enact a Religious Discrimination Act'? *Public Law 1978*, p. 379, cited by Thüsing 2003, p. 200, note 42.

151 *Seide v. Gillette Industries Ltd* [1980] IRLR 427 (EAT).

152 *Mandla v. Dowell Lee* [1983] 2 AC 548 (HL).

153 *Crown Suppliers (PSA) Ltd v. Dawkins* [1993] ICR 517 (CA).

154 *J.H. Walker Ltd v. Hussain* [1996] IRLR 11 (EAT).

155 See Opinion 2005-162. In that particular case, however, the ETC merely established *prima facie* indirect discrimination on grounds of religion which could not be objectively justified.

156 The Muslims in the case at hand descended from particular areas and therefore, the 'ethnic origin' aspect was determinative and a case of unlawful race discrimination was established.

157 Burnham and Cohen 2006, p. 5.

158 McColgan 2001, p. 228. See also, Bharania 2004, who has stressed that 'the obligations imposed on the state by [the ECHR] will be a relevant consideration for any court or tribunal'. And further: 'Even if the employer is not an emanation of the state, the courts and tribunals →

relevant ECHR framework was sketched in the foregoing parts and will not be repeated hereafter. However, given the importance of ECHR law in the application and interpretation of domestic law, it will be referred to at appropriate junctures in the upcoming analysis.

4.2. *The Meaning of 'Religion' and 'Belief'*

Similar to the EFD, the R&B Regulations do not contain a definition of the central concepts of 'religion' and 'belief'. Regulation 2(1) merely specifies that 'religion' or 'belief' means any religion, religious belief or similar philosophical belief. Further guidance can be found in the Advisory Conciliation and Arbitration Service (ACAS) guidance on the Regulations. This indicates that whilst assessing the meaning of 'religion' or 'similar belief', courts and tribunals are likely to consider 'things such as collective worship, a clear belief system, a profound belief affecting the way of life or view of the world'.[159] In the literature, it has been called into question whether Regulation 2(1) offers any legal protection to those explicitly denouncing of any religion or belief.[160] In deciding on this question Courts and Tribunals ought to follow the line adopted by the Strasbourg Court in the case of *Kokkinakis v. Greece*[161] in which, it is recalled, the Court held that Article 9 ECHR captures both theists and atheists. This reflects a logical stance, for one of the important roles of religious discrimination law should be to foster a diversity of approaches and to ensure that all, regardless of religion and belief, can work in dignity. In light of this it should not matter whether an act of discrimination is inspired by a person's religion or belief, or by the absence thereof. The intention to embrace atheists and other godless persons within the notion of 'similar philosophical belief' has also been expressed by the government in a debate in the House of Lords.[162] Any further doubt on this question has been taken away by the new definition of religion and belief introduced by the 2006 Equality Act which, once the Act enters into force,[163] will replace the existing definition in the Regulations. The new definition specifies that 'religion' means any religion' and that 'a reference to religion includes a reference to lack of

will have to interpret the Regulations under the Human Rights Act with the Article 9 [ECHR] jurisprudence in mind.'

159 The ACAS guidelines are available at <www.acas.org.uk/publications/pdf/religion/pdf>.

160 See, for example, Rubenstein 2003, p. 23: 'The definition refers to discrimination on grounds of religion or belief and it must be questionable whether this covers an absence of religion or belief, unless that takes the form of a positive philosophical belief such as atheism, agnosticism or humanism.'

161 *Kokkinakis v. Greece,* 14307/88 [1993] ECHR 20 (25 May 1993) (ECtHR). This case has been discussed earlier on in the analysis.

162 Hansard, HL, vol 649, col 786 (17 june 2003) and Hansard, HL, Vol. 649, col 792 (17 june 2003) both referred to by De Marco 2004, p. 13.

163 It is currently not yet clear when the Equality Act 2006 will enter into force. It will probably enter into force at different times for different parts. Ministerial orders are issued to declare when specific parts enter into effect. I am grateful to Dr. Mark Bell for providing me with this information.

STELLINGEN

Behorende bij het proefschrift van M.H.S. Gijzen

Selected Issues in Equal Treatment Law:
A Multi-Layered Comparison of European, English and Dutch Law

(1) Artikel 13 van het EG Verdrag, alsmede de uitspraak van het HvJEG in de zaak C-144/04 *Mangold t. Helm*, Jur. 2005, I-9981 vormen een weerspiegeling van een opkomend geconstitutionaliseerd gelijkheidsprincipe in de Communautaire rechtsorde.

(2) De introductie in het EG recht van de nieuwe discriminatiegronden vervat in Artikel 13 EG heeft ertoe geleid dat het concept van indirecte discriminatie thans berust op het *individual justice* in plaats van het *group justice* model. Deze verschuiving doet afbreuk aan de theoretische fundering van het concept zelf.

(3) Hoewel de *top-down* invloed van Europees op nationaal recht ten goede komt aan de coherentie van het recht *tussen* de lidstaten kan het een corrosief effect hebben op de eenheid van het recht *in* de lidstaten.

(4) In de beslechting van hoofddoekjeszaken die zich voordoen in een publieke context dient het HvJEG juridische terughoudendheid te betrachten; wat de toepasselijke verhouding is tussen godsdienst en Staat dient beantwoord te worden door de nationale constitutionele rechter die beter dan de supranationale rechter in staat is het geschil in zijn historische, maatschappelijke en culturele context te plaatsen.

(5) Het relatieve of comparatieve gelijkheidsmodel ondermijnt het vermogen van het gelijkheidsbeginsel om te fungeren als een *social engineering* mechanisme.

(6) Een recht op gratis kinderopvang bevordert niet slechts gelijkheid tussen de seksen, maar is tevens economisch efficiënt.

(7) De wijze van distributie van de subsidies onder het Europees landbouwbeleid doet geen recht aan een materiële gelijkheidsgedachte.

(8) Het pleidooi voor volledige vestiging van het Europees Parlement in Brussel heeft niets van doen met een ongelijke behandeling van Frankrijk, maar berust bovenal op het democratiebeginsel.

(9) Een goed begin is niet het halve werk.

(10) Dat de discussie over *global warming* is losgebroken tegen het einde van de koude oorlog wekt geen bevreemding.

Duty of accommodation - p294

Headscarf debate in Netherlands - p297

'Sole ground' + relig orgns discrim on grnds of S.O. p315.

Read chapter in conjunction w UK chapter + Europe comparison

religion'. This definition applies *eo ipso* for the ground 'belief'.[164] In all, the Regulations appear to cover traditionally accepted religions (Christianity, Islam, Judaism, Hinduism, etc), more 'unconventional' faiths and religious cults (e.g. Zoroastrianism, Rastafarianism), those adhering to a 'similar philosophical belief' (such as for example pacifists, humanists),[165] as well as non-believers (such as atheists and the unconcerned). In contrast, mere political beliefs fall outside the scope of the Regulations (e.g. communism and fascism). Lastly, in light of Article 9 ECHR, domestic religious discrimination law must offer protection both to discrimination on grounds of having a belief (*forum internum*), and on grounds of manifesting such a belief (*forum externum*). As discussed before this is also the applicable approach in the context of Dutch law.

4.3. *Aspects of Direct and Indirect Discrimination*

Similar to the RRA and SDA,[166] the R&B Regulations *inter alia* contain a legal prohibition of direct and indirect discrimination on grounds of religion and belief. Like the EFD, the Regulations also prohibit religious related harassment. What was stated before in sections 3.3.2 and 3.3.3 on, respectively, direct and indirect discrimination also applies in the context of English law, although it is currently not clear how both prohibitions of discrimination will be applied by the courts in concrete cases. At the time of writing no judicial authorities exist on direct or indirect religious discrimination law, or on harassment. In addition to what was stated earlier in the context of EC law a number of specific issues and peculiarities regarding the various concepts of discrimination in the context of the R&B Regulations deserve our attention at this juncture. A first point concerns the relationship between direct discrimination and the instruction to discriminate. The latter is prohibited by Article 1(4) EFD. The prohibition of instruction to discriminate has not, however, been transposed into the R&B Regulations. This gap is, however, filled by existing case law which has arisen in the fields of race and sex discrimination law. It is submitted that *Showboat*[167] must be the applicable legal authority, in order to cover the prohibition of instruction to discriminate.

In *Showboat* the alleged victim had refused to comply with racially based instructions given by the employer. In essence, he had been instructed to exclude blacks from the entertainment centre. In the absence of an explicit provision in the RRA 1976 prohibiting from the instruction to discriminate, the EAT considered the case on the basis of Section 1(1)(a) RRA 1976. This contains the prohibition of direct discrimination. It provides that 'person discriminates against another in any circum-

164 'Belief' means any religious or philosophical belief. A reference to belief includes a reference 'to lack of belief'. See Section 44 in Part 2 of the Equality Act 2006.

165 See also Rubenstein 2003, p. 23, who has referred to vegetarianism as a possible example of a belief protected by the Regulations.

166 It is recalled from Chapter 2 that the DDA 1995 (as amended) rests upon an asymmetrical framework and therefore deviates in some but not all respects from the legal frameworks of the SDA and the RRA. This point will be considered in further detail in Chapter 8.

167 Showboat Entertainment Centre Ltd v. Owens [1984] IRLR 7 (EAT).

stances relevant for the purposes of any provision of this Act if on racial grounds he treats that other less favourably than he treats or would treat other persons'. The question was, however, whether the rubric 'on racial grounds' *also* captures discrimination against a person, *not* by reason of his own racial features, but by reason of the racial features of others. Adopting a teleological interpretation of Statute, the EAT answered this question in the affirmative. It concluded an instance of unlawful direct race discrimination.

The legal reasoning by the EAT in *Showboat* was subsequently affirmed by the CA in *Weathersfield Ltd v. Sargent.*[168] It was held that Mrs Sargent, a white employee, was discriminated against 'on racial grounds' when she resigned from her job as a reaction to her employer's instruction not to hire vehicles to coloured persons or Asians. Most recently, *Showboat* and *Weathersfield* have been affirmed by the EAT in *Redfearn.*[169] In all, these authorities make clear that the prohibition of direct discrimination is sufficiently ample to capture discrimination on grounds of *another person's* race, sex, religion, etc. including discrimination of a person by reason of his (her) refusal to abide by discriminatory instructions given by the employer.

The prohibition of direct discrimination is contained in Regulation 3 of the R&B Regulations. It specifies as follows:

> 3(1) For the purposes of these Regulations, a person ('A') discriminates against another person ('B') if-
> (a) on grounds of religion or belief, A treats B less favourably than he treats or would treat other persons
> (...)
> 3(2) The reference in paragraph (1) (a) to religion or belief does not include A's religion or belief.

The convoluted formulation in Regulation 3(2) essentially seeks to prevent a person from lodging a complaint on the basis of the R&B Regulations for acts of discrimination which find their source in an aspect of that person's identity, which is *not* related to 'religion' or 'belief' but, for example, to 'sexual orientation' or 'sex' and which clashes with the religion or belief of the alleged perpetrator. Matters can be illustrated on the basis of the following example. A strict Catholic employer refuses to employ a woman whom he knows has undergone an abortion. The woman in question cannot challenge the employer's behaviour under the R&B Regulations, due to the legal restriction contained in Regulation 3(2). She could nonetheless base her claim on the SDA 1975 and argue that the employer's conduct constitutes unlawful direct sex discrimination. It should be noted that, for purposes of clarification, the definition of 'direct discrimination' in the Regulations has been amended by the 2006 Equality Act which provides as follows: 'A person ('A') discriminates against another ('B')

168 *Weathersfield (t/a Van and Truck Rentals) v. Sargent* [1999] IRLR 94 (CA).

169 *Redfearn v. Serco LTD t/a West Yorkshire Transport Service* [2005] IRLR 744. The outcome in this case is rather controversial given that the RRA 1976 offered protection to the applicant, who himself held particularly racist views and who was standing as a candidate for the right-wing British National Party in the forthcoming local elections.

(...) if on grounds of the religion or belief of B, or of any other person except A (...) A treats B less favourably than he treats or would treat others (...)'.[170]

It is clear from these definitions that the concept of direct discrimination rests upon the comparative justice model, for it requires proof of 'less favourable treatment' of one person, relative to another person, who finds herself in a comparable situation. It is submitted that a number of legal authorities, which have been established under the SDA and RRA in relation to the concept of direct discrimination, are likely to be extrapolated to comparable cases that arise under the R&B Regulations. Hence, it has, for example, been established by the House of Lords in a sex discrimination case that the mere deprivation of a person's *choice* constitutes 'less favourable treatment' for purposes of the Statute.[171] It moreover follows from *Simon v. Brimham Associates,*[172] that acts of discouragement may also amount to 'less favourable treatment'. It has further been held by the Law Lords, that motive and intention are no material ingredients for establishing a case of direct discrimination.[173] Lastly, it follows from the case law that direct discrimination is also an effective instrument to address discrimination by way of 'stereotyping'.[174] Stereotyping occurs where a person is discriminated against because of assumptions about the group of persons (defined by, e.g. religion) and to whom the (alleged) victim belongs.

Another point worth mentioning concerns the artificial construction of direct discrimination cases as indirect discrimination cases. According to Regulation 3(1)(B) of the R&B Regulations, indirect discrimination occurs where

> 'A applies to B a provision, criterion or practice which he applies or would apply equally to persons not of the same religion or belief as B, but- (i) which puts or would put persons of the same religion or belief as B at a particular disadvantage when compared with other persons, (ii) which puts B at that disadvantage, and (iii) which A cannot show to be a proportionate means of achieving a legitimate aim.'[175]

170 Section 45 of Part 2 of the Equality Act 2006.

171 *Equal Opportunities Commission v. Birmingham City Council,* [1989] 1 ALL ER 769 (HL). In this case the Equal Opportunities Commission (EOC) challenged the Council's discriminatory allocation of grammar school places. The House of Lords (per Lord Goff) held that in order to establish 'less favourable treatment' the applicant needed not show that grammar school education was *better* (my emphasis) than alternative education. In contrast, the mere deprivation of a person's choice may amount to 'less favourable treatment': '...it is enough that by denying the girls the same opportunity as the boys, the Council is depriving them of a choice which is valued by them, or at least by their parents, and which (...) is a view obviously valued, on reasonable grounds by many others'. The phrase 'on reasonable grounds' reflects an objective interpretation of the notion of 'less favourable treatment'.

172 *Simon v. Brimham Associates,* [1987] IRLR 307 (CA).

173 *James v. Eastleigh Borough Council,* [1990] 2 All ER, 607 (HL). This case was discussed in Chapter 3 in relation to the grounds 'sex' and 'race'.

174 *Solowo-Coker v. Highways Agency* (2001 ET 2300595/00) racial stereotyping amounted to direct discrimination. *Coleman v. Skyrail Oceanic Ltd* [1981] ICR 864 (stereotyping and sex discrimination). See also *Horsey v. Dyfed CC* [1982] ICR 755 (EAT).

175 The notion of indirect discrimination in the context of English law was extensively dealt with in Chapter 3.

It should be noted that the 2006 Equality Act omits the 'proportionality requirement' in the final sentence of the provision and simply states 'which A cannot reasonably justify by reference to matters other than B's religion or belief'.[176] It has been seen in the context of Dutch law that constructing 'direct discrimination cases' as 'indirect discrimination cases' is one of the techniques employed by the ETC to circumvent the rigidities of the 'closed' model of anti-discrimination law. It is likely that, where necessary, English courts and tribunals will also avail themselves of this technique, whilst, e.g. deciding on headscarf cases in the context of the R&B Regulations.

In sections 3.3.4.1 and 3.3.4.2 above I, respectively, outlined the approach adopted in Dutch equal treatment law with respect to religious disputes arising from 'dress-requirements',[177] and from requests for time off from work. Hereafter, I will discuss the legal approach adopted in English law in parallel cases. The analysis hereafter begins with 'time off from work cases', whereby references will also be made to relevant ECHR law. I will subsequently consider disputes over religious dress. It should be emphasised that the English case law to be discussed hereafter has arisen *outside* the context of the R&B Regulations.

Time off from work cases: Ahmad, Stedman, Kosteski and Copsey

The approach adopted by the Dutch Supreme Court in the *Sugarfeast* case (section 3.3.4.2 above) can be contrasted with the legal outcome in parallel cases that have arisen in English law, as well as in ECHR law. In *Ahmad*[178] the facts were as follows.

The applicant was a Muslim schoolteacher who wished to leave 45 minutes earlier from work on Fridays in order to enable him to pray at the Mosque. The employer took the view that Ahmad's contract of employment required him to work on Fridays. The applicant was offered a four and a half days contract with which he, however, disagreed. At the domestic level, the Court of Appeal rejected Ahmad's claim for unfair dismissal by a 2-1 majority (Denning (LJ) and Orr (LJ) judged in favour of the employer and Scarman (LJ) dissented in favour of Ahmad, essentially with reference to a rejection of the formal justice model. In the view of Scarman (LJ) Ahmad had a right to be accommodated.) In deciding on the case within the framework of the ECHR,[179] the European Commission of Human Rights took the view that the applicant's rights under Article 9 of the Convention had not been breached, given that Ahmad had agreed with the conditions of employment including working on Fridays. In addition, the applicant had not complained of this condition or asked for earlier leave on Fridays in the first six years at work. Furthermore, the Commission pointed out that the applicant remained free to resign if and when he found that his teaching duties were in conflict with his religious observance. In

176 It is submitted that this formulation is not in conformity with the concept of 'objective justification' in EC law which clearly does contain a proportionality test (which consists of the elements of 'appropriateness' and 'necessity'). For a further and more detailed analysis, I refer to Chapter 3.

177 See moreover section 3.3.5 which examined so-called 'headscarf cases' decided on by the ECtHR.

178 *Ahmad v. Inner London Education Authority* [1978] 1 All ER 574 [CA].

179 *Ahmad v. UK* (1981) 4 EHRR 126 (CD).

summary: the freedom of contract took precedence over religious freedom. The Commission decided that the case was inadmissible.[180]

The outcome in *Ahmad* is comparable to the one in *Stedman v. UK.*[181]

Mrs Stedman was dismissed by her employer for refusing to work on Sundays. The applicant maintained that her Christian religion prevented her from working on that day of the week. She resigned rather than complying with the request to work. The European Commission of Human Rights took the view that no breach of the Convention had occurred. The dismissal was rooted in the applicant's refusal to abide by the contractual working hours and not in her religious belief. Like in *Ahmad*, the case was ruled to be inadmissible.

Most recently, the modus of legal reasoning adopted in *Ahmad* and *Stedman* was affirmed by the ECtHR in the similar (albeit in various respects distinguishable) case of *Kosteski.*[182]

In casu, the applicant stayed off from work with a view to celebrating a Muslim feast thereby, however, ignoring the instructions of his superior who had prohibited this. The Strasbourg Court held that

> '(...) while it may be that [Mr Kosteski's; MG] absence from work was motivated by the applicant's intention of celebrating a Muslim festival it is not persuaded that this was a manifestation of his beliefs in the sense protected by Article 9 of the Convention or that the penalty imposed on him for breach of contract in absenting himself without permission was an interference with this right'.[183]

In other words, according to the ECtHR in *Kosteski*, an employee's unauthorised absence from work in order to celebrate a religious feast is, in principle, *not* protected under Article 9 of the Convention.[184] This line of reasoning differs from that of the

180 See also *Konttinen v. Finland,* 24949/94 [1996] (03 December 1996) 87-A DR 86 (CD) in which the conclusion was drawn that the applicant's claim was 'manifestly ill founded': 'The Commission recalls that Article 9 primarily protects the sphere of personal convictions and religious beliefs. In addition, it protects acts which are intimately linked to these attitudes, such as worship or devotion which are aspects of the practice of a religion or belief in a generally recognized form (...) the applicant was not dismissed because of his religious convictions but for having refused to respect his working hours. This refusal, even if motivated by his religious convictions, cannot as such be considered protected by Article 9(1). Nor has the applicant shown that he was pressured to change his religious views or prevented from manifesting his religion or belief.' In summary: the view was adopted that the applicant had not been forced to change his religious convictions or prevented from manifesting them: having concluded that his hours of work were in conflict with his religious views, the applicant was free to relinquish his job.

181 *Stedman v. UK* (1997) 23 EHRR 168 (CD)

182 *Kosteski v. the former Yugoslav Republic of Macedonia* EHRC 2006, 73 (with a case comment by Gerards).

183 Paragraph 38 of the Court's judgment. See also *Kalac v. Turkey*, judgment of 1 July 1997, *Reports of Judgments and Decisions* 1997-IV, paragraph 27; *Konttinen v. Finland,* 24949/94 [1996] (03 December 1996) 87-A DR 86 (CD); *Stedman v. UK* (1997) 23 EHRR 168 (CD) to which the Court referred.

184 In addition to the question whether an employee's absence from work for religious reasons constitutes an expression of his or her belief that is protected under Article 9 ECHR, the

→

Dutch Supreme Court in *Sugarfeast* according to which requests for time off from work for religious reasons have in principle to be granted by the employer. This will only be different, if granting the request would seriously disturb the state of affairs at work.

The cases of *Ahmad, Stedman* and *Kosteski* show clear tensions between two important legal values, namely contractual freedom *v.* the freedom of religion. Essentially, it follows from these cases that an employee cannot claim a breach of his right under Article 9 of the Convention when he has accepted by his own will to enter into a contractual agreement with his employer. In the present author's view, the legal outcomes in the aforementioned three cases reflect an artificial approach. Obviously, the refusal by a religious employee to abide by his (her) contractual working hours is inherently grounded in the basic tenets of his (her) religion (although, admittedly, this was less clear-cut in the *Kosteski* case).[185] In other words, such a refusal cannot reasonably be *detached* from the applicants' religion and belief. Furthermore, the decisions in these cases are difficult to reconcile with the fundamental character of the freedom of religion, the exercise of which was *de facto* made dependent upon the acceptance by the applicants to quit their work (or to pay a disciplinary fine).

The last case to be mentioned in the present context is the case of *Copsey v. WWB Devon Clays Ltd.*[186]

Kosteski case concerned the vexed issue of having to *prove* one's religion, as condition for legal protection from discrimination. The employer, as well as the domestic courts, had cast serious doubts on Mr Kosteski's claim that he was a citizen of the Muslim faith. Under the applicable law in Macedonia, only citizens of the Muslim faith had the right to have a day off on the *in casu* contested dates. Mr Kosteski was suspected of not being a 'genuine' Muslim by reason of the following: the applicant had been registered as a Macedonian without any mention of being a Muslim; he had moreover celebrated the Christian religious holidays; his parents were (also) Christians and his way of life and diet showed that he was of the Christian faith. Finally, Mr Kosteski had *refused* to substantiate his claim that he was really of Muslim faith. In proceedings before the Strasbourg Court, Mr Kosteski claimed that the requirement of having to *prove* his Muslim faith constituted an interference with his inner sphere of belief and thus a breach of Article 9 of the Convention (as well as Article 9 in conjunction with Article 14 ECHR, given that other Muslim believers were not required to prove their religion). The Court rejected this argument, although it did acknowledge that 'the notion of the State sitting in judgment on the state of a citizen's inner and personal beliefs is abhorrent and may smack unhappily of past infamous persecutions'. However, held the Court, '(...) [it is not unreasonable] that an employer may regard absence without permission (...) as a disciplinary matter. Where the employee then seeks to rely on a particular exemption, it is not oppressive or in fundamental conflict with freedom of conscience to require some level of substantiation when that claim concerns a privilege of entitlement not commonly available and, if that substantiation is not forthcoming, to reach a negative conclusion'. (paragraph 39).

185 See footnote 182 *supra.*

186 *Copsey v. WWB Devon Clays Ltd* [2005] EWCA Civ 932, available at <http://www/bailii.org/ew/cases/EWCA/Civ/2005/932.html>. It should be noted that the judgment in this case was rendered on 25 July 2005, however, the dismissal of the employee had taken place prior to the entering into force of the R&B Regulations and therefore the latter (and neither the EFD itself) could be relied upon. See paragraph 8 of the judgment, in which the CA (per Lord Justice Mummery) made it clear what the case was *not* about. See for a case comment also European Anti-Discrimination Law Review 2006, p. 87.

The applicant, Mr Stephen Copsey, was dismissed by his employer, Devon Clays by reason of his refusal to work on Sundays. The applicant had made it clear to his employer that by reason of his Christian faith he was prevented from working on Sundays on a regular basis, although he would be prepared to help his employer on Sundays in a case of emergency. The applicant claimed that he was dismissed for a reason related to his religious beliefs, contrary to Article 9 ECHR. This view was contested by the employer, who argued that Mr Copsey had been dismissed by his refusal to agree to a contractual variation in his hours with the effect that he would work 7 days a week, including Sundays, if necessary. The applicant brought proceedings for unfair dismissal under the 1996 Employment Rights Act. The question was what impact Article 9 of the ECHR possibly had upon the alleged unfair dismissal claim by Mr Copsey against his private employer. The ET and the EAT had decided against Mr Copsey by holding that the dismissal was fair in the circumstances of the case at hand.[187] The views expressed by the ET and the EAT were subsequently upheld by a unanimous Court of Appeal. It was essentially held that the decisions by the European Commission of Human Rights in *Ahmad* and *Stedman* and *Konntinen*[188] needed to be continued to be applied by employment tribunals, until these cases are overruled by the Strasbourg Court or by the House of Lords, notwithstanding that all three judges in the Court of Appeal showed themselves to be concerned about the Commission's stance in these cases. Thus, as Lord Justice Mummery opined in paragraph 35 of the judgment:

> 'the rulings are difficult to square with the supposed fundamental character of the rights. It hardly seems compatible with the fundamental character of Article 9 [ECHR] that a person can be told that his right has not been interfered with because he is free to move on, for example, to another employer, who will not interfere with his fundamental right, or even to a condition of unemployment in order to manifest the fundamental right'.

However, it was also held that even if it were accepted that the applicant's complaint fell within the ambit of Article 9(1) ECHR, the dismissal would have been justified under paragraph 2 of that same Article:

> 'Devon Clays had compelling economic reasons which made it necessary to change the working practices of its workforce to a 7 day shift. The alternatives to dismissal were fully explored with Mr Copsey. No sensible alternative to dismissal could be found. The Tribunal found that Devon Clays had done everything that they could to accommodate Mr Copsey's wish not to work on Sundays. In such circumstances the tribunal would be entitled to conclude that the dismissal was justified.'[189]

[187] See paragraphs 17 and 18 ('decision of the employment tribunal') and 19-21 ('decision of the Employment Appeal Tribunal') of the judgment by the CA.

[188] See footnotes 179, 180 and 181 *supra*.

[189] Paragraph 41 of the judgment (per Lord Justice Mummery).

Disputes over religious dress: Shabina Begum

Another recently decided and important judgment is that of *R (on the application of SB) v. Headteacher and Governors of Denbigh Highschool,*[190] which concerned a dispute over religious dress. Issues regarding *discrimination* on grounds of religion did formally not constitute part of the complaint *in casu.* Nonetheless, the facts, legal reasoning and outcome of the case under review do bear an impact questions regarding religious discrimination.

The applicant (Shabina Begum) was a Muslim girl who attended Denbigh High School, a Secular school characterised by a very diverse ethnic and religious student population. According to the applicable uniform regulations girls should (among other things) wear a skirt, trousers or a Shalwar Kameeeze. The Shalwar consists of loose trousers tapered at the ankles; the Kameeze is a sleeveless smock-like dress with a square neckline that reveals a student's collar and tie. Shabina Begum contented that maturing Muslim girls are required by reasons of their religion to wear the Jiljab. This is a dress worn by Muslim women that hides the shape of her arms and legs and that is full-length. Shabina Begum was refused entrance to the school, unless she would wear the Shalwar Kameeze. In the school's view, there were a number of important reasons for its uniform policy namely, the fact that the school was multi-cultural, multi-faith and secular and that the uniform policy was vital in promoting a positive ethos and a sense of communal identity. Moreover, the policy guaranteed that no particular religion was favoured or disfavoured and it moreover protected Muslim girls from being pressurised to wear the Jiljab. In the school's view, the uniform guaranteed that students dressed in a way that was safe, practical and appropriate for learning. Moreover, it ensured that students did not become outcasts for wearing the 'wrong' clothes. In designing its uniform policy the school had widely taken into account the advice given to it by the Muslim community. The administrative court in the first instance had decided against the applicant.[191] She appealed against that decision to the Court of Appeal seeking a declaration that her rights under Article 9 ECHR had been violated. Hence, she did not pursue a claim for damages but the case concerned a point of principle. Brooke (LJ)[192] indicated that three main questions had to be analysed before such a declaration could be made: *(i)*

190 *R (on the application of SB) v. Headteacher and Governors of Denbigh Highschool* [2005] EWCA Civ 199; [2005] 2 All E.R. 396 (CA). For a case comment of the CA's judgment, I refer to Poole 2005, p. 685-695. The CA's judgment has recently been overruled by the House of Lords in its judgment in *R (on the application of Begum (by her litigation friend, Rahman (Respondent) v. Headteacher and Governors of Denbigh High School (Appellants)* [2006] UKHL 15 of 22 March 2006. The viewpoints adopted by both the CA and the House of Lords will be discussed in the main text to follow.

191 [2004] EWHC 1389 (Admin).

192 With whom Lord Justice Mummery and Lord Justice Scott Baker agreed. Mummery LJ did, however, add that the present case fell to be distinguished from the cases of *Ahmad v. UK* (1981) 4 EHRR 126 (CD) and *Stedman v. UK* (1997) 23 EHRR 168 (CD) (both earlier discussed in the main text above) and which concerned *employees* relying on Article 9 ECHR. He held that 'it is irrelevant to the engagement of Article 9 that the claimant could have changed to a school which accommodated her religious beliefs about dress. Education at the school or at another school was not a contractual choice'.

was the claimant excluded from the school? (ii) if yes, was it because her rights under Article 9(1) ECHR were being limited? *(iii)* if yes, were they being justifiably limited pursuant to Article 9(2) ECHR? The first question was answered in the affirmative,[193] as well as was the second question.[194] The court then turned to the last question which essentially focused upon the 'necessity' element. Against the background of *Leyla Sahin* the Court insisted that '[t]he United Kingdom is very different from Turkey. It is not a secular state, and although the Human Rights Act is now part of our law we have no written Constitution'. It held that the school had *ab initio* failed to recognise that Shabina had a right guaranteed by English law, namely the right to have and manifest her religion, and that the burden should have been on the part of the school to justify an interference with that right. In contrast, the school took as a starting point that its uniform policy had to be complied with and if not, she had the option of attending another school.[195] Hence, in the court's view

> '(…) because [the school] approached the issues in this case from an entirely wrong direction and did not attribute to the claimant's beliefs the weight they deserved, the school is not entitled to resist the declarations she seeks, namely: (1) that it unlawfully excluded her from the school, (ii) that it unlawfully denied her the right to manifest her religions, (iii) that it unlawfully denied her access to suitable and appropriate education.'

The following comments can be made with regard to the legal reasoning of the CA. First, it should be emphasised that the Appeal Court did not give a substantive ruling on the issues at stake. Instead, it (merely) held that the applicant had received unlawful treatment, given that the school had approached the issues at stake from the wrong (procedural) direction. In other words, the CA did not decide the alleged interference with the applicant's right to religion on its merits. Of course, by doing so, it prevented itself from taking up a position in highly contentious questions. In the CA's view, the (mere) fact that a wrong procedural approach had been adopted did not by itself mean that the school's uniform policy constituted a breach of Article 9(1) of the Convention. As stressed by Brooke LJ in paragraph 81 of the judgment, '[n]othing in this judgment should be taken as meaning that it would be impossible for the School to justify its stance if it were to consider its uniform policy in the light of this judgment and were to determine not to alter it in any significant respect'.[196]

193 See paragraph 24 of the judgment: 'The school undoubtedly did exclude the claimant. They told her, in effect: "Go away, and do not come back unless you are wearing proper school uniform".'

194 See the eventual conclusion in paragraph 49 of the judgment. The CA reached this conclusion only after an in-depth analysis of two main schools of thought amongst Muslims. It is submitted that the CA should have refrained from such an extensive religious analysis, as courts should become as little as possible involved in questions regarding the interpretation of the concept of religion *in se*.

195 See paragraph 76 of the judgment.

196 See also Lord Justice Mummery: '(…) it would still be possible for the School, on a structured reconsideration of the relevant issues, including the Article 9 right of a person in the position of the claimant, to justify its stance on the school uniform policy. If it could, there would be no breach of the Article 9(1) right.' (paragraph 87). See with similar effect Scott Baker (LJ) in paragraph 92 of the judgment.

Hence, the CA essentially instructed the school to reconsider its procedural approach to the applicant's insistence upon wearing the jiljab, whereby it gave detailed judicial guidance as to how it should do so. It should be noted that the school is a public body for the purposes of Article 6(1) HRA[197] and it is therefore required to act compatibly with the rights and freedoms contained in the Convention. In the view of the CA, for the school to follow the right procedural approach, it ought to *inter alia* reflect on the question whether the interference is prescribed by law, whether it pursues a legitimate aim and whether it is proportional.[198] The CA's formalistic approach in *Shabina Begum* has been rightfully criticised by Poole. Poole had argued that the CA was wrong to extrapolate a judicial review test, which has to be applied by the courts whilst reviewing (*ex post*) decisions made by public authorities, to the decision-making process carried out by these authorities themselves (*ex ante*).[199] As Poole has correctly argued, the decision in *Denbigh High School* '(...) seeks to impose a test on primary decision-makers that has no obvious relevance outside the context of judicial decision-making'.[200]

This criticism has eventually been shared by a unanimous decision by the Lordships on appeal.[201] In the view of Lord Hoffman '(...) the whole approach [adopted by the CA; MG] seems (...) a mistaken construction of Article 9 [of the ECHR; MG] (...) Article 9 is concerned with substance, not procedure.[202] In deciding the case on its merits entailing an assessment of the *proportionality* (rather than, e.g. the 'reasonableness', which would have amounted to a less strict judicial scrutiny test)[203] of the

197 Section 6(1) HRA provides that 'it is unlawful for a public authority [including courts and tribunals; MG] to act in a way which is incompatible with a Convention right'. See also the explanatory comments at the outset of Part IV, which gave an explanation on the relationship between English and ECHR law.

198 See paragraph 75 of the judgment.

199 Poole 2005, p. 685-695, notably p. 690.

200 Poole 2005, p. 685-695, notably p. 694.

201 *R (on the application of Begum (by her litigation friend, Rahman (Respondent) v. Headteacher and Governors of Denbigh High School (Appellants)* [2006] UKHL 15 of 22 March 2006 (HL).

202 Paragraph 68 of the judgment. See also in particular the opinion by Lord Bingham of Cornhill who advanced the following three reasons why the procedural approach adopted by the CA was mistaken: (1) the purpose of the HRA 1998 is to enable the rights and remedies of persons in the United Kingdom to be asserted and enforced before the domestic courts and not only before the ECtHR (paragraph 29 of the judgment); (2) the Convention requires the national courts to adopt a greater intensity of judicial review than that which has traditionally been employed in a purely domestic setting. Domestic courts are required to make a normative judgment, by reference to the circumstances prevailing at the relevant material time (paragraph 30 of the judgment); (3) The guidance given by the CA to the school, would be a commendable guidance to be given to a lower court or legal tribunal but not to a head teacher or to the governors of a school. This last point parallels the criticism by Poole outlined in the main text above.

203 See in this respect the following observation by Lord Hoffman in paragraph 68 of the judgment: 'In domestic judicial review, the court is usually concerned with whether the decision-maker reached his decision in the right way rather than whether he got what the court might think to be the right answer [such an approach amounts to a judicial 'reasonableness test'; MG]. But Article 9 is concerned with substance, not procedure. It confers no right to have a decision made in a particular way. What matters is the result: was the right to manifest a →

school's interference with Shabina's right to manifest her religious belief by wearing the jiljab in school, the Law Lords decided in favour of the school.[204] It was *inter alia* held that the school 'had taken immense pains to devise a uniform policy which respected Muslims beliefs but did so in an inclusive, unthreatening and uncompetitive way'.[205] Moreover, importance was given to the fact that Shabina could have been transferred to other schools in the Luton area which would allow her to wear a jiljab, however, she had not taken up the chance of doing so.[206] Moreover, the school's objective of fostering a sense of community and social cohesion within the school was considered to be an important element in encouraging persons of diverse races, religions and cultures to live harmoniously together.[207]

4.4. *Exceptions*

A triad of exceptions to the central prohibition of discrimination on grounds of religion and belief can be found in the R&B Regulations. These are the following: (1) the genuine occupational requirement exception in Regulation 7; (2) the national security exception in Regulation 24, which seeks to transpose Article 2(5) EFD and (3) an exception for positive action in Regulation 25. It should furthermore be noted that according to Regulation 26, Sikhs cannot lawfully be compelled to wear a safety helmet at construction sites. Hereafter, I will only deal with the GOR exception in Regulation 7 of the R&B Regulations.[208]

Regulation 7(2) transposes Article 4(1) of the EFD. It contains a genuine and determining occupational requirement exception that calls for a clear link between the discriminatory job requirement, on the one hand, and the effective performance of the job, on the other. Both religious and non-religious employers may invoke it. Unlike the EFD, Regulation 7(2) of the R&B Regulations does not provide that the

religious belief restricted in a way which is not justified under Article 9.2.?' See also paragraph 30 of the judgment where it was explicitly held by Lord Bingham 'that the court's approach to an issue of proportionality under the Convention must go beyond that traditionally adopted to judicial review in a domestic setting'.

204 It should be noted that 2 of the 5 Law Lords (namely Lord Nicholls of Birkenhead and Lady Hale of Richmond) expressed a slightly different opinion from the one shared by the majority as to whether the applicant's rights under Article 9 of the Convention had been interfered with. According to the majority of the law lords, the applicant's rights under Article 9(2) of the Convention had *not* been interfered with given that it had been Shabina's choice to attend this particular school and given that she could have moved to another, more appropriate school where she would be allowed to wear the jiljab. However, even if it were accepted that Shabina's rights had been interfered with, this interference was justified under Article 9(2) ECHR. However, according to Lord Nicholls and Lady Hale of Richmond, the school's refusal to allow Shabina Begum to wear a jiljab at school *did* interfere with her Article 9(2) ECHR right but the school's decision could be justified.

205 Paragraph 34 of the judgment per Lord Bingham of Cornhill.

206 Paragraph 89 of the judgment, per Lord Scott of Foscote.

207 Paragraph 97 of the judgment, per Lady Hale of Richmond.

208 Positive action was dealt with in Chapter 5. The public security exception will be touched on in Chapter 7 in the context of sexual orientation law. The exception contained in Regulation 26 warrants no further discussion.

objective pursued by the imposition of the contested job requirement must be 'legitimate'. Therefore, this element of the test must be 'read in' by tribunals and courts in light of requirements of EC law. For the remainder, implementation of Article 4(1) EFD has correctly occurred. Regulation 7(3) aims to transpose Article 4(2) EFD. It follows from this provision that a discriminatory job requirement must be genuinely imposed with the aim of preserving the organisation's ethos and it must be in conformity with the proportionality principle. Like Article 4(2) EFD, the requirement need not be a decisive (i.e. *determining*) job requirement. Earlier on in the analysis, Article 4(2) EFD was examined in light of the applicable law in the Netherlands. The Dutch approach could be of judicial assistance in the application and interpretation of Regulation 7(3) of the R&B Regulations, if the ECJ feels 'bottom-up' inspired by this approach. After all, the approach by the ECJ would then cross-fertilise into English law. It is argued that the UK government has fallen short of its obligations under EC law by its failure to implement the requirement in Article 4(2) EFD, namely that the imposition of a religious job requirement may not lead to discrimination on another forbidden ground, e.g. sexual orientation. An instance of sexual orientation discrimination can, however, be challenged on the basis of the S.O. Regulations to be discussed in Chapter 7. Regulation 7(3) neither transposes the 'loyalty clause' found in Article 4(2) EFD.[209] This, it is argued is, however, in conformity with EC law, given that this omission merely *reduces* the scope granted by the law to religious employers for the imposition of discriminatory job requirements, rather than extending it. A final comment regards the relationship between the R&B Regulations, on the one hand, and the 1998 School Standards and Framework Act (SSFA), on the other. According to Regulation 39 of the R&B Regulations, the Regulations are without prejudice to Sections 58-60 of the SSFA, which basically concern the appointment and dismissal of teachers (but not of other staff) by faith schools. It should be stressed that the relevant provisions in the SSFA do *not* provide that religious job requirements imposed upon teachers must be 'genuine', 'legitimate' and 'justified' in light of the school's religious founding principles, and, that such requirements may (in principle) not justify discrimination on another forbidden ground.[210] In summary, the broad formulation of this exception appears to be in breach of the UK's obligations under the Framework Directive and courts and tribunals are therefore under a legal duty to interpret these provisions in light of applicable EC law.

5. Conclusions

This Chapter examined the concepts of equality and non-discrimination in respect of religion and belief on the basis of a multi-layered comparison. This triggered 'cross-ground', 'top-down', 'bottom-up' and 'cross-country' perspectives. Reference was moreover made to the case law arisen in the context of Article 9 ECHR. The analysis

209 It is recalled that this clause provides that the EFD '(…) shall thus not prejudice the right of churches and other public or private organisations, the ethos of which is based on religion or belief, acting in conformity with national constitutions and laws, to require individuals working for them to act in good faith and with loyalty to the organisation's ethos'.

210 See the analysis in section 3.4.3 above.

of the underlying logic of the discrimination grounds 'religion' and 'belief' *inter alia* stressed that both grounds play a vital role in shaping the identity of the individual believer, as well as the group to which (s)he belongs. In this respect, 'religion' and 'belief' show commonalities with other choice-grounds, notably 'sexual orientation'. With reference to the values inherent to the grounds 'religion' and 'belief', it was argued that one of the prominent tasks of the law should be to foster religious pluralism and diversity. At the same time, due regard should be given to the historical and socio cultural context when framing and interpreting the law. Having examined the elemental nature of the discrimination grounds religion and belief, the discussion proceeded with an analysis of EC religious discrimination law. This analysis was embedded in a comparative law analysis whose aim was to illustrate how the Luxembourg Court could interpret relevant provisions in the EFD in future cases that come before it. It is clear from the comparative law analysis that the interpretation of alleged instances of discrimination in the public sphere is highly dependent on the socio cultural context and on prevailing interpretations of the notions of secularism and state neutrality. Although the 'positive neutrality approach' reflects an apposite legal stance in the particular socio cultural context in the Netherlands, this is not necessarily the case in other European states. This explains why the ECJ is unlikely to feel inspired by the judicial approach in Dutch law concerning Muslim headscarf disputes in a public setting, including public employment. The present author is in favour of the positive neutrality approach in the Dutch legal context. Nonetheless, she contends that the ECJ should not necessarily follow this approach, given that a supranational court cannot and ought not to brush aside highly divergent interpretations across the EC Member States on the proper relationship between religion and the state. It is submitted that this relationship is historically, socially and culturally determined and therefore the ECJ's stance should be deferent and subsidiary. Hence, the Court should leave a great scope of judicial discretion to the domestic courts in the context of an assessment of 'objective justification' of indirect discrimination cases on grounds of religion/belief.

The analysis also illustrated that EC religious discrimination law has arguably been bottom-up inspired by domestic approaches. It was contended that the EC legislator has presumably been influenced by Dutch law whilst framing the exception to the prohibition of discrimination contained in Article 4(2) of the Framework Directive. This provision incorporates legal language that closely resembles what is known in Dutch law as the 'sole ground construction' (*enkele feit constructie*). In the present author's view the Dutch approach reflects a proper balance between the right to religious freedom (and freedom of education), on the one hand, and the right to be free from discrimination on a forbidden ground, on the other. It was argued that the legal approach in the Netherlands sets a good example for the Luxembourg Court in the interpretation of the Article 4(2) EFD exception in future case law.

The analysis in this Chapter also showed that EC law has exerted a far-reaching top-down influence on the English anti-discrimination framework. By virtue of EC law, English law has been enriched with a legal prohibition of discrimination on grounds of religion/belief in employment. The discussion of English religious discrimination law was ingrained with references to legal approaches and interpretations in Dutch and ECHR law. Dutch and English law show divergences with respect to the interpretation of the notion of 'race' in cases where 'race' was closely connected with 'religion'. The legal interpretation of 'religion' and 'belief' appears, however, to be similar in both jurisdictions, although no cases have yet arisen before the English courts. The cross-country comparison also illustrated that in 'time off from work' cases, the Dutch Supreme Court and the ETC have given much less importance to the freedom of contract, in comparison with judicial approaches in English, as well as Strasbourg Convention law. Recent English case law appears, however, to acknowledge that an unconditional preference for contractual freedom over religious freedom is hard to square with the fundamental nature of the latter right. Towards the end of the analysis in Chapter 5, an analysis was made of the first case that has arisen in the context of English law concerning a dispute over religious dress in a public school. It is hard to predict on the basis of a single case, whether the English legal approach differs from that adopted by the Dutch ETC in parallel cases. In any case, both the latter and the House of Lords have adopted a strict proportionality test in the assessment of the lawfulness of dress requirements where such requirements allegedly impinge on a person's right to freedom of religion.

Chapter 7

SEXUAL ORIENTATION

1. Introduction

In Chapter 6 we saw that the statutory anti-discrimination framework in England has been enriched with a new legal framework governing religious discrimination in employment. In addition to this the English anti-discrimination framework has been enriched with a series of governmental Regulations which prohibit sexual orientation discrimination in employment.[1] These Regulations were adopted on 26 June 2003 under Section 2(2) of the European Communities Act 1972 and they entered into force on 1 December 2003. They constitute the legal transposition of the EFD into domestic law insofar as the discrimination ground 'sexual orientation' is concerned.[2] The present Chapter will be similar in fashion and scope as Chapter 6. Indeed, a comparison of the Religion and Belief Regulations[3] with the S.O. Regulations instantly shows that both sets of Regulations have been framed in congruent legal language. Therefore, a research approach analogous to the one adopted in Chapter 6 will underpin the discussion to follow. Like in Chapter 6 the analysis to follow will illustrate the top-down influence exercised by EC law upon the scope of domestic anti-discrimination law. Indeed, were it not for reason of supranational equality guarantees calling for transposition into the domestic anti-discrimination framework, a clear-cut prohibition in English law of sexual orientation discrimination in employment would be more apparent than real.[4] The discussion to follow will be

1 S.I. 2003, No. 1661, The Employment Equality (Sexual Orientation) Regulations 2003. For the sake of convenience, they will hereafter be referred to as the 'S.O. Regulations' or simply, 'the Regulations'.

2 'Regulations', in contrast to Parliamentary Acts or Statutes, are 'secondary' (as opposed to 'primary') legislation. The implementation of EC law by means of 'Regulations' instead of the (more democratically informed) route of primary legislation has the practical effect of adopting a *de minimis* approach to the implementation of EC law: transposition of an EC Directive (in casu the Article 13 EFD) may not go beyond what is strictly required by the Directive. See Section 2(2) of the 1972 European Communities Act. See generally Chapter 2.

3 See Chapter 6.

4 The judicial House of Lords has not adopted an active stance in deciding on cases regarding employment related sexual orientation discrimination. See *Macdonald (Appellant) v. Advocate* →

presented in the following way. In section 2 hereafter, I will first make a number of theoretical comments on sexual orientation as a ground of discrimination. This section will be functional to the 'cross-ground' analysis in Chapter 10, which will highlight the underlying values of different grounds of discrimination. In section 3, I will outline the legal state of affairs regarding EC sexual orientation and equality law, both *ex ante* and *ex post* the adoption of the Article 13 Framework Directive. I will subsequently examine the English sexual orientation law framework in section 4. Naturally, this will include a detailed examination of the Regulations but it will also embrace a discussion of the first important judicial case that has arisen in the context of the S.O. Regulations and the EFD. On 26 April 2004 the High Court of Justice, per Mr Justice Richards, delivered its judgment in the case of *Amicus v. Secretary of State for Trade and Industry* in which the claimant and six trade unions challenged a number of provisions contained within the S.O. Regulations.[5] While discussing the domestic legal framework particular attention will be paid to possible pitfalls in the implementation of supranational equality standards and to the overall effectiveness of the new law in banning instances of homophobia and discrimination in employment. Brief conclusions will be drawn in section 5. The analysis as a whole will be ingrained, wherever appropriate, with relevant elements of Dutch sexual orientation law and ECHR law.[6]

2. Sexual Orientation as a Ground of Discrimination

2.1. *The Underlying Logic of 'Sexual Orientation': Cross-Ground Perspectives*

The presentation of the present chapter in sequence after the analysis regarding the grounds 'religion' and 'belief' provides for interesting insights into the distinct but related realms of sexual orientation and religious discrimination law. Various commentators have taken the view that both grounds denote a common character ('cross-ground comparison'). Wintemute, for example, has cited in this context the case of *Egan v. Canada,* in which the Canadian Supreme Court has taken the following view:

> '[s]exual orientation is (…) demonstrated in an individual's conduct by the choice of a partner. The Charter [i.e., the Canadian Charter of Rights and Freedoms; MG] protects religious beliefs and religious practice as aspects of religious freedom. So, too, should it be

General for Scotland (Respondent) and Pearce (Appellant) v. Governing Body of Mayfield School (Respondents) [2003] UKHL 34 (judgment of 19 June 2003). It was held by the House of Lords that 'sex' in the 1975 SDA was not wide enough to encompass sexual orientation discrimination and therefore the Act was held to be limited to gender discrimination. See for a critique Wintemute 2003, p. 267-281.

5 See *R. v. Secretary of State for Trade and Industry, ex parte Amicus – MSF Section, et al.* 2004 EWHC 860 (Admin), per the honourable Mr Justice Richards, available at <http://www.courtservice.gov.uk/judgmentsfiles/j2476/amicus-v-ssti.htm>.

6 The reasons why Strasbourg Convention law is discussed in Chapters 6 and 7 but not in the remainder of this book have been indicated in the preliminary issues at the outset of Part IV.

> recognized that sexual orientation encompasses aspects of 'status' and 'conduct' and that both should receive protection'.[7]

A comparison of sexual orientation with other grounds of discrimination involves looking for analogies, dissimilarities and tensions. This will be done hereafter. A fully-fledged cross-ground analysis will moreover be made in Chapter 10.

a. Analogies

Via the vehicle of the so-called *immutable status argument* attempts have been made to analogise the civil rights movement striving for gay rights, on the one hand, with similar movements calling for racial and gender equality, on the other.[8] These attempts have been founded upon a view that the disadvantages suffered by gays and lesbians, by racial minorities and by women are all rooted in the immutability of a personal characteristic. In the context of sexual orientation, the immutability argument draws on studies which have argued that sexual orientation is biologically explicable.[9] However, as Richards has argued,

> '(...) sexual orientation, even if it were biologically explicable [which he himself firmly denies; MG], is not a fact like race and gender but a complex system of psychological propensities (thoughts, fantasies, desires, vulnerabilities, deeply rooted in our imaginative lives as persons).'[10]

Thus, Richards has contrasted race and sex as grounds of discrimination, with sexual orientation as far as the immutability argument is concerned. However, he has analogised sexual orientation with the former two grounds by seeking recourse to, what he has called, the 'moral slavery argument'. As Richards explains 'moral slavery' condemns structural injustices which are featured by two inter-related assets, namely, (1) the curtailment of the basic human rights of a class of persons, in casu, gay persons as compared with women and black persons, and (2) the rationalisation of this curtailment on unjust grounds, mirroring a history of unequal treatment and disadvantage and involving the 'dehumanization of the group'.[11] In Richards' analysis it was argued that 'moral slavery' essentially hampers the free development of a person's self and her identity. It should be noted that the denial of rights to persons belonging to a particular group on the basis of unjust grounds, which are linked with a history of disadvantage, results in self-entrenched inequality, given that the history of disadvantage is effectively kept alive.

7 *Egan v. Canada* [1995] 2 S.C.R. 513, at paragraph 175, cited by Wintemute 2000, p. 608 and footnote 24.

8 Richards 1999, p. 7 *et seq*. Richards has shown himself to be an opponent of making this analogy.

9 See the various scientific studies referred to by Richards 1999, p. 7 footnote 8. Richards himself has heavily criticised the, what he has called, 'biological story' as the vehicle via which analogies could be drawn between 'sexual orientation' *v.* 'race' and 'sex' (Richards 1999, p. 7-10).

10 Richards 1999, p. 9.

11 Richards 1999, p. 3.

Richards has argued that, although via the 'moral slavery argument' commonalities could be drawn between sexual orientation on the one hand, and race and sex, on the other, sexual orientation is in fact best analogised with religious freedom:

> 'Both the advocacy and opposition to gay rights suggest the distinctively illuminating power of the religious analogy in understanding the case for gay rights. The constitutional protection of religion never turned on its putative and salient character (people can and do convert, and can and do conceal religious convictions), but on the traditional place of religion in the conscientious reasonable formation of one's moral identity in public and private life and the need for protection, consistent with the inalienable right to conscience, of persons against state impositions of sectarian religious views.'

Gays, Richards argues, make a similar claim to 'a self-respecting personal and moral identity (...) through which they may reasonably express and realize their ethical convictions of the moral powers of friendship and love (...)'.[12]

In other words, if the immutability argument can be easily applied to race and sex, this is not true for the grounds of religion and sexual orientation. Richards has argued that the essential commonality between the last two grounds is that both call for the protection of, and equal respect for, the 'conscientious ethical claim' to gay, or for that matter, religious identity. In other words both religious and gay identity come about by making an ethical claim of conscience and thus, these grounds of discrimination cannot be explained in terms of immutability.

Wintemute has argued too, that same-sex relationships are essentially a matter of choice no matter how compelling, arduous or obligatory.[13] Wintemute has convincingly argued that it cannot be denied that most judicial controversies which have emerged in the context of sexual orientation law involve *chosen* conduct (my emphasis).[14] As shown in Chapter 6, this holds equally true for the discrimination grounds religion and belief. Hence, the intrinsic nature of both the latter two grounds, and sexual orientation enfolds a dual dimension, namely the *forum internum* and the *forum externum*, i.e. the right to, respectively, *have* a particular sexual orientation/ attraction/faith and the right to *behave* accordingly.[15] This has also been recognised by the Dutch ETC which has taken the view that the notion of homosexual (or hetero-

12 Richards 1999, p. 93.

13 Wintemute 1997, p. 232-248.

14 He mentions the examples of same-sex sexual activity or partnerships. Wintemute 2004, p. 370-371 and footnote 18.

15 Bonini-Baraldi 2004, p. 30 with reference to the case decided by the ECtHR in *Dudgeon v. the United Kingdom*, 7525/76, 22 October 1981 available at <http://www.echr.coe.int/echr> and which concerned sexual behaviour. The *Dudgeon case* concerned the criminalisation by Northern Irish law of certain homosexual acts between consenting adult males. Hence, it concerned the *forum externum* of sexual orientation. The *forum internum* was *inter alia* at stake in the *Karner* case (*Karner v. Austria* EHRC 2003, 83) concerning Austrian legislation which prohibited unmarried cohabitating same-sex partners from succeeding a deceased partner in the tenancy of the house, whereas such a right was granted to unmarried cohabitating different-sex couples. The *Karner* case will be discussed in more detail in the passages to follow in the main text. Cases relating to the grounds 'religion' and 'belief' have been cited and commented upon in the previous chapter.

or bisexual) orientation ('*gerichtheid*') is broader than preference ('*voorkeur*'). As such, the former notion also covers 'concrete conduct which is generally regarded as being a logical consequence of one's homosexual (or heterosexual [or, bisexual]) orientation'.[16]

b. Dissimilarities

In other respects, however, the grounds sexual orientation and religion and belief show dissimilarities. Many aspects of sexual orientation, arguably more than is the case with other grounds, are intrinsically linked with issues concerning a person's private (and family) life. Indeed, in the context of the ECHR, cases regarding a person's sexual orientation have been decided on the basis of Article 8 of the Convention, which secures a person's right to private life[17] (sometimes in conjunction with Article 14 ECHR). One could argue that the linkage[18] of Article 14 ECHR, on the one hand, with a substantive Convention right, on the other, fosters the human rights dimension of the principle of equality. It has been held by the Strasbourg Court that sexual conduct concerns 'a most intimate part of an individual's private life'[19] and that restrictions placed on a person's sexual conduct call for 'particularly serious reasons'[20] by way of justification. Moreover, differences based on sexual orientation also call for 'particularly serious reasons' in order to be justified.[21] With reference to a growing common consensus on the illegitimacy of employing 'sexual

16 See for example paragraph 5.3 of Opinion 2003-113: '*De term gerichtheid is daarmee ruimer dan de term voorkeur (...) concreet gedrag, dat algemeen wordt beschouwd als uitvloeisel van de homoseksuele (of heteroseksuele) gerichtheid van een persoon, [wordt] door de AWGB beschermd.*' (translated by the author in English in the main text above). See also Opinion 2003-150, paragraph 5.3.

17 See for a general analysis of Article 8 ECHR, Heringa 2004. Examples of concrete cases in which sexual orientation was perceived in the context of Article 8 of the Convention are *Dudgeon v. the United Kingdom,* 7525/76, 22 October 1981 available at <http://www.echr.coe.int/echr> (separate examination under Article 14 in conjunction with Article 8 ECHR was not deemed necessary); *L and V v. Austria,* EHRC 2003, 18 (Article 14 in conjunction with Article 8 ECHR); *Salgueiro da Silva Mouta v. Portugal* EHRC 2000, 16 (Article 14 in conjunction with Article 8 ECHR); *Smith* and *Grady v. the United Kingdom,* 33985/96 and 33986/96, 27 September 1999 (available at <http://www.echr.coe.int/echr> (Article 8 ECHR; no separate examination under Article 14 in conjunction with Article 8 ECHR); *Lustig-Prean* and *Beckett v. the United Kingdom,* 31417/96 and 32377/96, 27 December 1999 available at <http://www.echr.coe.int/echr> (Article 8 ECHR; no separate examination under Article 14 in conjunction with Article 8 ECHR).

18 It was explained in the preliminary issues at the start of Part IV that this linking exercise is no longer required for those States Parties to the Convention which have signed and ratified Protocol No. 12 to the Convention.

19 *Dudgeon v. the United Kingdom,* 7525/76, 22 October 1981 available at <http://www.echr.coe.int/echr>, paragraph. 52; *Smith* and *Grady v. the United Kingdom,* 33985/96 and 33986/96, 27 September 1999 (available at <http://www.echr.coe.int/echr> paragraph 89 (with reference to the Court's judgment in *Dudgeon,* paragraph 52). See for a discussion also Sottiaux 2003, p. 614-615.

20 *Smith* and *Grady v. the United Kingdom,* 33985/96 and 33986/96, 27 September 1999 (available at <http://www.echr.coe.int/echr> paragraph 89; *L and V v. Austria,* EHRC 2003, 18, paragraph 45.

21 *L and V v. Austria,* EHRC 2003, 18, paragraph 45 and *Karner v. Austria* EHRC 2003, 83, paragraph 37 of the judgment.

orientation' as a factor in the decision-making process, the Court regards this ground as a 'suspect' classification.[22] This brings with it that the state is only afforded a minimal margin of appreciation in cases concerning an interference with rights linked with a person's sexual orientation, including the right to be free from discrimination on this ground.[23] The present author contends that the fact that sexual orientation is regarded by the Strasbourg Court as a suspect classification works as a catalyst for the effective protection by the law from sexual orientation discrimination, both at the domestic level and at the level of the EC.

The fact that sexual orientation is so closely related with privacy, testifies to an intrinsic logic underpinning this ground of discrimination which is different from other grounds. 'Sexual orientation', writes Oliver, 'is unique in being a "hidden" characteristic, which is not generally obvious to an outside observer'.[24] More than is the case with religion, which often calls for a 'difference approach' towards achieving equality at work, a person's sexual orientation appears largely irrelevant in employment-related decision-making processes.[25] In other words, formal equality appears to fit better with sexual orientation than, e.g. with religion.

Sottiaux[26] has criticised a (merely) 'privacy oriented' approach to sexual orientation. He has argued that the right to privacy is a negative right, which requires abstinence on the part of the state and which is particularly apt in claims concerning the criminalisation of certain sexual acts. However, in his view, it is not an appropriate basis for equal treatment claims. Sottiaux has moreover criticised the privacy approach to sexual orientation for being too individualistic and, notably, for failing to emancipate sexual minorities. In light of this, he has argued that this approach fails to eliminate the untrue stereotypes linked with homosexuality: 'privacy arguments do not question homophobic views but, at most, they set boundaries to the role of the state in guarding the community moral'.[27] The present author agrees with the views expressed by Sottiaux and stresses the need for a fully-fledged equality law framework which aims at the following: (1) the eradication of stereotypical views on homosexuality and of gender-role-typing. Gender-role-typing refers to conventional (and deeply embedded) ideas about what is 'proper' social behaviour of women and of men; (2) fostering the development of a person's identity which is (or at least may

22 See for a general discussion on the hierarchy between 'suspect' and 'non-suspect' grounds in the context of the ECHR, Gerards 2004.

23 *Dudgeon v. the United Kingdom,* 7525/76, 22 October 1981 available at <http://www.echr.coe.int/echr>, paragraph 52.

24 Oliver 2004, p. 5. It is acknowledged that this is, however, only true for a person's sexual preference (and some behavioural aspects), not for the coming out aspects of 'sexual orientation'. See also Bonini-Baraldi 2004, p. 26, who has noted that '[s]ilence and hiding (...) might have a negative impact on a person's self-perception as equally worthy of consideration and respect, and on the possibility of developing a fulfilling life in all of its social and relational dimensions'.

25 Oliver 2004, p. 6.

26 Sottiaux 2003, p. 619 with further references.

27 Sottiaux 2003, p. 619 (with reference to the work by Kane): *'Privacy argumenten stellen homofobe opvattingen niet in vraag, maar bakenen hoogstens de rol af van de staat in het behoeden van de gemeenschapsmoraal.'*

be) shaped by a person's sexual orientation; (3) promoting equal concern and respect for heterosexual, homosexual and bi-sexual persons alike. A similar viewpoint has been aired by Fredman who has argued that protection from sexual orientation discrimination flourishes best in those legal systems, which ingrain the equality principle within the paradigms of 'dignity' and the 'free development of the person'.[28]

c. Tensions

In addition to the cross-ground analysis above, the intersections between the grounds 'sexual orientation' and 'religion' and 'belief' can be demonstrated with reference to the fact that both grounds often clash in legal proceedings. In Chapter 6 this has already been illustrated with reference to the classic example of the right of a homosexual teacher to non-discrimination *v.* the right of denominational schools to freedom of religion. Hence, legal tensions easily emerge where one person claims her right to be free from discrimination on grounds of sexual orientation, whereas another simultaneously relies upon her right to freedom of religion. In the context of Dutch law it has, for example, been questioned whether the appointment of a civil servant may be refused on grounds of objections of conscience against the conclusion of a marriage between two persons of the same sex.[29] The possibility of clashes between the above-mentioned rights has been taken account of by the EC, English and Dutch legislative frameworks governing discrimination on the grounds religion and belief, and sexual orientation.

2.2. *Conclusions*

In the above, analytical remarks have been made in respect of the intrinsic nature of sexual orientation as a ground of discrimination. The cross-ground comparison has revealed analogies, dissimilarities and tensions. Like religion, sexual orientation involves, to speak with Richards' words, 'an ethical decision of conscience' which thus reflects an element of choice, rather than an immutable status, and which (may) largely define a person's identity. Unlike other grounds, sexual orientation is intrinsically linked with privacy issues but, as has been seen, a mere privacy approach is too circumscribed for the achievement of equal dignity for all, as well as for the liberation of oppressed sexual minorities. Lastly, it has been observed that sexual orientation and religion as grounds of discrimination are not always easy bed-fellows. The tensions between religion and sexual orientation have been illustrated in much detail in Chapter 6. Therefore, they will not be repeated in the analysis to follow. A fully-fledged comparative analysis of the different logics and intricacies underpinning different grounds of discrimination will be made in Chapter 10. Hereafter, I will proceed with a discussion of sexual orientation discrimination in the context of EC law.

28 Fredman 2002a, p. 18.

29 See Opinion 2002-25 in which the ETC concluded a case of indirect discrimination of the civil servant on grounds of religion (which could not be justified). See also Opinion 2002-26 (*idem*) and Opinion 2002-24 (inadmissibility decision).

3. Discrimination, Sexual Orientation and EC Law

In this section, I will sketch the state of affairs regarding sexual orientation discrimination in EC law, both prior to and after the adoption of the Framework Directive. At appropriate junctures, I will make references to the law stemming from the ECHR and to Dutch sexual orientation discrimination law.

3.1. *Legal Framework Ex Ante the EFD*

Prior to the adoption of the Framework Directive, the ECJ's focus on the wrong comparator, in combination with a 'subsidiarity' approach, has essentially frustrated adequate legal protection from discrimination to gay and lesbian (and bisexual) persons. The lack of an explicit legal framework containing a prohibition of discrimination on grounds of sexual orientation has led to attempts to shoehorn claims of sexual orientation discrimination into existing EC sex equality law. However, the ECJ's cautious stance, inspired by its fear not to take up the role of Community legislator in this 'sensitive' area of the law, has thwarted these attempts. The absence of a civil rights and dignity approach in the Court's case law on the rights of homosexual persons has resulted in fallacious[30] legal reasoning.[31] The wealth of academic commentaries show that Community law avails itself of many divergent conceptions of equality[32], ranging from formal equality (which is traceable in the Court's case law on positive action), to substantive equality (e.g. underlying pregnancy discrimination claims), to equality in terms of dignity (gender reassignment case law). The key words, however, which characterise the ECJ's line of reasoning in its jurisprudence on the rights of homosexual persons are 'comparative justice' (wrongly applied) and 'subsidiarity'.

In *Grant v. Southwest Trains*[33] the ECJ principally held that discrimination against the lesbian applicant did not constitute discrimination on grounds of *sex* contrary to Community law.[34] In casu, Lisa Grant was denied travel concessions by her employer, *South-West Trains,* in respect of her female partner, whereas such concessions were granted to (un)married opposite sex partners. In other words, travel concessions were only given by the employer to a cohabitee of the opposite sex (whether or not married), but not to a cohabitee of the same sex. The question whether the impugned rules constituted discrimination based directly on the sex of the worker concerned was answered by the ECJ in the negative. A negative outcome was inevitable due to

30 Admittedly, the adoption of a formal equality approach and the ECJ's cautious stance in sexual orientation cases before the adoption of the Framework Directive is understandable from a political, rather than a legal, point of view. This point will be further elaborated upon in the main text to follow.

31 See also Barnard 1998, p. 353-366, especially p. 356.

32 The adoption of shifting conceptions of equality discloses the lack of a cohesive theoretical framework underpinning European equality law. See McCrudden 2003a, p. 1-38.

33 *Grant v. South West Trains* (Case C-249/96) [1998] ECR I-621.

34 The *Grant* case has not been deprived whatsoever of academic commentary and critique. See for example: Koppelman 2001, p. 623-633; Stychin 2003, p. 75-92; Bamforth 2000, p. 694.

the Court's choice of the legal equivalent with whom Lisa Grant fell to be compared. The Court portrayed this equivalent as being 'same sex couples of the opposite sex (i.e., a gay couple to whom the beneficiary travel concessions would equally have been denied) rather than as being heterosexual couples (to whom the concessions were and would have been afforded)'.[35] In other words, the ECJ found that no discrimination had occurred, given that travel concessions were equally denied to male and female homosexual couples. An interesting and convincing argument has been voiced by Bamforth, who has noted that the Court's insistence upon a comparison between one 'oppressed' group (lesbians) with another 'oppressed' group (gays) frustrates an important conceptual aspect of non-discrimination law, namely the aim of such law to correct imbalances between the 'disempowered' and the 'empowered'. Hence, in view of this, Bamforth has rightfully argued that a comparison should have been drawn with an opposite sex couple.[36]

A second question posed in *Grant* was whether Community law requires that stable relationships between two persons of the same sex should be perceived by employers as being equivalent to marriage, *or,* to unmarried relationships between persons of the opposite sex. In answering this question, the ECJ felt negatively inspired by a number of (early) cases decided by the European Commission of Human Rights which warrant the conclusion that homosexual relationships do not fall within the ambit of Article 8 ECHR.[37] In light of these, and with reference to the laws of the Member States, the ECJ pointed at a lack of a European consensus on the question in issue.[38]

The approach adopted by the Court in *Grant* has been criticised for at least three reasons. Firstly, critiques have been voiced by those who firmly defend the so-called 'sex discrimination argument',[39] i.e. the argument that discrimination against

35 See paragraphs 27 and 28 of the judgment: (Paragraph 27) '(...) Thus travel concessions are refused to a male worker if he is living with a person of the same sex, just as they are to a female worker if she is living with a person of the same sex. (Paragraph 28) Since the condition imposed by the undertaking's regulations applies in the same way to female and male workers, it cannot be regarded as constituting discrimination directly based on sex.' It is worth noting that Advocate General (AG) Elmer had reached the opposite conclusion: (Paragraph 24) '(...) Travel concessions for a male cohabitee may only be obtained if the employee is a woman. Travel concessions for a female cohabitee may only be obtained if the employee is a man. (Paragraph 25) The fact that (...) the (...) Regulations [do] not refer to a specific sex as the criterion for discrimination, but lay down a more abstract criterion ('opposite sex') can, in my view, make no difference, since the decisive point, as laid down in *P v. S* is whether discrimination is exclusively or essentially based on sex, whereas the fact that the discrimination is, de jure or de facto, on the basis of a specific sex cannot be decisive. (Paragraph 26) (...) it is my view that a provision in an employer's pay regulations under which the employee is granted travel concessions for a cohabitee of the opposite sex to the employee but refused such concessions for a cohabitee of the same sex as the employee constitutes discrimination on the basis of gender which falls within the scope of Article 119 of the Treaty.'

36 Bamforth 2000, p. 703.

37 See paragraph 33 of the judgment in *Grant.*

38 See paragraphs 32-34 of the judgment in *Grant,* with an eventual conclusion (on the lack of a European consensus) in paragraph 35 of the judgment.

39 This notion has been used by Wintemute. See e.g. Wintemute 2005, p. 183.

lesbians, gays and bisexuals (whether individually, or as couples) constitutes *both sexual orientation discrimination and sex discrimination.*[40] For divergent reasons, most courts[41] have not shown judicial sympathy for the 'sex discrimination argument',[42] including thus the ECJ in *Grant*. The Court, in its judgment in *Grant*, did refer to the view adopted by the Human Rights Committee, set up under Article 18 of the International Covenant on Civil and Political Rights (ICCPR) according to which the notion of 'sex' in Article 26 of the Covenant (i.e. the non-discrimination clause) does embrace sexual orientation.[43] Moreover, the sex discrimination argument had been accepted by Elmer (AG) in his Opinion to the Court in the *Grant* case.[44] The present author also shows sympathy for the argument. As Wintemute has insisted, the sex discrimination argument rests upon pristine logic. Wintemute has advanced a formalistic argument, which basically says that discrimination of a gay man, who is in an emotional and sexual relationship with another man, constitutes sex discrimination (in addition to sexual orientation discrimination), the reason for this being that, if he were a woman, he would not have been discriminated against.[45] In addition, there is what Bamforth has labelled the 'social argument'.[46] This argument summarises the academic work done by Koppelman and Sunstein to which Bamforth refers. It establishes the link between sexual orientation and sex discrimination as follows. Instances of gay and lesbian discrimination buttress the 'normative stereotype' that certain types of social conduct (*e.g.* kissing a man) are acceptable for members of one sex (namely, a woman) to the exclusion of members of the other sex (namely, a man). The social argument renders the interconnection between 'sex' and 'sexual

40 Proponents of this argument are *inter alia* Wintemute (see for example Wintemute 2003 and Wintemute 1997a); Bamforth (e.g. Bamforth 2000, p. 694); Koppelman (e.g. Koppelman 1994, p. 197); Farrel 2004, p. 605-704. Amongst the opponents are: Gardner 1998, p. 180.

41 See, for example, the decision by the House of Lords in *Macdonald (Appellant) v. Advocate General for Scotland (Respondent) and Pearce (Appellant) v. Governing Body of Mayfield School (Respondents)* [2003] UKHL 34 (judgment of 19 June 2003) in which it was held that 'sex' does not embrace 'sexual orientation'. The Dutch ETC has followed the stance adopted by the ECJ in Grant (see Opinion 98-98, Opinion 98-110, Opinion 98-137 and Opinion 99-08). It should be noted that sexual orientation discrimination has been outlawed by the Dutch GETA since 1994. Hence, in Dutch law, cases of sexual orientation discrimination have not been in need of being perceived as sex discrimination cases. However, the same cannot be said with regard to EC and English law which have only prohibited sexual orientation discrimination since 2000 and 2003 respectively.

42 Wintemute 2003, p. 277-279, where he has indicated the reasons why courts hesitate to conform to the argument. These reasons are both practical, conceptual and institutional in kind.

43 See Communication No. 488/1992, *Toonen v. Australia*, views adopted on 31 March 1994, 50th session, point 8.7., referred to by the ECJ in *Grant*, paragraph 43. However, the ECJ stressed that the Human Rights Committee is not a judicial body capable of giving binding views. It is noted that in the case *Baehr v. Lewin* 852, P 2d 44 (Hawa 1993), decided by the Constitutional Court of Hawaii, the sex discrimination argument has equally been accepted. This case has been referred to by Sottiaux 2003, p. 617-618.

44 See footnote 33 above.

45 See *inter alia* Wintemute 2003.

46 Others have referred to it as the 'ideological argument', see Farrell 2004, footnote 7 at p. 608. The argument is elaborated on p. 618-621 of Farell's Article. See also Sottiaux 2003, p. 614, with reference to the work by Heinze.

orientation' visible in terms of 'gender-role-typing' which is one of the harms that anti-discrimination law aims to combat. The gender-role-typing argument has recently decisively been used by the Dutch ETC in a so-called 'dancing competition case'. The exclusion of two persons of the same sex from professional dancing competitions had up until recently been construed by the ETC as constituting indirect discrimination against homosexuals. In Opinion 2004-116 the Commission has, however, substituted the indirect discrimination analysis by a direct discrimination analysis, both on grounds of sex and sexual orientation discrimination, *inter alia* with reference to the gender-role-typing argument. Opinion 2004-116 and the Commission's legal reasoning will be discussed in further detail later on in the analysis.

Secondly, critiques[47] regard the Court's ambivalent, if not inconsistent, approach in deciding *Grant* in view of its earlier decision in the case of *P v. S and Cornwall County Council.*[48] The latter case concerned strictly spoken gender namely, gender reassignment, discrimination, rather than 'sexual orientation' discrimination.[49] The case is nonetheless discussed within this Chapter, in order to illustrate its relationship with the *Grant* case. In *P v. S* the Court was sufficiently confident to take the view that discrimination by an employer against a transsexual person constitutes direct discrimination on grounds of sex contrary to Community law: 'discrimination arising (...) from the gender reassignment of the person concerned (...) is based, essentially if not exclusively, on the sex of the person concerned'.[50] In *P v. S* the Court clearly adopted a 'dignity approach'[51] to issues of equality and non-discrimination by holding that 'to tolerate such discrimination would be tantamount, as regards such a person, to a failure to respect the dignity and freedom to which he or she is entitled, and which the Court has a duty to safeguard'.[52] In essence, whereas *P v. S* was decided from a fundamental rights and dignity perspective, *Grant* was moulded into a wrongly analysed comparative exercise as a consequence of which an approach founded on a dignity model of equality was ruled out.

Thirdly, the ECJ's approach in *Grant* has been criticised on a more general level, namely, for failing to protect the human rights of European citizens in a 'progressive and proactive manner'.[53] Gerards has contrasted the ECJ's approach in *Grant* (1998) with the ECtHR's stance in the case of *Salgueiro v. Portugal* (1999).[54] In this case the homosexual applicant complained before the Strasbourg Court about a

47 For example Bell 1999, p. 63; Koppelman 2001, p. 632 with references to Bell.

48 *P v. S v. Cornwall County Council* (Case C-13/94) [1996] ECR I-2143. In order to give effect to this judgment the UK government made an amendment to the SDA by the enactment of the 1999 Sex Discrimination (Gender Reassignment) Regulations 1999, SI 1999, No. 1102.

49 In Dutch law discrimination on grounds of gender-reassignment has also been treated as sex discrimination. See e.g., Opinions 99-107; 00-73; 01-54; 02-195; 02-196; 03-139. The same approach is followed in English law; see the Sex Discrimination (Gender Reassignment) Regulations 1999 S.I. 1999, No. 1102 amending the SDA 1975.

50 Paragraph 20-21 of the judgment.

51 See more generally Fredman 2000, p. 17-19.

52 Paragraph 22 of the judgment. See for a discussion, Barnard 1997, p. 59-79.

53 Gerards 2003, p. 775.

54 *Salgueiro da Silva Mouta v. Portugal* EHRC 2000, 16 (Article 14 in conjunction with Article 8 ECHR), with a case comment by Gerards.

judgment rendered by the Lisbon Court of Appeal and as a result of which parental responsibility of the applicant's child was granted to the mother. In the applicant's view this constituted a breach of Article 8 of the Convention alone and in conjunction with Article 14. The Court agreed with unanimity. The facts of the case indicated that the applicant's homosexuality had been a *decisive* factor (my emphasis) in the domestic court's decision to award parental responsibility to the mother. A distinction which is exclusively based on sexual orientation is, in the view of the ECtHR, 'unacceptable under the Convention'.[55]

It is submitted that from the view-points of legal logic and normative justice the ECJ's stance in *Grant* deserves to be criticised in light of what was stated above. However, admittedly, politically perceived the Court's approach is more cognisable. As Bell has observed, the group of lesbians and gays constitutes a 'larger' minority group compared with the group of transsexuals and therefore, any 'sex-based' reasoning which concomitantly affords equal treatment to lesbians and gays bears a much greater legal and social impact than similar judicial reasoning in the context of gender-reassignment'.[56] Moreover, the *Grant* judgment was decided prior to a number of significant decisions decided by the Strasbourg Court, including *Salgueiro* discussed above.

In the literature[57] a connection has been established between *Grant*, on the one hand, and the judgments by the ECtHR in the cases of *Smith and Grady v. UK* and *Lustig Prean and Beckett v. UK*,[58] on the other. The Strasbourg Court held in these cases that the UK's Ministry of Defence Policy of excluding all gays and lesbians from serving in the armed forces, was contrary to Article 8 of the Convention.[59] The applicants in these cases had been dismissed from employment in the Royal Air Force/Royal Navy, on the ground of their homosexuality. Bamforth[60] has interpreted the 'armed forces cases' by the ECtHR in a broad fashion, in that they appear to lay down the principle that dismissal of public sector employees on grounds of sexual orientation is in breach of Articles 8 ECHR in itself, as well as in conjunction with Article 14 of the Convention. The last point is still of relevance for those States, including the UK, which have not signed up to Protocol No. 12 to the Convention. It is argued that the ECJ in cases such as *Grant* ought to apply a standard of protection

55 Paragraph 36 of the judgment.

56 Bell 1999, p. 74-75.

57 See notably Bamforth 2000.

58 *Smith* and *Grady v. the United Kingdom,* 33985/96 and 33986/96, 27 September 1999 (available at <http://www.echr.coe.int/echr> (Article 8 ECHR; no separate examination under Article 14 in conjunction with Article 8 ECHR); *Lustig-Prean* and *Beckett v. the United Kingdom,* 31417/96 and 32377/96, 27 December 1999 available at <http://www.echr.coe.int/echr> (Article 8 ECHR; no separate examination under Article 14 in conjunction with Article 8 ECHR).

59 No separate issues had arisen from the combined application of Articles 8 and 14 ECHR. Wintemute has moreover indicated that the fact that the Strasbourg Court in *Smith and Grady* and *Lustig Prean Beckett* explicitly drew a parallel between discrimination on grounds of 'race', on the one hand, and 'sexual orientation' on the other (see paragraphs 97 and 90 of the respective judgments) leads to the conclusion that the ECtHR regards sexual orientation discrimination 'very seriously'. See Wintemute 2005a, p. 185.

60 See Bamforth 2000.

that matches with the one adopted by the Strasbourg Court in cases such as the ones mentioned above (i.e. *Salgueiro* and the 'armed forces cases').

It is to be noted that with the adoption of the EFD it is no longer a vexed issue that dismissal on the ground of sexual orientation is in contravention of Community law. This holds true, both for private and public sector employees. Strasbourg case law remains nevertheless relevant, both for the interpretation of unanswered questions which may arise under the EFD, and in respect of cases which fall outside the scope of the Directive but potentially within the scope of Community *sex* discrimination law (e.g. discrimination against homosexuals in the provision of goods and services[61] or in the realm of social security[62]). At this juncture, another important case decided by the ECtHR must be discussed with which *Grant* can be effectively contrasted.[63]

In *Karner v. Austria*[64] the applicant[65] challenged a provision in the Austrian rent Act which, like in *Grant*, discriminated against same-sex couples, in comparison with married or unmarried opposite sex couples.[66] Under the impugned Austrian law, (*inter alia*)[67] unmarried and married opposite sex couples were entitled to succeed to the tenancy of the house, after the main tenant had deceased. In contrast, this right was denied to same-sex couples. In the view of the Supreme Court (*Oberster Gerichtshof*) the notion of 'life companion' in the vexed provision of the Rent Act was not to include persons of the same sex. The ECtHR reiterated its stance expressed in previous sexual orientation cases namely, that 'differences based on sexual orientation require particularly serious reasons by way of justification'.[68] This means that the state enjoys only a narrow margin of appreciation in justifying interference. The Court considered that the aim pursued by the contested rules, namely protection of the

61 Directive *2004/113/EC* of 13 December 2004 implementing the principle of equal treatment between men and women in the access to and supply of goods and services, *OJ* L 373, of 21 December 2004.

62 Equal Treatment in social security matters is regulated in the following Directives: Directive 79/7/EEC on Equal Treatment for Men and Women in matters of social security, *OJ* 1979, L 6/24 and Directive 86/378/EEC on Equal Treatment for Men and Women in Occupational Social Security Schemes, *OJ* 1986, L 225/40, as amended by Directive 96/97 *OJ* 1997, L 46/20.

63 Also Gerards 2003, p. 773, who has noted that the ECJ's outcome in *Grant* is 'diametrically opposed' to that of the Strasbourg Court in *Karner v. Austria* EHRC 2003, 83.

64 *Karner v. Austria* EHRC 2003, 83 with a case comment by Gerards 2003.

65 It should be noted that the applicant died whilst legal proceedings were pending. This fact constituted a separate legal issue in the case at hand, namely, the question as to whether or not the Court had jurisdiction in deciding on the case. This part of the case will not be dealt with in the present discussion.

66 An equivalent case has arisen in the context of English law, see *Ghaidan (appellant) v. Godin-Mendoza (FC) (respondent)* [2004] UKHL 30 (4-1, Lord Millett dissenting). This case has been discussed in the preliminary issues at the outset of Part IV. It is called to mind that in *Ghaidan* it was held by the majority in the House of Lords that the clause 'a person who was living with the original tenant as his or her wife or husband', contained in the 1977 Rent Act, must be judicially construed as to embrace *both* unmarried opposite *and* same-sex partners, for any other conclusion would be contrary to Articles 8 and 14 of the ECHR.

67 In addition, relatives in the direct line, including adopted children, and siblings of the former tenant were entitled to succeed to the tenancy under certain by the law prescribed conditions (Article 14(3) *Mietrechtsgesetz* (Rent Act).

68 Paragraph 37 of the judgment.

traditional family unit, was legitimate.[69] However, the government's justifiability defence nonetheless failed for non-compliance with the necessity requirement which forms part of the proportionality test:

> 'The principle of proportionality does not merely require that the measure chosen is in principle suited for realising the aim sought. It must also be shown that it was necessary to exclude persons living in a homosexual relationship from the scope of application of (…) the Rent Act in order to achieve that aim. The Court cannot see that the Government has advanced any arguments that would allow of such a conclusion.'[70]

It ultimately held that the differential treatment of same-sex couples, compared with opposite (married or unmarried) different-sex couples, constitutes a breach of Article 14 of the Convention in conjunction with Article 8.[71]

It should be noted that in reaching this conclusion the Strasbourg Court did not unequivocally indicate on which ground discrimination had occurred. In its reasoning the Court made reference both to the grounds of sex and sexual orientation. *Karner* is a ground-breaking judgment, for it requires that States that are Parties to the Convention afford equal treatment to same-sex partners who are in a loving and meaningful relationship, on the one hand, compared with unmarried (or married)[72] different sex partners, on the other.

The EFD does certainly require that, in cases which fall within its material scope, same-sex cohabitating partners are treated on a par with different-sex unmarried cohabitating partners. However, and for reasons to be explained hereafter, it is not fully clear whether the EFD also forbids unequal treatment between *unmarried* same-sex couples, compared with *married* opposite sex partners. An affirmative answer to this question is the more pressing in light of the fact that marital status is not an independently protected ground of discrimination in EC law. As will be seen below, (non-binding) Recital 22 of the Directive may, however, frustrate treating unmarried same-sex couples on an equal par with married opposite-sex couples.

Another case decided by the ECJ prior to the EFD concerns that of *D* and *Sweden v. Council*[73] in which the applicant appealed against a judgment initially decided on by the Court of First Instance (CFI).[74] Basically, *D*, who was in a registered partnership with his same-sex partner under Swedish law, challenged certain provisions of the Community's staff regulations (*D* being a Council official) which reserved certain

69 Paragraph 40.

70 Paragraph 41.

71 See also the case of *Salgueiro da Silva Mouta v. Portugal* EHRC 2000, 16 in which the Court held (by unanimity) that the denial on grounds of homosexuality of parental responsibility to the father, constituted an infringement of Article 14 in conjunction with Article 8 of the Convention.

72 The requirement that unmarried same-sex couples should be treated equally to married couples is, however, limited to situations where unmarried opposite-sex couples are already treated equally to married couples.

73 See joined cases C-122/99 P and C-125/99 P of 31 May 2001, [2001] ECR I-4319.

74 See Case T-264/97 [1999] Reports of European Community Staff Cases (ECR-SC) II-1, available at <http://www.europe.eu.int>.

benefits for *married* couples only.[75] In essence, and without much elaboration, the ECJ decided that 'marriage' cannot be compared with 'legal situations distinct from marriage'[76] and that it had not been *D's sex* but rather his *civil status* which triggered the differential treatment complained of. The Court rejected the claim whereby it followed the Opinion expressed by AG Mischo in the case at hand.[77]

Another case worth mentioning is that of *K.B. v. National Health Service Pensions Agency and another*.[78] Like *P v. S* this case regards unequal treatment in the context of transsexualism (gender) rather than homosexualism (sexual orientation). K.B. claimed an instance of discrimination with regard to pay, contrary to Article 141 EC and Council Directive 75/117/EEC (the Equal Pay Directive). The factual basis for her claim lay in the refusal by the NHS Pensions Agency to award a widower's pension to K.B.'s transsexual partner. According to the applicable Regulations a widower pension may only be granted to a person *married* to the scheme member. However, the marriage requirement could not be met by K.B. and her transsexual male partner, given that English legislation only permitted marriage between two persons of the opposite sex. In addition, under English law, a transsexual person who had undergone gender-reassignment could not alter her birth certificate so as to reflect the change in sex legally and officially.[79] In all, marriage was a *conditio sine qua non* for being awarded a widower's pension, however, at the same time, English law prevented the applicant from fulfilling this requirement. In the ECJ's view legislation which, contrary to the Strasbourg Convention, prevents a couple such as K.B. and her transsexual partner from fulfilling the marriage requirement, which must be complied with in order for one of them to be able to benefit from part of the pay of the partner, is in principle not compatible with Article 141 EC. In rendering this judgment the ECJ made reference to the case of *Goodwin* and *I v. the United Kingdom*,[80] in which the Strasbourg Court decided that the failure by the State to provide legal recognition of a person's gender-reassignment constitutes an infringement of Article 8 of the Convention. In addition, the EctHR concluded a breach of Article 12 of the Convention which secures the right to marry:

> 'While it is for the Contracting State to determine inter alia the conditions under which a person claiming legal recognition as a transsexual establishes that gender reassignment has been properly affected or under which past marriages cease to be valid and the

75 The facts thus differed from those in the *Grant case*, where the travel concessions were awarded to married couples and to unmarried couples of the opposite sex. In D, the impugned provisions made a distinction between persons in a registered partnership *v.* married persons.

76 See paragraph 37 of the judgment where the Court held that '(...) the Community judicature cannot interpret the Staff Regulations in such a way that legal situations distinct from marriage are treated in the same way as marriage'.

77 The ECJ's outcome in *D* has been contrasted with the more liberal approach in regard to the notion of marriage adopted by the ECtHR in the case of *Christine Goodwin v. the United Kingdom*, 28957/95, 11 July 2002 (Grand Chamber). See Gerards 2003, p. 775.

78 Case C-117/01, EHRC 2004, 10 with a case note by van der Velde.

79 This has changed with the entering into force of the Gender Recognition Act 2004.

80 *Christine Goodwin v. the United Kingdom*, 28957/95, 11 July 2002 and *I. v. United Kingdom*, 25680/94, 11 July 2002 (Grand Chamber).

> formalities applicable to future marriages (...), the Court finds no justification for barring the transsexual from enjoying the right to marry under any circumstances'.[81]

The ECJ, in reliance on *Goodwin* and *I* referred the matter back to the domestic court, for it was for the Member States to determine the conditions for giving legal recognition to the change of a person's gender. Simply put, it was the domestic court's rather than the ECJ's prerogative to decide on whether or not a person who finds herself in the applicant's circumstances can rely on Article 141 EC, in order to gain recognition of her right to nominate her transsexual partner as the beneficiary of a survivor's pension.

The judicial approach in *K.B.* is featured by caution. The ECJ did not on the basis of Community law stretch the notion of 'marriage' but left the matter for the national court to decide. The judgment does, however, affirm that a transgendered person has the right to be recognised by the law as being of the sex as it is post-gender reassignment (*in casu*: male).[82] As will be seen below, it is not completely clear whether or not Community law forbids differential treatment on grounds of marital status given that it may simultaneously result in direct or indirect sexual orientation (or, as argued, perhaps even sex) discrimination. This point will be further elaborated on in section 3.3 to follow.

3.2. *Conclusions*

The previous passages have revealed that, prior to the adoption of the Framework Directive, the ECJ's persistence on a comparative exercise has been detrimental to the effective protection against discrimination offered by the legal framework to gays and lesbians. Although it would not have been inconsistent had the ECJ adopted in *Grant* a similar 'deontological' equality approach to that adopted in *P v. S,* the Court effectively refrained from doing so. Due to conceiving Lisa Grant's claim in terms of comparative justice, the ECJ blocked the route to substantive justice for sexual minorities. Moreover, the ECJ has shown a cautious stance with respect to stretching the notion of 'marriage' beyond the conventional meaning of the word. However, as the analysis has sought to illustrate, developments in European Convention law potentially pave the way for a more 'rights-based approach' towards sexual orientation discrimination under Community law. This is of importance both in respect of the

81 See paragraph 103 of the judgment.

82 See in the context of English law the decision by the House of Lords in *A (Respondent) v. Chief Constable of West Yorkshire Police (Appellant) and another* of 6 May 2004 (available at <http://www.publications.parliament.uk/pa/ld200304ldjudgmt/jd040506/chief-1htm.>. This case concerned Ms A, who was a transgendered person (male to female). She had been refused by the Chief Constable of West Yorkshire Police to join the force as a woman, given that, according to the applicable rules, as a man she could not carry out routine searches upon women and, as a person who has the appearance of a woman, she could not search men. In light of this the Chief Constable had argued that a person's ability to carry out searches constitutes a genuine occupational requirement for the office of Constable. The House of Lords, however, unanimously held that A's refusal had been discriminatory under EC sex discrimination law which entitled her to be recognised in her reassigned gender.

legal application and (liberal) interpretation of sexual orientation discrimination cases which *are* covered by the Article 13 Framework Directive, on the one hand, and, cases which fall outside the scope of the Framework Directive but (possibly) within the ambit of Community sex discrimination law, on the other.

3.3. *The Legal Framework Ex Post the EFD*

3.3.1. Introduction

It has been illustrated in the above that, prior to the adoption of the EFD, Community law did not prohibit differential treatment between unmarried gays and lesbians (whether individually or in pairs) on the one hand, and married or unmarried straight persons, on the other (*Grant* case, which must, however, nowadays be perceived in light of *Karner* discussed above). Moreover, as follows from *D v. Council* (discussed above) no legal protection from discrimination is given by Community law to gay and lesbian registered partners, compared with married straight persons. Lastly, given that in the Netherlands, Belgium and Spain the law permits same-sex marriage, cases may arise in which a married gay couple is discriminated against, compared with a married different-sex couple.[83] Furthermore, discrimination may occur in respect of a person's sexual preference, behaviour and/or coming out. Which of these various forms of discrimination are presently prohibited under the EFD? The answer will become apparent in the analysis hereafter. In what follows, a detailed examination will be made of sexual orientation law in the EFD. Attention will be paid to the different prohibitions of discrimination, which will not be dealt with in a general fashion but rather within the specific context of sexual orientation law. Moreover, regard will be had to relevant exceptions and to the notion of 'sexual orientation' itself. Wherever appropriate, cross-references will be made to legal approaches and practices in the Netherlands which has a (relatively) long-standing tradition of dealing with sexual orientation discrimination complaints. At the end of the analysis some tentative conclusions will be drawn.

3.3.2. Concepts of Discrimination: a Tailor-Made Analysis in the Context of Sexual Orientation Law

As is known, the Directive contains four distinct prohibitions of discrimination: 'direct discrimination', 'indirect discrimination', the 'instruction to discriminate' and 'harassment'. Hereafter, these four concepts will be discussed (to a greater or lesser degree) in relation to the ground 'sexual orientation'.

Direct discrimination calls for an actual, past or hypothetical comparison of gay, or lesbian, or bisexual persons (whether alone or in pairs), with heterosexual persons (or *vice versa*). But for the aspect of 'sexual orientation', the legal comparator with whom the applicant has to be compared must find himself in an otherwise similar situation. Article 2(2)(a) EFD provides as follows: 'direct discrimination shall be

83 Waaldijk and Bonini-Baraldi 2006, p. 115.

taken to occur where one person is treated less favourably than another is, has been or would be treated in a comparable situation, on any of the grounds referred to in Article 1 [including 'sexual orientation'; MG]'. Given that Article 2(2)a EFD does not make a reference to 'persons' it also covers behaviour and relationships.[84] An instance of discrimination such as that suffered by Lisa Grant constitutes nowadays direct sexual orientation discrimination namely, 'less favourable treatment' of unmarried same-sex partners compared to unmarried opposite sex partners, contrary to Community law.[85] If, however, a benefit is granted on the condition of being *married*, the legal situation will be less clear-cut. Surely, this would constitute direct discrimination on grounds of 'marital status', however, as is known this ground of discrimination is not protected by the EFD. Generally perceived, discriminatory conduct that is based on 'marriage', might also be analysed on the basis of *indirect* discrimination on grounds of 'sexual orientation', given that the marriage requirement is neutrally applied but has in practice a disproportionate impact on gay and lesbian persons, who are legally precluded from marriage (save in the Netherlands, Belgium and Spain). Some authors have moreover argued that a marriage requirement constitutes *direct* sexual orientation discrimination, given that in nearly every EC Member State such a requirement affects 100% of the group of gay and lesbian persons.[86] Put differently, on this view, a marriage requirement constitutes a 'sexual orientation based criterion', analogous to 'pregnancy' which is 'gender-based'. Put differently, these authors argue that discrimination on grounds of marriage is no more than convenient shorthand for direct sexual orientation discrimination.[87] Whether or not marriage discrimination is at all captured by the protective scope of the Framework Directive will be discussed further below.

Case law in the Netherlands indicates that in order to establish a case of direct sexual orientation discrimination, 'sexual orientation' need not be the decisive factor which has resulted in the act of discrimination complained of.[88] It moreover follows from the interpretation of the relevant Dutch law that an employer may not ask a job applicant questions about his or her sexual orientation or about the sex of his or her partner. In fact, as can be deduced from Opinion 2004-104, an applicant may lawfully hide his or her sexual orientation and may even lie about it. In the view of

84 I am grateful to Dr. Kees Waaldijk for drawing my attention to this point.

85 Unless, of course, one of the exceptions to 'direct discrimination' applies. Exceptions will be discussed in section 3.3.4 hereafter.

86 Bell 2001b, p. 668.

87 Such an approach would dovetail with the ECJ's approach in pregnancy cases (e.g. *Dekker v. Stichting Vormingscentrum voor Jong Volwassenen* (Case C-177/88), [1990] ECR I-3941) and from which it follows that discrimination on grounds of pregnancy constitutes direct sex discrimination. See also the House of Lord's approach in the case of *James v. Eastleigh Borough Council,* [1990] 2 All ER, 607 (discussed in Chapter 3).

88 This is a general element of the ETC's case law which applies to all grounds of discrimination covered by Dutch equal treatment law. See for example Opinion 95-15; Opinion 96-10 and Opinion 2002-127.

the Commission, doing so does not warrant any conclusions as to the trustworthiness of the person (e.g. a job applicant) concerned.[89]

The prohibition of direct discrimination in the EFD is wide enough to cover instances of 'associated discrimination', for example, discrimination against a person by reason of his or her association with a gay or lesbian person. This follows from the absence of the words 'his' [sexual orientation; MG] or 'her' [sexual orientation; MG] in the legal definition of direct discrimination contained in Article 2(2) EFD.[90] The Directive also covers instances of discrimination on grounds of a false assumption regarding a person's sexual orientation. This is also the applicable approach in Dutch law.[91] Coverage of discrimination on grounds of a falsely assumed status is important, for an alleged discriminator could otherwise defend himself by stating that discrimination on grounds of (e.g.) 'homosexuality' has not (and could not have) occurred, if the alleged victim subsequently turned out to be a heterosexual person.

With respect to the prohibition of 'indirect discrimination' in relation to 'sexual orientation' the following remarks can be made. One of the specifics worth mentioning is the relaxation by the EFD of the insistence upon collecting statistical evidence. The legal implications of this have already been discussed in much detail in Chapter 3. As Bell has clarified, the gathering of statistical evidence in relation to the numbers of gay, lesbian or bisexual people in order to establish 'disproportionate impact'[92] poses problems, both in the sense that employees tend to mask their sexual preferences out of fear for existing prejudices and taboos, and by reason of privacy-related rights.[93] Moreover, from the perspective of the intrinsic logic of 'sexual orientation' as a ground of discrimination, it can be questioned whether the collection of statistical data is altogether feasible. Oliver has argued, with reference to so-called 'Queer Theory',[94] that sexual orientation is a volatile rather than fixed concept.[95] It can there-

89 Paragraph 6.13 of the Commission's Opinion. The Commission's approach dovetails with the stance adopted by the ECJ in *Tele Danmark* (Case C-109/00) [2001] ECR I-6993 (decided on by the ECJ in the context of EC sex discrimination law). In *Tele Danmark* a women had omitted to tell her employer that she was pregnant, even though the post for which she applied concerned a temporary post for only six months. The employer dismissed her but the ECJ found that the dismissal constituted direct sex discrimination contrary to Community law. See the analysis by Bonini-Baraldi 2004, p. 36, who has drawn this analogy. See Also Waaldijk 2005a, p. 66-67.

90 Waaldijk and Bonini-Baraldi 2006, p. 45.

91 See Opinion 02-84 in which the ETC referred to relevant case law by the Dutch Supreme Court. Opinion 02-84 concerned the ground 'political opinion', however, the ETC's line of reasoning can be easily extrapolated to the other grounds of discrimination covered by Dutch equal treatment law.

92 It is recalled from Chapter 3 that prior to the adoption of the AETD, the Burden of Proof Directive in sex discrimination cases required an applicant to prove disproportionate impact on the basis of statistical evidence. For a fully-fledged analysis of the concept of indirect discrimination in EC law, pre- and post- the adoption of the RD, EFD and AETD, the reader is referred to Chapter 3.

93 Bell 2001b, p. 659-660.

94 'Queer Theory' is a theoretical approach which has explained the nature of sexual orientation as a ground of discrimination, in the same way as this has, for example, been done by feminist legal theory in relation to 'sex' and by the 'medical' and 'social' models in relation to 'disability'. →

fore be very difficult for a person, if not impossible, to establish within which 'fixed category' he or she belongs at a given moment in time. Indeed, an individual's capability of establishing his or her sexual orientation would necessarily have been one of the very assumptions had the Directive enshrined a definition of indirect discrimination which insisted upon statistical evidence.[96]

In the Netherlands the ETC has sometimes artificially construed cases of direct sexual orientation discrimination ('distinction'; *onderscheid*) as cases of indirect sexual orientation discrimination.[97] Arguably, the ETC has done so, given that this technique allows the Commission to embark upon the analysis of the objective justification defence for a *prima facie* case of indirect discrimination.[98] Indeed, the 'closed model' of anti-discrimination law[99] would prevent the ETC from doing so, if the case were analysed on the premise of direct discrimination. In other cases, and as earlier touched on, the Commission has shifted its approach from 'indirect discrimination', in favour of 'direct discrimination'. The so-called 'dancing competition cases' illustrate that the borderlines between direct and indirect discrimination are not always palpable. In 1997, the ETC qualified a prohibition of same-sex couples to participate in dancing competitions as an instance of 'indirect (sexual orientation) discrimination'.[100] In the Commission's view, the requirement that a dancing couple consists of a woman and a men reflected a 'neutral' standard which, however, disproportionately affected homosexual persons. This approach must be criticised, because the contested requirement is not 'neutral' whatsoever but instead it incorporates the dominant heterosexual moral.[101] The Commission has recognised this criticism and has accordingly shifted its approach from 'indirect discrimination' to 'direct discrimination'. Hence, in Opinion 2004-116 the Commission decided in an equivalent case, that the exclusion of homosexual couples in dancing competitions constituted direct sexual orientation discrimination, as well as direct sex discrimination. The Commission *inter alia* considered that the norm was not neutral but indeed biased in favour of the heterosexual majority. The Commission moreover clarified that 'sexual orientation' differs from other grounds of discrimination in the sense that the manifestation of one's 'sexual orientation' gets first and foremost meaning in relation to others. Therefore,

Time and space have prevented the author from considering Queer Theory in further detail. For further analysis, the reader is referred to Whittle 2005 and to Cossman 2004.

95 Oliver 2004, p. 18: 'The concept of sexual orientation is (...) a very fluid one. Sexual orientation will often change over time, as people try out different sexual experiences. Although many individuals clearly define themselves as heterosexual or homosexual, many others may not, and still have had experiences in the past that depart from their present sexual identity.'

96 The difficulty of obtaining statistical date in relation to 'sexual orientation' also poses itself in the context of positive action law. Positive action law

97 This point was also made in light of relevant case law in Chapter 6 in the context of 'religion' and 'belief'. See in the particular context of 'sexual orientation' the following Opinions by the ETC: Opinion 98-137, Opinion 98-139 and Opinion 00-95. See moreover Waaldijk 2004, p. 356.

98 The objective justification defence for indirect discrimination cases has extensively been discussed in Chapter 3.

99 See generally Chapter 2.

100 Opinion 1997-29.

101 See Bamforth's 'social argument' referred to earlier on in the analysis.

in the ETC's view, the theoretical possibility that a homosexual man could participate in dancing competitions provided he danced with a female partner, was not a convincing factor for analysing the case on the basis of 'indirect discrimination'. Direct sex discrimination was established, given that a *man's* participation in a dancing competition was dependent on the participation of a woman, and *vice versa*, which constitutes a direct reference to 'sex'.[102]

In the above, we considered issues relating to the concepts of 'direct' and 'indirect discrimination'. Hereafter, our attention will be focused on the following. It was already indicated earlier that it is not very clear whether the Framework Directive also covers acts of discrimination on the ground of marriage. Attention must be drawn to the non-binding provision captured by Recital 22 of the Directive which stipulates that 'this Directive is without prejudice to national laws on marital status and the benefits dependent thereon'. It is not obvious whether this Recital will withhold the ECJ and domestic courts from taking the view that (direct) differential treatment on the ground of marriage, constitutes simultaneously direct or indirect discrimination on the ground of sexual orientation. It should be noted that this question is particularly pertinent in jurisdictions which do not prohibit discrimination on grounds of 'marriage' or 'civil status'.[103] In the Netherlands, the ETC has held that discrimination on grounds of marriage also constitutes *indirect* discrimination on grounds of sexual orientation.[104] However, since the opening up in 2001 of marriage to same-sex couples this mode of legal reasoning has become redundant, given that discrimination of gay married couples nowadays constitutes direct discrimination on grounds of 'marital status' (which is a protected ground under Dutch non-discrimination law, but not under Community law).[105] It should be stressed that Recital 22 of the EFD is non-

102 See also the outcome of an equivalent case recently decided by the District Court in the Hague in summary proceedings (*Kort Geding*) (26 July 2006, AY5005). The court, like the CGB, did accept that the exclusion of same sex partners in dancing competition cases constitutes direct discrimination on grounds of *sex*, given that 'the participation of a woman will only be possible if a man also participates, and vice versa' (paragraph 3.5. of the judgment). In casu, it could, however, not be established whether this (*prima facie*) instance of direct sex discrimination could be justified on the basis of the exception enshrined in the Equal Treatment Decree (*Besluit Gelijke Behandeling*, adopted on the basis of the GETA), namely that differences in treatment between women and men may be lawful in the context of sports activities, where it can be proven that there is a relevant difference in the average performance of men, compared to women (see Article 1(g) of the Equal Treatment Decree). The Court observed that an analysis of this question would require further examination which was, however, prevented by the nature of the legal proceedings concerned (i.e. 'summary proceedings'). Unlike the ETC, the court did, however, not also conclude a case of direct *sexual orientation* discrimination. The court argued that a homosexual man or woman was not precluded from participating in a dancing competition with a person of the opposite sex. Regrettably, the court therefore did not recognise that the contested regulations reflected a heterosexual dominant norm which operated to the disadvantage of homosexual persons. Unlike the ETC, the Court apparently did also not acknowledge that a person's 'sexual orientation' gets first and for all meaning in relation to others.

103 Also Bell 2001b, p. 668.

104 Waaldijk 2004, p. 358 with reference to the relevant Dutch case law.

105 Waaldijk 2004, p. 358.

binding and that a counterpart exception to that contained in it cannot be traced within the material provisions of the Directive itself. As will be seen hereafter, the UK legislator has implemented Recital 22 of the Directive by inserting a clear-cut exception into the national implementing legislation, with the effect that the legislation shall be without prejudice to limiting certain benefits to married persons only.[106] This provision has passed the 'legal test' in a decision by the English High Court which did, however, not refer any preliminary questions to the ECJ under the Article 234 EC procedure. This decision will be commented upon in greater detail in the analysis of English sexual orientation law in section 4 hereafter.

Upon consideration, it appears that Recital 22 of the EFD could have four possible legal effects.[107] Firstly, it could have the effect of precluding the courts from finding an instance of discrimination on grounds of sexual orientation altogether. In other words, since marriage discrimination, it could be argued, has been exempted from the Directive's scope of application this effectively stops any subsequent legal analysis of sexual orientation discrimination that flows from the imposition of the marriage requirement. Secondly, Recital 22 could be read to mean that *prima facie* indirect sexual orientation discrimination, resulting from the application of a marriage requirement, is *per definition* objectively justified. *De facto*, the practical result of both the first and second effects would be identical. Thirdly, Waaldijk and Bonini-Baraldi have argued that Recital 22 EFD constitutes one of the factors to be taken into account in the legal assessment of 'justification' of *prima facie* cases of indirect sexual orientation discrimination.[108] Fourthly, and with reference to the non-binding nature of the Recital and the binding nature of the prohibition of discrimination, the ECJ could conclude a case of direct or indirect sexual orientation discrimination. Admittedly, the conclusion of an instance of direct or indirect sexual orientation discrimination is discouraged by the ECJ's restrictive stance in *D* (discussed above) in which the Court adopted the view that 'legal situations distinct from marriage' cannot be treated in the same way as marriage. In contrast, however, the aforementioned judicial stance would be supported by the ECJ's judgment in *K.B.* In that case the Court held that making benefits dependent on a marriage requirement, notwithstanding that the couple concerned is legally prevented from marrying, is in principle in contravention of EC sex discrimination law. This line of reasoning could then be extrapolated to the realm of sexual orientation discrimination law.[109] Construing discrimination on grounds of marital status in terms of indirect sexual orientation discrimination is also supported by the legal approach adopted by the Dutch ETC, notwithstanding that in the particular legal context in the Netherlands this mode of legal reasoning has no longer been necessary since the opening up of 'same sex marriage' in 2001. If the ECJ feels inspired by domestic approaches in future case law, this will amount to 'bottom-up' influence.

[106] Although, as will be referred to below, the exception was largely abolished in December 2005 when the Civil Partnership Act and additional legislation took effect.

[107] Also Bonini-Baraldi 2004, p. 33-35 and Wintemute 2004b, p. 496.

[108] Waaldijk and Bonini-Baraldi 2006, p. 42-43.

[109] Wintemute 2005a, p. 191.

In addition to the concepts of 'direct discrimination' and 'indirect discrimination', the EFD contains a prohibition of harassment and the instruction to discriminate. 'Harassment' has been extensively discussed in Chapter 4 in relation to the grounds 'sex', 'race' and 'disability'. Much of what was stated in that chapter could be extrapolated to the ground 'sexual orientation'. It has been argued in Chapter 4 that the blanket prohibition of harassment by the Directive reflects a deontological model of equality that can be contrasted with the comparative equality model. The following point is worth calling to mind. The concept of harassment in the EFD is textually limited to 'hostile work environment' harassment to the exclusion of '*quid pro quo* harassment'.[110] In '*quid pro quo* harassment' cases the perpetrator usually demands sexual favours in turn for e.g. a promotion or for being hired for the job. Save with regard to 'sexual orientation', '*quid pro quo* harassment' is not at a premium in relation to the grounds covered by the EFD although, as discussed in Chapter 4, it is highly relevant in relation to sex.[111] In other words, unlike e.g. a person's 'disability' or 'religion', his or her 'sexual orientation' can easily trigger *quid pro quo* scenarios at work. In the absence of relevant case law by the ECJ, it cannot be said with certainty whether the Court will interpret the prohibition of 'hostile work environment harassment' in the EFD broadly, so as to encompass claims of '*quid pro quo* harassment'. A teleological interpretation of the law should induce the ECJ to answer this question in the affirmative.

Comments on the last-mentioned prohibition of discrimination, i.e. the prohibition of instruction to discriminate can be very short. The well-known example is that of an employer instructing a recruitment agency to only seek personnel belonging to the community of straight people (whereby I leave aside the perceived practical and theoretical difficulties of classifying persons within fixed categories of sexual identity).

3.3.3. The Notion of 'Sexual Orientation'

The Directive prohibits discrimination on the ground of 'sexual orientation' rather than for example discrimination against gay, lesbian or bisexual orientations, which reflects the symmetrical framework upon which it rests. Hence, theoretically, the Directive also prohibits discrimination of a straight person *vis-à-vis* a homosexual person although such a scenario clearly does not reflect the social phenomenon of homophobia which the law essentially aims to address. The Directive specifies nothing beyond the bare reference to 'sexual orientation'. In Dutch law, the notion of sexual orientation (*seksuele gerichtheid*, to be distinguished from *seksuele voorkeur*, meaning sexual preference) has been interpreted broadly. According to the Parliamentary History to the GETA 'sexual orientation' relates to a person's orientation in sexual and love feelings, expressions and relationships.[112] In fact, the Dutch legislator has

110 For further explanation of this point, I refer to Chapter 4. In that Chapter, I have also elucidated the meaning of 'hostile work environment harassment' and of '*quid pro quo* harassment'.

111 This has been recognised by EC law, given that the AETD does regulate *quid pro quo* harassment.

112 For example Opinion 2003-113, paragraph 5.3. with reference to *Parliamentary Documents* II, 1990-1991, 22 014, no. 3., p. 13. See also Opinion 2003-150, paragraph 5.3. The original Dutch →

intentionally opted for the term 'orientation', rather than 'preference' in order to leave no doubt that both the *forum internum* and *externum* are captured. In other words: 'orientation' is a broader notion than 'preference'.[113] Both in English and Dutch law, 'sexual orientation' embraces heterosexuality, homosexuality and bisexuality, to the exclusion, however, of practices such as sadomasochism and paedophilia. The European Commission, in its explanatory memorandum to the EFD,[114] expressed the view that the Directive covers sexual orientation, but not sexual behaviour. Clearly, such an interpretation undermines the protective potential of the legal prohibition of sexual orientation discrimination, for it renders the right to equality of sexual preference extremely shallow. On the one hand, a person is permitted to *have* homosexual or bisexual feelings and thoughts but, on the other, he or she is prevented from *acting* in conformity therewith. Bell has rightly criticised the Commission's approach for being 'misplaced' as well as for being unduly wide in its interpretative scope. In his view, the Commission's statement must solely be understood in the context of a political rush, in order to secure that acts of paedophilia fall outside the scope of sexual orientation.[115] Indeed, any other interpretation would counteract established case law by the ECtHR. The Strasbourg Court has acknowledged that sexual orientation also includes sexual behaviour which in principle is protected by Articles 8 (and 14) of the Convention.[116]

3.3.4. Exceptions to the Central Norm

There are various exceptions to the prohibition of discrimination (excluding the prohibition of 'harassment' which is prohibited by the Directive *per se*)[117] contained within the EFD. Exceptions will be discussed henceforth, with the exception of positive action, which was extensively discussed in Chapter 5. Moreover, objective justification of indirect discrimination will not be examined either, given that this has been done in depth in Chapter 3.

Article 2(5) of the Directive provides that 'this Directive shall be without prejudice to measures laid down by national law which, in a democratic society, are necessary for public security, for the maintenance of public order and the preven-

formulation reads as follows: '[*hetero- of homoseksuele (of bi-seksuele; MG) gerichtheid*] *(…) ziet op de gerichtheid van een persoon in seksuele en liefdesgevoelens, -uitingen en relaties*'. See also Waaldijk 2004, p. 349-351.

113 See paragraph 5.3 of both Opinion 2003-113 and Opinion 2003-150. See also *Parliamentary Documents* II, 1991-1992, 22 014, no. 5, p. 21. See furthermore Waaldijk 2004, p. 349-351.

114 COM(1999) 565 (25 November 1999), *OJ* [2000] C 177/E/42.

115 Bell 2001b, p. 658.

116 *Salgueiro da Silva Mouta v. Portugal* EHRC 2000, 16. *L and V v. Austria*, EHRC 2003, 18; *Karner v. Austria* EHRC 2003, 83. See also Bonini-Baraldi 2004, who has argued that the Directive's concept of 'sexual orientation' embraces both feelings and conduct which can *inter alia* be deduced from the national security exception contained in Article 2(5) EFD (to be discussed hereafter in the main text). If sexual orientation merely saw at the *forum internum*, a national security exception would be *of little or no use*, for it is hard to see how mere feelings could constitute a threat to overriding interests of national security or the rights of others.

117 This point has been explained in detail in Chapter 4.

tion of criminal offences, for the protection of health and for the protection of the rights and freedoms of others'. It should be noted that no counterpart exception can be found in the RD and in the AETD.[118] It is not quite clear under what kind of circumstances employment-related sexual orientation discrimination can be legitimately upheld in reliance upon the exception contained in Article 2(5) EFD.[119] Outside employment (thus, in areas to which the Directive does not apply) one may think of precluding men, who have had sex with other men, from being a blood or sperm donor in light of, respectively, an increased risk of being HIV infected, or, of being infected with a sexually transmissible disease (STD).[120]

Article 4(1) of the Directive contains the genuine occupational requirement exception (GOR). This exception has already been examined in Chapter 6 in relation to the ground 'religion' and 'belief'. For both factual and theoretical reasons the application of the Article 4(1) EFD exception to sexual orientation cases it not obvious. Factually, it is difficult to imagine the types of jobs the essential requirements of which are best fulfilled by persons who are homosexual (or lesbian, or heterosexual or bisexual, as the case may be). In Dutch law, no cases have arisen on the matter, given that Dutch law does not contain a GOR exception in relation to 'sexual orientation'. In the already discussed cases of *Smith and Grady v. UK* and *Lustig Prean and Beckett v. UK* (decided by the ECtHR), heterosexuality was effectively struck down as being a decisive job requirement for serving in the army. Sexual orientation is indeed not covered by Article 3(4) EFD which provides that 'Member States may provide that this Directive, in so far as it relates to discrimination on the grounds of disability and age, shall not apply to the armed forces'. Within employment it might be the case that certain counselling jobs, or certain forms of service provision, which are specifically targeted at members of, for instance, the homosexual community may lawfully be confined to homosexual persons. A person's sexual orientation could be a GOR for the position of a welfare officer or counsellor for (e.g.) Moroccan homosexual boys. It follows that Article 4(1) EFD may restrict the call for equality for the sake of meeting demands of cultural empathy. Nonetheless, it being an exception to the prohibition of discrimination, domestic courts and the ECJ ought to apply Article 4(1) EFD restrictively.[121]

118 See, however, also Article 39(3) EC which contains a similar exception to the free movement of workers in the context of EC nationality discrimination law.

119 Waaldijk and Bonini-Baraldi 2006, p. 48 have warned for the risk that 'in contrast with case law of the European Court of Human Rights making it clear that homosexual conduct per se cannot be criminalised (with reference to Dudgeon) [Article 2(5) EFD] will be relied upon to place particular limitations in sensitive areas, such as the armed forces'.

120 In Opinion 1998-139 decided by the Dutch ETC the respondent was a fertility laboratory and sperm bank that excluded all men who had an increased risk of being infected with a STD from donating sperm. This neutrally applied criterion had the effect of disproportionately affecting men who had recently had sex with other men. The Commission concluded a case of indirect discrimination which could be objectively justified. See also Opinion 1998-137 in which the Commission adopted a similar legal approach with respect to the donation of blood.

121 This clearly follows from the ECJ's own case law on genuine occupational requirements in the area of gender discrimination. See, for example, Case 222/84, *Johnston v. Chief Constable of the Royal Ulster Constabulary* [1986] ECR 1651.

From a theoretical perspective, the Article 4(1) EFD exception has been criticised by Oliver with reference to a *Queer Theory* analysis. *Queer Theory* was touched on earlier in this chapter.[122] According to Oliver

> '(...) a queer theory analysis can be used to challenge the binary opposition of the categories heterosexual and homosexual, such that [citing the work done by Stychin[123]] 'sexual identities might be conceived as multiplicitous, shifting, fluid and fragmented'. If a queer theory approach is applied to a GOR [Genuine Occupational Requirement; MG], it appears to become impossible to state with any certainty whether a person is of a 'particular' sexual orientation (...)'.

In other words, the application of the GOR exception of Article 4(1) EFD presupposes the altogether possibility of categorising people's sexual orientations and identities into 'fixed categories'. It is this possibility which at an abstract and theoretical level has been challenged by the *Queer Theory*. *Queer Theory* would arguably challenge the same presupposition in the contexts of positive action (the possibility granted by anti-discrimination law to afford preferential treatment to, for example, homosexuals, presupposes the possibility of delineating the target group) and indirect discrimination (disparate impact upon the group of homosexuals presupposes the possibility of delineating this group).[124] In this sense, therefore, the application of the *Queer Theory* in law and in practice can be problematic, for it has the potential of undermining some of the legal tools which can be adopted to secure greater equality for sexual minorities.

Article 4(2) EFD contains the thorniest exception. This Article seeks to balance the competing rights of equal treatment and religious freedom. Given that this Article was extensively discussed in Chapter 6 it will not be scrutinised at this juncture.

3.3.5. Conclusions

The analysis of EC sexual orientation discrimination law, *ex post* the adoption of the Framework Directive, warrants the following concluding remarks. First, although the Directive contains clear-cut prohibitions of direct and indirect sexual orientation discrimination, it is currently opaque what legal impact these will have in cases of discrimination on grounds of 'marriage'. Non-binding Recital No. 22 of the EFD provides that the Directive is without prejudice to marriage requirements. This might have the effect that discrimination on grounds of marriage is altogether excluded from the EFD's scope of application. In other words, notwithstanding its non-binding nature, Recital 22 could prevent the intersection of marriage discrimination and sexual orientation discrimination from being prohibited under EC law. Alternatively, Recital No. 22 could have the effect that marriage discrimination results in indirect sexual

122 See for further references footnote 94 above.

123 C. Stychin, *Law's desire: Sexuality and the Limits of Justice* (New York: Routledge, 1990) at 141 and 153, cited by Oliver 2004, footnote 85.

124 It should, however, be recalled from Chapter 3 that the group dimension of indirect discrimination has been mitigated by the legal definition of indirect discrimination contained in the EFD.

orientation discrimination, which is *a priori* justified. Recital No. 22 could furthermore be interpreted as constituting one of more factors that are taken into account in the assessment of the 'justifiability' of acts of indirect discrimination on grounds of sexual orientation. Yet differently, given that the Recital is non-binding (as opposed to the EFD's prohibitions of (direct and indirect) discrimination!), the Court may conclude that marriage discrimination constitutes direct or indirect sexual orientation discrimination. The latter approach would arguably be supported by the case law of the ECtHR, as well as by legal approaches in the Netherlands. However, admittedly, if marriage discrimination is construed as simultaneously being a form of sexual orientation discrimination, it will not be clear what the added legal value is of Recital No. 22 EFD. In any case, the Recital should bear no impact on cases concerning the differential treatment of a married homosexual couple, compared to a married heterosexual couple. After all, this would amount to direct sexual orientation discrimination, for the only distinguishing factor is the 'sexual orientation' of the persons concerned.

The Directive also protects from discrimination on the ground of a falsely perceived sexual orientation, as well on the ground of being in association with a gay, lesbian, bisexual or heterosexual person. The analysis also showed that the intrinsic nature of 'sexual orientation' renders it difficult to collect statistical data in respect of this ground. The reasons for this difficulty are practical, legal and theoretical in kind. In light of this, the EFD has taken on a flexible approach with regard to the collection of statistical evidence in indirect discrimination cases. With regard to the concept of harassment, it as argued that a deliberate interpretation of the law should secure that so-called '*quid pro quo* scenarios' are covered by the Directive. After all, 'sexual orientation', unlike the other grounds covered by the EFD, easily triggers instances of '*quid pro quo* harassment'. The analysis moreover examined the meaning of 'sexual orientation' in the EFD, in light of Dutch and ECHR law. It has been argued that, notwithstanding indications to the contrary, 'sexual orientation' in the Directive captures both, the *forum internum* and the *forum externum*. Lastly, exceptions to the central norm were considered. It is currently not clear what kind of scenarios could be covered by the public security exception which, in any case, should be interpreted restrictively. Moreover, it was illustrated that perceived difficulties in delineating the group of gay, lesbian, bisexual or heterosexual persons might become manifest in relation to the GOR exception. This has arguably been recognised by Dutch law which is short of a GOR exception in relation to 'sexual orientation'.

4. Legal Novelties in English Non-Discrimination Law

4.1. *Introduction*

In the foregoing sections an analysis has been made of sexual orientation law in the context of EC law. Hereafter, I will proceed with an examination of the top-down influence of EC law upon English law in this area. It is recalled from the introduction to this chapter that the English legislator has transposed the sexual orientation law framework contained within the Article 13 EC Framework Directive by adopting the 2003 S.O. Regulations.[125] The Regulations prohibit sexual orientation discrimination in the areas of employment and vocational training. It is worth noting that Section 81 of the 2006 Equality Act which has recently been enacted contains an enabling provision permitting the government to introduce Regulations to outlaw discrimination on grounds of sexual orientation in the fields of access to goods, facilities and services.[126] Sexual orientation discrimination outside employment, which is currently not prohibited by English law (and neither by EC law) will not be dealt with in the discussion to follow.

With the adoption of the Regulations discrimination on grounds of sexual orientation has for the first time been expressly regulated by English statutory law. Before the entering into force of the Regulations applicants attempted to seek judicial relief from alleged instances of sexual orientation discrimination via the route of domestic *sex* discrimination law (*i.e.* via the SDA 1975) albeit with little success. Both in *MacDonald v. Advocate General for Scotland* (sexual orientation discrimination in the Royal Air Forces) and in *Pearce v. Governing Body of Mayfield School*[127] (harassment of a lesbian teacher by pupils in a school) the House of Lords refused to regard instances of sexual orientation discrimination as being also cases of unlawful sex discrimination under the 1975 SDA. Like the ECJ in *Grant* the Law Lords have dealt with these cases within a framework of comparative justice. They have drawn the legal comparison with a homosexual person of the opposite sex, rather than with a heterosexual person. Both cases have meant that gay men and lesbian women, who were victims of sexual orientation discrimination in employment were short of legal protection, unless a gay man, or a lesbian woman, could prove a case of 'less favourable treatment' compared with a lesbian woman, or a gay man, respectively.[128] As we have seen throughout this chapter the law flowing from the ECHR has positively contributed to the legal protection of homosexual persons both within and outside employment.[129] With the entry into force of the 1998 HRA in 2000 this positive influence is likely to percolate into the domestic equality law framework. However, as explained at the outset of Part IV, European human rights law creates itself a schism in legal protection, given that only public sector employees can directly rely upon Articles 8 and 14 of the Convention.[130] Their private sector peers can only do so indirectly via the legal mechanisms explained in the preliminary issues to Part IV. The S.O. Regulations apply to public and private sector employment, including the

125 See Statutory Instruments 2003 No. 1661, The Employment Equality (Sexual Orientation) Regulations 2003.

126 Equality Act 2006, Part 3, Section 81. The Act has been accompanied by a set of Explanatory Notes which comment upon each Section within the Act in more detail.

127 *Macdonald (Appellant) v. Advocate General for Scotland (Respondent)* and *Pearce (Appellant) v. Governing Body of Mayfield School (Respondents)* [2003] UKHL 34 (judgment of 19 June 2003);

128 See for a comment the Law Reports in EOR No. 98 July/August 2001, p. 39-40 See also Wintemute 2003, p. 267-281.

129 See also de Marco 2004, p. 6.

130 See in this respect also the 'armed forces' cases of the ECtHR earlier referred to.

armed forces. They moreover apply to vocational training including most types of university education.[131]

In the passages to follow a detailed analysis will be made of the S.O. Regulations whereby cross-references will be made to the applicable provisions in the EFD. The emphasis will be on particularities arising in the specific context of sexual orientation and a repetition of the analysis of the concepts of direct, indirect discrimination, harassment and the instruction to discrimination will largely be avoided. The analysis will not cover 'positive action', given that this was discussed separately in Chapter 5. In discussing the content of the Regulations, I will also pay attention to the first judicial case (arisen before the High Court) that has been adjudicated on within the context of the Regulations. This case sheds light upon the material meaning of a number of (sub) regulations contained in the S.O. Regulations.

4.2. *The Scope of 'Sexual Orientation'*

Regulation 2(1) of the S.O. Regulations specifies that sexual orientation means a sexual orientation towards *(1)* persons of the same sex, *(2)* persons of the opposite sex or (3) persons of the same sex and of the opposite sex. This provision thus reflects the symmetry principle where it affords legal protection from unlawful instances of sexual orientation discrimination to gays, lesbians, heterosexual men and women, and bi-sexuals alike. However, according to the explanatory comments to the S.O. Regulations the notion of sexual *orientation* does not embrace sexual practices, conduct or preferences (*e.g.* sadomasochism and paedophilia).[132] It is submitted that, as observed earlier in the context of EC law, a blanket exclusion from the Regulations' scope of application of the *forum externum,* (as opposed to the *forum internum*) runs counter to established case law by the Strasbourg Court in the context of Articles 8 and 14 ECHR. In the absence of case law, it is foggy whether the S.O. Regulations *in se* prohibit, for instance, discrimination by the employer against a gay worker who holds hands with another male worker while walking to the lunch canteen. It should, however, be highlighted that whilst drawing up the S.O. Regulations, the British legislator was under a legal obligation to act compatibly with the rights and freedoms contained in the Convention. This follows from Section 6(1) of the HRA 1998 which has been discussed in the preliminary issues at the outset of Part IV. Moreover, the Regulations must be read and given effect to in a manner which accords with ECHR law 'so far as it is possible to do so' (Section 3(1) HRA 1998). It thus follows that the Regulations have to be interpreted by courts and tribunals so as to offer protection from both *having* a sexual orientation and from *manifesting* it.

131 For a detailed overview of the protective scope of the S.O. Regulations, I refer to de Marco 2003, Chapter 3.

132 Rubenstein 2003, p. 26. See in this context the following criticism by Wintemute: '[t]he (...) *Explanatory Memorandum* (...) states misleadingly that sexual orientation 'does not extend to sexual practices and preferences (e.g. sadomasochism and paedophilia). The Memorandum should instead have stated that sexual orientation: 'does not extend to aspects of sexual practices and preferences other than the fact that the practices and preferences involved are same-sex, opposite sex or both.' (Wintemute 2004b, p. 493).

4.3. *Concepts of Discrimination*

The S.O. Regulations prohibit discrimination on grounds of sexual orientation in employment and occupation, including vocational training. The prohibition of discrimination is fourfold and includes: 'direct discrimination', 'indirect discrimination', 'harassment' and discrimination by way of 'victimisation'.[133] Like the R&B Regulations, discussed in Chapter 6, the S.O. Regulations have failed to transpose the prohibition of the instruction to discrimination. As argued in Chapter 6, the prohibition of 'direct discrimination' is, however, sufficiently ample to fill this lacuna, notably in light of existing judicial authorities in the context of race.[134] The definition of 'direct discrimination' in Regulation 3(1)(a) refers to less favourable treatment 'on grounds of sexual orientation'. This is sufficiently broad as to encompass (1) discrimination based on a person's sexual orientation, (2) on a false assumption or perception about a person's sexual orientation, (3) on the basis of being in association with a gay, lesbian, heterosexual or bisexual person, (4) as well as for failing to comply with an instruction to discriminate.[135] Direct discrimination cannot be justified save in very limited circumstances outlined within the Regulations themselves. Exceptions will be dealt with henceforth in section 4.4.

The prohibition of 'indirect discrimination' is contained in Regulation 3(1) (b), which stipulates that

> '(…) a person ('A') discriminates against another person ('B') if-
> A applies to B a provision, criterion or practice which he applies or would apply equally to persons not of the same sexual orientation as B, but-
> i) which puts or would put persons of the same sexual orientation as B at a particular disadvantage when compared with other persons,
> ii) which puts B at that disadvantage, and
> iii) which A cannot show to be a proportionate means of achieving a legitimate aim.

This provision requires that the person who complains about indirect sexual orientation discrimination has suffered an actual personal detriment, a requirement that is absent in Article 2(2)(b) EFD. It thus follows that under English law it appears to be insufficient that the person concerned *risks* suffering a disadvantage as a result of the application of a neutrally applied standard. Unlike direct discrimination, indirect discrimination may be objectively justified which has extensively been explained in chapter 3.

Regulations 5(1) and 5(2) cover the prohibition of harassment. The legal conditions for establishing a case of ground-related harassment, as well as the theoretical vision of equality which informs this concept in provisions of positive law, were discussed in Chapter 4. That Chapter moreover considered issues relating to the liability

133 See Part I of the Regulations under 'General'.

134 *Showboat Entertainment Centre Ltd v. Owens* [1984] IRLR 7 and *Weathersfield (t/a Van and Truck Rentals) v. Sargent* [1999] IRLR 94. See also *Redfearn v. Serco LTD t/a West Yorkshire Transport Service* [2005] IRLR 744. The aforementioned cases were discussed in Chapter 6.

135 DTI Explanatory Notes for the S.O. Regulations and the R&B Regulations 2003, p. 5-6, available at <http://www/dti.gov.uk/er/equality/so_rb_longexplan.pdf>.

for harassment. It is briefly recalled that the harm of ground-related harassment at work manifests itself through a violation of the person's dignity *and* (EC law imposing cumulative conditions)/*or* (English law merely imposing alternative conditions) through the creation of a hostile work environment. Importantly, post-implementation of EC law harassment is no longer perceived as a *species* of the *genus* direct discrimination. The huge practical advantage of this is that the law no longer requires that a comparison be drawn with a relevant real or hypothetical comparator. Hence, for example, a gay worker who is the victim of acts of harassment by co-workers, or by his employer, needs (merely) to establish that the acts complained of are connected to sexual orientation, that they infringe his dignity, *or*, that they create an intimidating or hostile work environment. However, unlike the situation pre-transposition of the EFD, it is no longer a legal requirement to prove a case of 'less favourable treatment' of (e.g.) a female lesbian worker *vis-à-vis* a male gay worker.[136] Similarly, it is no longer a legitimate defence for an employer to submit before a court that direct discrimination has not occurred given that the same evil or disadvantageous treatment would have been meted out to a gay person of the opposite sex (the so-called 'levelling down defence' which is not precluded by the formal equality model). In short: the prohibition of harassment presently rests upon a deontological, rather than a comparative vision of justice. This conceptual change is laudable for, as is the case with pregnancy discrimination law, the limits of comparative justice can easily be detained in a context of the law on harassment, given that relevant comparators are not readily available.

Lastly, discrimination by way of 'victimisation' is prohibited by Regulation 4. It is to be noted that the Framework Directive does not regard 'victimisation' as a form of discrimination but instead it deals with this concept within the context of remedies and enforcement. Hence, English law departs from this conceptual approach. One of the practical advantages this seems to entail is that the partially reversed burden of proof contained in Article 10 EFD equally applies in victimisation cases.

4.4. *Exceptions to the Prohibition of Sexual Orientation Discrimination*

In this section the focus will be on the circumstances which may justify an infringement of the principle of non-discrimination on grounds of sexual orientation. Summarised, these circumstances are the following: Regulation 7 (genuine occupational requirement exception), Regulation 24 (national security exception); Regulation 25 (exception for benefits dependent on marital status), Regulation 26 (exception for positive action). Moreover, Regulation 3(1)(b) contains a general objective justification exception for *prima facie* instances of indirect sexual orientation discrimination. The latter has been extensively discussed in Chapter 3 and will not be repeated at this juncture. The same applies with respect to the positive action exception which was examined in depth in Chapter 5.

136 As discussed in section 4.1 a female lesbian worker was prevented from comparing herself with a female heterosexual worker under the SDA 1975.

The exceptions contained in Regulations 7(2), 7(3) and 25 have been the object of judicial proceedings in the first case decided in the context of the S.O. Regulations. The case of *Amicus and others v. Secretary of State for Trade and Industry*[137] was decided by Mr Justice Richards for the High Court of Justice.[138] The case was brought by *Amicus* and six other trade unions (the claimants) against the Secretary of State for Trade and Industry (the defendant) with a number of religious organisations as interveners to the case. Judgment was delivered on 26 April 2004. The case will be discussed at appropriate junctures in the discussion to follow.

Regulation 24 contains the public security exception. It gives effect to Article 2(5) of the EFD, which was earlier discussed. Regulations 7(2) and 7(3), read in conjunction with Regulation 7(1), concern exceptions for occupational requirements. Let me first analyse Regulation 7(2). This Regulation seeks to implement Article 4(1) of the EFD. It provides as follows:

> 7(2) This paragraph applies where, having regard to the nature of the employment or the context in which it is carried out –
> (a) being of a particular sexual orientation is a genuine and determining occupational requirement;
> (b) it is proportionate to apply that requirement in the particular case; and
> (c) either
> (i) the person to whom that requirement is applied does not meet it, or
> (ii) the employer is not satisfied, and in all the circumstances it is reasonable for him not to be satisfied, that that person meets it,
> and this paragraph applies whether or not the employment is for purposes of an organised religion.

The circumstances in which an employer may lawfully discriminate are outlined in Regulation 7(1), namely with regard to 'recruitment', 'promotion', 'training' and 'dismissal'. It follows from the *Amicus* case (earlier referred to) that the proportionality requirement implies (notwithstanding that this is not explicitly stated in Regulation 7(2) of the S.O. Regulations) that by imposing a GOR the employer must pursue a legitimate aim. This requirement explicitly also flows from Article 4(1) EFD. A more pertinent point concerns, however, the question whether the ending clause of Regulation 7(2) namely, 'or the employer is not satisfied, and in all the circumstances it is reasonable for him not to be satisfied, that that person meets [the imposed GOR; MG]' has been lawfully imposed or not. In the Amicus case the ending clause of Regulation 7(2) was challenged for a number of reasons. An important objection forwarded by the claimants was the potential of this clause to foster 'social stereotyping'. After all, albeit within the limits of 'reasonableness', the clause permits the employer to act on the basis of assumptions about a job applicant's sexual orientation. Moreover, the fear was expressed that, given the need for the employer to take reasonable steps before reaching his conclusion as to whether or not a person meets the imposed GOR, the employer would possibly engage in intrusive questioning about a person's sexual orientation. This could interfere with a person's privacy rights secured by

137 *Amicus v. Secretary of State for Trade and Industry* [2004] EWHC 860 Admin.
138 Queens Bench Division, Administrative Court.

Article 8 of the ECHR. However, the claimants' arguments were decisively dismissed by Mr Justice Richards, who held that

> '(...) Regulation 7(2) (c) (ii) has a sensible rationale. In those cases where being of a particular sexual orientation is a genuine and determining occupational requirement, it cannot be right that an employer, having asked the plainly permissible initial question whether a person meets that requirement, is bound in all circumstances to accept at face value the answer given or is precluded from forming his own judgment if no answer is given.' [139]

Leaving aside the problems related to the delineation of the group of, for example, gay or lesbian persons, the present author agrees with this view,[140] despite the risk of social stereotyping indicated by the claimants (a risk which arguably decreases in the light of the requirement of 'reasonableness'). It is submitted that the range of employment-related scenarios in which being of a given sexual orientation (be it gay, lesbian, heterosexual or bi-sexual) is already very narrow in itself. Not only is it much harder to imagine cases where a person's 'sexual orientation' (as opposed to a person's 'sex' for example) can be essential for a given job, it should also be borne in mind that the GOR provision constitutes an exception to the central norm. It follows from settled case law by the ECJ that all exceptions to the principles of equality and non-discrimination must be interpreted strictly.[141] Hence, in those very limited circumstances where a person's sexual orientation could legitimately be regarded as necessary for the performance of the job (for example, a gay rights organisation might insist that a person doing the job of gay rights activist must be gay) the employer must be in a position to form a reasonable and objective assessment as to whether or not this requirement is met. Arguably, the fact that Regulation 7(2) affords this right to the employer prevents, rather than that it encourages intrusive questioning about a person's sexual orientation.

As stated above, the GOR exception contained in Regulation 7(2) may be imposed by *any* kind of employer. In contrast, the exception in Regulation 7(3) only applies in the context of employment which is 'for the purposes of an organised religion'. Regulation 7(3) seeks to implement Article 4(1) of the Directive, rather than Article 4(2) EFD which permits discrimination by religious employers on the grounds of religion or belief (where being of a particular religion or belief constitutes a GOR).[142] The compatibility of Regulation 7(3) with the EFD was the object of judicial scrutiny in the *Amicus* case. Regulation 7(3) reads as follows:

> 7(3) This paragraph applies where-
> (a) the employment is for the purposes of an organised religion;
> (b) the employer applies a requirement related to sexual orientation-
> (i) so as to comply with the doctrines of the religion, or

139 See paragraph 80 of the judgment.

140 For an opposite view see Oliver 2004, section 4.

141 See for example *Johnston v. Chief Constable of the Royal Ulster Constabulary* (Case 222/84) [1986] ECR 1651.

142 The Article 4(2) EFD exception was extensively discussed in Chapter 6.

> (ii) because of the nature of the employment and the context in which it is carried out, so as to avoid conflicting with the strongly held religious convictions of a significant number of the religion's followers; and
> (c) either-
> (i) the person to whom that requirement is applied does not meet it, or
> (ii) the employer is not satisfied, and in all the circumstances it is reasonable for him not to be satisfied, that that person meets it.

Regulation 7(3) was added to the S.O. Regulations at the last moment and had originally not been foreseen in the draft Regulations. Its insertion intended to meet the concerns expressed by representatives of Churches who intended to secure the right of religious freedom which, in their view, could be jeopardised by the S.O. Regulations.[143] Regulation 7(3) has been challenged in legal proceedings for being too wide in scope. In contrast to Regulation 7(2), Regulation 7(3) does not stipulate that the vexed requirement (i.e. the requirement regarding a person's sexual orientation) must be 'genuine' and 'determining' and may only be imposed provided that 'proportionality' is respected. Proportionality generally requires that the imposition of the GOR is both an 'appropriate' and 'necessary' means for reaching the (legitimate) objectives pursued. Moreover, a proportional balance must be struck between the imposition of the GOR, on the one hand, and the interference with a person's right to be free from discrimination on grounds of sexual orientation, on the other. It does not follow from Regulation 7(3) what is meant by the notion of an 'organised religion' and what the relationship is between this concept and the concept of 'ethos based employers'. The last-mentioned rubric is used in Regulation 7(3) of the R&B Regulations. Neither is it clear-cut what is meant by a 'significant number of the religion's followers'. Both the Parliamentary History and the judicial outcome in *Amicus* essentially emphasise that the scope of Regulation 7(3) is to be taken as being exceptionally narrow. Only a narrow interpretation of this Regulation secures legal compatibility with the Framework Directive. Hence, both in political and legal circles it is firmly denied that Regulation 7(3) enshrines a blanket exception to the principle of non-discrimination on grounds of sexual orientation. In its reply to the Parliamentary debates on the S.O. Regulations in the House of Lords, Lord Sainsbury of Turville for the government took the following view:

> 'it became clear that with the Regulations as [originally] drafted the Churches would have some difficulty upholding the doctrine and teaching of their faith in relation to particular posts. ... [W]e do not believe that these Regulations should interfere with religious teachings or doctrine, nor do we believe it appropriate that doctrine should be the subject of litigation in the civil courts. ... This is not a question of extreme positions. Article 4(1) of the European Directive is quite clear that religious considerations can be taken into account. What we are debating this evening is exactly where that line is drawn. Under these circumstances I believe that Government need to take a lead- and we did that in preparing Regulation 7(3). It resolves the problem of interfering with doctrine and teachings while remaining consistent with the Directive. We believe that Regulation 7(3) is lawful because it pursues a legitimate aim of preventing interference with a religion's doctrine and teaching and it does so proportionately because its narrow

[143] See paragraph 90 of the *Amicus* judgment.

> application to a small number of jobs and the strict criteria which it lays down. ... When drafting Regulation 7(3) we had in mind a very narrow range of employment: ministers of religion, plus a small number of posts outside the clergy, including those who exist to promote and represent religion. The words on the page reflect our intentions. ... First, this is no 'blanket exception'. It is quite clear that Regulation 7(3) does not apply to all jobs in a particular type of organisation. On the contrary, employers must be prepared to justify any requirement relating to sexual orientation on a case by case basis. The rule only applies to employment which is for the purposes of 'organised religion', not religious organisations. There is a clear distinction in meaning between the two. A religious organisation could be any organisation with an ethos based on religion or belief. However, employment for the purposes of an organised religion clearly means a job, such as a minister of religion, involving work for a church, synagogue or mosque. A care home run by a religious foundation may qualify as a religious organisation, for example. ... but I believe that it would be very difficult under these Regulations to show that a job of a nurse in a care home exists 'for the purposes of an organised religion'. I would say exactly the same in relation to a teacher at a faith school. Such jobs exist for the purposes of health care and education. Regulation 7(3) does not stop there. Even if an employer can show that the job exists for the purposes of organised religion, and that is a significant hurdle, he may only apply a requirement related to sexual orientation if one of two further tests are met. In the first test the requirement must be applied to comply with the doctrines of the religion. We do not believe that that test would be met in relation to many posts. It would be very difficult for a church to argue that a requirement related to sexual orientation applied to a post of cleaner, gardener or secretary. Religious doctrine rarely has much to say about posts such as those. If the first test is not met, what about the second? ... Both elements have to be satisfied before the second test can be met. It is, therefore, a very strict test and one that will be met in very few cases.'[144]

The above statement by Lord Sainsbury of Turville can operate as a '*Pepper v. Hart Statement*'[145] which means that it can be relied upon in judicial proceedings as an aid to the proper statutory interpretation and construction of Regulation 7(3).

Bearing in mind the observations by Lord Sainsbury of Turville, Justice Richards (in the *Amicus* case) while deciding on the compatibility of Regulation 7(3) with the Directive took the following view:

> 'The main question, as it seems to me, concerns the scope of the exception (...) I think it clear from the Parliamentary material that the exception was intended to be very narrow; and in my view it is, on its proper construction, very narrow. It has to be construed strictly since it is a derogation from the principle of equal treatment; and it has to be construed purposively so as to ensure, so far as possible, compatibility with the Directive. When its terms are considered in the light of those interpretative principles, they can be seen to afford an exception only in very limited circumstances.'[146]

Eventually, he concluded that 'Looking at Regulation 7(3) as a whole, and bearing in mind what I have said about its terms and the strict construction that they must

144 This statement has been quoted from paragraph 91 of the *Amicus* judgment.

145 See the case of *Pepper v. Hart* [1993] AC 593 by the House of Lords.

146 Paragraph 115 of the judgment.

be given, I take the view that the exception is a lawful implementation of Article 4(1) of the Directive.'[147]

Lastly, the following was observed

> 'the exception [in Regulation 7(3); MG] involves a legislative striking of the balance between competing rights. It was done deliberately in this way so as to reduce the issues that would have to be determined by the courts or tribunals in such a sensitive field. As a matter of principle, that was a course properly open to the legislature (...).'[148]

In light of the emphasised narrowness of the exception, it appears that much of the initial fears surrounding the Regulation 7(3) exception have largely been taken away. The present author observes that Article 3 of the Dutch GETA provides that the Act does not apply to the internal affairs of churches or other religious communities or of associations of a spiritual nature.[149] Unlike Regulation 7(3), this Article has not been the object of controversy in the process of transposing the EFD into Dutch law.[150] It follows from Article 3 GETA that, e.g. the professions of priest, rabbi and imam are exempted from the scope of the Act. Hence, if a Roman Catholic Church refuses to install a homosexual person for the function of priest this cannot be challenged on the basis of the GETA. The present author finds this a correct legal approach, for Article 3 GETA reflects the right to freedom of religion which is secured by Article 6 of the Dutch Constitution. Via the HRA 1998, this right is *eo ipso* secured in the context of English law. Moreover, Article 3 GETA reflects the principle of separation of Church and State. This principle is also, albeit to a lesser extent, mirrored by Regulation 7(3) and by the observations by Lord Sainsbury of Turville stated above.[151] However, whereas the Dutch ETC is prevented *altogether* from considering a complaint of discrimination on grounds of sexual orientation by, e.g. a Church,[152] the English courts may still engage in a balancing exercise on the basis of Regulation 7(3).[153] In this context it should be noted that in the recent decision by the House or Lords in *Percy v. Church of Scotland Board of National Mission* it was held that persons

147 Paragraph 115 of the judgment.

148 Paragraph 123 of the judgment.

149 Article 3 provides as follows: 'This Act shall not apply to (a) legal relations within religious communities and independent sections thereof and within other associations of a spiritual nature; (b) the office of minister of religion.' Article 3 GETA is strictly spoken not an *exception* to the central prohibition of making a distinction. It rather constitutes a boundary to the material scope of the GETA.

150 See, however, Waaldijk 2004, p. 363-364, who has argued that the Article 3 GETA exemption is 'unconditional and (...) therefore too wide'.

151 Notably where it is observed that the government believes that 'Regulation 7(3) is lawful because it pursues a legitimate aim of preventing interference with a religion's doctrine and teaching and it does so proportionately because its narrow application to a small number of jobs and the strict criteria which it lays down'.

152 This is, however, not the case with respect to situations that are covered by Article 5 GETA (see Chapter 6).

153 This also applied for the Dutch Courts if the case at hand falls within the scope of Article 5 GETA. See Chapter 6.

who are employed as religious ministers are entitled to bring claims of discrimination (*in casu*: sex discrimination) in an employment tribunal.[154]

The last exception to be dealt with here is contained in the brief but vexed provision in Regulation 25 of the S.O. Regulations. Regulation 25 (in its original format) reads as follows: 'Nothing in Part II or III [i.e., regarding 'employment' and 'other unlawful acts', respectively; MG] shall render unlawful anything which prevents or restricts access to a benefit by reference to marital status'.

Basically, this Regulation means that employment-related benefits that are granted by reference to marital status are not unlawful under the Regulations, although as will be explained since 05-12-05 employers have been prohibited to afford differential treatment to persons in a civil partnership compared with married persons.

Regulation 25 forms a transposition of non-binding Recital 22 EFD, which was discussed earlier in the analysis. Regulation 25 was yet another contentious provision challenged by the claimants in the *Amicus* case for being incompatible with the Framework Directive and/or with Article 8 in conjunction with Article 14 ECHR. In the claimants' view, making employment benefits dependent upon a marriage requirement constitutes direct or indirect sexual orientation discrimination, given that English law excludes same sex couples from the social institution of marriage. As far as EC law was concerned, the claimants argued that, but for a non-binding Recital, the EFD does not contain a provision such as that contained in Regulation 25 of the S.O. Regulations. Therefore, the latter was alleged to be *ultra vires*. Nonetheless, Mr Justice Richards took the view that Regulation 25 was in conformity with the requirements imposed upon the British legislator by the EFD.[155] Firstly, and although he did acknowledge that 'the troubling feature about recital (22) is that it is only a recital and (…) it has no parallel in the substantive provisions of the Directive',[156] he nevertheless accepted that it intends to limit the scope of the Directive in such a way as Regulation 25 dictates, for 'to hold otherwise would be to frustrate the legislative intention as it appears in recital 22'.[157] Moreover, a case of direct sexual orientation discrimination was rejected for 'the ground of the difference in treatment is marriage, not sexual orientation'.[158] And, stating the ECJ's authorities in the cases of *Grant, D v. Sweden* and *K.B.* (all discussed above) the claim of indirect sexual orientation discrimination was equally rejected. According to the ECJ in the aforementioned cases there is a perceived lack of comparability between, on the one hand, married couples and couples having engaged in other kinds of relationships, on the other. What is more, Mr Justice Richards submitted that the exclusion of benefits payable by reference to marriage was 'objectively justified' in light of overriding aims of the UK's social policy (namely, the desire to promote marriage and the elimination of the risk of a very great increase in costs).

154 *Percy v. Church of Scotland Board of National Mission* [2006] IRLR 195 (House of Lords by 4:1 with dissenting opinion by Lord Hoffman).

155 For reasons which will not further be outlined here the High Court did neither conclude incompatibility with Articles 8 and 14 of the ECHR. See moreover Wintemute 2004b, p. 415.

156 Paragraph 158 of the judgment.

157 Paragraph 159 of the judgment.

158 Paragraph 162 of the judgment.

At this juncture and as referred to earlier it should be highlighted that the Civil Partnership Act 2004 came into effect on 05-12-05 together with the Civil Partnership Act 2004 (Amendments to Subordinate Legislation) Order 2005.[159] This Order has amended Regulation 25 of the S.O. Regulations with the effect of prohibiting employers to afford unequal treatment to a married employee compared with an employee in a civil partnership.[160]

It will have to be seen how instance of discrimination on grounds of marriage will be dealt with by the ECJ (and thus by the domestic courts) in future cases. It might be that the Luxembourg Court feels inspired by Mr Justice Richard's legal approach in *Amicus*. Alternatively, the ECJ might use *Karner* as a tool for judicial interpretation. The requirement in *Karner* namely, that unmarried same-sex couples were to be treated equally to married couples was, however, limited to situations where unmarried opposite-sex couples were already treated equally to married couples. What is interesting is the acknowledgement by the High Court that Recital No. 22 is non-binding and that it is not substantiated by any binding provision in the Directive. Hence, it was admitted that although a Recital can serve as an interpretative tool in constructing the legal meaning of a substantive provision in a Directive, it is quite a different matter if a recital is transposed into national law with the effect of considerably narrowing the law's scope of application. The court found no legal authority which could be of assistance in this regard and in light of this it would have been appropriate, had it referred a preliminary question under Article 234 EC. If the case had gone on appeal, or if a similar matter formed the object of legal proceedings in another case, this fundamental question could well lead to a different outcome.

4.5. *Conclusions*

In the above, a top-down analysis was made which examined the influence of EC law upon English sexual orientation law. Moreover, references were made to Strasbourg Convention law, as well as to legal approaches in the Netherlands. As result of the adoption of the Framework Directive domestic law has been supplemented with a new legal framework prohibiting sexual orientation discrimination in employment and occupation. Like the ECJ, the English Courts had adopted a comparative

159 S.I. 2005, no. 2114 The Civil Partnership Act 2004 (Amendments to Subordinate Legislation) Order 2005.

160 See Schedule 17 of the 2005 Order which provides in Regulation 7(3) as follows:
For Regulation 25 [of the S.O. Regulations; MG] (exception for benefits dependent on marital status) substitute-
'25. Exception for benefits dependent on a person's status
Nothing in Part II or III shall render unlawful-
(a) anything which prevents or restricts access to a benefit by reference to marital status where the right to the benefit accrued or the benefit is payable in respect of periods of service prior to the coming into force of the Civil Partnership Act 2004;
(b) the conferring of a benefit on married persons and civil partners to the exclusion of all other persons.'

approach to alleged instances of sexual orientation discrimination prior to the introduction of the S.O. Regulations. In practice, this meant that sexual minorities were unprotected by domestic sex discrimination law. Like the EFD, English sexual orientation discrimination law reflects the principle of symmetry. This means that both the 'sexual majority' and 'sexual minorities' are covered. It was argued that the HRA 1998 requires courts and tribunals to offer legal protection from discrimination on the ground of having a sexual orientation (*forum internum*) and on the ground of manifesting it (*forum externum*). The analysis of concepts of discrimination *inter alia* showed that in respect of 'indirect discrimination', the English approach is arguably deviant from the required EC law approach, given that an actual personal detriment must be established. The discussion also showed that, like EC law, the S.O. Regulations protect from discrimination on grounds of a falsely presumed sexual orientation, as well as on grounds of being in association with a person of a given sexual orientation. A number of exceptions to the prohibition of discrimination were also considered. This was done in light of the *Amicus* decision by the English High Court. The argument was made that in the confined range of circumstances in which being of a given sexual orientation constitutes a 'GOR', the employer must be in the position to form an objective assessment as to whether or not this requirement is met. The *Amicus* case, perceived in light of a number of Parliamentary comments, moreover showed that the exception contained in Regulation 7(3) of the S.O. Regulations (i.e. the GOR exception 'for the purposes of an organised religion') must be interpreted strictly. This being the case, the present author agrees with the legal outcome in *Amicus,* given that Article 7(3) of the Regulations reflects the freedom of religion and (to a lesser extent) the principle of separation of Church and State. A similar 'exception' (or rather a boundary to the law's scope of application) is enshrined in the Dutch GETA. A highly interesting issue that was at stake in the *Amicus* case concerned the weight to be given to Recital No. 22 of the EFD. Notwithstanding its non-binding nature, the Recital has been transposed as a 'hard law' exception in English law. In the view of the English judge this does not constitute a breach of EC law, however, it would certainly have been commendable, had the domestic court referred a preliminary question to the ECJ in order to clarify the matter once and for all.

5. Concluding Remarks

In the above a comparative analysis was made of sexual orientation discrimination law in the context of employment. This involved an analysis of 'cross-ground', 'top-down', 'cross-country' and 'bottom-up' dimensions, to a greater or lesser degree. Moreover, Strasbourg Convention law was embedded at appropriate junctures in the analysis. Given that fully-fledged conclusions were made throughout the analysis as a whole, the present section can be brief. The analysis stressed that amongst the thorniest questions which arise in the interpretation and application of EC sexual orientation law is the question as to the legal status of non-binding Recital No. 22 of the Directive. Whether the ECJ will analyse instances of marriage discrimination as being beyond the boundaries of the Directive's scope of application, or, as an instance of (*prima facie*) indirect or direct sexual orientation discrimination, remains currently unclear. The Court may either feel inspired by the more liberal approach adopted by the Strasbourg Court (and in Dutch law), or by the more conservative stance adopted by the English High Court in the *Amicus* case. Future case law will have to be awaited in order to know which approach will be followed. Arguably, either approach will have implications of a more general, constitutional kind, for it will tell us something about the degree of impact which non-binding Recitals in Directives may have upon the interpretation of Community law.

Chapter 8

DISABILITY

1. Introduction

In the previous two chapters we saw that the anti-discrimination law framework in England has been expanded with new legal frameworks governing discrimination on grounds of religion and belief (Chapter 6) and sexual orientation (Chapter 7). This expansion has been a direct result of the implementation of the EFD into domestic law (top-down influence). We also saw that both EC and English anti-discrimination law on these grounds leave many unanswered questions which have not yet been resolved through judicial interpretation. It has been suggested that (semi) judicial approaches and practices in the Netherlands may serve as a source of inspiration for the ECJ (bottom-up influence), and possibly for the English courts while dealing with alleged instances of discrimination on the aforementioned grounds. If the ECJ feels inspired in future case law by domestic approaches and practices, this will amount to bottom-up influence. Ultimately, this will have a cross-fertilisation effect upon all 25 Member States, for all Member States will have to comply with the relevant ECJ judgment. In Chapters 6 and 7, I have moreover made short excursions into the law stemming from the ECHR. Why I have done so, and why I will not do so in the present (or indeed any other) chapter, has been explained in the preliminary issues at the outset of Part IV. It has been argued that Strasbourg Convention law could have a considerable impact upon judicial application and interpretation by the ECJ of the provisions contained in the Article 13 EC Framework Directive. Moreover, it has been argued that the case law of the ECtHR constitutes an important interpretative tool for English domestic courts in legal proceedings concerning the Religion and Belief Regulations and the Sexual Orientation Regulations. In Chapters 6 and 7, I have furthermore examined the grounds religion and belief and sexual orientation from a theoretical perspective. Providing theoretical insights into the various grounds of discrimination shall be instrumental to the cross-ground comparison which will be drawn in Chapter 10.

In the present chapter the research approach will be largely similar to the one adopted in Chapters 6 and 7. The way in which the upcoming analysis will be presented differs, however, slightly from the way this has been done in the previous two chapters. In the analysis to follow, I will look at disability discrimination law from a multi-layered comparative perspective. This includes a top-down, a cross-country and a cross-ground analysis. Once domestic approaches and practices in combating disability discrimination have been analysed, one could speculate on possible bottom-up influence. The analysis hereafter will be presented as follows.

First, I will make a theoretical analysis of disability as a ground of discrimination (section 2). In that analysis, I will examine the intricacies of disability as a ground of discrimination whereby comparisons will be drawn with other grounds. Moreover, I will examine various theoretical models which seek to rationalise the nature and causes of discrimination on grounds of disability. In section 2, I will moreover establish links with the notions of formal and substantive equality. In section 3, I will examine various aspects of disability discrimination in the context of EC law. The aim will not be to discuss the legal framework governing disability discrimination in the EC in an exhaustive fashion. Rather, I have prioritised three aspects which are of particular importance in the context of disability. These aspects are the following: (1) the principles of symmetry and asymmetry; (2) the definition of disability, and, (3) the concept of reasonable accommodation. Reasonable accommodation was touched on in Chapters 3 and 6 but a fully-fledged analysis of this concept will be made in this chapter in the context of disability. It follows from the foregoing that the various concepts of discrimination (direct discrimination, indirect discrimination, harassment and the instruction to discriminate) shall not be discussed in this chapter.[1] The analysis of EC law in section 3 will be functional to the top-down analysis to be carried out in section 4. In section 4, I will examine the principles of symmetry and asymmetry, the definition of disability and the notion of reasonable accommodation in the context of both Dutch and English law. These analyses will be made in light of the Framework Directive (top-down analysis). Moreover, the Dutch approach will be compared with the English approach (cross-country analysis). It is to be noted that the adoption and subsequent implementation of the EFD into domestic law has meant that Dutch equal treatment law has been complemented with a new legal framework governing disability discrimination in employment. The Act on Equal Treatment on grounds of Disability and Chronic Disease entered into force on 1 December 2003.[2] This Act will hereafter be referred to as the DETA (Disability Equal Treatment Act).

In contrast, English disability discrimination law has existed since 1995.[3] Given that the DDA has existed for more than a decade and given that, as will be seen, it is

1 Indirect discrimination and harassment have extensively been discussed in Chapters 3 and 4 respectively. In Chapter 3, I have also made reference to the concept of direct discrimination, which has moreover been discussed in Chapter 6 (religion and belief) and Chapter 7 (sexual orientation). The prohibition of the instruction to discriminate is self-explanatory and does not call for an in depth analysis.

2 Act of 3 April 2003 concerning the establishment of the Act on Equal Treatment on the grounds of disability or chronic disease [*Wet Gelijke Behandeling op grond van Handicap en Chronische ziekte*], *Stb.* 2003, 206 [*Law Gazette* 2003, 206]. See generally also Chapter 2.

3 The DDA 1995 entered into force on 2 December 1996. The Act applies in fact to England, Wales, Scotland and Northern Ireland (hence, to the whole of the United Kingdom) although with regard to Northern Ireland the Act applies with certain modifications (See Schedule 8 of the Act).

premised upon a radically different conceptual framework than the DETA, it will form a fruitful source for the comparative law analysis. Tentative conclusions will be drawn in section 5.

2. Equality, Non-Discrimination and Disability: Mapping the Theory

2.1. *Introduction*

A theoretical discussion on disability in relation to the principles of non-discrimination and equality embraces at least three distinct but closely inter-related theoretical strands. Firstly, one can analyse disability as a ground of discrimination *in se*. This involves the examination of the intrinsic values and logic underpinning this discrimination ground. In such an analysis disability can be compared with other discrimination grounds. Secondly, and inter-related, one can interlink the specifics inherent to the ground 'disability' on the one hand, with the theoretical discourse on formal and substantive equality, on the other. As is known, formal equality requires equal treatment of equal cases, whereas substantive equality also requires different treatment of materially different cases. A study into the inherent nature of disability as a ground of discrimination can be informative to the question whether disability discrimination law should be designed on the basis of a formal or substantive justice paradigm.[4] Thirdly, one can theorise the very underlying causes (or sources) of the disadvantages suffered by disabled persons in social life. The theories regarding the causes of disability-related disadvantage are essentially two-fold. On one side of the spectrum stands the so-called medical model of disability, and on the other side the so-called social model. Eventually, one could also establish a nexus between these two models on the one hand, and the concepts of formal and substantive equality on the other. It will be seen that the medical model echoes the philosophy of formal equality, whereas the social model is underpinned by substantive equality concerns.

In the passages to follow the just outlined theoretical approaches will be taken a step further. In section 2.2, I will first study the characteristics of disability as a ground of discrimination. Differences and commonalities with other grounds of discrimination shall be referred to, although a fully-fledged cross-ground analysis will only be made in Chapter 10. In section 2.3, I will subsequently analyse the medical and social models of disability-based disadvantage. Whilst doing so, I will make links with the concepts of formal and substantive equality. Tentative conclusions will be drawn in section 2.4.

4 See also Waddington, who has argued that a study into the different geneses of different discrimination grounds has an impact upon the formulation of policy and legislation. (Waddington 1995, p. 41 *et seq*.).

2.2. *The Underlying Logic of 'Disability': Cross-Ground Perspectives*

As stated earlier, differences and commonalities may be found between 'disability' and other grounds of discrimination.[5] Together with 'race' and 'gender' (not 'sex'), Schiek has categorised disability into the category of grounds which exist as 'mere ascriptions'.[6] Thus, like gender, which reflects a socio-cultural construction of women and men, and like race, which mirrors a similar construction of black persons *vis-à-vis* whites, disability reflects the socio-cultural construction of disabled persons *versus* those who are defined by the dominant norm of ableism or able-bodiedness. Ascriptive criteria are often uncontrollable, in the sense that persons cannot discard their status which, in combination with societal attitudes, is the root of disadvantage. This is, however, in a sense different with respect to 'disability', given that a disabled person can become non-disabled as a result of medical treatment or rehabilitation.[7] Hence, disability is a fluid concept in the sense that being or not being disabled may fluctuate over time. Hendriks has illustrated the ascriptive nature of disability in reference to the difficulty of delineating who *is* and who *is not* disabled which, he argues, is not so much a result of a medical or a biological cause but rather of a (random) 'social exercise'.[8] This argument goes to the heart of the social model of disability which will be discussed in section 2.3 hereafter.

Schiek has furthermore classified disability within the group of grounds which have a biological footing, just like age and sex.[9] It *might*[10] be that for biological[11] reasons, the employability of disabled persons (or women or elderly persons) gets reduced, either by reason of temporary unavailability[12] for the job, or as a consequence of temporary or permanent inability to carry out the duties attached to the job.[13] A person's employability could moreover be reduced by the fact that (s)he cannot perform the job in a standard manner.[14] What amounts to 'standard' job-per-

5 See for a detailed analysis also Waddington 1995, p. 41-53.

6 See Schiek 2002, p. 309.

7 Waddington 1995, p. 41. This is, however, only true for some disabled persons. Others are and remain disabled forever.

8 Hendriks 1999, p. 181-194.

9 See Schiek 2002, p. 309-310.

10 I emphasize this, for I want to avoid false presumptions and stereotyping about the capacity of disabled persons at work.

11 It is acknowledged that the causes of a person's inability to perform a job or her temporary unavailability for the job need not per definition be biological in kind. The exclusion of disabled persons from work is often not traceable to biological reasons but rather the result of 'social determinism' (Quinn 2004) over-emphasising the reduced work capacity of disabled persons. This point shall be taken further in the discussion of the social model of disability hereafter.

12 In the context of the ground 'sex' the pivotal example being a woman's absence from work as a result of pregnancy.

13 Bell and Waddington 2003, p. 361. See also Quinn 2004, p. 12. Quinn has rightly observed that the reduction of what he has called 'use value' is embedded within the notion of disability itself: 'Take disability. Here the reduction of "use value" is implicit in the very word "disability". So the resulting exclusion (...) appears even more natural.'

14 Bell and Waddington 2003, p. 361.

formance tends however to be determined on the basis of the dominant norm of ableism.[15] Although as a matter of fact a disabled person's employability might be reduced for a certain reason, we should be careful not to operate on the basis of false assumptions or stereotypes. Hence, argues Quinn, '(...) disability [and age] tend to mask an underlying reality of personal capacity. So the key task with respect to those grounds is to create space for a more rational appreciation of individual worth behind the mask'.[16] In other words, the law's objective must be to address stereotyping and stigma, such as for instance the stereotypical view that disabled persons constitute a barrier to economic efficiency and competitiveness. In addition to the foregoing aims, the legal framework must be aimed at ensuring that actors, such as employers, do not fail to see disability as a material difference.[17] The just outlined objectives could be pursued by the introduction of legal prohibitions of direct and indirect discrimination and notably by the imposition upon the employer of a duty to make reasonable accommodation. The legal concept of reasonable accommodation seeks not only to show respect for material differences, but also to actively accommodate difference, e.g. by making an adaptation to the workplace or by allowing for alterations in the scheme of work hours.[18]

Quinn has furthermore observed that with disability[19] a discriminating agent is not very likely to be driven by a personal resentment against the disabled person, such as is more likely to be the case with sexual orientation. Rather, writes Quinn, the agent who discriminates against a disabled person is '(...) likely to unthinkingly repeat a pattern or practice once considered 'normal'.[20] Hence, a workplace design which does not show sympathy for the needs of disabled persons does not intend to discriminate against disabled persons, although it clearly has this effect in practice. Once the exclusionary effects of the notion of 'normality' are accepted the legal framework should seek to address these effects via the prohibition of indirect discrimination and via a duty to adjust.

In the above it was stated that a person's disability may in certain circumstances prevent him or her from being at work, from carrying out certain aspects of the work or from carrying out the work in the same way as non-disabled persons or as persons with a different disability. In this regard 'disability' thus differs from other statuses such as 'race' and 'sexual orientation' and, pregnancy aside, from 'sex'. However, 'disability' resembles 'religion' and 'age', given that these grounds may equally hamper availability (e.g. in light of praying times), ability (e.g. an old employee may not

15 Just like for example in the context of 'sex' the dominant norm is the male norm and with respect to 'sexual orientation' it is heterosexualism.

16 Quinn 2004, p. 13.

17 Degener 2004, section 3, who has in this regard spoken of disability as a 'human difference'.

18 Quinn 2004, p. 12. The concept of reasonable accommodation has already been touched on in Chapters 3 and 6 and will be discussed in further detail in the analyses regarding EC, Dutch and English disability discrimination law in the passages to follow.

19 As well as with 'age'.

20 Quinn 2004, p. 13.

be able to lift heavy objects)[21] or standard job performance (e.g. a religious nurse may refuse to assist with an abortion).

Bickenbach has argued that 'disability' and other grounds of discrimination cannot truly be compared.[22] He has pointed to the rather different responses by society to different mental and physical impairments. Indeed, the group of disabled persons cannot truly be established given its great diversity and given the lack of a common experience and common sentiments of solidarity.[23] This cannot be said of, for example, women or black persons whose group is much more 'fixed'. Thus, whereas a person with minor sight or hearing problems and a person who suffers from a leg impairment are both 'disabled persons', the latter arguably faces many more barriers to social inclusion and participation as well as to employability, compared with the former.[24] In all, the group of disabled persons lacks a common identity given its vast heterogeneity and given the fluid status of the group of disabled persons.[25]

Furthermore, as observed by Van den Langenbergh, disabled persons, compared with persons of other minority groups, are often disproportionately dependent upon social insurance and assistance measures.[26] Indeed, up until very recently, the legal approach to disability was solely based upon State support for those in need, rather than upon a civil rights approach.[27] Therefore, whereas sex and race have appeared to lend themselves for being regulated within (formally oriented) first generation equality laws[28], this has not been the case with respect to disability. Both in the UK and in the Netherlands, disability has only relatively recently been regulated by the anti-discrimination framework. The anti-discrimination framework should however not act as a substitute for measures adopted within the framework of national social policy. As observed by Quinn and Quinlivan disability, more palpably than is the case with other grounds of discrimination, cannot merely be addressed by the non-discrimination framework which, in itself, appears to be insufficient (though crucial) to

21 Although, admittedly, it will not always be apparent whether an older employee is unable to lift a heavy object by reason of his or her age or rather by reason of a disability related to ageing.

22 In his view, the '(…) the analogy between racial minorities and disabled people [breaks] down at many important points'. Bickenbach 1999, p. 106.

23 Bickenbach 1999, p. 106; similarly, Waddington 1995, notably p. 46-48.

24 See also Hendriks 1999, p. 208.

25 See also Van den Langenbergh 2003, 578.

26 Van den Langenbergh 2003, p. 578.

27 As Quinn and Quinlivan have noted, disability '(…) is the latest field in which the shift to the civil rights framework of reference is making its presence felt'. See Quinn and Quinlivan 2003, p. 215. See also Hendriks 2005, p. 187 and in more detail section 3. Also Degener and Quinn, who have examined the 'rise and influence of the rights-based approach to disability throughout the world' (p. 1).

28 It is argued that 'race' has received early attention by the anti-discrimination framework both because of the historical legacy of race discrimination and because of a large flux of immigrants coming from former colonies to the European continent (see also Chapter 2). Within Community law, sex has been regulated as a source of discrimination in the early stages for economic reasons of competition, which were not at a premium with respect to race and disability. Outside the context of Community law, sex has also received early attention by law and policy-makers by virtue of the success of the women's movement in post-war Europe, most notably in the late 1960s and the 1970s.

realise equality.[29] The same could be said for certain other grounds of discrimination. For instance, sex discrimination law cannot substitute for important social measures in the areas of parental leave and childcare facilities. The successfulness of anti-discrimination law in creating greater equality for persons who belong to a disadvantaged group depends moreover on the conceptual premises underlying the law. Perhaps most pressingly with regard to disability, anti-discrimination law must be based upon the notion of substantive equality. Disability discrimination law must go beyond the principle of consistency of treatment. Rather, it ought to reconstruct the dominant norm of normality in favour of those who cannot comply with it.

As stated, prior to the insight that disability must (additionally) be perceived within a context of civil rights, the law's approach was foremost premised upon a 'need and charity approach'. In this respect, Fredman has drawn a parallel with the discrimination ground 'sex'. As she has observed:

> '(...) [the] restriction of [protective legislation, e.g. with respect to working hours or working underground] to women inevitably disadvantaged them in the labour market as well as characterising women as weak and in need of protection' (....) [s]imilarly, for many decades disabled persons were depicted 'not as subjects with legal rights, but as objects of welfare, health and charity programs'.[30]

As shall be seen hereafter, the charity approach appears to be a direct consequence of the medical model of disability, whereas a civil rights and equality approach reflects the social model of disability. Henceforth I shall shed further light on this point.

In the above, reference has been made to the great heterogeneity of the group of disabled people. The question arises whether this group can be altogether defined. Disability appears to be a fluid characteristic in the sense that a disabled person may become non-disabled, either by virtue of social accommodation, or by means of medical treatment or as a result of rehabilitation.[31] Conversely, a non-disabled person can suddenly become disabled. Moreover, the range of disabilities is hugely diverse. In all, disability differs from race and sex, for the dividing line between 'ability' and 'disability' is harder to draw, compared with 'men' *v.* 'women' and 'black persons' *v.* 'white persons'.[32] In sum, disability is not immutable, nor can it be categorised as a choice-ground, like 'sexual orientation' and 'religion' for example. In light of the foregoing, it becomes clear that the identification of the class of disabled persons is

29 Quinn and Quinlivan 2003, p. 125 where they have warned that '[i]t is not enough to break down doors into the mainstream- it is also important to equip people with the wherewithal to enter the mainstream through education and to enable them to prosper whilst in the mainstream through adequate social support'. See also Hendriks 2005, who has indicated that social welfare laws and equality and non-discrimination laws should not be regarded as being mutually exclusive but rather complements to one another.

30 Fredman 2005, p. 202 in reference to Degener and Quinn, p. 3.

31 This is, however, only true for some disabled persons. Other disabled people will become and remain disabled forever.

32 Also Degener 2004, p. 4.

essentially a random exercise. As Fredman has argued, '(...) the borderline between 'we' and 'they' is not only arbitrary but shifting'.[33]

Bickenbach has advanced a similar argument where he has emphasised the variable character of disability as a source of discrimination.[34] As he has noted:

> '[n]o human has a complete repertoire of abilities, suitable for all permutations of the physical and social environment. Scientifically speaking, there are no inherent or intrinsic boundaries to the range of variation in human abilities; ability-disability is a continuum and the complete absence of disability, like the complete absence of ability, is a limiting case of theoretic interest only.'[35]

The difficulties of demarcation (i.e. of deciding who is 'in' and 'out') have furthermore been highlighted by Hendriks.[36] The fact that disability is a fluid concept and that the group of disabled persons is far from homogeneous raises questions of symmetry and asymmetry. Would it be more desirable if the legal framework applied 'symmetrically' (thus granting protection to persons who are discriminated against on grounds of disability *and* on grounds of *not* having a disability) or 'asymmetrically'? If asymmetry is taken as a starting point how then must the group of 'disabled persons' be defined for purposes of the law? These and related questions will be further dealt with in the analysis hereafter.

In the above, a number of intrinsic features of disability as a ground of discrimination have been analysed. It has been seen that disability is often no more than a social construction although, in certain circumstances, biological factors might impede a disabled person from being available for work, or from altogether being able to do the work, or from doing the work in a standard manner. It has also been seen that disability based disadvantage is often not the result of a resentful act by the discriminator. It is rather to be explained in terms of systemic discrimination which is created by the fact that, arguably quite unconsciously, the normality standard underpins decision-making processes. Alternatively, the discriminating act could result from paternalistic feelings, i.e. the discriminator could feel that (s)he is actually helping the disabled person, rather than placing her at a disadvantage. It has furthermore been highlighted that in contrast with other grounds of discrimination, it is inherently difficult to delineate the group of disabled people, given its vast heterogeneity which, in turn, fosters the lack of a group identity. Lastly, disability differs from most other grounds (save 'sex') in the sense that it has traditionally been approached by the law from a charity-based perspective, rather than from a civil rights perspective. As previously stated, the intrinsic features of the various grounds of discrimination discussed in Chapters 6-9 will be subjected to further comparative analysis in Chapter 10. At this juncture I will proceed with an analysis of the various models that attempt to explain the locus of disadvantage felt by disabled persons in daily and working life.

33 Fredman 2002, p. 58.
34 See moreover Waddington 1995, p. 41-46.
35 Bickenbach 1999, p. 112.
36 Hendriks 2000.

2.3. *The Medical and Social Model of Disability: Antagonistic Approaches to the Locus of Disadvantage*

2.3.1. Introduction

Just as 'sex' has been theorised in an insular fashion by the feminist movement, disability as a ground of discrimination has also been theorised in a discrete manner, which cannot easily be applied to other grounds of discrimination. Hereafter, disability will be looked at from the perspective of, broadly spoken, two antagonistic models: the medical and social model of disability. The former reflects an orthodox intra-personal angle to the locus of disadvantage, whereas the latter, in a more modern fashion, highlights the exclusionary effects of environmental attitudes. As shall be seen, within these two opposing models further refinements can be made. Throughout the discussion, the medical and social model of disability will be interlinked with the opposing paradigms of formal and substantive equality.

2.3.2. The Medical Model of Disability and its Relationship with the Principle of Equality

2.3.2.1. *The Medical Model of Disability*

The medical model argues that the problems and disadvantages which a disabled person faces in day-to-day life, including working-life, are a direct cause of the person's impairment as such, that is to say, of 'intra-personal' factors.[37] Put differently, according to this model, disability is caused by a physical, a mental or other 'aberration' from what society believes and engineers as 'normal'. This model is called the medical model, for it emphasises, not only that the decision as to whether or not one is 'disabled' should be diagnosed by medical means, but also, for it assumes that many (although certainly not all impairments) can be 'corrected' by medical intervention to an extent that the correction amounts (to the highest possible degree) to 'normality'. The medical model has also been referred to as the 'functional limitation model' or as the 'biological inferiority' model of disability.[38] Yet others have labelled it the 'individual' or 'biomedical' model.[39] In short, the medical model denies the existence of a causal connection between, on the one hand, the disadvantages faced by disabled persons, for example in the labour market and, on the other, their surrounding physical and social environment.

37 See for example Boorse, 'On the distinction between Disease and Illness', 5 *Philosophy and Public Affairs*, p. 49, and Boorse, 'Health as a Theoretical Concept', 44 *Philosophy of Science*, p. 542, both cited by Bickenbach 1999, p. 101. See also Barnes 2000, p. 448 and Wells 2003, p. 257.

38 See Waddington 1995, p. 33-34. Also, Janoff-Bulman and Frieze, 'A Theoretical perspective for understanding reactions to victimization', *Journal of Social Issues*, 1983, 39(2), p. 1-17, cited by Waddington 1995, p. 33.

39 Hendriks 2000.

A sub model of the medical model is the economic model of disability.[40] This model also rests upon a medical analysis of the impairment. Klosse has explained that according to the economic model 'disability' can be equated with a human harm, which results in a reduced earning capacity.[41] This is in its turn compensated for either by way of rehabilitation, with a view to counteracting or curing existing impairments, or, alternatively, by an adaptation of the working environment or, yet differently, by way of social welfare support which ultimately seeks to compensate for the reduced income.[42]

The medical model is inherently problematic for a number of reasons. Firstly, the medical model is intrinsically negative, as it stresses the distinctness of disabled persons (perceived against the standards of normality) by focusing upon what is wrong with disabled persons.[43] In other words, consciously or subconsciously, the medical model buttresses the perception (which precisely should be taken away) that disabled persons have a reduced productivity capacity. It thus not only reinforces the idea of inability, but with that, it perpetuates prejudice, stigmatisation and exclusion. In its core, it perceives disabled persons as persons in need, rather than as holders of rights. Secondly, and closely related to the first point, the medical model tends to compensate for disadvantage by way of social assistance measures,[44] rather than by the introduction of measures which empower disabled persons. The medical model therefore dovetails with a 'help' or 'charity' approach to disability, rather than with a civil rights approach. Whereas charity approaches keep disabled persons distinct from mainstream society,[45] the more contemporary civil rights approach emphasises equality of opportunities, as well as equal respect for every person's dignity and worth.

In light of the foregoing it is argued that discrimination and equality law in the realm of disability ought not to be underpinned by the philosophies of the medical model, for this would hamper the law's effectiveness in unravelling power structures in society as a whole, including the labour market.[46] After all, if it is the dominant group itself which determines what amounts to 'normality', the law's objective of dismantling power structures is inherently endangered. Related to this argument is that the protective scope of the law will be reduced, if the question as to what amounts to a disability for purposes of the law is determined on the basis of a medically focused approach. Such an approach risks excluding a large number of potential victims of disability based discrimination, for example, because they have only a minor disability, or because they have been discriminated against on grounds of a falsely

40 Also Waddington 1995, p. 33 with further references.

41 Klosse 1989, cited by Hendriks 2000. The economic model is clearly in tension with civil rights strategies. The latter seek to combat prejudice and stereotyping and seek to empower disabled persons, rather than making them dependent upon charity based means.

42 Klosse 1989, cited by Hendriks 2000.

43 Wells 2003, p. 258.

44 It seems that this is also implied in the analysis by Waddington 1995, p. 34.

45 Apart from when they are used as a complementary policy-approach to the civil rights approach.

46 See Goldschmidt 1997, who has emphasised that an important role of equality and non-discrimination law is to combat power structures with the aim of protecting non-dominant groups.

assumed disability.[47] Hence, a medical definition of disability has an exclusionary effect, for many instances of disability-based discrimination will not easily fit within the medically focused straightjacket of the law. Issues relating to the legal definition of disability shall be discussed further on in the analysis.

2.3.2.2. *Reconciling the 'Medical Model' with the Discourse on 'Formal Equality'*

The theoretical approach to disability enshrined in the medical model shows affinity with the ideas underlying the concept of formal equality.[48] Earlier discussions stated that formal equality equates to sameness of treatment, regardless of the question whether relevant differences between people call for inconsistency of treatment, with a view to accommodating these differences. In fact, treating two persons the same notwithstanding that each finds herself in a different starting position, necessarily results in the affirmation of the dominant norm. For instance, a rule by the employer which provides that an assessment test takes place in writing, works to the disadvantage of persons who suffer from restricted manual dexterity. Unless this material difference is accommodated (e.g. by permitting an oral exam) the dominant norm, namely that people can write without insurmountable problems gets reinforced.[49] This in turn reinforces the perception by the majority that those who cannot comply with the dominant standard of normality are inferior.[50] In all, and exactly like the medical model of disability discussed above, formal equality appears to perpetuate existing power structures rather than dismantling these in favour of disadvantaged groups. The limits of formal equality are stressed by the substantive equality paradigm which seeks to accommodate differences with a view to achieving *de facto* equality. To speak with Fredman's words: substantive equality 'reconfigure[s] the norm itself'.[51] A similar process can precisely be discerned with respect to the theoretical discourse on disability. Rather than defining the notion of disability in reference to perceived 'normality', as the medical model seeks to do, a model was called for which 'reconfigured' the notion of disability itself. Such reconfiguration ought to promote the accommodation of difference, just like substantive equality seeks to do, and most importantly, it ought to result in an adaptation of environmental attitudes.[52] The

47 Wells 2003, p. 258. A falsely assumed disability can refer to two situations: (1) the case where an individual has no impairment whatsoever and (2) the case where an individual has an impairment (e.g. a facial disfigurement) but where this does not lead to a disability.

48 This argument has been inspired by Fredman 2005, p. 199-218.

49 That formal equality reinforces the dominant norm has also been illustrated in respect of 'sex' and 'race' (see Chapter 3), 'religion' (Chapter 6) and 'sexual orientation' (Chapter 7). It will moreover be illustrated in Chapter 9 in respect of 'age'.

50 See Fredman 2005, section 2.1, in which she has analysed the notion of 'difference as inferiority'.

51 Fredman 2005, p. 203.

52 It is worth observing that a link has been established in the literature between the social model of disability on the one hand, and the distinction made by feminists between 'sex' and 'gender', on the other. It is recalled that 'sex' concerns biological differences, whereas 'gender' refers to a socio-cultural construction of men and women. Thus writes Shakespeare, with reference to Oakley 1972, the 'social model understanding borrows the feminist distinction between →

model called for is the social model of disability which shall be discussed immediately henceforth.

2.3.3. The Social Model of Disability

2.3.3.1. General Analysis of the Social Model

In the previous section it was argued that the central tenets of substantive equality can be associated with the premises underlying the social model of disability. This argument will be taken further hereafter. Since the 1960s, a shift[53] can be discerned in the theoretical explanation of the disadvantageous position of disabled persons. Whereas hitherto the locus of disadvantage had been found in intra-personal factors (medical model), the social model has relocated the source of disadvantage and exclusion in environmental and cultural circumstances.[54] Hence, according to the social model, the notion of disability is very much constructed by environmental design and by social attitudes which, in interaction with a person's impairment, account for the disadvantages felt by disabled persons in daily life.[55] Thus, by way of illustration, the social model argues that a person who uses a wheelchair because (s)he cannot walk is disadvantaged, not so much by reason of her leg impairment but rather due to the interaction of the physical impairment, on the one hand, and the societal reaction to it, on the other. Hence, not the impairment *in se* but, for example, the absence of a lift at work constitutes the very source of disadvantage. Clearly, the absence of a lift reflects the unintentional and unconscious assumption by those in the dominant pool that all can walk. Although this is a simple example it does illustrate the pivotal role played by environmental design and attitudes in constructing disability. It follows that the social model fiercely denies that the marginalisation[56] of disabled persons can be explained in reference to medically informed intra-personal factors. It rather argues that disability is simply a social construct. This essentially means that it is society itself, which constructs disability by taking as a point of departure the 'able-bodied' norm. Necessarily, a disabled person cannot comply with this norm, at least not on an equal footing with a non-disabled person. The

biological sex and social gender, and recreates it in the impairment [which is biological; MG]/ disability [which is socially constructed; MG] dyad'. See Shakespeare 1999, p. 25.

53 This must, however, not be taken to mean that medical aspects become entirely redundant in a theoretical discourse on disability. Most scholars do indeed agree that certain aspects of disablement can be medically explained. Thus, as Waddington has observed, '(...) the problems related to disability do not arise solely from the environment; there remains the impairment which can be a source of difficulty itself' (Waddington 1995, p. 34). However, the focal point of analysis has shifted from a medically oriented approach, to an environmental approach. In other words, those who adhere to the social model of disability claim that the locus of disadvantage suffered by disabled persons can *largely* (although perhaps not entirely) be traced back to environmental and attitudinal factors.

54 Barnes 2000, p. 441.

55 See for example also Drake who has referred to 'social, environmental and industrial barriers' (Drake 2000, p. 431).

56 Picking 2000, p. 11-27, notably at p. 13.

ultimate net result is a situation of dependency and exclusion, rather than a strengthening of the rights of disabled persons.[57]

So far, it has been explained that the social model argues that disability is the end product of disabling attitudes and a disabling environment, rather than of the medical impairment as such. In fact, the disabled person's environment is 'polluted', not only by a concealed assumption that disabled persons ought to assimilate to normality but also, and closely related to that, by an omission to accommodate society, including the labour market, to the legitimate needs of disabled persons. The lack of accommodation reinforces prejudiced ideas about the productivity and ability of disabled persons, given that they are not granted the opportunity in the first place to demonstrate their abilities and capacities. The very emphasis upon the need for a legal duty to make reasonable accommodation for disabled persons echoes the positive orientation of the social model, which can be contrasted with the negative approach underpinning the medical model.

Once it is recognised that the locus of disadvantage can be found in the social and attitudinal environment, this has an impact upon the preferable approach to be adopted in law and policy.[58] The law should strive for a change in attitudes and minds which can most effectively be realised by a duty imposed upon employers to bring about reasonable accommodation for disabled persons. It can moreover be accomplished via the prohibition of indirect discrimination, although this is a more reactively oriented concept. Lastly, it could be fostered by the introduction of a so-called 'positive duties' and mainstreaming approach which seeks to incorporate the element of 'disability' within all policy-making processes that are ongoing in a particular organisation (e.g. the EU, the national state, or a company).[59]

The social model rejects the idea that a solution for the disadvantages faced by disabled persons can (solely) be found in traditional welfare approaches. Instead, it places a strong emphasis upon the need for effective anti-discrimination and equality laws which fit within a civil rights strategy. The anti-discrimination framework should foster the inclusion of disabled persons in mainstream jobs, thus obviating (in part) the need for compensation for exclusion by means of social insurance measures.

In the above, the central tenets of the social model have been explained. As stated previously further refinements can be made. Indeed two important, and in

57 See for further in depth analysis Oliver 1990 and Oliver 1996. See also Shakespeare, who has observed as follows: 'Disability, in this approach (i.e. the cultural or social approach; MG) is a product of social context, not the attribute of an individual' (Shakespeare 1999, p. 25). A sound analysis has also been made by Jones and Basser Marks 1999, p. 3-24. Jones and Basser Marks have argued that the objective of what they have called the 'social constructionist approach' is '(...) to uncover the subtle societal factors which interplay with personal experiences and together create and reinforce and potentially perpetuate the subordination of people with disabilities' (p. 3). Furthermore, they have observed that '[t]he social constructionist approach to disability highlights the role of the environment, social policy and institutions, ideology and law play in disadvantaging various sectors of the community. The concern is to bring about systemic change by removing artificial barriers which limit the lives of people with disabilities' (p. 5).

58 Waddington 1995, p. 34. See also Bickenbach 1999, p. 102.

59 See also the preliminary issues to Part III.

some respects contrasting, sub models can be discerned, namely the minority rights model and the universalist model.[60] Simultaneously, these models also have a number of important things in common. Thus, both models clearly rebuff the medical model and both call for social, legal and political change. The parallels and differences between the minority rights model and the universalist model shall be outlined in more detail directly below.

2.3.3.2. Sub Models of the Social Model of Disability

2.3.3.2.1. The Minority Rights Model of Disability[61]

Following prior discussions, the minority rights model is a sub model of the social model of disability.[62] According to this model, disabled persons (no less than, e.g. black persons, religious minorities, women, etc) are a distinct minority group[63] which suffers from status-based discrimination, segregation, stigmatisation and prejudice. A vivid proponent of the minority rights model is Hahn. In his academic work, Hahn has pointed at the analogy between disabled persons and other minority groups, notably ethnic groups, by arguing that '(...) physically disabled people comprise a minority group with many of the same problems as other disadvantaged ethnic or racial segments of the population'.[64] These problems lie foremost in the reality of systemic discrimination which, according to advocates of the minority rights analysis, can be addressed most effectively through law and civil rights instruments.[65] In short, the minority model argues that, like other minorities, disabled persons constitute a disadvantaged and disempowered group whose disadvantages mainly flow from a discriminatory and exclusionary environment and which can most effectively be addressed by law.

As indicated earlier, an effective anti-discrimination framework is indeed vital in the quest for equality and inclusion of disabled people. At the same time, one should be wary of the possible limits of the law in realising greater *de facto* equality for disabled people. The (potential) limits of the law can be appreciated in light of (*inter alia*) the following. It is to be stressed that discrimination suffered by disabled people is often as invidious as subtle. Thus, patterns of discrimination have become institutionalised and systemic discrimination is difficult to eradicate through a statu-

60 Bickenbach 1999, p. 102.

61 For a very detailed account of this model I refer to Bickenbach 1999, p. 102-110 with multiple references.

62 Hendriks 2000.

63 Women cannot be said to constitute a minority group in the numerical sense of the word. However, they can be said to be a 'minority' group in the social sense of the word, namely in the sense that they are clearly disadvantaged. Hence, minority should in this context be understood as equating to 'non-dominant'.

64 Hahn, 'Toward a Politics of Disability: Definitions, Disciplines, and Policies', internet publication available at <www.independentliving.org/docs4/hahn2.html> (last viewed on 15-04-06). Also Fredman 2005, section 3.2. Fredman, in contrast with Hahn, has however not shown herself an explicit proponent (or opponent) of the minority rights analysis.

65 Bickenbach 1999, p. 104-105 with further references.

tory framework of discrimination law, particularly if the legal framework is 'negatively' and 'formally' oriented.[66] Thus, argues Scotch, '(...) as we have experienced in race and gender equity issues, changing cultural values and social relationships that have become institutionalised in the informal patterns of everyday life, may be beyond the capacity of statutory mandates'.[67]

Similarly, Bickenbach has noted that disability discrimination is often not about intentional discrimination by an identifiable discriminating agent, but rather the result of systemic social forces resulting in the denial of opportunities and the unjust distribution of resources. As Bickenbach has argued

> '(...) [b]ecause discrimination is an indignity, compensation to the victim of the insult is meaningful and appropriate. But where neutral forces such as economic factors create the disadvantage, there is no insult, because there is no insulter. There is a social evil; there is injustice and inequality. But of a different sort'.[68]

Precisely in light of the systemic nature of disability discrimination Bickenbach regards the universalist model of disability, which will be discussed in section 2.3.2.2.1 hereafter, as being more effective.

It is submitted that systemic discrimination can merely be eradicated if the substantive justice approach infiltrates disability discrimination law. If we wish to achieve *de facto* equality for disabled persons, we will need to design the law in such a way that it contributes to the reconfiguration of the notions of normality and ableism. The substantive justice approach calls *inter alia* for a prohibition of indirect disability discrimination and for a legal duty to make reasonable accommodation. Notably these notions have the potential of dismantling the systemic nature of disability-based discrimination, although this can arguably only very gradually be achieved. The law must moreover operate proactively in the sense that it should encourage employers and other agents to prevent disadvantage from occurring, rather than remedying disadvantage *ex post*. Proactive stances could be nourished by the adoption of a positive duties and mainstreaming approach which seeks to ingrain 'disability' in all policy considerations and processes.

At this juncture, our attention should be drawn to the following perceived paradox. As previously already stated, the minority rights model of disability forms a sub model of the social model of disability. However, it might become unduly intertwined with the medical model of disability, given that it calls for the extraction of the group of disabled persons. If the group of disabled persons is defined on the basis of a medical model of disability, as is the case in English law, there will be a risk that the minority rights model underscores conspicuous aspects of the medical model. In other words, both models risk becoming intersected. This outlined paradox

66 Although true minority rights legislation is often not so designed. Indeed, a formal, symmetrical framework tends to underpin legislation which is premised not upon a minority rights analysis but rather upon the principle of individual justice for all. See also Fredman 2005, section 3.1, where she has outlined the problems connected to the individual justice approach. These have also been outlined in Chapter 3 in the context of the concept of indirect discrimination.

67 Scotch 2000, p. 222.

68 Bickenbach 1999, p. 109.

could be resolved in two ways, namely either by designing the disability discrimination framework in a symmetrical fashion which would obviate the need of extracting the group, or, if asymmetry is taken as a starting point, by avoiding a medically focused approach to the definition of disability. Both options will be elaborated later on in the analysis. Henceforth, I will first analyse the universalist model of disability.

2.3.3.2.2. The Universalist Model[69]

The universalist model of disability recognises the heterogeneous and variable character of disability. This model does therefore not perceive disability as a fixed quality of a particular group but rather as a variable condition. Thus, writes Bickenbach, '(...) disability should not be viewed as a human attribute that demarcates one portion of humanity from another (as gender does, and race sometimes does), but rather as an infinitely various but universal feature of the human condition'.[70]

Thus, in simple words, all at least risk becoming disabled, but not becoming black, female, Muslim, etc. The variable character of disability shows commonalities with age as a ground of discrimination, given that all 'risk' becoming old. Essentially, those who adhere to a universalist approach call for policies which respect difference and diversity and which broaden the range of 'normality'. Thus, on this view, a building ought to be designed in such a way that the widest range of potential users may have access to it. The universalist model does not contest that for social and political purposes boundaries might need to be drawn with the effect that some are and others are not 'disabled'.[71] However, the model stresses that such boundaries may fluctuate in a democratic society.[72] The kernel of the universalist approach is that it seeks to demystify the 'distinct characteristics' of disability with the ultimate aim of bringing about greater equal opportunities for all and a fairer distribution of resources.[73] According to the universalist model, the narrower our interpretation of normality is, the less likely it is that opportunities are fairly distributed.

2.4. *Interim Conclusions*

In the above a theoretical analysis has been made of disability as a ground of discrimination. Attention has been paid to the intrinsic logic underpinning this ground, which has been contrasted and compared with that of other grounds. Prime features of disability are its fluid and heterogeneous character and as a consequence of which

69 For an in depth account of this model, I refer to Bickenbach 1999, p. 111-113 with further references. See also Fredman 2005, section 3.3.

70 Bickenbach 1999, p. 112 in reference to Zola 1989.

71 Bickenbach 1999, p. 112.

72 Bickenbach 1999, p. 112 where he has observed that boundaries are drawn '(...) for social and political purposes, and as such are not facts of the world- like gravity- but negotiable political and economic stances which, in a democratic setting, should always be open to challenge, debate and revision'.

73 Fredman 2005, p. 207, who has argued that '[c]entral [to the universalist approach] is the call for justice in the distribution of resources and opportunities'.

the group of disabled persons lacks a common identity. Moreover, disability differs from some other grounds of discrimination in the sense that it may have an impact upon availability for a job, or upon the way in which a job is performed (which may deviate from what is perceived as standard job performance). It has also been seen that disability-based disadvantage occurs often quite unconsciously, simply because the normality standard is dominant in daily decision-making processes.

In the above, I have moreover explored various models of disability. These models each seek to discern the exact source of disadvantage suffered by disabled persons. This is important, for tracing the locus of disadvantage forms an important yardstick in assessing the preferable legal and policy approach. Whereas the medical model argues that the source of disadvantage is to be found in the individual impairment as such, the social model emphasises the link between discrimination and disadvantage on the one hand, and societal attitudes and environmental design, on the other. In the present author's view, the medical model should not be taken as a starting point for a legal framework that aims at reducing disability related disadvantage and exclusion. This is so, for the medical model buttresses the dominant norm of normality, which is subsequently compensated for by a reliance upon help and charitable approaches. The social model, in contrast, has the effect of empowering disabled persons, for it acknowledges the nexus between disadvantage, on the one hand and implied assimilation to able-bodiedness, on the other. Hence, the social model seeks to dismantle the systemic nature of disability discrimination. As such it reflects a proactive substantive justice model which, it has been argued, should underpin the legal framework of disability discrimination.

3. Discrimination, Disability and EC Law[74]

3.1. *Shifting Theoretical Bedrocks*

With the adoption of the EFD, discrimination on grounds of disability in the realm of employment has for the first time become a matter of binding Community law. As shall be argued below, the Directive, insofar as the ground disability is concerned, appears to be founded upon a minority rights analysis, whereas with respect to the other grounds of discrimination it reflects elements of the individual justice model. The latter model seeks to grant protection from discrimination to discernible individuals rather than to disadvantaged groups.[75] The Directive's purpose is comparatively limited,[76] but nonetheless ambitious. Its prime aim is to strengthen the opportunities of *inter alia* disabled people in the labour market (including vocational training),

74 For an extensive analysis of EU law and disability I refer to Waddington 1995, Quinn 1999; Mabbett and Bolderson 2001. For a specific and detailed analysis of the EFD in relation to disability, I refer to Whittle 2002, p. 303-326.

75 The tenets of the models of individual and group justice have been analysed in Chapter 3 in the context of the concept of indirect discrimination.

76 In the sense that Article 13 EC Treaty upon which the Directive is based would have permitted for a more extensive protection from discrimination (*inter alia*) on grounds of disability. See generally Chapter 2.

without however transcending the principle of meritocracy.[77] Hence, although employers cannot be compelled on the basis of the Directive to reserve certain jobs for disabled persons only[78] (which would effectively amount to 'results equality', or 'equality of outcome'), they are under a legal duty to ensure that disabled persons are treated on an equal footing with non-disabled persons. As shall be seen, with respect to 'disability' the Directive most clearly infuses the principle of equality with concerns over substantive, and not merely formal, justice.

Prior to the adoption of the Directive there were already a number of EC soft law provisions concerning the rights of disabled people. In the early years, EC soft law regarding the employment position of disabled persons in the Community clearly reflected a medically focused approach.[79] This approach has however been departed from in favour of the social (environmental) model of disability discussed above. This has explicitly been recognised in a recent Commission Communication regarding the rights of disabled people which states as follows:

> '(...) the circumstances of people with disabilities and the discrimination they face, are socially created phenomena which are not directly related to their impairments per se. While the medical approach is often characterised as locating the 'problem' of disability within the person, the social approach locates the problem of disability in the environment, which fails to accommodate people with disabilities.'[80]

Furthermore, the Commission has observed that

> '(...) from seeing people with disabilities as the passive recipients of compensation, society has come to recognise their legitimate demands for equal rights and to realise that participation relates directly to insertion. Contributing to shaping society in a fully inclusive way is therefore the overall EU objective: in this respect, the fight against discrimination and the promotion of the participation of people with disabilities into the economy and society play a fundamental role'.[81]

77 Whittle 2002, p. 305.

78 It should be noted that Article 7(1) EFD does permit the Member States to adopt positive action measures for *inter alia* disabled persons. However, as we saw in Chapter 5, the ECJ's case law on positive action in the context of sex shows that such measures may not overstep the boundaries of the equality of opportunities paradigm. Whether the ECJ will extrapolate its case law on gender positive action measures to the realm of 'disability' is currently unclear, given the absence of cases. It could well be that the Court will permit quota systems for disabled persons, whereas it has struck down such systems in the context of gender.

79 See notably the Council Recommendation of 24 July 1986 on the Employment of Disabled People in the Community (86/379/EEC) *OJ* L, 12 August 1986, 225, 43 which stipulates as follows: '(...) for the purposes of this Recommendation, 'disabled people' includes all people with serious disabilities which result from physical, mental or psychological impairments'.

80 Communication from the Commission 'Towards a United Nations Legally Binding Instrument to Promote and Protect the Rights and Dignity of Persons with Disabilities', COM(2003) 16 final 24 January 2003.

81 Communication from the Commission, *Equal Opportunities for people with disabilities: A European Action Plan,* Brussels, 30-10-2003, COM (2003) 650 final. This matches with the stance adopted by the Commission in earlier Communications. See, for example, the Commission's Communication on Equal Opportunities for Disabled People of 30 July 1996, COM (96) 406 →

It therefore follows that EC equality and non-discrimination law in the context of disability takes as a starting point the social model of disability rather than the (old-fashioned) medically focused approach. The social model is also underlying the legal framework contained in the EFD. This *inter alia* follows from the more general fact that the Directive aims to foster the civil rights and equal opportunities of disabled persons in the context of employment, rather than supporting them by way of social insurance and assistance measures.[82] Given that the Directive arguably only offers protection from discrimination to disabled persons (broadly defined), and not to persons who claim an instance of discrimination on the ground of *not being disabled*, it echoes the tenets of the minority rights model, rather than the universalist model. As explained in section 2.3.3, the minority rights model is a subset of the social model of disability. The latter is patently mirrored in the concept of reasonable accommodation enshrined in Article 5 EFD. In the section to follow, the Directive shall be analysed in further depth from the specific angle of disability. It is to this that I shall turn now.

3.2. *The EFD and Disability: a Tailor-Made Analysis*

3.2.1. Introduction

Hereafter, I shall examine the EFD in the particular context of disability. My aim shall not be to examine every single provision of the Directive in depth, but rather to focus upon these concepts and provisions in the Directive which are at a premium in a disability rights context and which have not yet been analysed in other chapters in this book. Thus, given that direct discrimination, indirect discrimination, harassment and the instruction to discriminate have all (to a greater or lesser degree) been examined in previous chapters, a repetitive analysis should be avoided. Hereafter, I will focus upon the following concepts: (a)symmetry, the definition of disability and the concept of reasonable accommodation. It is to be noted that up until now, no

final, which states as follows: 'The old medical-centred approach is now giving way to a social one which puts much stronger emphasis on identifying and removing the various barriers to equal opportunities and full participation in all aspects of life for people with disabilities.' See moreover, Communication from the Commission 'Towards a Barrier Free Europe for People with Disabilities', COM (2000) 284 final, 12/05/2000, which provides that 'The approach endorsed by the European Union acknowledges that environmental barriers are a greater impediment to participation in society than functional limitations. Barrier removal through legislation, provision of accommodations, universal design and other means, has been identified as the key to equal opportunities for people with disabilities'. See also Communication from the Commission 'Towards a United Nations Legally Binding Instrument to Promote and Protect the Rights and Dignity of Persons with Disabilities', COM 2003, 16 final of 24 January 2003.

82 It might be worth noting that on the basis of Article 7(2) EFD the Member States may adopt social policy measures which are aimed at creating or maintaining provisions or facilities for safeguarding or promoting the integration of disabled persons into the working environment.

disability discrimination cases have emerged before the ECJ,[83] although these are likely to arise in the future.[84]

3.2.2. (A)symmetry?

With regard to religion and belief, sexual orientation and age it is abundantly clear that the EFD is premised upon a symmetrical model of anti-discrimination law. The legal framework thus offers the same degree of protection from discrimination to persons in the dominant pool (e.g. Christians, heterosexuals and young people) compared with persons in the disadvantaged pool (e.g. Muslims, homosexuals and the elderly). Matters are less clear-cut with regard to the ground disability. Some scholars have argued that the Directive reflects the principle of asymmetry in the specific context of disability. On this reading the Directive merely offers legal protection from discrimination to 'disabled persons', whereby it remains unclear who exactly are covered by this notion. Thus, argues Skidmore, '(...) with regard to disability the Directive does not operate in the same symmetrical fashion as provisions on sex and race do. It only discriminates on grounds of disability and not "non-disability" which is prevented by the Directive'.[85] Skidmore's argument is primarily based on the Directive's definition of indirect discrimination.[86] This states expressly that only persons 'having a particular disability' can be the victim of indirect discrimination.[87] Furthermore, and logically, the duty to make reasonable accommodation merely applies with respect to disabled persons. Waddington has nevertheless referred to the fact that other provisions in the Directive might be interpreted symmetrically. She refers to the prohibition of direct discrimination.[88] The latter requires proof of less favourable treatment 'on the ground of disability'.[89] In *abstracto*, I agree with

83 See, however, the Opinion by Geelhoed (AG) in *Sonia Chacón Navas v. Eurest Colectividades SA*, Case C-13/05 of 16 March 2006. In this case the Spanish *Juzgado de lo Social* referred a preliminary question to the ECJ on the meaning of 'disability' in the Framework Directive.

84 While this book was finalised for publication, the ECJ gave judgment in the case of *Sonia Chacón Navas v. Eurest Colectividades SA*, Case C-13/05, 11 July 2006. In casu, it was (*inter alia*) held that 'disability' in the Framework Directive does not cover 'sickness' and that 'sickness' could neither be brought within the scope of the Directive through an expansion of the list of grounds that are covered by the EFD. In casu, the ECJ interpreted the concept of 'disability' on the basis of a medical approach. With reference to section 3.1 above and section 3.2.3 to follow, this reflects a wrong stance, given that the EC Commission's approach to the rights of disabled persons clearly takes the social model as a starting-point for analysis and policy-making. Furthermore, the EFD mirrors a civil rights approach to the rights of disabled persons which cannot sensibly be reconciled with the outdated medical model of disability. It is regretted that time has precluded the author from analysing the aforementioned case in further detail.

85 Skidmore 2001, p. 131.

86 The concept of indirect discrimination has extensively been discussed in Chapter 3.

87 Article 2(2) 'b' reads as follows: 'indirect discrimination shall be taken to occur where an apparently neutral provision, criterion or practice would put persons having a (...) particular disability (...) at a particular disadvantage compared with other persons unless (...)'.

88 Waddington 2005, p. 114-115.

89 The less favourable treatment has to be assessed relative to the treatment meted out to a present, past or hypothetical comparator. Perhaps superfluous, Article 2(2) 'a' EFD provides →

Waddington that the latter rubric is ample enough to be interpreted both symmetrically and asymmetrically. However, perceived in context and notably in light of the asymmetrical application of both 'indirect discrimination' and the 'duty to accommodate', it is argued that the principle of legal consistency requires that only 'disabled persons' may rely upon the prohibition of direct discrimination. The present author therefore agrees with Skidmore that with regard to 'disability' the EFD applies asymmetrically. Whether this is indeed the case is ultimately a matter for the ECJ to decide.

3.2.3. The Definition of Disability

What does it mean in practice, if only 'disabled persons' can rely upon the protective framework of the EFD? The Directive remains silent on the definition of 'disabled person'. Indeed, whether or not defining this notion and, if so, *how* was purposefully left a matter for the Member States to decide.[90] Hence, it is currently unclear whether persons with minor disabilities, future disabilities, past disabilities, persons who have received discriminatory treatment by reason of their association with a disabled person, persons who have been discriminated against on grounds of a falsely assumed disability etc., are in fact covered by the legal framework.

Ultimately, the definition of disability has to be interpreted by the ECJ. Indeed, it is important that the Court, in future case law, indicates at least a number of parameters as to how to define disability. If it does not do so, a person might be legally disabled in Member State *x* but not in Member State *y*.[91] This would undermine, not only the effectiveness of the Directive itself, but might moreover constitute an impediment to free movement rights and equal competition in the internal market.[92] If, in future case law, the Court is endowed with the task of defining disability, it should be aware that EC disability law echoes the tenets of the social model of disability. Any narrowly medically focused interpretation of disability must therefore be avoided, given that this would shift our attention away from the *discriminatory treatment* (which should stand central), to the physical or mental *impairment* as such.[93] In other words, a medically focused approach unduly concentrates on the nature of the impairment (e.g. is the impairment sufficiently severe to be captured by the definition of disability?), rather than on the societal response to that very impairment. If the medical model is taken as a starting point for judicial analysis, the Court will risk becoming unduly involved in medical issues whereas the real concern, namely the combat against disability-based discrimination risks becoming an ancillary matter.

that 'direct discrimination shall be taken to occur where one person is treated less favourably than another is, has been or would be treated in a comparable situation on any of the grounds referred to in Article 1 (i.e. religion and belief, sexual orientation, disability and age)'.

90 Degener 2004, section 5.

91 Quinn and Quinlivan 2003, p. 234.

92 Quinn and Quinlivan 2003, p. 234. See also Waddington 2005, p. 117-119. Also Wells 2003, p. 262.

93 See also Waddington 2005, p. 117 who has indicated that 'one could even envisage the unhappy situation where an almost unending series of preliminary questions are referred to the Court asking if individuals, each with a slightly different impairment, are covered by the Directive'.

Perhaps superfluous, an adherence to the social model should not prevent the Court from establishing a link between 'disability' and 'impairment'. After all without the impairment there will be no 'cause' which interacts with societal attitudes and hence there will be no disability based discrimination.[94] If, however, the Court acts on the premises of the social model of disability it will recognise that it is the very combination of the impairment *and* the social environment which constitutes disability based disadvantage. This insight should prevent the Court from launching a definition of disability which mirrors the notions of capacity *v.* incapacity, or which is confined to coverage of severely disabled persons only or which merely covers persons with an actual disability.[95] If protection from disability based discrimination is to be effective all of the examples which have been listed at the outset of this section will have to be captured by the notion of 'disabled person'. In the author's view, this is moreover required by the nature of the EFD which is about non-discrimination and equality rather than about social assistance and help. As Degener has written, the legal definitions of 'disabled person' ought to be different in the context of equality law, compared with social assistance law: 'the distribution of social benefits has to be needs based in order to be rational. Equal treatment as a right not a benefit should not be offered only to those in need but to all persons potentially affected by discrimination'.[96]

3.2.4. The Concept of Reasonable Accommodation[97]

Article 5 of the Directive provides as follows:

> 'In order to guarantee compliance with the principle of equal treatment in relation to persons with disabilities, reasonable accommodation shall be provided. This means that employers shall take appropriate measures, where needed in a particular case, to enable a person with a disability to have access to, participate in, or advance employment, or to undergo training, unless [emphasis; MG] such measures would impose a disproportionate burden on the employer. This burden shall not be disproportionate when it is sufficiently remedied by measures existing within the framework of the disability policy of the Member State concerned.'

94 Degener 2004, p. 6: 'The impairment may be visible or invisible, it may be real or imputed, but it is always the reference of discriminative treatment.'

95 See Degener 2004, p. 6-7, who has illustrated that the exercise of defining disability by reference to 'impairment' does not contradict with the premises of the social model of disability. Problems do however arise, if the definition of disability depicts disabled persons as being helpless and in need, if the definition is narrowly designed so as to cover merely those with a severe disability, or if not all persons who are adversely affected by disability based discrimination (e.g. those who receive discriminatory treatment by reason of their association with a disabled person) are covered.

96 Degener 2004, section 2.

97 See also Chapter 3 in which reasonable accommodation has been discussed in relation to the concept of indirect discrimination. For an extensive analysis of anti-discrimination and the concept of reasonable accommodation, I refer to Jolls 2005.

As Barnard has noted, this Article had been lobbied for by the European Disability Forum, whereby the DDA 1995 was used as a template.[98]

Article 5 is placed in further detailed context by a number of Recitals contained in the Directives' Preamble:

> Recital 16
> 'The provision of measures to accommodate the needs of disabled people at the workplace plays an important role in combating discrimination on grounds of disability.'
>
> Recital 17
> 'This Directive does not require the recruitment, promotion, maintenance in employment or training of an individual who is not competent, capable and available to perform the essential functions of the post concerned or to undergo the relevant training, without prejudice to the obligation to provide reasonable accommodation for people with disabilities.'
>
> Recital 20
> 'Appropriate measures should be provided. i.e. effective and practical measures to adapt the workplace to the disability, for example adapting premises and equipment, patterns of working time, the distribution of tasks or the provision of training or integration resources.'

Moreover, Recital 21 provides as follows:

> 'To determine whether the measures in question give rise to a disproportionate burden, account should be taken in particular of the financial and other costs entailed, the scale and financial resources of the organisation or undertaking and the possibility of obtaining public funding or any other assistance.'

With regard to the above provisions the following could be said. The concept of reasonable accommodation clearly moves beyond the comparative anti-discrimination framework which underpins the prohibitions of direct and indirect discrimination contained in the EFD. The concept of reasonable accommodation requires that the decision-making agent (e.g. the employer) actively takes account of a disabled person's impairment which, in interaction with the environmental or social attitude to that impairment, places a disabled person in a materially different position relative to a non-disabled person, or compared with a differently disabled person. If the employer[99] fails to make reasonable accommodation, the legal consequence of this failure should be an act of disability-based discrimination.[100] I shall come back to this point hereafter.

It follows from the previous, that the notion of reasonable accommodation is ill-placed within the equality as consistency paradigm which calls for sameness of

98 Barnard 2001, p. 972.

99 As shall be explained hereafter the law sets limits upon an employer's duty to make reasonable accommodations. In other words, in certain circumstances it is not unlawful if the employer does not make a reasonable accommodation. This point will be taken further in the passages to follow in the main text.

100 The argument that the legal consequence of a failure to accommodate results in an act of disability-based discrimination cannot however directly be derived from the wording of Article 5 EFD. As stated, I will come back to this point later on in the analysis.

treatment.[101] In contrast, reasonable accommodation reflects substantive justice, for it conveys a message that persons who find themselves in a materially different position (disabled persons) compared with others (non-disabled persons or persons with a different disability), should not be afforded consistent but rather different treatment. Only in this way can equality be achieved in practice, rather than merely in form.

The essential aim of the legal duty to make reasonable accommodation is to eradicate barriers which prevent disabled persons from competing on an equal footing with non-disabled persons or differently abled persons in the labour market.[102] Hence, reasonable accommodation is a tool to advance, rather than to guarantee, the employability of disabled people. Indeed, as follows clearly from Recital 17 of the Directive, employers are not under a legal duty to hire persons who do not have the required merit for the job concerned.[103] However, importantly, whether or not a person has the required merit for the post has to be assessed in light of the employer's duty to accommodate. In other words, merit must be assessed *ex post* the conclusion on whether reasonable accommodation could or could not be made. From what has been said so far, it is clear that the notion of reasonable accommodation correlates with an equal opportunities, rather than with an equality of results, paradigm. Thus, writes Whittle, reasonable accommodation does not seek to treat disabled persons in a *preferential* way, compared with non-disabled persons.[104]

In the above, it has been argued that unlawful failure to accommodate amounts to an act of discrimination. However, admittedly, that unlawful failure to accommodate results in discriminatory treatment does not explicitly (and perhaps not even implicitly) follow from Article 5 EFD. In fact, the duty to accommodate has not been enshrined within Article 2 of the Directive entitled 'concepts of discrimination'. Article 2 merely refers to direct and indirect discrimination, harassment and the instruction to discriminate.[105]

It follows from the extensive comparative law report on reasonable accommodation drawn up by Waddington that various scholars regard reasonable accommodation as a sub form of positive action.[106] The concept of positive action was extensively discussed in Chapter 5. We saw that positive action, if perceived within a substantive equality paradigm could be regarded as being part of the principle of equality itself. The same holds true for the duty to make reasonable accommodation. Further, depending on its exact format, positive action as well as reasonable accommodation may be aimed at bringing about equality of opportunity. Despite the just-mentioned

101 Also Waddington 2004a, p. 7, who has referred to the 'sameness' model of discrimination.

102 Whittle 2002, p. 313.

103 I may be argued that 'merit' is a notion which is biased in itself, for 'merit' tends to be assessed on the basis of the dominant norm of normality. Hence, the principle of merit tends to favour those in the dominant group.

104 Whittle 2002, p. 313-314.

105 It is a sign of bad legal drafting that the last paragraph of Article 2 contains a general public security exception which in fact has nothing to do with the definitional concept of discrimination as such (see Article 2(5) EFD).

106 Waddington 2004a, under III (p. 30 *et seq.*) in reference to *inter alia* Doyle, 'Enabling Legislation of disassembling law? The Disability Discrimination Act 1995', 60 *Modern Law Review* 1997, 64 at 74.

commonalities between both notions the present author agrees with Waddington that both concepts should be distinctly understood.[107] At least four reasons could be advanced to support this argument. First, unlike the adoption of positive action measures which are allowed but not *required*, an employer is under a legal duty to consider the possibility of making a reasonable accommodation.[108] In other words, if an employer *a priori* fails to do so, he will act in contravention of the Framework Directive. This does, however, not mean that the employer is under an unconditional obligation to realise an accommodation. As shall be seen below, the duty to accommodate is not unlimited but the possibility of making an accommodation must always be examined. Secondly, as observed by Waddington, reasonable accommodation is an 'individualised notion' in the sense that realising such an accommodation offers a tailor-made solution to the obstacles faced by a particular individual.[109] Thirdly, the duty to adjust is not limited in time. In contrast, as we saw in Chapter 5, the quintessence of positive action is to redress the disadvantaged position of the *group* of persons (defined by race, sex, etc.) up until the moment in time, that it can no longer be upheld that the group concerned is disadvantaged. In sum, whereas reasonable accommodation forms an individualised notion, positive action is a group concept. And, whereas the latter ought to be accompanied by limitations in time, this does not hold true with regard to the former. Fourthly, reasonable accommodation seeks to provide an effective answer to the problems faced by a disabled person[110] which stem from the concealed and often unintended interplay between a physical or a mental impairment on the one hand, and the societal reactions to this impairment, on the other. Hence, unlike positive action measures and policies, reasonable accommodation requires some kind of adaptation to the work environment, e.g. by being flexible in respect of a rostering requirement, or by means of amending the physical features of the workplace.

As referred to earlier, Article 5 EFD does not stipulate that failure to accommodate results in disability-based discrimination. The Article does however explicitly state that reasonable accommodation shall be provided 'in order to guarantee compliance with the principle of equal treatment'. It is argued, however, that the principle of non-discrimination forms the negatively framed *subset* of the wider, positively oriented, principle of equality. In this way, Article 5 could be interpreted as implying a notion of discrimination, which however goes beyond the conventional dichotomy of direct and indirect discrimination.[111] The argument is moreover supported by Recital 16 of the EFD which states that 'the provision of measures to accommodate the needs of disabled people at the workplace plays an important role in combating discrimination on grounds of disability'.

107 Waddington 2004a, p. 31 where she has observed that '(...) it seems inappropriate to view the reasonable accommodation requirement found in the Framework Employment Directive in this light [i.e. in the light of positive action; MG].'

108 Also Waddington 2004a, p. 31.

109 Waddington 2004a, p. 30.

110 Although certainly, the duty to make reasonable accommodation could be extended to notably the grounds of age, religion and sex. See Waddington and Hendriks 2002.

111 Waddington and Hendriks 2002.

The question as to what exact form of discrimination a failure to accommodate amounts has been neatly analysed by Waddington and Hendriks.[112] They have argued that

> '[d]ifferent from direct and indirect discrimination, reasonable accommodation discrimination typically emerges in response to the failure to make an adaptation to ensure equal opportunities and commonly does not follow from differentiation on a forbidden or seemingly neutral ground - a distinction which is sometimes difficult to apply with respect to groups in need of adaptation'.

In this light, they have contended that reasonable accommodation discrimination cannot fit with the dual, conventional, classification of direct *v.* indirect discrimination. Hence, Waddington and Hendriks have concluded that reasonable accommodation discrimination constitutes a *sui generis* form of discrimination featured by its own specifics. The present author agrees with this view, since reasonable accommodation cannot be integrated within the comparative model of discrimination which underpins both the notion of direct and indirect discrimination. Moreover, direct discrimination has traditionally developed within the consistency model of discrimination.[113] Although indirect discrimination, like reasonable accommodation, reflects a 'difference model' it cannot reasonably be maintained that reasonable accommodation discrimination is the result of the application of a neutral provision, criterion or practice which has a disproportionate impact upon the group of disabled persons. In fact, as argued before, the latter cannot truly be discerned given the great heterogeneity of disabled persons. In light of the foregoing it must be concluded that although both 'indirect discrimination' and 'reasonable accommodation' ingrain the equality as difference approach, only indirect discrimination has traditionally been perceived as a group-oriented notion.[114] In contrast, the duty to make reasonable accommodations aims to offer a tailor-made solution to the particular barriers faced by a particular disabled person. Hence, reasonable accommodation rests upon an individualised approach.[115]

In the above it has been noted already that only the *unlawful* failure to accommodate results in a breach of the Framework Directive. Indeed, the duty to make accommodations is not unlimited. First, only *reasonable* accommodation must be made. Whittle has interpreted this notion as being linked to the question as to whether the accommodation would amount to a disproportionate burden on the part of the

112 See for further discussion also Tobler 2003 p. 17-18, who has perceived the right to a reasonable accommodation as a specific right, rather than as fitting within the non-discrimination paradigm which rests upon comparative justice.

113 With the exception of discrimination on grounds of pregnancy. See e.g. *Dekker v. Stichting Vormingscentrum voor Jong Volwassenen* (Case C-177/88), [1990] ECR I-3941; *Webb v. EMO Air Cargo* (Case C-32/93), [1994] ECR I-3567.

114 Although the EFD, RD and AETD have softened the group-oriented nature of the concept. See for further discussion the analysis of indirect discrimination in EC law made in Chapter 3.

115 See also Whittle 2002, p. 310. He has stressed that the successfulness of a claim of indirect discrimination, has a beneficial effect not only upon the individual applicant but in fact upon all who belong to the same group as the individual applicant. The same does, however, not apply with respect to the successfulness of a claim of reasonable accommodation discrimination.

employer.[116] Waddington, in contrast, has argued that the notion of reasonableness in Article 5 EFD should not be confused with the 'disproportionate burden defence' also contained in that Article. In her view, and with reference to relevant U.S. law, 'reasonableness' in Article 5 equates to 'effectiveness' or 'practicability'. In other words, reasonable accommodation is accommodation that enables the individual disabled person concerned to effectively carry out the functions attached to a post.[117] The present author agrees with Waddington's view, notably also in light of Recital 20 of the Directive (referred to above), which stresses the need for effectiveness and practicality of the accommodation sought and which, in addition, lists examples of reasonable accommodation that could be considered. The disproportionate burden defence is placed in context in a separate Recital (Recital no. 21 of the EFD). It is submitted that if 'reasonableness' equated with the employer's disproportionate burden defence, it would have been unnecessary to explicitly refer to both of these concepts within a single Article (i.e. Article 5 EFD). It would moreover have been redundant to draw up two separate Recitals, namely one contextualising 'reasonableness', and one qualifying the disproportionate burden defence. It shall be seen below that Dutch law also draws a distinction between the notions of 'reasonableness' and 'disproportion'. This differs, however, from the approach adopted in English law.

The disproportionate burden defence seeks to balance the right of the disabled person to a reasonable accommodation on the one hand, with the employer's target of cost-efficiency, on the other. One could argue that the disproportionate burden defence immediately transmits a negative message, namely that making reasonable accommodation is necessarily cost-*in*efficient. However, if the best candidate for the job happens to be disabled, hiring her/him may nonetheless be economically efficient in the longer run.[118] Once this is acknowledged, making a reasonable accommodation and hiring disabled persons does not per definition show tensions with a cost-efficiency model. The delicate and fair balancing of the relevant interests at stake in disability discrimination claims is far from being an easy exercise. As observed by Mummery LJ for the CA in the context of the English DDA

> '[t]he whole subject [i.e. disability discrimination law; MG] presents unique challenges to legislators and to tribunals and courts, as well as to those responsible for the day to day operation of the Act in the workplace. Anyone who thinks that there is an easy way of achieving a sensible, workable and fair balance between the different interests of disabled persons, of employers and of able-bodied workers, in harmony with the wider public interests in an economically efficient workforce, in access to employment, in equal treatment of workers and in standards of fairness at work, has probably not given much serious thought to the problem'.[119]

116 Whittle 2002, p. 314.

117 Waddington 2005, p. 125. Also Waddington 2004a, where she has observed that '[in the relevant U.S. law; MG] the reasonableness of the accommodation did not refer to its limited cost or inconvenience to the employer, but rather to its potential to provide equal opportunity, reliability and efficiency.' (p. 63).

118 See also Wells 2003, p. 264.

119 *Clark v. TDG t/a Novacold* [1999] IRLR 318 (CA).

The disproportionate burden defence is captured by Article 5 itself. It is further qualified by Recital 21 of the EFD. In any case, the burden on the employer shall not be deemed to be disproportionate when it is sufficiently remedied by measures adopted by the Member State within the framework of national (or regional) disability policy (see Article 5). Thus, Article 5 embeds the link between a civil rights strategy to bring about equal opportunities for disabled people on the one hand, and state social insurance strategies, on the other.[120] This link is also reflected in Recital 21 of the Directive which makes it clear that 'proportionality' must be assessed on a case by case basis, taking into account the financial or other costs entailed by making the accommodation, the scale and financial capacity of the employer and the possibility of receiving external state funding or other assistance for the realisation of the accommodation.

Given the lack of case law on the notion of reasonable accommodation, it remains currently unclear if, and to what degree, the ECJ will grant the Member States a margin of discretion in carrying out the above balancing exercise in concrete cases, or whether it will be the Court itself which effectively keeps control over the disproportionate burden defence. As seen in Chapter 3, the ECJ has adopted a relatively strict and structured test of 'objective justification' in indirect discrimination cases in which the alleged indirectly discriminatory act was caused by the employer's policy (rather than by state policies or state legislation). It is submitted that, if the prime aim is to bring about equal opportunities for disabled persons, the Court should not easily let cost considerations prevail over equality concerns. As previously stated,, we must however await whether the Court

> '(…) will be inclined to enforce a certain level of reasonable accommodation as part of the fundamental right of non-discrimination, or whether it will take the view that subsidiarity should govern the determination of levels of accommodation: in other words, that member states should determine what is reasonable or proportionate in the light of their social policies'.[121]

Obviously, if the matter is left for the Member States to decide, the legal protection from disability discrimination will arguably vary considerably within the EU as a whole. Such diversity would not truly be reconcilable with the fundamental nature of the rights in issue.

3.2.5. Conclusions

In the above, the Framework Directive has been analysed in the context of disability, whereby the focal point has been on the (a)symmetrical application of the Directive, the definition of disability and the duty to make reasonable accommodation. It has been argued that the Directive, by way of exception, is premised upon asymmetry as far as the ground 'disability' is concerned. This should, however, not prevent the ECJ from defining 'disability' broadly and along the lines of a social model of dis-

120 Hendriks 2005, p. 191.
121 Mabbett 2003, p. 12.

ability. The concept of reasonable accommodation reflects deontological justice, in the sense that it is not dependent upon a 'like for like comparison'. In this respect, the concept of making reasonable accommodation differs from the notions of direct and indirect discrimination. It has been argued that reasonable accommodation cannot easily be analysed around the conventional axes of direct and indirect discrimination. The present author agrees with the view expressed by Waddington and Hendriks that reasonable accommodation discrimination constitutes an independent form of discrimination, which goes moreover accompanied by its own distinctive judicial balancing exercise. The nature of this balancing exercise is currently undefined and needs to be elaborated upon by the ECJ in future case law. In certain circumstances, a right to a reasonable accommodation might be trumped by financial considerations of costs which, as seen, is however less likely to happen if the employer is granted state subsidies flowing from national social assistance schemes. The close interplay between civil rights strategies and social welfare policies is thus reflected in the wording of Article 5 EFD.

4. Comparative Law Analysis

4.1. *Introduction*

In the above disability discrimination law has been examined in the context of the EC. The analysis of EC law is instrumental to the analysis in section 4 as a whole, which will *inter alia* examine the impact of supranational law upon domestic approaches and practices. This amounts to an analysis of top-down influence. Section 4 moreover seeks to compare legal approaches in the Netherlands with legal approaches in England. This amounts to the cross-country comparison. The top-down analysis and the cross-country comparison will be made with respect to the notions of 'symmetry' and 'asymmetry' (section 4.3), the definition of disability (section 4.4) and the concept of reasonable accommodation (section 4.5). Wherever appropriate, I will also make references to (potential) bottom-up influence. Throughout the analysis I will establish links with the medical and social models of disability discussed above. Tentative conclusions will be drawn in section 4.6. Before starting the comparative law analysis it seems useful to explain in brief certain general elements of Dutch and English disability discrimination law. This will be done in section 4.2 to follow which partially recalls a number of issues which have also been explained in Chapter 2.

4.2. *Domestic Disability Discrimination Law in a Nutshell*

4.2.1. The DETA 2003

The adoption of the Framework Directive turned out to be an effective means for fast-tracking the adoption of specific equal treatment law on grounds of disability and chronic disease in the Netherlands. As stated in section 1 above equal treatment law concerning the grounds disability and chronic disease has existed in the Netherlands since 1 December 2003 when the DETA[122] entered into force.[123] This Act currently only applies to the areas of employment and occupation.[124] The Act stands separately from the GETA[125] which covers most grounds of discrimination, apart from 'disability', 'age' and, partially, 'sex'. This was explained in Chapter 2. The reason why the grounds 'disability' and 'chronic disease' have been regulated outside the framework of the GETA is political expediency. In other words, the separate regulation of these grounds does not reflect a principled legislative stance.[126] Implementation of the relevant provisions of the EFD in Dutch law has occurred in two stages.[127] In the first stage, the disability specific provisions of the Directive were implemented by the enactment of the DETA. This included, for example, the implementation of the concept of reasonable accommodation. In the second stage, the DETA was amended by the 2004 EC Implementation Act[128] whose aim it was to transpose the so-called 'common provisions' of the Directive. These are provisions which are applicable to all grounds of discrimination, including for example the concepts of discrimination, general exceptions, etc.[129] It follows from the previous observations that the Dutch Act mirrors the EC dimension of disability discrimination law. However, EC law has not been the only catalyst behind the adoption of the Act, although it has clearly accelerated the legislative process. Prior to the adoption of the EFD the need for regulating equal treatment for disabled persons had been widely debated in the Dutch Parliament.[130] It is worth stressing that the legislative

122 See footnote 2 above. A concise but integral analysis of the Act has been made by Hendriks 2003. See also Gijzen 2003.

123 Before that date, issues of discrimination, equality and disability in employment were only indirectly captured via constitutional law, general employment law and civil law. Moreover, a number of laws already existed (and they still do) which seek to promote the employability of disabled persons but which must be perceived within the context of social welfare law, rather than civil rights law. An important example of social welfare laws for disabled persons is the Act on the Reintegration of Disabled People in Employment (*Wet op de (re)integratie Arbeidsgehandicapten*), 23 April 1998, *Law Gazette* 290, most recently amended by the Act of 15 December 1999, *Law Gazette* 564. These measures shall not be discussed hereafter. See Waddington and Gijzen 2004, p. 4-7 and p. 21-23 (with further references).

124 Articles 7 and 8 of the Act regard the area of social transport but with regard to these areas the Act has not yet entered into force. See for a brief discussion of the expansion of the Act with new areas of social life (beyond employment), Kroes 2005, section 2.

125 General Equal Treatment Act. See generally Chapter 2.

126 See Chapter 2. See for a discussion of the advantages and disadvantages of a disability specific Act and a general Act covering a multitude of grounds including disability, Waddington 2005, p. 129-131.

127 See also Waddington and Gijzen 2004.

128 See Chapter 2.

129 See the *Explanatory Memorandum* to the EC Implementation Act, Second Chamber of Parliament, 2002-2003, 28 770, no. 3, p. 7. For a more extensive overview of the background to the Act and the implementation process, I refer to Gijzen 2003 and to Waddington and Gijzen 2004.

130 The DETA 2003 was preceded by a so-called 'proeve van wet' (i.e. a provisional preliminary model for legislation) which addressed disability discrimination in a number of areas of social life, including recruitment and selection in employment (see *Parliamentary Documents* II, 1997-1998, 24 170, no. 36). With reference to Waddington and Gijzen 2004, the aim of this document was to explore the social consequences of disability discrimination legislation and →

proposals that existed prior to the entry into force of the EFD envisaged a prohibition of discrimination with respect to disability *in* and *outside* employment.[131] Given that the DETA 2003 merely applies to employment the 'top-down' influence exercised by EC on national law apparently has also had a *restraining* impact on the development of domestic equal treatment law. All in all, the Dutch Act must be perceived as reflecting both the mandatory implementation of EC law and as an elaboration of Article 1 of the Dutch Constitution[132] in horizontal relations (i.e. relations between private individuals).[133] Article 1 of the Constitution does not specifically mention 'disability' in the list of grounds it contains. Disability is, however, implied within this list via the open-ended formula 'or on any other ground'. What has been stated so far is not merely a matter of semantics. That the Act also conveys a constitutional law dimension is important, for it should encourage the government to go beyond what is strictly required by EC law.[134] The latter has paradoxically both inhibited and promoted the development of Dutch disability equal treatment law.

The DETA prohibits direct and indirect discrimination, harassment and the instruction to discriminate in employment. It moreover contains a duty to make reasonable accommodation for disabled persons. The DETA applies to both disabled and non-disabled persons and thus echoes the principle of symmetry. This means that the Act does not need to define the notion of a disabled person. This point shall be explained in further detail in section 4.3 hereafter. The DETA also contains a number of exceptions including a positive action exception, an exception for the adoption of protective social policies that are aimed at ameliorating the disadvantaged position of disabled persons and a health and safety exception.

So far, the DETA has been explained in a nutshell. Not all aspects which I have just touched on shall be subjected to the comparative law analysis to follow hereafter. As is known, the analysis to follow will be confined to (1) symmetry and asymmetry; (2) the definition of disability and (3) the concept of reasonable accom-

to reflect on the question whether legislation was the most effective means to achieve full participation of disabled persons in employment and social life. The 'proeve' resulted in the adoption in 2000 of a bill concerning the equal treatment of disabled persons and persons with a chronic disease (see *Parliamentary Documents* 1999-2000, 24 170, no. 55). The function of the 'proeve' as a paragon for an intended Act on disability discrimination was ultimately taken over by the EFD which has inspired the contents of the DETA in its present format. See for further analysis also Kroes 1999 and Asscher-Vonk 1998a.

131 The envisaged legislation were to cover (1) recruitment and selection in employment; (2) contracts and the provision of goods and services in the context of sports; (3) the design and maintenance of public areas (see: *Parliamentary Documents* II, 1999-2000, 24 170, no. 55). Also, Kroes 1999, p. 2052-2053.

132 The Constitutional equality clause. See generally Chapter 2.

133 Given that the Constitutional equality clause is meant to apply in vertical relations, i.e. in relations between private individuals and the State.

134 The Act is a so-called *'aanbouwwet'* which means that its scope is intended to be expanded in years to come. Currently, the Act merely applies with regard to the areas of employment, occupation and training. However, Articles 7 and 8 also render the Act applicable in the area of public transport, although these two Articles have not yet entered into force. See for further discussion Kroes 2005, section 2.

modation. I will, however, first consider a number of general aspects of English disability discrimination law. It is to this that I shall turn now.

4.2.2. The DDA 1995 as Amended

Legal protection from disability discrimination in the United Kingdom has existed since 1995.[135] Unlike sex discrimination law, which has traditionally been influenced by EC law, disability discrimination law has developed independently although the DDA 1995 has been inspired by U.S. disability discrimination law. It has been seen in Chapter 3 in the context of indirect discrimination that the RRA 1976 has sometimes been influenced indirectly by EC law, given that the RRA is generally treated *in pari materiae* with domestic sex discrimination law. After all, the SDA and RRA are premised upon the same conceptual model of discrimination law. Both Acts prohibit discrimination on grounds of sex and race respectively, and thus apply symmetrically. However, the DDA 1995 deviates from the conceptual framework which underpins the SDA and RRA.[136] The DDA 1995 applies asymmetrically which means that it specifically aims at the amelioration of the disadvantaged position of disabled people. The conceptual differences between the SDA/RRA and the DDA have been made explicit in the case law. In *Clark v. Novacold* Mummery (LJ) for the Court of Appeal held as follows:

> 'contrary to what may be reasonably assumed, the exercise of interpretation [of the DDA 1995; MG] is not facilitated by familiarity with the pre-existing legislation prohibiting discrimination in the field of employment (and elsewhere) on the grounds of sex (SDA 1975) and race (RRA 1976). Indeed, it may be positively misleading to approach the 1995 Act with assumptions and concepts familiar from experience of the workings of the 1975 Act and the 1976 Act.'[137]

Another difference between the DDA and the other two Acts is that it does not contain a prohibition of indirect discrimination (neither pre- nor post-implementation of EC law). The DDA seeks to fill this gap by imposing upon employers a duty to make reasonable adjustments. Furthermore, the DDA adopts a different approach with respect to the prohibition of direct discrimination.[138] The DDA is not so much premised

135 The DDA prohibits discrimination against disabled people in the areas of employment, goods and services and the sale or rental of property. However, the present analysis shall be confined to employment. The employment related provisions of the Act are contained in Part II DDA. Prior to the adoption of the Act disability issues fell predominantly within the realm of social security laws. For a recent and exhaustive overview of the DDA 1995 as amended I refer to McColgan 2005, notably Chapter 8.

136 Fredman 2005, section 5.

137 *Clark v. Novacold* [1999] IRLR 322 (CA per Mummery LJ], paragraph 30. See also Baroness Hale of Richmond in the case of *Archibald v. Five Council* [2004] ICR 954 (HL), paragraphs 47 and 48.

138 Before the implementation of the EFD the DDA 1995 only contained a prohibition of less favourable treatment related to a person's disability. This could (and can still be) justified. Post-implementation of EC law (i.e. as of October 2004), this prohibition has been expanded (not substituted by) with a prohibition of direct discrimination which cannot be justified. In short, post implementation, a two-fold conceptualisation of 'direct discrimination' features →

upon the comparative justice model, at least not in the sense that it requires 'like for like comparisons' as is the case with the SDA and RRA.[139] In other words, the DDA more than is the case with the SDA and RRA reflects a substantive equality approach. However, and as will be explained in great detail hereafter, substantive equality is often not achieved due to a restrictive interpretation of the notion of a 'disabled person'. Implementation of the EFD into domestic law has resulted in a partial amendment of the Act. Amendments have occurred by the adoption of the Disability Discrimination Act 1995 Amendment Regulations 2003 (hereafter: 'the Disability Regulations', or 'Regulations').[140] The Regulations entered into force on 1 October 2004.[141] Insofar that this is relevant for the subject matter to be discussed hereafter, these amendments will be commented upon throughout the discussion to follow. In addition to Community law, domestic developments have blown a fresh wind through the existing English disability discrimination law framework. The adoption of the DDA 2005 imposes a positive equality duty upon public sector authorities and, moreover, it amends in certain respects the definition of disability. Public sector duties will not be discussed in this chapter but amendments to the definition of disability will be examined in the analysis to follow.

It is clear from the foregoing that the genesis of English disability discrimination law is fundamentally different from domestic race and sex discrimination law. Moreover, English disability discrimination law is conceptually different from Dutch disability discrimination law. This last point will be illustrated in greater detail hereafter in the context of the comparative law analysis.

4.3. *The Principles of Symmetry and Asymmetry*

As argued above, the EFD is likely to apply asymmetrically with respect to the discrimination ground 'disability'. It has also been argued that the concept of disability must be broadly defined by the ECJ in order to replicate the social model of disability discussed in section 2.3.3 above. In sharp contrast with EC law, the Dutch DETA applies symmetrically. One could argue that the Dutch approach reflects a somewhat artificial stance, given that disability is by itself not a neutral notion.[142] The Dutch approach implies in practice that both disabled and non-disabled persons are covered by the legal framework. In short, the Act may be invoked by disabled

the DDA 1995. The introduction of a dual concept of direct discrimination reflects however a complicated and muddled approach. It would have been easier had the DDA adopted a singular concept of direct disability discrimination analogous to the one contained in the EFD. For reasons of space and time, I have not been able to analyse direct disability discrimination in the context of the DDA in much further detail. For a comprehensive analysis I refer to McColgan 2005, Chapter 5, p. 581-589.

139 See *Clark v. Novacold* [1999] IRLR 322 (CA per Mummery LJ]. See Fredman 2005, p. 211-212.

140 Disability Discrimination Act 1995 Amendment Regulations 2003, SI 2003, 1673.

141 In contrast with the Netherlands, the UK has made use of the possibility granted by Article 18 EFD of the extended deadline for implementation of the EFD's provisions disability and age. Although the regular deadline lapsed on 2 December 2003, this deadline could be extended with a maximum of three years for the grounds disability and age.

142 Degener 2004, p. 10.

persons, who claim discrimination *vis-à-vis* non-disabled persons, and by non-disabled persons who claim discrimination *vis-à-vis* disabled persons. However, reasonable accommodation can merely be required by disabled persons.[143] This is logical, for the concept of reasonable accommodation seeks to actively take account of the materially different position of disabled persons which has been caused by the interplay between the individual impairment and the societal reaction to that impairment. It follows that, with the exception of reasonable accommodation, the DETA reflects an individual justice approach and not a group-justice approach. Dutch law seems to differ in this respect from the approach adopted in the EFD. However, Dutch law is in common with the latter in that both are premised upon the social model of disability. This has the practical advantage that the discriminatory treatment complained of is the centrepiece of judicial analysis, rather than the medical impairment as such. This point shall be taken further in the discussion concerning the definition of disability hereafter.

The symmetrical framework underpinning the Dutch Act parallels the overarching genesis of Dutch equal treatment law which is centred around the neutral notion of distinction (*onderscheid*), rather than around the asymmetrical concept of discrimination (*discriminatie*). The different conceptual meanings of both hypotheses have been explained in Chapter 2.

From the viewpoint of formal equality the Dutch approach appears to go beyond the Directive's requirements, given that the range of protected persons in Dutch law is wider than in EC law. As shall be seen in more detail below, the symmetrical framework bears the advantage that a litigant need not, by way of preliminary legal exercise, establish that he or she belongs to the 'protected class'. Put differently, the symmetrical framework frees an individual from proving that (s)he has a disability and, with that, a potentially medically focused legal approach by the courts is *a priori* avoided. Indeed, as will be clarified in further detail in section 4.4 below, in English disability discrimination law an applicant is frequently denied the chance to argue a case of discrimination on its merits, given that the claim at hand is rejected at an early stage, by reason of the applicant's failure to establish that (s)he is disabled for purposes of the DDA. In other words, due to the need to prove disability, the discriminatory aspect of the claim at hand, it is often precluded from being considered.[144] It is particularly in this respect, that the Dutch symmetrical approach is to be preferred over the asymmetrical framework underlying the DDA 1995.

From the perspective of substantive justice the Dutch approach constitutes, however, an impediment to the quest for greater *de facto* equality for disabled persons.

143 *Parliamentary Documents* II 2001/2002, 28 169, no. 3, p. 9. Moreover, positive action measures operate a-symmetrically in the sense that such measures can only be adopted to the benefit of disabled persons. However, and as shall be seen below, the symmetrical framework implies that the lawfulness of positive action measures for disabled persons can judicially be challenged by non-disabled persons.

144 Recent research has indicated that the most usual ground for rejecting an applicant's claim under the DDA 1995 is the applicant's failure to *prove* his or her disability. See Monitoring the Disability Discrimination Act (Phase 2) by Leverton et al., IDS, February 2002.

De facto equality is boosted, not only via the vehicles of indirect discrimination and reasonable accommodation but also, and importantly, via the adoption of positive action measures and policies. This we saw in Chapter 5. It should be stressed that the DETA treats positive action as an exception to the central prohibition of making a distinction. Therefore, a non-disabled person can challenge positive action measures which have been adopted to the benefit of a disabled person. After all, as we saw in Chapter 5, although positive action is permitted by the law, it must remain within the limits set by the law. If it is accepted that the EFD cannot be relied on by a non-disabled person, who claims that (s)he has been discriminated against in comparison with a disabled person, the Dutch symmetrical approach is arguably in breach of the Directive. Whether this is a correct account of the law must be decided by the ECJ in future case law.

The symmetrical model of anti-discrimination law underpinning the DETA, contrasts with the asymmetrical framework underlying the DDA 1995 (as amended).[145] Given that the DDA is explicitly aimed at benefiting disabled persons, positive action measures cannot be challenged before the courts by non-disabled persons. In all, the symmetrical framework bears the advantage that positive action measures for disabled persons are regarded by the law as being unproblematic. Moreover, a symmetrical model is conceptually purer than an asymmetrical model, because 'disability' is an asymmetrical concept *per se*. On the other hand, the Dutch approach bears the advantage that 'disability' need not be defined. As will be seen in section 4.4 defining disability by law bears a risk that the medical model of disability creeps into the judicial analysis. This has the consequence that the effective protection by law against disability-based disadvantage gets frustrated. The possible pitfalls of defining disability will be considered below. It will be argued that, if an asymmetrical model is taken as a starting point, the exercise of defining disability will have to be premised upon the social model.

4.4. *Defining Disability*

4.4.1. Preliminary Issues

As we have seen in section 3.2.3 above, the EFD is short of a definition of disability and defining this notion has been left as a task for the ECJ. It has also been argued in section 3.2.3 that the Court ought to define disability in line with the spirits of the social model of disability. Given that the Dutch DETA applies symmetrically, defining disability becomes logically redundant.[146] Not defining disability bears various disadvantages notably, as seen above, that proving disability is *a priori* unnecessary (save with respect to the notions of reasonable accommodation and positive action). Therefore, a discrimination complaint can immediately be assessed on its merits. The Dutch

145 It is to be noted that the provisions regarding victimisation in the DDA 1995 (as amended) do however apply symmetrically.

146 This immediately explains the absence of Dutch case law on the matter. However, the right to a reasonable accommodation can only be claimed by a disabled person even under the Dutch symmetrical model of discrimination law.

DETA explicitly stipulates that those who are discriminated against on the basis of a (falsely) assumed disability or chronic disease are covered too.[147]

The Dutch approach stands in sharp contrast with the English approach which does define disability. The mere fact that disability is defined does not conflict with the requirements of the Framework Directive. The latter leaves a discretionary choice to the Member States as to whether or not to define disability.[148] However, it is argued that those Member States who have decided to define disability, including the UK, must do so on the premise of the social model of disability. If disability is narrowly defined and in line with the medical model of disability, the domestic approach will be likely to falling short of the Directive's requirements. Hereafter, the DDA's approach to disability shall be studied in closer detail. It is to be noted that the definition of disability has been partially amended by the DDA 1995. These amendments will be commented upon in the analysis to follow.

4.4.2. The Definition of Disability in the DDA 1995 as Amended by the DDA 2005

4.4.2.1. The Statutory Test for Defining 'Disability'

It is stressed at the outset that the notion of disability in the DDA 1995 (as amended) is underpinned by the individual, medical model discussed in section 2.3.2 above. In the government's view the DDA would lose its credibility and would be open for abuse if those who are not 'fairly and generally regarded as disabled' were covered too.[149] Others have however argued that the true reason for the medically focused approach has been a desired reduction of the costs for employers which, it was feared, would rise with the adoption of the Act.[150] Presently, one can legitimately question whether the medically focused approach to the definition of disability is in line with the legal requirements stemming from the EFD. I will argue that it is not and that tribunals and courts will have to attach a 'Directive conforming' interpretation to the notion of disability in cases that appear before them.

In order to decide who is and who is not covered by the Act the following legal sources are of relevance: (1) Schedules 1 and 2 of the DDA 1995, as amended by the DDA 2005; (2) the Meaning of Disability Regulations;[151] (3) the 1996 (non-

147 Article 1(b) of the DETA provides that a 'direct distinction' is 'a distinction between persons on the ground of an actual or an assumed disability or chronic disease'. The word 'assumed' has superfluously been added to the definition given that both the Dutch Supreme Court and the ETC have taken the view that also the false ascription of a discrimination ground is protected under Dutch equal treatment legislation. See Opinion 02/84 of the ETC with reference to the judgment by the Dutch Supreme Court of 26-02-1993, *NJ* 1993, 507.

148 See also Waddington 2005, section 3.2, and Wells 2003, p. 255.

149 Minister for Social Security and Disabled People, Mr William Hague, HC Debs Standing Committee E, 1995, vol 235, col's 73 and 148, referred to by Hamilton 2000, p. 209, notably footnote 15.

150 Hamilton 2000, p. 209.

151 The Disability Discrimination (Meaning of Disability) Regulations 1996, SI 1996/1455, available at <http://www.drc-gb.org> (last visited on 15-04-06).

binding) Guidance issued by the Secretary of State,[152] which will soon be overtaken by a revised Guidance;[153] (4) the 2004 (non binding) Code of Practice;[154] (5) case law by courts and tribunals. Although the Guidance and the Code of Practice are no binding legal authorities, a failure to take account of it could be raised in legal proceedings as 'unreasonable practice'.[155]

Section 1(1) of the DDA 1995, which is subject to Schedule 1 of the Act, defines the notion of disabled person as follows: 'A person has a disability for the purposes of this Act if he has a physical or mental impairment which has a substantial and long-term adverse effect on his ability to carry out normal day-to-day activities'.

In *Goodwin v. the Patent Office* Mr Justice Morison for the EAT dealt with this definition on the basis of a four-limb test:[156]

1. Does the applicant have an impairment which is either mental or physical?
2. Does the impairment affect the applicant's ability to carry out normal day-to-day activities and does it have an adverse effect?
3. Is the adverse condition (upon the applicant's ability) substantial?
4. Is the adverse condition (upon the applicant's ability) long term?

152 Guidance on matters to be taken into account in determining questions relating to the definition of disability. The Guidance has been issued by the Secretary of State under Section 3 of the DDA 1995. The Guidance has been published by HMSO and is available from the HMSO Publications Centre, PO Box 276, London SW8 5DT. The Guidance has gained statutory effect as from 31 July 1996.

153 The Revised Guidance on matters to be taken into account in determining questions relating to the definition of disability will come into force on 1 May 2006. The 1996 Guidance will on that date be revoked. However, the 1996 Guidance shall remain applicable with regard to claims arising out of an act of discrimination which occurred before 1 May 2006. See for further information and for the material contents of the Revised Act the website of the Disability Rights Commission at <http://www.drc-gb.org>(last visited on 15-04-06).

154 Disability Discrimination Act 1995 Code of Practice- Employment and Education 2004. The revised Code of Practice is available at <http://www.drc-gb.org.documents/employment_occupation.pdf > (last viewed 01-05-06). This Code has replaced the 'Code of Practice for the elimination of discrimination in the field of employment against disabled persons or persons who have had a disability' issued in 1996.

155 Cooper 2004. See also DDA 1995, Sections 53(4) -53(7) and DDA 1995 Section 3. The importance of taking note of the Guidance and of the Code of Practice has been stressed in the case law. In *Ridout v. TC Group* [1998] IRLR 628, the EAT held as follows: 'We do criticise the Industrial Tribunal for not making specific reference to the Code of Practice. It seems to us that as the case law develops in relation to the Disability Discrimination Act, Industrial Tribunals will build up a knowledge of how the Act should be applied in practice. At the period of development, it is particularly important (...) that Industrial Tribunals should also refer to the relevant provisions of the Code of Practice as they are required to do under Section 53.' (paragraph 28 of the judgment). See also *Goodwin v. the Patent Office* [1999] IRLR 4 (EAT), paragraph 23. In contrast, in *Goodwin the Patent Office* also recognised that '(...) in many cases the question whether a person is disabled within the meaning of the Act can admit of only one answer. In such clear cases it would be wrong to search the Guide and use what it says as some kind of extra hurdle over which the applicant must jump' (paragraph 23). Similarly, the EAT in *Vicary v. British Telecommunications plc* [1999] IRLR 680 held that 'the Guidance (...) will only be of assistance in what might be described as marginal cases'. (paragraph 11).

156 *Goodwin v. the Patent Office*, [1999] IRLR 4 (EAT), paragraph 26.

In *Goodwin* it was stressed that 'with social legislation of this kind [i.e. the DDA 1995; MG] a purposive approach to construction should be adopted'.[157] However, as will be seen below, due to the medical model underpinning the law the modus of legal interpretation has been narrow and formal. This must be criticised on principle, as well as in light of the Framework Directive. In what follows an analysis will be made of each of the sub questions referred to above in light of the relevant case law.

Ad. 1. Does the applicant have an impairment which is either mental or physical?
The concept of impairment has not been defined by the law. A side-step route has been followed in the sense that an impairment will be discerned, if it adversely affects a person's ability to carry out normal day-to-day activities. What this entails will be examined hereafter. Before the entering into force of the DDA 2005, Section 1(1) of Schedule 1 of the DDA provided that a 'mental impairment' includes an impairment resulting from or consisting of a mental illness *only* if the illness is 'clinically recognised'. This fell to be determined on the basis of medical expert evidence which clearly echoes the tenets of the medical model.[158] In *Morgan v. Staffordshire University,*[159] the EAT took the view that the applicant's recourse to occasional references of 'anxiety', 'stress' and 'depression' in medical notes, as well as in the WHO's[160] International Classification of Diseases, without any well-briefed medical evidence beyond that did not amount to sufficient evidence of a mental impairment for the purposes of the Act. In *Goodwin v. the Patent Office* the EAT encouraged first instance tribunals '(...) to ascertain whether the illness described or referred to in the medical evidence is mentioned in the WHO's International Classification of Diseases'.[161] The requirement that a mental illness must be 'clinically well recognised' has recently been repealed by the DDA 2005 which does justice to the social model of disability.

In the joint cases of *Rugamer* and *McNicol*[162] the EAT held that a physical impairment will only be covered, if it does not find its cause in psychological factors. This view was overruled by Mummery LJ for the CA. The CA held that it was not necessary to analyse the cause of an impairment.[163] This reflects a correct approach, for it should not matter how exactly an impairment has been caused but rather what are its discriminatory effects (perceived in conjunction with social reactions to it) upon a disabled person's life.

The cause of the impairment was however decisive for the judgment by the EAT in *Murray*.[164] The facts were as follows. Mr Murray suffered from paranoid schizophrenia and had been imprisoned in the past for stabbing a neighbour. He had

157 Paragraph 22.

158 Wells 2003, p. 256. See also *Abadeh v. British Telecommunications plc* [2001] ICR 156 (EAT).

159 *Morgan v. Staffordshire University* [2002] IRLR 190 (EAT).

160 World Health Organisation.

161 Paragraph 33.

162 *Rugamer v. Sony Entertainment UK Ltd and McNicol v. Balfour Beatty Rail Maintenance Ltd* [2001] IRLR 644 (EAT); [2002] IRLR 711 (CA).

163 The CA had nevertheless dismissed the claim upon appeal, for the claimant had failed to establish that his impairment had been the result of either a physical or a mental impairment. See McColgan 2005, p. 574.

164 *Murray v. Newham Citizens Advice Bureau Ltd. (no. 2)*, [2003] IRLR 340 (EAT).

applied for a voluntary job with Newham Citizens Advice Bureau (the respondent). He was rejected for the job, for the employer feared that as a result of stress caused by the fact of being employed, the applicant would engage in violent conduct. The employer's fear had not been mitigated by the applicant's contention that a psychiatric diagnosis had guaranteed that stress was not a meaningful factor in his illness. In deciding the case, the ET referred to Section 4(1)(c) of the meaning of disability Regulations. This provides that persons who have a tendency to physical or sexual abuse of others are not covered by the Act. In its view, the applicant could therefore not rely on the Act, notwithstanding that it had been recognised in medical circles that the stabbing had been a direct consequence of the applicant's mental illness for which he had been treated. The EAT disagreed with this reasoning. It held that a person who has a tendency to physical or sexual abuse is only excluded from legal protection, if that tendency amounts to a freestanding condition. Since the applicant suffered from paranoid schizophrenia and, as a direct consequence thereof, had a tendency to violence, he was not *a priori* excluded from the Act's protective scope.

The approach by the EAT in *Murray* raises serious objections. It could be questioned whether tendencies to physical or sexual abuse can ever be 'freestanding' conditions, as the EAT suggested. Moreover, the Section 4(1)(c) exception has been undermined by the EAT by deciding as it did. It has been rightfully suggested in the literature that the EAT should have concluded that Mr Murray's recourse to violence in the past had been a single incident act and hence, could not be said to amount to a 'tendency'.[165]

It follows from the case law that persons suffering from Chronic Fatigue Syndrome (CFS, or ME) are in principle covered by the Act.[166]

Ad. 2. Does the impairment affect the applicant's ability to carry out normal day-to-day activities and does it have an adverse effect?

The requirement that an impairment must have an adverse effect upon a person's ability to carry out normal day-to-day activities shifts the judicial analysis away from a complaint about discrimination, to the nature of the impairment. Hence, the second requirement also mirrors the medical model of disability. Section 4(1) of Schedule 1 of the Act provides as follows:

> 'An impairment is to be taken to affect the ability of the person concerned to carry out normal day-to-day activities only if it affects one of the following: a. mobility, b. manual dexterity, c. physical co-ordination, d. continence, e. ability to lift, carry or otherwise move everyday objects, f. speech/ hearing/eyesight, g. memory or ability to concentrate/ learn/understand, h. perception of the risk of physical danger.'

The adjective 'normal' has been interpreted as meaning what is normal for most people. This means that this notion must not be interpreted restrictively by solely looking at the precise circumstances of the case at hand. Thus, in *Abadeh v. British*

165 See IRLR 'Highlights' 2003, cited by McColgan 2005, p. 573.

166 *O'Neill v. Symm & Company Limited* [1998] 481 (EAT).

Telecommunications plc[167] the EAT held that the first instance tribunal had erred in law where it had held that travelling by underground was not a 'normal day-to-day activity', for the applicant did not live and work in London and, that flying was not a 'normal day-to-day activity', for the applicant's work did not involve travelling by plane.

The notion of 'normal day-to-day activity' has also been interpreted in the case of *Epke v. Commissioner of the Police of the Metropolis.*[168] In that case, the EAT emphasised that

> '(...) what is normal cannot sensibly depend on asking the question whether the majority of people can do it. The anti-thesis for the purposes of the Act is between that which is 'normal' and that which is 'abnormal' or 'unusual' as a regular activity, judged by an objective population standard (...) what is 'normal' [may] best be understood by defining it as anything which is not abnormal or unusual (or (...) 'particular' to the individual applicant'.[169]

In the case at hand, the first instance tribunal decided that Mrs. Epke's impairment to her hand did not have an adverse effect on her ability to carry out normal day-to-day activities. The tribunal in deciding as it did adopted a positive approach in the sense that it focused upon what Mrs Epke could do, rather than on what she could not do. However, it subsequently used this against the applicant by concluding that her ability to carry out normal day-to-day activities had not been affected. Hence, the EAT held that in deciding on the issue at hand, the focus must be on what an applicant cannot do, rather than on what she can do.[170] Paradoxically, the 'positive approach' adopted by the ET diminished the scope of legal protection, whereas a judicial focus upon 'inability' appeared to extend this scope. On principle, the emphasis upon what is wrong with disabled persons must be condemned, for this has the effect of reinforcing prejudice, stigmatisation and discrimination. Moreover, the requirement to prove 'disability' by means of medical expert evidence entails significant costs.[171]

It also follows from *Epke* that whether something amounts to a 'normal day-to-day activity' must not be assessed by looking at whether more or less than 50% of the population would do it. The first instance tribunal had held that Mrs. Epke's inability to put rollers into her hair and to apply make-up fell outside the notion of a 'normal day-to-day activity', given that these activities are only carried out by women. The EAT rightfully held that

> '[t]his reasoning is plainly wrong. The logic would exclude anything done by women rather than men, or vice versa, as not being normal. What would strike the person in the

167 Abadeh v. British Telecommunications [2001] IRLR 23 (EAT).

168 Epke v. Commissioner of the Police of the Metropolis [2001] IRLR 605 (EAT).

169 Paragraph 32 of the judgment.

170 Paragraphs 37 and 38 of the judgment.

171 Cooper 2004.

street as entirely normal behaviour- doing up the zip on her dress, for a woman; shaving for a man- would not be classed as a normal day-to-day activity'.[172]

Ad. 3. Is the adverse effect substantial?

The Guidance[173] provides that '[a] substantial effect is one that is greater than the effect which would be produced by the sort of physical or mental conditions experienced by many people which have only 'minor' or 'trivial' effects.' Once again, the law adopts a negative angle by focusing upon the applicant's inability. This negative angle is also evident from an analysis of the case law.[174] It follows from the case law that 'substantial' means 'more than minor or trivial',[175] or, alternatively phrased, 'anything which is more than insubstantial'.[176] Also in *Leonard v. Southern Derbyshire Chamber of Commerce*,[177] the EAT took the view that the employment tribunal had misguided themselves by taking examples from the Guidance of what the applicant could do (e.g. to eat and drink, to catch a ball) and had subsequently inappropriately balanced that against what she could not do, e.g. negotiating pavement edges safely. The EAT considered this the wrong approach, for the things that the applicant could do (e.g. catching a ball) did not diminish her inability to negotiate pavement edges safely.

It is recalled that in establishing whether or not an impairment exists, medical expert evidence can be conclusive. However, it follows from *Abadeh v. British Telecommunications plc*,[178] that whether or not an impairment is 'substantial' remains a question of fact which has to be decided on exclusively by the first instance tribunal. This is a problematic approach, for the higher courts cannot overrule questions of fact which have been decided on by lower courts and which may be detrimental for the success of the claim at hand.[179]

Ad. 4. Is the adverse effect long term?

This element of the legislative test is elaborated upon by Schedule 1 of Section 2 of the DDA. The effect of an impairment constitutes a 'long-term effect' for purposes of the law if: (a) it has lasted at least 12 months; (b) the period for which it lasts is likely to be at least 12 months; (c) it is likely to last for the rest of the life of the person

172 Paragraph 39 of the judgment. It should be noted that legal confusion is created by the Guidance which states in Section C under C2 that the notion of 'normal day-to-day activities' is not intended to include activities which are normal only for a particular person or group of people.

173 See footnotes 152 and 153 above.

174 See e.g. *Goodwin v. the Patent Office* [1999] IRLR 4 (EAT); *Vicary v. British Telecommunications plc* [1999] IRLR 680 (EAT); *Leonard v. Southern Derbyshire Chamber of Commerce*, [2001] IRLR 19 (EAT).

175 *Goodwin v. the Patent Office* [1999] IRLR 4 (EAT).

176 *Epke v. Commissioner of Police of the Metropolis* [2001] IRLR 605.

177 *Leonard v. Southern Derbyshire Chamber of Commerce* [2001] IRLR 19.

178 *Abadeh v. British Telecommunications plc* [2001] IRLR 23.

179 Wells 2003, p. 256-257. Wells has moreover pointed at the lack of expertise on the part of tribunals in deciding accurately on the question as to whether or not the adverse effect is 'substantial'.

affected. The Guidance moreover clarifies matters in further detail. It is for example not required that the effect of the impairment is the same throughout the relevant period of time. It follows from *Greenwood v. British Airways plc*[180] that courts and tribunals in their assessment of the existence or not of a 'long-term effect' ought not to solely concentrate upon the state of the applicant's medical condition on the date of the alleged discriminatory act. In contrast, in deciding as to whether the impairment's effect is likely to endure for at least 12 months, the adverse effect of the applicant's condition must be assessed up to and including the employment tribunal hearing. This means that events which occur after the date of an alleged discriminatory act are of importance in the legal assessment as to whether an applicant is 'disabled' for the purposes of the law.[181]

With regard to so-called 'recurring effects', Section 2(2) of Schedule 1 of the DDA provides that 'where an impairment ceases to have a substantial adverse effect on a person's ability to carry out normal day-to-day activities, it is to be treated as continuing to have that effect if that effect is likely to recur.' According to the Guidance conditions which recur only sporadically or for short periods of time, e.g. epilepsy, can nevertheless amount to a DDA impairment.[182]

So far, I have considered the statutory test which governs the legal assessment of whether a person is a 'disabled person' for the purposes of the law. It should be noted that there are a number of conditions or situations for which special provision is made. These will be looked at immediately henceforth.

4.4.2.2. Situations which Are Expressly Covered or for which Special Provision is Made

A number of conditions are *a priori* excluded from the protective scope of the DDA. These include certain anti-social disorders, such as a tendency to start fires, a tendency to steal, a tendency to physical or sexual abuse, exhibitionism and voyeurism.[183] Moreover, addiction to alcohol, nicotine or any other substance does not amount to an 'impairment' for the purposes of the Act, unless the addiction has stemmed from medically prescribed drugs or other medical treatment.[184] Impairments which stem from, e.g. an addiction to alcohol (such as a liver function impairment) or nicotine (e.g. a lung function impairment) are, in contrast, covered. In this regard, the Guidance makes it clear that 'it is not necessary to consider how an impairment was caused'. However, the *Murray* case[185] (discussed above) shows that the cause of an impair-

180 *Greenwood v. British Airways plc* [1999] IRLR 600.

181 See however, *Cosgrove v. Caesar & Howie* [2001] IRLR 654. In that case, the EAT took the view that 'it seems to us [i.e. EAT] that the appropriate time at which to adjudicate whether a person is disabled or not is the date of the unfavourable treatment alleged to have been dealt to him or her'.

182 Explicitly excluded from this grouping is however seasonal allergic rhinitis ('hay fever') unless this aggravates the effects of an existing condition. See Guidance, Under B 'Long Term'.

183 Meaning of disability Regulations 1996, SI 1996/1455, para. 4(1).

184 Meaning of disability Regulations 1996, SI 1996/1455, para. 3.

185 *Murray v. Newham Citizens Advice Bureau Ltd. (no. 2)*, [2003] IRLR 340 (EAT).

ment might nonetheless be an important factor in the decision whether or not a particular impairment 'qualifies'.

Special provision is made for persons with 'severe disfigurements' (Schedule 1, Section 3 DDA). Persons with severe disfigurements (e.g. scars, birthmarks, limb or postural deformation or skin diseases) are treated by the law as being covered by the notion of 'disabled person'. However, this does not apply with regard to disfigurements which consist of a tattoo or body piercing.[186]

The DDA 2005 has guaranteed that a person who has cancer, HIV infection or Multiple Sclerosis (MS) is deemed to be a disabled person for the purposes of the Act.[187] The DDA 2005 has, however, not generally extended legal protection to persons who suffer from asymptomatic conditions, or to persons who are genetically predisposed to acquire certain conditions in the future. It follows from Section 8 of Schedule 1 of the Act that persons who suffer from asymptomatic progressive conditions fall outside the protective scope of the law (e.g. a person who is genetically predisposed to get cancer in the future).[188] A person with a 'progressive condition' (e.g. cancer, MS) is only covered if, as a result of that condition he has an 'impairment' which has or had some effect of that person's ability to carry out day-to-day activities, and, if that impairment is likely to have a 'substantial' effect in the future.[189] Case law shows that the courts have adopted an unduly narrow approach with respect to legal protection from discrimination to persons with progressive conditions.

In *Mowat Brown v. the University of Surrey*[190] the applicant had been diagnosed with MS since 1995. Since medical expert evidence indicated that Mr Mowat Brown was 'not more probable than not' to suffer from any adverse substantial effects in the future, the EAT affirmed the decision by the ET that the claimant was not a 'disabled person' for the purposes of the Act. The EAT rejected the argument made by the claimant that the assessment as to whether a progressive condition is likely to have a 'substantial adverse effect' in the future, should be answered by looking at the impairment in *abstracto* (objective approach), rather than by looking at the particular case at hand (subjective approach). In other words, it must be shown that the condition in the applicant's case, is more 'probably than not' to result in a substantial adverse effect in the future.

The EAT's approach in *Mowat Brown* must be criticised, given that discriminatory treatment by employers is very often the result of stereotypical assumptions about the capabilities of disabled persons. These assumptions exist, regardless of whether or not an applicant will or will not suffer from an adverse effect upon his

186 Article 5 of the meaning of disability Regulations.

187 See Section 18 of the DDA 2005. However, by way of Regulations certain forms of cancer may be excluded from automatically amounting to a disability for purposes of the law.

188 The European Disability Forum has noted that since genetic diagnosis is becoming increasingly usual, an increased number of people are aware of their future state of health. See their website at <www.edf-feph.org>. See for further legal comment in the context of the DDA also McColgan 2005, p. 575 *et seq*.

189 See Section 8 of Schedule 1 DDA and Cooper 2004.

190 Mowat-Brown v. University of Surrey [2002] IRLR 235.

ability to carry out normal day-to-day activities in the future. Once again, in *Mowat Brown*, the Act was interpreted in an unduly medically focused fashion.

The intervention of medical treatment, prosthesis or aids treating or correcting the effect of an impairment does not necessarily prevent a person showing that (s)he has a disability.[191] The question to be assessed in such cases is whether, 'but for' the correction or medical intervention, there would be a disability in terms of the DDA.

4.4.2.3. *Discrimination on Grounds of a Past Disability, a Perceived Disability and 'Associated Discrimination'*

Persons who are the victim of discrimination by reason of a past disability are covered by the Act (see Schedule 2 of the Act). However, and this has not changed with the entry into force of the DDA 2005, those who are discriminated against by reason of a falsely presumed disability are not protected. This is another clear difference between English and Dutch disability discrimination law. It is also a consequence of the medically focused approach to disability. The social model places the emphasis upon the discriminatory treatment which, in this context, has been caused by the false presumption(s) of a person's disability, on the one hand, and the societal reactions to it, on the other. Unlike the medical model, the focus is thus not upon the existence or not of the individual impairment. Due to the adherence to the medical model, people who are discriminated against by reason of their association with a disabled persons are not covered either (e.g. the spouse of somebody who is HIV infected). This has not changed with the adoption of the DDA 1995.

Some might contend that the asymmetrical model that underpins the DDA precludes legal protection from discrimination to those who have been discriminated against on grounds of a falsely presumed disability, or to those who have received discriminatory treatment on grounds of their association with a disabled person. This, I argue, is a deceptive way of reasoning. What the asymmetrical model aims to preclude is that a person would be protected under the Act from instances of discrimination on the ground of 'not being disabled' (e.g. a non-disabled person who claims an act of disability discrimination because he has been refused for a job by an employer who wishes to employ a disabled person). Obviously, those who receive discriminatory treatment on grounds of false presumptions as to their 'disability' are not discriminated against 'on grounds of not being disabled'. The same applies to those who have been a victim of 'associated discrimination'. All in all, it cannot legitimately be maintained that an asymmetrical model a priori excludes the coverage of the aforementioned two categories of (potential) victims.

4.4.3. Conclusions

It is clear from the above analysis that English disability discrimination law transmits a highly medically focused approach with regard to the definition of disability. The DDA 1995 excludes, without good reason, a wide range of potential victims

[191] Schedule 1, Sections 6(1) and (2) of the DDA.

from its protective scope. This regrettable situation has not been mended with the transposition of the EFD into domestic law, nor with the entry into force of the DDA 2005. The English approach can be contrasted with the 'inclusive' and flexible approach which features Dutch disability discrimination law. Given that Dutch law applies symmetrically, the risk of a medically focused approach to the disability question has *a priori* been avoided. Consequently, in Dutch law the legal attention is duly focused upon the act of discrimination, rather than upon the individual impairment. It is nonetheless submitted that the symmetrical approach need not be adopted *per se*, in order to avoid the problems connected with defining disability. However, if disability is defined, this will have to be done on the premises of the social model of disability. The law should state explicitly that persons who have suffered from an actual, a past or a future disability are covered, as well as persons who have been discriminated against on the ground of their association with a disabled person. Moreover, the law should grant protection to those who have been the victim of discrimination on the ground of a falsely perceived disability. Furthermore, both 'major' and 'minor' disabilities ought to be covered, as well as persons who have been discriminated against on grounds of an asymptomatic condition. Since the medical model thwarts such extensive coverage it should not function as a template for the design of disability discrimination law. It has also been argued that, from a conceptual point of view, the asymmetrical model underlying the DDA would not be in tension with such an approach, for the trigger of disadvantage is always 'disability-related'. *A fortiori*, it is argued that English law as it currently stands falls short of the requirements imposed upon the government by the Framework Directive. Since the Directive takes as a starting point the social model of disability, the English medically focused approach can no longer be upheld.

4.5. *The Concept of Reasonable Accommodation*

4.5.1. Introduction

Hereafter, I will analyse the concept of reasonable accommodation from the perspective of comparative law. In section 4.5.2, I will first examine how the legal duty to make reasonable accommodation for disabled persons has been applied and interpreted in the context of the Dutch DETA. This will be done in light of the requirements stemming from the Framework Directive ('top-down comparison'). The same will be done in section 4.5.3 with respect to English disability discrimination law. In section 4.5.4 the two domestic approaches will be compared ('cross-country' analysis) and tentative conclusions will be drawn.

4.5.2. Reasonable Accommodation in Dutch Law: Top-Down Comparison[192]

The reasonable accommodation duty of Article 5 EFD has been transposed in Article 2 of the DETA which reads as follows:

[192] This section partially draws on Waddington and Gijzen 2004, Gijzen 2003 and Gijzen 2004.

> 'The prohibition of making a distinction also includes that the person to whom this prohibition is addressed must make effective accommodations, according to need, unless these would place a disproportionate burden upon that person.'[193]

Unlike the overall genesis of the DETA, Article 2 of the Act applies asymmetrically. It is clear from this provision that failure to accommodate is regarded by the legal framework as a form of distinction (*onderscheid*).[194] That reasonable accommodation discrimination constitutes a *sui generis* form of distinction, meaning that it is distinct from direct and indirect discrimination, has been explicitly recognised by the Dutch ETC in its non-binding case law.[195]

Whereas Article 5 EFD places a duty upon employers (and upon others to whom the Directive is addressed) to make reasonable accommodation for disabled persons,[196] Article 2 of the Dutch DETA uses the term 'effective accommodation' (*doeltreffende aanpassing*). In the government's view, 'effectiveness' expresses better than 'reasonableness' that the accommodation must have the pursued effect.[197] This is a correct view for, as explained before, the notion of reasonableness gets easily mixed up with the 'disproportionate burden defence' which may be invoked by the employer. As argued before, the adjective 'reasonable' in Article 5 of the Directive must be taking to equate with 'effective' or 'practicable'. If this is accepted, the Dutch and the EFD's approach will be materially identical.

Article 2 of the DETA does not define in further detail what is meant by 'effective' accommodation. However, guidance is found both in the Explanatory Memorandum to the Act and in the ETC's non-binding case law. It follows from these sources that an accommodation is effective, if it is both 'appropriate' and 'necessary'. It is in principle for the disabled person to show that the accommodation sought meets both of these requirements. The applicant's point of view can subsequently be rebutted by the employer.[198] 'Appropriateness' implies that the accommodation must be an 'appropriate' or 'suitable' means to eradicate the barriers faced by a disabled person in an individual case. Put differently, the accommodation will be appropriate, if it enables the disabled person to participate and integrate in social life.[199] In the context of employment this implies that it must enable the disabled person to

193 'Het verbod van onderscheid houdt mede in dat degene tot wie dit verbod zich richt gehouden is, naar gelang de behoefte, doeltreffende aanpassingen te verrichten, tenzij deze voor hem een onevenredige belasting vormen' (translation by the author).

194 The conceptual differences between 'distinction' ('*onderscheid*') and 'discrimination' ('*discriminatie*') have been explained in Chapter 2.

195 See Opinion 2004-140 by the Dutch ETC, paragraph 5.11 where it held as follows: ('it [reasonable accommodation discrimination; MG] concerns an independent form of discrimination which is (currently) non-existent in the remainder of equal treatment law' [*'het betreft een op zichzelf staande vorm van onderscheid die in the overige gelijkebehandelingswetgeving (nog) niet voorkomt;* translation by the author].

196 It is recalled that both the Directive and the Dutch DETA apply a-symmetrically as far as the notion of 'reasonable accommodation' is concerned. See section 4.2 above.

197 *Explanatory Memorandum* to the DETA, 2001-2002, 28 169, no. 3, p. 25.

198 See for example Opinion 2004-59, paragraph 5.5.

199 See Opinion 2004-140, paragraph 5.12 in reference to the *Explanatory Memorandum* to the DETA, 2001-2002, 28 169, no. 3, p. 25.

perform the essential duties attached to a post. It is however not required, that the accommodation enables a disabled person to carry out all job-related duties. In Opinion 2006-35 the facts were as follows. The applicant suffered from a hearing impairment. She had applied for a practical training position for the job of nurse. However, by reason of her disability she was prevented from performing night duties. The respondent considered that working the night duties constituted an essential part of the practical training and therefore refused to take on the applicant. In the applicant's view night duties did not form part of the essentials of the job. It is plain from the ETC's line of reasoning that it is for the employer to prove that a function *x* constitutes an essential part of the job concerned. *In casu*, the respondent had failed to prove this and as a result the Commission concluded a case of direct disability distinction. The Commission moreover held that even *if* the respondent had proven that night duties belonged to the essentials of the practical training concerned, it had nonetheless failed to investigate the possibility of making an effective accommodation. Hence, in any case, the respondent would have breached Article 2 of the DETA.

The requirement of 'necessity' means that the same objective, i.e. enabling the disabled person to perform the job, cannot be reached with other (possibly less expensive) means.[200] The Commission has taken the view that medical expert advice may play an important role in assessing the effectiveness of an accommodation in the concrete case at hand.[201] It is in this regard that the medical model of disability creeps into the equation. However, at the same time, the Commission has held that the views of the disabled person herself play an important role in the analysis of the 'effectiveness requirement'.[202]

Only after it has been concluded that an accommodation is both 'appropriate' and 'necessary', the disproportionate burden defence comes into play. The latter can trump the elements of appropriateness and necessity, in the sense that, even if these two requirements are met, realisation of the accommodation will not be necessary if doing so would place a disproportionate burden upon the employer. The balancing exercise between the interests of the disabled person, on the one hand and those of the employer, on the other, must be assessed in light of so-called open norms of civil and general employment law. These include in particular the employer's duty to act as a good employer (*goed werkgeversschap*) and the principle of equity (*'redelijkheid en billijkheid'*).[203] Although this is not expressly regulated in Article 2 DETA, it follows from the Parliamentary History that if the employer has a possibility to receive state funding, the realisation of the accommodation will in principle not be regarded as placing a disproportionate burden on the employer.[204] The Commission's case law makes it clear that the employer is under a legal duty to investigate the possibilities of state compensation, for example under social assistance schemes.[205] The fact that

200 *Explanatory Memorandum* to the DETA, 2001-2002, 28 169, no. 3, p. 25. See for example also Opinion 2004-140, paragraphs 5.12 and 5.13. Also Opinion 2005-18, paragraph 5.4.

201 See Opinion 2004-140, paragraph 5.13 in reference to the Parliamentary History to the DETA.

202 Opinion 2004-140, paragraph 5.11.

203 *Explanatory Memorandum* to the DETA, 2001-2002, 28 169, no. 3, p. 25-30.

204 *Explanatory Memorandum* to the DETA, 2001-2002, 28 169, no. 3, p. 28.

205 Opinion 2004-140, paragraph 5.22.

the law provides for a disproportionate burden defence implies that *the employer* is regarded by the law as being the prime cost bearer of making the accommodation. This has been made explicit by the ETC in Opinion 2004-140. *In casu*, an anti-discrimination bureau in the Netherlands initiated legal proceedings against an association which administered examinations for the hotel and restaurant branch (the respondent). The respondent offered special examinations to candidates with a reading disability. However, the price of such a special examination was ninety Euros extra compared to the price for a regular examination. The Commission held that notwithstanding that effective accommodation had been made, the respondent had nonetheless acted in breach of Article 2 of the DETA by shifting the expense of the accommodation on to disabled persons. The facts of the case could not convince the Commission that the respondent would be disproportionately affected, if the costs were either paid by the educational establishment itself or, alternatively, were divided among all candidates (i.e. both disabled and non-disabled candidates) wishing to sit for the exam.

What other factors beyond the possibility of public funding can be taken into account in deciding on the disproportionate burden defence? Nothing is said with respect to this in the DETA itself. However, the Parliamentary comments and the Commission's case law indicate the following: (1) the size of the organisation and the number of people working for it; (2) the costs involved in the realisation of the accommodation; (3) the technical feasibility of realising the accommodation and (4) the financial strength of the organisation concerned.[206] According to the government, in the employment context account may also be taken of (5) whether the (future) employee is (or will be) hired on the basis of a fixed-term or a permanent contract of employment.[207] This, however, may result in an unlawful distinction on grounds of employment duration. It could also trigger instances of unlawful indirect distinction on grounds of sex, if it can be proven that women are more likely than men to be employed on the basis of a fixed-term contract. The duty to make effective accommodation can also be trumped by the health and safety rationale.[208] Article 3(1) indent *a* of the DETA, in parallel with Article 7(2) of the Framework Directive, provides that the prohibition of distinction shall not apply if the distinction serves the interests of health and safety.[209] This sees to the health and safety of both the disabled person and of others. However, as with any exception, the health and safety exception should

206 *Explanatory Memorandum* to the DETA, 2001-2002, 28 169, no. 3, p. 29.

207 *Explanatory Memorandum* to the DETA, 2001-2002, 28 169, no. 3, p. 29.

208 See Article 3(1) DETA which explicitly contains a health and safety exception. The government has moreover indicated that an accommodation, which interferes with the health and safety rationale, can anyhow not be considered as being an 'effective accommodation', given that the aims of participation and of integration cannot be reached. See *Explanatory Memorandum* to the DETA, 2001-2002, 28 169, no. 3, p. 29: *('[het kan niet zo zijn; MG] dat een aanpassing wordt gevergd wanneer, ondanks of dankzij de aanspassing, de veiligheid en de gezondheid van de gehandicapte of chronisch zieke zelf of van personen in zijn directe omgeving in gevaar zouden komen. Een dergelijke aanpassing kan overigens al moeilijk gekwalificeerd worden als 'doeltreffend', omdat het doel van participatie en integratie er niet echt mee kan worden bereikt.'*

209 It is noted that under the Dutch 1998 Act on Working Conditions (AWC) and under Dutch general private employment law the employer is under a duty to eliminate and/or reduce much as possible any risk to the health and well-being of employees.

be interpreted restrictively. It follows from the Parliamentary History that a high threshold is set for any successful reliance on this exception. If an employer claims that a reasonable accommodation ought not to be realised by reason of health and safety requirements, he will be required to duly motivate this contention. If it is possible to take away health and safety risks by means of making an effective accommodation, the exception can logically not be relied upon.

The employer's duty to make effective accommodation under Article 2 DETA is neither a general, nor an anticipatory duty. Indeed, one of the prime features of reasonable accommodation is that it seeks to offer a tailor-made solution to the particular barriers which the disabled person faces in the specific case at hand.[210] Hence, reasonable accommodation, unlike the concept of indirect distinction, it not a powerful tool to tackle underlying power structures which cause and keep the disadvantage alive.[211] That the duty to accommodate is not meant to be either general or anticipatory also follows from the wording of Article 2 DETA. The rubric 'according to need' (*'al naar gelang de behoefte'*) of Article 2 of the Act implies that it must be clear for the employer *that* accommodation is needed and *what form* of accommodation.[212] The government has indicated that it is the responsibility of the disabled person to discuss the need for accommodation. The government expects that in practice both the need and the kind of accommodation required will be decided on in consultation between the employer and the future user.

The last matter concerns the principle of meritocracy. In line with the Directive, the ETC's case law and the Parliamentary History to the DETA indicate that the Article 2 duty can never transcend the principle of merit.[213] The principle that the best person for the job must be hired forms the starting point of all Dutch equal treatment legislation. The onus of proving merit lies upon the disabled person and can be challenged by the employer in legal proceedings. If the employer can prove that even with a reasonable accommodation, the disabled person will not be able to perform the essentials of the job, the employer will not act in contravention of his duties under Article 2 of the DETA.[214]

In the above, an analysis has been made of the concept of reasonable accommodation in Dutch law, in light of EC law. The analysis makes it clear that the approach in Dutch law is in conformity with the requirements placed upon the government by the EFD. Immediately henceforth a similar analysis will be made of reasonable accommodation in English law. Eventually, both approaches will be compared and commented upon towards the end of section 4.

210 See also Opinion 2005-18, paragraph 5.11 with further reference to the Parliamentary History to the DETA.

211 Waddington and Hendriks 2002, p. 415.

212 See for example paragraph 5.14. of Opinion 2004-21 and paragraph 5.2. of Opinion 2005-140. Also *Explanatory Memorandum* to the DETA, 2001-2002, 28 169, no. 3, p. 26.

213 See for example Opinion 2005-18, paragraph 3.6 in reference to Opinions 2005-78; 2004-139 and 2005-44.

214 See for example Opinion 2005-18, paragraph 5.4. Also Opinion 2004-59, paragraph 5.5.

4.5.3. Reasonable Accommodation in English Law: Top-Down Comparison

Rather than employing the notion of an 'effective accommodation', as Dutch law does, English law imposes a duty upon employers to make 'reasonable adjustments'. It has been argued before that 'effectiveness' in Dutch law is synonymous with the EFD's notion of 'reasonableness'. However, 'reasonableness' in English disability discrimination law does not equate to 'effectiveness' or 'reasonableness' in Dutch and EC law, respectively. This point will be elaborated later on in the analysis. Similar to the approach in the Dutch DETA, Section 3A of the DDA 1995 leaves no doubt that the unlawful failure to adjust amounts to discrimination: '[f]or the purposes of this Act, a person also discriminates against a disabled person if he fails to comply with a duty to make reasonable adjustments imposed on him in relation to the disabled person'.[215]

How has the duty to adjust been defined by the law? New Section 4A 1 DDA 1995, which was inserted into the Act by the 2004 Disability Discrimination Regulations[216] provides as follows:

> 'where-
> (a) a provision, criterion or practice applied by or on behalf of the employer, or
> (b) any physical feature of premises occupied by the employer,
> places the disabled person concerned at a substantial disadvantage in comparison with persons who are not disabled, it is the duty of the employer to take such steps as it is reasonable, in all the circumstances of the case, for him to have to take in order to prevent the provision, criterion or practice, or feature, having that effect.'

What may amount to a 'reasonable adjustment' is set out in Section 18(B) (2) DDA. This Article contains a list with illustrations of reasonable adjustments: making adjustments to premises; altering hours of work or training; allowing the person to be absent from work, for rehabilitation, assessment or treatment; transferring the disabled person to an existing vacancy, etc. The transfer of a disabled person to an existing vacancy was at stake in the House of Lords' judgment in *Archibald v. Five Council*,[217] a case to be discussed hereafter. Detailed guidance as to what may be a reasonable adjustment is

215 The DDA, different from the SDA and RRA, contains a three-fold notion of discrimination, namely (1) a notion of direct discrimination which cannot be justified, (2) a notion of so-called 'less favourable treatment discrimination for a reason which relates to the disabled person's disability and (3) failure to make reasonable adjustments. Harassment is deemed to be a form of discrimination, although it is captured in a separate Article 3B of the Act.

216 It is recalled that with the adoption of these Regulations the government has sought to transpose the EFD in relation to the discrimination ground 'disability'. See section 4.1 above and Chapter 2. The adoption of the Regulations has *inter alia* had an impact on the legal duty to make reasonable adjustments. It is to be noted that the enactment of the 2005 Disability Discrimination Act has not had an impact upon the provisions on reasonable adjustment in the DDA 1995.

217 *Archibald v. Five Council* [2004] ICR 954 (HL).

also given in the Revised Code of Practice which has to be consulted by tribunals and courts.[218]

New Section 4A DDA 1995 has replaced former Section 6 of the Act which captured the duty to adjust prior to the transposition of the Framework Directive. In what respects the provisions concerning the duty to adjust have been changed as a result of the transposition of the EFD into domestic law will become clear throughout the passages to follow. In *Morse v. Wiltshire County Council*,[219] a case decided on the basis of old Section 6 DDA, the EAT explained that Tribunals must examine three sequential steps when judging on claims regarding the duty to adjust. These are the following:

1. it must be analysed whether the duty to adjust has been triggered at all in the case at hand. In other words: does the employer in the particular case at hand owe the applicant a reasonable adjustment? In order to decide this, the Tribunal must analyse whether there is an '*arrangement*' made by or on behalf of the employer, or a physical feature of premises which places the disabled person concerned at a substantial disadvantage compared with persons who are not disabled;
2. if it has been established that the duty is triggered it must subsequently be examined whether, in light of the circumstances in the case at hand, the employer has taken reasonable steps so as to prevent the disabled person concerned from being placed at a substantial disadvantage compared with non-disabled persons;
3. examination of the justification defence.

The aforementioned three steps reflect the legal limbs of the Section 6 duty as it stood pre-implementation of the Directive. Post-implementation the law has changed in some but not all respects.[220] Essentially, with regard to the duty to adjust, the DDA 1995 has been amended in two chief ways. These will be discussed immediately below.

The first amendment

The first amendment regards the first step outlined by the EAT in *Morse* (discussed above). The law as it stands post-implementation of the EFD still requires Tribunals to examine, as a first step, whether the duty to adjust is triggered at all in the particular case at hand. This will be the case, if the disabled person concerned has suffered a 'substantial disadvantage' relative to persons who are not disabled and which has been caused by a 'provision, criterion or practice' applied by the employer (or by a physical feature of the premises). This is a much wider formulation than that contained in Section 6 DDA pre-implementation of the Directive. Section 6 DDA did not

218 The importance of the Code was once again stressed by the Law Lords in *Archibald* (cited in footnote 217 above); as stated earlier I will discuss this case in further detail in the main text to follow.

219 *Morse v. Wiltshire County Council* [1998] IRLR 352 (EAT).

220 For a fully-fledged account I refer to McColgan 2005, Chapter 8, notably p. 589-601.

provide that the disadvantage was caused by a 'provision, criterion or practice' but by an 'arrangement' made by the employer (or by a physical feature of the premises). Furthermore, restrictions were contained in Section 6(2) of the Act which stipulated that an 'arrangement' only referred to arrangements for determining to whom employment should be offered (in short: the recruitment and selection procedure) and to any term, condition or arrangement on which employment, promotion, a transfer, training or any other benefit was offered or afforded (in short: the employee's working conditions). The notion of 'arrangement' has been subject to judicial interpretation. A restrictive (albeit not unreasonable) interpretation was employed by the EAT in *Kenny v. Hamshire Constabulary*.[221] *In casu*, the EAT held that 'arrangement' only covered job-related arrangements to the exclusion therefore of matters which are personal to the disabled person. The applicant in *Kenny* had cerebral palsy. The EAT held that the future employer had not discriminated against the applicant by not providing him with personal assistance for going to the toilet. Although the EAT did acknowledge that this approach might be disadvantageous to disabled persons it found that 'a line must be drawn somewhere'. The EAT substantiated its view by indicating that the Code of Practice remained silent on the question as to whether or not personal assistance falls within the ambit of the employer's duty to adjust. Hence, it held that Parliament could not have intended that matters which are personal to the person concerned are also covered.

In contrast, the House of Lords in *Archibald v. Five Council* attached a liberal meaning to the notion of 'arrangement'.[222] The facts were as follows. Ms Archibald was a road sweeper working for Five Council. She used to be physically fit to walk and sweep but as a result of minor surgery she had become severely disabled. She could no longer perform the job of road sweeper and her disability compelled her to do a sedentary job. The employer retrained her to do office work and it turned out that Ms Archibald was more than capable to perform such work. The sedentary jobs that were available within the organisation were however of a slightly higher grade. According to the applicable redeployment rules all persons who wished to obtain a sedentary job had to undergo a competitive interview. The applicant had applied for over 100 jobs but none of these had been given to her. She was eventually dismissed. In essence she claimed that the employer's duty to adjust entailed that she should have been exempted from the rule that competitive interviews should be held, if she could demonstrate her aptitude for the job concerned. Simply put, she claimed that once it was clear that she was capable of doing the job, the duty to adjust required that the job should have been given to her. Her claim had been rejected by the ET. The tribunal had pointed at [old] Section 6(7) DDA (now, Section 18D(1) DDA) according to which employers are not required to treat disabled persons more favourably than non-disabled persons.[223] In light of this, it had taken the view that the statutory duty to adjust had not been triggered. Albeit for different reasons, the

221 *Kenny v. Hamshire Constabulary* [1999] IRLR 76 (EAT).

222 *Archibald v. Five Council* [2004] ICR 954 (HL). This case was decided on the basis of the DDA 1995 as it stood pre-implementation of the EFD.

223 Post implementation this is contained in Section 18D(1) DDA.

EAT and the Court of Session had equally held that the employer did not owe Ms Archibald a duty to adjust. Leave was granted to the House of Lords which *inter alia* considered the meaning of 'arrangement'.

In deciding on what 'arrangement' was at stake in the case at hand, Lord Rodger of Earlsferry held as follows:

> 'Ms Archibald never swept a road after she became unfit. What actually happens if an employee becomes so disabled that she cannot perform the essential functions of her job is that, under her contract of employment, she is liable to be dismissed. That is the substantial disadvantage she suffers. The contractual term, whether express or implied, which provides for her dismissal in these circumstances constitutes the relevant 'arrangement' for the purposes of Section 6(1). That arrangement places the disabled person at a substantial disadvantage by comparison with persons who are not disabled because she is liable to be dismissed on the ground of disability whereas they are not.'[224]

This view was affirmed by Baroness Hale of Richmond where she held that 'also included [in the notion of] arrangement is the liability of anyone who becomes incapable of fulfilling the job description to be dismissed'.[225]

As correctly argued by Rubenstein, the teleological approach adopted by the House of Lords in Archibald had the effect of '[shifting] the focus of reasonable adjustment in an employment context from physical features to an employer's policies and practices'.[226] A similar approach was subsequently also adopted by the CA in *Smith v. Churchills Stairlifts plc*.[227] In present times much of the controversy has been taken away, given that the notion of 'arrangement' has been substituted by the 'provision, criterion or practice'. This includes, for example, determining to whom employment should be offered, conditions on which a promotion or a benefit is offered, interview procedures, etc.[228]

Merely establishing that a disabled person has suffered a substantial disadvantage caused by a 'provision, criterion or practice' (or according to the old approach an 'arrangement') or by a physical feature is by itself not enough to trigger the duty to adjust. In addition the applicant must establish that non-disabled persons have *not* suffered this disadvantage (i.e. the comparative exercise). The need for making a comparative exercise remains intact also post-implementation of the Directive. What the correct comparative exercise is in cases concerning the duty to make adjustments

224 See paragraph 42 of the judgment. See also the speech by Lord Hope of Craighead which has a similar effect (paragraph 11 of the judgment).

225 See paragraph 62 of the judgment.

226 Rubenstein 2006, p. 1.

227 *Smith v. Churchills Stairlifts plc*, [2006] IRLR 41 (a case decided on the basis of the old Section 6 duty). In *Smith* the CA accepted the submission made by counsel for the applicant that the fact that the offer of a place on a training course was subject to an implied condition that the applicant was able to carry a 25 kilogramme full-sized sample radiator cabinet and that he would not be offered the place on the training course if he was unable to carry such a cabinet amounted to an 'arrangement' for the purposes of Section 6(1) DDA. See paragraphs 30 (submission made by counsel) and 34 (acceptance by the CA).

228 Further guidance on the meaning of 'provision, criterion or practice' is also provided by the Revised Code of Practice. See Chapter 5 of the Code, section 5.8.

depends on the circumstances of the particular case at hand. As Lord Rodger of Earlsferry observed in *Archibald* 'Section 6(1) envisages a comparison, but its exact nature is not spelt out'.[229] In any case, as was recognised by the Law Lords in *Archibald*, '[the DDA] does not require the "like for like" comparison which is involved in the Sex Discrimination and Race Relations Acts'.[230] This is logical in light of the diverging conceptual frameworks underpinning the DDA, on the one hand, and the SDA and RRA, on the other. This point has already been explained in section 4.2.2 above. In *Archibald*, Lord Rodger held that Ms Archibald fell to be compared with 'other employees of the employer who are not disabled, can therefore carry out the essential functions of their jobs and are, accordingly, not liable to be dismissed on the ground of disability'.[231] Baroness Hale put is as follows: '(...) the duty is triggered where an employee becomes so disabled that she can no longer meet the requirements of her job description.'[232] This approach was subsequently also adopted by the CA in *Smith v. Churchills Stairlifts plc*.[233] The first Instance Tribunal in *Archibald* had held that the duty to adjust was not triggered in the case at hand, for Section 6(7) DDA (new Section 18D(1) DDA) prevents employers from treating disabled persons more favourably, compared with other persons. However, in the view of the Law Lords, the Tribunal by deciding as it did had erred in law given that Section 6(7) DDA was *itself* subject to the legal duty placed upon the employer to make reasonable adjustments. Hence, the Tribunal had misconstrued Section 6(7) duty which had prevented it from considering whether the employer had taken reasonable steps to prevent Ms Archibald from being placed at a substantial disadvantage. The House of Lords held that the applicable redeployment rules, which distinguished between the same or lower grade jobs for which no competitive interviews had to be undergone, on the one hand, and higher grade jobs which did require such interviews, on the other, could generally be said to be reasonable. However, in cases such as the one at hand, 'it might be reasonable to expect a small modification either in general or in the particular case to meet the needs of a well-qualified and well-motivated employee who has become disabled'.[234] In taking this view, account was had of the fact that the positions concerned were general positions which could be carried out by a vast range of people. Moreover, the House of Lords has taken the view that employers might have to take into account that, in the case of a transfer of a disabled manual worker to a sedentary office job, she is likely to face discrimination by reason of her manual background.[235] Whether the employer must do so depends, however,

229 Paragraph 35 of the judgment.

230 Per Baroness Hale of Richmond, paragraph 64 of the judgment. See also Lord Rodger of Earlsferry, at paragraph 38 of the judgment: '(...) various factors suggest that the comparison in Section 6(1) DDA need not be with fit people who are in exactly the same situation as the disabled person'.

231 Paragraph 42 of the judgment.

232 Paragraph 64 of the judgment.

233 *Smith v. Churchills Stairlifts plc*, [2006] IRLR 41 (decided on the basis of the (old) Section 6 DDA duty). See notably paragraph 40 of *Smith*.

234 Paragraph 70 (per Baroness Hale of Richmond).

235 'There is no law against discriminating against people with a background in manual work, but it might be reasonable for an employer to have to take that difficulty into account when →

on the concrete facts of a particular case. In light of the foregoing the case was remitted to the Employment Tribunal which has to reconsider the case in light of the Law Lords' guidance.

Before proceeding with a discussion of the second major change to the legal duty to adjust post implementation of EC law the following is worth observing. As stated the notion of 'arrangements' has been replaced by that of a 'provision, criterion or practice'. The latter rubric immediately reminds discrimination lawyers of the concept of indirect discrimination. This concept has extensively been dealt with in Chapter 3. It is recalled that the DDA, both pre- and post-implementation of the EFD, lacks a concept of indirect discrimination. The government has sought to fill the lacuna via an adaptation to the provision on the duty to adjust. In Chapter 3 it has already been explained that the UK whilst negotiating the Directive exercised bottom-up pressure, so as to guarantee that the concept of indirect discrimination, contained in the Framework Directive, could be transposed into domestic law via a duty to adjust. However, such an approach fails to implement the Directive correctly. It is stressed again that the concept of indirect discrimination has the potential of tackling underlying power structures which, if successful, has a beneficial impact upon all persons who belong to the group of the applicant. Hence, in indirect discrimination procedures there are a lot of 'free riders' whose legal situation will be improved, if an individual complainant succeeds in an indirect discrimination complaint. This is not the case with the duty to adjust which, as stated before, is individual in kind. Reasonable adjustment seeks to offer a tailor-made solution to an individual applicant in the case at hand. Moreover, McColgan has rightly argued that the duty to adjust will only be triggered, if the disabled person concerned is placed at a 'substantial' disadvantage, whereas the notion of indirect discrimination, as used by the EFD, speaks of a 'particular disadvantage'.[236] The latter appears to set a lower threshold to the benefit of the alleged victim.

The second amendment

The second major change that has occurred in relation to the duty to adjust post-implementation of EC law concerns the abolition of the justification defence. In its post-implementation format the DDA no longer grants an employer an escape route in the form of a separate justification defence.[237] This does, however, not mean that the employer's duty to adjust is currently unconditioned. Although the third step outlined by the EAT in *Morse* needs no longer be considered in the judicial analysis, the second step (i.e. 'reasonableness') has become more important than ever. Currently there are two main restrictions to the employer's duty to adjust. First, an employer will *not* be under a duty to adjust, if he does not know and can neither reasonably

considering the transfer of a disabled worker who could no longer does that type of work. I only say 'might' because it depends on all the circumstances of the case.' [paragraph 70, per Baroness Hale of Richmond].

236 See for further criticism in regard to the UK government's omission to insert a concept of indirect disability discrimination into the DDA Wells 2003.

237 The justification defence for a failure to adjust used to be contained in Sections 5(2) 'b' DDA in conjunction with Section 5(4) DDA.

be expected to know that the person concerned is disabled and that she is placed at a substantial disadvantage compared with others.[238] Secondly, an employer is not required by law to make *any* possible form of adjustment. He is only required to make 'reasonable' adjustments. We have already seen that in Dutch law the notion of 'effectiveness' relates to the practicability of the accommodation and equates to the concept of 'reasonableness' employed by Article 5 EFD. Therefore, in EC and in Dutch law the notions of, respectively, 'reasonableness' and 'effectiveness' have to be distinguished from the employer's cost defence. However, since the DDA does not make reference to a 'disproportionate burden defence' this defence is *ingrained* within the notion of 'reasonableness'. It follows that 'reasonableness' in the DDA is not synonymous with 'reasonableness' in the EFD and in Dutch law.[239] New Section 18B(1) DDA, which has partially amended old Section 6(4) DDA, sheds light on how 'reasonableness' has to be assessed. It states that the following factors are to be taken into account: (1) the extent to which taking the step would prevent the effect in relation to which the duty is imposed; (2) the extent to which it is practicable for the employer to take the step; (3) the financial and other costs which would be incurred by the employer in taking the step and the extent to which taking it would disrupt any of his activities; (4) the employer's financial and other resources; (5) the availability to the employer of financial or other assistance; (6) the nature of the employer's activities and the size of his undertaking. It moreover follows from the case law that has arisen in relation to the old Section 6 DDA duty that the test of 'reasonableness' is an objective test.[240] This means that it is for the Employment Tribunal to decide on 'reasonableness' whereby it disregards the subjective views of the alleged discriminator. Another factor which might be taken into account in deciding on 'reasonableness' is the risk involved by making the adjustment to the health and safety of the disabled person concerned or of others.[241] Tribunals and courts must, however, guard that this (alleged) risk is duly substantiated by the employer in light of the particular circumstances of the case at hand.

4.5.4. Reasonable Accommodation: Cross-Country Comparison

Having compared Dutch and English reasonable accommodation law in light of EC law I will hereafter compare domestic approaches and practices. First, it can be concluded that both Dutch and English law conceive, respectively, the failure to make an effective accommodation and a reasonable adjustment as a *sui generis* form of

238 See Section 4A (3) under 'b' DDA 1995. This has moreover been affirmed in the case law, see *Ridout v. TC Group*, 1998, IRLR 628. See for further comment also EOR 98, July/August 2001, p. 17-18.

239 Wells 2003, p. 268.

240 See most recently Smith *v.* Churchills Stairlifts plc, [2006] IRLR 41 in which the EAT held that 'there is no doubt that the test required by S6(1) is an objective test. The employer must take 'such steps as it is reasonable, in all the circumstances of the case.' This had been held already in earlier cases. See e.g. *Morse v. Wiltshire County Council* [1998] IRLR 352 and *Collins v. Royal National Theatre Board Ltd* [2004] EWCA 144. See also Wells 2003, p. 267.

241 Cohen 2005, p. 24 in reference to the Management of Health and Safety and Work Regulations 1999. No specific health and safety exceptions are, however, contained in the DDA itself.

disability discrimination. However, the DDA's duty to adjust bears a bigger legal mandate in practice in the sense that it is supposed to also cover these acts of disability discrimination that would otherwise be captured by the prohibition of indirect discrimination. After all, the DDA is short of a concept of indirect discrimination which, it has been argued, constitutes a breach of the Directive, given that reasonable accommodation is an individualised concept, whereas indirect discrimination is a group-oriented notion. Neither Dutch nor English law regard, respectively, the duty to make an 'effective accommodation' and a 'reasonable adjustment' as an anticipatory or general obligation that is placed upon the employer. In Dutch law it must be known to the employer that and what form of accommodation is required, whereas in English law the employer should know that the person concerned is disabled and that she is placed at a substantial disadvantage. In both legal systems the principle of meritocracy remains unchallenged, although merit has to be assessed *after* having considered the possibility of making an accommodation. The analysis has moreover shown that in English law a disabled applicant must prove more in order to trigger the duty to adjust than is the case in Dutch law. The DDA requires that in deciding on the question whether in a particular case at hand the employer owes the disabled person a reasonable adjustment it must be demonstrated that: (1) by reason of the application of a 'provision, criterion or practice', or, by reason of a physical feature of premises the disabled applicant is placed at a (2) 'substantial' disadvantage, (3) compared with persons who are not disabled. None of these conditions are imposed by Dutch law which therefore reflects a more flexible approach. It follows from the foregoing that the English DDA preserves the comparative exercise meaning that the duty to adjust remains premised upon the comparative justice model. The Dutch approach is in contrast founded on a freestanding model, given that it does not emphasise the need for a legal comparison. The analysis has also shed light on the differences in terminology adopted in the DETA compared with the DDA. It has been shown that the notion of 'effectiveness' in Dutch law equates to 'reasonableness' in Article 5 of the Framework Directive. 'Effectiveness' sees to the practicability of an accommodation and enshrines the notions of 'appropriateness' and 'necessity'. It is, however, distinct from the employer's disproportionate cost defence. In contrast, 'reasonableness' in English law is a broader concept. It captures both the practicability/effectiveness of an accommodation and the disproportionate burden defence. Notwithstanding that Dutch law separates the former from the latter the legal end result remains the same. The legal yardsticks for assessing the legitimacy of the employer's cost defence are *grosso modo* the same in Dutch and English law. In both legal systems regard is (*inter alia*) given to the following: (a) the size of the undertaking; (b) the financial or other costs involved; (c) the possibility of receiving external funding; (d) the financial strength of the undertaking; (e) the technical/practical feasibility of realising the accommodation/adjustment; (f) health and safety concerns. Judicial bodies must supervise that the employer involved in legal proceedings duly substantiates all of these factors. In carrying out the balancing-exercise of the interests of all the stakeholders in a particular case at hand the courts (and semi-judicial bodies) must bear in mind the human rights nature of the legal duty to make reasonable accommodation.

5. Conclusions

In this chapter disability discrimination law has been analysed through the prism of comparative law. This involved a 'cross-ground', 'top-down', 'cross-country' and, to a lesser degree, a 'bottom-up' analysis. The cross-ground analysis involved looking at the intrinsic logic that underpins the discrimination ground 'disability'. It has been argued that 'disability' is not only a social construct (like, e.g. 'race' and 'sex') but also a highly fluid and shifting notion. This renders it difficult, if not arbitrary, to delineate the group of disabled persons. Moreover, the analysis showed that 'disability' tends to cover a person's merit and capacities, although admittedly a person's disability *can* have a (decisive) impact on a person's employability and job performance. With respect to 'disability' one of the key tasks of the legal framework should be to accommodate difference, as well as to address stereotyping and stigma. Only a difference-approach can counteract the dominant norms of 'normality' and 'able-bodiedness' which govern daily decision and policy-making processes. The analysis examined a number of theoretical models of disability which have been linked to both the intrinsic nature of disability as a ground of discrimination and to the notions of formal and substantive equality. It has been illustrated that the medical model of disability locates disability-based disadvantage in intra-personal factors, whereas the social model argues that disability-based disadvantage stems from the inter-relationship between the individual impairment, on the one hand, and societal reactions to the impairment, on the other. The argument has been made that the medical model amalgamates with formal equality, whereas the social model dovetails into substantive equality. Given that 'disability' (often) reflects 'difference' it has been argued that the social model should be taken as a starting point in both the design, the interpretation and the application of the legal anti-discrimination framework. The top-down and cross-country comparisons have been illustrated with reference to (1) the notions of 'symmetry' and 'asymmetry', (2) the definition of disability and (3) the concept of reasonable accommodation. In the context of the EFD the argument has been made that the Directive applies asymmetrically in respect of 'disability'. This should, however, not preclude the ECJ from defining disability in a liberal and extensive fashion. The exercise of defining disability must be entrenched with the logic underlining the social model of disability. The Directive reflects substantive, rather than comparative justice in respect of the duty to make reasonable accommodation. The analysis of EC law has been functional to the top-down comparison. Particularly in the Netherlands has EC law exercised a great deal of top-down influence on domestic disability equal treatment law. Paradoxically, EC law has had both an accelerating and a regressive effect on the development of Dutch law. As the discussion has shown the implementation of the EFD fast-tracked the legislative process on equal treatment law for disabled persons. However, simultaneously, EC law has had the effect that the material scope that was initially envisaged by the legislative process *prior* to the adoption of the Directive was narrowed down, so as to merely include the area of employment. It has been explained that the Dutch DETA applies symmetrically which bears the advantage that the group of disabled persons need not be defined. It, however, also brings with it that positive action measures that are adopted in favour of disabled persons can be challenged in legal proceedings by persons who are not disabled. The English approach differs fundamentally from the Dutch approach, given that the DDA is premised upon asymmetry. Consequently, disability needs to be legally defined. This brings with it the risk that the medical model of disability dominates the judicial interpretation of the anti-discrimination framework, a risk that has clearly manifested itself in the context of English law. The English DDA, both pre-and post-implementation of EC law, reflects an unduly medically focused framework which undermines the effective judicial protection from disability-based disadvantage. This must not only be criticised as a matter of principle but also in light of EC law. Since the EFD takes the social model of disability as a starting point for judicial analysis, the medically focused approach which features in English law can no longer be regarded as reflecting the correct approach. In order to be in conformity with EC law the DDA should define disability on the basis of the social model, so as to include (*inter alia*) discrimination on grounds of a perceived disability and on grounds of a person's association with a disabled person.

Finally, the analysis compared the domestic approaches with respect to the legal duty to make reasonable accommodations. It has been seen that the DETA reflects substantive justice approach in the sense that the law places little emphasis upon the comparative exercise. Dutch law reflects a flexible approach and the legal threshold for triggering the duty to make a reasonable (i.e. effective) accommodation is low. Although the legal threshold for triggering the duty to adjust in English law has been lowered post-implementation of the EFD, in the sense that 'arrangement' has been replaced by the wider notion of a 'provision, criterion, practice', English law nonetheless imposes a higher burden of proof compared with Dutch law. Although a 'like for like' comparison is (logically) not called for, the comparative exercise does remain an important factor in the judicial analysis. It has also been illustrated that the 'duty to adjust' in the context of English law seeks to compensate for the lack of a prohibition of indirect discrimination in the DDA. This has been the result of 'bottom-up' influence exercised by the UK government in the process of negotiation of the Directive. Since divergent theoretical premises underlie the concepts of 'reasonable accommodation', on the one hand, and 'indirect discrimination', on the other, the English approach cannot be said to be in conformity with EC law. Lastly, it has been seen that the notions of 'effectiveness' and 'reasonableness' in, respectively, Dutch and English law are not synonymous, although in practice they lead to a corresponding legal analysis. The DETA and the DDA appear to set similar limits on the employer's duty to adjust. Both legal frameworks preserve the principle of merit, both do not perceive the duty to make an 'effective accommodation'/'reasonable adjustment' as a generic duty and both apply the same yardsticks in the legal assessment of the employer's cost defence. Although in English law the hitherto existing justification defence for a failure to adjust has been repealed post-implementation of EC law this defence seems currently ingrained within the judicial assessment of 'reasonableness'.

Chapter 9

AGE

1. Introduction

According to the full Luxembourg Court (sitting as a Grand Chamber) in *Mangold v. Helm*[1] – the first substantive ruling that has been made by the Court in the context of the EFD[2] – 'the principle of non-discrimination on grounds of age must be regarded as a general principle of Community law'.[3] The objective of the present chapter is to analyse how the legislative frameworks of the EC and the Netherlands deal with discrimination on grounds of age, which is a relatively new element in anti-discrimination and equality law.[4] Hence, English law will not be considered in this chapter for the practical reason that the *Age Regulations*, which seek to implement the Framework Directive insofar as the discrimination ground 'age' is concerned, do not take effect until 1 October 2006.[5] The prohibition of age discrimination in employment

1 *Mangold v. Helm* (Case C-144/04) of 22 November 2005 available at <www.europa.eu.int>. See also the Opinion of Advocate General Tizzano delivered on 30 June 2005 in *Mangold v. Helm* (Case C-144/04). This Opinion is also available at <www.europa.eu.int>.

2 A number of infringement proceedings have been brought against various Member States. See most recently *Commission of the European Communities v. Luxembourg* (Case C-70/05) judgment of 20 October 2005, *OJ* 10-12-2005/C315-07, in which the Court held that Luxembourg had failed to comply with its legal obligations to implement the EFD into national law.

3 Paragraph 75 of the judgment.

4 This is perhaps not surprising given that age discrimination law forms a concrete reaction to changing demographic trends and an ageing population. See in this respect Fredman and Spencer 2003, p. 1, who have observed the following in this context: 'Life expectancy both at birth and at retirement age continue to lengthen and fertility rates remain very low. Europeans live longer but have far fewer children and grandchildren to replace them than previous generations. The result is that in less than 15 years, the number of Europeans in the 20-29 age band will fall by 20 percent, the number in the 50-64 age group will increase by 25 percent and the number of people aged 80 and over will increase by 50 percent. By 2015 one-third of those of working age will be 50 years and over.' For an in depth analysis of age discrimination and the implications of ageing, I refer to the analysis by Grimley Evans 2003.

5 The final version of the Age Regulations has only recently been published at <http://www.opsi.gov.uk/si/si2006/uksi_20061031_en.pdf>. It should be noted that the UK has availed itself of the possibility of an extended implementation deadline granted by the EFD to the →

will have profound implications for the lawfulness of recruitment and dismissal procedures, employment conditions, pension provision etc. The prohibition of age discrimination by Community and domestic law raises more questions than it answers: in what circumstances may an employer impose experience requirements upon its future employees? May an employer make benefits dependent on a length of service requirement? In what circumstances may job advertisements be directed to young workers only? May age criteria be used in the calculation of pension provision? These are only a handful of questions that are likely to arise in the context of age discrimination law. The analysis in this chapter will proceed along the following stages. In section 2 hereafter, I will first give a brief commentary on the intrinsic values of age as a ground of discrimination. This will be functional to the cross-ground comparison to be drawn in Chapter 10. I will subsequently proceed with a discussion of age discrimination in the context of EC law (section 3), whereby particular attention will be paid to the ECJ's legal reasoning in *Mangold v. Helm* (referred to above). In section 4 Dutch equal treatment law in respect of age will be examined in light of EC law ('top down comparison'). This involves a consideration of the legal framework, which will be placed in context through an analysis of the case law by the courts and by the ETC. The supranational legal dimension will be embedded in the discussion. It is submitted that the Dutch approach could set an example for the modus of legal reasoning to be adopted (or not to be adopted) by the Luxembourg Court. If the ECJ feels inspired by domestic approaches and interpretations, this will amount to bottom-up influence of EC law by national law. This would subsequently result in a cross-fertilisation of legal norms, for the ECJ's line of reasoning would spread its wings across the European Member States which are all bound by the Court's judgment. Given that since 1 May 2004 (the date on which Dutch age discrimination law entered into force), until the time of writing,[6] 140 Opinions have been given by the ETC, I will make no attempt to provide an exhaustive overview of the case law in the Netherlands. The abundant number of cases shows, however, that age discrimination is in vogue and it might form an indication of the amount of labour which is still in store for the ECJ in this area of non-discrimination law. Tentative conclusions will be drawn in section 5.

2. The Intrinsic Values of Age as a Ground of Discrimination

It has been argued that 'age' unlike, for example, 'race' and 'sex' cannot be characterised as an *a priori* suspect ground of discrimination.[7] This view has recently also

Member States in respect of the grounds 'age' and 'disability'. See Article 18 EFD. Drawing a legal comparison between the regulatory approaches in the United Kingdom and in the Netherlands with respect to age discrimination in employment will be one of the themes which call for future research by the author. An early analysis of the law-making possibilities of which the UK legislator could avail itself in regulating age discrimination has been made by Meenan 2000.

6 i.e. until 27-05-06.

7 This view was explicitly expressed by the Dutch government while implementing EC age discrimination law. See *Explanatory Memorandum* to the Act concerning the equal treatment on grounds of age in employment, occupation and vocational training [*Wet gelijke behandeling* →

been aired by the Dutch Supreme Court.[8] In the literature a number of reasons have been given to support this point of view. First, it has been argued that age classifications are required by the principle of legal certainty and by the need to structure society efficiently.[9] Hence, for example, it seems perfectly permissible to subject the right to vote to an age requirement or to confine the possibility of obtaining a driving licence to persons of 18 years or older.[10] Gerritsen has contended that general (objective) age classifications could be upheld by the idea of formal equality, given that sometimes the fact that one has adopted the correct procedure is more important than the outcome of that procedure.[11] If all within a particular age band are afforded consistent (equal) treatment the principle of formal equality is met. Secondly, it has been asserted that age classifications are needed with a view to protecting vulnerable groups, especially young children and the elderly.[12] Thus, for example, in *Mangold* (referred to above) the Luxembourg Court accepted that the aim pursued by the vexed provisions namely, the vocational integration of unemployed older workers who encountered considerable difficulties in finding work, constituted a legitimate aim.[13] Thirdly, 'age' has been contrasted with other grounds of discrimination, notably 'race' and 'sex', in the sense that 'age' is not a permanent benchmark but one that transforms by itself.[14] In this respect 'age' could be paralleled with 'disability'[15] and with 'sexual orientation'[16] which are also fluid (or shifting) concepts.

op grond van leeftijd], *Parliamentary Documents* II, 2001-2002, 28 170, no. 3, p. 12. See also Jacobs 1992, p. 183, who has argued that only in a limited number of circumstances age classifications can amount to discrimination in a pejorative sense. See moreover Loenen 2003, p. 612. See, however, differently, Heerma van Voss 2002, p. 63-64.

8 *Eisers (16 piloten) tegen Martinair Holland N.V. en de Vereniging van Nederlandse Verkeersvliegers* (No. C03/077HR) 8 October 2004 (HR), (paragraph 3.4.2.) and *Eiser tegen Koninklijke Luchtvaartmaatschappij N.V. en de Vereniging van Nederlandse Verkeersvliegers* (NO. C03/133HR), 8 October 2004 (HR), paragraph 3.4.2.

9 Verhoogt 1990. Also Evenhuis 2001, p. 18.

10 Van Maarsseveen (1988, p. 631) has argued that '[a]ge like race and sex is an absolutely involuntary and immutable characteristic'. It is, however, submitted that the character of the aforementioned grounds is not truly comparable. For example, subjecting the right to vote to an age requirement is fundamentally different from confining the right to vote to men or to white persons.

11 Gerritsen 1994, p. 165-166.

12 See the view expressed by the Dutch government in the *Explanatory Memorandum* to the Act concerning the equal treatment on grounds of age in employment, occupation and vocational training [*Wet gelijke behandeling op grond van leeftijd*], *Parliamentary Documents* II, 2001-2002, 28 170, no. 3, p. 12. See in this respect also the analysis by Herring 2003. See moreover Evenhuis, who has drawn an analogy between 'protection' arguments in the context of 'age' with similar arguments in the context of 'sex'. She has (rightfully) pointed out that arguments stressing the need for the protection of women have (at times) resulted in the *exclusion* of women and that these experiences should be born in mind in the legal assessment of age classifications (see Evenhuis 2001, p. 19-21).

13 As will become clear in section 3 hereafter this, however, did not mean that the contested provisions were consequently lawful.

14 See, for example, Groenendijk 1988, p. 623 and Heringa 1990, p. 58.

15 See Chapter 8.

16 See Chapter 7.

Moreover, 'age' and 'disability' have in common that these characteristics may prevent a person from being available for particular work or from doing that work in a conventional manner. As with disability this might be caused by biological or genetic factors (i.e. by intrapersonal factors) or by the interaction of ageing, on the one hand, and environmental reactions (or the absence thereof) and attitudes, on the other. Another analogy between 'age' and 'disability' is that the disadvantageous effects which stem from a person's disability (in conjuncture with environmental attitudes) and from senescence (i.e. the process of decline with age)[17] could possibly be mitigated by medical intervention.[18] On the basis of the so-called 'life-cycle argument' *('levensloop argument')* one may contend that age classifications are easier to digest than, for example, race classifications, given that rights which cannot be enjoyed in present times can be exercised at a later stage in life and, *vice versa*, rights which must be relinquished at an older age have been enjoyed in earlier life times. The life-cycle argument thus uses time and, inherent to that, age classifications, as a mechanism for the distribution of resources, e.g. paid employment, conditions of employment, retirement benefits, etc.[19] Thus, for example, the idea that old employees should leave the labour market in order to create labour opportunities for younger people could be rationalised on the basis of this argument. The analysis thus far prompts the following interim comments. Notwithstanding material differences between 'age' and other forbidden grounds age criteria, not dissimilar from classifications based on, for example, race and sex may result in severe forms of social and economic exclusion.[20] Such classifications may form an impediment to the effective enjoyment of basic social rights, including the right to free choice of employment.[21] Moreover, like acts of discrimination on other forbidden grounds differential treatment on grounds of age is often the result of stereotyping and stigmatisation. Hence, whereas young people are often appreciated for being energetic, productive and flexible, elderly people are conceived of in opposite terms. Stereotyping, however, conceals an individual's personal capacities and worth with the result that a large group of people are denied access to the labour market due to mere reliance upon an individual criterion which reveals nothing about a person's merit for the job.[22] Therefore, one of the objectives of the legal framework should be to expose these capacities by addressing stereotyping, stigmatisation and prejudice through, for example, prohibitions of direct and indirect discrimination and through raising positive awareness of the exclusionary effects of age based discrimination. It is argued that if

17 Hepple 2003, p. 72.

18 Hepple 2003, who in addition to medical intervention has mentioned diet and lifestyle as factors which decelerate senescence. It is, however, acknowledged that it is certainly not always the case that disadvantage which stems from an individual impairment (in conjunction with the societal reactions to that impairment) can always be removed by means of medical treatment. The present author recognises that many disabled persons become and remain disabled forever. This point applies also in respect of ageing.

19 Evenhuis 2001, p. 21-23 and Gerritsen 1994, p. 162. Both authors have, however, disagreed with the philosophy underpinning the life cycle argument.

20 Evenhuis 1999, p. 45.

21 See for example Article 19(3) of the Dutch Constitution.

22 See also Geers 1997, p. 311 and Van Maarsseveen 1988.

individual merit is assessed on a more rational and balanced basis, rather than merely in reference to 'age', this will (1) foster the social inclusion and participation of persons hitherto excluded, (2) preserve human dignity and (3) optimise economic effectiveness, given that the employer can choose from a large pool of potential talent.[23] Another objective of the law should be to guarantee equality in individual cases. Indeed, one of the objections that can be raised to the earlier discussed life-cycle argument is that it merely secures equality at 'macro-level', rather than in concrete individual cases (equality at 'micro-level').[24] However, in order to give real effect to the equality principle classifications at macro-level ought to reduce as much as possible inequality at the level of the individual.[25]

Up until now it has been shown that gauging the 'suspicion' of age as a ground of discrimination calls for caution. On the one hand, age classifications can find their source in legitimate policy objectives or in the principle of legal certainty. In other words, more than is the case with other grounds, 'age' can form a rational factor in the decision-making process.[26] This being the case the legal test for justification may be differently applied compared with other grounds so as to reflect the intrinsic values of this ground of discrimination. However, on the other hand, age classifications can be the mere result of irrational prejudice fostering as such the isolation and marginalisation of (especially) elderly persons.[27] Furthermore, discrimination on grounds of age may intersect with discrimination on other grounds, for example, 'sex' and 'disability'.[28] All in all, although justifiability might be *differently* appraised in the context of age this should certainly not reduce the alertness of (semi) judicial bodies in reviewing age classifications. It is argued that such classifications should only be allowed for provided that they pursue a legitimate aim and provided that due regard is had to the principle of proportionality. As will be seen below this strict approach is also reflected in the ECJ's judicial stance in *Mangold*. A strict test of judicial review has moreover been applied by the Dutch ETC in the large amount of cases with which the Commission has dealt up until present times.

23 See in this respect also Fredman 2003a.

24 Heringa 1990, p. 58. Another objection which can be raised to this argument is that it presupposes that the chance that benefits will be enjoyed at a later stage in life and, *vice versa*, that benefits have already been enjoyed in an earlier life time, remains stationary. However, this chance can, for example, be influenced by changes in the legal framework. In addition, the life-cycle argument presupposes that all will indeed experience all stages in life (i.e. youth, adolescence, adulthood and old age).

25 Heringa 1990, p. 58. Also Huizer 1991.

26 See in this context also the study by van den Bogaart, de Lange and van Poppel 2005, concerning the desirability or not of making distinctions on grounds of age. This study is available in Dutch at <http://www.cgb.nl/_media/downloadables/rapport%20IVA%20leeftijdsonderscheid.pdf>.

27 More than with any other ground is it difficult to establish who is the oppressed/ dominant group in the context of age discrimination. The reason for this is, as observed by Veldman, that with regard to 'age' one may distinguish between many different groups (50+/50-/25+/30-/young people/old people). See Veldman 2003, p. 363.

28 Also Evenhuis 2000, p. 77-90. Also, for example, Opinions 2002-63, 2002-67, 1997-106 and 1997-108 by the Dutch ETC.

3. Age Discrimination in EC Law[29]

3.1. *Translating the Intrinsic Values of 'Age' into Provisions of EC Law*

The insertion of 'age' in Article 13 EC amidst traditional grounds such as race, sex and religion, reflects a common agreement by the Member States that unjustified differences in treatment on grounds of age should be regarded morally unjust. This assertion gathers weight by the fact that age discrimination has been regulated by the Article 13 EC Framework Directive, which was adopted on the basis of a unanimous political stance by the Member States. The ethical cause for age discrimination is also reflected in Recital No. 6 of the Directive which refers to the Community Charter of the *Fundamental* (emphasis; MG) Social Rights of Workers which 'recognises the importance of combating every form of discrimination, including the need to take appropriate action for the social and economic integration of elderly (…) people'. Moreover, the participation rationale, which underpins age discrimination legislation, is reflected in Recital No. 8 EFD. This Recital makes a reference to the European Employment Guidelines for 2000[30] which *inter alia* emphasised the need 'to pay particular attention to supporting older workers, in order to increase their participation in the labour force'.[31] In the context of the Employment Guidelines the participation rationale reflects both economic and ethical concerns. Promoting the employability of old and young people increases labour supply whereas at the same time the social exclusion and marginalisation of (especially) older workers is combated. Moreover, resisting age discrimination in employment fosters the diversity in the workforce which again meets both a moral and an economic concern.[32] In section 2 above it was argued that age discrimination is no less important than discrimination on other grounds, although the elemental nature of age as a ground of discrimination brings with it that age classifications may be *differently* appreciated by the legal framework than classifications on other grounds. This point is also reflected in the language employed by the Framework Directive in respect of 'age'. Hence, Recital No. 25 of the Directive provides that

> '(…) differences in treatment in connection with age may be justified under certain circumstances and therefore require specific provisions which may vary in accordance with

29 A sound and in-depth analysis of age discrimination and European law has also been made by O'Cinneide 2005.

30 See Council Decision of 13 March 2000 on guidelines for Member States' employment policies for the year 2000 (2000/228/EC) *OJ* L 072, 21-03-2000 P. 0015-0020. The guidelines have been adopted within the context of the European Employment Strategy (EES) laid down in Title VIII of the EC Treaty. It should be noted that these guidelines are currently no longer in force.

31 See Recital 8 EFD. These guidelines are currently no longer in force. However, the Employment Guidelines 2005-2008 equally emphasise the need to pay (*inter alia*) special attention to 'the low employment rates of older workers and young people'. See Council Decision of 12 July 2005 on Guidelines for the employment policies of the Member States (2005/600/EC) *OJ* L 205/21, 06-08-2005.

32 See also Recital 25 EFD which *inter alia* stipulates as follows: 'the prohibition of age discrimination (…) [encourages; MG] diversity in the workforce (…)'.

the situation in the Member States. It is therefore essential to distinguish between differences in treatment which are justified, in particular by legitimate employment policy, labour market and vocational training objectives, and discrimination which must be prohibited'.

Moreover, and crucially, this point is reflected in the main text of the Directive, namely in Article 6 which reflects an 'open model'[33] of anti-discrimination law in respect of the ground age. Unlike all other grounds contained in Article 13 EC *both direct and indirect* age discrimination is susceptible for objective justification.[34] Article 6 EFD provides as follows:

6(1) Notwithstanding Article 2(2), [from which it inter alia follows that only indirect but not direct discrimination can be 'objectively justified'; MG] Member States may provide that differences of treatment on grounds of age shall not constitute discrimination, if, within the context of national law, they are objectively and reasonably justified by a legitimate aim, including legitimate employment policy, labour market and vocational training objectives, and if the means of achieving that aim are appropriate and necessary. Such differences of treatment may include, among others:
(a) the setting of special conditions on access to employment and vocational training, employment and occupation, including dismissal and remuneration conditions, for young people, older workers and persons with caring responsibilities in order to promote their vocational integration or ensure their protection;
(b) the fixing of minimum conditions of age, professional experience or seniority in service for access to employment or to certain advantages linked to employment;
(c) the fixing of a maximum age for recruitment which is based on the training requirements of the post in question or the need for a reasonable period of employment before retirement.[35]
6(2) Notwithstanding Article 2(2), Member States may provide that the fixing for occupational social security schemes of ages for admission or entitlement to retirement or invalidity benefits,[36] including the fixing under those schemes of different ages for employees or categories of employees, and the use, in the context of such schemes, of age criteria in

33 See Chapter 2.

34 In addition to the 'tailor-made' exceptions contained in Article 6 EFD that will be discussed in the main text to follow the Directive contains the genuine occupational requirement exception in respect of age (Article 4(1) EFD) and the positive action exception (Article 7(1) EFD). Moreover, the Directive provides that 'Member States may provide that [the] Directive, in so far as it relates to discrimination on the grounds of disability and age, shall not apply to the armed forces'. (Article 3(4) EFD). Strictly perceived, Article 3(4) of the Directive forms no *exception* to the principle of non-discrimination but sets a boundary to the Directive's scope of application. See in this respect moreover Recital No. 19 to the EFD. None of the just-mentioned exceptions (boundaries) will be dealt in further detail in this Chapter. The genuine occupational requirement exception was examined in Chapter 6 in respect of 'religion' and 'belief'. Positive action was analysed in depth in Chapter 5.

35 Some authors have argued that it is ironic to find that the archetypal example of why age discrimination law has been necessary in the first place has been explicitly listed as an exception in Article 6(1)(c) EFD (see e.g. Waddingon and Bell 2001, p. 599). However, as the analysis of the Dutch case law hereafter will illustrate the Article 6(1)(c) EFD exception is necessary in certain circumstances in order to avoid unfair legal outcomes.

36 See moreover Recital No. 14 of the EFD which provides that '[t]his Directive shall be without prejudice to national provisions laying down retirement ages'.

> actuarial calculations, does not constitute discrimination on grounds of age, provided this does not result in discrimination on the grounds of sex.

It follows from Article 6(1) EFD that differences of treatment on grounds of age may be 'objectively justified' provided that such differences pursue a legitimate aim and provided that the means of achieving that aim are appropriate and necessary. In other words, the mere establishment that the aim pursued by a particular age classification is *benevolent* is by itself not sufficient for upholding it, for the requirements of both 'appropriateness' (is the alleged discriminatory act a *suitable* means for reaching the objectives pursued?) and 'necessity' (can the pursued objectives not be achieved by other, less discriminatory means, and, is there a proportional balance between, on the one hand, the objectives pursued and, on the other, the contested age classification?) must also be complied with. In other words: age classifications adopted on the basis of Article 6(1) EFD are subject to a strict judicial scrutiny test which supports the view that the regulation of age discrimination in EC law is (*inter alia*) rationalised by ethical and moral concerns. This point has recently been affirmed by the ECJ in *Mangold* as will be illustrated in section 3.2 hereafter. Article 6 (1) paragraphs *(a)-(c)* EFD mention in a *non-exhaustive* fashion a number of aims which are deemed to be legitimate by the Community legislator. However, the 'appropriateness' and 'necessity' of a particular act of age discrimination seeking to attain (one of) these aims has to be assessed by the domestic courts, and ultimately by the ECJ, on the basis of the facts of the concrete case at hand.

The provision contained in Article 6(2) EFD has been differently formulated compared with its sister provision in Article 6(1) of the Directive. In light of this, I submit that the provision in Article 6(2) EFD does not contain an exception to the principle of non-discrimination on grounds of age but rather sets a limit to the Directive's scope of application. According to the wording of Article 6(2) EFD acts of discrimination on grounds of age, which fall within the ambit of this provision, '[do] not constitute discrimination on grounds of age'. The only qualification to this is that such acts of discrimination may not result in (direct or indirect) sex discrimination. In sum, once it has been determined that a certain act of discrimination falls within the scope of Article 6(2) EFD no *prima facie* case of direct or indirect age discrimination can be established. However, domestic courts and the ECJ will have to examine whether the contested age distinction results in an instance of (direct or indirect) sex discrimination. The just-sketched interpretation of Article 6(2) EFD must clearly be distinguished from the scenario in Article 6(1) EFD which, it is argued, should be interpreted to mean that acts of discrimination on grounds of age in principle constitute unlawful age discrimination, unless they can be justified. Whether that is the case has to be assessed in light of the elements of 'legitimacy', 'appropriateness' and 'necessity'.

The analysis of the domestic law in the Netherlands hereafter will elucidate how the exceptions contained in Article 6 EFD have been employed in practice both by the legislator and by the ETC. It will be argued that the approach adopted by the Dutch legislator with regard to the implementation of Article 6 EFD is not fully in line with the Directive's requirements. At this juncture, however, it will be necessary first to discuss in depth the ECJ's judgment in *Mangold v. Helm* which forms the first indication of how EC age discrimination law must be appreciated. It is to an analysis of this judgment that I will turn henceforth.

3.2. *The ECJ's Judgment In Mangold v. Helm*[37]

The *Mangold* case, decided on by the Luxembourg Court in 2005 (GC)[38] has been referred to at various junctures above. *Mangold* concerned the following.[39] According to the German Law on Part-time Working and Fixed-Term Contracts (hereafter: *TzBfG*)[40] the conclusion of fixed-term contracts must be based on an objective reason. Moreover, in the absence of an objective reason, a fixed-term contract can only last for two years and, within these two years, the contract can be renewed for a maximum of three times. These provisions aimed to prevent employers from abusing the use of successive fixed-term employment contracts in accordance with the objectives sought by the EC Framework Agreement on fixed-term work.[41] However, Paragraph 14(3) of the *TzBfG* also stipulated that the just-outlined legal restrictions to the conclusion of fixed-term contracts did *not* apply if the worker has reached the age of 52 by the time that the fixed-term contract takes effect, unless there exists a close connection with a previous employment contract of indefinite duration concluded with the same employer. The exception regarding older workers pursued a benign aim namely, promoting their integration into the labour market and stimulating their prospects for employment. The applicant, Mr Mangold, concluded a fixed-term contract with Mr Helm, the respondent, in 2003 when Mr Mangold was 56 years old. Article 5 of the contract specified in unambiguous terms that the contract was based upon Paragraph 14(3) *TzBfG*, given that Mr Mangold was older than 52. In addition, Article 5 provided clearly that any other statutory ground which, in principle, permits the conclusion of fixed-term contracts was outside the scope of the employment contract. Mr Mangold maintained that albeit Article 5 of the contract was in conformity with Paragraph 14(3) *TzBfG* it constituted a breach of (*inter alia*) Article 6(1) of the Article 13 EC Framework Directive.[42] In the context of legal pro-

[37] The ECJ's judgment in *Mangold* has *inter alia* also been analysed by Schiek 2006; Schiek 2006a; Schmidt 2005 and Szyszczak 2006, p. 478.

[38] The fact that the case was decided on by a full Court renders its outcome all the more important.

[39] This case has *inter alia* also been commented upon by Schmidt 2005, by the Anti-discrimination Law Review 2006 (p. 42-47) and by the Editorial in the *Common Market Law Review* (43) 2006, p. 1-8.

[40] *Gesetz über Teilzeitarbeit und befristete Arbeidsverträge und zur Änderung und Aufhebung arbeitsrechtlicher Bestimmungen* – TzBfG) (BGBL. 2000, p. 1966) which entered into force on 1 January 2001. The TzBfG was the domestic implementing measure for transposing Directive 1999/70/EC of 18 June 1999 concerning the Framework Agreement on fixed-term work concluded by ETUC, UNICE and CEEP (*OJ* 1999 L 175, p. 43).

[41] *Ibid.*

[42] Mr Mangold moreover claimed that Article 5 of the employment contract was in conflict with Directive 1999/70/EC giving effect to the Framework Agreement on fixed-term work (see footnote 40 above). However, both Tizzano (AG) and the ECJ disagreed with the applicant in this respect. See paragraphs 36-79 of the Opinion of Tizzano (AG) and paragraphs 40-54 of the judgment by the Court. In summary: Directive 1999/70/EC had not been breached. Since this Chapter deals with age discrimination law I will not elaborate in further detail on those →

ceedings before the *Arbeitsgericht München* the following preliminary questions were amongst others referred to the ECJ:

> 'Is Article 6 [of the EFD; MG] to be interpreted as precluding a provision of national law which, like the provision at issue in this case [i.e. Paragraph 14(3) TzBfG; MG] authorises the conclusion of fixed-term employment contracts, without any objective reason, with workers aged 52 and over, contrary to the principle requiring justification on objective grounds?'
> '[If this question; MG] is answered in the affirmative, must the national court refuse to apply the provision of domestic law which is contrary to Community law and apply the general principle of internal law under which fixed terms of employment are permissible only if they are justified on objective grounds?'

The ECJ analysed both of these questions in conjunction.[43] It first emphasised the benign rationale behind Paragraph 14(3) *TzBfG*, namely (it is recalled) enhancing the employability of unemployed older workers. However, the Court's test of review did not end with this. In addition, the Court stressed that the legitimacy of the aim is not sufficient for upholding the lawfulness of the contested provision of domestic law. In addition, Paragraph 14(3) TzBfG must meet the requirements of 'appropriateness' and 'necessity'.[44] Although the Court observed that '(...) the Member States arguably enjoy a broad discretion in their choice of the measures capable ['capable' refers in my view only to the element of 'appropriateness', not 'necessity'; MG] of attaining their objectives in the field of social and employment policy, it subsequently adopted a strict necessity test in it assessment of the lawfulness of the contested provision at stake. Put differently, provisions which are allegedly in contravention of Article 6(1) EFD are subjected to a strict proportionality test which, in the view of the Court, was not complied with by the contested exception in *Mangold:*

> '(...) application of national legislation such as that at issue in the main proceedings leads to a situation in which all workers who have reached the age of 52 without distinction, whether or not they were unemployed before the contract was concluded and whatever the duration of any period of unemployment, may lawfully, until the age at which they may claim their entitlement to a retirement pension, be offered fixed-term contracts of employment which may be renewed an indefinite number of times. This significant body of workers, determined solely on the basis of age, is thus in danger, during a substantial part of its members' working life, of being excluded from the benefit of stable employment

aspects in the *Mangold* case which concerned the alleged breach of Directive 1999/70/EC. For further analysis I refer to Schmidt 2005, p. 511-513.

43 Paragraphs 55-78 of the Court's judgment.

44 Paragraph 61 of the judgment in which the Court held that 'an objective of that kind [i.e. a legitimate public-interest objective such as the one in issue in the proceedings at hand; MG] must as a rule, therefore, be regarded as justifying, 'objectively and reasonably', as provided for by the first subparagraph of Article 6(1) of Directive 2000/78, a difference of treatment on grounds of age laid down by the Member States'.

> which, however, as the Framework Agreement makes clear, constitutes a major element in the protection of workers.'[45]

In other words, although the contested exception did boost the employment prospects for older workers the downside of this was that workers of 50 years[46] and older were in principle permanently excluded from the benefit of stable permanent employment.[47] In other words, Paragraph 14(3) *TzBfG* went beyond what was 'appropriate' and 'necessary' to reach the objectives pursued and hence the principle of proportionality had not been duly observed. In the view of the ECJ

> 'observance of the principle of proportionality requires every derogation from an individual right to reconcile, so far as is possible, the requirements of the principle of equal treatment with those of the aim pursued. Such national legislation [i.e. Paragraph 14(3) TzBfG; MG] cannot, therefore, be justified under Article 6(1) of Directive 2000/78'.[48]

This conclusion formed the affirmative answer to the first question referred to above. However, the Court subsequently needed to determine what were the legal effects of this affirmative answer for the resolution of the dispute[49] between Mr Helm and Mr Mangold (i.e. the second question referred to above). In respect of the second question it is essential to stress that (i) the dispute at hand concerned a dispute between two privately acting individuals and that (ii) the implementation deadline imposed upon Germany for transposing Article 6 EFD only expires on 02-12-06.[50] However, in the ECJ's view, the last-mentioned fact did not thwart its finding that Paragraph 14(3) *TzBfG* was in breach of the Directive. The Court substantiated this view in reference to two arguments. First, it highlighted that 'during the period prescribed for transposition of a Directive, the Member States must refrain from taking any measures liable seriously to compromise the attainment of the result prescribed

45 Paragraph 64 of the judgment. See for the same conclusion also the observations by Tizzano (AG) in paragraphs 94 and 95 of his Opinion to the Court.

46 Rather than 52 years old, given that a fixed-term contract could be concluded with a worker of 50 years old in the absence of an objective reason provided that such a contract did not last for more than 2 years and had not been renewed more than 3 times. See the starting lines of section 3.2 above.

47 See paragraph 64 of the judgment of the Court and paragraph 95 of Tizzano's (AG) Opinion to the Court.

48 Paragraph 65 of the judgment in reference to *Lommers* (Case C-476/99) [2002] ECR I-2891, paragraph 39), as case which was discussed in detail in Chapter 5.

49 It can be questioned whether there was really a 'dispute' between the applicant and the respondent, given that the facts of the case and notably the way in which the employment contract between the two parties had been drafted suggested that the dispute at hand was contrived. This, however, had not led to the inadmissibility of the reference for a preliminary ruling by the domestic court. See paragraphs 32-39 of the judgment of the Court. Similarly, paragraphs 22-35 of the Opinion by Tizzano (AG).

50 Like the United Kingdom, Germany has used the possibility granted to the Member States by Article 18 of the Directive for an extended deadline for the implementation of the EFD in respect of 'age' and 'disability'.

by that Directive'.[51] Whilst holding so, the Court considered it of importance that if a Member State opts for an extended implementation deadline by virtue of Article 18 EFD it will be under an obligation to report annually to the European Commission on the steps it is taking to combat age discrimination and on the Member State's progress in this respect.[52] However, held the Court, this provision would become inessential, if in the meantime Member States were allowed to act contrary to the spirit of the Directive.[53] At this juncture it should be noted that Paragraph 14(3) *TzBfG* was only to apply until 31 December 2006, a couple of weeks after the deadline for transposition of the Directive expired.[54] However, as the Court observed in a substantive fashion, this would not be of help to Mr Mangold and others who are in a similar position, for by that time he will have reached the age of 58 years old, i.e. the applicable age after 31-12-2006. Secondly, and crucially, the Court held that the source underlying the Article 13 EC Framework Directive namely, the principle of non-discrimination, is found 'in various international instruments and in the constitutional traditions common to the Member States'.[55] In other words, the Framework Directive is merely a concrete manifestation of a 'meta-juridical principle' (namely, the principle of equal treatment). It went on by holding in very clear terms that 'the principle of non-discrimination on grounds of age must be regarded as a general principle of Community law'.[56] In the Court's view

> 'observance of the general principle of equal treatment, in particular in respect of age, cannot as such be conditional upon the expiry of the period allowed to the Member States for the transposition of a Directive intended to lay down a general framework for combating discrimination on the grounds of age (...). In those circumstances it is the responsibility of the national court, hearing a dispute involving the principle of non-discrimination in respect of age, to provide, in a case within its jurisdiction, the legal protection which individuals derive from the rules of Community law and to ensure that those rules are fully effective, setting aside any provision of national law which may conflict with that law'.[57]

The judicial outcome in *Mangold* is far-reaching. The Court permitted a private individual to rely *directly* on the (meta) principle of equal treatment in respect of age against another private individual. *De facto* this meant that Article 6(1) of the Frame-

51 Paragraph 67 of the judgment in reference to the ECJ's earlier case law in Inter-Environnement Wallonie (Case C-129/96) [1997] ECR I-7411, paragraph 45.

52 See Article 18 EFD and paragraph 71 of the Court's judgment.

53 See paragraph 72 of the Court's judgment.

54 In the editorial comments in the *Common Market Law Review* (43) 2006, p. 1-8 it has been noted that 'it might have been objected that the result prescribed by Directive 2000/78 was hardly likely to be compromised seriously by a national measure due to expire less than a month after the final date for the Directive's implementation' (p. 6). However, as will be illustrated in the main text above, this argument would arguably not have convinced the Court.

55 Paragraph 74 of the judgment.

56 Paragraph 75 of the judgment.

57 Paragraph 76 and 77 of the judgment in reference to the Court's earlier case law in *Simmenthal* (Case 106/77) [1978] ECR, 629, paragraph 21, and *Soldred* (Case C-347/96) [1998] ECR I-937, paragraph 30.

work Directive could be invoked by Mr Mangold against Mr Helm (horizontal application of Community Directives), *notwithstanding* the fact that the deadline for implementation had not yet expired.[58] I submit that the ECJ's legal reasoning in *Mangold* cannot be interpreted as establishing the principle of direct effect of EC Directives in 'horizontal' legal proceedings. This would run counter to established case law by the Court.[59] In *Mangold* the Court permitted an individual to rely upon a general ('meta-juridical') principle of EC law against another individual with the *de facto* but, in my view, not *legal* effect that Article 6 EFD was directly applicable in a horizontal dispute.[60] Put differently, it is submitted that *Mangold* restricts the direct applicability of provisions in EC Directives in private party disputes to those provisions whose content is materially identical to a general (constitutional) principle of EC law.[61] It is not, however, certain whether the direct effect of Directives in the circumstances just sketched is *fully* independent of whether or not the deadline for implementation has expired. In the view of the ECJ, observance of the principle of

58 According to established case law by the Court domestic law must be interpreted in light of Community Directives *Von Colson and Kamann v. Land Nordrhein-Westfalen* (Case 14/83) [1984] ECR 1891, paragraph 26 and, *Marleasing SA v. La Comercial Internacionale de Alimentacion SA* (Case 106/89) [1990] ECR I-4135. See more recently also *Pfeiffer* (joined Cases C-397/01 to C-403/01 [2004] ECR I-8835, paragraphs 113, 115, 116 and 118). The duty to interpret national law in line with the spirit of Community Directives exists in any case once the deadline for transposition of the Directive into domestic law has expired (*Marleasing SA v. La Comercial Internacionale de Alimentacion SA* (Case 106/89) [1990] ECR I-4135, paragraph 8). In *Mangold* the ECJ has tightened the duty imposed upon domestic courts by EC law, namely to interpret national law in conformity with EC Directives, by holding that this duty exists even *before* the deadline for transposition of a Directive has lapsed. Tizzano (AG) had also endorsed this view (see paragraphs 115 and 120 of the Opinion of Tizzano (AG) to the Court). Moreover, the same legal view has been taken by Kokott (AG) in his Opinion (delivered prior to the ECJ's judgment in *Mangold*) in *Konstantinos Adeneler and Others* (Case C-212/04) of 27 October 2005 (available at <http://www.europa.eu.int>), paragraphs 43-54 and by Kokott (AG) in his (earlier) Opinion in *Nicole Wippel v. Peek & Cloppenburg GmbH & Co KG* (Case C-313/02) delivered on 18 May 2004, paragraphs 58-63.

59 See in particular *Marshall v. Southhampton & South-West Hampshire Area Health Authority (Teaching)* (Case 152/84) [1986] ECR 723 (paragraph 48); *Faccini Dori* (Case C-91/92) [1994] ECR I-3325 (paragraph 20); *Wells* (Case C-201/02) [2004] ECR I-723 (paragraph 56). See generally also Chapter 2.

60 See especially also paragraph 84 of the Opinion of Tizzano (AG) in which he held as follows: 'As a comparison between them shows, both requirements- the specific requirement of the Directive [i.e. the requirement that discrimination on grounds of age is in principle prohibited under EC law; MG] and the general requirement just described- are essentially identical, so that the analysis of the compatibility of a rule such as the German one could be carried out in the light of either requirement with similar results. The better option is perhaps to use the principle of equality (...) since, *being a general principle of Community law imposing an obligation that is precise and unconditional, it is effective against all parties and, unlike the Directive, could therefore be relied upon directly by Mr Mangold against Mr Helm and could be applied by the Arbeitsgericht in the main proceedings* [italics; MG].'

61 See also Schmidt 2005, who has assumed that horizontal direct effect of provisions in Directives 'may be limited to those constituting fundamental rights' (p. 521). The present author observes, however, that this might be a too broad formulation given that not every fundamental right constitutes also a general principle of EC law.

equality *in particular* in respect of age cannot be conditional upon the expiry of the deadline. What did the Court mean by 'in particular'? I submit that this rubric must *not* be taken to mean that equality in respect of age has a higher priority than equality on other grounds. In other words, 'in particular' says nothing on the normative value of age equality, compared with equality on other grounds. Rather, by using this rubric the Court apparently gives importance to the fact that the *regular* deadline of implementation of the Directive had already expired. After all, but for the grounds 'age' and 'disability', the Article 13 EC Framework Directive obliges the Member States to finalise implementation into domestic law by 02-12-03 at the latest.[62] However, only with respect to 'age' and 'disability' may the Member States avail themselves of a prolonged deadline for implementation, namely until 02-12-06.[63] In other words, it is not unlikely, but neither certain, that had the *Mangold* case come before the Court at a point in time on which the *regular* deadline for implementation of the EFD had not yet expired (e.g. on 02-12-02), the case would have generated less far-reaching effects. Future case law by the Court will have to clarify whether this legal argumentation is valid.

Lastly, it is emphasised once again that the Court in *Mangold* has bolstered the moral character of the principle of equality in Community law. What the Court held in relation to 'age' can easily be extrapolated to discrimination on another ground listed in Article 13 EC.[64] *Mangold* supports the assertion that the principle of non-discrimination can be directly relied on by individual *x* against individual *y* in domestic legal proceedings. It is for the domestic courts, which are under a duty to secure the full effectiveness of EC law, to set aside national law that is in conflict with the general principle of non-discrimination on grounds of age secured by EC law. *De facto*, although with caution, namely via the legal detour of equality as a general principle of EC law, the Court seems to have granted Article 13 EC direct legal effect analogous to the direct legal effect of Article 141 EC.

4. The Principle of Equal Treatment in Respect of Age in Dutch Law[65]

4.1. *Introduction*

The aim of this section is to provide an analysis of Dutch equal treatment law in respect of 'age' perceived in light of EC law. This comprises both 'top-down' and 'bottom-up' perspectives. The Act on Equal Treatment on grounds of Age (henceforth, AETA)[66] implements the EFD (insofar as the ground 'age' is concerned) into domes-

62 Article 18 EFD.

63 *Ibid.*

64 Also European Anti-Discrimination Law Review 2006, p. 46.

65 This part draws on Gijzen 2004. See for a comment on the AETA also van Drongelen 2004.

66 Act of 17 December 2003 concerning the equal treatment on grounds of age in employment, occupation and vocational training [*Wet gelijke behandeling op grond van leeftijd*], *Staatsblad* 2004, 30 [*Law Gazette* 2004, 30]. Hereafter, his Act will be referred to as the 'AETA' (Age Equal Treatment Act). See generally also Chapter 2.

tic law.[67] Before the entry into force of the AETA age discrimination could merely be challenged on the basis of Article 1 of the Constitution which contains an open-ended equality and non-discrimination guarantee often in combination with Article 26 ICCPR.[68] Both provisions are directly applicable in both horizontal and vertical legal proceedings before the domestic courts.[69] It should be noted that 'age' is not explicitly mentioned in Article 1 of the Constitution.[70] This is regrettable, not only from the point of view of legal consistency with other grounds that *are* explicitly covered (i.e. religion, belief, political opinion, race, sex), but also because domestic courts tend to apply a less strict judicial scrutiny test in respect of alleged instances of discrimination on grounds that are *not* explicitly covered.[71] The fact that Article 13 EC places 'age' in the midst of other more conventional grounds of discrimination is yet another reason why Article 1 of the Constitution should be complemented with this ground.

As will be explained hereafter, the way in which age discrimination has been regulated in domestic law has been highly influenced by developments in EC law ('top-down' influence).[72] Conversely, it will be argued that experiences and practices

67 It is worth noting that the *Explanatory Memorandum* refers only obliquely and in second resort to Article 1 of the Dutch Constitution (see *Explanatory Memorandum* to the AETA, II, 2001-2002, 28 170, no. 3, p. 3). Evenhuis has argued that Article 1 of the Constitution has not served as a teleological tool in the interpretation of (openly phrased) provisions of the EFD. See Evenhuis 2002, p. 6.

68 Article 26 ICCPR provides as follows: 'All persons are equal before the law and are entitled without any discrimination to the equal protection of the law. In this respect, the law shall prohibit any discrimination and guarantee to all persons equal and effective protection against discrimination on any ground *such as* [italics; MG] race, colour, sex, language, religion, political or other opinion, national or social origin, property, birth or other status.'

69 *Codfried,* judgment of 13 January 1995, *NJ* 1995, 430 (HR). This case will be discussed in the main text hereafter. See also paragraph 2.4. of the Conclusion by Keus (AG) in his advisory opinion to joined cases *Eisers (16 piloten) tegen Martinair Holland N.V. en de Vereniging van Nederlandse Verkeersvliegers* (No. C03/077HR) 8 October 2004 (HR), (paragraph 3.4.2.) and *Eiser tegen Koninklijke Luchtvaartmaatschappij N.V. en de Vereniging van Nederlandse Verkeersvliegers,* (NO. C03/133HR) 8 October 2004 (HR), paragraph 3.4.2. These joined cases will be discussed in further detail hereafter. It is recalled from Chapter 2 that the Netherlands adhere to a monist theory of international law which means that international law standards form part and parcel of domestic law.

70 Article 1 of the Constitution is 'open-ended' and provides as follows: 'All who are in the Netherlands shall be treated equal in equal circumstances. Discrimination on the grounds of religion, belief, political opinion, race, sex or any other ground shall be prohibited'. Hence, the Constitutional prohibition of age discrimination is latently covered by the rubric 'or any other ground'. See generally also Chapter 2. Age as a ground of discrimination is neither expressly mentioned in Article 26 ICCPR (nor in Article 14 ECHR).

71 Mainly for these two reasons the ETC advised the government in 2004 to extend Article 1 of the Constitution with the following grounds: disability, nationality, hetero- or homosexual orientation, marital status and age. See *Advies 2004-03 van de Commissie Gelijke Behandeling over Artikel 1 Grondwet* [Advice 2004-03 of the Equal Treatment Commission with respect to Article 1 of the Constitution] 2004, available at <http://www.cgb.nl/_media/ downloadables/ advies%202004%2003.pdf>. This advice has not been followed.

72 It should be noted that the bill preceding the AETA as it currently stands has constituted the third legislative proposal since 1997. The first bill in 1997 merely applied with regard to the →

in the Netherlands can set an example (good or bad) for the application by the Luxembourg Court of EC anti-discrimination law on grounds of age. This would amount to 'bottom-up' influence and would eventually result in the cross-fertilisation of judicial approaches across the Community. As will be elucidated the Dutch ETC adopts a strict judicial scrutiny test whilst assessing the lawfulness of differences of treatment on grounds of age. This, it is argued, reflects the constitutional character of 'age' as a ground of discrimination. This strict approach interlocks with the ECJ's judicial stance in *Mangold* discussed above. The strict approaches by the ECJ and by the ETC can be contrasted with the more deferent approach adopted by the Dutch Supreme Court in the context of Article 1 Constitution and Article 26 ICCPR, prior to the adoption of the AETA. I submit that as a result of the insertion of age in Article 13 EC, and notably in light of the *Mangold* judgment, the argument that 'age' is not *a priori* suspect calls for reconsideration. In the analysis to follow, I will first make an analysis of the AETA in light of EC law (section 4.2). This involves an analysis of the legal framework of the AETA in a general fashion, as well as a more specific examination of a number of exceptions contained within the Act. The discussion in section 4.2 will be perceived in light of EC law and in light of the case law by the Dutch courts prior to the entry into force of the AETA. In section 4.3, I will elucidate the AETA in a practical fashion, namely through a discussion of the case law by the ETC.[73]

4.2. *The AETA*

4.2.1. General Overview of the AETA

Like 'disability', 'age' has been regulated outside the framework of the General Equal Treatment Act (GETA).[74] The separate regulation of the ground age (as well as disability and partly also sex) fosters a fragmented legal approach to the regulation of the principles of equality and non-discrimination. Therefore, the government currently contemplates to integrate these grounds into the GETA.[75] Implementation of the EFD in respect of 'age' has been achieved by the adoption of a separate Act, namely the AETA, which took effect on 1 May 2004.

The Act's material scope covers the broad area of employment, including self-employment, vocational training and the membership of employers' organisations,

recruitment and selection process in employment and was premised upon an 'open model' of equal treatment law. The second bill was proposed in 1999 and reflected a 'closed' model of equal treatment law. The 1999 bill was ultimately overhauled by fast-moving developments in EC law. These induced the government to adopt a third bill in 2001. This bill culminated into the AETA in its current format.

73 It is recalled from Chapter 2 that the ETC has solely jurisdiction in respect of the AETA to the exclusion of Article 1 of the Constitution.

74 See also Chapter 2, section 3.1.

75 See Chapter 2.

trade unions and other professional organisations.[76] This is in line with Articles 3(1) and 3(3) EFD. In conformity with Article 3(4) EFD, Article 17 AETA provides moreover that the Act shall not be applicable to the military service until 01-01-2008 at the latest.[77]

Like the GETA, the DETA[78] and the AET w/m[79], the AETA applies symmetrically. This means that it offers legal protection from unlawful distinction (*onderscheid*)[80] on grounds of age to young and old people alike.[81] In another important respect, however, the AETA's conceptual framework deviates from that underpinning the three aforementioned Acts. Whereas the GETA, DETA and AET w/m are founded upon a 'closed' model[82] of equal treatment law, the AETA reflects a 'half open' model. In conformity with Article 6 EFD, direct (as well as indirect) age distinction may be objectively justified.[83] Given that the AETA contains a number of exceptions which are *deemed* (by the legislator) to be 'objectively justified'[84] the underlying model of the AETA should be characterised as '*half* open'.[85]

Article 1(1) AETA defines the concept of 'distinction' (onderscheid) as follows: '(...) distinction shall mean distinction on the grounds of age or on the grounds of other characteristics or conduct which results in a distinction on grounds of age'.[86]

76 See Articles 3-6 of the Act. For a detailed discussion of the Act's material scope against the background of the relevant provisions of the EFD, I refer to Gijzen 2004, section 3.2.

77 This is thus only a temporary limitation to the AETA's material scope which, however, was not required by Article 3(4) EFD.

78 Disability Equal Treatment Act. See generally Chapter 2 and specifically Chapter 8.

79 Act on Equal Treatment between Men and Women (as amended). See generally Chapter 2.

80 The conceptual difference between the notions of '*discriminatie*' (discrimination) and '*onderscheid*' (distinction) has been explained in Chapter 2.

81 More than with any other ground is it difficult to establish who is the advantaged or disadvantaged group in the context of age discrimination. See footnote 27 above.

82 See Chapter 2. It should, however, be noted that the GETA, DETA and AET w/m are 'open' with respect to the objective justification test for *prima facie* cases of indirect distinction (*indirect onderscheid*). This was discussed in Chapter 3.

83 It is worth noting that the conceptual framework underpinning the AETA parallels with the one underlying the Act on the Prohibition of Distinction on grounds of Employment Duration [*Wet Onderscheid Arbeidsduur*: *WOA*] of 1996 which equally allows for the 'objective justification' of instances of both direct and indirect distinction. This Act is contained within Article 7:648 of the Civil Code (*Burgerlijk Wetboek*) and in Article 125g of the Civil Servants Act (*Ambtenarenwet*). The 'open model' is furthermore reflected in the Act on the Prohibition of Distinction on grounds of the employee's fixed-term or permanent contract [*Wet onderscheid bepaalde en onbepaalde tijd*: *WOBOT*] of 2002 (Article 7: 649 of the Civil Code). The WOA and the WOBOT will be discussed in no more detail.

84 The viewpoint adopted by the government, namely that a number of exceptions contained in the AETA are *a priori* objectively justified will be elaborated on and criticised in the main text to follow. It will be argued that this viewpoint is not in conformity with the spirit of Article 6 EFD, notably perceived in light of *Mangold* (earlier discussed).

85 For a discussion of 'open' and 'closed' models in the context of the legal regulation of discrimination on grounds of age, I refer to Heringa 1998, p. 118-119.

86 The original Dutch text of Article 1(1) AETA reads as follows: '*Onder onderscheid wordt in deze wet verstaan: onderscheid op grond van leeftijd of op grond van andere hoedanigheden of gedragingen dat onderscheid op grond van leeftijd tot gevolg heeft*' (unofficial translatation by the author in the main text above).

This Article transposes Articles 2(1)(a) and 2(1)(b) of the EFD which, respectively, contain the prohibition of direct and indirect discrimination.[87]

The prohibition of distinction on grounds of age also captures the prohibition of giving an instruction to make a distinction,[88] as well as the prohibition of harassment.[89] In addition, the broad formulation in Article 1(1) AETA covers discrimination on grounds of a wrongly assumed age,[90] as well as discrimination based on the association with persons with a particular age. Article 9 of the AETA specifies that, if an age classification is made in an advertisement for employment the grounds for doing so will have to be stated explicitly.[91]

Unlike the GETA, the DETA and the AET w/m, the AETA does *not* draw the conventional distinction between the prohibition of direct and indirect distinction. The government deemed this unnecessary,[92] given that the Directive anyhow allows for the objective justification of both types of prohibitions.[93] This stance assumes that the objective justification test in cases of direct and indirect age discrimination is

87 See *Explanatory Memorandum* to the AETA, II, 2001-2002, 28 170, no. 3, p. 4. For a detailed and technical discussion of Article 1(1) AETA in light of the requirements contained in the EFD, I refer to Gijzen 2004, section 2.2 under B and section 2.3 under A.

88 See, for example, Opinions 2005-113 and 2005-114. These concerned an employer's instruction to a recruitment agency to give preference to students while recruiting candidates for the job of computer expert. The Commission concluded a case of unlawful age distinction both by the recruitment agency (Opinion 2005-113) and by the employer (Opinion 2005-114).

89 See Article 1(2) AETA and Article 2 AETA, respectively. These Articles will be discussed in no more detail. The law on harassment was extensively discussed in Chapter 4 in relation to 'race', 'sex' and 'disability'.

90 This is in line with the approach adopted in the GETA, DETA and AET w/m. See also the decision by the Dutch Supreme Court of 26-02-1993, *NJ* 1993, 507.

91 See, for example, Opinion 2006-58. *In casu*, the advertisement for employment *inter alia* stated that applicants 'may not be older than 40 years'. The advertisement remained, however, silent on the reasons for this explicit age requirement. The ETC concluded a case of unlawful direct age distinction contrary to Article 9 of the Act. This conclusion remained unaltered by the employer's argument that it had not intended to discriminate against older workers. That intention is not a material condition for establishing a case of unlawful distinction is established case law by the Commission. See *inter alia* also Opinion 2004-13 and Opinion 1999-16 to which the Commission referred. See also *Advies 2005-06 van de Commissie Gelijke Behandeling inzake leeftijdsonderscheid in advertenties* [Advice 2005-06 of the Equal Treatment Commission with respect to the usage of age classifications in advertisements for employment], available in Dutch at <http://www.cgb.nl/_media/downloadables/advies% 202005%2006.pfd>.

92 The ETC advised the Dutch government that it should draw the conventional schism between direct and indirect distinction, given that depending on the type of distinction at stake the test of judicial review may be differently applied. Moreover, the type of distinction may bear an impact upon the burden of proof. See *Commentaar 2001-04 van de Commissie Gelijke Behandeling inzake het voorstel voor een Wet gelijke behandeling op grond van leeftijd* (2001) [Commentary 2001-04 by the Equal Treatment Commission on the Bill for the Act on Equal Treatment on the ground of age (2001)] available at <http://www.cgb.nl/media_downloadables/advies%202001%2004.pdf>. The government did, however, not follow the ETC's advice. See *Parliamentary Documents* II, 2001-2002, 28 170, no. 5 (*Nota naar aanleiding van het verslag*), p. 26-27. See for a critique Grapperhaus 2002.

93 See Articles 2(2)(b) under *i* EFD (objective justification of indirect age discrimination) and Article 6 EFD (objective justification of direct age discrimination).

identical,[94] an assumption that has been confirmed both by the ECJ in *Mangold* and by the case law of the ETC. As earlier explained, in *Mangold* the ECJ required compliance of the vexed provisions in the *TzBfG* with the principles of 'legitimacy' (the aim pursued must be legitimate), 'appropriateness' and 'necessity'. The judicial stance in *Mangold* reflects the Court's earlier approach in indirect sex discrimination cases.[95] Thus, in deciding on a case of direct age discrimination the Court effectively drew on its earlier experiences in indirect sex discrimination law. This constitutes an example of 'cross-fertilisation' of legal standards between two distinct grounds of discrimination, as well as between two different concepts of discrimination, i.e. direct and indirect discrimination.

For the same reason as that mentioned above the government also deemed it superfluous to insert a genuine occupational requirement exception (GOR) into the AETA,[96] which would, however, have been permitted by Article 4(1) EFD. Classifying the GOR exception under the general exception of Article 6 EFD is, however, conceptually confusing, for it presumes that the former exception is a species of the latter which is not the case.[97] The positive action exception contained in Article 7(1) EFD has not been transposed into the AETA. As explained in Chapter 5, Dutch equal treatment law merely permits the adoption of positive action measures and policies with respect to the grounds 'race', 'sex' and 'disability'. Article 6 EFD has been transposed into domestic law via Articles 7 and 8 of the AETA. Given the crucial role these two Articles play in the (semi) judicial resolution of cases concerning direct and indirect distinctions on grounds of age, I will examine these two Articles separately. This will be done in light of Article 6 EFD. It is to this analysis that I will turn now.

94 This view has *inter alia* been contested by Grapperhaus 2002, notably at pages 359-361. He has argued that the objective justification test for *direct* age distinction contains four constituent elements: (1) a 'legitimate aim', (2) 'appropriateness', (3) 'necessity' and (4) that the exception to the prohibition of age discrimination is explicitly provided for by domestic law. Grapperhaus infers this fourth element from the rubric 'within the context of national law' contained in Article 6(1) EFD. In other words, on this view, the objective justification test for cases of direct age discrimination is stricter compared to the one of indirect age discrimination. An identical view to that of Grapperhaus was taken by the *Democrats 66* (a Dutch Parliamentary party) in the course of the parliamentary proceedings leading to the adoption of the AETA. The government already at that point in time rejected this view. See *Parliamentary Documents* II, 2001-2002, 28 170, no. 5 (*Nota naar aanleiding van het verslag*), p. 33. This view has also been rejected by the ECJ as follows from the *Mangold* judgment.

95 Waddington 'Recent developments and the Non-Discrimination Directives: *Mangold* and More', *Maastricht Journal (forthcoming)* with reference to the ECJ's approach in *Bilka Kaufhaus GmbH v. Karin Weber von Hartz* (Case 170/84) [1986] ECR 1607 (discussed in detail in Chapter 3).

96 *Explanatory Memorandum* to the AETA, II, 2001-2002, 28 170, no. 3, p. 35.

97 Grapperhaus 2002, p. 362.

4.2.2. The Exceptions of Articles 7 and 8 AETA Examined in the Light of Article 6 EFD

4.2.2.1. Article 7 AETA

Article 7 AETA provides as follows:

> 7(1) The prohibition of distinction shall not apply if the distinction:
> (a) is based on employment or labour market policies seeking to promote employment in certain age categories, provided that such policies are laid down by or pursuant to an Act of Parliament.
> (b) relates to the termination of an employment relationship by reason that the person concerned has reached the pensionable age under the Statutory Old Age Pensions Act (henceforth: OAPA)[98] [i.e. the age of 65; MG], or an age higher than that [however, not lower!; MG] which has been laid down by or pursuant to an Act of Parliament, or, which has been agreed on by the parties concerned.
> (c) is otherwise objectively justified by a legitimate aim and the means used to achieve that aim are appropriate and necessary.

The exceptions under Article 7(1)(a)-(c) all fall within the scope of Article 6(1) EFD.[99] Hereafter, each of these exceptions will be scrutinised in further detail. This will be done in the light of the parliamentary comments to this Article, as well as in the light of existing case law by the Dutch courts[100] and against the background of EC law.

(i) The Exception under 7(1)(a) AETA

The exception under Article 7(1)(a) AETA is the one that was at stake in *Mangold* earlier discussed. In that case the ECJ affirmed that enhancing the employability of older workers constitutes a legitimate aim for purposes of the test of objective justification.[101] Nothing suggests that this would be different in respect of measures seeking to encourage the participation of young workers in the labour market. In this context the government has referred to the Governmental Regulation on a minimum youth wage (*Besluit minimumjeugdloonregelingen*) which seeks to enhance the employability of persons up until 23 years old. It permits an employer to pay a lower wage to persons under 23 years old in order to compensate the employer for the lack of

98 Algemene Ouderdomswet (AOW).

99 This is obvious with respect to Article 7(1)(a) and (c) AETA, given that they contain similar language as that contained in Article 6(1) EFD. The government has explicitly stated that Article 7(1)(b) AETA is also premised upon Article 6(1) EFD, rather than on Article 6(2) EFD. See in this respect *Explanatory Memorandum II*, 2001-2002, 28 170, no. 5 (*Nota naar aanleiding van het verslag*), p. 31. That Article 7(1) AETA as a whole should be perceived in light of Article 6(1) EFD also follows from the *Explanatory Memorandum* to the AETA, II, 2001-2002, 28 170, no. 3, p. 7 and p. 24-36.

100 The case law of the Dutch ETC will be discussed in section 4.3 hereafter.

101 As the Court held in *Mangold*: 'The purpose of [the vexed legislation; MG] is plainly to promote the vocational integration of unemployed workers, insofar as they encounter considerably difficulties in finding work (paragraph 59). The legitimacy of such a public-interest objective cannot reasonably be thrown in doubt, as indeed the Commission itself has admitted.' (paragraph 60).

experience of young persons in working life and their (presumed) lower productivity as a result of this. In other words, without the *Besluit minimumjeugdloonregelingen* the government believes that employers would be less likely to fill vacancies by employing young persons.[102]

In its explanatory comments to Article 7(1) AETA the government expressly aired the view that the exception under Article 7(1)(a) is *a priori* objectively justified, obviating thus the need for a *judicial* review of 'objective justification'.[103] This view is also implicit in the word 'otherwise' employed in Article 7(1)(c) AETA. However, *Mangold* has shown that the government's view reflects an incorrect understanding of the law. In *Mangold* the ECJ's test of review did not end with the acceptance that the aim pursued was legitimate. In addition, the Court went on by assessing the 'appropriateness' and 'necessity' of the vexed provision in the *TzBfG*. With regard to the element of appropriateness the ECJ held that 'the Member States arguably enjoy broad discretion'.[104] However, as explained in section 3 above, the Court does not readily accept the compliance with the necessity requirement.[105] *Mangold* shows that the assessment of 'objective justification' has to be carried out by the domestic courts which are under a legal duty to 'guarantee the full effectiveness of the general principle of non-discrimination in respect of age'.[106] Ultimately, 'objective justification' is a matter for the ECJ to decide on. In summary, objective justification calls for a *judicial* rather than for a *political* assessment contrary to what the Dutch government seemingly suggests.

(ii) The Exception under 7(1)(b) AETA

By virtue of Article 7(1)(b) AETA the dismissal of a worker by reason that he or she has reached the age of 65 or an agreed higher age is not unlawful. This exception must also be understood in the context of Article 6(1) EFD. It should be noted that Article 6(2) of the Framework Directive merely concerns an exception to the prohibition of age discrimination in respect of the admission or entitlement to retirement benefits to the exclusion, however, of age-based dismissals.[107] The government has advanced

102 *Explanatory Memorandum* to the AETA, II, 2001-2002, 28 170, no. 3, p. 28.

103 *Explanatory Memorandum* to the AETA, II, 2001-2002, 28 170, no. 3, p. 7 ('(...) Artikel 7, eerste lid, onderdelen a en b van het wetsvoorstel [somt] een aantal situaties op van onderscheid naar leeftijd dat volgens de regering objectief gerechtvaardigd is, zodat in deze gevallen toetsing per geval achterwege kan blijven'). See also van Drongelen 2004, p. 47, who has furthermore observed that legislation which employs age classifications is reviewed by the government as to its conformity with the principles of 'legitimacy', 'appropriateness' and 'necessity' in the context of Article 16 EFD. This Article provides that 'Member States shall take the necessary measures to ensure that (a) any laws, regulations and administrative provisions contrary to the principle of equal treatment are abolished' (Article 16(a) ETD).

104 Paragraph 63 of the judgment, which refers to the measure *capable* of attaining the pursued objectives.

105 Paragraph 65 of the judgment.

106 Paragraph 78 of the judgment.

107 See in this respect *Parliamentary Documents* II, 2001-2002, 28 170, no. 5 (*Nota naar aanleiding van het verslag*), p. 31. See also Lutjens 2003, p. 219. Article 6(2) EFD will be dealt with in further detail in section 4.2.2.2 hereafter, in the discussion of Article 8 of the AETA.

a number of reasons which, in its view, render the exception in Article 7(1)(b) AETA *a priori* 'objectively justified'.[108] These are the following:

1. the application of an objective criterion, namely the age of 65 is preferable to a system that requires an individual assessment, on a case-by-case basis, as to whether the worker concerned is still capable of performing the job effectively. In the government's view such an individual assessment might even entail an element of humiliation for the worker concerned;
2. the age classification of 65 enjoys great public support;
3. the age of 65 also underpins the national social security system. In other words, albeit a person no longer receives income through paid employment at the age of 65 this loss will be compensated for by an income under a state social security scheme, namely the OAPA;
4. dismissal at the age of 65 fosters and sustains the inflow of younger workers into the labour market.

For the same reasons the Supreme Court has hitherto equally rejected claims concerning the alleged unlawfulness of dismissal at the age of 65 under Article 1 of the Constitution and Article 26 ICCPR.[109] Moreover, the same stance has been adopted by the highest court in cases concerning claims by civil servants (i.e. the *Centrale Raad van Beroep*).[110] In its 1995 judgment in *Codfried*[111] the Supreme Court left open the possibility that dismissal at the age of 65 might be unlawful in the future depending on social developments.[112] However, in *Op 't Land-Wulfelé v. ESS*[113] this possibility was decisively ruled out by that same Court. The Supreme Court did so *inter alia* in light of Article 7(1)(b) of the bill for the GETA which contained unambiguous language[114] and which was allowed for under Article 6 EFD.[115] Although one may disagree on principle with the lawfulness of dismissals at the age of 65,[116] it is submitted that the Supreme Court's stance in *Op 't Land-Wulfelé v. ESS* is correct, given that the Court could simply not ignore (and neither should it have done so)

108 *Explanatory Memorandum* to the AETA, II, 2001-2002, 28 170, no. 3, p. 31, where the government has explicitly assessed the exception in light of the requirements of 'legitimacy', 'appropriateness' and 'necessity'. See also *Parliamentary Documents II*, 2001-2002, 28 170, no. 5 (*Nota naar aanleiding van het verslag*), p. 31.

109 *Codfried*, judgment of 13 January 1995, *NJ* 1995, 430 (HR), paragraph 3.6. See also *Op 't Land-Wulffelé v. ESS* No. C01/076/HR, judgment of 1 November 2002, paragraph 3.4.2. The last-mentioned case is also published in the NJCM Bulletin, 28 (2003), no. 5 (with a case comment by Loenen).

110 *Van Maarsseveen*, 4 November 1993, *TAR* 1994, 6 (CRvB).

111 *Codfried*, judgment of 13 January 1995, *NJ* 1995, 430 (HR).

112 See paragraph 3.6. of the judgment.

113 *Op 't Land-Wulffelé v. ESS* No. C01/076/HR judgment of 1 November 2002.

114 The wording of Article 7(1)(b) of the bill for the GETA is identical to the wording of the equivalent Article in the GETA as it currently stands.

115 See 3.4.2 of the judgment.

116 For example, Heerma van Voss 2002. His criticism will be outlined in the main text to follow.

the clear-cut language in Article 7(1)(b) of the bill for the GETA.[117] At the material moment in time (i.e. at the end of 2002) the (regular) deadline for implementation of the EFD had not yet expired. Neither had the ECJ rendered its judgment *Mangold*. I will come back to this point hereafter. Heerma van Voss has correctly argued that the adoption of the AETA has somehow led to a reduced level of protection granted to older workers, given that Article 7(1)(b) AETA currently blocks the possibility not yet entirely precluded by the Supreme Court in *Codfried*, namely that compulsory dismissals at 65 might be unlawful in the future.[118] The Court's decision in *Op 't Land-Wulfelé v. ESS* is clear evidence for this. It would nonetheless be a step too far to argue[119] that the Supreme Court's judgment in *Op 't Land-Wulfelé v. ESS* and the adoption of Article 7(1)(b) constitutes a breach of the non-regression clause in Article 8(2) EFD, given that in *Codfried* the Supreme Court had merely left the door open for a *potentially* different judicial outcome in future cases. In *Op 't Land-Wulfelé v. ESS* the applicant had also argued that the dismissal was unlawful, given that she was not entitled to an occupational pension scheme on top of her state pension. The Supreme Court, however, rejected this argument for

> 'any other outcome would mean that (...) de facto a general obligation was placed on the employer (...) to make provision for a pension scheme for all employees, an obligation which was apparently not foreseen [by the bill for the AETA]. Such an obligation does neither flow from the [Employment Framework] Directive.[120]

At this juncture the following interim observations must be made. It is clear from the above that under domestic law dismissal at the age of 65+ is not considered unlawful. This is also the prevailing view in the literature.[121] As was earlier explained, the government has deemed the exception in Article 7(1)(b) of the AETA *a priori* justifiable. This consequently precludes a *judicial* assessment of a '65+ dismissal' as to its conformity with the three-stage test of 'objective justification'. For the same reasons as stated above in the discussion of the Article 7(1)(a) AETA exception, I submit that the *a priori* conclusion by the legislator, namely that Article 7(1)(b) is anyhow 'objectively justified' is contrary to Community law in light of *Mangold*.[122]

117 See also Loenen 2003, who has correctly argued that, had the Supreme Court decided that the vexed dismissal was unlawful, it would have interfered with the role of the legislator and thus with the *trias politica*. The need for a deferent stance had also been stressed by the Supreme Court itself in *Codfried* (paragraph 3.5.) and was reiterated by the Supreme Court in *op 't Land-Wulffelé v. ESS* (paragraph 3.4.2.).

118 Heerma van Voss 2002, p. 64.

119 This argument has not been made by Heerma van Voss but is an observation by the present author.

120 Paragraph 3.4.3. of the judgment *'Een andere opvatting zou ertoe leiden dat langs deze weg in feite voor de werkgever of the bedrijfstak een algemene verplichting tot het treffen van een pensioenregeling voor alle werknemers in het leven zou worden geroepen, hetgeen klaarblijkelijk niet de bedoeling van het onderhavige wetsvoorstel is. Een dergelijke verplichting vloeit ook niet uit de Richtlijn voort.'* (translated in the main text above).

121 See for example Lutjens 2003, p. 217 and Heemskerk 2003, p. 302.

122 It should be noted that Recital No. 14 EFD does not bear an impact upon this. This Recital provides that the EFD 'shall be without prejudice to national provisions laying down →

Mangold supports the view that such a dismissal can be challenged before the domestic courts, both in 'horizontal' and 'vertical' legal proceedings, in direct reliance upon the principle of non-discrimination on grounds of age which is a general principle of EC law. This *does not* mean that such a dismissal is necessarily unlawful under EC law. It *does* mean that the dismissal must be subjected to *judicial scrutiny* by the domestic courts in light of the spirit of the Framework Directive *and* in light of the ECJ's decision in *Mangold*. With a view to securing the full effectiveness of the principle of non-discrimination on grounds of age as guaranteed by EC law, the domestic courts are under a duty to assess the lawfulness of '65+ dismissals' on the basis of a strict proportionality test. This implies that they will have to go beyond the more deferent test adopted by the Supreme Court in *Codfried* and *Op 't Land-Wulfelé v. ESS*. In these two cases the Supreme Court merely required a 'reasonable and objective justification' for the vexed dismissal.[123] In line with this, the Supreme Court moreover stressed the need for a different approach in light of the respective roles of the courts and the legislator within the *trias politica*. *Mangold* suggests that it will be ultimately for the ECJ to decide on the lawfulness of '65+ dismissals' under Community law. The ECJ may decide in a future case that the reasons advanced by the Dutch government in support of Article 7(1)(b) AETA do *not* pass the test for 'objective justification' under EC law[124]. It must however be stressed that this outcome is not inevitable and the opposite could well be true. It is submitted that the outcome of a given case is largely dependent on the concrete circumstances of the case at hand which fall to be perceived on the basis of the three-limb test of 'legitimacy', 'appropriateness' and 'necessity'.

So far, the discussion has focused on the lawfulness of '65+ dismissals'. It has been argued that these are not *a priori* in conformity with EC age discrimination law.

retirement ages'. However, this Recital says nothing on the lawfulness under Community law of age-based *dismissals*. It should in this context also be noted that Dutch law does not *require* that a worker leaves employment once he has reached the age of 65.

123 Heerma van Voss 2002, p. 63. See paragraph 3.6. of the Supreme Court's judgment in *Codfried* and paragraph 3.4.2. of the Supreme Court's decision in *Op 't Land-Wulfelé*.

124 See in this light the criticism expressed by Heerma van Voss in respect of almost all of the arguments given by the government in support of the lawfulness of 65+ dismissals. Heerma van Voss has merely agreed with the first-mentioned reason by the government, i.e. that 'age' constitutes an objective criterion, to the exclusion, however, of that element relating to the alleged humiliating effect of individual assessments which he has characterised as 'paternalistic'. With respect to the argument that older workers should make room for younger workers, Heerma van Voss has opined that this can no longer be reconciled with the ageing of the population and with the increased cost of pension provision. In addition, in his view this reason sends off a fundamentally wrong message, namely that a person's right to take up paid employment is conditional upon being younger than 65 years old. He has regarded this as inherently discriminatory on grounds of age. With respect to the reason stated by the government that paid income through employment is substituted for by an income under a state social security scheme, Heerma van Voss has argued that this will not always be sufficient for the worker concerned which, as seen above, is substantiated by the facts in *Op 't Land-Wulfelé v. ESS*. The ECJ, in case it would be asked for its opinion on the lawfulness of Article 7(1)(b) AETA, might give more importance to these counterarguments than to the arguments advanced by the government, although this need not necessarily be the case.

The next logical question concerns the lawfulness of dismissals by reason that the worker has reached an age which is *lower* than 65 years old (henceforth: '65-*dismissals*'). In respect of these dismissals the law is clear. '65- dismissals' are in any case not captured by the language of the exception in Article 7(1)(b) AETA. In addition, Article 16 of the Act[125] merely contains a *temporary* boundary to the Act's scope of application in respect of provisions (contained in, for example, a private or collective employment agreement) providing for the dismissal at an age lower than 65, provided that this was agreed on prior to the entry into force of the AETA.[126] Article 16 AETA prescribes that after 02-12-06 such dismissals will have to be objectively justified. This means that they will be subject to judicial scrutiny by the courts in the context of the exception contained in Article 7(1)(c) EFD.[127] This is not only fair in light of the non-discrimination principle but also logical. After all, although a '65-dismissal' does foster the flow of younger workers into the labour market, it is not supported by any of the other reasons advanced by the government in support of the exception contained in Article 7(1)(c) AETA (i.e. 'age as an objective criterion', 'public support' and 'the link with the social security system').[128] Hereafter, I will discuss the exception under Article 7(1)(c) AETA. In that discussion, I will proceed with the discussion on the lawfulness of '65- dismissals'.

(iii) The Exception under 7(1)(c) AETA

This exception reflects most clearly the open model of the AETA. Like the exceptions under (a) and (b), this exception is also premised upon Article 6(1) EFD. Any form of differential treatment on grounds of age which allegedly falls within the scope of this exception is subject to a strict proportionality review by the courts. The latter are under a duty to act in conformity with the general principle of non-discrimination on grounds of age secured by Community law. What kind of age-based distinctions might be captured by Article 7(1)(c) AETA? As illustrated above, *inter alia* 65-dismissals might be uphold by Article 7(1)(c) AETA. This will be elaborated on henceforth in light of relevant case law by the courts. In addition, I will examine a number of other circumstances that were explicitly stated by the government in the course of

125 This Article had initially not been foreseen by the original text of the bill for the AETA. During the parliamentary proceedings which led to the adoption of the Act an amendment was proposed by de Grave (MP) to the effect that '65- dismissals' should also be covered by the exception in Article 7(1)(b) AETA (with a view to securing that the prohibition of age distinction would not be applicable in respect of such dismissals). However, rather than amending the AETA to this effect, the temporary provision contained in Article 16 was inserted into the Act. See in this context also *Parliamentary Documents*, I, 2003-2004, 18 170, C, p. 2.

126 Article 16 of the AETA thus contains a transitional provision of law in order to grant time to employers and the social partners to streamline existing provisions in employment contracts and pension regulations with the law contained in the AETA. See also Veldman 2003, p. 364.

127 See also *Explanatory Memorandum* to the AETA, II, 2001-2002, 28 170, no. 3, p. 32. Also Lutjens 2003, p. 218.

128 Heemskerk 2003, p. 299. See, however, for a different view van Gemerden 2002, who has defended the lawfulness of 65- dismissals under the AETA (notably p. 353).

the Parliamentary proceedings leading to the adoption of the Act.[129] Matters will be presented under headings *(a)-(f)* hereafter.

(a) The usage of age-based distinctions by reason of health and safety arguments[130]
Health and safety rationales underpin, for example, certain provisions in the Act on Working Conditions *(Arbeidsomstandighedenwet)* that regulate the performance of hazardous labour by young persons. Such provisions might thus be challenged for being in breach with the test for proportionality.

(b) 'Functional age dismissal'[131]
This refers to the dismissal of a person by reason that he or she has reached a certain age (usually 55 years or older) in view of a presumed correlation between, ageing, on the one hand, and effective job performance, on the other.[132] In other words, it is assumed that certain jobs (e.g. the job of fireman to which the government has explicitly referred)[133] cannot be effectively performed at a certain age, also in light of requirements of health and safety. However, in the so-called *Referee case*, decided on by the Amsterdam Appeal Court,[134] the court did not uphold the lawfulness of the dismissal of a number of referees, employed by the Royal Dutch Football Association, by reason of having reached the age of 47, and 49, respectively. In the Court's view medical fitness for the job could be assessed on the basis of a broad range of instruments (including medical tests, fitness tests, knowledge tests, etc.) which meant that the imposition of an age classification went beyond what was necessary with a view to reaching the pursued objective (i.e. guaranteeing fit referees).

129 *Explanatory Memorandum* to the AETA, II, 2001-2002, 28 170, no. 3, p. 32-36.
130 *Explanatory Memorandum* to the AETA, II, 2001-2002, 28 170, no. 3, p. 32-33.
131 *Explanatory Memorandum* to the AETA, II, 2001-2002, 28 170, no. 3, p. 33.
132 This presumption has recently been affirmed by the recent expert research carried out by Van den Bogaart, De Lange and Van Poppel, 2005. The question as to whether there is a relationship between the burden of labour that can be placed on an employee, on the one hand, and age, on the other, has on average been answered in the affirmative (in the sense that this burden declines with age). It has, however, also been concluded that the nexus between 'age' and the burden of labour which can be put on somebody is individually determined and moreover depends on the type of job performed. See also *Advies 2006-04 van de Commissie Gelijke Behandeling inzake Seniorenregelingen als onderdeel van leeftijds(fase)bewust personeelsbeleid* [Advice 2006-04 of the Equal Treatment Commission on Seniorityprovisions as part of an age conscious personnel policy] available at <http://www.cgb.nl/_media/downloadables/advies%202006%2004.pdf>, p. 6.
133 *Explanatory Memorandum* to the AETA, II, 2001-2002, 28 170, no. 3, p. 33-34.
134 Hof Amsterdam [Amsterdam Appeal Court] 13 January 2000, KG 2000, 42; *NJ* 2000, 43. This case has explicitly been referred to by the government in its explanatory memorandum to the AETA (p. 33).

(c) Seniority provisions[135]

Seniority refers to the number of years of service of an employee with the same employer or within a certain job. Employment contracts and collective labour agreements often make employment conditions (for instance, the amount of holiday, pay, participation in a pension scheme) dependent on the number of years that an employee has worked (for the same employer). Furthermore, seniority can be a factor in dismissal decisions, including dismissals induced by the financial situation of the company (*ontslag om bedrijfseconomische redenen*).[136] Seniority requirements amount to *prima facie* indirect age discrimination, given that in practice such requirements tend to disproportionately affect younger workers (the older one gets, the more years of service one is likely to have). However, an employer who grants all persons in the age band of 50-55 years old 3 extra days of holidays discriminates *directly* on grounds of age, given that 'age' is explicitly used as a criterion in the decision-making process. The lawfulness of seniority requirements is subject to judicial scrutiny and thus depends on the concrete circumstances of the case at hand. That application of seniority criteria may be objectively justified also follows from Article 6(1)(b) of the Framework Directive.

(d) Age classifications and 'pressing business needs' (zwaarwegend bedrijfs- of dienstbelang)[137]

Sometimes age classifications might be necessary for the sake of the continuity of the undertaking or the operational management of the enterprise. Thus, an employer might deem it necessary to recruit employees within certain age bands, so as to secure a fairly represented management team.[138] Once again, this will be subject to judicial scrutiny.

(e) Age classifications in light of the training requirements for the post in question[139]

These might also be objectively justified under Article 7(1)(c) AETA. This example of a possibly justifiable exception is also expressly stated in Article 6(1) EFD (under (c)).

(f) '65- dismissals'

As we saw, these will have to be justified on the basis of Article 7(1)(c) AETA as from 02-12-06.[140] As clarified under point *(b)* above, according to the government

135 *Explanatory Memorandum* to the AETA, II, 2001-2002, 28 170, no. 3, p. 33-34. See also Advies 2006-04 van de Commissie Gelijke Behandeling inzake Seniorenregelingen als onderdeel van leeftijds(fase)bewust personeelsbeleid [Advice 2006-04 of the Equal Treatment Commission on Seniority provisions as part of an age conscious personnel policy] available at <http://www.cgb.nl/ _media/downloadables/advies%202006%2004.pdf>. This Advice will be elaborated on in section 4.2.4 hereafter. In that section I will also analyse a number of cases decided on by the ETC regarding the (un)lawfulness of seniority provisions.

136 *Explanatory Memorandum* to the AETA, II, 2001-2002, 28 170, no. 3, p. 33.

137 *Explanatory Memorandum* to the AETA, II, 2001-2002, 28 170, no. 3, p. 34-35.

138 *Explanatory Memorandum* to the AETA, II, 2001-2002, 28 170, no. 3, p. 35.

139 *Explanatory Memorandum* to the AETA, II, 2001-2002, 28 170, no. 3, p. 335-36.

such dismissals could be lawful if they are 'functional' to the need for securing effective job performance (so-called 'functional age dismissals'), provided that 'appropriateness' and 'necessity' are met. In addition, '65-dismissals' which pursue the objective of securing the flow of young workers into the labour market have been held by the courts to be objectively justified.[141]

4.2.2.2. *Article 8 AETA*

According to Articles 8(2) and 8(3) of the AETA the prohibition of distinction on grounds of age shall not apply:

> 'to ages for admission or entitlement to retirement benefits contained in retirement schemes, nor to the fixing of different pensionable ages for employees or categories of employees'. (Article 8(2))
> 'to actuarial calculations in the context of retirement schemes which take the factor 'age' into account'.[142] (Article 8(3))

According to Article 8(1) AETA the above-mentioned exceptions only apply in relation to occupational pensions, to the exclusions of pensions under a state social security scheme (i.e. the AOPA).[143] It follows from Article 8(2) AETA that fixing an age for admission to retirement benefits which is under the age of 65 (e.g. 62) is not unlawful. However, on the other hand, this does not automatically warrant compul-

140 For further discussion of the lawfulness of 65- dismissals decided on by the lower courts prior to the entry into force of the AETA, I refer to the following contributions: Van Gemerden 2002; Heemskerk 2003; Lutjens 2003.

141 District Court Haarlem, 19 November 2002, *JAR* 2002/290; Amsterdam Court of Appeal, 04 December 2003, *JAR* 2004, 12; *Eisers (16 piloten) tegen Martinair Holland N.V. en de Vereniging van Nederlandse Verkeersvliegers* (No. C03/077HR) 8 October 2004 (HR), (paragraph 3.4.2.) and *Eiser tegen Koninklijke Luchtvaartmaatschappij N.V. en de Vereniging van Nederlandse Verkeersvliegers,* (NO. C03/133HR) 8 October 2004 (HR) (in the context of Article 1 of the Constitution and Article 26 of the ICCPR). See, however, in contrast Opinion 2005-226 by the ETC which was decided on the basis of the AETA.

142 Unofficial translation by the author. The original Dutch language text reads as follows: Article 8(1) AETA: *'Het verbod van onderscheid is niet van toepassing op in pensioenvoorzieningen vastgelegde toetredingsleeftijden en op pensioengerechtigde leeftijden, alsmede op de vaststelling van verschillende toetredings- en pensioengerechtigde leeftijden voor werknemers of voor groepen of categorieën van werknemers.'*
Article 8(2) AETA: *'Het verbod van onderscheid is niet van toepassing op actuariële berekeningen bij pensioenvoorzieningen waarbij met leeftijd rekening wordt gehouden.'*

143 Article 8(1) AETA provides that 'pension scheme' shall mean a pension scheme applying to one or more persons solely in connection with their activities in a company, branch of industry, occupation or public service, which supplements a pension provided for under a state social security scheme and, in case it applies to a person, has not been arranged privately by the person concerned' (unofficial translation by the author). The original Dutch language text reads as follows: *'Voor de toepassing van dit Artikel wordt verstaan onder pensioenvoorziening: een pensioenvoorziening ten behoeve van een of meer personenen, uitsluitend in verband met hun werkzaamheden in een onderneming, bedrijfstak, tak van beroep of openbare dienst, in aanvulling op een wettelijk stelsel van sociale zekerheid en, in geval van een voorziening ten behoeve van een persoon, anders dan door die persoon zelf tot stand gebracht.'*

sory dismissal at the age of 62 because, as we saw, such a dismissal must be 'objectively justified' on the basis of Article 7(1)(c) AETA.[144] Article 8 AETA implements Article 6(2) EFD. The latter Article must moreover be perceived in light of Recital No. 14 EFD, which states that the EFD 'shall be without prejudice to national provisions laying down retirement ages'. Just like Article 6(2) EFD sets a limit on the scope of application of the EFD, Article 8 AETA sets a limit to the AETA's scope of application. Once it has been concluded that a certain act falls within the ambit of Article 8 AETA, no *prima facie* case of distinction on grounds of age can be established. Such an act can merely be reviewed as to its conformity with the principle of non-discrimination on grounds of sex.[145] This interpretation is not only supported by the wording of Articles 6(2) EFD and 8 AETA but also by the *travaux préparatoires* to the latter Article.[146]

4.2.3. Interim Conclusions

In sections 4.1 and 4.2 above an overview was, respectively, given of the AETA generally and of the exceptions contained in Articles 7 and 8 of the Act. This was done, not only in light of existing case law by the Dutch courts, but also in light of EC law and specifically in light of the ECJ's decision in *Mangold.* It was argued in particular that the stance adopted by the Dutch government in relation to Article 7(1)(a) and 7(1)(b) AETA, namely that the exceptions contained within these Articles are *a priori* objectively justified, falls short of EC law requirements perceived in light of *Mangold.* That is, however, not to say that the exceptions in these Articles are necessarily in breach of EC law. Deciding on this question is a matter for the courts, and ultimately for the ECJ, on the basis of a strict proportionality test which has to be applied on a case-by-case basis. The analysis thus far also showed that '65-dismissals' will only be lawful, if the requirements contained in Article 7(1)(c) AETA are met. Article 8 AETA seeks to implement Article 6(2) EFD. Article 8 AETA sets a boundary to the Act's scope of application and acts of distinction on grounds of age which are covered by this Article can only be reviewed for compliance with the principle of gender equality.

4.3. *The AETA and the Case Law by the ETC*

As stated at the outset of this chapter the ETC has rendered a tremendous amount[147] of case law regarding alleged unlawful distinctions on grounds of age. Hereafter, I

144 Lutjens 2003.

145 Such a review would take place on the basis of the AET m/w, not on the basis of the AETA. This has explicitly also been stated by the government. See *Explanatory Memorandum* to the AETA, II, 2001-2002, 28 170, no. 3, p. 8.

146 *Explanatory Memorandum* to the AETA, II, 2001-2002, 28 170, no. 3, p. 37.

147 As stated in the Introduction to this Chapter from 01-05-04 until 27-05-06 the Commission has decided on 140 cases concerning differences in treatment on grounds of age. This can, for example, be contrasted with only 8 cases from 01-01-04 until the time of writing concerning the discrimination ground sexual orientation. On 27-05-06, 68 cases exist concerning the →

will give an illustrative overview of how the ETC has applied and interpreted the AETA in practice.

4.3.1. Seniority Provisions

In Opinion 2004-118 an employer asked the ETC whether three seniority provisions contained in the employees' terms of employment were in conformity with the AETA.

One of the provisions granted extra days of holidays to employees of 45 years and older with a view to maintaining their availability for work. Whilst assessing the question of justifiability on the basis of Article 7(1)(c) AETA, the Commission considered as follows. In the ETC's view the aim pursued was not legitimate. The Commission relied on an expert study[148] showing only a weak nexus between 'age' on the one hand, and the health and availability for work of older employees, on the other. The provision in issue did also not meet the 'appropriateness' requirement: the employer had been unable to show that granting extra days of holidays had actually contributed to a disburdening of employees. Neither had the employer established that there was a difference in sickness absence between persons in different age categories. Furthermore, the jobs performed within the company were not physically demanding. The employer's arguments, namely that extra days had been granted for the past 20 years, that employees regarded this as a positive rule, and that the rule had been introduced on the basis of a social trend were all held to be too general in kind to justify differentiation on the ground of age.[149] No objective justification was found.

A second provision granted extra days of holidays to employees with 10, 15 or 20 years of employment within the company. This provision constitutes a *prima facie* case of indirect distinction on grounds of age. The aim pursued by the second provision was to motivate employees to work, to limit staff turnovers and to reward the knowledge, expertise and loyalty of employees. With reference to the parliamentary records the ETC concluded that these aims were legitimate. They were moreover 'appropriate'. However, they were not 'necessary': other means could be used to reach the same objectives. Examples given were, respectively, a yearly trip out with colleagues; attractive conditions of employment and an increase of salaries; a system of bonuses related to an employee's expertise and knowledge. Once again there was no objective justification.

A third provision provided for a reduction in the hours of work for employees of 60 years and older. Such a provision amounts to *prima facie* direct age distinction. The employer's objectives were to keep older employees in employment, to realise a gradual transfer of job responsibilities and to prepare employees of 60+ for a life

discrimination ground disability, although the DETA entered into force 5 months earlier than the AETA.

148 Nauta, de Bruin, Cremer, *De Mythe doorbroken, gezondheid en inzetbaarheid oudere medewerkers*, 2004 TNO Arbeid.

149 In reference to *Ingrid Rinner-Kühn v. FWW Spezial-Gebaudereinigung GmbH & Co.KG* (Case 171/88) [1989] ECR 2743 and the *Explanatory Memorandum* to the AETA, II, 2001-2002, 28 170, no. 3, p. 25.

with more leisure time. Since none of the employees actually made use of the provision in issue, and only a few had made use of it in the past, there was no real need for the employer to reduce working hours for employees of 60 years and older. Since the contested provision was optional for employees the objective sought did not serve a real need and thus the aim was not legitimate. No objective justification was found.

In a comparable case (Opinion 2004-150) the employer asked the ETC whether a 'gradually reduced working time arrangement' for older workers (*afbouwregeling*) and an arrangement regarding the allocation of extra holidays to older workers (henceforth: the 'extra holidays arrangement') contravened the AETA. In addition, a separate Opinion of the ETC was requested on a 'length of service requirement'. This requirement was a yardstick used by the employer to determine whether or not an employee could take advantage of the gradually reduced working time arrangement. If an employee chose to participate in the gradually reduced working time arrangement, this meant that he worked less and received 50% of his gross salary for the time he did not work. Concretely, under the employer's arrangement that meant that an employee of 57,5 years old could choose to work half a day less per week and be paid 95% of his gross monthly salary. An employee aged 60 could opt to work one day less per week against 95% of his gross monthly salary. An employee aged 62,5 could choose to work 2 days less per week against 80% of his monthly gross salary. Importantly, in order to be eligible for the arrangement an *additional and decisive criterion* was that an employee had to be continuously employed by the employer for 10 years (the 'length of service requirement').[150] The rationale underlying the arrangement in issue was to enable older workers to gradually step back from the labour market and to prepare them for retirement. With respect to the length of service requirement in particular, the employer noted that in the absence of this requirement it would be economically disadvantageous for the employer to recruit older employees where young employees were also available. The ETC held that the vexed arrangement made a distinction between persons over and under the age of 57,5. This therefore constituted a *prima facie* direct distinction on grounds of age. It then continued with an assessment of justifiability under Article 7(1)(c) AETA. The Commission found that the aims were legitimate, however, it held that the appropriateness requirement had been breached. This was so, given that older employees who did not meet the length of service requirement might have as much a need to be prepared for withdrawal from the labour market, compared with employees who did meet this requirement. Hence, the arrangement in issue was not objectively justified. The Commission was of the view that, even if the length of service requirement was not taken into account, the 'necessity' requirement could not be met, since a special preparatory course could be an alternative means which would be less (if not, not) discriminatory. Moreover, the Commission indicated that no proportionate relationship existed between the means used and the objective sought: those aged over 57,5 were eligible but in the ETC's view a person would not need 7,5 years (until 65) to prepare for pensionable age.

150 The arrangement also applied to part-time workers (*pro rata* of the amount of hours worked).

The Commission gave a separate Opinion on the length of service requirement. The ETC with reference to the *travaux préparatoires* indicated that a length of service requirement such as the one in question may constitute unlawful '*indirect* age distinction'. After all, older workers fulfil such a requirement more easily than younger workers. However, since the 10 years of service requirement was made in addition to[151] the requirement that an employee be over 57,5 there was no distinction between *younger* and *older* workers, but between workers over 57,5 who *did meet* the 10 year requirement *and* those who *did not*. In the Commission's view this did not in itself constitute a distinction on the ground of age. Hence, the 'length of service requirement' was held to be compatible with the AETA.

Finally, the Commission assessed the lawfulness of the 'extra holiday arrangement'. Under this arrangement extra days of holiday were granted to persons aged 50 or over. Persons aged 50-55 were granted one extra day; those of 55-60 were granted two extra days and those over 60 were given three extra days. The employer indicated that the rationale for this was to alleviate the pressure of work on older employees. The ETC pointed out that the arrangement made a distinction between persons under 50 and persons over 50. This was thus a direct distinction on the grounds of age. With reference to the *travaux préparatoires* the ETC pointed out that the above rationale could constitute a legitimate aim, since it could prevent sickness absence. However, on the basis of the patterns of sickness absence within the company, and in reference to external expert research,[152] the ETC concluded that other factors (e.g. lifestyle, long-term physical burden) rather than age had an impact upon older employees' availability for work. It therefore held that the aim pursued was not legitimate and it concluded a breach of the AETA.

The above two cases show that the Commission does not readily accept the by employers alleged link between age, on the one hand, and the need for reduced pressure of work, on the other. Although more favourable conditions of employment for older workers could work to the benefit of these workers they can also have a downside effect, namely supporting the idea that older workers are less capable to perform the job than other workers.[153] Moreover, if older workers are entitled to many extra days of leave by reason of their age this might be an incentive for the employer *not* to employ them.[154] Nonetheless, the Commission was not sure as to whether its outcome in the above cases reflected a correct stance. It therefore commissioned

151 In other words: the length of service requirement was not used as an 'autonomous' yardstick for participation in the 'gradually reduced working time arrangement'.

152 Nauta, de Bruin, Cremer, *De Mythe doorbroken, gezondheid en inzetbaarheid oudere medewerkers*, 2004, TNO Arbeid.

153 See also *Advies 2006-04 van de Commissie Gelijke Behandeling inzake Seniorenregelingen als onderdeel van leeftijds(fase)bewust personeelsbeleid* [Advice 2006-04 of the Equal Treatment Commission on Seniority provisions as part of an age conscious personnel policy] available at <http://www.cgb.nl/_media/downloadables/advies%202006%2004.pdf>, p. 3.

154 See Opinions 2005-45 and 2006-34. See also Advies 2006-04 van de Commissie Gelijke Behandeling inzake Seniorenregelingen als onderdeel van leeftijds(fase)bewust personeelsbeleid [Advice 2006-04 of the Equal Treatment Commission on Seniority provisions as part of an age conscious personnel policy] available at <http://www.cgb.nl/_media/downloadables/advies%202006%2004.pdf>, p. 3.

new expert research to examine whether a correlation exists between 'age' and the need for a reduced work pressure.[155] This question has recently been answered in the affirmative.[156] In light of this the Commission has decided to stay proceedings of all questions regarding the lawfulness of measures seeking to alleviate the burden of work of older workers until after 02-12-06.[157] By doing so, the ETC gives the necessary time to the social partners to reflect on the advisability for such provisions.[158]

In Opinion 2006-26 the applicant was older than 65.[159] The employment contract between him and his employer entered into force on 1 March 2004. The applicant received less payment than he should receive according to the applicable collective labour agreement. He also received less payment than colleagues, who were younger than 65. The employer rationalised the reduction in payment with reference to the applicant's reduced pace and productivity in carrying out the job. Moreover, the applicant had informed the employer that his wish to work was not so much rationalised by financial reasons, but rather by reason of being able to remain in work. It was not disputed between the parties that the applicant's age had not been the sole reason for the difference in payment. In its assessment of the claim the Commission held that, in order to conclude a *prima facie* case of age distinction, 'age' need not be the exclusive reason for a difference of treatment.[160] Therefore it concluded a case of *prima facie* age distinction contrary to Article 3(e) of the AETA. In conjunction with Article 1 AETA this forbids distinctions on grounds of age with respect to the conditions of employment, including pay. The Commission subsequently analysed the question of justifiability under Article 7(1)(c) of the Act. It concluded that the aim pursued was not legitimate, given that the individual employment contract expressly declared the applicability of the collective labour agreement. The

155 In the meanwhile the Commission was continuously asked to give its opinion on the lawfulness of seniority provisions. However, the Commission stayed proceedings in these cases until the conclusions of the external research would become apparent. See Opinions 2005-110 and 2005-66. In Opinion 2005-110 the employer (*inter alia*) afforded workers of 50+ three extra days of holidays and workers of 55+ four extra days of holidays. In Opinion 2005-66 the employer asked the Commission whether a provision in the terms of employment providing that workers of 60+ years old were exempted from working overtime, and were entitled to extra days of holidays as well as to reduced working hours was in conformity with the AETA.

156 See footnote 132 above. The research by the independent experts is accompanied by a checklist which will be an aid to the Commission whilst deciding on the lawfulness of seniority provisions in future cases. See Institute for Labour Studies, *Regelingen voor oudere werknemers – checklist voor de Commissie Gelijke Behandeling* [Regulations for older workers – checklist for the Equal Treatment Commission]. This checklist is available at <http://www.cgb.nl/_media/downloadables/checklist%20bij%advies%202006%2004.pdf>.

157 Provided, of course, that the employer/the organisation of employers together with the representatives of the employees/the trade unions reflect on the necessity and desirability or collective seniority regulations.

158 *Advies 2006-04 van de Commissie Gelijke Behandeling inzake Seniorenregelingen als onderdeel van leeftijds(fase)bewust personeelsbeleid* [Advice 2006-04 of the Equal Treatment Commission on Seniority provisions as part of an age conscious personnel policy] available at <http://www.cgb.nl/_media/downloadables/advies%202006%2004.pdf>, p. 7-9.

159 The applicant was born on 09-05-1927; the Commission's judgment was rendered on 21-02-2006. In other words, at the time that the judgment was given the applicant was 79 years old.

160 This is established case law by the Commission. See also Opinion 2006-10; 2005-240; 2005-122.

latter contained binding provisions on payment, which could not be deviated from by the individual contract of employment. The Commission concluded a breach of the AETA.

The question arises how the above case would have been decided on in the absence of the collective labour agreement? Future case law must answer this question. *In casu*, the reduced wages had been mutually agreed on by the parties in light of the presumed link between the applicant's age and his lowered labour productivity. As we saw this link has recently been confirmed by independent expert research.

4.3.2. Recruitment and Selection

In Opinion 2005-179 the applicant was 18 years old.[161] He claimed an instance of unlawful distinction on grounds of age by the respondent, a chain of supermarkets, by reason of the latter's refusal to transform the applicant's fixed-term contract into a permanent one. The applicant had worked for the respondent as a temporary worker since June 2003. The employment contract had been renewed for the maximum amount of two times and therefore the option for a maximum of two consecutive renewals prior to an automatic extension into a permanent contract was fully utilised in November 2004. According to established case law by the Commission the refusal to renew a fixed-term contract, or to transform it into a permanent contract, amounts to a decision concerning recruitment.[162] Such a refusal can therefore be assessed on the basis of Article 3(a) in conjunction with Article 1 AETA, which prohibit age distinction in the recruitment and selection procedure. The employer rationalised its refusal in a three-fold manner: (1) the employer was in need of keeping its workforce flexible, in order to take account of its fluctuating market position; (2) offering the applicant a permanent contract would entail that the employer would be required to pay the minimum youth wage.[163] Since there is a great difference in pay between a 14 year old worker compared with an 18 year old worker, employing the applicant would counter the business needs of the enterprise; (3) workers under 18 years old will be longer available to the employer, given that they tend to attend secondary school. In its assessment of objective justification on the basis of Article 7(1)(c) AETA the Commission held as follows. In respect of the first-mentioned rationale it found that this did not correspond with a 'real need' on the part of the undertaking, given

161 See for a similar case also Opinion 2006-27. In that case the employer (i.e. a chain of supermarkets) applied a less favourable policy regarding the renewal of contracts to temporary workers compared with part-time and full-time workers. The Commission concluded a *prima facie* case of indirect distinction on grounds of age (given that the group of part-time workers was mainly composed of young persons). The distinction could not be objectively justified.

162 See, for example, Opinion 1997-101; Opinion 2000-25; Opinion 2004-130. See also Opinion 2006-27 in which the Commission expressly held that the employer's freedom not to renew a contract under the 'Act on Flexibility and Security' (*Wet Flexibiliteit en Zekerheid*, or *Flexwet*, *Stb.* 1998, 332; this Act entered into force on 01-01-1999) was limited by equal treatment law. The employer's reason for not renewing a contract may not be based on a forbidden ground (see paragraph 5.3. of Opinion 2006-27).

163 The employer is required to do so on the basis of the Governmental Regulation on a minimum youth wage (*Besluit minimumjeugdloonregelingen*), referred to earlier on in the analysis.

that the employer had failed to substantiate its fluctuating market position. Moreover, in relation to the second-mentioned rationale, the Commission referred to established case law by the Supreme Court and the by ECJ, according to which financial considerations *in se* are in principle insufficient to objectively justify a difference of treatment.[164] Moreover, held the ETC, the employer's refusal to hire the applicant ran counter to the purposes behind the minimum youth wage, namely *promoting the employability* of young workers.[165] The refusal by the employer under the last mentioned rationale did not pass the test of objective justification: a refusal to renew was not an appropriate means to secure longer availability.

Case law like this warrants caution. Firstly, it is likely to constitute an incentive for employers not to hire staff in the first place or, at least, to hire less staff than they would otherwise do. Moreover, case law like this runs counter to the promotion of employment of young workers. Secondly, the facts *in casu* ought to be distinguished from those in *Mangold.* Admittedly, both applicants in these cases were excluded from the safeguards that go with permanent employment. Unlike Mr Mangold, however, the applicant *in casu* was only 18 years old and was still attending secondary school. As such it is unlikely that he, unlike Mr Mangold, would be excluded from the benefits of stable employment for a substantial part of his working life. Thirdly, the facts *in casu* should be distinguished from the scenario where an employer refuses to renew the employment contract of a woman, or a black person, for business-related reasons.[166] Given the immutable status of being female or black it is likely that a malicious employer would not employ a female or black job applicant in the first place. The applicant *in casu,* however, had enjoyed the benefit of working for the employer ('life cycle argument'). The facts of the case showed that the employer had been satisfied with the applicant's performance in the job. In the author's opinion it cannot be maintained that by not renewing the applicant's contract the employer had infringed his dignity or equal worth. This would be different in such cases where a person's race or sex constitutes the ground for a refusal to recruit.

Opinion 2005-174 concerned the following. The applicant was 61 years old and had applied for the position of expert in practical driving performance with the respondent. It concerned a job for two days per week. Prior to the commencement of the job the candidate would have to undergo a training period. The applicable collective labour agreement provided that a worker retired at the age of 65. It moreover provided that pre-retirement at the age of 62 was possible on a voluntary basis. The

164 The ETC referred to the ECJ's judgment in *de Weerd, neé Roks and Others* (Case C-343/92) [1994] ECR I-571 and to the decision by the Dutch Supreme Court of 24-04-1992, *NJ* 1992, 689, as well as to its own established case law (Opinions 2002-165 and 2005-83. This would only be different, if the requirement to treat people equally would result in a disproportionate burden for the employer. The Commission explained that if financial considerations by themselves could constitute an objective justification, the rationales of equal treatment law would be largely undermined. See also Opinion 2005-186.

165 The employer had in this context argued that not the applicant's age, but the fact that *as a result of the minimum youth wage regulations* the employer was compelled to pay a higher wage, had been the reason for the vexed refusal.

166 For example, by reason that the woman may become pregnant or, with respect to the black person, for example as a result of 'customer preference'.

applicant was rejected for the job by reason that, had he been accepted, there would have been a disproportionate balance between the duration (5 months) and cost (€50.000) of the training, on the one hand, and its cost-effectiveness, on the other. With reference to Article 6(1)(c) EFD, which provides that differences in treatment can (*inter alia*) be objectively justified where a maximum recruitment age is fixed by reason of the training requirements of the post or the need for a reasonable period of employment before retirement, the ETC reviewed the contested age distinction as to its conformity with the elements of 'legitimacy', 'appropriateness' and 'necessity'. The aim pursued was both legitimate and appropriate. It was moreover considered necessary: the applicant would not have finished the training before June 2005. Hence, depending on whether the applicant would retire at the age of 62 or at that of 65, he would be employed for a minimum of 6 months until a maximum of three and a half years, for only 2 days a week.

The above case shows that the exception in Article 6(1)(c) EFD is necessary to avoid unreasonable outcomes in equal treatment cases on grounds of age. Furthermore, it shows that if a distinction on grounds of age falls within the ambit of the list of examples contained in Article 6(1)(a)-(c) of the Directive, the ETC will nevertheless apply the objective justification test to the facts of the case at hand. By doing so, the Commission acts in conformity with the ECJ's approach in *Mangold.*

In Opinion 2005-134, the applicant asked the ETC for its opinion on the lawfulness of experience requirements. *In casu*, a recruitment agency had advertised for the jobs of Line Manager and 'International Sales Talent' on the authority of a principal. The job advertisements specified that candidates should have 2-4 years, or at any rate, 6-8 years of experience.[167] The applicant was 54 years old and in search of work. He had applied for the just-mentioned jobs but was not short listed because he was considered to be overqualified. The Commission examined whether the applicant had been discriminated against on grounds of age with respect to recruitment and selection for the job (Article 3(a) AETA), as well as with respect to employment mediation (Article 3(b) AETA).[168] The ETC, with reference to the *travaux préparatoires*, indicated that requirements of job experience may constitute an instance of indirect distinction on grounds of age depending, however, on the size of the group which is liable to be affected by such requirements by reason that it cannot comply with them. The size of the group of 'non compliers' must be perceived in relation to the size of the group that can comply with the vexed requirements.[169] The Commission held

167 The job advertisement specified that a maximum of 2-4 years of experience was required for the job of International Sales Talent. Initially, the advertisement specified a maximum of 6-8 years of experience for the job of Line Manager which had subsequently been reduced to a maximum of 2-4 years.

168 Since the prohibition of distinction is directed at both principals/employers and those who mediate between candidates and employers (e.g. recruitment agencies), the recruitment agency *in casu* could not free itself of its legal responsibilities under the AETA. See paragraph 5.9 of Opinion 2006-01.

169 Paragraph 5.8 of Opinion 2006-01. It is recalled from Chapter 3 that the prohibition of indirect discrimination under Article 2(2)(b) EFD does not require that a *group of persons* is disproportionately affected, given that this Article merely refers to 'persons'. On the other hand, Recital No. 15 EFD provides that 'the appreciation of the facts from which it may be inferred →

that, *in casu*, the vexed provisions on job experience not only laid down *minimum* experience requirements but also *maximum* experience requirements. As a consequence, a large group of persons namely, persons with more than 4, or at any rate, 8 years of experience were excluded from the job. This resulted in *prima facie* discrimination against older candidates (such as the applicant). The ETC held that this was not objectively justified: other than the fact that the agency had acted in conformity with the wishes of the principal, no further reasons were advanced to justify the application of experience requirements. The ETC moreover observed that it could not reasonably be maintained that a person with a surplus of relevant work experience is a less adequate, let alone an inadequate, candidate for the job. The ETC concluded an instance of unlawful age distinction.

4.3.3. Education and Vocational Training

In Opinions 2005-235 and 2005-236 the question was whether a University is allowed under the AETA to charge a higher entry fee to students who on 01-09-05 were younger than 30 years old, compared with students who on that date were 30 years or older. Part-time students of younger than 30 years old were charged €1,260 compared with €1,740 for students aged 30 and older (Opinion 2005-235). Similarly, full-time students of younger than 30 years old were charged €1,496 compared with €1,980 for full-time students of 30+ (Opinion 2005-236). Article 1 AETA, in conjunction with Article 5(b) of the Act, prohibits age distinction with respect to providing entry to education directed at the entry to and the functioning in the labour market. According to earlier case law by the Commission the AETA applies to Universities.[170] Differences in treatment in respect of charging an entrance fee fall within the scope of Article 5(b) AETA.[171] Having established a *prima facie* case of direct distinction on grounds of age, the ETC considered the question of justifiability under Article 7(1)(c) AETA. The respondent had indicated that the contested differences in treatment on grounds of age pursued the following aims: (1) securing the accessibility to university education; (2) encouraging students to graduate within a foreseeable time frame; (3) maximising financial resources. In respect of the first-mentioned aim, the respondent had referred to the *travaux préparatoires* to the AETA.[172] These explicitly state that the age classification of 30 years old is contained in the 2000 Statutory Act on Student Grants (*Wet Studiefinanciering*), as well as in the Statutory Act on Higher Education and Academic Research (*Wet op het Hoger Onderwijs en Wetenschappelijk Onderzoek*). The *travaux préparatoires* furthermore indicate that it is desirable to link

that there has been direct or indirect discrimination is a matter for national judicial or other competent authorities, in accordance with rules of national law or practice. Such rules may provide, in particular, for indirect discrimination to be established by any means including on the basis of statistical evidence'. For further in-depth discussion of the concept of indirect discrimination in EC and in Dutch law, I refer to Chapter 3.

170 See, for example, Opinion 2005-96.

171 *Ibid.*

172 *Parliamentary Documents*, II, 2001-2002, 28 170, no. 5, p. 29-30. Also paragraph 4.9 of both Opinion 2005-235 and Opinion 2005-236.

one's right to a student grant, on the one hand, with the obligation to pay a university entrance fee, on the other. In other words, the payment of the lower fee should be limited to those younger than 30 years. According to the government this serves a legitimate aim, namely guaranteeing that all youngsters who have sufficient capabilities to attend university ought to be able to do so, regardless of the financial means of the parents. In the government's view, this falls within the scope of its responsibilities. The Commission agreed that the first-mentioned aim was a legitimate aim,[173] however, it disagreed on the appropriateness of the contested age classification to reach this aim. It considered that charging a higher entry fee to those of 30+ had no impact upon the accessibility to university education for those younger than 30.[174] Moreover, 5 of the 13 Universities in the Netherlands did not differentiate on grounds of age with respect to the entrance fee. The Commission held that the second pursued aim was also legitimate. However, the respondent had been unable to prove that the amount of the entry fee had had an impact upon the pace of graduating. Therefore, the contested age distinction was held to be an inappropriate means for reaching the pursued objectives. The third aim (i.e. maximising financial resources) was held to be an illegitimate aim, given that mere financial considerations cannot in principle by themselves form the ground of justifiability. In light of the foregoing the ETC concluded an instance of unlawful age distinction.

4.3.4. Conditions of Employment and Pension Provision

In Opinion 2004-122 a pension insurance asked the ETC whether it would act in breach of the AETA, if it executed the following two[175] pension schemes:

1. a so-called (mitigated) final salary pension scheme (*gemitigeerde eindloonregeling*) according to which at a certain age an employee's increase in salary would not be taken into account in the calculation of his/her pension;
2. a final salary pension scheme which, once the employee reaches a certain age, would be replaced by a so-called 'indexed'[176] average pay pension scheme (*geïndexeerde middelloonregeling*).

Before proceeding with the analysis of the case at hand it seems useful to explain the general meaning of a 'final salary pension scheme' and of an 'average pay pension scheme'. A final salary pension scheme secures that every year of service entitles the employee to a fixed percentage of the salary (s)he earns when (s)he retires. In practice this means that after 35[177] years of service the employee is entitled to 70%

173 Paragraph 4.10 of both Opinions.

174 Paragraph 4.11 of both Opinions, reference to Opinion 2005-96.

175 The Commission was moreover asked for its Opinion on a third scheme and although it did not differ that much from the other two pension schemes, the ETC considered it necessary to render a separate Opinion on it. See Opinion 2004-123 which shall not be further discussed here.

176 This means that the accumulated pension right increases with the inflation rate.

177 The pension build up in the Netherlands is in current times on average 35, rather than 40 years. I am grateful to Professor Raymond Luja for this point.

of his or her last earned salary. A final salary scheme is, however, disadvantageous for the employer by reason of the following. Every time that an employee's salary increases (e.g. every 5 or 10 years) his or her pension claim also increases with retrospective force. This increase in the employee's pension claim will have to be paid retroactively by the employer, that is to say, for all the preceding years calculated as from the year that the employee entered employment. This is known as the employer's *back service duty* (*backservice verplichting*). Especially when an employee's salary increases considerably and at a relatively high age a final salary pension scheme will be very costly for the employer. In order to mitigate the negative effects flowing from the employer's backservice duty, final salary pension schemes often provide that, from a certain age, an employee's increase in salary will not be taken into account for the purposes of pension calculation. If this is done, we will speak of a 'mitigated final salary pension scheme' (*gematigde eindloonregeling*).

A pension scheme based on an employee's average, rather than final salary, is not characterised by retrospective backservice duties. After all, an employee's pension is not calculated on the basis of the last earned salary but on the basis of the employee's *average* salary throughout his career. Average pay pension schemes are therefore more favourable to employers and less favourable to workers.

In its assessment of the two pension schemes in issue in Opinion 2004-122 the Commission considered as follows. With reference to earlier case law[178] it held that (mitigated) final salary pension schemes which, for the purposes of pension calculation, ignore an employee's increase in salary as from a certain age result in an instance of direct age distinction on grounds of age. The same conclusion applies to the second pension scheme in issue which uses 'age' as a decisive factor in establishing when the final salary pension scheme will be replaced by the 'indexed average pay pension scheme.' The ETC subsequently examined whether the pension schemes in issue could be objectively justified on the basis of Article 7(1)(c) AETA. In this context it first held that it is for the alleged discriminator to come up with an objective justification, and especially with possible alternatives which, in the applicant's view *in casu*, could not be employed in order to reach the pursued objectives. In addition, the ETC itself is entitled to come up with possible alternatives in its assessment of the 'necessity requirement'. Both schemes in issue pursued a twin aim, namely (1) avoiding high pension costs and *(2)* avoiding so-called 'pension promotions' (given the employer's backservice duty). The Commission deemed these aims legitimate: both aims were sufficiently weighty and they corresponded to a real need on the part of the organisation.[179] Moreover, given that both aims could be reached by means of the pension schemes in issue, the 'appropriateness requirement' was also met.[180] The Commission lastly assessed both pension schemes in light of the necessity requirement. A number of non or less-discriminatory alternatives were considered by means of which the pursued aims could also be achieved. For example, (a) the applicant could execute a scheme according to which the maximum pensionable salary would

178 Opinion 2004-46.

179 Paragraph 4.5 of Opinion 2004-122.

180 Paragraph 4.6 of Opinion 2004-122.

be linked with a certain job category; (b) the applicant could also introduce an indexed average pay pension scheme, because such a scheme (as we saw above) does not discriminate on grounds of age; (c) he could moreover establish a final pay pension scheme which, as from a certain maximum salary (rather than as from a certain age) would be replaced by an indexed average pay pension scheme. The applicant had indicated that the last-mentioned alternative would not reduce the employer's costs as a result of back service duties. However, argued the Commission, this will depend on the *level* of the maximum salary which would be employed. The applicant had moreover argued that the alternative under (c) would be likely to result in indirect discrimination against older workers (because they are more likely than younger workers to have reached the applicable maximum salary). However, held the Commission, in the current situation the final salary pension would be replaced by an average pay pension scheme *for every older worker* who had reached a certain age. Hence, the pension scheme as it currently stood resulted in direct age distinction. Per definition this was less beneficial for older workers than a pension scheme which (merely) hit older workers who had reached a certain maximum salary. In other words, the alternative under (c) was considered less discriminatory compared with the pension scheme as it then stood. Yet another alternative (d) would be to introduce a pension scheme which provided that increases in salary would only be taken into account for the purposes of pension calculation up until a certain percentage, or, which specified that the increase in an employee's pensionable salary was set at a maximum percentage. The applicant had indicated that such schemes are relatively costly in practice by reason that they require a lot of administration. However, once again, it was held that mere financial considerations can in principle not uphold a distinction on grounds of age. This will only be different, if the applicant can prove that increased costs result in a disproportionate burden on the part of the organisation.

Given that final salary schemes, which are currently most frequently used,[181] in practice operate to the disadvantage of employers they are increasingly replaced by indexed average pension schemes. As this case shows, it is currently no longer permitted under equal treatment law to mitigate a final salary scheme with reference to 'age'. *In casu*, one of the alternatives suggested by the ETC was to replace the mitigated final salary scheme by an indexed average pay pension scheme. Certainly, this will not be more advantageous for the worker concerned, given that even a mitigated final salary scheme will generate a higher pension compared with an indexed average pay pension scheme. After all, the latter does not at all increase a worker's pension with retroactive force, given that the pension build up takes place per year.

5. Conclusions

In this chapter a comparative law analysis has been made of discrimination on grounds of age in the context of EC and Dutch law. This triggered aspects of cross-

181 This information was gained from the following website: <http://www.orpension.nl/1b2.htm> (last visited on 29 May 2006).

ground, bottom-up and top-down influence although the focus has been on top-down influence. The analysis of the intrinsic logic of age as a ground of discrimination has revealed that age is different from other grounds, in the sense that age can form a rational factor in the decision-making process. In most instances this cannot be said with respect to the other discrimination grounds, unless the substantive equality model is taken as a starting point. Although the usage of 'age' can be rational, differences in treatment on grounds of age can also have the effect of social exclusion and stigmatisation. In this sense 'age' is not dissimilar from other grounds. It is therefore important to distinguish cases in which 'age' classifications result in unlawful discrimination, from those instances in which age constitutes a sound criterion in the decision-making process. This, it has been argued, must be done on the basis of a strict judicial scrutiny test. The courts, rather than the legislator, ought to determine whether a particular act of discrimination meets the requirements of legitimacy, appropriateness and necessity in the context of Article 6(1) EFD. Given the different nature of 'age' compared with other grounds, the half-open model which features both EC and domestic age discrimination law is a proper model for the regulation of discrimination on this ground. The analysis of EC law has paid attention to the way in which the intrinsic nature of 'age' has been converted into the supranational equality law framework. As has been seen, only in respect of age does Community non-discrimination law allow for a justifiability defence in respect of both direct and indirect acts of discrimination. In the analysis of Article 6 EFD emphasis has been placed upon the different geneses of paragraph 1, compared with paragraph 2, of this Article. Whereas the former should be conceived of as an exception to the principle of non-discrimination on grounds of age, Article 6(2) EFD sets a boundary to the Directive's scope of application. Bearing this distinction in mind is important while assessing the conformity of national age discrimination law with Community law. The analysis of the EFD has also shown that (some of) the for 'age' relevant provisions in the Directive can be interpreted as reflecting both an economic and a human rights rationale. The ethical cause of age equality was, however, clearly at the fore in the ECJ's ground-breaking judgment in *Mangold v. Helm.* By holding that the principle of equality on grounds of age is a 'general principle of Community law', and by allowing Mr Mangold to rely directly upon this principle in a private party dispute against Mr Helm, notwithstanding that the deadline for implementation of the Framework Directive had not yet expired, the Court went far beyond its established case law. However, as argued, the effects of Mangold are confined to those provisions in EC Directives which are in fact legal translations of general principles of EC law. While the ECJ was prudent not to grant direct applicability to Article 13 EC, *de facto* this Article was given direct effect via the vehicle of equality as a general principle of EC law. Mangold allows for the conclusion that the right to non-discrimination on grounds of age ought to be regarded as a basic human right, which can only be interfered with if the principles of 'legitimacy', 'appropriateness' and 'necessity' are met.

Subsequent to the analysis of EC law the Dutch legal framework was analysed in light of this. EC law has exercised a great top-down influence upon national law, given that the AETA is largely the result of the implementation of the Framework Directive. While interpreting the AETA in concrete cases the ETC has adopted a strict proportionality test in cases concerning alleged distinctions on grounds of age. By doing so, the Commission acts in conformity with the stance adopted by the ECJ in *Mangold*. It has been illustrated that, prior to the entry into force of the AETA, the Dutch courts had adopted a more deferent approach in cases of age discrimination in the context of Article 1 of the Dutch Constitution and Article 26 ICCPR. The view expressed by the Supreme Court, namely that 'age' is less suspect than other grounds will have to be revised in light of EC law and notably, in light of *Mangold*. In the analysis of the AETA particular attention has been paid to the exceptions in Article 7 and 8 of this Act. In the context of Article 7(1) and 7(2) AETA, it has been argued that the *a priori* declaration by the government that certain acts of age distinction are anyhow 'objectively justified' is neither in conformity with Article 6(1) EFD, nor with the ECJ's judgment in *Mangold*. This means, *inter alia*, that dismissals at the age of 65 may be contrary to EC law, although this will depend upon the application of the objective justification test in the particular case at hand. With respect to Article 8 AETD the Dutch government has transposed the Directive correctly. Like Article 6(2) EFD, Article 8 of the AETA constitutes a limit to the scope of application of the law. Finally, the ETC's case law has been examined in an illustrative fashion. It has *inter alia* been seen that seniority rules have not readily been accepted, however, in light of recent expert research the Commission's stance might be different in the future. It has moreover been illustrated how the exception contained in Article 6(1)(c) EFD may operate in concrete cases in order to avoid inequitable outcomes. The ETC's case law with regard to an employee's pension rights has illustrated the many alternatives which may be employed instead of applying age classifications as a means to reduce costs. However, some of the alternatives suggested by the Commission are far more disadvantageous (albeit non-discriminatory) for workers than the application of 'age' as a factor in the calculation of pensions.

PART V

CONCLUDING OBSERVATIONS

Chapter 10

CONCLUSIONS

1. General Concluding Observations

In this book the emerging equality principle in EC law has been analysed from a multi-layered comparative law perspective. This involved drawing a multi-facetted comparison namely, a 'top-down' comparison, 'bottom-up' comparison, 'cross-country' comparison and 'cross-ground' comparison. Whereas the top-down and bottom-up comparisons formed the hinges of the analysis concerning the interrelationship between EC and domestic law, the cross-country analysis examined how 'equality' and 'non-discrimination' are protected in national law and whether Member States differ in their approach. The cross-ground comparison sought to analyse and compare the nature of the various grounds of discrimination contained in Article 13 EC, with a view to evaluating the regulation by law of discrimination on these grounds. In addition, in the areas of religious and sexual orientation discrimination law, comparisons were drawn between EC and domestic law, on the one hand, and Strasbourg Convention law, on the other.

Clearly, the insertion in 1999 of Article 13 into the EC Treaty has given an enormous impetus to combating 'discrimination' and bringing about 'equality' in the context of Community law. At the same time, it has posed new challenges at different but inter-related levels. In Chapter 2, whose objective it was to provide the necessary context for this research it was explained that Article 13 EC confers on the Community legislator the competence to act in the realms of 'equality' and 'non-discrimination' with respect to the grounds 'sex', 'racial and ethnic origin', 'religion' and 'belief', 'disability', 'age' and 'sexual orientation' whereby due respect is to be given to the principle of attributed powers. It was argued that one of the principal virtues of Article 13 EC is that it strengthens the constitutional (human rights) rationale for equality in EC law. The latter can be contrasted with the economic, or market-based approach to equality. This approach informed the introduction of EC sex discrimination law[1] and EC nationality discrimination law[2] in the early stages of European

1 See especially old Article 119 EC (now Article 141(1) and (2) EC) concerning the principle of equal pay between the sexes.

integration. The economic approach to the principles of equality and non-discrimination rationalises the need for EC non-discrimination law with reference to the effective functioning of the internal market. A constitutional or rights based model aims on the other hand to foster the basic rights of people who are marginalised, excluded or otherwise put at a disadvantage for arbitrary reasons related to a forbidden ground. The adoption of Article 13 EC has meant that the significance and the role of 'equality' and 'non-discrimination' in EC law have prospered markedly quickly. On the basis of Article 13 EC the Community legislator swiftly adopted a number of equality Directives, including the Race Directive[3] and the Employment Framework Directive[4] both of which have had a significant impact on the development of national law.[5] Synergies have furthermore occurred and are likely to continue to occur between the Article 13 EC *acquis*, on the one hand, and EC sex discrimination law, on the other.[6] The discussion in the preceding chapters focused on substantive, rather than procedural issues in equality and non-discrimination law. The various substantive themes were moreover perceived in their appropriate theoretical context. Theoretical insights were given both into the meaning of 'equality' and 'non-discrimination' as legal and philosophical principles and into the different grounds of discrimination contained in Article 13 EC. The analysis showed amongst other things that the elemental nature of a particular ground of discrimination provides information as to the apposite role of the law in addressing acts of discrimination on that ground. As clarified in Chapter 1, the essence of the multi-layered comparison was captured by three main and two minor research questions which will be addresssed in detail below. For the purpose of clarity, I will hereafter call to mind the research questions referred to in Chapter 1 and deal with each of them in a separate fashion. While doing so, the aim will be to draw general overall conclusions, rather than repeating the specific conclusions found at the end of each of the preceding chapters and to which the reader is additionally referred.

2 The principle of non-discrimination on grounds of nationality is contained in Article 12 EC and merely applies to the citizens of the EU. See also Articles 39-42 EC (free movement of workers); Articles 43-48 (freedom of establishment) and Articles 49-55 EG (freedom of service provision) as well as secondary EC law based on these Articles.

3 Council Directive 2000/43/EC of 29 June 2000 implementing the principle of equal treatment between persons irrespective of racial or ethnic origin, *OJ* L 180/22, 19 July 2000.

4 Council Directive 2000/78/EC of 27 November 2000 establishing a general framework for equal treatment in employment and occupation, *OJ* L 303/16, 02 December 2000.

5 Council Directive 2004/113/EC of 13 December 2004 implements the principle of equal treatment between men and women in the areas of access to and supply of goods and services (*OJ* L 373, 21 December 2004). Like the RD and EFD it has been adopted on the basis of Article 13 EC. This Directive goes beyond the scope of employment and has therefore not been discussed in the present book. See generally Chapter 1.

6 See especially also Council Directive 2002/73/EC of 23 September 2002 *OJ* L 269/15, 23 September 2002. This Amended Equal Treatment Directive (AETD) streamlined existing EC sex discrimination law in light of equivalent legal guarantees contained in the RD and EFD. See generally Chapter 2.

2. Conclusions with respect to the Research Questions

Question 1

If, and in what respects has the process of constitutionalisation of equality and non-discrimination in EC law forced changes in domestic equal treatment law and to what degree has this created shifts in domestic approaches and practices? This question concerns 'top-down' effects that can be evidenced in domestic equal treatment laws when comparing their shape pre and post-implementation of EC law.

The mandatory, top-down, influence of EC equal treatment law on domestic law has brought about important changes to both the English and Dutch equality law frameworks. The consequences of top-down influence are both positive and negative in kind. On the positive side is that by virtue of EC law, new legal frameworks have been introduced at the domestic level offering protection from discrimination in employment on grounds previously not covered (see Chapters 6-9). The constitutionalised nature of 'equality' and 'non-discrimination' in EU law is *inter alia* reflected in the fact that the list of discrimination grounds protected in EC law currently goes beyond 'sex' and 'nationality'. As this book has argued, moral, rather than economic concerns were at the basis of the adoption of Article 13 EC and the RD and EFD. In English law the expansion of the list of grounds at the supranational level has led to the adoption of new legal frameworks governing discrimination in employment on grounds of religion and belief and sexual orientation. It is noteworthy that the development does not stop there. As of 1 October 2006, age discrimination in the employment sector will be prohibited too. The research showed that but for supranational equality law a number of disadvantaged groups would currently be short of legal protection in English statutory anti-discrimination law Dutch law, for its turn, has been enriched with new legal frameworks outlawing acts of distinction (*onderscheid*) on grounds of disability and chronic disease and age. Admittedly, the need for a statutory prohibition of discrimination on grounds of disability and age had been acknowledged in Dutch political circles before the adoption of Article 13 EC and the EFD. This therefore mitigates the top-down influence of EC on Dutch law in the aforementioned areas.With respect to Dutch disability discrimination law the EFD has both had an accelerating and a regressive impact on the development of national law. On the one hand, the DETA has been adopted sooner than would have been the case in the absence of a supranational prohibition of discrimination on grounds of disability. On the other hand, the Act's originally foreseen scope was reduced in the process of implementation of the EFD, given that the Directive imposed less requirements. A beneficial effect of EC top-down influence has occurred in the area of the law on harassment.

Chapter 4 illustrated that the prohibition of (sexual) harassment in EC law extends beyond the comparative model of equality to the benefit of a 'deontological'[7] approach. The latter, unlike the former, accords a substantive connotation to

[7] Quinn 2004.

'equality' in the sense that it does not accentuate the fact that a ground-related disadvantage is to be evaluated with reference to the disadvantage suffered by a legal comparator. Post-implementation of EC law the freestanding approach to harassment has been introduced in both of the domestic legal systems considered. The autonomous approach to (sexual) harassment in EC law has, however, had a particularly constructive effect on the legal approach and interpretation regarding this concept in English statutory law. The reasons for this will become apparent hereafter. With respect to Dutch law it is worth noting that the case law of the Equal Treatment Commission before the implementation of the RD and the EFD, required that an applicant proves ground-related harassment on the basis of (by the law) alternatively imposed conditions. Post-implementation, however, a complainant must prove cumulative conditions in order to establish a case of ground-related harassment (except for 'sexual harassment'). The introduction of cumulative conditions is to be criticised for constituting a breach of the Directives' non-regression clauses. As noted earlier, the independent (freestanding) approach to harassment in EC law has been of particular benefit to the approach in English law. As was explained in Chapter 4, prior to the transposition of the EFD into national law, both the English courts and the Dutch Equal Treatment Commission (ETC) analysed alleged instances of (ground-related) harassment on the basis of a direct discrimination complaint. However, differently from the ETC, which has given little importance to the need for drawing a legal comparison in these cases, the judicial House of Lords has taken an opposite stance. Like in ordinary direct discrimination proceedings the Law Lords have insisted on the 'comparative exercise' in harassment cases with the effect of thwarting the effective legal protection from this social mischief. Post implementation of EC law the need for drawing a comparison in ground-related harassment cases in employment has largely been abolished under English statutory anti-discrimination law. This has not only enhanced the successfulness of proving a claim of harassment. At a broader level it has meant that English statutory anti-discrimination law which was traditionally characterised by a comparative equality model has been enriched with a freestanding approach to the non-discrimination principle.

Another advantageous effect of EC top-down influence has been the simpli*fication of indirect discrimination law which, once again, has had a particularly* positive effect on English law (see Chapter 3). The major lacuna in English indirect discrimination law, the '*Perera* loophole',[8] has largely been abolished by virtue of EC top-down influence. As a consequence both absolute bars and (mere) job preferences can currently be challenged in legal proceedings. This was already the case in Dutch indirect discrimination law. All in all, English indirect discrimination law reflects a flexible stance post implementation of EC law.

In addition to the positive effects of EC top-down influence a number of negative consequences have to be mentioned. In the first place, and as touched on earlier, the top-down influence of EC law can both have an accellerating and a regressive

8 *Perera v. Civil Service Commission & the Department of Customs & Excise* [1982] IRLR 147 (EAT); [1983] IRLR 166 (CA).

effect on the development of domestic non-discrimination law. This was illustrated in Chapter 8 in the context of the discussion of Dutch disability discrimination law whose originally foreseen scope was reduced in the process of implementation of EC disability discrimination law. Secondly, a major downside effect of top-down influence has been 'fragmentation'. Despite the EC Commission's green paper entitled 'Equality and Non-Discrimination in an Enlarged European Union', according to which '[t]he adoption of Article 13 [EC] reflected the growing recognition of the need to develop a coherent and integrated approach towards the fight against discrimination'[9] this book has highlighted the following paradox: the quest by supranational law for a convergence of legal standards in the areas of equality and non-discrimination *across* the Member States risks resulting in a disruption of the internal coherence of the legal framework *within* a Member State. Nothing suggests that similar effects do not also occur in areas other than equal treatment law. The corrosive effects of EC top-down influence have become particularly visible in the context of English anti-discrimination law. The latter is featured by a speckled framework due to the *de minimis* approach adopted by the UK government to the process of implementation of EC equality Directives. English anti-discrimination law has therefore developed in an unsystematic fashion. Unlike Dutch law, which has emerged out of a Constitutional equality guarantee, English anti-discrimination law has been the result of either (top-down imposed) EC law or the wish to redress a particular social problem in an instant fashion. As this book explains, the transposition of the RD, the EFD and the AETD in English law has occurred by means of governmental Regulations, rather than by way of Acts of Parliament. In practice this means that implementation of the relevant EC norms may not go beyond that what is strictly required by EC law.[10] The method of implementation by Regulations has created schisms in legal protection from discrimination in the context of English race discrimination law. Post implementation of EC law the RRA 1976 as amended is characterised by a dual approach, given that the discrimination grounds 'colour' and 'nationality' are still governed by the law (including the case law) as it stood pre-implementation of the RD. In contrast, the other grounds that are covered by the RRA (i.e. 'race', 'ethnic origin' and 'national origin') have become subject to the law as it stands post-implementation of EC law. The latter provides a much more beneficial framework. This was illustrated in Chapters 3 and 4 in the legal analysis of indirect discrimination and harassment, respectively. In summary, depending on the exact ground of discrimination on which a complaint is based the RRA 1976 as it stands post-implementation of the RD provides more or less judicial protection from discrimination. This scenario must be criticised as a matter of principle, given that the aforementioned divergences in legal protection cannot be explained with reference to rational factors (such as, for example, the different nature of different grounds of discrimination). The patchy framework of English race discrimination law furthermore complicates claims of intersectional discrimination, i.e. claims of discrimination on two or more protected grounds.

9 *'Equality and Non-Discrimination in an Enlarged European Union'*, Green Paper, European Commission, Employment and Social Affairs, May 2004, p. 10.

10 See Chapter 2.

Further (irrational) irregularities were found in the area of English positive action law discussed in Chapter 5. The discussion revealed that positive action law with respect to 'race' and 'sex' is dominated by the principle of symmetry. The latter leaves little room for the adoption of positive action measures. This was contrasted with positive action law in the context of the grounds 'religion' and 'belief' and 'sexual orientation', which reflects a more flexible stance. The irregularities in English positive action law are due to the absence of a holistic and thorough approach to the process of implementation of the Directives. With a view to creating a uniform framework, English positive action law with respect to 'race' and 'sex' ought to have been streamlined with reference to the equivalent provisions in the R&B and S.O. Regulations.

Corrosive effects as a result of the transposition of EC law have been much less in the context of Dutch law, notwithstanding that separate equal treatment Acts have been adopted for the grounds 'disability', 'chronic disease' and 'age' (see Chapters 8 and 9, respectively). Unlike the UK legislator, the Dutch legislator has rendered EC equality norms applicable in areas where this was not strictly required. Put differently, EC law was 'voluntarily' applied in areas that fall outside the scope of EC but within the scope of Dutch equality law. This has meant that, unlike the sitation in English law, no grounds of discrimination were carved out from the implementation process. For the sake of legal consistency, clarity and fairness, and in order to optimise legal protection from (intersectional) discrimination, the UK legislator should have adopted a similar approach. This implies that implementation of the Directives should have occurred by means of Statutory Acts of Parliament. Another option would be to merge existing English non-discrimination law into a single equality Act, whereby room should be left for tailor-made approaches and interpretations for different grounds of discrimination. This point will be addressed in further detail below in the discussion of the cross-ground comparison. Similarly, the legal guarantees contained in the Dutch DETA and AETA should be transferred to the general equal treatment framework contained in the GETA (which is currently contemplated by the Dutch government).[11]

Question 2

To what extent do national legal approaches differ from one another pre and post-implementation of EC law? This question involves a 'cross-country' comparison of English and Dutch equal treatment law, against the background of supranational equality standards.

Before providing a concrete answer to the second research question it seems useful to submit a number of observations of a more general kind, so as to put the question in context. It is clear that the bulk of EC equal treatment law is captured by EC Directives, rather than by EC primary law or EC Council Regulations. This has the effect in practice that it remains within the Member States' discretion to choose the most appropriate form of implementation of the various provisions contained in Equality Directives, although due attention has to be paid to the objectives pursued by supranational

11 This was touched on in Chapter 2.

EC law. This explains why even post-implementation of EC law national approaches can (and are likely to) differ from one another. Given that issues of 'non-discrimination' and 'equality' are closely linked to the sociocultural tradition in a given State (which often is historically determined), including prevailing views on diversity, multiculturalism and tolerance, the method of working with Directives is considered positive. This is so, for it strikes a fair balance between the sovereignty of the Member States in regulating a sensitive area of social and employment policy, on the one hand, and the goals pursued by EC equality and non-discrimination law, on the other. Furthermore, that the Member States have a certain margin of policy discretion with respect to the implementation of EC equal treatment Directives does justice to the divergent legal contexts within which domestic equal treatment law ought to be appreciated. As illustrated in Chapter 2, Dutch equal treatment law has been the result of a legislative elaboration of the Constitutional equality guarantees. English non-discrimination law on the other hand has flourished in the context of employment law, given the absence in the UK of a written Constitution.

One of the striking differences between English and Dutch law in the areas of equality and non-discrimination is that the former, more than the latter, operates in a framework of comparative equality. The highest courts have consistently emphasised the need for drawing a comparison with a legal equivalent in English anti-discrimination law proceedings. Pre-implementation of EC law, the comparative equality law approach in combination with a grammatical interpretation of the statutes has led to particularly unsatisfactory outcomes in harassment and sexual orientation discrimination cases (see Chapters 4 and 7, respectively). In line with the Continental legal tradition judicial interpretation of equality and non-discrimination the Netherlands has adopted a more teleological approach which has resulted in less emphasis on the need for drawing a legal comparison in equal treatment, including harassment cases.

Among the most noticeable differences between statutory English and Dutch non-discrimination law is the legal approach that these legal systems adopt to discrimination on grounds of disability. English disability discrimination law rests upon an asymmetrical framework. As a result of this the legal framework only offers protection from discrimination to the group of disabled persons to the exclusion of persons who have been discrimination against on grounds of *not having* a disability (i.e. non-disabled persons). This means in practice that the group of disabled persons is in need of being legally defined. As illustrated in Chapter 8, in English law the legal definition of disability has been dominated by the tenets of the medical model of disability, rather than by the social model of disability. The medical model argues that it is the individual impairment itself which hampers the participation of disabled persons in social life, including employment. In contrast, the social model takes the view that the source of disability-based disadvantage is to be found in the interaction between the individual impairment, on the one hand, and the societal reactions to that impairment, on the other. The (case law) analysis of English disability discrimination law shows that many potential victims of discrimination on this ground have been and remain unprotected by the legal framework. This, I argue, is not so much caused by the asymmetrical framework in itself, but rather by the legal interpretation of this framework on the basis of the medical model of disability. Put differently, an asymmetrical framework of disability discrimination law is capable of affording adequate protection from disability discrimination provided that it is informed by the philosophy underpinning the social model of disability. Alternatively, the legislator may opt for the adoption of a symmetrical model of disability discrimination law. Such a model offers protection from discrimination to both disabled and non-disabled persons, that is to say, to both persons who have been discriminated against on grounds of having and not having a disability. In practice this means that in order to rely on the protective scope of the law, an applicant need not first prove his or her disability. This is the applicable approach adopted in the Netherlands where disability equal treatment law is short of a legal definition of disability. In general, the fact that disability need not be legally defined has the advantage in practice that the judicial analysis in discrimination law proceedings is immediately focused on the act of discrimination, rather than on the (preliminary) question whether the applicant is 'sufficiently disabled' to qualify for legal protection. The analysis in Chapter 8 showed that the Dutch approach with respect to discrimination on grounds of disability is more flexible and inclusive compared to the English approach, although it bears the disadvantage that positive action measures in favour of disabled persons, including quota, can be challenged in judicial proceedings by non-disabled persons (see Chapter 5). A further difference between Dutch and English disability discrimination law is that the latter is short of a definition of 'indirect discrimination'. The English DDA 1995 has traditionally approached instances of indirect disability discrimination on the basis of the legal duty to make reasonable adjustments. This has not changed post-implementation of the EFD. It is submitted that the omission on the part of the UK government to transpose the concept of indirect discrimination of the EFD into domestic disability discrimination law constitutes a breach of the government's obligations under EC law. The Directive requires the Member States to insert into their legal frameworks both a prohibition of indirect discrimination and a duty to make reasonable accommodation. Both concepts reflect different strategies to achieving equality, in the sense that the former seeks to tackle underlying power structures, whereas the latter proffers an individualised solution for the disabled person concerned. The conceptual differences between indirect discrimination and the duty to make reasonable adjustments ('accommodations') were discussed in Chapter 3 and Chapter 8.

Differences between English and Dutch law were also discerned in Chapter 6 in the context of the discrimination grounds religion and belief. Although no English case law exists at present regarding complaints of discrimination arisen under the R&B Regulations, case law with respect to 'religion' and 'belief' has emerged in the contexts of unfair dismissal and human rights law. The discussion of so-called 'time off from work cases' exhibited the tensions between the opposing values of contractual *v.* religious freedom. In English law, the former has trumped the latter which, as I will note below, contrasts with the approach in the Netherlands. The English approach parallels the stance adopted by the Strasbourg Convention institutions (i.e. the Commission and the ECtHR) in equivalent cases. Most recently, in *Kosteski*,[12] the Strasbourg Court held that an employee's unauthorised absence from work in order

12 Kosteski v. the former Yugoslav Republic of Macedonia EHRC 2006, 73 (ECtHR).

to celebrate a religious feast is, in principle, not protected under Article 9 ECHR. The Dutch Supreme Court has adopted an approach that, in the view of the present author, correlates better with the fundamental rights character of the freedom of religion. In Dutch law an employee's request for time off from work may only be refused, if abiding by the request would lead to a serious disturbance of the state of affairs at work. Hence, unlike in English law, an employee's right to freedom of religion has not been made dependent on his acceptance to quit the job. The Dutch ETC has followed the same stance as that adopted by the Supreme Court in its interpretation of the prohibition of discrimination on grounds of religion contained in the GETA 1994. The analysis of sexual orientation discrimination law in Chapter 7 highlighted *inter alia* the contentious issue of according employment-related benefits on the condition of being married. In Dutch law this constitutes direct discrimination on grounds of marital status, a ground which is explicitly covered by the GETA 1994. Prior to the opening up of same-sex marriage in the Netherlands in 2001, the Dutch ETC also accepted that direct discrimination on grounds of marriage simultaneously constitutes indirect discrimination on grounds of sexual orientation, given that the marriage requirement has a disproportionate impact on same-sex couples. This approach has not been followed in the English S.O. Regulations which form the legal transposition of the EFD as far as the ground 'sexual orientation' is concerned. In their original format, the Regulations provided explicitly that the prevention or the restriction of access to a benefit by reference to marital status was *not* unlawful. Since December 2005, however, the legislation has been partially amended with the effect that employers have to afford equal treatment to an employee in a civil partnership compared with a married employee. This was discussed in Chapter 7.

Given that at the time of writing, English law was short of a prohibition of age discrimination law in employment no 'cross-country' comparison was made in Chapter 9. The legal comparison of English and Dutch age discrimination law is therefore still in need of future research.

Question 3

What are the intrinsic values underlying the different grounds of discrimination that are covered in this book? Do these values differ from one another? If so, what consequences do or should such differences have for the regulatory approach of 'equality' and 'non-discrimination' in relation to these different grounds? ('cross-ground' comparison).

(A) Preliminary Observations

Each of the chapters contained in Part IV regarding, respectively, 'religion' and 'belief' (Chapter 6), 'sexual orientation' (Chapter 7), 'disability' (Chapter 8) and 'age' (Chapter 9) started off with a theoretical analysis concerning the underlying values of the different grounds of discrimination considered. The time has now come to present an integrated overview thereof ('cross-ground' comparison). This will be done under section (B) hereafter. The synthesised analysis of the values of different grounds sheds light on the question why the law does or should adopt different approaches to 'equality' and 'non-discrimination' for different target groups. It is submitted that the intrinsic nature of the different discrimination grounds is or should be instructive to the choices of legislators and policy-makers when framing anti-discrimination law. The link between the nature of the grounds, on the one hand, and the design of equal treatment law, on the other, will be explored in greater detail in section (C) hereafter.

(B) Comparing the Elemental Nature of Different Grounds: an Integrated Overview

As argued in Chapter 6, unlike the discrimination grounds 'race', 'ethnicity' and 'gender', the grounds 'religion' and 'belief' do not express a putative status but rather a conscious adherence to a process of thought that is often shared with others. It has been argued that 'religion' and 'belief' can be important earmarks of a person's (moral) identity and conscience and that they bear a great impact on intra-community relations. Hence, these grounds of discrimination cannot be explained with reference to immutability or in terms of biological factors. Rather, and as argued by Schiek, these grounds reflect a 'chosen lifestyle'[13] which, is was stressed, goes (far) beyond a simple preference. With reference to this last point one can easily draw an analogy with 'sexual orientation' which, like 'religion' and 'belief', is a 'choice-ground' that, however, goes beyond a mere preference and which triggers issues of a person's way of life and his identity. The intrinsic nature of 'religion', 'belief' and 'sexual orientation' explains why the right to non-discrimination with respect to these grounds embraces both the so-called '*forum internum*' and '*forum externum*', i.e. the right *to have* a particular religion/belief/sexual orientation and the right *to act* in accordance therewith (although clearly, a person may equally choose to hide his or her religious or sexual preference/identity). The foregoing makes clear that an analogy can be drawn between the grounds religion and belief and sexual orientation. These discrimination grounds also intersect in a 'negative' way in the sense that these grounds often compete with each other in legal proceedings. In other words, the legal claim to conscience and identity by a religious believer often infringes on the rights of sexual minorities and *vice versa*. The application of anti-discrimination law in concrete cases therefore calls for a balancing exercise of competing priorities.

The aforementioned distinction between the *forum internum* and *forum externum* cannot be made with respect to the other discrimination grounds listed in Article 13 EC. Another characteristic of the grounds 'religion' and 'belief' is that they may impede a worker from being available for a particular job, for example, by reason of worship or praying duties. In this respect these two grounds of discrimination resemble the grounds 'sex', more specifically 'pregnancy' given that a pregnant worker is equally (temporarily) unavailable for (paid) labour, and 'disability'. Furthermore, the aforementioned grounds as well as the ground age can bear an impact on (typical) job performance.[14] A contrast can be made in this respect with the grounds 'sexual orientation' and 'race' which hardly ever bear an impact on the availability for work or on the manner in which the work is performed. In this sense these grounds can be purged purged relatively easy from the (employer's) decision-making process,

13 Schiek 2002.

14 Waddington and Bell 2003.

whereas the grounds religion and belief, sex, disability and age call for taking into account material differences between persons.

In Chapter 7 it was argued that the ground 'sexual orientation' has a close relationship with privacy rights. However, as rightfully argued by Sottiaux[15] a mere focus by the law on privacy issues in relation to sexual orientation fails to foster the emancipation of sexual minorities.

In Chapter 8, the elementary nature of 'disability' was considered. A person's individual impairment could be analogised with 'sex' (being male/female) and 'race' (being e.g. black or white) in the sense that they all share an (often) uncontrollable character.[16] On the other hand, given the fact that the real cause of disability-based disadvantage is not so much the individual *impairment*, but rather the interaction between the impairment, on the one hand, and the societal reactions to it, on the other, disability is in fact a *'social construct'*. This means that 'disability' is often *created* by the disabling attitudes of others (rather than by the impairment as such). In Chapter 8, the medical and social models of disability were discussed. The medical model argues that it is the (medical) impairment *in se* that hinders a disabled person's participation in social life. This model therefore 'individualises' the locus of disability-based disadvantage in the sense that the problems that disabled persons face in daily life are attributed to a medical condition. This can be contrasted with the philosophy underlying the social model. The latter stresses the intrinsic link between the impairment *and* the setup of society, which fails to accommodate the different needs of disabled persons (compared with non-disabled people or with people with a different disability). For example, in the context of work, the notion of 'standard' job performance is in fact dominated by the notions of 'normality' and 'ableism' which place disabled persons at a disadvantage. Disability based discrimination is often systemic, given that the (unconscious) insistence by society on 'normality' prevents a disabled person from exposing her real merit and capabilities.[17] Disability therefore calls for a 'difference' approach to equality. This lies at the heart of the legal duty to make 'reasonable accommodation'. In Chapter 8 it was also stressed that 'disability' is a heterogeneous notion. This brings with it that the group of disabled persons cannot easily be established. Thus, as argued by Hendriks, 'disability' entails problems of demarcation i.e. of defining who is 'in' and who is 'out'.[18] Hence, unlike the case with other groups that are defined by a protected status (e.g. women or black persons) feelings of solidarity are not always present among disabled persons.[19] In short, unlike, e.g. 'sex' and 'race', 'disability' is not a fixed category which as a concequence hampers feelings of *group identity*.

15 Sottiaux 2003.

16 Although clearly, and in this sense 'disability' differs from 'race' and 'sex' (save gender-reassignment), a disabled person can become non-disabled as a result of medical treatment and rehabilitation. See Chapter 8. In this sense, 'disability' is also a fluid concept just like 'age' (and to a lesser extent 'sexual orientation' and 'religion').

17 Quinn 2004.

18 Hendriks 2000.

19 Bickenbach 1999.

The intrinsic values of 'age' were expounded in Chapter 8. On the one hand, the discussion showed that, perceived from the viewpoint of formal equality, 'age' arguably more than is the case with other grounds can be a rational factor in the decision-making process. In light of this, academic commentary has shown that 'age' is often not conceived as a suspect ground of discrimination. This view is also endorsed by those who favour the 'life-cycle argument' according to which age classifications are more acceptable than categorisations on other grounds, given that rights which cannot be exercised in current times can be enjoyed later, and *vice versa*. This is so, given that 'age' is not 'fixed' but self-changing. On the other hand, like any other ground of discrimination, 'age' classifications can result in social exclusion and stigmatisation. Like 'disability', 'age' often obscures 'merit'.[20] Moreover, like 'disability', 'age' might prevent a person from doing particular work in a standard way or from doing it altogether. This might be caused by biological factors, however, it can also be the result of the interaction of ageing and environmental attitudes. With reference to the intrinsic logic of 'age' it was argued that the legal analysis of age discrimination warrants judicial vigilance. Judicial scrutiny exercises may be carried out differently in the context of age discrimination, compared to other grounds, but should not be characterised by less concern.

(C) *The Nature of the Grounds and the Design and Interpretation of Equal Treatment Law*

At various junctures it was highlighted that inconsistencies in the regulatory framework of equality and non-discrimination can be rational in the sense that they can be explained with reference to the intrinsic nature of different grounds. In the above (under *B*) an amalgamated (theoretical) analysis was presented of the characteristics of the different grounds of discrimination considered ('cross-ground' comparison). Hereafter, a link will be established between these characteristics, on the one hand, and their implications for the legal regulation or interpretation of the equality principle, on the other. It was argued at various occasions that the underlying values of different grounds of discrimination have been or should be instructive to the design of (both EC and domestic) anti-discrimination law.

First, as shown in Chapter 3, the regulatory approach adopted by the EC legislator to the prohibition of indirect discrimination in the Article 13 EC Directives has changed compared to the hitherto existing legislative approach to indirect sex discrimination (based on Article 141 EC). This regulatory shift was explained with reference to the cross-ground comparison. The theoretical discourse on indirect discrimination showed that this concept correlates with group-justice, in contrast to direct discrimination, which reflects the tenets of individual justice. The group-rationale of indirect discrimination has, however, been undermined in the legislative definitions of this concept contained in the Article 13 EC Directives, as well as in the AETD.[21] In

20 See the work by Quinn 2004.

21 As discussed in Chapter 3 the definition of indirect sex discrimination in the AETD was streamlined with the definitions of this concept in the RD and EFD for reasons of legal consistency, rather than for principled grounds.

contrast with the legislative definition of 'indirect discrimination' enshrined in the Burden of Proof Directive, which reflects a statistical evidence approach to proving 'disparate impact', the RD, EFD and AETD have softened this approach in light of the following. Unlike the ground 'sex', which can be captured easily by statistical data, this is not the case for 'disability' and 'sexual orientation', given the intrinsic nature of these grounds. As stated earlier, disability is a heterogeneous (and sometimes fluid) concept and therefore the group of disabled persons cannot be discerned easily. The same applies to 'sexual orientation' as a ground of discrimination, which is not only fluid but often also hidden. The latter ground shows clear links with privacy matters, which explains that statistical data concerning this ground cannot readily be collected. As far as the grounds 'race' and 'ethnicity' are concerned some Member States furthermore regard the collection of statistical data with respect to these grounds a racist act in itself. All in all, the cross-ground comparison has shed light on the reasons for the introduction of a new legislative definition of indirect discrimination in EC law. A negative effect of the redefined approach to indirect discrimination has been that the theoretical foundations of this concept have been eroded. There is currently no cognitive link between the theoretical premises of 'indirect discrimination', and the formulation of this concept by positive EC equality law. It is argued that the group rationale of indirect discrimination could and should have been preserved in EC equal treatment law, given that proof of 'disparate impact' can occur by means other than statistics. Put differently, from a conceptual point of view the legislative approach to indirect discrimination in the RD, EFD and AETD reflects a wrong stance, for the departure from 'statistics' has falsely been equated to a departure from 'group-justice'.

Secondly, the cross-ground comparison leads to the conclusion that some discrimination grounds flourish well in a formal equality law framework, whereas others require a 'difference' approach. 'Sexual orientation' and 'race'/'ethnicity', for example, can be ignored relatively often in the decision-making process, in the sense that both grounds hardly ever bear an impact on the worker's job performance or on his or her availability for work. As mentioned before, in this respect the afore mentioned grounds can be contrasted with 'disability', 'religion'/'belief', 'sex' and 'age' which, to a greater or lesser extent, demand the decision-maker to take account of relevant differences. Arguably, the substantive equality approach is needed most in the context of disability discrimination law. The social model argues correctly that disability-based disadvantage is often the result of environmental attitudes, which ignore the different position of disabled people. It was argued in Chapter 8, with reference to the work by Fredman that the tenets of the social model of disability correspond with the philosophy underpinning the substantive approach to 'equality'. In order to render disability discrimination law effective in practice, law and policy-makers, as well as the courts, should frame and/or interpret disability discrimination law on the basis of a substantive equality paradigm. Only in this way can the law accommodate 'difference', and can it expose the merit and capabilities of disabled persons in the labour market. The substantive equality approach is clearly present in both EC and domestic disability equal treatment laws, which impose a duty upon employers to make reasonable accommodations for disabled persons. The latter duty is, however, absent in the law governing discrimination on grounds of 'religion' and 'belief', as well as 'age'. We saw that these grounds of discrimination may equally bear an impact on a person's performance of a job and/or on his or her availability for labour.[22] Case law in the Netherlands indicates that the prohibition of indirect discrimination has played a vital role in the creation of religious pluralism in the workplace. In other words, in the absence of a reasonable accommodation duty, the accommodation of religious difference could also be achieved on the basis of an indirect discrimination approach. By means of judicial creativity, the duty to accommodate could even be read in the legal prohibition of indirect discrimination, namely when interpreting the 'necessity' element of the 'objective justification' test (for cases of *prima facie* indirect discrimination). 'Necessity' requires that the aim(s) pursued by a *prima facie* indirectly discriminatory measure cannot be reached by other, non-discriminatory or less discriminatory means that could include 'reasonable accommodation'. At the same time, however, the successfulness of the prohibition of indirect discrimination in bringing about diversity can be relative. This largely depends on whether the courts are indeed willing to adopt a strict scrutiny test while assessing 'objective justification'. Furthermore, the willingness of the courts to foster religious diversity is closely connected to the prevailing socio-cultural climate in the particular State concerned. This point will be taken further in the answer to research question no. 5 hereafter.

Thirdly, the intrinsic values of the discrimination ground 'age' have induced the Community legislator to frame the prohibition of discrimination on this ground on the basis of an 'open' model of anti-discrimination law. Hence, the EC and domestic law approach to age discrimination is conceptually different from that adopted with respect to the other grounds of discrimination contained in Article 13 EC, which are all governed by a 'closed' framework. It is submitted that the different regulatory approach to age discrimination adopts a proper stance. In Chapter 9 it was argued that 'age', more than other grounds of discrimination frequently forms a rational factor in the decision-making process of (e.g.) an employer. At the same time, it was, however, acknowledged that discrimination on grounds of age could result in stigmatisation and exclusion. With a view to reconciling the at times innocuous and suspect nature of age classifications the courts should be granted room to review both direct and indirect acts of age discrimination on a case-by-case basis. This should be done on the basis of strict scrutiny, so as to reflect the constitutionalised nature of 'equality' in contemporary EC law.

Clearly, and as already indicated, the cross-ground comparison also sheds light on the judicial interpretation and application of the concept of equality with respect to different grounds of discrimination. In the absence of (sufficient) case law on the Article 13 EC Directives it is currently unclear whether the ECJ will interpret the principles of equality and non-discrimination differently for different target groups. This question is therefore in need of future research. In Chapter 5 it was, for example, questioned whether the approach adopted by the ECJ in positive action cases for women sets an appropriate example for the interpretation of future equivalent cases in the context of other grounds of discrimination. The analysis of Dutch

22 Bell and Waddington 2003.

positive action law indicated that the ETC in the Netherlands has extrapolated the judicial boundaries set by the ECJ in positive action cases regarding 'sex' to similar cases regarding 'race' and 'ethnicity'. Nonetheless, the ECJ may decide in future cases that the legal limits of positive action measures for women are different compared to the legal limits of similar measures that are adopted in favour of other disadvantaged groups. The decision on this issue will depend on the degree of disadvantage suffered by different out-groups, which can be measured by sociological research. Furthermore, if the ECJ decides that, as I argued, the EFD applies asymmetrically in relation to 'disability' positive action measures for disabled persons cannot be legally challenged. This would match with the approach adopted by English disability discrimination law which, as illustrated, is centred on the principle of 'asymmetry'.

It was argued in Chapter 6 that the Court's role in religious discrimination proceedings should be to foster religious diversity, with a view to accommodating the needs of members of different religious groups. While deciding on religious disputes in the context of public life the Court should, however, not lose sight of divergent interpretations across the Member States as to the apposite relationship between religion and the State. How to reconcile 'secularism' and 'religion' should rather be a matter for the national (constitutional) courts. The latter are in a better position than the ECJ to assess the particular case in its proper socio-cultural and historical context.

A dignity approach to equality should be informative to the Court's case law in sexual orientation disputes. It was illustrated in Chapter 7 that prior to the adoption of the EFD the ECJ could deal with sexual orientation discrimination complaints merely in the context of European *sex* discrimination law. The Court's case law on sexual orientation discrimination was flawed due to the ECJ's focus on the wrong legal equivalent as well as its subsidiary (deferent) stance. This has been contrasted with the ECJ's case law on gender reassignment complaints which reflects a human rights and dignity approach.

The Framework Directive must be appraised for reflecting a 'difference', rather than 'sameness' approach in relation to the ground 'disability'. As argued in Chapter 8, only a substantive equality approach will be capable of counteracting the dominant norm of 'normality', which hinders the participation of disabled persons in employment. Already prior to the implementation of the Framework Directive the English courts had acknowledged that the DDA 1995 could not be treated *in pari materiae* with the SDA 1975 and the RRA 1976, which are both moulded in a formal equality framework. It is argued that in deciding on disability discrimination complaints, the ECJ and the domestic courts ought to focus on the act of discrimination rather than on the medical impairment. Hence, the social rather than medical model of disability should be instructive to the judicial interpretation of disability discrimination disputes. The obstructive effects of the medical model of disability-based disadvantage were highlighted with reference to English law. This point will be taken further hereafter in the analysis of Question no. 4 (regarding 'bottom-up' influence).

As was earlier indicated, 'age' is more often than other grounds a rational factor in the decision-making process. This, however, should not lessen the strictness of judicial review in age discrimination cases. A strict judicial scrutiny approach featured the ECJ's first case on age discrimination law. In *Mangold v. Helm* the Court held that the principle of age discrimination is a general principle of Community law the breach of which requires a high threshold for justification. *In casu*, the general principle of equality in respect of age could be directly invoked by a private individual (*Mangold*) against another private actor (*Helm*), regardless of the fact that at the material time the deadline for implementation of the Framework Directive had not expired. It was argued in Chapter 9 that via the route of equality as a general principle of EC law the Court granted a *de facto* (not *legal*) direct effect to Article 13 EC. The ECJ's stance in *Mangold* corresponds with the constitutionalised nature of equality and non-discrimination at the EU level which warrants that these principles go beyond the aims of market integration (as argued in Chapter 2). Moreover, the *Mangold* judgment is also interesting from the perspective of 'cross-fertilisation'. *In casu*, the ECJ's objective justification test designed in the context of indirect sex discrimination law cross-fertilised into the realm of direct age discrimination law. Whether such a cross-fertilisation of standards will also occur in other realms of the law is currently not known, given the lack of relevant case law.

The foregoing portrayal concludes the reflection on the above three major research questions of this book. In addition, this book considered two minor research questions[23] which will hereafter be dealt with.

Question 4

Has EC equal treatment law been inspired, or should it be inspired in the future, by (long-standing) national approaches and practices? This question involves a 'bottom-up' analysis of EC equal treatment law in light of domestic law ('bottom-up' comparison).

The interaction between supranational and national equality law extends beyond the conventional top-down influence. It was argued that the shaping of supranational equality standards has been, or could be, equally influenced by prevailing national approaches and practices. EC equal treatment law can be 'bottom-up' influenced both at the stage of law making and in the process of judicial interpretation of the legal framework by the ECJ. Chapter 3 illustrated a clear example of the influence of domestic law on EC law at the level of the law-making process, namely when the EC legislator introduced a second justification defence for *prima facie* instances of indirect disability discrimination. The discussion showed that, in addition to the conventional 'objective justification' defence (Article 2(2)(b)(i) EFD), *prima facie* acts of indirect discrimination on grounds of disability can be justified by making 'reasonable accommodation' (Article 2(2)(b)(ii) EFD). With reference to the legislative history of the Framework Directive, it was argued that the introduction of this second possibility for justification has *not* been the result of a principled approach adopted by the EC legislator, but rather of 'bottom-up' pressure exercised by the

23 The reasons why the two questions to be addressed in the main text to follow are only minor research questions have been outlined in Chapter 1 and at the outset of Part IV. They will not be repeated at this juncture.

UK government in the process of negotiation that led to the adoption of the Framework Directive. By doing so, the government presumably aimed to protect its own legislative interests, namely that it intended to preserve the hitherto applicable approach in English disability discrimination law. After all, both pre and post-implementation of EC law, English disability discrimination law was and is short of a prohibition of indirect discrimination. Instead it focuses on the 'duty to make reasonable adjustments'. Arguably, where the U.K. government called for an insertion of the reasonable accommodation approach into the EFD's definition of indirect disability discrimination, it intended to avoid being obliged under Community law to complement the DDA 1995 with a legal prohibition of indirect discrimination. As Chapter 3 showed, the UK government has interpreted Article 2(2)(b)(ii) EFD in conjunction with Article 5 EFD which contains the reasonable accommodation duty. According to the government, both Articles in conjunction grant a discretionary choice to the Member States to the effect that domestic governments may either introduce a legal prohibition of indirect disability discrimination in domestic law, or design national legislation that imposes a duty on employers to make reasonable adjustments (accommodations) for disabled persons. Intermingling the concepts of 'reasonable accommodation' and 'indirect discrimination' reflects, however, a wrong stance, both in terms of legal theory and in terms of EC law. It is argued that, whereas the undercurrent of indirect discrimination is a 'group-justice' rationale, the concept of reasonable accommodation ingrains the elements of 'individual justice'. Moreover, from a legal point of view, Article 2(2)(b) EFD ('indirect discrimination') and Article 5 EFD ('reasonable accommodation') each impose *distinct* legislative obligations on the Member States. Implementation of the former ought to bear no impact on a Member State's obligations under the latter, and *vice versa*.[24] In short, the present author argues that the absence of the concept of indirect discrimination in the DDA 1995 is in contravention of EC equality law.

Another possible example of 'bottom-up' influence at the stage of law making was given in Chapter 6 in the discussion of religious discrimination law. EC equality law with respect to the grounds religion and belief reflects a balancing exercise of rival rights, namely the right to religious freedom and the right to non-discrimination on a forbidden ground (notably, 'sexual orientation' and 'sex'). It was shown that an identical balancing exercise features in Dutch equal treatment law which (unlike English law) has developed in a constitutional rights context. Arguably, the so-called 'sole ground construction' (*'enkele feit constructie'*), which is characteristic of Dutch equal treatment law in the context of 'religion' and 'belief', has been a source of inspiration for the EC legislator whilst framing the exception contained in Article 4(2) EFD. In the present author's view, the Dutch approach evidences a proper balance between freedom of religion, on the one hand, and the right to equality and non-discrimination, on the other. The Dutch approach therefore sets a good example for the

24 See also the criticism voiced by the House of Lords Select Committee on European Union (2000). As stated in Chapter 2, and with reference to Fredman 2003, English non-discrimination and equality law has evolved in the context of labour relations rather than within a constitutional setting.

ECJ in the interpretation of future complaints that emerge in the context of Article 4(2) EFD.

As stated before, bottom-up influence can also occur at the stage of legal interpretation of Community equality law by the ECJ. Domestic interpretations of 'equality' and 'non-discrimination' can set both good and bad examples for the ECJ while interpreting supranational equal treatment law. A particularly bad example is set by the English courts' interpretation of the concept of 'disability'. In order to render EC disability discrimination law effective the ECJ ought to refrain from the 'medicalised' interpretation of 'disability' which has dominated the judicial analysis in English disability discrimination cases. The discussion in Chapter 8 of the relevant English case law illustrated that, by taking the medical model as a starting point for judicial analysis, a wide range of potential victims of disability-based disadvantage have remained unprotected. In light of this it is highly regrettable that the definition of disability, designed by the ECJ in *Sonia Chacón Navas v. Eurest Colectividades SA*[25] reflects the tenets of the medical model of disability. It is much hoped that in future case law the ECJ will shift its approach in favour of the 'social model' with the effect of including persons who have suffered discrimination on grounds of an actual, past and future disability, discrimination on grounds of being associated with a disabled person, discrimination on grounds of a falsely perceived disability, discrimination on grounds of both major and minor disabilities, as well as discrimination on grounds of an asymptomatic condition. Given that such an extensive coverage will be precluded if the medical model is followed, the latter should not function as a template for judicial analysis.

The analysis of Dutch age discrimination law in Chapter 8 gave insights into the way in which the Dutch ETC has interpreted domestic age discrimination law. In general, it can be concluded that the ETC adopts a strict test in its review of age classifications, thereby implying that 'age' is not *a priori* regarded as less suspect a ground of discrimination compared to other grounds. The Dutch approach sets a proper example for the ECJ which would be advised to adopt a similar stance. The ECJ has indeed done so in its first decision on age discrimination, i.e. the *Mangold* case earlier referred to.

Question 5

If and in what respects could EC and domestic equal treatment law draw inspiration from the fundamental rights approach adopted by the Strasbourg Court in the context of the ECHR (and vice versa)?

This question was merely examined in Chapters 6 and 7 regarding discrimination on grounds of religion and belief, and sexual orientation, respectively. Chapter 6 highlighted the radically different stances adopted by the Dutch ETC, on the one hand, and the ECtHR, on the other in Muslim headscarf cases. The ETC has adopted a

25 *Sonia Chacón Navas v. Eurest Colectividades SA*, (Case C-13/05), 11 July 2006. This is the first case given by the ECJ on EC disability discrimination law.

'positive neutrality approach'[26] to headscarf (and other religious dress) cases in both *public* and *private* employment (and schools). This approach reconfigures the (traditional) notion of 'secularism' in the sense that it does *not* call for a *laïcité* approach (i.e. for a 'negative neutrality approach'), but on the contrary for bringing about religious pluralism (rather than eradicating 'religion' from public life). In the resolution of headscarf disputes the ETC has not drawn inspiration from the legal analysis by the Strasbourg court in similar cases. Indeed, the latter has shown a much more deferent stance so as to respect the highly divergent views across the States Parties to the Convention on the proper relationship between 'religion' and the State. Put differently, given the lack of a *common ground* on the proper interpretation of 'secularism' in the different States concerned the Strasbourg Court has granted a wide 'margin of appreciation' to the State involved in judicial proceedings. The role of the ECtHR is to determine whether a State Party to the Convention has violated a particular Convention right or freedom whereby, depending on the existence or absence of a European consensus on a given matter, it leaves more or less discretion to the State involved in legal proceedings. In contrast, the Dutch ETC seeks to (actively) resolve religious disputes in concrete cases whereby it performs this task in a climate of multiculturalism. In summary, the divergent stances by the ETC and the ECtHR in headscarf cases can be explained with reference to (1) the different judicial mandates of these (semi)judicial bodies and, related to that, (2) by the different socio-cultural contexts in which the religious dispute must be perceived. The aforementioned aspects also explain why the ECJ is likely to follow a stance that is similar to the cautious one adopted by the Strasbourg Court. It is argued that if the ECJ is invited to give its assessment on a religious discrimination dispute in the context of public life the Court ought to adopt a reserved stance. The question as to the proper relationship between 'religion' and public life ought to be largely a matter for the national constitutional courts. They are in a better position than the ECJ to place the case at hand in its historical and socio-cultural context.

In Chapter 7 EC and domestic sexual orientation discrimination law was analysed in light of relevant ECHR law. Prior to the implementation of the EFD the ECJ dealt with sexual orientation complaints on the basis of EC sex discrimination law. This proved to be of little assistance to alleged victims, given that the ECJ refused to accept that discrimination on grounds of sexual orientation is also sex discrimination (i.e. the 'sex discrimination argument'). The analysis in Chapter 7 showed that pre-implementation of the EFD the ECJ's approach in cases concerning the rights of sexual minorities was conservative (mainly due to a focus on the wrong comparator and the Court's subsidiary stance). The same point can be made with respect to the English courts. Both the ECJ and courts and tribunals in the UK should draw inspiration from the case law by the Strasbourg Court. The latter regards 'sexual orientation' as a suspect classification which therefore calls for a strict judicial scrutiny exercise.

26 This notion has been used by Zoontjens 2003.

Samenvatting

THEMA'S IN HET GELIJKEBEHANDELINGSRECHT: EEN VEELLAGIGE RECHTSVERGELIJKENDE ANALYSE VAN HET EUROPESE, ENGELSE EN NEDERLANDSE RECHT

Al in 1957, toen het Verdrag tot oprichting van de Europese (Economische) Gemeenschap werd ondertekend, kende het Communautaire recht het verbod van ongelijke behandeling bij de beloning van mannelijke en vrouwelijke werknemers (Artikel 141 EG; Artikel 119 oud). Daarnaast is het verbod van ongelijke behandeling op grond van nationaliteit (tussen de burgers van de EU) neergelegd in Artikel 12 EG.[1] De grondgedachte achter deze bepalingen was niet zozeer van een ethische of morele aard, maar stoelde vooraleer op economische gronden te bezien binnen de doelstellingen van de Interne Markt.[2] Pas in 1999, bij de inwerkingtreding van het Verdrag van Amsterdam, werd het Gemeenschapsrecht verrijkt met een algemene non-discriminatie bepaling die, zo betoogt dit boek, een uiting is van een opkomend geconstitutionaliseerd gelijkheidsprincipe in de Communautaire rechtsorde. Voorgenoemde bepaling is neergelegd in Artikel 13 EG, dat niet zozeer is ingegeven door economische, als wel door morele gronden. Artikel 13 EG verleent de juridische bevoegdheid aan de Gemeenschapswetgever om maatregelen te nemen om discriminatie op grond van geslacht, ras of etnische afstamming, godsdienst of overtuiging, handicap, leeftijd of seksuele geaardheid te bestrijden (waarbij het principe van 'gebonden bevoegdheden'[3] overigens niet mag worden geschonden). In 2000, zeer kort na de adoptie van Artikel 13 EG, nam de gemeenschapswetgever op basis van dit Artikel twee[4] belang-

1 Zie ook de Artikelen 39-42 EG (vrij verkeer van werknemers), Artikelen 43-48 EG (vrijheid van vestiging) en Artikelen 49-55 EG (vrijheid tot het verrichten van diensten) alsmede relevante secundaire regelgeving.

2 Alhoewel dit ten dele is gemitigeerd in de rechtspraak van het HvJEG. Dit is besproken in hoofdstuk 2 onder verwijzing naar de relevante jurisprudentie van het Hof.

3 Artikel 5 EG bepaalt dat 'de Gemeenschap handelt binnen de grenzen van de haar door [het] Verdrag verleende bevoegdheden en toegewezen doelstellingen'. Artikel 13 EG refereert expliciet aan dit beginsel in de specifieke context van 'non-discriminatie'.

4 In 2004 werd op basis van Artikel 13 EG tevens Richtlijn 2004/113/EG van de Raad van 13 december 2004 houdende toepassing van het beginsel van gelijke behandeling van vrouwen en mannen bij de toegang tot en het aanbod van goederen en diensten aangenomen (*Publi-*
→

rijke Richtlijnen aan te weten, Richtlijn 2000/43/EC (de 'Rasrichtlijn')[5] en Richtlijn 2000/78/EC (de 'Kaderrichtlijn').[6] Bij aanvang van dit onderzoek moesten beide Richtlijnen nog worden geïmplementeerd in het nationale recht van de lidstaten wat inmiddels is gebeurd.[7] Eerstgenoemde Richtlijn bevat een verbod van discriminatie op grond van ras en etniciteit op een groot aantal maatschappelijke terreinen waaronder 'arbeid en beroep'. Laatstgenoemde verbiedt discriminatie op grond van godsdienst en overtuiging, handicap, leeftijd en seksuele geaardheid en is gelimiteerd tot het arbeidsterrein. Naast voornoemde Richtlijnen is het Communautaire recht (onder meer) rijk aan een scala van secundaire regelgeving betreffende de gelijke behandeling van mannen en vrouwen, zowel binnen als buiten de arbeid.[8] Het sinds oudsher bestaande principe van gelijkheid tussen de seksen is bovendien veelvuldig geïnterpreteerd in de jurisprudentie van het Hof van Justitie (hierna: HvJEG). Ditzelfde geldt overigens niet voor het gelijkheidsbeginsel betreffende de nieuwe discriminatiegronden neergelegd in Artikel 13 EG.[9]

Bovenstaande maakt duidelijk dat het gelijkheidsbeginsel in het Communautaire recht volop in ontwikkeling is. Deze ontwikkeling wordt in dit boek in kaart gebracht op basis van een veellagige rechtsvergelijkende analyse. Zoals uiteengezet in hoofdstuk 1 staan binnen deze analyse drie primaire en twee secundaire vraagstellingen centraal welke hierna kort worden uitgewerkt. In de eerste plaats wordt in dit boek een analyse gemaakt van de 'top-down' invloed die het Communautaire recht uitoefent op het recht van de lidstaten. Hiertoe wordt de juridische regulering van het gelijkheidsbeginsel in het Engelse en het Nederlandse recht bestudeerd alsmede de interpretatie van dit beginsel door (quasi) judiciële organen. Het nationale recht wordt vergeleken met het Communautaire gelijkebehandelingsrecht teneinde een antwoord

katieblad no. L 373 van 21/12/2004, p.. 0037-0043). Deze Richtlijn wordt niet in dit boek behandeld.

5 Richtlijn 2000/43/EG van de Raad van 29 juni 2000 houdende toepassing van het beginsel van gelijke behandeling van personen ongeacht ras of etnische afstamming *Publikatieblad* no. *L 180 van 19/07/2000, p. 0022-0026.*

6 Richtlijn 2000/78/EG van de Raad van 27 november 2000 tot instelling van een algemeen kader voor gelijke behandeling in arbeid en beroep *Publikatieblad* no. *L 303 van 02/12/2000, p. 0016-0022.*

7 De implementatietermijn van de Rasrichtlijn is verstreken op 19-07-03 (vgl. Artikel 16 Rassenrichtlijn) en die van de Kaderrichtlijn op 2 December 2003 (vgl. Artikel 18 Kaderrichtlijn). Een uitzondering wordt gemaakt in de Kaderrichtlijn voor de implementatie van de Richtlijn wat betreft de gronden 'handicap' en 'leeftijd' die uiterlijk op 02-12-06 in het nationale recht moeten zijn omgezet.

8 Richtlijn 2006/54/EG van het Europees Parlement en de Raad van 5 juli 2006, betreffende de toepassing van het beginsel van gelijke kansen en gelijke behandeling van mannen en vrouwen in arbeid en beroep (*Publikatieblad nr L 204 van 26/07/2006, p. 0023-0036)* consolideert de bestaande bepalingen betreffende het gelijkheidsbeginsel tussen de seksen uit reeds bestaande Richtlijnen alsmede vaste rechtspraak van het HvJEG in één tekst (zie hoofdstuk 2). Deze Richtlijn staat bekend als de z.g. 'Recast Directive'.

9 Tot op heden is er geen rechtspraak voorhanden betreffende Richtlijn 2000/43/EG (de 'Rasrichtlijn') en heeft het HvJEG slechts twee zaken gewezen in de context van Richtlijn 2000/78/EC (de 'Kaderrichtlijn), namelijk *Mangold v. Helm* (Zaak C-144/04) van 22 november 2005 (HvJEG) en *Sonia Chacón Navas v. Eurest Colectividades SA,* (Zaak C-13/05) van 11 July 2006 (HvJEG). Beide zaken zijn respectievelijk besproken in hoofdstukken 9 en 8.

te bieden op de vraag of het nationale recht in overeenstemming is met de eisen die voortvloeien uit het Gemeenschapsrecht ('top-down' vergelijking). In de tweede plaats wordt in dit boek een vergelijking getrokken tussen het Engelse en Nederlandse gelijkebehandelingsrecht, zowel vóór als ná de implementatie van EG recht ('cross-country' vergelijking). Hierboven was al opgemerkt dat de lidstaten onder het Communautaire recht verplicht zijn om EG Richtlijnen om te zetten in het nationale recht binnen een daartoe vastgestelde termijn. Zij hebben echter een discretionaire bevoegdheid ten aanzien van de vraag *hoe* zij dit willen doen, mits het door de Richtlijn vastgestelde doel wordt bereikt. Met andere woorden, zelfs na de implementatie van EG recht kunnen er verschillen zijn in de juridische benadering van 'gelijkheid' in de wetgeving van verschillende lidstaten (*in casu*: het Verenigd Koninkrijk en Nederland). In de derde plaats wordt in dit boek een vergelijking gemaakt tussen de onderliggende waarden van de verschillende discriminatiegronden neergelegd in Artikel 13 EG te weten geslacht, ras of etnische afstamming, godsdienst of overtuiging, handicap, leeftijd of seksuele geaardheid ('cross-ground' vergelijking). Het is van belang om inzicht te verwerven in de logica van de verschillende discriminatiegronden, nu deze een belangrijke leidraad vormen voor de vraag hoe de wetgevende en rechtsprekende macht discriminatie op een bepaalde grond dienen te reguleren, c.q. interpreteren. Immers, zoals dit boek laat zien, het gelijkheidsbeginsel kent meerdere 'gezichten' welke meer of minder opgeld doen ten aanzien van (een) bepaalde discriminatiegrond(en), vergeleken met (een) andere. In het voorgaande heb ik de drie hoofdvragen geschetst die in dit boek centraal staan. Op een tentatieve wijze wordt in dit boek tevens aandacht besteed aan een vierde vraag, namelijk of en in welk opzicht het Communautaire gelijkebehandelingsrecht is beïnvloed (of zou beïnvloed moeten worden) door het nationale recht ('bottom-up' vergelijking). De invloed die het nationale recht uitoefent op het EG recht en die het EG recht heeft op het recht in de lidstaten vormen samen de scharnieren van de wisselwerking tussen Communautair en nationaal recht. Een laatste, secundaire, vraag is of en in welke opzicht EG en nationaal recht lessen kunnen trekken uit de rechtspraak van het Europese Hof voor de Rechten van de Mens aangaande de rechten van seksuele minderheden en de vrijheid van godsdienst (zie hoofdstukken 6 en 7).

Bovenvermelde vergelijkingen worden in dit boek getrokken binnen de context van de arbeid en ten aanzien van geselecteerde thema's uit het gelijkebehandelingsrecht. Na een uiteenzetting van de evolutie van het gelijkheidsbeginsel in de Communautaire, Britse en Nederlandse rechtsorde (hoofdstuk 2), behandelt hoofdstuk 3 het concept van 'indirecte discriminatie' op basis van de uiteengezette veellagige rechtsvergelijkende analyse. Hetzelfde wordt gedaan in hoofdstukken 4 en 5 met betrekking tot, respectievelijk, de concepten '(seksuele) intimidatie' en 'positieve actie'. De bespreking van de theorie omtrent 'indirecte discriminatie', '(seksuele) intimidatie' en 'positieve actie' is ingebed in de hiervoor genoemde hoofdstukken wat als voordeel heeft dat de theoretische verhandeling over 'gelijkheid' direct wordt gekoppeld aan de analyse van positiefrechtelijke vraagstukken. Hoofdstukken 6 tot en met 9 behandelen het gelijkheidsbeginsel in relatie tot, respectievelijk, godsdienst, seksuele oriëntatie, handicap en leeftijd op basis van de veellagige rechtsvergelijking. Zoals eerder vermeld wordt in de analyse van de gronden godsdienst en overtuiging (hoofdstuk 6) en seksuele oriëntatie (hoofdstuk 7) tevens aandacht besteed aan relevant recht voortvloeiende uit de Artikelen 8 en 9 (al dan niet in combinatie met Artikel 14) van het EVRM. Het is, zoals dit boek aangeeft, niet onwaarschijnlijk dat het HvJEG (alsmede nationale rechtsprekende organen) bij de interpretatie van de gelijkebehandelingsnorm ten aanzien van 'godsdienst' en 'seksuele oriëntatie' word(t)(en) geïnspireerd (zowel positief als negatief) door relevante rechtspraak van het Hof in Straatsburg. Als direct gevolg van de adoptie van de Kaderrichtlijn is het Engelse gelijkebehandelingsrecht uitgebreid met een verbod van discriminatie op grond van godsdienst en overtuiging, seksuele oriëntatie en leeftijd[10]. Met uitzondering van de grond leeftijd waren deze gronden al sinds 1994 gereguleerd in de Nederlandse Algemene Wet Gelijke Behandeling (AWGB). Vice versa, waar het Engelse recht al sinds 1995 wetgeving kende op het gebied van discriminatie van gehandicapten is dergelijke wetgeving in Nederland pas ingevoerd in 2003. Dit is grotendeels gebeurd onder invloed van het EG recht. Hetzelfde geldt voor de in 2004 ingevoerde wetgeving inzake leeftijdsdiscriminatie. Al met al vormen de nationale rechtssystemen een vruchtbare bron voor wederzijdse rechtsvergelijking gezien hun respectievelijke ervaring met betrekking tot verschillende gronden van discriminatie.

De veellagige rechtsvergelijkende analyse die in dit boek is toegepast leidt tot de volgende (belangrijkste) conclusies.

Conclusies met betrekking tot onderzoeksvraag 1

Wat betreft de 'top-down' vergelijking was hierboven al aangegeven dat het bereik van de nationale gelijkebehandelingswetgeving is uitgebreid met nieuwe gronden als (direct) gevolg van EG regelgeving. Het onderzoek heeft echter vastgesteld dat deze positieve ontwikkeling tevens twee negatieve bijgevolgen heeft gehad. In de eerste plaats heeft de implementatie van het relevante EG recht een corrosief effect gehad op het wettelijke stelsel van gelijke behandeling in het Engelse recht. In deze context moet worden benadrukt dat de adoptie van Artikel 13 EG 'een weerspiegeling [vormde] van het groeiend besef dat er een samenhangende en geïntegreerde aanpak nodig was om discriminatie te bestrijden'.[11] Het onderzoek heeft echter een paradox vastgesteld, namelijk dat het zoeken naar coherentie in de regelgeving inzake 'gelijkheid' *tussen* de lidstaten kan leiden tot een ontwrichting van de coherentie in de regelgeving *binnen* een lidstaat. Dit negatieve effect heeft zich duidelijk gemanifesteerd in het Engelse recht, met name in de Engelse *Race Relations Act* die, post implementatie van het EG recht wordt gekenmerkt door een tweespaltige vorm van rechtsbescherming. De reden waarom de implementatie van de Europese gelijkebehandelingsrichtlijnen een minder eroderend effect heeft gehad op de coherentie van de Nederlandse regelgeving is dat de Nederlandse wetgever, vaker dan de Engelse, bereid is

10 De regulering van leeftijdsdiscriminatie in het Engelse recht werd onlangs pas voltooid (op 01-10-06) toen de zogenaamde *Employment Equality (Age) Regulations 2006* (S.I. 2006 No. 1031) inwerking zijn getreden. De *Age Regulations* zijn niet meer behandeld in dit boek gezien hun late inwerkingtreding.

11 Equality and Non-discrimination in an Enlarged European Union, Green Paper [Groenboek] May 2004, p. 10.

om de Communautaire regel tevens toe te passen op gebieden waar dit juridisch bezien niet hoeft.

Het tweede negatieve effect dat is vastgesteld op basis van de 'top-down' vergelijking is dat het EG recht tegelijkertijd een versnellend en regressief effect kan hebben op de ontwikkeling van nationale regelgeving. Dit is in dit onderzoek geïllustreerd aan de hand van de Nederlandse regelgeving inzake discriminatie op grond van handicap. Enerzijds is deze regelgeving veel vlugger aangenomen dan het geval zou zijn geweest zonder de EG-rechtelijke verplichtingen die voortvloeien uit de Kaderrichtlijn. Anderzijds heeft de Richtlijn tevens tot gevolg gehad dat de voorstellen voor regelgeving op dit terrein die reeds bestonden vóór de adoptie van het relevante EG recht qua (materieel) bereik hebben ingeboet als gevolg van het implementatieproces (aangezien de Kaderrichtlijn tot minder verplichtte).

Als gevolg van de top-down invloed van het EG recht op het nationale recht is het recht inzake indirecte discriminatie en (seksuele) intimidatie versoepeld en biedt het een ruimere mate van rechtsbescherming aan slachtoffers van discriminatie, c.q. intimidatie. Deze positieve invloed van het EG recht is met name waar te nemen in het Engelse recht. Als gevolg van de implementatie van het EG recht is de noodzaak om indirecte discriminatie te bewijzen op grond van (niet altijd voorhanden zijnd) statistisch bewijsmateriaal gemitigeerd. Dit geldt voor zowel Nederlands als Engels recht. Wat het Engels recht betreft is bovendien als gevolg van de implementatie van EG recht het zogenaamde '*Perera*-gat' grotendeels gedicht. Dit betekent dat in de huidige situatie zowel mandatoire als niet mandatoire job criteria in een indirecte discriminatie procedure kunnen worden aangevochten. Bescherming tegen (seksuele) intimidatie is nieuw in het Gemeenschapsrecht. Pre-implementatie van de Richtlijnen werd (seksuele) intimidatie in zowel Engels als Nederlands recht behandeld onder de noemer van directe discriminatie c.q. direct onderscheid. Het comparatieve element dat het verbod van 'directe discriminatie' kenmerkt leidde met name in het Engelse recht tot onbevredigende uitkomsten. Het feit dat het EG recht '(seksuele) intimidatie' conceptualiseert als een autonoom kwaad wordt in dit onderzoek als positief gekwalificeerd.

Conclusies met betrekking tot onderzoeksvraag 2

In meer algemene zin heeft de 'cross-country' vergelijking onder meer nadruk gelegd op het feit dat het Nederlandse gelijkebehandelingsrecht bezien dient te worden in het licht van een constitutionele gelijkheidsgedachte die is verwoord in Artikel 1 van de Grondwet, terwijl 'gelijkheid' in het Engelse recht met name is geëvolueerd in de context van het arbeidsrecht en tegen de achtergrond van een implementatieplicht die voortvloeit uit het Communautaire recht. Engels recht kent immers geen geschreven Constitutie. Daarnaast laat dit boek op verschillende plaatsen zien dat het Engelse recht meer dan het Nederlandse recht is ingegeven door een comparatief gelijkheidsmodel (zie met name de analyse in hoofdstuk 4 en (in mindere mate) hoofdstuk 7). Meer specifiek heeft de 'cross-country' vergelijking principiële verschillen aangetoond in de regulering van discriminatie op grond van handicap in het Engelse vergeleken met het Nederlandse recht (zie hoofdstuk 8). Waar de Engelse regelgeving inzake handicap is gestoeld op een asymmetrisch gelijkheidsprincipe neemt de

Nederlandse wetgeving een symmetrische gelijkheidsgedachte als uitgangspunt. Dit betekent dat onder het Engelse recht een klager alleen een beroep kan doen op de wet vanwege het feit dat hij of zij is gediscrimineerd *'op grond van handicap'*. Het Nederlandse recht biedt tevens bescherming aan mensen die zijn gediscrimineerd omdat ze juist *geen* handicap hebben. Het praktische en tegelijkertijd onwenselijke gevolg van de Engelse benadering is dat de groep van 'gehandicapte mensen' nauwkeurig door het recht moet worden gedefinieerd hetgeen overbodig is onder het symmetrische (Nederlandse) model. De noodzaak tot definiëring heeft er in het Engelse recht toe geleid dat de interpretatie van de DDA 1995 wordt gedomineerd door het medische model van handicap en niet door het sociale model. Beide modellen pogen de bron van het nadeel dat gehandicapte mensen ondervinden in het dagelijkse leven in te lokaliseren. Kort gezegd ligt deze bron volgens het medische model in de individuele handicap zélf, terwijl deze volgens het sociale model ligt in de interactie van iemands individuele handicap en de reacties daarop uit de omgeving. Het medische model legt de nadruk op de *individuele handicap* en niet op de *discriminatoire behandeling* en dient daarom niet als uitgangspunt te worden genomen bij het ontwerp en de interpretatie van wetgeving inzake discriminatie met betrekking tot 'handicap'. Dit wil overigens niet zeggen dat het Engelse asymmetrische model op zichzelf genomen een onjuist uitgangspunt vormt. Het wil wél zeggen dat áls een asymmetrisch model wordt gevolgd de groep van 'gehandicapte mensen' ruim dient te worden gedefinieerd op basis van de uitgangspunten van het 'sociale model'.

Ook in de context van het discriminatieverbod op grond van godsdienst en overtuiging zijn er verschillen aangetoond tussen het Engelse en Nederlandse recht in deze. De vrijheid van godsdienst kan onder meer in conflict zijn met het principe van de contractuele vrijheid. Waar de Engelse rechtspraak godsdienstige geschillen tussen een werknemer en een werkgever pleegt te beslechten in het voordeel van de contractvrijheid is het omgekeerde het geval in het Nederlandse recht. Uit de Engelse rechtspraak blijkt dat de godsdienstvrijheid van een werknemer afhankelijk wordt gemaakt van diens aanvaarding om het dienstverband te verbreken. Een dergelijke benadering strookt echter niet met het fundamentele karakter van de vrijheid van godsdienst en verdient derhalve geen aanbeveling.

Conclusies met betrekking tot onderzoeksvraag 3

De derde laag van de vergelijkende analyse betreft een vergelijking van de onderliggende waarden van verschillende discriminatiegronden. De bespreking in hoofdstukken 6-9 van discriminatie in relatie tot, respectievelijk, godsdienst, seksuele oriëntatie, handicap en leeftijd begint steeds met een verhandeling van de theorie behorende bij deze gronden. Godsdienst, bijvoorbeeld, is niet *per se* een onveranderlijke status, zoals ras en sekse, welke beide biologisch zijn bepaald. Hetzelfde geldt voor seksuele oriëntatie dat een fluctuerend concept is, alsmede leeftijd dat een zichzelf transformerend concept is. In de literatuur zijn de gronden godsdienst en seksuele oriëntatie gecategoriseerd als zijnde een uitdrukking van iemands (gekozen) levensstijl welke echter lastig is te verklaren in termen van 'voorkeur'.[12] Zoals dit boek betoogt zijn beide gronden sterk verbonden met iemands *identiteit*. Bovendien kan ten aanzien van deze gronden een onderscheid worden gemaakt tussen het '*forum internum*' (dit is het recht om een bepaalde godsdienst/oriëntatie te *hebben*) en het '*forum externum*' (dis is het recht om zich te *gedragen* in overeenstemming daarmee). Dit onderscheid kan niet worden gemaakt ten aanzien van de andere gronden opgenomen in Artikel 13 EG. Een overeenkomst tussen godsdienst, zwangerschap (dat valt onder 'sekse') en handicap is dat al deze gronden een impact kunnen hebben op de mogelijkheid van de werknemer om (op tijd) beschikbaar te zijn voor werk en op de wijze waarop het werk wordt uitgevoerd.[13] Zo zou, bijvoorbeeld, een godsdienstige werknemer zijn werkgever kunnen vragen of hij tijdens bepaalde uren op het werk kan bidden en kan een gehandicapte werknemer vragen om een aanpassing van de werkplek teneinde het werk te kunnen uitoefenen. Voornoemde gronden verschillen in deze zin van ras en seksuele oriëntatie die vrijwel nooit enige impact hebben op 'aanwezigheid' of 'job performance'. Zo bezien past een formeel gelijkheidsmodel beter bij de twee laatstgenoemde gronden, terwijl de daarvoor genoemde gronden materiële gelijkheid vergen. Het materiële gelijkheidsmodel is het duidelijkst aanwezig in zowel Communautair als nationaal gehandicaptenrecht (zie hoofdstuk 8). Dit verplicht werkgevers 'redelijke aanpassingen' te maken voor gehandicapte werknemers, teneinde de verschillen tussen gehandicapte en niet gehandicapte werknemers te compenseren. De wettelijke verplichting tot het maken van redelijke aanpassingen is tevens een erkenning van het feit dat 'handicap' niet puur in biologische termen is te verklaren. Net als 'gender'[14] is handicap een sociale constructie in die zin dat de maatschappij/omgeving vaak 'handicap' *creëert* door de dominante *niet gehandicapte* norm[15] als uitgangspunt te kiezen. Een overeenkomst tussen handicap en leeftijd is dat het niet makkelijk is om de benadeelde groep te traceren, omdat beide heterogene begrippen zijn.[16] Leeftijd wordt over het algemeen niet gekwalificeerd als een verdachte grond, o.a. onder verwijzing naar het 'levensloop' argument. Dat leeftijd minder verdacht is dan andere gronden wordt ook tot uitdrukking gebracht door het feit dat, wat deze grond betreft, het EG en het nationale recht op een 'open' model van non-discriminatie zijn gestoeld. Dit betekent dat zowel directe als indirecte vormen van leeftijdsdiscriminatie algemeen gerechtvaardigd kunnen worden. Tegelijkertijd, zo is betoogd, moeten leeftijdsclassificaties door de rechter streng worden getoetst[17],

12 Zie Schiek 2002.

13 Dit laatste geldt tevens voor de grond leeftijd. Zie Waddington en Bell 2003.

14 'Gender' heeft betrekking op de sociale, culturele en psychologische aspecten van 'sekse', terwijl 'sekse' een biologisch concept is.

15 In genderstudies gaat het dan om de mannelijke norm die dominant is.

16 De moeilijkheid om ten aanzien van bepaalde gronden van discriminatie de benadeelde groep te traceren heeft ook een impact gehad op de juridische formulering van 'indirecte discriminatie' in de Kaderrichtlijn en de Rassenrichtlijn. Dit punt is behandeld in hoofdstuk 3.

17 Een strenge toets werd inderdaad door het HvJEG gehanteerd in de allereerste zaak aangaande EG leeftijdsdiscriminatierecht. Zie *Mangold v. Helm* (Zaak C-144/04) van 22 november 2005 (HvJEG). Deze zaak is van wijdere constitutionele betekenis en is uitvoerig besproken in hoofdstuk 9. Ook de Nederlandse CGB hanteert een strenge toets in de behandeling van zaken betreffende onderscheid op grond van leeftijd.

omdat zij lang niet altijd rationeel te verklaren zijn en dus kunnen leiden tot sociale uitsluiting en marginalisering.

Conclusies met betrekking tot onderzoeksvraag 4

De interactie tussen het EG enerzijds en het nationale recht anderzijds strekt verder dan de conventionele (mandatoire) invloed van supranationaal op nationaal recht. EG recht kan tevens van onderaf worden beïnvloed door het recht (inclusief de juridische interpretatie van dat recht) in de lidstaten. De 'bottom-up' vergelijking vormt de vierde laag van de rechtsvergelijkende studie. Deze laag wordt relatief marginaal bestudeerd vanwege de redenen uiteengezet in hoofdstuk 1. Een eerste vorm van 'bottom-up' invloed is ontwaard in hoofdstuk 3 in de context van de discussie over indirecte discriminatie op grond van handicap. Indirecte discriminatie kan slechts worden gerechtvaardigd op basis van de zogenaamde 'objectieve rechtvaardigingstoets'. Deze is door het HvJEG ontwikkeld in de context van sekse discriminatie. Ten aanzien van de grond 'handicap' bepaalt de Kaderrichtlijn echter dat indirecte discriminatie op deze grond tevens kan worden gerechtvaardigd indien de werkgever verplicht is krachtens nationale wetgeving om een redelijke aanpassing te maken. Betoogd is dat deze tweede rechtvaardigingsmogelijkheid is beïnvloed door de Engelse gehandicaptenwetgeving. Deze kent immers geen verbod van indirecte discriminatie hetgeen overigens in strijd is met de Kaderrichtlijn. Volgens de Britse regering daarentegen wordt deze omissie gecompenseerd door de plicht om redelijke aanpassingen te maken.

Een mogelijk tweede voorbeeld van invloed van onderaf is gegeven in hoofdstuk 6 in de context van discriminatie op grond van godsdienst. Het Communautaire recht met betrekking tot deze discriminatiegrond is een weerspiegeling van conflicterende rechten, in die zin dat het recht op gelijke behandeling op grond van godsdienst vaak op gespannen voet staat met de rechten van anderen (met name homoseksuelen en vrouwen). De 'balancing-exercise' tussen conflicterende rechten komt in de Kaderrichtlijn (onder meer) tot uiting in Artikel 4(2) van de Richtlijn. Kort gezegd bepaalt dit Artikel dat godsdienstige organisaties (bijvoorbeeld kerken of godsdienstige scholen) een onderscheid mogen maken op grond van godsdienst indien dit nodig is vanwege de aard van de beroepsactiviteit óf de context waarin deze wordt uitgeoefend. Dit betekent dat godsdienstige eisen dus ook mogen worden gesteld teneinde de godsdienstige ethos van de organisatie te beschermen, ook al zijn dergelijke eisen niet nodig voor een effectieve uitoefening van het werk in kwestie. Artikel 4(2) van de Richtlijn bepaalt echter tevens dat dergelijke godsdienstige eisen geen rechtvaardiging kunnen vormen voor discriminatie op een andere door het EG recht beschermde grond. Een vrijwel identieke constructie is eveneens neergelegd in de Nederlandse AWGB[18] en staat bekend als de zogenaamde 'enkele feit constructie'. Betoogd is dat

18 Algemene Wet Gelijke Behandeling. Deze wet dateert uit 1994 en is daarna op punten gewijzigd in het licht van supranationaal recht.

de wijze waarop deze constructie is geïnterpreteerd door de Commissie Gelijke Behandeling (CGB) als voorbeeld kan dienen voor het HvJEG in toekomstige zaken.[19]

De rechtspraak van het HvJEG kan tevens op een 'negatieve' manier worden geïnspireerd door nationale benaderingen, in die zin dat het Hof er bewust voor kan kiezen een bepaalde nationale benadering *niet* te volgen. Betoogd is onder meer dat het Hof zeker geen voorbeeld moet nemen aan de medische interpretatie van discriminatiewetgeving inzake handicap die gangbaar is in het Engelse recht. Het is bijzonder jammer dat het Hof deze medische benadering desalniettemin heeft gevolgd in het eerste arrest dat het heeft gewezen aangaande discriminatie op grond van handicap.[20]

Conclusies met betrekking tot onderzoeksvraag 5

Tot slot is in dit boek summier aandacht besteed aan de vraag in welk opzicht het HvJEG en de nationale rechtsprekende organen iets kunnen leren van de interpretatie door het Hof in Straatsburg van (mensenrechtelijke) geschillen betreffende 'godsdienst' en 'seksuele oriëntatie'. Deze vraag is slechts behandeld in hoofdstukken 6 en 7. In hoofdstuk 6 is onder meer aandacht besteed aan de uiteenlopende benaderingen van de Nederlandse CGB enerzijds en het Straatsburgse Hof anderzijds in zogenaamde hoofddoekjeszaken. De CGB pleegt deze zaken op te lossen onder verwijzing naar een positieve neutraliteitsgedachte. In praktijk betekent dit dat hoofddoekjes op de (publieke) werkplek en in (publieke) scholen in beginsel niet geweigerd mogen worden. Betoogd is dat deze benadering past in het socioculturele klimaat in Nederland dat multicultureel en pluriform is. Het Hof voor de Rechten van de Mens daarentegen lost hoofddoekjeszaken niet zelf actief op, doch beziet slechts of een staat die regels stelt omtrent de hoofddoek in strijd handelt met Artikel 9 (al dan niet in combinatie met Artikel 14) van de Conventie. Gezien de afwezigheid van een Europese consensus ten aanzien van het begrip 'seculiere staat' en daarmee de verhouding tussen 'religie' en 'staat' pleegt het Hof in hoofddoekkwesties een ruime beoordelingsvrijheid (*'margin of appreciation'*) toe te kennen aan de Verdragsrechtelijke staten. Kort gezegd, verschillende juridische benaderingen kunnen worden verklaard op grond van (1) de verschillende (quasi) judiciële taken van verschillende rechtsprekende organen en (2) de uiteenlopende socioculturele context waarin deze organen opereren. Betoogd is dat het HvJEG analoog aan het Straatsburgse Hof terughoudendheid dient te betrachten in hoofddoekkwesties die zich voordoen in een publieke context. De vraag wat de rol van godsdienst is in het publieke leven dient beantwoord te worden door de nationale (constitutionele) rechter die veel beter dan de supranationale rechter het geschil in zijn historische en socioculturele context kan plaatsen.

In hoofdstuk 7 is het Communautaire en nationale gelijkebehandelingsrecht ten aanzien van de grond 'seksuele oriëntatie' bezien in het licht van relevante Straatsburgse rechtspraak. Vóór de inwerkingtreding van de Kaderrichtlijn benaderde

[19] Dit is *en detail* besproken in hoofdstuk 6 waarnaar de lezer wordt verwezen.

[20] *Sonia Chacón Navas v. Eurest Colectividades SA*, (Zaak C-13/05) van 11 July 2006 (HvJEG).

het HvJEG klachten over discriminatie op grond van seksuele oriëntatie op basis van het Communautaire gelijkebehandelinsrecht tussen mannen en vrouwen. Een klager bleek hiermee weinig op te schieten aangezien het Hof weigerde om discriminatie op grond van seksuele oriëntatie tevens te kwalificeren als discriminatie op grond van geslacht.[21] De analyse in hoofdstuk 7 heeft aangetoond dat vóór de adoptie van de Kaderrichtlijn het Hof (alsmede het Engelse House of Lords) een conservatieve houding aannam ten aanzien van de rechten van seksuele minderheden. Dit was met name het gevolg van de keuze voor de foute maatman ('comparator') binnen het model van comparatieve (sekse) gelijkheid (zie hoofdstuk 7). Het Hof in Straatsburg behandelt 'seksuele oriëntatie' als een verdachte grond. Beweerdelijke discriminatie op deze grond wordt daarom strikt door het Hof getoetst. Het HvJEG dient in toekomstige rechtspraak eenzelfde strikte lijn te volgen.

21 Zie *Grant v. South West Trains* (Zaak C-249/96) [1998] ECR I-621.

LIST OF CASES

A (Respondent) v. Chief Constable of West Yorkshire Police (Appellant) and another [2004] (6 May 2004) (HL) available at <http://www.publications.parliament.uk/pa/ld200304ldjudgmnt/jd040506/chief-1htm>

Abadeh v. British Telecommunications plc [2001] ICR 156 (EAT)

Abrahammson and Anderson v. Fogelqfist (Case C-407/98) [2000] ECR I-5539 (ECJ)

Acas v. Taylor (EAT 788/97) unreported (11-02-1998) (EAT)

Ahmad v. Inner London Education Authority [1978] 1 All ER 574 (CA)

Ahmad v. UK [1981] 4 EHRR 126 (CD)

Allonby (appellant) v. Accrington & Rossendale College and others (respondents) [2001] IRLR 364 (EAT)

Allonby v Accrington & Rossendale College and others (Case C-256/01) [2004] ECR I- 9077 (ECJ)

Amicus v. Secretary of State for Trade and Industry [2004] EWHC 860 (High Court (Administrative Court))

Amsterdam Appeal Court, 13-01-2000, KG 2000, 42; NJ 2000/43 (Appeal Court)

(Appellant) v. (1) WC and (2) SPV (respondents) [1999] IRLR 410 (EAT)

Archibald v. Five Council [2004] ICR 954 (HL)

Arrowsmith v. UK 7050/75 [1978] (12 October 1978) 19 DR 5 (CD)

Badeck & Others v. Hessische Ministerpraesident and Landesanwalt beim Staatsgerichtshof des Landes Hessen (Case C-158/97) [2000] ECR I-1875 (ECJ)

Baehr v. Lewin 852 P 2d 44 1993 (Hawaii Supreme Court)

Balgobin and Francis (appellants) *v. London Borough of Tower Hamlets* (respondents) [1987] IRLR 401 (EAT)

Barber v. Guardian Royal Exchange Assurance (Case C-262/88) [1990] ECR I-1889 (ECJ)

Barry v. Midland Bank plc [1999] IRLR 581 (HL)

Bayoomi v. British Railways Board [1981] IRLR 431 (EAT)

Bilka Kaufhaus GmbH v. Karin Weber von Hartz (Case 170/84) [1986] ECR 1607 (ECJ)

Binderen v. Kaya, Hoge Raad 10 December 1982, NJ 1983/87 (HR)

Blaizot v. University of Liège and others (Case 24/86) [1988] ECR 379 (ECJ)

Bracebridge Engineering Ltd v. Darby [1990] IRLR 3 (EAT)

Brasserie dû Pêcheur SA v. Germany and *R. v. Secretary of State for Transport, ex parte Factortame Ltd. And others* (Case C-46/93 and C-48/93) [1996] ECR I-1029 (ECJ)

Briheche v. Ministre de l'Intérieur, Ministre de l'Education and Ministre de la Justice (Case C-319/03) [2004] ECR 0000 (ECJ)

British Telecommunications Plc v. Williams [1997] IRLR 668 (EAT)

Brook v. London Borough of Haringey [1992] IRLR 478 (EAT)

Brumfit v. (1) Ministry of Defence (2) Sergeant JJ Fitzpatrick Appeal UK EAT/1004/MAA (EAT)

Burton and Rhule v. de Vere Hotels [1996] IRLR 596 (EAT)

Buscarini and others v. San Marino 24645/94 [1999] ECHR 7 (18 February 1999) (ECtHR)

Caisse nationale d'assurance vieillesse des travailleurs salariés (CNAVTS) v. Evelyne Thibault (Case C-136/95) [1998] ECR I-2011 (ECJ)

Canniffe v. East Riding CC [2000] IRLR 555 (EAT)

Chief Constable of the Kent Constabulary v. Kufeji EAT 1135 00 (unreported) (EAT)

Christine Goodwin v. the United Kingdom 28957/95 11 July 2002 (ECtHR GC)

Clarke v. Ely (IMI) Kynoch Ltd [1982] IRLR 482 (EAT)

Clark v. TDG t/a Novacold [1999] IRLR 318 (CA)

Codfried, Hoge Raad 13-01-1995, NJ 1995/430 (HR)

Coker and Osamor (appellants) v. Lord Chancellor and Lord Chancellor's Department (respondents) [2001] IRLR 116 (EAT)

Coker and Osamor (appellants) v. Lord Chancellor and Lord Chancellor's Department (respondents) [2002] IRLR 80 (CA)

Coleman v. Skyrail Oceanic Ltd [1981] ICR 864 (CA)

Collins v. Royal National Theatre Board Ltd [2004] EWCA Civ 144 (CA Civil Division)

Commission for Racial Equality v. Dutton [1989] 1 All ER 306 (CA)

Commission of the European Communities v. Luxembourg (Case C-70/05) [2005] *OJ* 10-12-2005/C315-07 (ECJ)

Coote v. Granada Hospitality Ltd (Case C-185/97) [1998] ECR I-5199 (ECJ)

Copsey v. WWB Devon Clays Ltd [2005] EWCA Civ 932 (CA)

Cosgrove v. Caesar & Howie [2001] IRLR 654 (EAT)

Costa (Flaminio) v. ENEL (Case 6/64) [1964] ECR 585 (ECJ)

Cross and Others v. British Airways plc [2005] IRLR 423 (EAT)

Crown Suppliers (PSA) Ltd v. Dawkins [1993] ICR 517 (CA)

D v. Council T-264/97 [1999] Reports of European Community Staff Cases (ECR-SC) II-1 available at <http://www.europa.eu.int> (ECJ)

D and *Sweden v. Council* (Case C-122/99 P and C-125/99 P) [2001] ECR I-4319 (ECJ)

Dahlab v Switzerland [2001] ECHR 42393/98 (ECtHR)

Dawkins v. Department of the Environment [1993] IRLR 284 (CA)

Defrenne v. Sabena II (Case 43/75) [1976] ECR 455 (ECJ)

Defrenne v. Sabena III (Case 149/77) [1978] ECR 01365 (ECJ)

Dekker v. Stichting Vormingscentrum voor Jong Volwassenen (Case C-177/88) [1990] ECR I-3941 (ECJ)

De Souza v. Automobile Association [1986] IRLR 103 (CA)

Deutsche Telekom AG v. Lilli Schröder (Case C-50/96) [2000] ECR-I-743 (ECJ)

De Venhorst BV tegen Hayriye Inan, Hoge Raad 30 Maart 1984 NJ 1985/350 (HR)

De Weerd, née Roks, and others v. Bestuur van de Bedrijfsvereniging voor de Gezondheid, Geestelijke en Maatschappelijke Belangen and others (Case C-343/92) [1994] ECR I-571(ECJ)

Dr Helga Kutz-Bauer v. Freie und Hansestadt Hamburg (Case C-187/00) [2003] ECR I-2741 (ECJ)

Driskel v. Peninsula Business Services LTD and others [2000] IRLR 151 (EAT)

Dudgeon v. the United Kingdom, 7525/76, 22 October 1981 at <http://www.echr.coe.int/echr>.

Eiser tegen Koninklijke Luchtvaartmaatschappij N.V. en de Vereniging van Nederlandse Verkeersvliegers, Hoge Raad 8-10-2004, No. C03/133 (HR)

Eisers (16 piloten) tegen Martinair Holland N.V. en de Vereniging van Nederlandse Verkeersvliegers, Hoge Raad 6-10-2004, No. C03/077 (HR)

Epke v. Commissioner of the Police of the Metropolis [2001] IRLR 605 (EAT)

Enderby v. Frenchay Health Authority & the Secretary of State for Health (Case C-127/92) [1993] ECR I-5535 (ECJ)

Equal Opportunities Commission v. Birmingham City Council [1989] 1 ALL ER 769 (HL)

Erika Steinicke v. Bundesanstalt für Arbeit (Case C-77/02) [2003] ECR I-9027 (ECJ)

Faccini Dori v Recreb Srl. (Case C-91/92) [1994] ECR I-3325 (ECJ)

Falkirk Council v. White [1997] IRLR 560 (EAT)

Francovich & Bonifaci v. Italy (Cases C-6&9/90) [1991] ECR I-5357 (ECJ)

Freers and Speckmann v. Deutsche Bundespost (Case C-278/93) [1996] ECR I-1165 (ECJ)

Finanzamt Köln-Altstadt v. Roland Schumacker (Case C-279/93) [1995] ECR I-225 (ECJ)

Garbett and Others v. Sierotko, 2406815/97 (ET)

Garry v. London Borough of Ealing [2001] IRLR 681 (CA)

Gereformeerde Kerk Hasselt, Hoge Raad 15-02-1957, NJ 1957/201 (HR)

Ghaidan (appellant) v. Godin-Mendoza (FC) (respondent) [2004] 30 21-06-2004 (HL)

Goodwin v. the Patent Office [1999] IRLR 4 (EAT)

Grant v. South-West Trains (Case C-249/96) [1998] ECR I-621 (ECJ)

Gravier v. City of Liège (Case 293/83) [1985] ECR 593 (ECJ)

Greater Manchester Police Authority v. Lea [1990] IRLR 372 (EAT)

Greenwood v. British Airways plc [1999] IRLR 600 (EAT)

Griggs v. Duke Power Co. [1971] 401 US 424 (US Supreme Court)

Hampson v. Department of Education and Science [1988] IRLR 87 (EAT)

Hampson v. Department of Education and Science [1989] IRLR 69 (CA)

Hampson v. Department of Education and Science [1990] IRLR 302 (HL)

Handels- og Kontorfunktionaerernes Forbund I Danmark v. Dansk Arbejdsgiverforening acting on behalf of Danfoss (Case 109/88) [1989] ECR 3199 (ECJ)

Helga Nimz v. Freie und Hansestadt Hamburg (Case C-184/89) [1991] ECR I-297 (ECJ)

Hill and Stapleton v. Revenue Commissioners and Department of Finance (Case C-243/95) [1998] ECR I-3739 (ECJ)

Hoffman ECHR (23 June 1993) Series A Vol. 255-C (ECtHR)

Home Office v. Coyne [2000] IRLR 838 (CA)

Horsey v. Dyfed CC [1982] ICR 755 (EAT)

Hughes v. London Borough of Hackney (unreported 7 EOR 27 1986) (IT)

Hussein v. Saints Complete House Furnishers [1979] IRLR 337 (EAT)

Inge Nolte v. Landesversicherungsanstalt Hannover (Case C-317/93) [1995] ECR I-4625 (ECJ)

Ingrid Rinner-Kühn v. FWW Spezial-Gebaudereinigung GmbH & Co.KG (Case 171/88) [1989] ECR 2743 (ECJ)

Insitu Cleaning CO LTD and another v. HEADS [1995] IRLR 4 (EAT)

Inter-Environnement Wallonie ASBL v. Région wallonne (Case C-129/96) [1997] ECR I-7411 (ECJ)

Internationale Handelsgesellschaft mbH v. Einfuhr- und Vorratsstelle für Getreide und Futtermittel (Case 11/70) [1970] ECR 1125 (ECJ)

Irving and Anor v. The Post Office [1987] IRLR 289 (EAT)

J.H. Walker Ltd v. Hussain [1996] IRLR 11 (EAT)

J.P. Jenkins v. Kingsgate (Clothing Productions) Ltd (Case C-96/80) [1981] ECR 911 (ECJ)

James v. Eastleigh Borough Council [1990] 2 All ER 607 (HL)

Jämställdhetsombudsmannen v. Örebro Läns Landsting (Case C-236/98) [2000] ECR I-2189 (ECJ)

Jepson and Dyas-Elliott (applicants) v. The Labour Party and Others (respondents) [1996] IRLR 116 (EAT)

Johnston v. Chief Constable of the Royal Ulster Constabulary (Case 222/84) [1986] ECR 1651 (ECJ)

Jones v. University of Manchester [1993] IRLR 218 (CA)

Jørgensen v. Foreningen af Speciallæger, Sygesikringens Forhandlingsudvalg (Case C-226/98) [2000] ECR I-2447 (ECJ)

Julia Schnorbus v. Land Hessen (Case C-79/99) [2000] ECR I-10997 (ECJ)

K.B. v National Health Service Pensions Agency and Secretary of State for Health C-117/01 EHRC 2004 10 (ECJ)

Kalanke v. Freie Hansestadt Bremen (Case C-450/93) [1995] ECR I-3051 (ECJ)

Karaduman v. Turkey 16278/90 [1993] 74 DR 93 (CD)

Karner v. Austria EHRC 2003 83 (ECtHR)

Katharina Rinke v. Ärztekammer Hamburg (Case C-25/02) [2003] ECR I-2575 (ECJ)

Kenny v. Hamshire Constabulary [1999] IRLR 76 (EAT)

Kidd (appellant) v. DRG (UK) LTD (respondents) [1985] IRLR 190 (EAT)

Kingston and Richmond Area Health Authority v. Kaur [1981] ICR 631 (EAT)

Kokkinakis v. Greece 14307/88 [1993] ECHR 20 (25 May 1993) (ECtHR)

Konstantinos Adeneler and Others v Ellinikos Organismos Galaktos (ELOG), (Case C-212/04) [2005] available at <http://www.europa.eu.int> (ECJ) (*n.y.r.*)

Konttinen v. Finland, 24949/94 [1996] (03 December 1996) 87-A DR 86 (CD)

Kording v. Senator für Finanzen (Case 100/95) [1997] ECR I-5289 (ECJ)

Kowalska v. Freie und Hansestadt Hamburg (Case C-33/89) [1990] ECR I-2591 (ECJ)

Kuratorium für Dialyse and Nierentransplantation e.V. v. Johanna Lewark (Case C-457/93) [1996] ECR I-00243 (ECJ)

L v. United Kingdom 25680/94 11 July 2002 (ECtHR GC)

L and V v Austria EHRC 2003 18 (ECtHR)

Leonard v. Southern Derbyshire Chamber of Commerce [2001] IRLR 19 (EAT)

Leyla Sahin v. Turkey 44774/98 (10 November 2005) (ECtHR GC)

Leyla Sahin v. Turkey 44774/98 (29 June 2004) (ECtHR)

Lommers v. Minister van Landbouw, Natuurbeheer en Visserij (Case C-476/99) [2002] ECR I-2891 (ECJ)

London Borough of Lambeth v. CRE [1990] IRLR 231 (CA)

London Underground Ltd (appellants) v. Edwards (Respondent) [1995] IRLR 355 (EAT)

London Underground Ltd v. Edwards (No. 2) [1997] IRLR 157 (EAT)

London Underground v. Edwards (No 2) [1998] IRLR 364 (CA)

Lustig-Prean and *Beckett v. the United Kingdom* 31417/96 and 32377/96 (27 December 1999) (ECtHR) available at <http://www.echr.coe.int/echr>.

Luisa Sabbatini v. European Parliament (Case 20/71) [1972] ECR 00345 (ECJ)

MacCarthys Ltd. v. Smith Advel (Case 129/80) [1980] ECR 1275 (ECJ)

Macdonald (Appellant) v. Advocate General for Scotland (Respondent) and Pearce (Appellant) v. Governing Body of Mayfield School (Respondents) [2003] UKHL 34 (HL)

Mandla v. Lee [1983] 2 AC 548 IRLR 209 (HL)

Manchester University v. Jones [1992] ICR. 52 (EAT)

Mangold v. Helm (Case C-144/04) [2005] (ECJ) available at <http://www.europa.eu.int> (ECJ) (*n.y.r.*)

Marguerite Johnston v. Chief Constable of the Royal Ulster Constabulary (Case 222/84) [1986] ECR (ECJ)

Marleasing SA v. La Comercial Internacionale de Alimentacion SA (Case 106/89) [1990] ECR I-4135 (ECJ)

Marschall v. Land Nordrhein-Westfalen (Case C-409/95) [1997] ECR I-6363 (ECJ)

Marshall v. Southhampton & South-West Hampshire Area Health Authority (Teaching) (Case 152/84) [1986] ECR 723 (ECJ)

Martinez Sala v. Freistaat Bayern (Case C-85-96) [1998] ECR I-2691 (ECJ)

Meer v. Tower Hamlets LBC [1988] IRLR 399 (CA)

Megner and Scheffel v. Innungskrankenkasse Vorderplatz (Case C-444/93) [1995] ECR I-4741 (ECJ)

Morgan v. Staffordshire University [2002] IRLR 190 (EAT)

Morse v. Wiltshire County Council [1998] IRLR 352 (EAT)

Mowat-Brown v. University of Surrey [2002] IRLR 235 (EAT)

Murray v. Newham Citizens Advice Bureau Ltd. (no. 2) [2003] IRLR 340 (EAT)

Nicole Wippel v. Peek & Cloppenburg GmbH & Co KG (Case C-313/02) [2004] ECR I-09483 (ECJ)

Nold, Kohlen und Baustoffgrosshandlung v Commission of the European Communities (Case 4-73) [1974] ECR (ECJ)

O'Flynn v. Adjudication Officer (Case C-237/94) [1996] ECR I-2617 (ECJ)

Ojutiku and Oberoni v. Manpower Services Commission, [1982] IRLR 418 (CA)

O'Neill v. Symm & Company Limited [1998] 481 (EAT)

Op 't Land-Wulffelé v. ESS, Hoge Raad 1-11-2002 No. C01/076/ NJ 2003/28 (HR)

Opinion 1994-04 (ETC)

Opinion 1995-15 (ETC)

Opinion 1995-31(ETC)

Opinion 1995-35 (ETC)

Opinion 1995-47 (ETC)

Opinion 1996-10 (ETC)

Opinion 1996-23 (ETC)

Opinion 1996-88 (ETC)

Opinion 1996-109 (ETC)

Opinion 1996-118 (ETC)

Opinion 1997-04 (ETC)

Opinions 1997-07 (ETC)

Opinion 1997-15 (ETC)

Opinion 1997-23 (ETC)

Opinion 1997-25 (ETC)

Opinion 1997-29 (ETC)

Opinion 1997-45 (ETC)

Opinion 1997-46 (ETC)

Opinion 1997-70 (ETC)

Opinion 1997-82 (ETC)

Opinion 1997-91 (ETC)

Opinion 1997-101 (ETC)

Opinion 1997-105 (ETC)

Opinion 1997-106 (ETC)

Opinion 1997-108 (ETC)

Opinion 1997-122 (ETC)

Opinion 1997-138 (ETC)

Opinion 1997-147 (ETC)
Opinion 1997-149 (ETC)
Opinion 1998-38 (ETC)
Opinion 1998-98 (ETC)
Opinion 1998-110 (ETC)
Opinion 1998-119 (ETC)
Opinion 1998-123 (ETC)
Opinion 1998-137 (ETC)
Opinion 1998-139 (ETC)
Opinion 1998-151 (ETC)
Opinion 1999-01 (ETC)
Opinion 1999-08 (ETC)
Opinion 1999-16 (ETC)
Opinion 1999-18 (ETC)
Opinion 1999-31 (ETC)
Opinion 1999-32 (ETC)
Opinion 1999-38 (ETC)
Opinion 1999-48 (ETC)
Opinion 1999-49 (ETC)
Opinion 1999-50 (ETC)
Opinion 1999-72 (ETC)
Opinion 1999-103 (ETC)
Opinion 1999-106 (ETC)
Opinion 1999-107 (ETC)
Opinion 2000-25 (ETC)
Opinion 2000-51 (ETC)
Opinion 2000-60 (ETC)
Opinion 2000-64 (ETC)
Opinion 2000-67 (ETC)
Opinion 2000-73 (ETC)
Opinion 2000-95 (ETC)
Opinion 2001-09 (ETC)
Opinion 2001-54 (ETC)
Opinion 2001-83 (ETC)
Opinion 2001-88 (ETC)
Opinion 2001-131 (ETC)
Opinion 2001-143 (ETC)

Opinion 2002-24 (ETC)
Opinion 2002-25 (ETC)
Opinion 2002-26 (ETC)
Opinion 2002-63 (ETC)
Opinion 2002-67 (ETC)
Opinion 2002-84 (ETC)
Opinion 2002-127 (ETC)
Opinion 2002-161 (ETC)
Opinion 2002-195 (ETC)
Opinion 2002-196 (ETC)
Opinion 2003-01 (ETC)
Opinion 2003-09 (ETC)
Opinion 2003-10 (ETC)
Opinion 2003-41 (ETC)
Opinion 2003-75 (ETC)
Opinion 2003-91 (ETC)
Opinion 2003-113 (ETC)
Opinion 2003-114 (ETC)
Opinion 2003-138 (ETC)
Opinion 2003-139 (ETC)
Opinion 2003-150 (ETC)
Opinion 2004-08 (ETC)
Opinion 2004-10 (ETC)
Opinion 2004-11 (ETC)
Opinion 2004-13 (ETC)
Opinion 2004-21 (ETC)
Opinion 2004-36 (ETC)
Opinion 2004-46 (ETC)
Opinion 2004-59 (ETC)
Opinion 2004-82 (ETC)
Opinion 2004-112 (ETC)
Opinion 2004-122 (ETC)
Opinion 2004-123 (ETC)
Opinion 2004-130 (ETC)
Opinion 2004-140 (ETC)
Opinion 2004-143 (ETC)
Opinion 2004-145 (ETC)

Opinion 2004-148 (ETC)
Opinion 2004-170 (ETC)
Opinion 2004-173 (ETC)
Opinion 2005-18 (ETC)
Opinion 2005-21 (ETC)
Opinion 2005-28 (ETC)
Opinion 2005-31 (ETC)
Opinion 2005-45 (ETC)
Opinion 2005-65 (ETC)
Opinion 2005-66 (ETC)
Opinion 2005-77 (ETC)
Opinion 2005-96 (ETC)
Opinion 2005-110 (ETC)
Opinion 2005-113 (ETC)
Opinion 2005-114 (ETC)
Opinion 2005-144 (ETC)
Opinion 2005-153 (ETC)
Opinion 2005-154 (ETC)
Opinion 2005-162 (ETC)
Opinion 2005-186 (ETC)
Opinion 2005-187 (ETC)
Opinion 2005-225 (ETC)
Opinion 2005-226 (ETC)
Opinion 2005-235 (ETC)
Opinion 2005-236 (ETC)
Opinion 2006-01 (ETC)
Opinion 2006-27 (ETC)
Opinion 2006-34 (ETC)
Opinion 2006-58 (ETC)
Opinion 2006-61 (ETC)
Opinion 2006-98 (ETC)
P v. S and Cornwall County Council (Case C-13/94) [1996] ECR I-2143 (ECJ)
Panesar v. NESTLE Co. LTD ICR [1980] 144 (CA)
Pepper v. Hart [1993] AC 593 (HL)
Percy v. Church of Scotland Board of National Mission [2006] IRLR 195 (HL)
Perera v. Civil Service Commission & the Department of Customs & Excise [1982] IRLR 147 (EAT)
Perera v. Civil Service Commission & the Department of Customs & Excise [1983] IRLR 166 (CA)

Pfeiffer and others Deutsches Rotes Kreuz, Kreisverband Waldshut eV, (joined Cases C-397/01 to C-403/01) [2004] ECR I-8835 (ECJ)

Price v. The Civil Service Commission [1978] 1 All ER 1228 (HL)

Quereshi v. Victoria University of Manchester [1996] EAT/484/95 (EAT)

R (on the application of SB) v. Headteacher and Governors of Denbigh Highschool [2005] EWCA Civ 199 2 All E.R. 396 (CA Civil Division)

R (on the application of Begum (by her litigation friend, Rahman (Respondent) v. Headteacher and Governors of Denbigh High School (Appellants) [2006] 15 of 22 March 2006 (HL)

R v. Birmingham City Council ex Parte EOC [1989] 1 All ER 769 (HL)

R v. Secretary of State for Employment, ex parte Seymour Smith and Perez (Case C-167/97) [1999] ECR 1999 I-00623 (ECJ)

R. v. Secretary of State for Trade and Industry, ex parte Amicus – MSF Section, et al. [2004] EWHC 860 (High Court (Administrative Court))

R v. Secretary of State v. Unison [1996] IRLR 438 (EAT)

Rainey v. Greater Glasgow Health Board [1987] IRLR 26(HL)

Redfearn v. Serco LTD t/a West Yorkshire Transport Service [2005] IRLR 744 (EAT)

Reed and Bull Information Systems Ltd v. Stedman [1999] IRLR 300 (EAT)

Regina v. Secretary of State for Employment (Original Appellant and Cross Respondent) *Ex Parte Seymour Smith (A.P.) and Another* (Original Respondents and Cross-Appellants) [2000] 1 All ER 857 (HL)

Ridout v. TC Group [1998] IRLR 628 (EAT)

Rinner-Kühn v. FWW Spezial-Gebaudereinigung GmbH & Co.KG (Case 171/88) [1989] ECR 2743 (ECJ)

Ruckdeschel & Co. et Hansa-Lagerhaus Ströh & Co. v. Hauptzollamt Hamburg-St. Annen ; Diamalt AG v. Hauptzollamt Itzehoe (Joined Cases 117/76 and 16/77) [1977] ECR 1753 (ECJ)

Rugamer v. Sony Entertainment UK Ltd and McNicol v. Balfour Beatty Rail Maintenance Ltd [2001] IRLR 644 (EAT)

Rugamer v. Sony Entertainment UK Ltd and McNicol v. Balfour Beatty Rail Maintenance Ltd [2002] IRLR 711 (CA)

Rutherford and Bentley v. Secretary of State for Trade and Industry (no. 2) [2004] IRLR 892 EWCA (CA)

Salgueiro da Silva Mouta v. Portugal EHRC 2000 16 (ECtHR)

Seide v. Gillette Industries Ltd [1980] IRLR 427 (EAT)

Shamoon v. Chief Constable of the Royal Ulter Constabulary [2003] IRLR 285 (HL)

Showboat Entertainment Centre Ltd v. Owens [1984] IRLR 7 (EAT)

Sidabras and Dziautas v. Lithuania EHRC 2004 90 (ECtHR)

Sidhu v. Aerospace Composite Technology Ltd [1999] IRLR 683 (EAT)

Sidhu v. Aerospace Composite Technology Ltd [2000] IRLR 602 (CA)

Simon v. Brimham Associates [1987] IRLR 307 (CA)

Smith v. Churchills Stairlifts plc [2006] IRLR 41 (CA)

BIBLIOGRAPHY

Ahtela 2005
Ahtela, K., 'The Revised Provisions on Sex Discrimination in European Law, a Critical Assessment', *European Law Journal*, Vol. 11, No. 1, January 2005, p. 57-78.

Alkema and Rop 2002
Alkema, E.A. and Rop, A.C., 'Gelijk zijn en gelijk krijgen- aspecten van gelijkheid in de rechtspraktijk', in: Kroes, M., Loof, J.P. & Ten Napel, H.-M. Th.D. (eds.), *Gelijkheid en Rechtvaardigheid Staatsrechtelijke Vraagstukken om Minderheden*, Deventer: Kluwer, 2002, p. 31-77.

Alkema 2004
Alkema, E.A., 'Gelijkheid binnen het recht - enkele beschouwingen over het gelijkheidsconcept en zijn effecten', in: Holtmaat, R., (ed.), *Gelijkheid en (andere) grondrechten*, Deventer: Kluwer, 2004, p. 53-66.

Alston and De Schutter 2005
Alston, Ph. and De Schutter, O. (eds.), *Monitoring Fundamental Rights in the EU The Constribution of the Fundamental Rights Agency*, Oxford, 2005.

Apostolopoulou 2004
Apostolopoulou, Z., 'Equal Treatment of People With Disabilities in the EC, What does "equal" mean'?, Jean Monnet Working Paper, 09/04, available at <http://www.jeanmonnetpro gram.org/papers/04/040901.pdf>.

Asscher-Vonk 1998
Asscher-Vonk, I.P., 'Gelijke Behandeling in Vier Vragen', *Sociaal Recht*, 1998-4, p. 112-116.

Asscher-Vonk 1998a
Asscher-Vonk, I.P., 'Gelijke Behandeling van Gehandicapten', *SMA*, 1998, 7/8, p. 301-304.

Asscher-Vonk 1999
Asscher-Vonk, I.P., 'Conclusie Juridische Analyse', in: Asscher-Vonk, I.P. en Groenendijk, C.A. (eds.), *Gelijke Behandeling, Regels en Realiteit*, Den Haag: Sdu Uitgevers, 1999, p. 301-319.

Asscher-Vonk 2001
Asscher-Vonk, I.P., 'Gelijke Behandeling, Richtlijnen, de Bomen en het Bos', *SMA*, 2001, 4, p. 191-195.

Asscher-Vonk and Monster 2002
Asscher-Vonk, I.P. and Monster, W.C., *Gelijke Behandeling bij de Arbeid*, Deventer: Kluwer, 2002.

Asscher-Vonk and Wentholt 1994
Asscher-Vonk, I.P. and Wentholt, K., *Wet Gelijke Behandeling van Mannen en Vrouwen*, Deventer: Kluwer, 1994.

Bacik 2003
Bacik, I., 'Harassment', in: Costello, C. and Barry, E. (eds.), *Equality in Diversity, The New Equality Directives*, Irish Centre for European Law, 2003, p. 151-176

Bakirci 1998
Bakirci, K., 'Sexual harassment in the workplace in relation to EC legislation', *International Journal of Discrimination and the Law*, 1998, Vol. 3, p. 3-28.

Bamforth 1996
Bamforth, N., 'Setting the Limits of Anti-Discrimination Law, Some Legal and Social Concepts', in: Dine, J. and Watt, B. (eds.), *Discrimination Law, Concepts, Limitations and Justifications*, London and New York: Longman, 1996, p. 49-62.

Bamforth 1999
Bamforth, N., 'The Application of the Human Rights Act 1998 to Public Authorities and Private Bodies', *Cambridge Law Journal*, 58(1), March 1999, p. 159-170.

Bamforth 2000
Bamforth, N., 'Sexual Orientation Discrimination After *Grant v Southwest Trains*', *The Modern Law Review*, September 2000, p. 694-720.

Bamforth 2004
Bamforth, N., 'Conceptions of Anti-Discrimination Law', 24 *Oxford Journal of Legal Studies*, No. 4, 2004, p. 693-716.

Barbera 2002
Barbera, M., 'Not the Same? The Judicial Role in the New Community Anti-Discrimination Context', *Industrial Law Journal*, Vol. 31, No. 1, March 2002, p. 82-91.

Barnard 1996
Barnard, C., 'Gender and Commercial Discrimination', in: Dine, J. and Watt, B. (eds.), *Discrimination Law. Concepts, Limitations, and Justifications*, London/New York: Longman, 1996, p. 63-76.

Barnard 1996a
Barnard, C., 'The Economic Objectives of Article 119 EC', in: Hervey, T. and O' Keeffe, D. (eds.), *Sex Equality Law in the European Union*, Chichester: Wiley, 1996, p. 320-334.

Barnard 1997
Barnard, C., '*P. v. S.*, Kite flying or a new constitutional approach'?, in: Dashwood, A. and O'Leary, S. (eds.), *The Principle of Equal Treatment in EC Law*, London: Sweet and Maxwell, 1997, p. 59-79.

Barnard 1997a
Barnard, C., 'The United Kingdom, the Social Chapter and the Amsterdam Treaty', 26 *Industrial Law Journal*, 1997, p. 275-282.

Barnard 1998
Barnard, C., 'The Principle of Equality in the Community Context, *P*, *Grant*, *Kalanke* and *Marshall*, four uneasy bedfellows?', *Cambridge Law Journal*, 57, 2, July 1998, p. 352-373.

Barnard 1999
Barnard, C., 'Article 13 EC, Through the Looking Glass of Union Citizenship', in: O'Keeffe, D. and Twomey, P. (eds.), *Legal Issues of the Amsterdam Treaty*, Hart Publishing, 1999, p. 375-394.

Barnard 2000
Barnard, C., *EC Employment Law*, 2nd edition, OUP, 2000.

Barnard 2001
Barnard, C., 'The Changing Scope of the Fundamental Principle of Equality?', *McGill Law Journal,* 2001, p. 955-977.

Barnard, Deakin and Kilpatrick 2002
Barnard, C., Deakin, S., Kilpatrick, C., 'Equality, Non-discrimination and the Labour Market in the UK', 18/2, *The International Journal of Comparative Labour Law and Industrial Relations,* 2002, p. 129-147.

Barnard and Hepple 1999
Barnard, C. and Hepple, B., 'Indirect Discrimination, Interpreting Seymour Smith', 58(2), *Cambridge Law Journal,* 1999, p. 399-412.

Barnard and Hepple 2000
Barnard, C. and Hepple, B., 'Substantive Equality', *Cambridge Law Journal,* 59 (3), November 2000, p. 562-585.

Barnard and Hervey 1998
Barnard, C. and Hervey, T., 'Softening the approach to Quotas, positive action after Marshall', 20, *Journal of Social Welfare and Family Law,* 1998, p. 333-352.

Barnes 2000
Barnes, C., 'A Working Social Model? Disability, work and disability politics in the 21st century', *Critical Social Policy,* 2000, p. 441-457.

Bell 1999
Bell, M., 'Shifting Conceptions of Sexual Discrimination at the Court of Justice, from *P. v. S.* to *Grant v. SWT*', 5 *European Law Journal,* 1999, p. 63-81.

Bell 1999a
Bell, M., 'The New Article 13 EC Treaty, a Sound Basis for European Anti-Discrimination law?', *Maastricht Journal of European and Comparative Law,* 1999, p. 5-23.

Bell 2000
Bell, M., 'Article 13 EC, the European Commission's Anti-Discrimination Proposals', *Industrial Law Journal,* Vol. 29, 2000, p. 79-84.

Bell 2000a
Bell, M., 'Equality and Diversity, Anti Discrimination Law After Amsterdam', in: Shaw, J. (ed.), *Social Law and Policy in an evolving European Union,* Hart Publishing, 2000 p. 157-170.

Bell 2001
Bell, M., 'Mainstreaming Equality Norms into European Union Asylum Law, 26, *European Law Review,* 2001, p. 20-34.

Bell 2001a
Bell, M., 'Meeting the Challenge? A Comparison between the EU Racial Equality Directive and the Starting Line', in: Chopin, I. and Niessen, J., *The Starting Line and the Incorporation of the Racial Equality Directive into the National Laws of the EU Member States and Accession States,* Migration Policy Group (MPG), London/Brussels: Belmont Press, 2001, p. 22-54.

Bell 2001b
Bell, M., 'Sexual Orientation Discrimination in Employment, An Evolving Role for the European Union', in: Wintemute, R. and Andenas, M. (eds.), *Legal recognition of same sex couples, a study of national, European and international law,* Oxford Portland, Oregon: Hart Publishing 2001, p. 653-676.

Bell 2002
Bell, M., *Anti-Discrimination Law and the European Union,* OUP, 2002.

Bell 2002a
Bell, M., 'Beyond European Labour Law? Reflections on the EU Racial Equality Directive', *European Law Journal*, 8, No. 3, September 2002, p. 384-399.

Bell 2003
Bell, M., 'The Right to Equality and Non Discrimination', in: Hervey, T. and Kenner, J. (eds.), *Economic and Social Rights under the EU Charter of Fundamental Rights, a legal Perspective*, Oxford-Portland, Oregon: Hart Publishing, 2003, p. 91-110.

Bell 2003a
Bell, M., 'Diversity of religion and belief at work- a new legal framework', in: McColgan A. (ed.), *Achieving Equality at Work*, Institute for Employment Rights, 2003, p. 49-68.

Bell 2004
Bell, M., 'A Patchwork of Protection, The new Anti-Discrimination Law Framework', *The Modern Law Review*, 67:3, 2004, p. 465-477.

Bell 2004a
Bell, M., 'Equality and the European Union Constitution', *Industrial Law Journal*, 33, September 2004, p. 242-260.

Bell and Waddington 2003
Bell, M. and Waddington, L., 'Reflecting on Inequalities in European Equality Law', 28, *European Law Review*, June, 2003, p. 349-369.

Beveridge, Nott and Stephen 2000
Beveridge, F., Nott, S. and Stephen, K., 'Addressing Gender in National and Community Law and Policy-making', in: Shaw, M. (ed.), *Social Law and Policy in an evolving EU*, 2000, p.135-154.

Bharania 2004
Bharania, M., *Law Gazette*, Vol. 101, no. 21, 2004.

Bickenbach 1999
Bickenbach, J.E., 'Minority Rights or Universal Participation, The Politics of Disablement', in: Jones and Basser Marks (eds.), *Disability, Divers-ability and legal change*, Martinus Nijhoff Publishers, The Hague/ London/ Boston, 1999, p. 101-115.

Bindman 1985
Bindman, G., 'Reforming the Race Relations Act – II', *New Law Journal*, 1985, p. 1167-1169.

Bindman 1992
Bindman, G., 'Proof and Evidence of Discrimination', in: Hepple, B. and Szyszczak, E. (eds.) *Discrimination, the Limits of Law*, Mansell, 1992, p. 50-66.

Blumenthal 1998
Blumenthal, J., 'The Reasonable Woman Standard, A Meta-Analytic Review of Gender Differences in Perceptions of Sexual Harassment', 22, *Law and Human Behavior*, No. 1, 1998, p. 33-57.

Boerefijn, Coomans, Holtmaat and Wolleswinkel 2003
Boerefijn, I., Coomans, F., Goldschmidt J., Holtmaat R., Wolleswinkel R., *Temporary Special Measures Accelerating de facto Equality of Women under Article 4(1) UN Convention on the Elimination of All Forms of Discrimination against Women*, Anwerpen-Oxford-New York, 2003.

Bolger 2003
Bolger, M., 'Discrimination on grounds of religion', in: Costello, C. and Barry, E., *Equality in Diversity the New Equality Directives*, Irish Centre for European law, 2003, p. 371-390.

Bonini-Baraldi 2004
Bonini-Baraldi, M., 'Combating sexual orientation discrimination in employment, legislation in fifteen EU member states', Report of the European Group of Experts on Combating Sexual Orientation Discrimination about the implementation up to April 2004 of Directive 2000/78/EC establishing a general framework for equal treatment in employment and occupation, 2004, available at, <http://ec.europa.eu/employment_social/fundamental_rights/pdf/aneval/sexoreulaw.pdf>.

Bosse 2000
Bosse, C., 'Richtlijn inzake Bewijs van Discriminatie', 55, *Sociaal Maandblad voor de Arbeid*, 2000, p. 64-67.

Bossuyt 1998
Bossuyt, M., 'Het Discriminatieverbod en 'Positieve Actie', *Rechtskundig Weekblad*, 1998-1999, 8, 24 October 1998, p. 241-246.

Bossuyt 2002
Bossuyt, M., 'Prevention of Discrimination, the concept and practice of affirmative action', *Final Report for the UN Economic and Social Council*, E/CN.4/Sub.2/2002/21, 17th June 2002, p. 1-40.

Bowers and Moran 2002
Bowers, J. QC and Moran, E., 'Justification in Direct Sex Discrimination Law, Breaking the Taboo', *Industrial Law Journal*, Vol. 31, No. 4, December 2002, p. 307-320.

Buckley 1997
Buckley, L., 'Vicarious Liability and Employment Discrimination', *Industrial Law Journal*, Volume 26, June 1997, p. 158-166.

Burnham and Cohen 2006
Burnham, U. and Cohen, B., 'A New Vision for Equality Law', *Discrimination Law Association*, Briefings 391-404, 2006, p. 3-6.

Burrows and Robison 2006
Burrows, N. and Robison, M. (eds.), 'Positive Action for Women in Employment, Time to Align with Europe?', *Journal of Law and Society*, Volume 33, No. 1, March 2006, p. 24-41.

Caruso 2002
Caruso, D., *Limits of the Classic Method, Positive Action in the European Union after the New Equality Directives*, Jean Monnet Working Paper, 10/2002 p. 1-57.

Chalmers, Hadjiemmanuil, Monti and Tomkins 2006
Chalmers, D., Hadjiemmanuil, C., Monti G., and Tomkins A., *European Union Law*, Cambridge, 2006.

Chopin and Niessen 2001
Chopin, I. and Niessen, J. (eds.), *The Starting Line and the Incorporation of the Racial Equality Directive into the National Laws of the EU Member States and Accession States*, Migration Policy Group (MPG), London/Brussels: Belmont Press, 2001.

Choudhury 2006
Choudhury, T., 'New Protection from Discrimination for Religion and Belief', *Discrimination Law Association*, Briefings 391-404, 2006, p. 13-17.

Clarke 2006
Clarke, L., 'Harassment, Sexual Harassment, and the Employment Equality (Sex Discrimination) Regulations 2005, *Industrial Law Journal*, 35, 2006, p. 161-178.

Clayton 1998
Clayton, A., 'Comment, *Hellmut Marschall v. Land Nordrhein-Westfalen*, Has Equal Opportunity Between the Sexes Finally Found a Champion in European Community Law?', 16, *Boston University International Law Journal*, 423, 1998, p. 1-23.

Cliteur 2002
Cliteur, P., *Moderne Papoea's Dilemma's van een Multi-Culturele Samenleving*, Amsterdam/Antwerpen: De Arbeiderspers, 2002.

Cohen 2005
Cohen, B., *Report on Measures to Combat Discrimination Directives 2000/43/EC and 2000/78/EC*, 2005, (66 p.) available at, <http://europa.eu.int/comm/employment_social/fundamental_rights/pdf/legnet/nlrep05_en.pdf>.

Cohen 2005a
Cohen, B., UK Executive Summary of the Report on Measures to Combat Discrimination, 2005, (9 p.), available at <http://europa.eu.int/comm/employment_social/fundamental_rights/pdf/legnet/nlrep05_en.pdf>.

Collins 2003
Collins, H., 'Discrimination, Equality and Social Inclusion', 2003, *Modern Law Review*, Vol. 66, issue 1, p. 16-43.

Connolly 1996
Connolly, M., 'How an ECJ decision on Equal Pay May Affect British Indirect Discrimination Law', Web Journal of Current Legal Issues, 1996, 1, available at, <http://webjcli.ncl.ac.uk/1996/issue1/connolly1.html>.

Connolly 2000
Connolly, M., 'Freedom from Discrimination – *R v. Secretary of State for Employment, ex parte Seymour-Smith*, Case C-167/97, [1999] All ER (EC) 97 ECJ, [2000] 1 All ER 857 HL', 5, *J.C.L.*, 2000, p. 212-222.

Connolly 2002
Connolly, M., 'Subjective Hiring Practices, Quotas and Plantation Economies, What is the New Definition of Indirect Race Discrimination Supposed to Challenge?', 7, *J.C.L.*, 141, 2002, p. 129-142.

Connolly 2004
Connolly, M., 'Affirmative Action', in: Townshend-Smith, R. (ed.), *Discrimination Law, text, cases and materials*, second edition, London/Sydney/Portland, Oregon: Cavendish Publishing Ltd., 2004, p. 571-581.

Cooper 2004
Cooper, J., Disability, United Kingdom Report, 2004, (20 p.) available at, <http://europa.eu.int/comm/employment_social/fundamental_rights/pdf/legnet/nlrep05_en.pdf>.

Cossman 2004
Cossman, B., 'Sexuality, Queer theory, and 'Feminism After', Reading and Rereading the Sexual Subject', *McGill Law Journal*, 49, 2004, p. 847-876.

Costello 2003
Costello, C., 'Positive Action', in: Costello, C., and Barry, E., *Equality in Diversity, the New Equality Directives*, Irish Centre for European Law, 2003, p. 177-212.

Costello 2003a
Costello, C., 'Gender Equalities and the Charter of Fundamental Rights of the European Union', in: Hervey, T. and Kenner, J., *Economic and Social Rights under the EU Charter of Fundamental Rights, a legal Perspective*, Oxford-Portland, Oregon: Hart Publishing, 2003, p. 111-138.

Craig and De Búrca 2003
Craig, P. and De Búrca, G., *EU Law- Text, Cases and Materials,* third edition, OUP, 2003.

Cremers-Hartman 1999
Cremers-Hartman, E., 'Werkingssfeer AWGB (Art. 3, 4 sub c, 5 lid 1, 6, 7 lid 1 AWGB', in: Asscher-Vonk, I.P. and Groenendijk, C.A., *Gelijke Behandeling, Regels en Realiteit*, The Hague: Sdu Uitgevers, 1999, p. 29-88.

Crenshaw 1989
Crenshaw, K., 'Demarginalizing the Intersection of Race and Sex, A Black Feminist Critique of Anti-Discrimination Doctrine, Feminist Theory and Anti-Racist Politics', 1989, *U. Chi Legal F.*, 139, 1989, p. 139-167.

Crenshaw, Gotanda, Peller and Thomas 1995
Crenshaw, K., Gotanda, N., Peller, G. and Thomas, K. (eds.), *Critical Race Theory*, The New York Press, 1995.

Cumper 1996
Cumper, P., 'Religious Liberty in the United Kingdom', in: Van den Vyver, J.D. and Witte, J. Jr. (eds.), *Religious Human Rights in Global Perspective, Legal Perspectives*, The Hague-London-Boston: Martinus Nijhoff Publishers, 1996, p. 205-241.

Curtin 1984
Curtin, D., 'Ongewenste Intimiteiten op het Werk, de Keuze van Rechtsmiddelen', *NJCM - Bulletin*, 9, 1984, p. 419-431.

Curtin and Geurts 1996
Curtin, D. and Geurts, M., 'Race Discrimination and the European Union Anno 1996, From Rhetoric to Legal Remedy', in: *The Netherlands Quarterly of Human Rights*, Vol. 14/2, 1996, p. 147-171.

De Búrca 1997
De Búrca, G., 'The role of Equality in European Community Law', in: Dashwood, A. and O'Leary, S. (eds.), *The Principle of Equality in EC Law*, London, 1997, p. 13-34.

De Marco 2004
De Marco, N., *Blackstone's Guide to the Employment Equality Regulations 2003*, Oxford (OUP), 2004.

De Schutter 2001
De Schutter, O., *Discriminations et Marché du Travail- Liberté et égalité dans les rapports d'emploi*, Peter Lang, 2001.

De Schutter 2003
De Schutter, O., 'Methods of Proof in the Context of Combating Discrimination', in: Cormack, J. (ed.), 2003, *Proving Discrimination The Dynamic Implementation of EU Anti-Discrimination Law, the Role of Specialised Bodies*, Report of the First Experts' Meeting, 14-15 January 2003, p. 23-37.

De Schutter 2005
De Schutter, O., *The Prohibition of Discrimination under European Human Rights Law, Relevance for EU Racial and Employment Equality Directives*, European Commission, Employment and Social Affairs, 2005.

De Schutter 2005a
De Schutter, O., 'Reasonable Accommodations and Positive Obligations in the European Convention on Human Rights', in: Lawson, A. and Gooding, C. (eds.), *Disability Rights in Europe, from Theory to Practice*, Hart Publishing, 2005, p. 35-63.

De Schutter and Alston 2005
De Schutter, O. and Alston, Ph. (eds.) *Monitoring Fundamental Rights in the EU, The Contribution of the Fundamental Rights Agency*, Oxford, 2005.

De Schutter and Alston 2005a
De Schutter, O. and Alston, Ph., 'Introduction, Addressing the Challenges Confronting the EU Fundamental Rights Agency', in: Alston, Ph. and De Schutter, O. (eds.), *Monitoring Fundamental Rights in the EU, The Contribution of the Fundamental Rights Agency*, Oxford, 2005, p. 1-21.

De Winter 1996
De Winter, R., 'Godsdienst als Alibi', *Nederlands Juristenblad*, 1, 1996, p. 1-8.

Deakin 1996
Deakin, S., 'Labour Law as Market Regulation, the Economic Foundations of European Social Policy', in: Davies, P. et al. (eds), *European Community Labour Law, Principles and Perspectives. Liber Amicorum Lord Wedderburn of Charlton,* Oxford: Clarendon Press, 1996, p. 63-94.

Defeis 2004
Defeis, E.F., 'Equality and the European Union', 32, *Ga. J. Int'l & Comp. L*, 2004, p. 74-98.

Degener 2004
Degener, T., 'Definition of Disability', EU Network of Experts on Disability Discrimination, Paper presented at the Conference *Equality and Disability, Exploring the Challenge and Potential of Framework Directive 2000/78/EC'*, Louvain-la-Neuve, Belgium, 29-30 April 2004.

Degener and Quinn
Degener, T. and Quinn, G., A Survey of International Comparative and Regional Disability Law Reform from principles to practice, an International Disability Law and Policy Symposium, available at, <http://www.dredf.org/international/degener_quinn.html>.

Dine and Whatt 1995
Dine, J. and Whatt, B., 'Sexual harassment, Moving away from Discrimination', *The Modern Law Review*, 58:3, 1995, p. 343-363.

Drake 2000
Drake, R.F., 'Disabled people, New Labour, benefits and Work', *Critical Social Policy*, 65, 20:4, 2000, p. 421-457.

Driessen-Reilly and Driessen 2003
Driessen-Reilly, M. and Driessen, B., 'Don't Shoot the messenger, a Look at Community Law relating to Harassment in the Workplace', 28 *European Law Review*, 2003, p. 493-507.

Duppert 2005
Duppert, O., 'Remedying the Past or Reshaping the Future? Justifying Race-Based Affirmative Action in South Africa and the United States', *Journal of Comparative Labour Law and Industrial Relations*, Volume 21, Issue 1, Spring 2005, p. 89-130.

Dworkin 1985
Dworkin, R., *A matter of Principle*, Cambridge, Massachusetts: Harvard University Press, 1985.

Dworkin 2000
Dworkin, R., *Sovereign Virtue, the Theory and Practice of Equality*, Harvard University Press, 2000.

EDF 2001
EDF, 'Analysis of the EU Directive on Equal Treatment in Employment and Occupation', July 2001, available from the author and at <www.edf-feph.org>.

Editorial Comments 2006
'Editorial Comments', *Common Market Law Review*, 43, 2006, p. 1-8.

Ehrenreich 1990
Ehrenreich, N., 'Pluralist Myths and Powerless Men, The Ideology of Reasonableness in Sexual Harassment Law', 99, *The Yale Law Journal*, April 1990, p. 1178-1234.

Ellis 1994
Ellis, E., case-note on *Enderby*, *Common Market Law Review*, 1994, p. 387-394.

Ellis 1994a
Ellis, E., 'The Definition of Discrimination in European Community Sex Equality Law', *European Law Review*, 1994, p. 563-580.

Ellis 1998
Ellis, E., *EC Sex Equality Law*, Second Edition, Oxford: Clarendon Press, 1998.

Ellis 1998a
Ellis, E., 'Recent Developments in European Community Sex Equality Law', *Common Market Law Review*, 1998, p. 379-408.

Epstein 1992
Epstein, R., *Forbidden Grounds, The Case against Employment Discrimination Laws*, Harvard University Press, 1992.

Equal Opportunities Review 2002
Equal Opportunities Review, 'ECJ endorses positive discrimination', No. 105, May 2002, p. 25-26.

Equal Opportunities Review 2002a
Equal Opportunities Review, 'Revised Equal Treatment Directive', No. 106, June 2002, p. 22-25.

European Anti-Discrimination Law Review 2006
European Anti-Discrimination Law Review, Issue No. 3, April 2006.

European Commission 2004
European Commission, *Comparative Study on the Collection of Data to measure the extent and impact of discrimination within the United States, Canada, Australia, the United Kingdom and the Netherlands*, August 2004.

Europese Commissie Jaarrapport 2003
Europese Commissie, Gelijkheid en Non Discriminatie Jaarrapport 2003, available at, <http://europa.eu.int/comm/employment_social/fundamental_rights/public/pubst_en.htm#annual>.

Europese Commissie Jaarrapport 2005
Europese Commissie, Gelijkheid en Non-Discriminatie Jaarrapport 2005, ISSN 1725-4760, available at, <http://europa.eu.int/comm/employment_social/fundamental_rights/public/pubst_en.htm#annual>.

Evans 1997
Evans, M.D., *Religious Liberty and International Law in Europe*, 1997, Cambridge University Press.

Evans 1999
Evans, M.D., 'Religious Liberty and Non Discrimination', in: Loenen, T. and Rodrigues, P. (eds.), *Non Discrimination Law, Comparative Perspectives*, The Hague/London/Boston: Martinus Nijhoff, Kluwer Law International, 1999, p. 119-131.

Evenhuis 1999
Evenhuis, C., 'Gender en leeftijd, verdere verkenningen', *Nemesis*, 2, maart/april 1999, p. 42-51.

Evenhuis 2000
Evenhuis, C., 'Samenloop, een ondergewaardeerd vraagstuk', in: De Wolff, D.J.B. (ed.), *Gelijke Behandeling, Oordelen en Commentaar*, Commissie Gelijke Behandeling, 2000, p. 77-90.

Evenhuis 2001
Evenhuis, C., 'Gij zult niet discrimineren- ook niet op grond van leeftijd', in: Quispel and Christ (ed.), *Ouder worden, een Kwestie van Leeftijd*, 2001, Landelijk Bureau voor Leeftijdsdiscriminatie, 2001, p. 17-29.

Evenhuis 2002
Evenhuis, C., *'Preadvies aan het LBL inzake het wetsvoorstel gelijke behandeling op grond van leeftijd bij de arbeid'*, januari 2002, p. 1-14 (available with the author)

Fahlbeck 2004
Fahlbeck, R., 'Ora et Labora - On Freedom of Religion at the Work Place, A Stakeholder cum Balancing Factors Model, *IJCLLIR*, Vol. 20/1, 2004, p. 27-64.

Fairclough 2001
Fairclough, N., 'Indirect Discrimination', *Solicitors Journal*, 2001, p. 1126-1127.

Farell 2004
Farrell, S., 'Reconsidering the Gender Equality Perspective for understanding LGBT rights', 13 *Law and Sexuality, Rev. Lesbian, Gay, Bisexual & Transgender Legal Issues*, 2004, p. 605-704.

Feldman 2002
Feldman, D., *Civil Liberties and Human Rights in England and Wales*, 2nd edition, OUP 2002.

Fenwick 1998
Fenwick, H., 'From formal to substantive equality, the place of affirmative action in EU sex equality law', 4, *European Public Law*, 1998, p. 507-516.

Fenwick and Hervey 1995
Fenwick, H. and Hervey, T.K., 'Sex equality in the single market, new directions for the European Court of Justice', *Common Market Law Review*, 1995, p. 443-470.

Finlay 2003
Finlay, M., 'Indirect discrimination and the Article 13 Directives', in: Costello, C. and Barry (eds.), *Equality in Diversity, the new Equality Directives*, 2003, p. 135-150.

Fisher 1990
Fisher, L., *Constitutional Rights, Civil Rights and Civil Liberties, Volume 2 of American Constitutional Law*, McGraw-Hill Publishing Company, 1990.

Fitzpatrick and Kilpatrick 2000
Fitzpatrick, B. and Kilpatrick, C., 'The EC Directive on Race Discrimination, Suprises, Possibilities and Limitations', 29 *Industrial Law Journal*, 2000, p. 416-423.

Flynn 1999
Flynn, L. 'The Implications of Article 13 EC- After Amsterdam, will some forms of discrimination be more equal than others?', *Common Market Law Review*, 1999, p. 1127-1152.

Franke 1998
Franke, K. M., 'Gender, Sex, Agency and Discrimination, A Reply to Professor Abrams', *Cornell Law Review*, 1998, p. 1245-1256.

Fredman 1992
Fredman, S. 'European Community Discrimination Law, a Critique', 21, *Industrial Law Journal*, 1992, p. 110-134.

Fredman 1994
Fredman, S., 'A Difference with Distinction, Pregnancy and Parenthood Reassessed', 110, *Law Quarterly Review*, 1994, p. 106-123.

Fredman 1994a
Fredman, S., 'Equal Pay and Justification', Case-127/92 *Enderby v Frenchay Health Authority*, [1993] IRLR 591 (ECJ), *Industrial Law Journal*, Vol. 23, No. 1 March 1994, p. 37-41.

Fredman 1996
Fredman, S., 'Less Equal than Others- Equality and Women's rights', in: Gearty, C. and Tomkins, A.(eds.), *Understanding Human Rights*, London/New York: Mansell, 1996, p. 197-217.

Fredman 1997
Fredman, S., 'Reversing Discrimination', 113, *The Law Quarterly Review*, October 1997, p. 575-600.

Fredman 1997a
Fredman, S., *Women and the Law*, Oxford: Clarendon Press, 1997.

Fredman 1999
Fredman, S., 'A Critical Review of the Concept of Equality in UK Anti-Discrimination Law', Independent Review of the Enforcement of UK Anti-Discrimination Legislation, *Working Paper* No. 3, 1999, p. 1-18 (available from the author).

Fredman 2000
Fredman, S., 'Affirmative Action and the European Court of Justice, A Critical Analysis', in: Shaw, J. (ed.), *Social Law and Policy in an Evolving European Union*, 2000, p. 171-195.

Fredman 2001
Fredman, S., 'Combating Racism with Human Rights, the Right to Equality', in: Fredman, S. (ed.), *Discrimination and Human Rights- the case of racism*, Vol. XI/1, 2001, OUP, p. 9-44.

Fredman 2001a
Fredman, S., 'Equality, a New Generation?', *Industrial Law Journal*, Vol. 30, No. 2, 2001, p. 145-168.

Fredman 2002
Fredman, S., *Discrimination Law*, Clarendon Law Series, OUP 2002.

Fredman 2002a
Fredman, S., 'The Future of Equality in Britain', *Working Paper Series* No. 5, Equal Opportunities Commission, 2002.

Fredman 2002b
Fredman, S., 'Why the UK Government Should sign and ratify Protocol No. 12', Equal Opportunities Review 2002, available from <http://www.justice.org.uk/images/pdfs/protocol12.pdf>.

Fredman 2003
Fredman, S., 'Discrimination', in: Cane, P. and Tushnet, M. (eds.), *The Oxford Handbook of Legal Studies*, 2003, Chapter 11.

Fredman 2003a
Fredman S., 'The Age of Equality', in: Fredman, S. and Spencer, S. (eds.), *Age as an Equality Issue*, Oxford Portland, Oregon, 2003, p. 21-69.

Fredman 2004
Fredman, S., 'Marginalising Equal Pay Laws, *Allonby v Accrington & Rossendale College*, Case C-256/01 [2004] IRLR 224 (ECJ)', *Industrial Law Journal*, Vol. 33, No. 3, September 2004, p. 281-285.

Fredman 2005
Fredman, S. 'Disability Equality, A Challenge to the Existing Anti-Discrimination Paradigm?', in: Gooding, C. and Lawson, A. (eds.), *Disability Rights in Europe*, Oxford Portland, Oregon, 2005, p. 199-218.

Fredman 2005a
Fredman, S., 'Changing the Norm, Positive Duties in Equal Treatment Legislation', 12, *MJ*, 2005, p. 369-397.

Fredman and Spencer 2003
Fredman, S. and Spencer, S., 'Introduction', in: Fredman, S. and Spencer, S. (eds.), *Age as an Equality Issue*, Hart Publishing, 2003, p. 1-9.

Fredman and Szyszczak 1992
Fredman, S. and Szyszczak, E., 'The Interaction of Race and Gender', in: Hepple, B. and Szyszczak, E. (eds.), 1992, p. 214-226.

Friedman and Whitman 2003
Friedman, G. and Whitman, J.Q., 'The European Transformation of Harassment Law, Discrimination *v.* Dignity', 9, *Colombia Journal of European Law*, Spring 2003, p. 241-274.

Gardner 1998
Gardner, J., 'On the ground of Her Sex(uality)', 18 *Oxford Journal of Legal Studies*, 168, 1998, p. 167-187.

Geddes and Guiraudon 2004
Geddes, A. and Guiraudon, V., 'Britain, France, and EU Anti-Discrimination Policy, The Emergence of an EU Policy Paradigm', *West European Politics*, 27, 2004, p. 334-353.

Gearty 1999
Gearty, C.A., 'The Internal and External 'Other' in the Union Legal Order, Racism, Religious Intolerance and Xenophobia in Europe', in: P. Alston (ed.), *The The EU and Human Rights*, Oxford University Press, 1999, Chapter 10, p. 327-358.

Geers 1996
Geers, A.J.C.M., 'Seksuele Intimidatie en het mensbeeld in het arbeidsrecht', in: Loonstra, C.J. (ed.), *Arbeidsrecht en Mensbeeld 1946-1996, Jubileumbundel Vereniging voor Arbeidsrecht*, Deventer: Kluwer, 1996, p. 155-167.

Geers 1997
Geers, A.J.C.M., 'Verbod leeftijdsdiscriminatie bij werving en selectie bij de arbeid', *Sociaal Recht*, 11, 1997, p. 311-312.

Geers 2003
Geers, A.J.C.M., 'Intimidatie op de werkplek', in: Van Maanen, G. (ed.), *De Rol van het Aansprakelijkheidsrecht bij de verwerking van persoonlijk leed*, Boom Juridische Uitgevers, 2003, p. 183-198.

Geers 2003a
Geers, A.J.C.M., 'Naar een nieuwe Intimidatiewet', *Sociaal Recht*, 2, 2003, p. 35-36.

Gerards 2002
Gerards, J., *Rechterlijke Toetsing aan het Gelijkheidsbeginsel, Een rechtsvergelijkend onderzoek naar een algemeen toetsingsmodel*, Den Haag: Sdu Uitgevers, 2002.

Gerards 2003
Gerards, case note on *Karner*, EHRM 24 Juli 2003, No. 40016/98, *Karner, European Human Rights Cases*, 2003, Vol. 9, p. 766-777.

Gerards 2003a
Gerards, J., 'Het toetsingsmodel van de CGB voor de beoordeling van indirect onderscheid', in: De Wolff, D.J.B. (ed.), *Gelijke Behandeling Oordelen en Commentaar 2002*, 2003, p. 77-95.

Gerards 2004
Gerards, J., 'Intensity of Judicial Review in Equal Treatment Cases', *N.I.L.R.*, 2004, p. 135-183.

Gerards 2004a
Gerards, J.H., 'The Application of Article 14 ECHR by the European Court of Human Rights', in: Chopin, I. and Niessen, J. (eds.), *The Development of Legal Instruments to Combat Racism in a Diverse Europe*, Leiden/Boston: Martinus Nijhoff Publishers, 2004, p. 3-60.

Gerards 2004b
Gerards, J., 'Grondrechten en het recht op gelijke behandeling', in: Holtmaat, R. (ed.), *Gelijkheid en (andere) Grondrechten*, Deventer: Kluwer, 2004, p. 97-120.

Gerards 2005
Gerards, J., ' Equality as Legal Argument', in: A. Peczenikand others (eds.), *IVR Encyclopaedia of Jurisprudence, Legal Theory and Philosophy of Law*, <http://www.ivr-enc.info/en/article.php?id=21> (2005).

Gerards 2005a
Gerards, J., *Judicial Review in Equal Treatment Cases*, Leiden/Boston: Martinus Nijhoff Publishers , 2005.

Gerards 2005b
Gerards, J., 'Descriptieve Representatie als Rechtvaardiging voor Voorkeursbeleid', VN-Mensenrechtencomité 17 augustus 2004 Jacobs t. België (CCPR/C/81/D/943/2000)' *NJCM Bulletin* 30, 2005, p. 626-641.

Gerards and Heringa 2003
Gerards, J. en Heringa, A.W., *Wetgeving gelijke behandeling*, Deventer: Kluwer, 2003.

Gerritsen 1994
Gerritsen, A.M., *Onderscheid naar leeftijd in het arbeidsrecht*, Deventer: Kluwer, 1994,.

Gijzen 2003
Gijzen, M., 'Het Nieuwe Gelijkebehandelingsrecht voor gehandicapten en chronisch zieken', in: De Wolff, D.J.B. (ed.), *Gelijke Behandeling Oordelen en Commentaar 2002*, Deventer: Kluwer, 2003, p. 97-108.

Gijzen 2004
Gijzen, M., Report on Measures to combat Discrimination (Dutch Country Report 2004), available at, <http://europa.eu.int/comm/employment_social/fundamental_rights/pdf/legnet/nlrep05_en.pdf>.

Gijzen and Waddington 2004
Gijzen, M.H.S., and Waddington, L.B., *Dutch Report on the Implementation of the Disability Provisions in the Framework Employment Directive*, Brussel, Europese Commissie 2004, p. 1-36, available at <http://ec/europa.eu/employment_social/fundamental_rights/pfd/aneval/disabfull_nl.pdf#search=%22waddington%20gijzen%22>.

Gill and Monaghan 2003
Gill, T and Monaghan, K., 'Justification in Direct Sex Discrimination Law, Taboo Upheld', 32, 2, *Industrial Law Review*, 2003, p. 115-122.

Goldschmidt 1997
Goldschmidt, J., 'Het gelijkheidsbeginsel; gelijk zijn en het gelijke krijgen zijn twee', *Justitiële Verkenningen*, Vol. 23, No. 9, 1997, p. 8-19.

Goldschmidt 2003
Goldschmidt, J., 'Gelijkheid als fundamenteel recht, de spanning tussen gelijke behandeling en sociale cohesie in een veranderende samenleving', in: Cliteur, P.B. & Ten Napel, H.-M.Th..D. (eds.), *Rechten, Plichten, Deugden*, AA Libri, 2003, p. 97-111.

Goldschmidt and Hendriks 2003
Goldschmidt, J.E. and Hendriks, A.C., 'Gelijkheid Anno 2003, het Gelijkheidsbeginsel en andere grondrechten in een veranderende samenleving', 78 *Nederlands Juristenblad*, 2003, p. 1277-1284.

Grapperhaus 2002
Grapperhaus, F.B.J., 'Het verbod op onderscheid op grond van leeftijd in arbeid en beroep', *Ondernemingsrecht*, 2002-12, p. 356-363.

Grimley Evans 2003
Grimley Evans, J., 'Age Discrimination, Implications of the Ageing Process', in: Fredman, S. and Spencer, S. (eds.), *Age as an Equality Issue*, Hart Publishing, 2003, p. 11-20.

Groenendijk 1988
Groenendijk, C.A., 'Ouderenrecht, functionele rechtsgebieden en discriminatie. Mobilisatie van recht door ouderen of mobilisatie van ouderen door recht?', *Ars Aequi*, 37, 1988, 10, p. 615-626.

Guild 2000
Guild, E., 'The European Union and Article 13 of the Treaty establishing the European Community', *Race Discrimination*, 2000, p. 65-79.

Hahn
Hahn, 'Toward a Politics of Disability, Definitions, Disciplines, and Policies' internet publication, available at, <www.independentliving.org/docs4/hahn2.html> (last viewed on 15-04-06).

Haibach 1998
Haibach, G., 'Die Rechtsprechung des EuGH zu den Grundsätzen des Verwaltungsverfahrens', *Neue Zeitschrift für Verwaltungsrecht*, 1998, p. 456-462.

Hailbronner 2001
Hailbronner, K., 'Die Antidiskriminierungsrichtlinien der EU', *Zeitschrift für Ausländerrecht und Ausländerpolitik*, 2001, p. 254-259.

Hale of Richmond 2005
Hale of Richmond, The Rt. Hon. Baroness, 'The Quest for Equal Treatment', *Public Law*, 2005, p. 571-585.

Hamilton 2000
Hamilton, J., 'Disability and Discrimination in the Context of Disability Discrimination Legislation, the UK and Australian Acts compared', *International Journal of Discrimination and the Law*, Vol. 4, 2000, p. 203-245.

Hannett 2003
Hannett, S., 'Equality at the Intersections, the Legislative and Judicial Failure to Tackle Multiple Discrimination', *Oxford Journal of Legal Studies*, Vol. 23, No. 1, 2003 p. 65-86.

Heemskerk 2003
Heemskerk, M., 'Vervroegd pensioen zonder dat de arbeidsovereenkomst eindigt?', *Sociaal Recht*, 10, 2003, p. 297-304.

Heerma van Voss 2002
Heerma van Voss, G.J.J., 'Leeftijdsdiscriminatie en Pensioenleeftijd', *Sociaal Recht*, 2002-3, p. 63-64.

Heirbout 2002
Heirbout, D., 'Minderheden, tolerantie en gelijkheid in historisch perspectief', in: Kroes, Loof & Ten Napel (eds.), *Gelijkheid en rechtvaardigheid, Staatsrechtelijke vraagstukken rondom 'minderheden*, Deventer: Kluwer, 2002, p. 13-30.

Hendriks 1999
Hendriks, A.C., 'Health Inequalities, Symptom of Medicalisation and Denial of Equal Opportunities?', in: Loenen, T. and Rodrigues, P. (eds.), *Non-Discrimination Law, Comparative Perspectives*, The Hague/London/Boston: Martinus Nijhoff Publishers, Kluwer Law International, 1999, p. 181-194.

Hendriks 2000
Hendriks, A.C., Different Definition- Same Problems- One Way Out?, Paper presented at the Symposium 'From Principles to Practice', an International Disability Law and Policy Symposium, October 22-26 2000 available at, <http://www.dredf.org.international/Hendricks.html>.

Hendriks 2005
Hendriks, A.C., 'Promoting Disability Equality after the Treaty of Amsterdam - New Legal Directions and Practical Expansion Strategies', in: Lawson, A., and Gooding, C. (eds.), *Disability Rights in Europe From Theory to Practice'*, Oxford: Hart Publishing, 2005, p. 187-195.

Hepple 1969
Hepple, B.A., 'The British Race Relations Acts, 1965 and 1968', *The University of Toronto Law Journal*, Vol. 19, No. 2, 1969, p. 248-257.

Hepple 1990
Hepple, B., 'Discrimination and Equality of Opportunity, Northern Irish Lessons', 10, *The Oxford Journal of Legal Studies*, 1990, p. 408-421.

Hepple 1997
Hepple, B., 'The principle of Equal Treatment in Article 119 EC and the Possibilities for Reform', in: Dashwood, A. and O'Leary, S., *The Principle of Equal Treatment in EC Law, Papers collected by the Centre for European Legal Studies*, Sweet and Maxwell Ltd, 1997, p. 137-145.

Hepple 2001
Hepple, B., 'Equality and the Prohibition of Discrimination', 2001, p. 1384/7, *Emp. Law R.* 40.

Hepple 2003
Hepple, B., 'Age Discrimination in Employment, Implementing the Framework Directive 2000/78/EC', in: Fredman, S. and Spencer, S. (eds.), *Age as an Equality Issue*, Hart Publishing, 2003, p. 71-96.

Hepple and Choudhury 2001
Hepple, B. and Choudhury, T., Home Office Research Study 221, *Tackling Religious Discrimination, Practical Implications for Policy Makers and Legislators*, Home Office Research, Development and Statistics Directorate, February 2001.

Hepple, Coussey and Choudhury 2000
Hepple, B., Coussey, M. and Choudhury, T., *Equality, a New Framework Report of the Independent Review of the Enforcement of UK Anti-Discrimination Legislation*, Oxford Portland, Oregon: Hart Publishing, 2000.

Heringa 1990
Heringa, A.W., 'De toelaatbaarheid van Leeftijdsonderscheid, constitutionele en verdragsrechtelijke aspecten', in: Doup, A.C.W.B. (ed.), *Leeftijdscriteria in het Arbeidsbestel, Bijdragen aan de Studiedag over het gebruik van leeftijdscriteria in het Arbeidsbestel*, 1990, Alphen aan de Rijn: Samson, p. 53-68.

Heringa 1998
Heringa, A.W., 'Onderscheid op grond van leeftijd, Over discriminatie, onderscheid, (objectieve) rechtvaardigingen, open en gesloten modellen, kortom hoe in de wetgeving om te gaan met (on)gelijke behandeling', *SMA*, 1998, p. 116-122.

Heringa 1999
Heringa, A.W., 'Standards of Review for discrimination, the scope of review by the courts', in: Loenen, T. and Rodrigues, P. (eds.), *Non-Discrimination Law, Comparative Perspectives*, Martinus Nijhoff Publishers, 1999, p. 25-37.

Heringa 1999a
Heringa, A.W., 'Het "consensus principle". De rol van "gemeenschappelijk recht" in de jurisprudentie van het EHRM', EVRM R&C, 2.6., Koninklijke Vermande, 1999.

Heringa 2004
Heringa, A.W., 'Privé-leven en gezinsleven', updated by, Janssen, H.L., *EVRM R&C*, aanvulling 63, 12-2004, Den Haag: Sdu Uitgevers, p. 1-49.

Heringa 2005
Heringa, A.W., 'Art. 14 Discriminatieverbod', updated by, Gerards, J.H., *EVRM R&C*, aanvulling 68, 4-2005, Den Haag: Sdu Uitgevers, p. 1-28.

Herring 2003
Herring, J., 'Children's rights for Grown Groups', in: Fredman, S. and Spencer, S. (eds.), *Age as an Equality Issue*, Hart Publishing, 2003, p. 145-173.

Hervey 1991
Hervey, T.K., 'Justification for Indirect Sex Discrimination in Employment, European Community Law and United Kingdom Law Compared', 40, *International Comparative Law Quarterly*, 1991, p. 807-826.

Hervey 1995
Hervey, T.K., 'Migrant workers and their families in the European Union, the pervasive market ideology of Community Law', in: Shaw, J. and More, G. (eds.), *New Legal Dynamics of European Union*, OUP, 1995, p. 91-110.

Hervey 1998
Hervey, T.K., *European Social Law and Policy*, Longman, 1998.

Hervey 2005
Hervey, T.K., 'Thirty Years of EU Sex Equality Law, Looking Backwards, Looking Forwards', Editorial in 12, *Maastricht Journal of European and Comparative Law*, 4, 2005, p. 307-325.

Hervey and O'Keeffe 1996
Hervey, T. and O' Keeffe, D. (eds.), *Sex Equality Law in the European Union*, Chichester: Wiley, 1996.

Hervey and Shaw 1998
Hervey, T.K. and Shaw, J., 'Women, Work and Care, Women's dual Role and Double Burden in EC Sex Equality Law', 8, *Journal of European Social Policy*, 1998, p. 43-63.

Hill 2001
Hill, H., *Blackstone's Guide to the Race Relations (Amendment) Act 2000*, OUP, 2001.

Hirsch Ballin 2003
Hirsch Ballin, E., 'Gelijk in Waardigheid, over de zin van Artikel 1 van de Grondwet', *RM Themis*, 2003, p. 196-206.

Holtmaat 1999
Holtmaat, R., 'Seksuele Intimidatie op de Werkplek, een onuitroeibaar kwaad'?, *Nederlands Juristen Blad*, 1999, p. 1724-1728.

Holtmaat 1999a
Holtmaat, R., Casenote to Opinion 99-48 by the CGB, 25 May 1999, *AB*, 1999, 353.

Holtmaat 1999b
Holtmaat, R., *Seksuele intimidatie op de Werkplek*, Nijmegen: Ars Aequi Libri, 1999.

Holtmaat 2001
Holtmaat, R., 'Uit de Keuken van de Europese Unie, de gelijkebehandelingsrichtlijnen op grond van Artikel 13 EG-Verdrag', in: Loenen, T. (ed.), *Gelijke Behandeling, Oordelen en Commentaar*, Deventer: Kluwer, 2001, p. 105-124.

Holtmaat 2003
Holtmaat, R., 'Stop de Inflatie van het Discriminatiebegrip! Een pleidooi voor het maken van onderscheid tussen discriminatie en ongelijke behandeling', 25, *Nederlands Juristenblad* 2003, p. 1266-1276.

Holtmaat 2004
Holtmaat, R., *Grenzen aan Gelijkheid*, Den Haag: Boom Juridische Uitgevers, 2004.

Holtmaat 2004a
Holtmaat, R., '(Seksuele) Intimidatie en (on)gelijke behandeling, nieuwe normen, nieuwe praktijken? Enkele overwegingen bij de nieuwe EG-Richtlijnen op dit terrein en de wijze waarop deze in Nederland worden geïmplementeerd', in: De Wolff, D.J.B. (ed.), *Gelijke Behandeling Oordelen en Commentaar 2003*, Deventer: Kluwer, 2004, p. 89-106.

Holtmaat and Tobler 2005
Holtmaat, R. and Tobler, C., 'CEDAW and the European Union's Policy in the Field of Combating Gender Discrimination', 12, *Maastricht Journal of European and Comparative Law*, 4, 2005, p. 399-427.

House of Lords Fourth Report 2000
House of Lords, Select Committee on European Union, Fourth Report, The EU Framework Directive on Discrimination, 19 December 2000, available at, <http://www.parliament.the-stationery-office.co.uk>.

House of Lords Ninth Report 2000
House of Lords Select Committee on European Union, Ninth Report, *EU Proposals to Combat Discrimination*, 2000.

Houtzager and Bochhah 2004
Houtzager, D.C. en Bochhah, N., 'Onderscheid op grond van ras bij de Arbeid, nieuwe Ontwikkelingen', *Sociaal Recht*, 7/8, 2004, p. 272-278.

Huizer 1991
Huizer, A., *De Verjaardag, een Overgewaardeerd Rechtsfeit*, Stichting Recht en Leeftijd, 1991.

IDS 1999
IDS, *Race Discrimination*, Employment Law Handbook, 1999.

Jacobs 1992
Jacobs, A.T.J.M., ' 'Leeftijdsdiscriminatie bij de Arbeid', in: Jacobs, A.T.J.M. *et al.* (eds.), *'Arbeid en Discriminatie, sociaal en arbeidsrechtelijke reeks'* 29,Kluwer Deventer 1992, p. 181-198.

Jolls 2001
Jolls, C., 'Anti-Discrimination and Accommodation', Discussion Paper No. 344, 12-2001, p. 1-46, available at <http://www.law.harvard.edu/programs/olin_center>.

Jones and Basser Marks 1999
Jones, M. and Basser Marks, L.A., 'Law and the social construction of disability', in: Jones, M. and Basser Marks, L.A. (eds.), *Disability, Divers-Ability and Legal Change*', Martinus Nijhoff Publishers 1999, p. 3-24.

Jowell 1994
Jowell, J., 'Is Equality a Constitutional Principle?', in: Freeman, M.D.A. and Halson, R., *Current Legal Problems*, Volume 47, Part 2, Collected Papers, OUP, 1994, p. 1-18.

Kahn-Freund 1974
Kahn-Freund, O., 'On Uses and Misuses of Comparative Law', *37 Modern Law Review*, 1974, p. 1-27.

Kakouris 1997
Kakouris, C.N., 'Do the Member States possess judicial procedural autonomy?', *Common Market Law Review*, 1997, p. 1389-1412.

Kilpatrick 1998
Kilpatrick, C., 'Community or Communities of Courts in European Integration? Sex Equality Dialogues between UK Courts and the ECJ', *European Law Journal*, Vol. 4, No. 2, June 1998, p. 121-147.

Kilpatrick 2001
Kilpatrick, C., 'Gender Equality, A Fundamental Dialogue', in: Sciarra, S. (ed.), *Labour Law in the Courts, National Judges and the European Court of Justice*, Oxford: Hart 2001, p. 31-131.

Konijn 1995
Konijn, Y., 'Seksuele Intimidatie', *Nemesis*, 3, 1995, p. 35-38.

Koppelman 1994
Koppelman, A., 'Why Discrimination Against Lesbians and Gay Men is Sex Discrimination', *New York University Law Review*, Volume 69, No. 2, May 1994, p. 197-287.

Koppelman 2001
Koppelman, A., 'The Miscegenation Analogy in Europe, or, Lisa Grant meets Adolf Hitler', in: Wintemute, R. and Andenas, M. (eds.), *Legal Recognition of same sex couples, a study of national, european and international law*, Oxford Portland, Oregon: Hart Publishing, 2001, p. 623-633.

Koukoulis-Spiliotopoulos 2001
Koukoulis-Spiliotopoulos, S., *From Formal to Substantive Gender Equality, The Proposed Amendment of Directive 76/207, Comments and Suggestions*, Brussels: Bruylant, 2001, p. 6-94.

Koukoulis-Spiliotopoulos 2005
Koukoulis-Spiliotopoulos, S., 'The Amended Equal Treatment Directive (2002/73), an Expression of Constitutional Principles/Fundamental Rights, 12, *Maastricht Journal of European and Comparative Law*, 4, 2005, p. 327-369.

Kroes 1999
Kroes, M., Kanttekeningen bij de Proeve van Wet gelijke behandeling mensen met een handicap of chronische ziekte', *Nederlands Juristenblad*, 10, 1999, p. 2051-2057.

Kroes 2005
Kroes, M., 'Handicap of Chronische Ziekte', in Burri, S. (ed.), *Gelijke Behandeling, oordelen en commentaar 2004*, Deventer: Kluwer, 2005, p. 79-90.

Küchold 2001
Küchold, K., '*Badeck* - The Third German Reference on Positive Action', European Developments, *Industrial Law Journal*, Vol. 30, No. 1, March 2001, p. 116-120.

Labuschagne 1999
Labuschagne, B.C., 'Accommodating Religious Diversity in Employment', in: Loenen, T. and Rodrigues, R. (eds.), *Non Discrimination Law - Comparative Perspectives*, The Hague/London/Boston: Martinus Nijhoff, Kluwer International Law, 1999, p. 133-142.

Lacey 1987
Lacey, N., 'Legislation against Sex Discrimination, Questions from a Feminist Perspective', *Journal of Law and Society*, Vol. 14, No. 4, Winter, 1987, p. 411-421.

Lacey 1992
Lacey, N., 'From Individual to Group?', in: Hepple, B. and Szyszczak, E. (eds.), *Discrimination, the Limits of Law*, Mansell, 1992, p. 99-124.

Lacey 2004
Lacey, N., 'The Constitution of Identity', in: Sarat (ed.), *The Blackwell Companion to Law and Society*, 2004, p. 471-486.

Lang 2003-2004
Lang, J.T., 'Developments, Issues, and new Remedies- the Duties of National Authorities and Courts under Article 10 of the EC Treaty', 27, *Fordham International Law Journal*, 2003-2004, p. 1904-1939.

Lawson 2005
Lawson, A., 'The Human Rights Act 1998 and Disabled People, a Right to be Human?', in: Harvey, C. (ed.), *Human Rights in the Community, Rights as Agents for Change*, Oxford and Portland, Oregon: Hart Publishing, 2005, p. 135-154.

Lenaerts and van Nuffel 2005
Lenaerts, K. and Van Nuffel, Piet, *Constitutional Law of the European Union*, (edited by Bray, R.), London: Thomson Sweet and Maxwell, 2005.

Lester 2004
Lester, A., 'The Human Rights Act 1998 - Five Years on', *EHRLR*, Issue 3, 2004, p. 258-271.

Lester and Bindman 1972
Lester, A.. and Bindman, G., *Race and Law*, Harmondsworth, Penguin Books, 1972.

Loenen 1992
Loenen, T., *Verschil in Gelijkheid, de conceptualisering van het juridische gelijkheidsbeginsel met betrekking tot vrouwen en mannen in Nederland en in de Verenigde Staten*, Zwolle: W.E.J. Tjeenk Willink, 1992.

Loenen 1993
Loenen, T., 'Voorkeursbehandeling of gewoon sociaal beleid'?, *Nederlands Juristenblad*, afl. 12, 1993, p. 403-407.

Loenen 1998
Loenen, T., *Het Gelijkheidsbeginsel*, Rechtstheorie deel 2, Nijmegen: Ars Aequi Libri, 1998.

Loenen 1999
Loenen, T., 'Indirect discrimination, Oscillating Between Containment and Revolution', in: Loenen, T. and Rodrigues, P. (eds.), *Non-Discrimination Law, Comparative Perspectives*, Martinus Nijhoff Publishers, 1999, p. 195-211.

Loenen 2000
Loenen, T., 'Ras en Nationaliteit', in: *Gelijke Behandeling; Oordelen en Commentaar 1999*, Deventer: Kluwer, 2000, p. 15-24.

Loenen 2001
Loenen, T., 'Hoofddoeken in de Klas en in de Rechtbank, op Weg naar een Multicultureel Publiek Domein?', *NJCM Bulletin*, 26, 2001, 7, p. 851-869.

Loenen 2002
Loenen, T., 'Voorkeursbehandeling Bij Kinderopvangvoorzieningen Toegestaan, Hof van Justitie van de EG, 19 maart 2002, *Lommers t. Ministerie van Landbouw, Natuurbeheer en Visserij* (zaak C-476/99)', *NJCM-Bulletin*, Vol. 27, No. 5, 2002, p. 598-605.

Loenen 2003
Loenen, T., 'Ontslag wegens bereiken pensioenleeftijd nog steeds gerechtvaardigd', *NJCM Bulletin*, 28, 2003, 5, p. 609-612.

Lord Lester of Herne Hill 1997
Lord Lester of Herne Hill, 'Making Discrimination Law Effective, Old Barriers and New Frontiers', 1997, *International Journal of Discrimination and the Law*, p. 167-181.

Lord Lester of Herne Hill 2001
Lord Lester of Herne Hill, 'Equality and United Kingdom Law, Past, Present and Future', *Public Law*, 2001, p. 77-96.

Lutjens 2003
Lutjens, E., 'Pensioenontslag. Het eindigen of beeindigen van de arbeidsovereenkomst bij pensionering, kan het nog?', *Ondernemingsrecht*, 2003-6, p. 217-222.

Mabbett 2003
Mabbett, D., 'The Development of Rights-Based Social Policy in the European Union', 2003, p. 1-16, available at, <www.brunel.ac.uk/depts/govn/research>.

Mabbett and Bolderson 2001
Mabbett, D. and Bolderson, H., A significant Step Forward? EU Social Policy and the Development of a Rights based Strategy for Disabled people, 2001, available at, <www.brunel.ac.uk/depts/govn /research>.

MacKinnon 1979
MacKinnon, C., *Sexual Harassment of Working Women*, New Haven: Yale University Press, 1979.

MacKinnon 1987
MacKinnon, C.A., *Feminism Unmodified- Discourses on Life and Law*, Harvard University Press, 1987,

MacKinnon 1990-1991
MacKinnon, C., 'Reflections on Sex Equality under Law', 100, *Yale Law Journal*, 1990-1991, p. 1281-1328.

Malik 2000
Malik, M., 'Faith and the State of Jurisprudence' in: Oliver, Douglas, Scott (eds.), *Faith in Law*, Oxford, 2000, p. 129-149.

Mancini 2000
Mancini, G.F., *Democracy and Constitutionalism in the European Union*, Hart Publishing, 2000.

Martinez-Torron 2001
Martinez-Torron, J., 'The European Court of Human Rights and Religion', in: O'Dair, R. and Lewis, A. (eds.), *Law and Religion, Current Legal Issues*, Vol. 4, OUP, 2001, p. 185-204.

Marshall 2006
Marshall, J., 'Freedom of Religious Expression and Gender Equality, *Sahin v Turkey*', *Modern Law Review*, 2006, p. 452-461.

Masselot 2004
Masselot, A., 'The New Equal Treatment Directive, Plus ça Change…', 2004, *Feminist Legal Studies*, p. 93-104.

McColdrick 1999
McColdrick, D., 'The European Union after Amsterdam, An Organisation with General Human Rights Competence?', in: O'Keeffe, D. and Twomey, P. (eds.), *Legal issues of the Amsterdam Treaty*, Hart Publishing 1999, p. 249-270.

McColgan 1995
McColgan, A., 'Sexual Harassment, Sex Discrimination and Unfair Dismissal', 24 *Industrial Law Journal*, No. 2, 1995, p. 181-186.

McColgan 2000
McColgan, A., *Discrimination Law, text, cases and materials*, Hart Publishing, 2000.

McColgan 2001
McColgan, A., 'Discrimination Law and the Human Rights Act 1998', in: Campbell, T., Ewing, K.D. and Tomkins, A., *Sceptical Essays on Human Rights*, 2001, OUP, p. 215-241.

McColgan 2005
McColgan, A., *Discrimination Law, Text, Cases and Materials*, Oxford and Portland, Oregon: Hart Publishing, 2005.

McCrudden 1982
McCrudden, C., 'Institutional Discrimination', 1982, 2, *Oxford Journal of Legal Studies*, p. 303-367.

McCrudden 1986
McCrudden, C., 'Rethinking Positive Action', in: Goodman, M.J. (ed.), *Industrial Tribunals Practice and Procedure*, Sweet and Maxwell, 1986, p. 219-243.

McCrudden 1993
McCrudden, C., 'The Effectiveness of European Equality Law, National Mechanisms for Enforcing Gender Equality Law in the light of European Requirements', 1993, 13, *Oxford Journal of Legal Studies*, p. 320-367.

McCrudden 1998
McCrudden, C., 'Merit Principles', 1998, 18, *Oxford Journal of Legal Studies*, p. 543-579.

McCrudden 2001
McCrudden, C., 'International and European Norms Regarding National Legal Remedies For Racial Inequality', in: Fredman, S. (ed.), *Discrimination and Human Rights, the Case of Racism*, Vol. XI/1, OUP 2001, Chapter 8, p. 251-307.

McCrudden 2003
McCrudden, C., 'The New Concept of Equality', Trier Conference Paper, 2-3 June 2003, p. 1-24 (available with the author in its original format). Also available at, <http://www.era.int/web/en/resources/5_1990_344_file.327.pdf>.

McCrudden 2003a
McCrudden, C., 'Theorising European Equality Law', in: Costello, C. and Barry, E. *Equality in Diversity The New Equality Directives*, Irish Centre for European Law, 2003, p. 1-38.

McCrudden 2004
McCrudden, C (ed.)., *Anti-Discrimination Law*, Ashgate, Dartmouth, 2004.

McCrudden 2004a
McCrudden, C., 'Introduction', in: McCrudden, C. (ed.), *Anti Discrimination Law*, Ashgate, Dartmouth, 2004, p. xi-xxxii.

McCrudden 2004b
McCrudden, C., 'Equality and Non-Discrimination', in: Feldman, D. (ed.), *English Public Law*, OUP, 2004, Chapter 11.

McCrudden 2005
McCrudden, C., 'Thinking about the discrimination Directives', in: *European Anti-Discrimination Law Review*, 2005, p. 17-21.

McCrudden 2006
McCrudden, C., 'Consociationalism, Equality and Minorities in the Northern Ireland Bill of Rights Debate, The Role of the OSCE High Commissioner on National Minorities' (Draft; 15 june 2006, provided to me by the author), forthcoming in Morison, J., McEvoy K., and Anthony G. (eds.), *Judges, Transition and Human Rights Cultures* (OUP, *forthcoming*).

McCrudden, Ford and Heath 2004
McCrudden,C, Ford, R and Heath, A., 'Legal Regulation of Affirmative Action in Northern Ireland, An Empirical Assessment.', *Oxford Journal of Legal Studies*, Vol. 24, No. 3, 2004, p. 363-415.

McCrudden, Smith and Brown 1991
McCrudden, C., Smith, D.J. and Brown, C., *Racial Justice at Work, the Enforcement of the Race Relations Act 1976 in Employment*, Policy Studies Institute Research Report, 717, 1991.

McInerney 2000
McInerney, S., 'Equal Treatment between persons irrespective of racial or ethnic origin, a comment', *25 European Law Review*, 2000, p. 317-323.

McInerney 2003
McInerney, S., 'Legal Protection Against Discrimination based on Racial and Ethnic Origin under European Union Law – Necessary But Not Sufficient?', *International Journal of Discrimination and the Law*, 2003, Vol. 6, p. 3-43.

Mead 2005
Mead, D., 'Rights, relationships and retrospectivity, the impact of Convention rights on pre-existing private relationships following *Wilson* and *Ghaidan*', 2005, *Public Law*, Autumn, Sweet and Maxwell and Contributors, p. 459-467.

Meenan 2000
Meenan, H., 'Age Discrimination, Law-Making Possibilities Explored', *International Journal of Discrimination and the Law*, Vol. 4, 2000, p. 247-292.

Michelman 1986
Michelman, F., 'The meanings of Legal Equality', 3, *Harvard Blackletter Journal*, 24, Spring 1986, p. 24-36.

Millett 1987
Millett, T., 'Sex Equality, The Influence of Community Law in Great Britain', *Yearbook of European Law*, Vol. 6, 1987, p. 219-246.

Monaghan and Javaid 1997
Monaghan, K. and Javaid, M., 'Racial Harassment, No Laughing Matter', *New Law Journal*, March 7 1997, p. 350-352.

Moon 2001
Moon, G., 'A wider view of detriment' *Garry v London Borough of Ealing* [2001] *IRLR*, 681, in Discrimination Law Association, Briefings 217-228, 2001.

Moon and Allen
Moon, G. and Allen, R. (QC) 'Substantive Rights and Equal Treatment in Respect of Religion and Belief, towards a better understanding of the rights and their implications', p. 1-31, available at, <http://www.justice.org.uk/images/pdfs/religiousdiscrim.pdf>.

Moore 2000
Moore, S., Case note on *Seymour Smith, Common Market Law Review*, 37, 2000, p. 157-165.

More 1993
More, G., 'Equal Treatment of the Sexes in European Community Law, What does 'equal' mean?', (1993), 1, *Feminist Legal Studies*, p. 45-74.

More 1999
More, G., 'The Principle of Equal Treatment, From Market Unifier to Fundamental Right?', in: Craig, P. and De Búrca, G. (eds.), *The Evolution of EU Law*, Oxford: Oxford University Press, 1999, 517-553.

Morris 1995
Morris, A.J., 'On the Normative Foundations of Indirect Discrimination Law, Understanding the Competing Models of Discrimination Law as Aristotelian Forms of Justice', 15, *Oxford Journal of Legal Studies*, 1995, p. 199-228.

Morris 2003
Morris, A.J., 'Embodying the Law, *Coker and Osamor v the Lord Chancellor and the Lord Chancellor's Department* [2002] IRLR 80 CA', *Feminist Legal Studies*, 11, 2003, p. 45-55.

Mulder 1999
Mulder, L., 'How positive can equality measures be?', in: Loenen, T. and Rodrigues, P. (eds.), *Non Discrimination Law, Comparative Perspectives*, The Hague/London/Boston: Martinus Nijhoff Publishers, Kluwer Law International, 1999, p. 65-75.

Mullaly 1996
Mullaly, S., 'Beliefs that discriminate, A Rights-Based Solution', in: Gearty, C. and Tomkins, A. (eds.), *Understanding Human Rights*, London-New York: Mansell, 1996, p. 480-506.

Niessen 2001
Niessen, J., 'The Further Development of European Anti-Discrimination Policies', in: Chopin, I. and Niessen, J., *The Starting Line and the Incorporation of the Racial Equality Directive into the National Laws of the EU Member States and Accession States*, London/Brussels: Migration Policy Group (MPG), Belmont Press, 2001, p. 7-22.

Note 1979-1980
'Note', 64 *Minn. L. Rev.*, 151, 1979-1980, p. 151-181.

Numhauser-Henning 2001
Numhauser-Henning, A., 'Swedish Sex Equality Law before the European Court of Justice, Case C-407/98 *Katarina Abrahamsson and others v. Elisabet Fogelqvist*', European Developments, *Industrial Law Journal*, Vol. 30, No. 1, March 2001, p. 121-126.

O'Cinneide 2005
O'Cinneide, C., 'Age discrimination and European Law', European Commission, Employment & Social Affairs, April 2005, 58 p.

O'Cinneide 2005a
O'Cinneide, C., 'A New Generation of Equality Legislation? Positive Duties and Disability Rights', in: Lawson, A. and Gooding, C. (eds.), *Disability Rights in Europe*, Oxford: Hart, 2005, p. 219-248.

O'Hare 2001
O'Hare, U., 'Enhancing European Equality Rights, a new Regional Framework', *Maastricht Journal of European and Comparative Law*, Vol. 8, No. 2, 2001, p. 133-165.

O'Leary 2000
O'Leary, S., 'Economic v. Social Policy Considerations in Indirect Sex Discrimination Cases', in: O'Leary, S., *Employment Law at the European Court of Justice, Judical Structures, Policies and Processes*, Chapter 4, Oxford: Hart, 2000.

Oliver 2004
Oliver, H., 'Sexual Orientation Discrimination, Perceptions, Definitions and Genuine Occupational Requirements', *Industrial Law Journal*, 33, No. 1, 2004, p. 1-21.

Oliver 1990
Oliver, M., *The Politics of Disablement*, Basingstoke, London: Macmillan Press Ltd, 1990.

Oliver 1996
Oliver, M., *Understanding Disability, from Theory to Practice*, London: Macmillan Press Ltd, 1996.

Palmer and Gill 2002
Palmer, C, Gill, T., *et al.*, *Discrimination Law Handbook,* Legal Action Group Education and Service Trust Ltd., 2002.

Parmar 2004
Parmar, S., 'The European Court of Justice and Anti-Discrimination Law, Some Reflections on the Experience of Gender Equality Jurisprudence for the Future Interpretation of the Racial Equality Directive', in: Chopin, I. and Niessen, J. (eds.), *The Development of Legal Instruments to Combat Racism in a Diverse Europe*, Leiden/Boston: Martinus Nijhoff Publishers, 2004, p. 131-154.

Picking 2000
Picking, C., 'Working in Partnership with Disabled People, new perspectives for professionals within the social model of disability', in: Cooper, J. (ed.), *Law, Rights and* Disability, Jessica Kingsley Publishers, 2000, p. 11-27.

Poole 2005
Poole, Th., 'Of headscarves and heresies, the *Denbigh High School* case and public authority decision-making under the Human Rights Act', Analysis, *Public Law*, Winter, Sweet and Maxwell and Contributors, 2005, p. 685-695.

Posner 1989
Posner, R.A., 'An Economic Analysis of Sex Discrimination Laws', 56 *U.Ch.LR*, 1989, p. 1311-1335.

Prechal 1996
Prechal, S., 'Case C-450/93, *Kalanke v. Freie Hansestadt Bremen,* [1995] ECR I-3051', 33, *Common Market Law Review*, 1996, p. 1245-1259.

Prechal 2004
Prechal, S., 'Equality of Treatment, Non Discrimination and Social Policy, Achievements in Three Themes', *Common Market Law Review*, 41, 2004, p. 533-551.

Quinn 2004
Quinn, G., ***Walking the Talk - Equal Rights in an Enlarged Union or The Importance of Talking While Walking, A Reflection Paper,*** Prague, 5 6 July, 2004, p. 1 18. Available at, <http://europa.eu.int/comm/employment_social/fundamental_rights/pfd/events/prag04quinspeech.pdf>.

Quinn and Quinlivan 2003
Quinn, G. and Quinlivan, S., 'Disability Discrimination, the need to amend the Employment Equality Act 1998 in light of the EU Framework Directive on Employment', in: Costello, C. and Barry, E. (eds.), *Equality in Diversity, the New Equality Directives,* Irish Centre for European Law, 2003, p. 213-242.

Rath 1991
Rath, J., *Minorisering, de Sociale Constructie van 'Etnische Minderheden'*, Amsterdam: Sua, 1991.

Rawls 1971
Rawls, J., *A Theory of Justice*, Harvard University Press, 1971.

Raz 1986
Raz, J., *The Morality of Freedom*, Oxford University Press, 1986.

Rees 1998
Rees, T., *Mainstreaming Equality in the European Union*, Routledge UK, 1998.

Richards 1999
Richards, D.A.J., *Identity and the Case for Gay Rights – Race-Gender-Religion as Analogies,* Chicago and London: The University of Chicago Press, 1999.

Roberts 2001
Roberts, P., 'Employers' Liability for Sexual and Racial Harassment, Developing the Reasonably Practicable Steps Defence', *Industrial Law Journal*, Vol. 30, 2001, p. 388-396.

Rodrigues 2000
Rodrigues, P.R., 'De Richtlijn tegen Rassendiscriminatie bezien vanuit Polderperspectief', *Nederlands Tijdschrift voor Europees Recht*, 2000, p. 279-284.

Rubenfeld 1997
Rubenfeld, J., 'Affirmative Action', *The Yale Law Journal*, Vol. 107, 1997, p. 427-472.

Rubenstein 1992
Rubenstein, M., 'Sexual harassment, European Commission Recommendation and Code of Practice', 1992, *Industrial Law Journal*, Vol. 21, No. 1.

Rubenstein 2001
Rubenstein, M., Discrimination- A Guide to the Relevant Case Law on Sex, Race and Disability Discrimination and Equal Pay, *Industrial Relations Law Reports Equal Opportunities Review*, Eclipse Group LTD, 2001.

Rubenstein 2003
Rubenstein, 'New Discrimination Regulations, an EOR Guide, Part 2, Race, Religion and Sexual Orientation', *Equal Opportunities Review*, No. 119, July 2003, p. 20-28.

Rubenstein 2006
Rubenstein, M., 'Highlights, January 2006', *Industrial Relations Law Report*, Vol. 35, No. 1, January 2006, p. 1-2.

Rutten 2003
Rutten, S.W.E., 'In Nederland levende Rechtsovertuigingen', in: *Recht en Religie*, juli-augustus 2003, Nijmegen: Ars Aequi Libri, p. 21-28.

Sacks 1992
Sacks, V., 'Tackling Discimination Positively in Britain', in: Hepple, B. and Szyszczak, E. (eds.), *Discrimination, the Limits of Law*, 1992, p. 357-385.

Schiek 1999
Schiek, D., 'Freedom of Contract and a Non-Discrimination Principle - Irreconcilable Antonyms?', in: Loenen, T. and Rodrigues, P. (eds.), *Non-Discrimination Law, Comparative Perspectives*, The Hague/London/Boston: Kluwer Law International, Martinus Nijhoff Publishers, 1999, p. 77-89.

Schiek 2000
Schiek, D., 'Equality as a Right, Lessons to be learned from EC Sex Equality Law for a Multi Dimensional EC Anti Discrimination Law', in: Appelt, E. and Jarosh, M. (eds.), *Combating Racial Discrimination, Affirmative Action as a Model for Europe*, Oxford New York, 2000, p. 239-258.

Schiek 2000a
Schiek, D., 'Positive Action before the European Court of Justice - New Conceptions of Equality in Community Law? From *Kalanke* and *Marschall* to *Badeck*, *The International Journal of Comparative Labour Law and Industrial Relations*, Vol. 16/3, 2000, p. 251-275.

Schiek 2002
Schiek, D., 'A New Framework on Equal Treatment of Persons in EC Law?', *European Law Journal*, Vol. 8, No. 2, 2002, p. 290-314.

Schiek 2002a
Schiek, D., 'Torn between Arithmetic and Substantive Equality? Perspectives on Equality in German Labour Law', *The International Journal of Comparative Labour Law and Industrial Relations*, 2002, p. 149-167.

Schiek 2005
Schiek, D., 'Broadening the Scope and the Norms of EU Gender Equality Law, Towards a Multidimensional Conception of Equality Law', 12 *Maastricht Journal of European and Comparative Law*, 2005, p. 427-466.

Schiek 2006
Schiek, D., 'Grundsätzliche Bedeutung der gemeinschaftsrechtlichen Diskriminierungsverbote nach der Entscheidung Mangold', *AuR* 5/2006, p. 145-150.

Schiek 2006a
Schiek, D., 'The ECJ Decision in *Mangold*, A Further Twist on Effects of Directives and Constitutional Relevance of Community Equality Legislation', *Industrial Law Journal*, 35, 2006, p. 329-341.

Schmidt 2005
Schmidt, M., 'The Principle of Non-Discrimination in Respect of Age, Dimensions of the ECJ's *Mangold* Judgment', *German Law Journal*, Vol. 7, No. 5, 2005, p. 505-524.

Schneider 2005
Schneider, H. (ed.), *Migration, Integration and Citizenship A Challenge for Europe's Future*, Volume I, 2005.

Schultz 1997-1998
Schultz, V., 'Reconceptualising Sexual Harassment', 107, *Yale Law Journal*, 1997-1998, p. 1683-1805.

Schultz 2000-2001
Schultz, V., 'Talking about Harassment', 9, *Journal of Law and Policy*, 2000-2001, p. 417-433.

Schwarze 1982
Schwarze, J., *Europäisches Verwaltungsrecht im Werden*, Baden Baden: Nomos Verlagsgesellschaft, 1982.

Schwarze 1992
Schwarze, J., *European Administrative Law* , London: Sweet & Maxwell, 1992.

Schwarze 1993
Schwarze, J., 'Developing Principles of European Administrative Law', *Public Law*, 1993, p. 229-239.

Schwarze 1996
Schwarze, J., *Administrative Law under European Influence*, London: Sweet & Maxwell, 1996.

Scotch 2000
Scotch, R. K., 'Models of Disability and the Americans with Disabilities Act', *Berkeley Journal of Employment and Labor Law*', 2000, p. 213-222.

Scott and Trubek 2002
Scott, J. and Trubek, D.M., 'Mind the Gap, Law and New Approaches to Governance in the European Union', 8 *European Law Journal*, 1, 2002, p. 1-18.

Sen 1992
Sen, A., *Inequality Re-examined*, Harvard University Press, 1992.

Sewandono 2001
Sewandono, I., 'De Rassenrichtlijn en de Algemene Wet gelijke behandeling', *SEW*, 6, June, 2001, p. 218-226.

Shakespeare 1999
Shakespeare, T., 'What is a disabled person?', in: Jones, M. and Basser Marks, L.A.(eds.), *Disability, Divers-Ability and Legal Change*', 1999, p. 25-34.

Shaw 2004
Shaw, J., 'Mainstreaming Equality and Diversity in European Union Law and Policy', 57, *Current Legal Problems*, 2004, p. 255-312.

Sinclair 1998
Sinclair, A., 'Harassment, Discrimination in Interpretation', Web Journal of Current Legal Issues, 1998, available at, <http://webjcli.ncl.ac.uk/1998/issue1/sinclair1.html>.

Skidmore 2001
Skidmore, P., 'EC Framework Directive on Equal Treatment in Employment, Towards a Comprehensive Community Anti Discrimination Policy?', *Industrial Law Journal*, Vol. 30, March 2001, p. 126-132.

Slater 2002
Slater, H., 'Making a positive difference, a legal guide to positive action', *Equal Opportunities Review*, 111, November 2002, p. 12-17.

Smits 2000
Smits, J.M., 'Multiculturalisme en Europees Privaatrecht, een Pleidooi', *NTBR*, 2000, p. 289-292.

Zoethout and Sloep 2000
Soethout, J. and Sloep, M., *Evaluatie Arbowet over seksuele intimidatie, agressie en geweld op het Werk, Eindrapport*, Ministerie van Sociale Zaken en Werkgelegenheid, Mei 2000.

Somek 1999
Somek, A., 'A Constitution for Anti-Discrimination, Exploring the Vanguard Moment of Community Law', 5 *European Law Journal*, 1999, p. 243-271.

Somek 2001
Somek, A., 'Equality and Constitutional Indeterminacy, An Interpretative Perspective on the European Economic Constitution, *European Law Journal*, Vol. 7, No. 2, June 2001, p. 171-195.

Sottiaux 2003
Sottiaux, S., 'De seksuele geaardheid als toegelaten/verboden criterium voor ongelijke behandeling', in: Het recht in de samenleving - Bijdragen van het Centrum Grondslagen van het Recht, Universiteit Antwerpen (UFSIA), *Vrijheid en Gelijkheid. De Horizontale Werking van het gelijkheidsbeginsel en de nieuwe antidiscriminatiewet*, 2003, p. 611-645.

Sperling 1996
Sperling, J., 'Lessen uit de Verenigde Staten over seksuele intimidatie', *Nederlands Juristenblad*, 16 February 1996, 7, p. 242-246.

Stychin 2003
Stychin, C., *Governing Sexuality, The Changing Politics of Citizenship and Law Reform*, Oxford and Portland, Oregon: Hart, 2003.

Szyszczak 1990
Szyszczak, E., Casenote to Case 171/89, *Rinner-Kuhn v. FWW Spezial-Gebaudereinigung GmbH and CO. KG* [1989] IRLR 493 (ECJ), 19 *Industrial Law Journal*, 1990, p. 114.

Szyszczak 1996
Szyszczak, E., 'Positive Action After *Kalanke, The Modern Law Review*, 59:6, November, 1996, p. 876-883.

Szyszczak 1999
Szyszczak, E., 'The new Parameters of European Labour Law', in: O'Keeffe, D. and Twomey, P. (eds.), *Legal Issues of the Amsterdam Treaty*, 1999, p. 141-155.

Szyszczak 2005
Szyszczak, E., 2005, available at, <www.littletonchambers.com>.

Szyszczak 2006
Szyszczak, E., 'III Social Policy', *International and Comparative Law Quarterly*, 55, 2006, p. 475-467.

Thüsing 2003
Thüsing, G., 'Following the U.S. Example, European Employment Discrimination Law and the Impact of Council Directives 2000/43/EC and 2000/78/EC', *The International Journal of Comparative Labour Law and Industrial Relations*, Vol. 19/2, 2003, p. 187-218.

Tobler 1998
Tobler, C., 'Het Verdrag van Amsterdam, Relevante wijzigingen in het kader van de rechtsgelijkheid van mannen en vrouwen', *Nemesis*, 1998, p. 5-12.

Tobler 2001
Tobler, C., 'Rechtvaardiging van direct onderscheid in het EG recht', *Nemesis*, 4, 2001, p. 121-127.

Tobler 2002
Tobler, C., *Positive Action under the Revised Second Equal Treatment Directive*, Paper presented at the European Congress on 'Gender Equality and Professional Life - Current Developments in Europe', organised by the European Women Lawyers Association (EWLA), Paris 2002, available at, <http://www.ewla.org/wf_dl/tobler.doc>.

Tobler 2002a
Tobler, C., 'Rechtsgelijkheid en Voorkeursmaatregelen in het EG Recht', *NJCM Bulletin*, Jaargang 27, 4, 2002, p. 360-374.

Tobler 2003
Tobler, C., 'How to use the Experience with Sex Discrimination for the Other Grounds?', in: Cormack, J. (ed.), *Protection Against Discrimination and Gender Equality- How to meet both Requirements?*, Migration Policy Group, 2003, p. 14-27.

Tobler 2005
Tobler, C., *Indirect Discrimination- A Case Study into the Development of the Legal Concept of Indirect Discrimination Under EC Law*, Antwerpen/Oxford: Intersentia, 2005.

Tobler 2005a
Tobler, C., *Remedies and Sanctions in EC Non-Discrimination Law*, European Commission, Employment & Social Affairs, 2005.

Townshend-Smith 1989
Townshend-Smith, R., *Sex Discrimination in Employment, law, practice and policy*, London: Sweet and Maxwell, 1989, p. 227-241.

Townshend-Smith 1997
Townshend-Smith, R., 'Justifying indirect discrimination in English and American law, how stringent should the test be?', *International Journal of Discrimination and the Law*, 1997, p. 103-129.

Townshend-Smith 2001
Townshend-Smith, R., 'Reform of United Kingdom Discrimination Law, Philosophy, Principle or Pragmatism?', *International Journal of Discrimination and the Law*, 2001, p. 39-70.

Tyson 2001
Tyson, A., 'The Negotiation of the European Community Directive on Racial Discrimination', *European Journal of Migration and Law*, 3, 2001, p. 199-229.

Ulrich Jessurun d'Oliveira 1999
Ulrich Jessurun d'Oliveira, H., 'Nationality and the European Union after Amsterdam', in: O'Keeffe, D. and Twomey, P. (eds.), *Legal Issues of the Amsterdam Treaty*, Hart Publishing, 1999, p. 395-412.

Van Bijsterveld 2001
Van Bijsterveld, S.C., 'Freedom of Religion, Legal Perspectives', in: O' Dair, R. and Lewis, A. (eds.), *Law and Religion*, Current Legal Issues, Vol. 4, OUP, 2001, p. 299-309.

Van den Bogaard, De Lange and Van Poppel 2005
Van den Bogaard, M., De Lange, W., Van Poppel, J., 'De wenselijkheid van het maken van onderscheid naar leeftijd', Tiburg, 2005, available at, <http://www.cgb.nl/_media/downloadables/rapport%20IVA%20leeftijdsonderscheid.pdf>.

Van den Langhenberg 2003
Van den Langenbergh, K., 'Discriminatie van gehandicapten bij aanwerving, een verkennende analyse', in: *Vrijheid en Gelijkheid, De horizontale werking van het gelijkheidsbeginsel en de nieuwe antidiscriminatiewet*, Maklu, 2003, p. 573-610.

Van Dijk and Van Hoof 1998
Van Dijk, P. and Van Hoof, G.J.H., *et al. Theory and Practice of the European Convention on Human Rights*, Kluwer Law International, 1998.

Van Drongelen 2004
Van Drongelen, J., *Wet gelijke behandeling op grond van leeftijd bij de arbeid, Tekst en toelichting*, Den Haag: Sdu Uitgevers, 2004.

Van Gemerden 2002
Van Gemerden, Y., 'Het verbod op onderscheid op grond van leeftijd bij beëindiging van het dienstverband, Is een pensioenleeftijd nog wel van deze tijd?', *Sociaal Recht*, 2002-12, p. 347-355.

Van Maarsseveen 1988
Van Maarsseveen, H., 'Leeftijd, differentiatie of discriminatie?', *Ars Aequi*, 37, 1988, p. 627-632.

Van Maarsseveen 1990
Van Maarsseveen, H., 'Seksuele Intimidatie en Arbeidsrecht', *Nederlands Juristenblad*, afl. 25, 1990, p. 987-994.

Vegter 2000
Vegter, M.S.A., 'Zwangerschap en discriminatie, de pijnpunten van het gesloten stelsel van discriminatie', *Nemesis*, 4, 2000, p. 118-125.

Vegter 2001
Vegter, M.S.A., 'Aansprakelijkheid werkgever voor psychische schade werknemer als gevolg van seksuele intimidatie van de werknemer', in: *Aansprakelijkheid, Verzekering en Schade*, 5, October 2001, p. 133-140.

Veldman 1998
Veldman, A., 'The Lawfulness of Women's Priority Rules in the EC Labour Market, Case C-409/95 *Hellmut Marschall v. Land Nordrhein-Westfalen* Judgment of 11 November 1997, [1997] ECR I-6363', 5, *Maastricht Journal of European and Comparative Law*, 1998, p. 403-414.

Veldman 1999
Veldman, A., 'Mainstreaming van gelijkheidsdoelstellingen in de regulering van de arbeidsverhoudingen, Van het Verbod op Sekseonderscheid naar arbeid- en zorgarrangementen', *Justitiële verkenningen*, 1999, p. 193-214.

Veldman 2001
Veldman, A., 'De nieuwe Europese arresten over voorkeursbeleid, *Abrahamsson* en *Schnorbus*', *Nemesis*, No. 4, 2001, p. 116-120.

Veldman 2003
Veldman, A., 'Wet leeftijdsdiscriminatie gooit veel overhoop', *Sociaal Recht*, 2003-12, p. 363-364.

Verhey 2004
Verhey, L., case note on *Leyla Sahin*, EHRM, 29 juni 2004, No. 44774/98, *European Human Rights cases*, afl. 8, 2004, p. 749-753.

Verhoogt 1990
Verhoogt, J.P., 'Leeftijdsdiscriminatie, twee kanten van een begrip', *Recht en Kritiek*, 1990, p. 82-84.

Verrijn Stuart 1990
Verrijn Stuart, H., 'Take back the Words', *Nemesis*, 1, 1990, p. 1-3.

Vick 2001
Vick, D.W., 'Disparate Effects and Objective Justifications in Sex Discrimination Law', 2001, 5, *International Journal of Discrimination and the Law*, p. 3-38.

Vickers 2003
Vickers, L., 'Freedom of Religion and the Workplace, the *Draft* Employment Equality (Religion or Belief) Regulations 2003', 2003, *Industrial Law Journal*, Vol. 32, No. 1, p. 23-36.

Vickers 2004
Vickers, L., 'Approaching Religious Discrimination at Work, Lessons from Canada', *IJCLLIR*, Vol. 20/2, 2004, p. 177-200.

Villiers and Woods 1997
Villiers, C. and Woods, L., 'Seymour-Smith, Problems in Procedures and Proof', *Modern Law Review*, 1997, p. 110-119.

Waaldijk 2004
Waaldijk, K., 'The Netherlands', Combating Sexual Orientation Discrimination in Employment, legislation in fifteen EU member states, Report of the European Group of Experts on Combating Sexual Orientation Discrimination, about the implementation up to April 2004 of Directive 2000/78/EC establishing a general framework for equal treatment in employment and occupation, chapter 13, 2004, Available at, <http://ec.europa.eu/employment_social/fundamental_rights/pdf/aneval/sexorfull_nl.pdf>.

Waaldijk 2004a
Waaldijk, K., 'Seksuele Gerichtheid en Burgerlijke Staat', in: De Wolff, D.J.B. (ed.), *Gelijke Behandeling; Oordelen en Commentaar 2003*, 2004, p. 65-76.

Waaldijk 2005
Waaldijk, K., 'Wanneer telt (on)gelijke behandeling van (on)gelijke gevallen als indirect onderscheid', in: Burri, S.D. (ed.), *Gelijke behandeling, oordelen en commentaar 2004*, Deventer: Kluwer, 2005, p. 149-160.

Waaldijk 2005a
Waaldijk, K., 'Seksuele gerichtheid en burgerlijke staat', in: Burri, S.D. (ed.), *Gelijke behandeling, oordelen en commentaar 2004*, Deventer: Kluwer, 2005, p. 63-70.

Waaldijk and Bonini-Baraldi 2006
Waaldijk, K., and Bonini-Baraldi, M., *Sexual Orientation Discrimination in the European Union, National Laws and the Employment Equality Directive*, The Hague: T.M.C. Asser Press, 2006.

Waddington 1995
Waddington, L., *Disability, Employment and the European Community*, Maklu, 1995.

Waddington 1999
Waddington, L., 'Article 13 EC, Mere Rhetoric or a Harbinger of Change?', in: Dashwood and Ward (eds.), *Cambridge Yearbook of European Legal Studies*, Hart 1999, p. 175-198.

Waddington 2000
Waddington, L., 'Tweede Generatie richtlijnen gelijke behandeling, de nieuwe Richtlijn inzake gelijke behandeling ongeacht ras of etnische afstamming en de Kaderrichtlijn gelijke behandeling in arbeid en beroep', *Sociaal Recht*, 2000, p. 357-362.

Waddington 2004
Waddington, L., 'Taking Stock and Looking Forward, The Commission Green Paper on Equality and Non-Discrimination in an Enlarged Union', *Industrial Law Journal*, Vol. 33, No. 4, December 2004, p. 367-373.

Waddington 2004a
Waddington, L., *Implementing and Interpreting the Reasonable Accommodation Provision of the Framework Employment Directive, Learning from Experience and Achieving Best Practice*, EU Network of Experts on Disability Discrimination, 2004, p. 1-91.

Waddington 2005
Waddington, L., 'Implementing the Disability Provisions of the Framework Employment Directive, Room For Exercising National Discretion?', in: Lawson, A. and Gooding, C. (eds.), *Disability Rights in Europe, From Theory to Practice*, Oxford: Hart, 2005, p. 107-134.

Waddington 2006
Waddington, L. 'Recent developments and the Non-Discrimination Directives, *Mangold* and More', *Maastricht Journal of European and Comparative Law*, 2006 (*forthcoming*).

Waddington and Bell 2001
Waddington, L. and Bell, M., 'More Equal than Others, Distinguishing European Union Equality Directives', *Common Market Law Review*, 38, 2001, p. 587-611.

Waddington and Hendriks 2002
Waddington, L. and Hendriks, A.C., 'The Expanding Concept of Employment Discrimination in Europe, From Direct and Indirect Discrimination to Reasonable Accommodation Discrimination', *The International Journal of Comparative Labour Law and Industrial Relations*, Vol. 18/3, 2002, p. 403-427.

Watson 1995
Watson, P., 'Equality of Treatment, A Variable Concept', 1995, *Industrial Law Journal*, Vol. 24, no. 1, March 1995, p. 33-48.

Wells 2003
Wells, K., 'The impact of the Framework Employment Directive on UK Disability Discrimination Law', *Industrial Law Journal*, Vol. 32, no. 4, December 2003, p. 253-273.

Wentholt 1999
Wentholt, K., 'Het verbod om onderscheid te maken', in: Asscher-Vonk, I.P. and Groenendijk, C.A. (eds.), *Gelijke Behandeling, Regels en Realiteit- Een juridische en Rechtssociologische analyse van de gelijke-behandelingswetgeving*, Den Haag: Sdu Uitgevers, 1999, p. 89-130.

Westen 1982
Westen, P., 'The Empty Idea of Equality', *Harvard Law Review*, Vol. 95, January 1982, No. 3, p. 537-596.

Wetzel 2002-2003
Wetzel, J.R., 'Improving Fundamental Rights Protection in the European Union, Resolving the Conflict and Confusion Between the Luxembourg and Strasbourg Courts', 71 *Fordham Law Review*, 2002-2003, p. 2823-2862.

Whittle 2002
Whittle, R. 'The Framework Directive for equal treatment in Employment and Occupation, an analysis from a disability rights perspective', 27, *European Law Review*, 2002, p. 303-326.

Whittle 2005
Whittle, S., 'Gender Fucking or Fucking Gender'?, in: Morland, I. and Willox, A. (eds.), *Queer Theory*, Palgrave MacMillan, 2005, p. 115-129.

Williams 2003
Williams, A., 'The Changing Face of Indirect Discrimination', *Business Law Review*, January 2003, p. 8-11.

Wintemute 1997
Wintemute, R., *Sexual Orientation and Human Rights, The United States Constitution, the European Convention, and the Canadian Charter*, OUP 1997.

Wintemute 1997a
Wintemute, R., 'Recognising New Kinds of Direct Sex Discrimination, Transsexualism, Sexual Orientation and Dress Codes', *Modern Law Review*, 60:3, May, 1997, p. 334-359.

Wintemute 2000
Wintemute, R., 'Lesbian and Gay Inequality 2000, The Potential of the Human Rights Act 1998 and the Need for an Equality Act 2002', *EHRLR*, Issue 6, 2000, p. 603-626.

Wintemute 2003
Wintemute, R., 'Sex Discrimination in *MacDonald* and *Pearce,* Why the Law Lords Chose the Wrong Comparators', 2003, *The King's College Law Journal*, p. 267-281.

Wintemute 2003a
Wintemute, R., 'Same-Sex Partners, 'Living as husband and wife', and Section 3 of the Human Rights Act 1998, *Public Law*, 2003, p. 621-639.

Wintemute 2004
Wintemute, R., 'Within the Ambit', How Big *Is* The 'Gap' in Article 14 European Convention of Human Rights'?, *European Human Rights Law Review*, Issue 4, 2004, p. 366-382.

Wintemute 2004a
Wintemute, R., 'Filling the Article 14 'Gap', Government Ratification and Judicial Control of Protocol No. 12 ECHR', *EHRLR*, Issue 5, 2004, p. 484-499.

Wintemute 2004b
Wintemute, R., 'United Kingdom', Combating Sexual Orientation Discrimination in Employment, legislation in fifteen EU member states, Report of the European Group of Experts on Combating Sexual Orientation Discrimination, about the implementation up to April 2004 of Directive 2000/78/EC establishing a general framework for equal treatment in employment and occupation, chapter 17, 2004, available at, <http://ec.europa.eu/employment_social/fundamental_rights/pdf/aneval/sexorfull_uk.pdf>.

Wintemute 2005
Wintemute, R., 'From 'Sex Rights' to 'Love Rights', Partnership Rights as Human Rights', in: Bamforth, N. (ed.), '*Sex Rights - the Oxford Amnesty Lectures 2002*', OUP 2005, p. 183-224.

Wintemute 2005a
Wintemute, R., 'Sexual Orientation and Gender Identity', in: Harvey, C. (ed.) *Human Rights in the Community Rights as Agents for Changes*, Oxford and Portland Oregon: Hart Publishing, 2005, p. 175-199.

Young 2005
Young, A.L., 'The Charter, Constitution and Human Rights, is this the Beginning or the End for Human Rights Protections by Community Law?', *European Public Law*, Vol. 11, Issue 2, 2005, p. 219-240.

Young 1990
Young, I.M., *Justice and the politics of difference*, Princeton University Press, 1990.

Yu and Chopin 2001
Yu, P. and Chopin, I., 'Introduction', in: Chopin, I. and Niessen, J., *The Starting Line and the Incorporation of the Racial Equality Directive into the National Laws of the EU Member States and Accession States,* London/Brussels: Migration Policy Group (MPG), Belmont Press, 2001, p. 5-6.

Zoontjens 2003
Zoontjens, P.J.J., 'Bijzonder en Openbaar Onderwijs', in: *Recht en Religie*, Nijmegen: Ars Aequi Libri, 2003, p. 563-568.

Zuleeg 1999
Zuleeg, M., 'Constitutional Equality, Gender Equality and Affirmative Action under the Law of the European Union', 5, *Columbia Journal of European Law*, 1999, p. 1-9.

Zweigert and Kötz 1998
Zweigert and Kötz, *An Introduction to Comparative Law*, Third Edition, Oxford: Clarendon Press 1998.

CURRICULUM VITAE

Marianne (Henriëtte Simone) Gijzen (1976) received her Dutch law degree from Maastricht University (NL) in 1999, with specialisations in European Law and Languages (English/French) and Constitutional and Administrative Law. She obtained an LL.M. degree in European Law from Nottingham University (UK) in 2000 (with distinction). From 2001-2006 she was working as a Ph.D. researcher at the Maastricht Institute for Transnational Legal Research (METRO, Maastricht University, School of Law). Her Ph.D. examines selected issues in EC, English and Dutch equal treatment law on the basis of a multi-layered comparative analysis. Part of her Ph.D. was carried out at King's College London and at Oxford University. In 2004-2005 she was the Dutch member of the Independent Network of Legal Experts in Anti-Discrimination Matters set up by the European Commission. From 2002-2004 she was one of the Dutch members of the Group of Independent Experts on Disability. Her research and teaching interests include the areas of European and comparative equality law, European labour and social law, European human rights law and European and comparative constitutional law.